A HISTORY OF
MODERN SINGAPORE
——— 1819–2005 ———

A **HISTORY** OF
MODERN SINGAPORE
——— 1819–2005 ———

C.M. Turnbull

NUS PRESS
SINGAPORE

© 2020 NUS Press
National University of Singapore
AS3-01-02, 3 Arts Link
Singapore 117569

Fax: (65) 6774-0652
E-mail: nusbooks@nus.edu.sg
Website: http://nuspress.nus.edu.sg

ISBN: 978-981-325-116-8 (paper)
Reprint 2025

National Library Board, Singapore Cataloguing in Publication Data

Name(s): Turnbull, C.M. (Constance Mary).
Title: A history of modern Singapore 1819–2005 / C.M. Turnbull.
Description: New edition. | Singapore : NUS Press, 2020. | "The first
    and second edition were published by Oxford University Press,
    1977, 1989. The third edition was published by NUS Press in 2009."
    --Title page verso. | Includes index.
Identifier(s): OCN 1135718902 | ISBN 978-981-325-116-8 (paperback)
Subject(s): LCSH: Singapore--History.
Classification: DDC 959.57--dc23

*The first and second edition were published by Oxford University Press, 1977,
1989. The third edition was published by NUS Press in 2009.*

Printed by: Integrated Books International

Contents

Preface

The first edition of this history was published in 1977, just two years after Singapore completed her first decade of independence. In that short space of time the new nation's leaders came to grips with economic and security problems that had hitherto seemed insuperable in making a viable state. The results were impressive, but the young republic still remained largely a collection of different ethnic groups.

A second edition brought the story up to the late 1980s. Compared with the excitement of the early days of independence, this was a period without major dramatic incident. Despite a short-lived economic setback in the mid-1980s, these were years of outstanding material progress, when the republic became one of the most stable and prosperous countries in a troubled world, enjoying more peace and quiet than at any time since the outbreak of the Second World War.

Re-examining the past now in the light of new information and the findings of recent scholarship, this edition continues the narrative up to the fortieth anniversary of independence in 2005. It covers the changes that occurred as the leaders who oversaw the transition from a colony to independence stepped aside and a younger generation took control. Their task was to shape a course that sustained the economic growth and social stability achieved by their predecessors. They were tested when Southeast Asia experienced a severe and prolonged financial crisis in the late 1990s and were threatened by international terrorism in the early years of the new century. They also faced a newly affluent and better educated citizenry, who chafed at the constraints of the past and sought more control over shaping their society.

Narrative history has fallen out of fashion of late, in favour of a thematic approach stressing patterns and issues, while partnership with the social sciences has enriched the understanding of Singapore, particularly in the post-independence period. But this does not displace the need for a chronological story, which gives due weight to each stage in turn and attempts to place individuals and events within a framework of evolution over time, allowing for vagaries of human frailty and "the law of unintended consequences".

For the first edition of this book, His Highness, the late Sultan Ismail of Johor, graciously arranged for a copy to be made of the photograph from his family collection of his great-grandfather, Temenggong Ibrahim. The late Eric Jennings generously allowed me to use photographs from his collection.

Earlier editions of this work paid tribute to the generosity of the Lee Foundation, and the helpfulness of the University (now the National University) of Singapore Library, the Institute of Southeast Asian Studies, the National Library and National Archives in Singapore, and the University of Hong Kong Library, and in England to the Public Record Office (now The National Archives), the India Office Library (now the India and Oriental Collection in the British Library), the Royal Commonwealth Society Library (now part of Cambridge University Library), and Rhodes House Library in Oxford. I am grateful to those institutions for their continuing help.

In the early stages of bringing the work up to date, much appreciated facilities were offered to me as Hatfield Fellow at the University of Durham in 1989, Archival Fellow at Churchill College, Cambridge University in 1993, and Visiting Professor at the School of Oriental and African Studies, London University, in 1995–96. I was also indebted to Cheong Yip Seng, then editor-in-chief, and Lye Choy Lean, formerly Chief Librarian of the *Straits Times*, for their immense support and encouragement during two years spent researching the 150-year history of the *Straits Times* in 1993–95. I am grateful for the help of Allen Packwood, Director of the Churchill Archives Centre, Cambridge, and for the continuing support over many years of Nicholas Martland, Southeast Asia Librarian at the School of Oriental and African Studies.

Subsequently I welcomed invitations to present papers and hold discussions with fellow scholars in the History Department and Centre of Asian Studies, University of Hong Kong, the Malaysian Heritage Society in Kuala Lumpur, the Penang Story conference organized by Khoo Salma Nasution and Neil Khor in Penang in 2002, and to meet former Straits Settlements students in formal and informal Hong Kong University alumni associations in Singapore, Kuala Lumpur, and Penang.

In recent years I am grateful for a fruitful visit to New Zealand and Singapore in 2006. First to present views at the Conference on Southeast Asia: Past, Present and Future, which was held at the University of Auckland in honour of Emeritus Professor Nicholas Tarling's seventy-fifth birthday; and subsequently to undertake research and present a seminar at the National University of Singapore under the auspices of the Asia Research Institute, for which I am indebted to Professor Anthony Reid, then Director, and Chee Heng Leng, Deputy Director. The opportunity for discussions with NUS History Department staff was appreciated, and I owe special thanks to Tim Yap Fuan, Curator of the Malaysia Collection in the National University of Singapore Library.

A lively "Narrating the Nation: Singapore 30 Years On" workshop, which was organized by Dr. Emma Reisz and Thum Ping Tjin at St Antony's College, Oxford University in 2007 and brought together mainly younger scholars from Singapore and elsewhere, stimulated fresh ideas. Later that year I welcomed the chance to look at Singapore history from other different angles when presenting papers at a seminar at the Universiti Sains

Malaysia in Penang, at the invitation of Dr. Ooi Keat Gin, and at a conference on Britain and the Malay World at the Royal Asiatic Society in London, arranged by Dr. Ben Murtagh.

Dr. John Bastin and Dr. Karl Hack very kindly read parts of the manuscript and offered valuable – and at times stringent – comments. Neither they, nor the numerous Singaporeans and others who have generously shared their expertise and provided encouragement, advice, and hospitality over many years, are responsible for any mistakes or judgements, for which I bear sole responsibility.

Above all my thanks go out to the staff of NUS Press for their forbearance and to my editor, Paul Kratoska, a man with the patience of a dozen jobs.

C. Mary Turnbull
Oxford, August 2008

Abbreviations

AMDA	Anglo-Malayan Defence Agreement
ANZUK	Australia, New Zealand, United Kingdom
ASEAN	Association of Southeast Asian Nations
BMA	British Military Administration
CAB	Cabinet Papers
CO	Colonial Office
COD	Colonial Office Despatches
EIC	East India Company
GD	Governor's Despatches
JIA	Journal of the Indian Archipelago
JMBRAS	Journal of the Malaysian Branch, Royal Asiatic Society
JSBRAS	Journal of the Straits Branch, Royal Asiatic Society
JSEAH	Journal of Southeast Asian History
JSEAS	Journal of Southeast Asian Studies
JSSS	Journal of the South Seas Society
MCA	Malayan Chinese Association (subsequently Malaysian Chinese Association)
MNC	Multinational Corporation
MP	Member of Parliament

MPAJA	Malayan People's Anti-Japanese Army
NCMP	Non-Constituency Member of Parliament
NMP	Nominated Member of Parliament
OECD	Organization for Economic Cooperation and Development
PAP	People's Action Party
PRO	Public Record Office
PUTERA	Pusat Tenaga Ra'ayat
SEATO	Southeast Asian Treaty Organization
SFP	Singapore Free Press
SSR	Straits Settlements Records
ST	Straits Times
UMNO	United Malays National Organization
WO	War Office

Introduction to the First Edition

Modern Singapore is unique in that she was founded in 1819 on the initiative of one individual, Sir Stamford Raffles, despite almost universal opposition. An unwanted child, foisted upon the English East India Company, Singapore managed to survive and flourish, but her story was not one of steady development and unchecked progress. Her prosperity and sometimes even her existence were threatened many times.

In 1824 the East India Company purchased control of the whole island and Britain's legal sovereignty over Singapore was acknowledged. Two years later she became part, and subsequently the capital, of the Company's Straits Settlements, which were converted into a British Crown Colony in 1867. Throughout these years Singapore's position remained precarious, but the opening of the Suez Canal in 1869 and the extension of British political influence over the rich hinterland of the Malay States in the last quarter of the century assured her permanent status as one of the world's wealthiest and busiest ports. She became a separate Crown Colony in 1946, acquired the first measure of self-government in 1955 and internal autonomy in 1959. In 1963 she achieved independence as part of the new Federation of

Malaysia but was expelled after two troubled years to become a fully independent nation.

Interest in the history of Singapore as a separate entity is a comparatively new phenomenon, and until recently her story has been treated as part of Malayan history. Early attempts at writing a history of Singapore made little progress. Raffles's own manuscripts and papers, from which he intended to compose an account of the station's origins and early administration, perished in a shipwreck in 1824. Thomas Braddell, later Singapore's first Attorney-General, planned a history of the settlement but published only a collection of official documents as "Notices of Singapore" in the *Journal of the Indian Archipelago* in the 1850s.

Britain's political intervention in the Malay States from 1874 onwards and the development of peninsular tin and rubber production diverted the attention of officials, developers and writers away from the Straits Settlements. An enterprising new generation of colonial officials became absorbed in the Malay States. Singapore acquired her own civil service only in 1954, eight years after she became a separate Crown Colony, and up to that time service in Singapore constituted only an interlude from which most adventurous officials were glad to escape to more challenging and exotic postings up-country. Furthermore, specialization in Chinese affairs, which was most appropriate to work in Singapore, generally blocked the path of officials to the highest appointments, so that most ambitious civil servants chose to study Malay, and those with an academic bent concentrated their research into the history, customs and literature of the Malay States.

Sir Richard Winstedt, the leading British colonial historian of Malaya, dismissed Singapore's history before 1941 as "a scene of peaceful commercial development, disturbed only for a few years by pirates who molested its sea traffic and by pitched battles among Chinese secret societies".[1] This is too simple a view. There have been many paradoxes and vicissitudes in Singapore's history, and much that has defied the laws of probability.

Modern Singapore's birth was an exciting individual triumph, while her post-War history has been full of colour and incident, the clash of personalities and ideologies. The long intermediate years of adolescence have usually been dismissed as being dull as ditchwater, but of course ditchwater is never dull. The apparently placid surface of Singapore life covered a ferment of mixing and change, which produced a unique society, so that Singapore, one of the world's smallest nations, now commands a commercial and political influence out of proportion to her physical size.

In recent years various factors have inhibited the attempt to write a history of Singapore. With nationhood unexpectedly thrust upon her in 1965, her attention has focused upon creating national consciousness and working for future prosperity. In building up loyalties to the new state, Singaporeans concentrated on the present and future, neglecting their history, which originated under European colonial rule, with many of its Asian traditions and values also stemming from alien cultures. But ultimately nation-building implies a need to establish an identity based upon national development as distinct from the interests of individuals.

This present account traces the story of Singapore from 1819, when the modern settlement was founded, up to 1975, which completed the first decade of independence. In most newly independent countries there is a time lag of several years between acquiring political independence and loosening colonial economic and security ties or shedding colonial-based attitudes. The last formal links with Malaysia were cut in 1973 with the separation of the currency, the Stock Exchange and the rubber market. The same year witnessed Britain's entry into the European Economic Community, the winding-up of the British Malaysia Association and the virtual folding-up of the Commonwealth security umbrella. The Sino-American detente beginning in 1972, the oil crisis of 1973–74, the Paris Peace Agreements on Indo-China of 1973, the triumph of communism and humiliating defeat of United States policy in Cambodia and South Vietnam two years later, all combined to force Singapore to seek a new image in a changed world. She had to forge links with her regional neighbours, to come to terms with hostile ideologies in the Far East and to face a new economic situation in which the terms of trade suddenly swung away from the advanced industrial nations, whose ranks she had aspired to join.

It is difficult to see that any "standard" history of Singapore can be written for some time to come, since the diversity of cultural background and experience is so great that no foreigner or Singaporean of any one community can speak for the society as a whole. The author offers this book as a sympathetic personal interpretation by one who lived and worked in Singapore and Malaysia for nearly twenty years. It is presented in the hope that its limitations, omissions and faults may spur historians, sociologists, political scientists, anthropologists and others to fill in the gaps and correct misconceptions, in order that we may ultimately come to a greater understanding of the background of this young nation.

Hong Kong
September 1975

Introduction

"Singapore has no history! Singapore's history begins now!" was a popular and proud slogan after Singaporeans suddenly found independence thrust upon them in August 1965. Since everything was to be fashioned anew, an immediate reaction, particularly among the young, was to reject past history as irrelevant. The portraits of former British governors were consigned to a basement, and there were calls for Raffles's statue to be dumped in the Singapore River.

The newborn republic did indeed face stark and urgent economic and security problems, and it also needed to create a feeling of nationhood where none had existed before. But denial of the past offered only a shaky foundation for constructing a confident identity. Hitherto Singapore had always been viewed as a part – or an attachment – of a larger entity: the Straits Settlements, the British Empire, or latterly the Federation of Malaysia. Now it was necessary to look at what made the island's experience unique and, with this in mind, I embarked on writing a history of Singapore. The first edition, which was published in 1977, traced the island's fortunes to the end of the first decade of independence. A second edition updated the story to the late 1980s. It is now time to look afresh at Singapore's past in the light of her forty years' experience as an independent nation, of

Singaporeans' changing attitudes to their history and of modern historiography.

Little was known about pre-colonial Singapore at the time of independence, and the first edition of this history opened with the arrival of Raffles in 1819, while looking back briefly to the legends and semi-legends of the island's shadowy past. For a quite different reason the PAP government also decided to begin Singapore's history in 1819 since, according to Foreign Minister Sinnathamby Rajaratnam, any attempt to create a united nation by tracing Singaporeans' disparate roots back to China, India, Indonesia, and the Middle East would have risked turning the city state into "a bloody battleground for endless racial and communal conflicts and interventionist politics by the more powerful and bigger nations from which Singaporeans had emigrated" and the government needed to "be careful about the kind of awareness of the past it should inculcate in a multi-cultural society".[1] Seeking a neutral icon, the government took an unexpected, and to many an unpopular, decision: not only was Raffles's statue reprieved but he was officially acknowledged as the founder of Singapore in a second memorial, which was installed at his landing place on the river bank. "Our decision to name Raffles the founder of Singapore is an example of the proper use of history…. We are accepting a fact of history."[2]

After taking over whatever else was considered useful from the colonial past and paying tribute to Asian pioneers' perseverance, Singapore then went full steam ahead into the future to reshape the economy, build up the armed forces and foster a "rugged society". The civil service recruited technocrats to spearhead modernization, rather than history graduates, who had been the traditional sources of administrators. And in 1972 history was dropped from the primary school syllabus in favour of subjects that were considered of more practical use for the work force of the future.

These were exciting and dynamic years of growing confidence, but the very success of the "economic miracle" of the 1970s began to breed doubts about this preoccupation with the present. The political leadership feared that ignorance of the past left the younger generation too ready to take stability, prosperity and racial harmony for granted, with no appreciation of how difficult these had been to achieve and how easily they could be lost. Throughout the 1980s government ministers' public speeches reiterated exhortations for constant vigilance and effort and for flexibility and renewal in order to meet fresh challenges and to avoid the fatal collapse of earlier wealthy societies. "It is easy to forget the past, amidst the affluence, the high standard of living and modernization which we have",[3] "the more a nation achieves, the greater the danger of decline and collapse",[4] "our future as a nation is not predestined but will depend on our commitment and preparedness to work for our common good".[5]

The 1985 economic slump, which was the republic's first serious setback since independence, provided the occasion for further attempts to shake young Singaporeans out of complacency. Lee Hsien Loong, then Acting Minister for Trade and Industry, warned, "We must know the story of how Singapore came to be what it is, so that we never forget what an unnatural fact our very existence is, and why the price of this continuing is constant vigilance".[6]

Vigorous modernization policies posed a threat to the very nation building and unity they were designed to foster. Promoting English-language administration and education risked creating a cultural void. The systematic destruction of *kampong* and of entire run-down urban neighbourhoods to make way for new towns and high-rise buildings blotted out the physical evidence of past community cohesion and old ways of life. "There is increasing concern that we may create a sparkling new Singapore with no trace of the past."[7] "It is important for us to preserve as much of our history as possible if we are not to become a rootless and transient society ... we have inherited at least sixteen decades of historical commitment to Singapore."[8] The term "new Asian" came into vogue, to describe an ideal Singaporean, who would combine Western modernity with "Asian values" derived from cultural roots: "Although Singapore is a young nation, we are an ancient people, whether we are Chinese, Indian, Malay or Eurasian. We must never lose this sense of our past because it is a great source of spiritual strength in a crisis".[9]

In 1991 a national ideology was laid down, which was based on "shared values" of nation before community and society above self, the family as the basic social unit, community support for the individual, consensus not conflict and racial and religious harmony. As the twentieth century drew to a close, the confidence that national cohesion could be achieved within one generation of independence faded, and it became official policy to make the nation – and particularly the young – aware of the "Singapore Story".[10] To commemorate the fiftieth anniversary of the fall of Singapore, in 1992 the National Museum staged a "When Singapore was Syonan-To" exhibition, and 15 February was designated Heritage Day to mark the legacy of the war, "which saw the beginning of an attachment to this land as different peoples on the island banded together".[11] The exhibition highlighted the gallant stand in the last battle for Singapore, which was made by Asians in the Malay Regiment, the Volunteers and Dalforce. As new war sites were opened up in the next few years, a "persistent theme of disappointed faith in others"[12] and the need for Singaporeans to unite in self-defence was driven home.

In 1997 Deputy Prime Minister Lee Hsien Loong, launched a National Education programme, giving history a prominent place in the school curriculum in order to dispel the ignorance of the young and encourage them to "band together as one nation". In 1998 Lee Kuan Yew published the first volume of his memoirs, entitled *The Singapore Story*, and later that same year the Singapore Heritage Board staged a mammoth multi-media exhibition, also called "The Singapore Story". Together these laid down what could be termed the "authorized version" of Singapore's modern history: the fall of Singapore as a catalyst, the Japanese Occupation unifying diverse communities in the face of common hardships and suffering, the efforts and sacrifices of the past generation overcoming hardship, poverty, left-wing violence and racial strife to transform Singapore into a stable, prosperous, harmonious society, which the young needed to bond together to defend. In opening the exhibition, Prime Minister Goh Chok Tong commented, "A recurrent threat that weaves through the story was Singapore's vulnerabilities and constraints. These vulnerabilities and constraints will always be there".[13]

Singaporeans were invited to contribute to this historical story, and there was a rush to dispute the authorized version. The first volume of Lee's memoirs, outspoken and unmellowed by the passage of several decades, sparked off an uproar in Malaysia. And a number of former political opponents, liberal Western academics and young Singaporeans challenged the PAP account as "history told by the victors" and called for an "alternative history" or sometimes a "counter history".

There is a rich – and growing – literature of alternative or supplementary accounts about Singapore's emergence as an independent country. Since most of the players on the earlier political scene had been young at the time, a good many survived to publish or to record their versions of the story or to speak for those who had recently died. Western universities offered hospitality to political exiles and opposition figures. Academic conferences studied movements that had gone adrift and individuals who had been significant in creating modern Singapore but had been swept aside or fallen by the wayside.[14]

While the PAP was primarily concerned with the post-Second World War era, challengers of the Singapore Story also sought to dislodge Raffles from his pedestal, sometimes reducing him to the status of a dubious adventurer. It was argued that his importance had been exaggerated and credit for the settlement's early success should be shared with William Farquhar and John Crawfurd, with the immigrant population, and with the Malay chiefs.

In the latter years of the twentieth century Singapore-based archaeologists and historians advanced a more Asia-centric view, in which Raffles and the British period became an episode in a longer story, dating back to fourteenth century Temasek/Singapura,[15] and the island "evolved from classical emporium to global port city".[16] This interpretation claimed a continuity of experience in a flourishing maritime region, with modern Singapore emerging as natural heir to the ancient Malay empires of Srivijaya, Melaka and Riau-Johor. And the Asian communities, rather than the colonial regime, were presented as the most important factors in determining the character of modern Singapore.

It is true that since time immemorial the Straits of Singapore lay at the heart of a rich trading region in which great Malay empires had flourished. The prosperity and stability of the whole region depended on a paramount power, which could offer security, orderly administration and fair trade. Modern Singapore fulfilled such a role in the high colonial period, as Srivijaya and Melaka had done in their heydays. Yet this glittering maritime empire, held together like her Malay predecessors by mutual commercial advantage rather than by military might, was destined to fall at the very height of her prosperity at the hands of a numerically inferior assailant.

The findings of careful archaeological work carried out in the late twentieth century at Fort Canning and near the Singapore River, together with a study of pre-colonial records, charts and maps, supplement but basically support the previously known story: namely that Temasek appeared and flourished for a few decades as one of a number of moderately prosperous ports in the region but came to a sudden, violent and mysterious end at the close of the fourteenth century, when its ruler fled to found the more successful Melaka. The rulers of Temasek/Singapura were a vital link in Malay royal tradition, but genealogy was more important than geographical location, and there is little sign of any continuing attachment to the actual place. It was never entirely abandoned, but the thorough investigations of the late twentieth century confirmed that, after the fall of Temasek, nothing of significance took place on the island until Raffles's party landed in 1819. While the idea of a lost ancient city state exerted a sentimental attraction, Raffles did not set out in January 1819 with the specific intention of establishing a station at Singapore. A trading post in an established port was preferred: Riau was the first choice and, when that proved politically unacceptable, his thoughts turned to the former Johor Lama. Up to the moment Raffles dropped anchor at the mouth of the Singapore River, he was still engaged in an exploratory mission with an open mind and a hazy knowledge of the state of Malay politics. He was immediately impressed by the excellent geographical location of the Singapore River, with an established Malay/*orang laut* village, a welcoming local chief and a compliant overlord, who could boast a credible claim to the throne, although hardly the clear-cut title indicated in Raffles's reassuring report to the Governor-General.

Considerable obscurity still surrounds the Riau-Johor succession dispute and exactly when and why Temenggong Abdur Rahman settled in Singapore. While his presence provided an opportunity for Raffles to negotiate a plausible title to the new station, there is as yet no hard evidence to support the theory of a prior understanding between William Farquhar and the *temenggong*, which was mooted by Christopher Wake and taken up by later scholars.[17]

No trustworthy eyewitness account exists of the preliminary discussions between the *temenggong*, Raffles and Farquhar to balance the contradictory reports that the parties sent to satisfy their respective superiors. Obviously the Malay chief was attracted by the immediate offer of money and the prospect of more to come in the form of gifts and trade dues. What is not clear is whether he saw the deal as paving the way for a solution to the disputed Malay succession and an opportunity to advance the cause of the passed-over elder claimant, his son-in-law Hussein.

The 1824 Crawfurd Treaty, whereby the Malay chiefs ceded Singapore to the East India Company, together with the Anglo-Dutch Treaty of the same year, which deprived them of all the remaining lucrative parts of their patrimony, were to bring the Malay chiefs to the brink of ruin. Their own fortunes continued to be linked with Singapore and were dramatically affected by it. The *temenggong*'s successors were prominent in the social and economic life of the colony and her relations with the peninsular states, but after 1824 they exerted little direct influence in determining the character and administration of the port.

The original grant in 1819 merely gave the East India Company permission to establish a trading post as tenants in a Malay settlement, with the Malay chiefs exerting judicial powers and sharing in trade revenues. This situation was accepted by the first Resident, William Farquhar, and may also have been Raffles's initial intention. His attitude changed dramatically when, worn down by ill health, family tragedy and the collapse of his wider ambitions, he returned three years later to find Singapore so vibrant. Raffles may have been mistaken in attributing this to free trade, which was by no means fully established in practice, rather than to Farquhar's success in attracting settlers from Melaka and to Riau trade being drawn to their chiefs in Singapore. Whatever his original intentions, during his eight months' stay in 1822–23 Raffles ousted the Malay chiefs, obtained possession of the whole island, broke with the model of ports that had been traditional in the Malay world and created a new beginning. He may not have been the glittering hero of Victorian times, but Raffles made Singapore happen. Together with Farquhar and John Crawfurd he laid her foundations, and he brought a new vision of Singapore as a beacon for free trade and the rule of law, a magnet for commerce, modern ideas, and intellectual enlightenment. His ideals were not always practical, and it needed men of more prosaic common sense, such as Farquhar to nurse the infant settlement and Crawfurd to convert his quasi-legal agreements into sound law, but neither Farquhar or Crawfurd had the vision that could inspire future generations.

Modern Singapore was not an adaptation or natural progression from an indigenous polity, nor one transplanted by Chinese or Indian settlers. The Chinese scholar, Wei Yuan, was in no doubt that British Singapore was a new and disturbing phenomenon, which threatened the peace and security of the traditional world order, in which China, as the Middle Kingdom and supreme overlord, expected tributaries to maintain concord in their regions and barbarians to keep in their place.[18] Whereas Srivijaya and Melaka had been peaceful support for stability in the Nanyang, Wei Yuan lamented that European naval aggression and a greedy obsession with trade and profit for its own sake had destroyed Asian commercial patterns and upset the traditional equilibrium. In his *Illustrated Treatise on the Sea Kingdoms*, completed in 1843, a few months after the end of the First Opium War, Wei Yuan warned, "The bases of the English barbarians encircle the world".[19] They had broken out of the Great Western Ocean, where they belonged, and created in Singapore "a new and unruly locus of power".[20]

It is sometimes argued that too much attention has been given to colonial government and to the expansion of British control, whereas the people themselves were the most important factor in the making of modern Singapore. The colonial time will become less prominent as the period itself shrinks in proportion to the longer expanse of Singapore's history, and it is possible to take the story more broadly into society as more is discovered about economic and social life and activities away from Government House. Nevertheless, Singapore's administration, judiciary, commercial institutions, education system and eventually the constitution of the independent republic derived from the colonial government and developed within it. Similarly the expansion of British control over the Malay hinterland established Singapore's role for many decades as the major outlet for the economy of "British" Malaya and as one of the foremost ports in the British Empire. In a *general* history, a framework of government remains essential to an understanding of the colonial era and its legacy.

For most of the British colonial period, light government and a *laissez-faire* economy encouraged the different communities to develop their own organizations and way of life. This was particularly true of the last fifty years of Indian rule leading up to the transfer of the colony to British government control in 1867. Once the foundations had been laid down by Raffles, Farquhar and Crawfurd, much of the momentum passed to the Asian and Western communities themselves. Indeed, rather appropriately, in the late 1850s, Government House was demolished and the Governor had to move into rented accommodation. Regarded by India as a useless and expensive burden, the Straits Settlements were ruled by a skeleton administration, with little means to enforce law or exert any control over immigration and labour, and knowing virtually nothing about the mass of the population.

Despite this, it was a formative, constructive time. Within the severe financial constraints, the Straits government employed convict labour to construct public buildings, bridges and roads. The Royal Navy took vigorous action against pirates in the South China Sea, while local piracy died down when an unwritten understanding between the Singapore authorities turned Temenggong Ibrahim from pirate to pirate-hunter and set him and his successors on course to concentrate on developing the resources of mainland Johor. The first marine surveys of the Straits of Singapore and nearby coasts were carried out. Lighthouses were constructed at the eastern and western approaches to the Straits of Singapore, vital links in what was to become a "chain of light" stretching the length of the Melaka Straits and into the South China Sea. For the first time in history, the notorious Singapore Straits and surrounding seas became safe for shipping – and most significantly for steamers. The Asian population expanded rapidly, and Chinese farmers opened up the interior of the island. Western and Asian merchants founded commercial institutions: the Singapore International Chamber of Commerce, the first banks, independent newspapers.

The period is under-researched and remains a tantalizing challenge for the historian. While there are many excellent works by contemporary Western observers, the Asian sources remain scanty.[21] In 1975 Christopher Wake wrote of this era, "the Asian communities possessed a corporate life of their own … which … flourished in full vigour under the mantle of British over-rule, each with its own ends, organisation and historical evolution. To what extent and in what manner this 'internal' history of the Straits communities can be recovered is a question which largely remains to be answered".[22] Thirty years later it is still unanswered.

By contrast a great deal has been researched and written about the high colonial era from 1867 to the First World War, when the population was brought within the pale of the administration and the law and Singapore was transformed from a precarious entrepôt into the confident hub of an expanding regional economy. An older generation had been largely preoccupied with official activities and problem solving: enforcing law and order, breaking the secret societies' hold over immigration and the labour market, and expanding British control into the Malay States. Later historians turned to more constructive aspects of social and economic life, and many studies were made about important external movements that affected Singapore deeply: notably in late Ch'ing China and in the Islamic world. The opening up of opportunities for research in southern China as well as Taiwan in recent years made it possible to investigate the ramifications of Singapore family businesses. In general the modern literature about this period tended to amplify, enrich and put flesh on the bones of earlier knowledge, rather than leading to a radical reassessment. James Warren presented his studies of rickshaw pullers and prostitutes as the underside or "people's history of Singapore"[23] as a counterweight to the more familiar "overside".

During the First World War much attention was given to Singapore's one flutter of excitement: the mutiny of the Indian garrison in 1915 and its significance for the future. Perhaps indeed rather too much has been read into this episode, from which at the time neither the British, the Japanese nor the local population appeared to have learned anything.

The inter-war years were largely taken up with the periodic "boom and bust", to which Malaya's economy was particularly vulnerable, and notably the Great Depression of the early 1930s. But a great deal was happening on the periphery or under the surface of public life, and of recent years historians have shown how many of the forces, which were to be so important in reshaping post-war Singapore and Malaya, were gathering in those years.[24] While the economic, social and cultural divide between and within the different ethnic groups remained strong, there was some interchange of radical ideas among the growing minority of intellectuals and dissidents who were drawn to the cosmopolitan port city. Singapore was the base for flourishing Asian-owned newspapers, representing an Asian and often anti-colonial viewpoint: the *Malaya Tribune*, the English-language paper with the largest circulation, founded in 1914; the Chinese dailies, the *Nanyang Siang Pau* and the *Sin Chew Jit Poh*, both started in the 1920s; and the Malay *Utusan Melayu* launched in 1939. While a small group of anglicized "King's Chinese" was associated with the colonial regime, the majority of politically minded Singapore Chinese were caught up in the Comintern's activities or in Kuomintang Nationalist China's ambitions to command the loyalty of the Nanyang Chinese. The Kuomintang's "golden age" in China[25] was unsettling to the Chinese in Malaya and even more so to the British colonial regime. Valuable studies have been published about the leadership and organization of the Chinese community in this period, and particularly the role of Tan Kah-kee.[26] But on the eve of the Pacific War, Pan-Malay feeling was only beginning to formulate. Communism had taken a series of beatings in Indonesia, China, Malaya, and Singapore itself, and Kuomintang China was fighting for survival against Japan. British imperial rule in Southeast Asia seemed set to stay for a long time, had there not been the jolt of the Japanese invasion.

The fall of Singapore was the most momentous event in the island's entire history, and the British government's decision not to hold an official enquiry into the circumstances leading to the disaster, either during the Second World War or in the years that followed, left the field open to endless speculation and debate, blame and justification. The events and policies leading up to the Pacific War and the Malayan campaign itself have generated an impressive body of literature, including a number of substantial works with extensive bibliographies,[27] while the largest academic conference ever held in Singapore met in February 2002 on the occasion of the sixtieth anniversary of the fall.[28] Despite this comprehensive coverage, the topic will undoubtedly continue to excite controversy. On one level it is possible to trace a seemingly inevitable collapse back to the 1880s, to the inherent weakness of an overstretched maritime empire. Others portray a chain of disaster from the 1920s in which long-term policies fell victim to unexpected changes in circumstance, and problems were compounded by misfortunes and errors of judgement in the actual campaign to lead to inexorable defeat. Yet at the very end, much depended on the character and ability of the two opposing commanders, and alternative decisions taken in the last few days or even in the final 24 hours might have produced a very different outcome.

Invariably the saga is presented as a humiliating British disaster, as it certainly was. There is as yet no comparable authoritative academic work on a brilliant Japanese victory to supplement the enlightening, but not entirely reliable, eyewitness account of Colonel Masanobu Tsuji. Concentrating on the ignominy of the British collapse has eclipsed the achievement of the Japanese forces and the outstanding ability of their commander, making their task appear much easier than it was. To chronicle the campaign from a Japanese viewpoint poses considerable problems: vital official Japanese archival sources were destroyed in Allied bombing raids; leading Japanese participants, including General Yamashita, were executed as war criminals; and Japanese historians have been understandably reluctant to tackle this painful subject: the anomaly of a spectacular triumph submerged within a greater defeat. Of recent years a greater attempt has been made to tell the Japanese side of the story, including a valuable paper based on Yamashita's diary, which was presented to the Sixty Years On conference by Yoji Akashi, one of the very few Japanese historians who has devoted many years to studying Japan's wartime role in Malaya.[29] It shows how the months that the "Tiger of Malaya" spent in Nazi Germany before the invasion of Malaya profoundly influenced his conduct in the peninsular campaign and particularly in the final battle for Singapore. There might be much to learn from the German records of Yamashita's mission.

For Winston Churchill, the fall of Singapore was the most devastating shock of the whole Second World War. It still left him perplexed in 1949 when he came to write *The Grand Alliance*, the third volume of his *History of the Second World War*, and he sought an explanation from Field Marshal Sir Henry Pownall. The disaster was a matter of personal concern to Pownall, since he had been directly involved in War Office planning and he would have been in command in Singapore, rather than the luckless Percival, but for a quirk of fate. Looking back in retrospect, Pownall concluded that the whole policy pursued since 1921, whereby land and air forces would hold off an enemy attack until the fleet arrived, had been thrown into the melting pot by the unexpected events of the two years leading up to Pacific War. "In those years there were so many more urgent and dangerous problems nearer home that Singapore did not, I fear, get a high priority in our thoughts or in our working time".[30]

The main interest for Singaporeans is focused on the final battle for the island itself. The commonly held view of the different elements of the Chinese community sinking old rivalries to co-operate with one another and with the British in resisting the Japanese needs to be modified in the light of later research. There were deep divisions between the Kuomintang and pro-communist supporters, and Tan Kah-kee, the most respected anti-Japanese leader and head of the Singapore Chinese Mobilization Committee, opposed the arming of Chinese civilians and would have nothing to do with it. For Tan, the defence of Singapore was the responsibility of the British army. The resistance was fierce, but there were in fact two separate battles being waged: the struggle for imperial Singapore, which was being defended by conventional British and Commonwealth forces, including the Malay Regiment and the Volunteers; and the last impassioned stand of the Overseas Chinese National Salvation Movement in the Sino-Japanese War, which was being fought by young Chinese in Dalforce.

A general consensus about the final surrender is that the fall of Singapore was almost inevitable but did not need to come so quickly. A better co-ordinated resistance and fewer mistakes in the peninsular campaign could have delayed the Japanese advance and prolonged the battle for Singapore. In his *Singapore 1941–1942*, published in 1977, Louis Allen revealed that the British surrender offer came at the very moment when the Japanese were so extended and running so short of ammunition that Yamashita's officers were advising him to pull back. Whether such a pause would have enabled the Japanese to gather strength and regain air support or whether equipment and reinforcements would have arrived in time for the defence to turn the tide, a prolonged battle would have inflicted terrible devastation on Singapore. In any event Yamashita had already decided to overrule his subordinates' advice and gamble on throwing all his men and resources into one last push through the middle of Singapore city to split the Commonwealth forces. Given the defenders' confusion and demoralization, Yamashita's bold plan would undoubtedly have worked. As Allen stressed in the second edition of his work,[31] the surrender was not unconditional but carried an agreement for an orderly handover. Singapore was fortunate in that the humane Percival was not prepared to sacrifice the civilian population in order to save his own reputation or fulfil Churchill's vision of going down in glory in a last-ditch stand and that Yamashita was happy to hold back his force, which saved him from exposing the weakness of his own position. Whatever the blow to British prestige and however great the suffering to come under the Japanese Occupation, Singapore was spared the indiscriminate slaughter of a final street-by-street battle and a repetition of the Rape of Nanjing.

The Japanese Occupation was such a traumatic experience for all who lived through those years that it resulted in a treasure trove of personal reminiscences and continues to do so. Initially the Occupation was treated as part of the history of the Second World War or the British Empire, and the field was dominated by Westerners. Many were former military prisoners of war, who were sent elsewhere in Asia as slave labour, and were thus largely detached from the experiences of the local population and civilian internees in Singapore. The few early Asian accounts were about misery and brutality, particularly by those who had suffered at the hands of the Kempeitai. For several decades Singaporeans showed a reluctance to write about their experience: in part wishing to block out distressing memories and in part perhaps embarrassed to acknowledge what passed for "normal" routine life during the Occupation. This attitude changed over the years, and a steady stream of reminiscences, together with the work of academic historians, has recreated a picture of everyday social life and economic activity.[32] This evidence shifts the emphasis on to local society and adds an extra dimension to the story without necessarily creating a radical new picture of the Occupation period itself. No new lasting institutions were created. While individual Singaporeans might find hidden talents and unexpected inner reserves of strength and character, these were years of shortage, hunger, deprivation and often fear, when everything was geared to the Japanese war economy, but post-war interpretations have changed a great deal.

The full details of the notorious *sook ching*, in which tens of thousands of male Singapore Chinese were taken away and secretly massacred in the first two weeks of the Occupation, will probably never be known. The over-speedy execution of Yamashita and the disappearance of his henchman, Tsuji, deprived the war crimes court of its principal defendants, and the absence of precise evidence at that time resulted in a verdict which the Chinese community resented as far too lenient. The eventual discovery of mass burials in the early 1960s came at a time of acute political crisis, and, in order to avoid the exploitation of a racial issue, the PAP government deliberately represented the *sook ching* as an atrocity against all the peoples of Singapore and not specifically the Chinese.[33] According to the "authorized" version of the Singapore Story all ethnic groups suffered equally during the Occupation and were brought together by their common tribulation, marking the *sook ching* as a significant turning point on the way to national unity. The evidence does not bear out this interpretation. While few Singaporeans benefited, the experience of the different communities varied widely, and these years were a divisive rather than a unifying experience.

Turning to the wider picture, in the early twenty-first century Christopher Bayly and Timothy Harper took a new approach in two scholarly volumes, which viewed the experience of the Asian populations through the tumultuous decades of the mid-twentieth century across the entire British imperial crescent from India through Burma and Malaya to Singapore.[34] Starting with the disparate anti-colonial movements in the 1930s and the Sino-Japanese and Pacific wars through to the final post-Second World War struggles for independence, they portrayed Asians being moulded by trial and suffering into taking charge of their own destiny to throw off British domination. It is a stimulating theory but overestimates the unity of local determination and initiative to resist the return of British rule in Malaya, nor does it take full account of how the colonial power itself had been changed by the Pacific War.

It is a truism that the fall of Singapore was a great shock to the Asian population, which shattered the prestige of British imperialism, but the disaster caused shock waves in Britain itself. Already uneasy about the anachronistic administration in Malaya and stung by American criticism, the Colonial Office was initially convinced that Singapore fell because the state itself was rotten. The restoration of British rule in Malaya was not designed to be "business as usual" but as the opportunity to carry out far-reaching constitutional reform.

The abrupt and unexpected ending of the Pacific War in August 1945 had a dramatic impact on the future course of Malaya and Singapore. The country was spared the immediate horrors of becoming an active battlefield, but there were even more important long-term political repercussions. Grievances and resentment against the British ran deep, but most of this discontent was still vague and uncoordinated. The sudden collapse threw the Japanese-sponsored Pan-Malay movement out of gear, and the Indian National Army was routed and its leader killed, leaving only two clearly formulated plans for the future: the Malayan Communist Party's Republic of Democratic Malaya and the British government's Malayan Union. Both parties had anticipated consolidating their positions during a long drawn-out liberation campaign: the Malayan Communist Party to emerge as heroic guerrilla leaders and the British government to conduct a thorough consultation. These expectations were dashed.

The British returned not only with a ready-made Malayan Union plan and a Malayan Planning Unit, which had prepared for the restoration of administration in meticulous detail, they were also backed by a daunting military force designed to drive the Japanese out of Southeast Asia. While the future communist leader, Chin Peng, later represented this as a lost opportunity, which was squandered by the treachery of the party's secretary-general,[35] for the time being prudence dictated that the Malayan Communist Party should choose the less risky path of outward co-operation in a united front, leaving the British to go ahead with introducing the Malayan Union.

It was this scheme that was the immediate catalyst in sparking off active nationalism in Malaya and the attendant separation of Singapore, which prompted the creation of the colony's first political party. Far from being insulated by the constitutional separation, Singapore was caught up in the political upheaval on the mainland and the ensuing communist insurgency.

The republic's character and future were determined in the two decades leading up to independence, which encompassed the entire campaign to win independence from colonial rule, the battle to the death between the moderates and extreme left, the realization and collapse of merger in Malaysia, and the decision to reorient the economy. Later singled out by the PAP leadership as essential study for the young, these years of turmoil and excitement have also increasingly engaged the attention of historians and social scientists.

The British archives in London continued to be the major official source for this period but a growing body of information became available in Singapore itself: from the Singapore National Archives, which was established in 1967 and the prolific recordings of its Oral History Unit, which was set up twelve years later; from research studies at the University of Malaya, which was founded in 1949, and up to the late 1950s was a single Singapore-based campus, serving the Federation of Malaya and the three British Borneo protectorates; from the speeches and radio talks of leading public figures; and from contemporary journalism. Alongside a vibrant local English-language and vernacular press, Singapore was the favoured Southeast Asian base for the foreign correspondents of leading Western newspapers, and from his personal contacts with those involved, journalist Dennis Bloodworth provided a unique picture of the Malayan Communist Party's methods of recruitment, infiltration and manipulation.[36]

Mid-twentieth century English-speaking society comprised a small world of close personal contacts and lively political discussion, which cut across ethnic divides. On one level the Westernized were well-informed and conscious of being part of a region in turmoil – in Indonesia, the Philippines, China and Vietnam – but they had only a shadowy appreciation of the pent-up emotions and frustrations among the vernacular-educated masses, of which the frequent labour strikes, student protests, mass rallies and general air of chaotic confusion were an outward manifestation.

By the time Singapore became an independent republic, the PAP was firmly in charge and moved to establish increasingly tighter state control. The precarious situation of the early 1960s quickly gave way to virtually unassailable PAP dominance. From 1968 to 1981 the party held a monopoly of parliamentary seats and thereafter faced only a handful of opposition members, who were never a serious challenge. Political history became largely a story of the PAP's steady accretion of power and control, and opposition disarray. The City Council had been abolished and its functions taken over by central government in 1959. A Land Acquisition Act of 1966 gave the state the right to acquire land for public purposes; labour legislation in the late 1960s substituted arbitration for strike action and sapped trade union power; tertiary education was brought under control, and in 1980 the two universities were united as the National University of Singapore; radio and television were state owned, and all local newspapers, whether English-language or vernacular, were eventually brought under the umbrella of Singapore Press Holdings; the work of the voluntary Singapore Family Planning Association was absorbed into an official Singapore Family Planning and Population Board, and civil society organizations withered as more and more initiative passed into state hands.

From the beginning the PAP appreciated the great deal of parliamentary power offered by the Westminster constitution they had inherited, and their former communist allies taught them a bitter lesson in how to ensure permanent central control of party organization. After the 1961 debacle the PAP was reconstructed as a cadre party, in which the cadres chose the central executive and the party leaders chose the cadres. In 1982 the PAP declared itself a national movement rather than a political party, claiming this made formal opposition unnecessary. Political opponents who sought to overturn official policy were relentlessly attacked as alleged threats to the national good. On its own terms the government admitted some independent voices with limited powers into Parliament as Nominated and Non-Constituency Members. It also steadily built up an elaborate machinery of alternative grassroots consultation through the People's Association, Citizens' Consultative Committees, Feedback Units, Community Centres and Town Mayors, and invited expert participation in discussing policy changes. However there was no obligation to accept advice: the government made decisions and laid down so-called out-of-bounds markers, which meant anything that would detract from efficiency, cause disharmony or lower the dignity of political leaders. Citizens could express opinions through the channels provided to them from above, but, unless they were willing to enter the political arena and form a political party, individual citizens were deemed to have no right to challenge policy making, which was the sole prerogative of those who had obtained a mandate to rule and were responsible to the electorate.

Faced with stark and unexpected difficulties, in the early years of independence measures that had aroused passionate objections in the past were accepted with little or no opposition, despite causing personal distress: compulsory national military service, tough labour laws, and population limitation. An ambitious industrialization programme was launched to transform the economy, since Singapore could no longer rely on her traditional role as an imperial entrepôt and staple port for the Malay Peninsula. Initially there was widespread international admiration for the infant republic's resilience in tackling her problems and for the spectacular success of her "economic miracle". But autocratic politics attracted increasing criticism from liberals overseas, particularly from academics and the Western press, and the PAP had no hesitation in entering the fray against these vocal adversaries.

The authorities were determined to prevent Singapore newspapers from falling under foreign ownership, and in 1971 they closed down three local newspapers which were accused of being backed by foreign funds. Insistence that the foreign press should not interfere in or influence domestic opinion led to a running battle with prominent American and Hong Kong journals through the 1980s, involving libel cases, restrictive legislation and banning newspapers or imposing quotas on their circulation and advertising.

Liberal academics mourned the decline of civil society, and denounced the harsh treatment of opposition politicians, the prolonged imprisonment of political detainees until they either recanted or were too old to be effective, and the refusal to repeal internal security legislation long after the disappearance of the widespread poverty, unemployment and deprivation that had fuelled subversion. Some critics accused the PAP of deliberately manipulating crises as an excuse to impose controls and then perpetuating a crisis mentality in order to justify further tightening of state control.[37] Certainly the PAP established a firm grip over the party and the government in response to crises. The crises were real: the paralysis of City Hall under Ong Eng Guan's incompetent administration, the near destruction of the party by the extreme left wing, the external menace from the Indonesian

Confrontation, China's Cultural Revolution, the escalating Indo-China war and the economic and defence hazards threatened by the accelerated British military pull-out.

The Workers' Party by-election victory in 1981, which broke the PAP's parliamentary monopoly, revealed how some segments of society had been left behind in the general rise in prosperity. The requirement to conform to the ever-increasing pace of modernization caused distress to others, particularly the Malays. After Singapore separated from Malaysia, the community felt neglected and marginalized since the PAP government no longer needed to cultivate Malay support.[38] Malay land reservations all over the island were cleared to make way for new industrial and residential estates, forcing villagers to abandon their traditional way of life and move into high-rise flats. There was also a simmering of discontent among Singaporeans who had prospered but felt that political restriction was out of keeping with the increasingly well-educated, affluent and sophisticated society of the late twentieth century. With the rapid expansion of education at all levels, including overseas tertiary education, and one of the world's most open economies, the Singaporean professional middle class was at the heart of globalization: cosmopolitan in outlook, well-travelled, open to outside international influences, familiar with the Internet. Restraint within out-of-bounds markers seemed incongruous.

Government response was uncertain and unpredictable. In 1987 it over-reacted to an alleged Marxist conspiracy involving Roman Catholic priests and social workers. Even under Goh Chok Tong's premiership in the last decade of the twentieth century, when censorship was relaxed on films and the arts, and civil society revived, political out-of-bounds markers remained in place. Organizations were often unclear about what constituted impinging on politics. Mild critical comment from writers or journalists could provoke disproportionate rebuke, while the relentless discrediting and holding to account of opposition politicians who challenged the PAP's fundamental policies continued.

For most Singaporeans criticism did not translate into active resistance or protest. There was no widespread desire to change the PAP government or its policies, no clamour to repeal the internal security legislation, no widespread demand for a welfare state, and no sign of wanting to rush into active politics.

For the first thirty years or so following independence, social scientists dominated the field in Singapore studies, producing a large body of literature on political, economic and social development in the new republic. Almost half of the team of Singapore academics who produced *A History of Singapore* in 1991 were non-historians, and the book was designed to "set contemporary Singapore in historical perspective and to enable readers to appreciate the forces which shaped the country's society, economy, and polity".[39]

The PAP government's campaign in the last years of the twentieth century to enlighten the younger generation about the nation's formative years came at a time when interest in studying the past was reviving. In the more relaxed intellectual atmosphere at the turn of the century, people of all political persuasions became more willing to write and talk frankly about that turbulent era. It was not customary for Singapore politicians to keep diaries, but Lee Kuan Yew's two volumes of memoirs were particularly revealing and provoked strong reaction. The opposition was very vocal too. By that time all political prisoners had been released from gaol. Some, such as Said Zahari, published their own accounts to supplement the earlier narratives of political exiles, such as Francis Seow and Tan Wah Piow. Others wrote about leading figures who had recently died, such as Lim Chin Siong and Jamit Singh. Western universities were happy to give academic hospitality to critics of the regime, such as Francis Seow and Chin Peng. An impressive collection of interviews recorded by Melanie Chew in 1996 ranged across a wide spectrum of political, economic and social life.[40] And the official British archives for the period were open to public view. Consequently, a very vivid picture emerged of those complicated times.

Some revelations led to a fundamental reappraisal of past events. The detailed knowledge that came to light over the years about Singapore's separation from Malaysia in August 1965, corroborated from very different viewpoints, shows that, while the separation came as a complete shock to Singaporeans and to the majority of government ministers in Singapore and Malaysia, it was no surprise to a tiny inner circle of PAP and Alliance leaders and that Lee Kuan Yew's apparent reckless brinkmanship was a calculated risk.

From the complexities of the mid-twentieth century academics began to develop an "alternative history", which challenged the orthodox PAP version and looked at different paths which Singapore might have chosen.[41] Modern scholars welcomed the "vibrant diversity" and intellectual excitement of the times, impressed by the passions, enthusiasms and self-sacrifice, nostalgic for lost ideals of youth, and mourning the heavy price often paid by individuals for devotion to a cause. Some, particularly among the younger generation, would go further. Sceptical of the authorized version, they called for a "counter" history, belittling the PAP's achievements and arguing not only that the crisis mentality was unnecessary but the crises themselves were not genuine. Such "vibrant diversity" was not music to the ears of investors, nor were the strikes, mass rallies, protest demonstrations and violence which accompanied it, and Singapore was to take the more prosaic path of eschewing ideology in favour of practical common sense in providing the security, jobs, housing, schools and other amenities of comfortable living.

Turning to Singapore's fortunes after independence, the historian faces different problems, relating both to source material and perspective. The change in the nature of official archives compounds the difficulty which is always experienced in examining any recent period before official archives are open. The British archives were no longer a fruitful source, except for defence and that only into the mid-1970s,[42] and the historian of the Republic of Singapore has to rely on the official archives of the National Archives of Singapore as and when the original correspondence is systematically released. Meanwhile there is an abundance of official publications, parliamentary papers, transcripts of oral interviews, memoirs, and also the impressive work of social scientists.

The question of perspective posed a more serious problem. While the story of the economy is clear and has generated numerous studies, the political and social picture is more fluid. Although the system of government remained unchanged into the twenty-first century and the out-of-bounds markers were not relaxed, there was a change in atmosphere. Singapore had not yet blossomed into the ideal multiracial state which had been envisaged at the time of independence, but many of the issues that divided society had ceased to stir the same passions. Chinese culture, language and education were no longer burning sources of contention, and dialect was no longer important. Practical co-operation with ASEAN had replaced emotional ideological identification with non-aligned nations and anti-colonial movements, the Chinese motherland or a Greater Malaysia.

English was the main language but no longer the language of the master race, and Chinese had become a useful commercial tool. The People's Republic of China was a trading partner, rather than the motherland or a fount of communism. The Singapore Chinese Chamber of Commerce had put dissensions and political ambitions behind it. The younger generation of Malays was largely reconciled to urban living and modernization. The local press accepted its role to report and inform, without aspiring to be a Fourth Estate, while the Western world became less critical, as other countries were forced to tighten their anti-terrorist laws and faced problems with their welfare states. Any threat to security no longer came from internal left-wing subversion or external physical attack but from extremist Muslim terrorism. While Singapore's racial composition and geographical position made the republic particularly vulnerable, she foiled a major terrorist plot in 2001, and she had the internal security laws already in place, together with organizations for consultation and preserving ethnic and religious harmony, which had been built up over many years.

The current situation looked stable: a clean efficient government in full control, with an excellent record in managing the economy and in the provision of housing and education. The republic had survived hardship and emerged stronger from the prolonged Southeast Asia regional slump at the turn of the century, during which the government's resounding victory in the general election of 2001 was an expression of trust in its tough measures to bring Singapore through the storm. It had mastered a second test in achieving a smooth and seamless transition of political leadership through two generations without losing momentum.

Yet the republic's very success carried risks: lacking land, water or natural resources but wedded to a dynamic economy, which must forever expand and can never relax. The PAP leadership was aware of the dangers awaiting their "artificial", "unnatural" and "accidental" creation. Being one of globalization's greatest beneficiaries made it vulnerable to worldwide recession or environmental disaster which may be beyond its control. It meant increasing population in an overcrowded island and growing disparities between rich and poor, with the danger of creating a self-perpetuating élite and losing the social mobility that had been one of the corner-stones of Singapore's success throughout her history.

Creating what was in effect a national government and sidelining political rivals enabled efficient administration without the distraction of an opposition, but also created long-term problems of how to maintain touch with the electorate, how to keep the affluent, well-educated middle class contented, and how to ensure a continuous succession of intelligent, dedicated and incorrupt leaders. The republic had resisted the pitfalls of the welfare state without a rousing overt resistance, but it was doubtful whether Central Provident Fund provisions would be sufficient to support an increasingly ageing population.

At the time of independence in 1965 cosmopolitanism was seen as inimical to nation building. Singapore was standing alone, and the stress was on resilience, survival and what made Singapore special and different. Four decades later Singapore had become an integral part of the ASEAN region and a global city. Attitudes to history changed too, and it fitted in with modern priorities both to set Singapore in the region's longer history and to see it as part of the wider international world. In 1992, before the political debate began, Singapore historian Albert Lau suggested, "The fashioning of her "national" history ironically may be possible only by 'internationalising' it."[43]

At the other end of the scale, there was a call for "people's history". Museum exhibits were designed to attract active participation, and in 2006 a state-sponsored website was launched to encourage citizens to exchange information about their family's past, fitting in with a worldwide trend for ordinary people to explore their roots.

Yet Singapore remains unique in many ways and merits her own national history. The republic does not conform to social science models and rules. It has one of the world's most open and successful economies but a disciplined political system, it has a large prosperous, well-educated middle class which is not agitating for political change, it is dominated by one personality but without a personality cult.[44] It follows Westminster constitutional rules to the letter but contrasts in spirit with the original. It defies modern theories, encouraging and nurturing an élite and being prepared to accept inequalities of outcome. The liberal West decries modern Singapore as undemocratic, yet might find much that could be instructive for their own ailing democracies.

Time will tell whether Singapore becomes the prototype for a new type of nation state or whether this "artificial", "unnatural", "accidental" country is condemned by human frailty and the passage of time to fade into becoming a decaying Venice of the Orient.

1

The New Settlement
1819–1826

M odern Singapore dates from 30 January 1819, when the local chieftain, the Temenggong of Johor, signed a preliminary treaty with Sir Stamford Raffles, agent of the East India Company, permitting the British to set up a trading post. On the following day, camped on the banks of the Singapore River, with the Union Jack flying within the crumbling ramparts of old Singapura, Raffles wrote contentedly to his friend, the distinguished Orientalist William Marsden, "in the enjoyment of all the pleasure which a footing on such classic ground must inspire". Sentiment and romantic yearnings after vanished glories played a part in bringing Raffles to this particular spot, whose fascination was all the more tantalizing because the past was so obscure. In 1819 few physical remains survived of the flourishing fourteenth century port, and the very name "Singapura" was a paradox, for no lion had ever set foot in this "Lion City".

Evidence pieced together by late twentieth century archaeologists and historians showed that Temasek/Singapura was a prosperous regional port for much of the fourteenth century,[1] but by 1819 few traces of the old settlement remained. An earth wall, some 16 feet broad at the base and 8–9 feet high, stretched from the sea about a mile inland along the Bras Basah stream to Fort Canning Hill, which was then known as Bukit Larangan, or Forbidden Hill, because it was the reputed burial place of Singapura's kings. While no grave was identified, an outline of terraces and some ruins of good quality brick survived, together with remnants of pottery and old Chinese coins, and a century later, in 1926, some jewellery of Javanese Majapahit origin was unearthed nearby. The only other relic, a huge stone about 10 feet high and 9–10 feet long, inscribed supposedly in ancient Sumatran characters was found at the river's mouth. Badly worn by the tides, it was to be blown up in 1843 by the government engineer to make way for new construction, leaving only fragments which can be seen in the Singapore museum.

From time immemorial the seas and islands at the southern tip of the Malay Peninsula were a magnet for commerce, in the heart of a region rich in natural resources, astride the busy sea route that linked the Indian Ocean, the South China Sea and the Indonesian archipelago. Yet records relating to Singapore Island in ancient times are fragmentary. It may have been the Sabana of the second-century cartographer Ptolemy's Golden Khersonese.[2] It could be P'u Luo Chung, a Chinese rendering of the Malay Pulau Ujong, or "island at the end of the peninsula", mentioned briefly by a Chinese envoy, K'ang T'ai, in the third century. According to this hearsay account, the inhabitants were reputed to be primitive cannibals with tails 5 or 6 inches long.[3] Singapore also might be the island of Ma'it, recorded by Arab sailors in the ninth century.[4]

Arab writers in the thirteenth century spoke of the neighbouring islands "from which armed black pirates with poisoned arrows emerge, possessing armed warships",[5] but the first indisputable evidence of a settlement on the island dates from the fourteenth century. The Javanese *Nagarakretagama* of 1365 named a settlement called Temasek on Singapore Island, and the first eyewitness description came from a Chinese trader, Wang Dayuan, who travelled extensively in the southern seas over a period of twenty years in the first half of the fourteenth century.[6] Writing about the year 1349, Wang Dayuan recorded that there were some Chinese in Temasek, living and dressing in native style, but the island was infertile and unproductive, a place of dread for traders since "everything the inhabitants possess is a product of their plundering of Chinese junks". Wang Dayuan told how westbound ships were allowed to pass without hindrance, but on the homeward run junks put up padded screens as protection against arrows and prayed for fair winds to carry them safely through the Longyamen or Dragon's Teeth Strait (the modern Keppel Harbour) past the Danmaxi (Temasek) pirates, who lurked in wait with as many as 200 or 300 boats.

Temasek appears to have been one of a number of small ports that emerged in the Malay world in the fourteenth century in response to a shift in the pattern of commerce. The Nanyang (Southern Ocean) had long been a transshipment point for trade in luxuries between the Middle East, the Indian Ocean and China, but from the late thirteenth century a new trade in more mundane products began to flourish, in which local tropical produce from the Nanyang was exchanged for ceramics, textiles, metals and foodstuffs from southern China.[7] The discovery of high-quality Chinese porcelain remains and coins in recent excavations at Fort Canning indicate that fourteenth century Temasek was a prosperous town with a wealthy élite,[8] but it was also a period of danger and instability.

As the ancient Srivijaya Empire centred on Palembang loosened its hold over the seas, the local chieftains and island peoples living to the south of the Malay Peninsula broke away and degenerated into piracy, and Temasek was laid open to attack from the rival expanding empires of Majapahit and Thailand. Temasek survived at least one drawn-out Thai siege and repelled early Javanese onslaughts in the mid-fourteenth century, but by 1365 Majapahit claimed the island as a vassal state. In the last years of the century it was rent apart by internal turmoil and destroyed by external attack. The accounts of this most exciting and bloodstained chapter of Temasek's history are confusing. There were no Chinese travellers to record events, since at that time the first Ming emperor forbade his subjects to trade privately in the Nanyang. Sixteenth-century Portuguese historians wrote extensively about the area but pieced their stories together more than a century after Temasek/Singapura ceased to be important. And their evidence conflicts in some important respects with the seventeenth century *Sejarah Melayu*, or *Malay Annals*, the earliest, most colourful and vivid of Malay histories and the only one purporting to give a full account of Temasek/Singapura's past.

According to the *Malay Annals*, Raja Chulan, mighty warrior-king of India and descendant of Alexander the Great, encamped at Temasek on his way to conquer China. The Emperor of China tricked him by sending to Temasek a boat carrying a cargo of rusty needles and trees in full fruit, manned by a crew of senile, toothless men, who pretended that they had aged from lusty youths, that the needles had rusted from iron bars and that the trees had matured from seeds on the long voyage. So Raja Chulan, deceived into thinking China was far away, gave up his enterprise and married the daughter of the god of the sea.

The *Malay Annals* tell how a son of this marriage, Sang Utama, "the Highest", became ruler of Palembang, heart of the great Malay maritime empire of Srivijaya, and took the title of Sri Tri Buana. While touring the nearby islands, Sri Tri Buana saw the gleaming white shore of Temasek and determined to explore it, but a great storm blew up, forcing him to jettison everything, including his crown, to save his ship. Landing at Kuala Temasek, an estuary of the present Singapore River, Sri Tri Buana encountered a strange beast with a red body, a black head and a white breast, which he took to be a lion. This good omen induced the prince to found a settlement at Kuala Temasek, which he called Singapura or Lion City.

The *Malay Annals* go on to boast how, under the wise government of Sri Tri Buana and his four successors, Singapura blossomed into a great trading city to which foreigners resorted in great numbers. Singapura's wealth, according to the *Malay Annals*, attracted the envy of the Javanese empire of Majapahit. The city succeeded in repelling the first Javanese raid, but during a subsequent attack a treacherous minister opened the gates to the Javanese. Blood flowed "like a river in spate" and dyed the soil of the Singapore plain red forever. The ruler Iskander, fleeing into the jungle with his faithful followers, escaped to the mainland and, after wandering for several years, eventually founded a new and more fortunate settlement at Melaka, which became the centre of a great maritime empire.

The primary purpose of the *Malay Annals* was to legitimize the Malay rulers' claim to trace their supposed descent through Melaka and Temasek/Singapura back to the ancient ruling house of Srivijaya/Palembang. The stories are not mere contrived romantic fancy and contain a kernel of solid historical truth. According to Portuguese accounts, the last ruler of Temasek, Parameswara, was an ambitious and aggressive chieftain from Palembang. About the year 1390, after deciding to cast off allegiance to Majapahit, he mounted a lion throne and staged a religious ceremony of consecration as a god-king, symbolizing the revival of Palembang's former claims over the Srivijaya Empire. In anger, the Javanese drove Parameswara out of Palembang. He fled first to Bintang, where he mustered the support of neighbouring island chiefs, and was then granted asylum in Temasek. According to Portuguese accounts, Parameswara murdered his host and assumed command himself,[9] but the usurper's triumph was short-lived, and about the year 1398 he was driven from Temasek by the ruler of Patani, who was a vassal of the rising Thai state of Ayuthia. The parallel between the activities of Sri Tri Buana and Iskander/Parameswara is so close that it has been suggested that the genealogist who composed the opening chapters of the *Malay Annals* attributed to the mythical Sri Tri Buana the career of the factual Iskander and invented the tale of Temasek's five kings in order to gloss over three centuries of inglorious Palembang history. The period when any ruler of note held sway in Temasek appears to have been short, possibly from the early 1390s, when Iskander seized control, to 1398, when the Thais attacked the settlement.

The name "Singapura" came to replace "Temasek" about the end of the fourteenth century, but the origin of the name remains a mystery. Possibly Parameswara wished to signify that he was reestablishing the lion throne that he had set up in Palembang, symbolizing his claims to independence. This is a more convincing explanation than attempts to link the name with Singosari in Java or with a religious sect, adherents of early Majapahit Bhairava Buddhism, who were known as lions because of their wild orgies. Certainly it is less fanciful than the common suggestion that the island was overrun with tigers that early settlers mistook for lions.

Malay and Portuguese accounts agree that Iskander/ Parameswara, the last ruler of Temasek/Singapura and founder of Melaka, was driven out by violence and the town was destroyed about the end of the fourteenth century. Modern archaeological work confirms that the affluent Fort Canning settlement was abandoned at this time, but the unearthing of low-quality porcelain sherds and other mundane artifacts at the mouth of the Singapore River and at Kallang shows that utilitarian trade and a small-scale settlement survived much longer, and that the island was not completely deserted after Iskander's flight. Under the Melaka Sultanate it became the base of a senior vassal and provided the sultan with fighting ships. After the Portuguese seized Melaka in 1511, the Malay *laksamana*, or admiral, fled to Singapura, and when the sultan established his new capital on the Johor River, he kept a *shahbandar*, or harbour master, at Kallang, whose office appears on the Portuguese Manuel d'Eredia's Map of 1604.[10] The Johor Malays were in perpetual conflict with the Portuguese, and in 1603, in alliance with the Dutch, they seized a richly laden Portuguese ship off the east coast of Singapore. Ten years later the Portugese reported burning a Malay outpost at the mouth of the river,[11] and in the early 1620s a Flemish merchant, Jacques de Coutre, submitted a memorial to the King of Spain and Portugal[12] recommending that forts be erected in the Singapore Straits to counter mounting Dutch threats.[13] From that time the island faded from view, apart from providing a backdrop to a naval battle between Johor and Siak in the Singapore River in 1767.[14]

From the end of the fourteenth century Singapore played only a peripheral role in Malay politics. Its successor state, Melaka, was not only a great commercial port but a centre for the dissemination of Islam, legal codes and political organization throughout the region. Claiming allegiance from the whole Malay Peninsula, much of eastern Sumatra and the Riau-Lingga archipelago, the sultanate's influence extended to Brunei and Java through trade and royal marriage alliances.

When the Portuguese seized Melaka in 1511, the ruler fled to set up his court elsewhere, and Malay sultans ruled from various capitals on the Johor River for some two hundred years and subsequently from Riau and Lingga. The Johor-Riau-Lingga Empire never succeeded in reviving the golden age of Melaka's wealth and power, and its fortunes were precarious, but in peaceful times it attracted trade and recovered the allegiance of former vassal states. Throughout the sixteenth and early part of the seventeenth century, Johor suffered a dark age, when her settlements on the Johor River were repeatedly destroyed either by the Portuguese or by the warlike Achinese from North Sumatra. For some years the Johor Malays had no base, and the empire virtually disappeared, but after they allied with the Dutch to oust the Portuguese from Melaka in 1641, the Malays re-established their capital and continued to profit from co-operation with the Dutch East India Company. Johor enjoyed half a century of commercial prosperity, becoming a bustling port with a cosmopolitan population of Indonesian, Indian, Arab, Chinese and a few European traders, and regaining suzerainty over the southern part of the Malay Peninsula, the Riau-Lingga archipelago and states in East Sumatra.

The sultanate succumbed to internal troubles, starting in 1699, when the *bendahara* (chief minister) assumed the throne after the leading nobles assassinated the young, childless Sultan Mahmud, a cruel and unpredictable pervert. This blatant murder broke the final blood link with the old Srivijaya-Temasek-Melaka house, dispelling the mystical aura from which the Johor Sultanate had claimed its prestige. Many vassals broke away, feeling no ties of personal allegiance to the new ruler. The Johor River base was abandoned, and the capital moved to Riau, but the kingdom was soon overwhelmed by civil war, in which Bugis warrior chiefs from Sulawesi were called in to help but went on to seize effective power for themselves. Eventually in 1722 peace was restored, and a new sultan was installed, with real power being exerted by a series of strong Bugis under-kings. Mid-eighteenth century Riau attracted Asian and European traders, but this fragile prosperity was shattered in 1783, when the Bugis came into violent conflict with their Dutch allies, leading in the following year to a treaty by which the sultanate became a Dutch vassal and a Dutch Resident and garrison were installed in Riau.

During the French Revolutionary Wars, the British removed the Dutch garrison but did not occupy Riau, giving more scope for the sultan and under-king to reassert some of their authority, but the death of Sultan Mahmud in 1812 plunged the empire into a succession dispute. Mahmud had no sons by his two royal wives but had two sons by his other two wives, who came from prominent Bugis families but were not of royal blood. Neither commanded confidence either by birth or personal ability, but Hussein, the elder, appears to have been favoured by his father, and suitable marriages were arranged with daughters of the *bendahara* and the *temenggong* (chief of justice). Since Hussein was in Pahang to attend his wedding when his father died, the Bugis faction took advantage of his absence to acclaim his shy, retiring half-brother, Abdul Rahman, as Sultan. Hussein returned to live in obscurity while the Bugis under-king in Riau ruled in the name of Abdul Rahman, who held court in Lingga. However Sultan Mahmud's aristocratic widow refused to give up the regalia, so the essential formal installation ceremony could not be held.

By this time the senior Malay vassals had withdrawn to their fiefdoms: the *bendahara* to Pahang and the *temenggong* to Johor. Mainland Johor was very thinly peopled, and the most valued source of wealth and manpower in the *temenggong*'s domain lay in islands to the south and west – notably Singapore, the Karimuns, Bulang, Batam, Rempang, Galang and Timiang – which were inhabited by a mixture of seafaring people: Malays, Bugis and *orang laut* (sea people).[15]

The *orang laut* of the Riau-Lingga archipelago belonged to different tribes or *suku*. Living on boats, they led a nomadic existence as fishermen, petty traders and pirates and performed duties for Malay overlords according to their status. High-ranking *suku*, such as the fierce Orang Galang from the south of the archipelago, were organized into pirate armadas led by Malay war boats and were feared throughout the archipelago. Their fleets followed an annual pattern, raiding eastward along the north Java coast, then around South Java, Palembang, Bangka and neighbouring coasts. Chiefs supplied arms and provisions in exchange for a share of the plunder and, as one of the two main pirate chiefs owing allegiance to the sultan of Johor-Riau-Lingga, the *temenggong* was said to be able to muster 1,200 men in 50 ships from his *orang laut* tribes. In the early nineteenth century, Temenggong Abdur Rahman set up a village near the mouth of the Singapore River, with a small band of Malays and a following of *orang laut* from the Orang Gelam tribe who probably came over from Bulang Island.

෨෨

Despite the busy maritime activity in the area, Singapore Island at this time was a backwater, and the passage through Keppel Harbour, which had probably once been the major route between the Melaka Straits and the South China Sea, had long been abandoned. The maze of reefs, shoals and "broken islands" made the seas at the southern tip of the Malay Peninsula a treacherous hazard, and the natural dangers were often compounded by war and piracy. The Portuguese in particular, finding the narrow entrance to Keppel Harbour blockaded by the Johor Malays and their ships under attack by the Dutch, were forced to seek alternative routes. From the late sixteenth century their ships sometimes followed a tortuous "Route of the Conception of our Lady" through the Riau-Lingga archipelago, south of Bintan, Rempang, Galang and Batam islands. A more direct but still dangerous passage, which was discovered by accident to the south of the present-day Sentosa Island and named Governor's Strait in honour of the Spanish governor of the Philippines, who first sailed through it in 1616, became the main highway in modern times.[16] By the early nineteenth century, Westerners had forgotten the very existence of the Keppel passage and were describing the Tebrau (Johor) Strait between the northern coast of the island and the Johor coast as "The Old Straits of Singapore",[17] and "the only route of the first European navigators".[18] The area was left to *orang laut* known as Celates – *orang selat* or Straits people – who led a nomadic existence in the waters round Singapore, sometimes trading with passing ships in fish and fruit or lying in wait to plunder craft that got into difficulties in the treacherous shoals and shallows nearby.

The *temenggong*'s settlement on the Singapore River was a typical Malay-ruled, *orang laut* village, consisting of his substantial wooden house, surrounded by a few Malay huts, with large numbers of boats clustered in the river nearby. The Orang Gelam acted as boatmen for the *temenggong* and supplied him with fish.[19] Their piratical activities were restricted to pillaging helpless craft and slaughtering their crews, which gave Singapore something of a bad reputation. Other more reclusive people lived on the island: the Orang Seletar, who roamed the northern creeks along the present Johor Strait, and the Biduanda Orang Kallang, who had lived in the swamps at the mouth of the Kallang River as far back as their traditions went. These river peoples were boat dwellers but avoided the open sea. Shy, timid, shunning contact with other people, they subsisted on fish and produce gathered from the jungle.[20] A few Chinese lived near the village of the *temenggong* under the charge of their own headman or Kapitan China, while others grew gambier on the nearby hills.[21]

Altogether in January 1819 Singapore Island had perhaps 1,000 inhabitants, consisting of some 500 Orang Kallang, 200 Orang Seletar, 150 Orang Gelam, other *orang laut* in the Keppel Harbour area, 20–30 Malays in the *temenggong*'s entourage and a similar number of Chinese. The inhabitants grew fruit but no rice and depended for their livelihood on collecting jungle produce, fishing, small-scale trading and piracy. In 1818 the Singapore Straits was reputed to be one of the regular rendezvous spots for the main Galang pirate fleet on its annual raiding expeditions. Captured boats were sometimes brought to the Singapore River, where in 1810 a British man-of-war retook a pirated European ship.[22] But the island of Lingga was the fleet's main mart for selling plunder, and the modest Singapore village did not attract the large numbers of Chinese, Bugis and others who flocked to more flourishing centres to trade in slaves, arms and loot.

Temenggong Abdur Rahman, however, may well have had a major interest in the Galang pirate fleet. Energetic, resourceful and shrewd, he was quick to recognize opportunities for acquiring wealth and influence and to appreciate the new horizons of ambition and power opened up by the unexpected arrival in Singapore of Sir Stamford Raffles.

৯৯

Thomas Stamford Bingley Raffles was an official of the English East India Company, which had settlements in Benkulu in West Sumatra and in Penang. Britain's main interest in Southeast Asia was to deny bases to the French and to safeguard the East India Company's monopoly of the increasingly lucrative China trade. The Company acquired the island of Penang from the Sultan of Kedah in 1786 and the strip of land on the opposite coast (Province Wellesley) in 1800, and five years later it elevated Penang to the status of an Indian Presidency, with rather grandiose and unfulfilled plans to create a naval base. During the French Revolutionary and Napoleonic wars the Company took temporary possession of Dutch colonies in the East, including Melaka and Java, and removed the Dutch Resident and garrison from Riau. Neither the British government nor the East India Company wished to extend their commitments in Southeast Asia, and in 1814, as war in Europe was drawing to a close, Britain and the Netherlands signed a convention which agreed to the restoration of Dutch overseas possessions, including Java and Melaka. In the interest of promoting harmony and co-operation between them in Europe, the two countries opened negotiations to remove all the long-standing sources of contention in the East. These included proposals to separate territorial interests in which Benkulu and possibly Penang would be exchanged for the remaining Dutch territories in India.

Private British merchants, who had expanded their commercial activities during the wartime disruption of Dutch rule, feared that the restored regime would revert to its traditional attempts to secure a stranglehold on regional trade by imposing punitive protective tariffs and forcing local rulers into exclusive commercial agreements. The rendition of Dutch territories was also a bitter disappointment to the East India Company officials on the spot, such as Major William Farquhar, British Resident of wartime Melaka, and Raffles, Lieutenant-Governor of occupied Java, who was the most inveterate opponent of Dutch restrictive policies.

Born in 1781, Raffles left school at the age of fourteen to join the East India Company in London as a clerk. In 1805 he was sent as Assistant Secretary to the newly formed Penang presidency. Despite the wealth of literature about Raffles, he remains an enigma, a man of fascinating contradictions. A frail, diffident youth, "meek as a maiden" in his own description, he nursed vast ambitions for himself and his country. His lack of formal education gave him an insatiable appetite for learning, and he was assiduous in studying the language, literature, history, flora and fauna of the Malay world. Coming from a background of genteel poverty, he revelled in the company of the rich, the powerful and the aristocratic. A man of deep friendships, magnanimous and generous, with a passion for liberty, he could still be capable of petty meanness and deceit in his dealings with subordinates and colleagues and of gullible favouritism in advancing the fortunes of relatives and friends. Above all, he was a man for whom life was a perpetual challenge and who acted with courage and resilience in face of the many disappointments and disasters which overtook him.

Raffles's personal ambitions and his concern to boost British trade were backed by a sense of messianic mission. He did not seek territorial aggrandizement for Britain but rather a blend of commercial and moral pre-eminence. Fascinated by the romance of faded civilizations, he saw his country's role in Southeast Asia as a crusade to free the peoples of the eastern archipelago from civil war, piracy, slavery and oppression, and to restore and revive their old cultures and independence under the influence of European enlightenment, liberal education, progressive economic prosperity, and just laws. He wished to use the wartime occupation as an opportunity to supplant the influence of the Dutch, whose ways of government and commercial monopoly he regarded as "contrary to all principles of natural justice and unworthy of any enlightened and civilized nation".

Appointed Lieutenant-Governor when the East India Company occupied Java in 1811, Raffles set out to reform the Dutch system. Like many dreamers who look beyond their own age, he was an impractical administrator. Modernizing the traditional Javanese agricultural economy resulted in a substantial loss of revenue, and, after selling off colonial lands, he was recalled to England under a cloud. On a personal level the visit was a great success: his two-volume *History of Java* was hailed with critical acclaim, he was elected a Fellow of the Royal Society, received at court, knighted by the Prince Regent, and acquired a wife, Sophia, who was to show him utter devotion in life and death.

The Company Directors absolved him from acting dishonourably and appointed him Lieutenant-Governor of Benkulen, but the British government's decision to return the Dutch possessions shattered Raffles's dream of using Java as a base to extend British influence throughout the Indies. Before he left England in 1817 he submitted a paper on "Our Interests in the Eastern Archipelago", urging the India Board of Control to establish a chain of stations in Aceh, West Sumatra, the Sunda Straits, the Riau archipelago and West Borneo, which would protect the Company's China trade and develop British commerce with the archipelago. The paper was ignored.

On his arrival at Benkulen in 1818, Raffles was appalled at what he saw as the expansion of Dutch influence in Sumatra and warned the Company's Directors, "The Dutch possess the only passes through which ships must sail into the Archipelago, the Straits of Sunda and Malacca; and the British have now not an inch of ground to stand upon between the Cape of Good Hope and China, nor a single friendly port at which they can water and obtain refreshment."

The British government repudiated Raffles's attempts to thwart Dutch expansion in South Sumatra, but Lord Hastings, the Governor-General of India, permitted him to visit Calcutta in 1818 and outline his ideas. Raffles failed to win Hastings over to his ambitious plans for diffusing British influence throughout Sumatra, but the Governor-General approved a more limited project for protecting Britain's trade route through the Straits of Melaka. Hastings appointed Raffles as Agent and commissioned him to secure an agreement with Aceh at the northern end and establish a post at Riau, Johor, or some other point at the southern end of the Straits, provided he did not bring the Company into conflict with the Dutch.

For this purpose Raffles was authorized to enlist the services of Major William Farquhar, who was preparing to return to Britain on long leave after nearly thirty years of service in the East. As an old friend, with long Malayan experience and an intimate knowledge of Riau-Lingga politics, Farquhar enjoyed Raffles's complete trust. He had joined the Madras Engineers in 1791 at the age of seventeen and took part in the 1795 expedition to seize Melaka, where he was to serve throughout most of the British occupation. Farquhar first met Raffles in Melaka in 1807 and later helped him prepare for the 1811 invasion of Java and fought in that campaign. He regretted having to hand Melaka back to the Dutch and shared Raffles's alarm at the vulnerability of the British position in Southeast Asia following the return of the other Dutch possessions. In October 1816 Farquhar advised the Penang government to form a new British settlement near the entrance to the Straits of Singapore, and in 1818 the newly appointed Governor of Penang, James Bannerman, commissioned him to make commercial treaties with Riau and other states to safeguard British trade against the revival of Dutch privileges. On 19 August 1818 Farquhar and the Bugis under-king Raja Ja'afar, acting on behalf of Sultan Abdul Rahman, signed a treaty in which Riau accorded the British most favoured nation status and undertook not to renew "any obsolete and interrupted treaties with other nations" nor grant any monopolies. After signing a similar treaty with Siak, Farquhar returned to Melaka in September 1818 to find the Dutch Commissioners waiting to take over. On learning that the Dutch planned to revive their position in Riau, Farquhar warned Calcutta and Raffles and sought permission from the Bugis under-king to survey the Karimun islands, which he considered strategically to be "a complete key to the Straits of Singapore".[23]

The Government of India's original instructions to Raffles, which were issued on 28 November 1818 and probably were drafted by him, favoured siting the new post at Riau, as an established port with a settled population and a friendly government. Provided the Dutch had not returned to Riau, Raffles was authorized to set up a station there and leave Farquhar in charge, but otherwise he was to "abstain from all negotiation and collision".[24] Supplementary instructions, issued a week later in face of rumours about Dutch activities, envisaged alternative arrangements with Johor if Riau proved impractical. But the Government of India insisted on caution, since it knew so little about the geography or politics of Johor and its relationship with the Dutch.[25]

Raffles reached Penang on 30 December 1818, to find that Farquhar had arrived the previous day, bringing news of the Dutch treaty with Riau, which made Raffles even more eager to press on with his plans. After collecting as much information as he could about the situation at the southern end of the Melaka Straits, on 16 January 1819 he assured Calcutta that, despite not being entirely clear about the situation in Johor, he was confident they could obtain the consent of a "competent authority" to set up an alternative post near the Johor River. This was "reputedly capacious and easy to defend", while Singapore in particular "seems in every respect most peculiarly adapted for our object".[26]

While Raffles was to remain in Penang to undertake the mission to Aceh, he instructed Farquhar to set sail at once for the Karimuns to link up with two survey ships, which had been sent to inspect the islands. Farquhar was forbidden to make a settlement there without further instructions, however favourable the surveyors' report, and he was then to proceed eastward to inspect Singapore and her environs. If the island was deemed suitable and no Dutchmen were there, Farquhar was then to go on to Riau, to "make such arrangements for securing to us the eventual Command of that important Station as circumstances … may dictate". In Riau Farquhar was commissioned to find out the state of the Johor Empire and its relations with the Dutch, how far it had been dismembered, "and in what degree its ancient capital [i.e., Singapura] may be considered under the immediate authority of its local Chief".[27]

On 18 January Farquhar set sail in the brig *Ganges*, together with a further survey vessel, an armed ship and a detachment of European artillerymen and Indian sepoys. Immediately after Farquhar had departed, Bannerman insisted that Raffles defer his Aceh expedition pending further reference to Calcutta, leaving him convinced that the Governor had deliberately schemed to prevent him from taking part in the expedition. To Bannerman's annoyance, Raffles seized the opportunity to slip out of Penang before daybreak aboard the *Indiana*, sailing with the schooner *Enterprize*, and hurry south.

On 26 January Farquhar met the survey ships off the Karimuns as arranged, and the next day they explored the terrain. Late that evening Raffles arrived to find Farquhar still enthusiastic but the rest of the party very glum about the prospects of the rocky, inhospitable, uninhabited islands. Daniel Ross,[28] commander of the East India Company's survey ship *Discovery*, then drew attention to a promising site at the mouth of the Singapore

River, which he had recently observed in passing, and the little fleet set off early on the morning of 28 January. When they anchored off St. John's Island that afternoon, messengers sent out by the *temenggong* brought the welcome news that there were no Dutchmen in Singapore, and Raffles and Farquhar went ashore that evening to meet the chief.[29] The following day they continued their talks and were fully briefed on the *temenggong*'s version of the Malay succession dispute, which favoured the claim of the elder rival, his son-in-law, Hussein. On 30 January 1819 a preliminary agreement was signed by Raffles and Temenggong Abdur Rahman, "in his own name and in the name of Sree Sultan Hussein Mahummud Shah, Rajah of Johore", permitting the East India Company to establish a factory in return for an annual payment of $3,000 to the *temenggong*.

While Farquhar was dispatched immediately in style with two ships and a party of forty European soldiers and sailors to seek the Bugis under-king's consent to the Singapore settlement, two of Hussein's kinsmen, who were living in the *temenggong*'s entourage, were sent to bring Hussein to Singapore.[30] Meanwhile, after landing the troops and erecting tents, Raffles made a half-hearted foray eastward but quickly gave up any attempt to look at the Johor River or Johor Lama.[31] Back in Singapore he began surveying the harbour and possible defence positions. The site seemed ideal. While the southwestern bank of the river was swampy, the ground on the northeastern side was level and firm. There was an abundance of drinking water, and the river mouth formed a natural sheltered harbour. Singapore was conveniently placed as a centre for trade with the eastern archipelago and only a few miles from the main sea route through the Straits to China.

Farquhar met with the expected rebuff in Riau, but Hussein came to Singapore, rather frightened and suspicious at this turn in his fortunes. On 6 February, Raffles signed a formal treaty with the *temenggong* and "His Highness the Sultan Hussein Mahomed Shah Sultan of Johore", confirming the East India Company's right to establish a post, subject to annual payments of $5,000 to Sultan

Hussein and $3,000 to the *temenggong*. The formalities were carried out with as fine a ceremony as circumstances permitted. The day was auspiciously clear and sunny, and Chinese planters arrived from the country to join the throng of Malay and *orang laut* spectators. Malay dignitaries came in their finery, British officials and soldiers were smartly turned out, the ships were dressed overall for the occasion, speeches were read, the treaty was formally signed and sealed, guns fired salutes and presents were exchanged. Raffles departed the following day, leaving Farquhar as Resident and Commandant, with responsibility to himself as Lieutenant-Governor of Benkulen, and Farquhar's son-in-law, Francis Bernard, was appointed Master Attendant.

২৯

Raffles was delighted with the foundation of Singapore. "It breaks the spell," he wrote from Penang on 19 February 1819, "and they (the Dutch) are no longer the exclusive sovereigns of the eastern seas." "This will probably be my last attempt," he wrote to Marsden from Singapore the day after his landing. "If I am deserted now, I must fain return to Bencoolen and become philosopher." As he feared, Dutch opposition and bitter hostility from the Company's administration in Penang combined to threaten Singapore's very existence. The infant settlement's survival was little short of a miracle, the result of courage and grit on the spot, slow communications, and a large measure of luck. Astrologers claim that modern Singapore was born under a lucky star. She needed good fortune in February 1819.

The *temenggong* and Sultan Hussein fully anticipated angry reactions from the rival faction. After shocking Raffles by suggesting the British should murder the Dutch in Riau, Hussein set out to safeguard his position. The new sultan wrote to his half-brother, Abdul Rahman and to the Bugis under-king, while the *temenggong* also wrote to the Riau authorities and to Dutch friends in Melaka, claiming that Raffles had intimidated them into making the agreement. The Dutch were furious, arguing

Singapore was part of Riau's territories and thus under their control. The Dutch Governor of Melaka protested to Penang and contemplated driving the British out of Singapore. Prompt military action would have easily ousted Farquhar's party, which comprised only thirty European military officers and civilians, with a hundred discontented Indian sepoys and one barely seaworthy gunboat. In face of rumours of an impending attack from Melaka, Farquhar appealed urgently to Penang for reinforcements, but the unsympathetic Bannerman urged him to evacuate Singapore to avoid any embarrassing clash and assured the Dutch that Raffles had acted on his own initiative at Singapore. Appealing to Calcutta, Bannerman criticized Raffles's impetuous behaviour and his apparent irresponsibility in leaving his new settlement almost defenceless, acting "like a man who sets a house on fire and then runs away".

The Dutch had good reason to believe that the British would repudiate Raffles's venture. In January 1819, on the day before Raffles dropped anchor off Singapore, the India Board of Control in London had dispatched instructions to Calcutta forbidding his mission to the East. At the same time the British Foreign Office had assured the Dutch government that Raffles was only the Company's commercial representative with no authority to make any political arrangements.

These instructions were issued too late to stop Raffles, but Godert van der Capellen, Governor-General of the Netherlands Indies, expected that Calcutta would immediately disavow Raffles's action without even needing to refer to London. Armed with Bannerman's assurances and with the claims from Hussein and the *temenggong* that they had acted under duress, van der Capellen couched his protest in moderate terms. By that time, however, Raffles's action had caused a stir in Calcutta. In March 1819 the *Calcutta Journal* welcomed the establishment at Singapore "as a fulcrum for the support of our commercial views and speculations". Bannerman unwittingly helped to ensure the survival of Singapore not only by lulling Dutch suspicions but also by aggravating the Governor-General of India into giving Raffles his support. While Hastings was irritated when Raffles carried on with his plans despite finding the Dutch had returned to Riau, he was even more angry at Bannerman's imputation against his authority and anxious to justify his own position in the face of any reprimands from London. Raffles's despatch to Calcutta, written on 13 February 1819, explaining his decision to establish a station at Singapore, lauded the superiority of this "ancient capital" over Riau or any other spot. It was easy to demonstrate its ideal location, so close to the main shipping route through the Straits of Singapore, but justifying the legality of the transaction required a masterly spin. Glossing over the awkward fact that Farquhar's Riau treaty had implicitly recognized Abdul Rahman as sultan, Raffles claimed that as "Raja of Riau" Abdul Rahman held authority only over his immediate territory, whereas Hussein was the rightful sultan, and the *temenggong* enjoyed undisputed possession of Johor, Singapore and the other islands.

The Governor-General assured Raffles, "The selection of Singapore for a post is considered as to locality to have been highly judicious," and he agreed provisionally to the arrangement pending London's approval. Meanwhile Hastings reproached Bannerman and ordered him to give every assistance to Singapore. Grudgingly, Bannerman sent 200 troops and some money to Farquhar, who had also succeeded in intercepting and diverting to Singapore 500 Indian troops returning from Benkulen to India. Farquhar's courage brought Singapore through her first crisis, and the Dutch lost the opportunity to destroy the vulnerable settlement, whose future would now be determined not by military force but by the outcome of a paper war between London and The Hague.

The news of Raffles's action in Singapore, which reached London in August 1819, came as an unpleasant shock to the Directors of the East India Company, who feared his action would jeopardize the success of the entire Anglo-Dutch negotiations in Europe. "If the Dutch should forcibly expel our garrison at Singapore we must either submit in silence or demand reparation at hazard of war which may involve all Europe." Despite this, Lord Castlereagh, the British Foreign Secretary, saw the commercial and strategic danger of leaving the Dutch "all the military and naval keys of the Straits of Malacca" and recognized the value of a British station to the south. While the British government would have preferred a less controversial post, no other site offered the same advantages. The British legal claim to Singapore was weak, but the island's potential attractions induced the British government to play for time by adding the question to the subjects already under discussion with The Hague. For the time being the negotiations were suspended, awaiting a full report from the Governor-General of India, which Hastings never supplied. The delay did not worry Raffles: the longer the negotiations dragged on, the stronger would be the case for keeping Singapore.

∽

Raffles left Farquhar with instructions to clear the ground, put up simple defence works, post a responsible European on St. John's Island to inform passing ships about the new settlement, and encourage trade by imposing no tariffs for the time being. He sent messages to Melaka seeking settlers and supplies. Attracted by the considerable profits to be made from selling foodstuffs and other necessities at inflated prices, many Melaka traders were prepared to defy a Dutch ban, and settlers were drawn by Farquhar's record as their wartime Resident. Popularly known as "Rajah of Malacca", he had taken a local mistress and spoke fluent Malay. A tall, soldierly figure, Farquhar commanded respect but was humane and kindly, always accessible and ready to hear complaints and judge disputes. He enjoyed a reputation for being honest, fair, and impartial to rich and poor alike.

The plain on the northeastern bank of the river was cleared and soon boasted a flourishing bazaar and a cantonment of temporary huts. The regular supplies from Melaka saved Singapore from the customary privations and malnutrition suffered by pioneer settlements. Within six weeks more than a hundred small Indonesian craft were anchored in the harbour, in addition to two European merchant ships and a Siamese junk.

When Raffles returned at the end of May 1819, bringing immigrants from Penang and welcome supplies of timber, tiles, and implements, he was thrilled with the settlement's progress. "My new Colony thrives most rapidly", he wrote to the Duchess of Somerset, adding with pardonable exaggeration, "We have not been established four months and it has received an accession of population exceeding five thousand, principally Chinese, and their number is daily increasing." To another correspondent, he wrote enthusiastically that Singapore "bids fair to be the next port to Calcutta … this is by far the most important station in the East; and, as far as naval superiority and commercial interests are concerned, of much higher value than whole continents of territory".

Raffles spent four weeks in Singapore on this second visit. He made a further agreement with Sultan Hussein and the *temenggong* in June 1819, defining the boundaries of the British settlement, which were to stretch from Tanjong Malang on the west to Tanjong Katong on the east and inland as far as the range of a cannon shot. His plan for the town was designed partly for aesthetic effect but primarily to ensure order and control by grouping the different communities in specified areas under their own headmen. Apart from the *temenggong*'s village, the left bank of the river and the plain were to be reserved for the military cantonment and official quarter, together with the land on the opposite bank at the river mouth. The European quarter was to be laid out east of the cantonment, the Chinese were to settle on the right bank of the river, and Farquhar was ordered to build a bridge to link the Chinese district with the Malay village and the cantonment.

The two Malay chiefs had authority over their own followers, while other Asians were put under the jurisdiction of their own *kapitan*, who would keep the peace and settle disputes among their own community. In conjunction with the sultan and *temenggong*, Farquhar held court once a week, when the *kapitan* presented grievances and reports, and their people could appeal against their judgments. The Resident made final decisions according to common sense.

༄

Raffles left Singapore for Benkulen in June 1819 and did not return for more than three years, a period when Singapore was largely left to fend for herself because communications were so poor. In March 1820, for instance, Farquhar complained to Raffles that he had heard nothing from Calcutta for nearly seven weeks and nothing from Benkulen for nearly three months.

Singapore's trade expanded rapidly. From Benkulen Raffles wrote to his cousin in July 1820, "My settlement continues to thrive most wonderfully; it is all and everything I could wish and if no untimely fate awaits it, promises to become the emporium and the pride of the East." To strengthen the case for retaining Singapore, he painted her successes in glowing colours to correspondents in England. There was no need to exaggerate her achievements because Singapore's convenient location and comparative orderliness contributed to her early success. The main reason for her spectacular growth was that she offered a unique outlet, free of tariffs, to an already well-developed regional trade. In addition to the ban on customs duties, port charges were kept to a minimum. The sultan and *temenggong* at first put pressure on *nakodah* (or ships' captains) to present them with "gifts", but in April 1820 the Master Attendant was instructed to impress on shipmasters that they were not obliged to offer any presents to the Malay chiefs.

Nevertheless in the early days the presence of Hussein and the *temenggong* were crucial to attracting trade. Hitherto Riau had been the headquarters for South Sumatra and Bugis trade and a prosperous centre of Chinese gambier production, but very quickly the bulk of this flourishing commerce was diverted to Singapore. The new port also drew junks from Siam, Cambodia, and Cochin-China, and Western shipping from India. The first

Amoy junk arrived in February 1821 and the first China trade vessel from Europe five months later. In the first two and a half years nearly 3,000 vessels came to Singapore. In that time, the import and export trade totalled $8 million, of which $5 million was carried in Asian craft and $3 million in European ships. Private merchants demonstrated their faith in Singapore at a time when her future was still doubtful to the British government.

Farquhar encouraged all comers to settle and by 1821 the cosmopolitan town had about 5,000 inhabitants, of whom nearly 3,000 were Malays, more than 1,000 Chinese, and 500 or 600 were Bugis, together with Indians, Arabs, Armenians, Europeans, Eurasians, and other minority groups. The Malay chiefs' new-found fortunes attracted a throng of followers, who settled in the *temenggong*'s village on the river or around the sultan's *istana* (palace) at Kampong Glam to the east of the town. Soon after the founding of the settlement Hussein brought his whole family and entourage over from Riau in hundreds of boats. Other Malays came in a steady influx from Melaka, the Riau islands and Sumatra, including Benkulen men, who built Kampong Benkulen on the Bras Basah stream.

Singapore was particularly attractive to the Nanyang Chinese, who for many years had operated a network of commerce in Riau, Melaka, Penang, Bangkok, Manila, Batavia and other Javanese ports and had settled throughout the region as traders, farmers and miners. The Chinese had no support from their own government, which officially prohibited emigration or private overseas trading, but they congregated where conditions were favourable. None of the earlier centres in the Nanyang was ideal. Penang was geographically inconvenient, and elsewhere alien traders were subject to heavy duties, erratic laws, irksome restrictions and extortion. The attractions of Singapore as the natural centre for Southeast Asian trade were immediately obvious to established Chinese, who moved there from other ports in the Nanyang. The first Chinese immigrants came from Riau and Melaka, many of them from long-settled families, who had inter-married with Malay women to form a distinct Baba Chinese community.

The most important Chinese pioneer was Tan Che Sang, who left his native Canton in 1778 at the age of fifteen, made his fortune in Riau, Penang and Melaka, and came to Singapore in 1819, where he built the first warehouse and was agent for the early Chinese junks. Known to Farquhar from his Melaka days, Tan Che Sang encouraged Chinese immigration by standing surety for newcomers who wanted to obtain goods on credit. When he died in Singapore in 1836, a huge crowd, said to be between 10,000 and 15,000, attended his funeral. But he had no social contact with the ruling community and was a strange withdrawn man, an inveterate gambler, obsessed with making money, and reputed to sleep with his money chests in his bedroom.

The Hokkien Choa Chong Long was the only Chinese who could rival Tan Che Sang's wealth in the early days of Singapore. Born in Dutch Melaka, where his father was the Kapitan China, Choa became head of the Hokkien *pang*, or guild, in Singapore and the first opium revenue farmer. In contrast to Tan Che Sang, Choa was an open-handed extrovert who entertained Europeans lavishly, such as the banquet that he staged in 1831 to celebrate his forty-fourth birthday. He was the government's most trusted go-between with the Chinese community until he left Singapore for China in 1836, but he was murdered by burglars in Macau.

Most of the influential early Asian settlers were already prosperous men when they arrived and did not fit the popular "rags to riches" success stories of penniless youths rising by hard work and acumen to wealth and eminence. The Hokkien Tan Tock Seng was an exception. Born in Melaka, he came to Singapore as a vegetable hawker in 1819 at the age of twenty-one and became one of the richest merchants.

For many years Bugis traders, who dominated the commerce of the eastern islands of the archipelago, had flocked to Riau, where their countrymen were strongly entrenched politically. The re-imposition of Dutch control in Riau threatened the Bugis' position and sparked off armed clashes in February 1820, after which 500 Bugis fled to Singapore with their chieftain, Arong Bilawa. The first appearance on the horizon of the fierce, warlike

Bugis fleet terrified the inhabitants of Singapore, who were relieved to find they came as settlers, bringing their women and children. This was the largest single body of immigrants, and the Resident was delighted to welcome a balanced community of families who would attract the prized Bugis trade. He refused to hand Arong Bilawa over to the Dutch envoy who demanded his extradition, and instead granted him asylum in Singapore, where the Bugis built their kampong on the Rochore River. The Dutch later permitted Arong Bilawa to return to Riau, but many Bugis remained in Singapore, which soon became the headquarters of Bugis trade in the western archipelago.

Most Indians in early Singapore were soldiers or camp followers, but there were also a few merchants, drawn mainly from Penang's large Indian mercantile community. The most notable was Naraina Pillai, who accompanied Raffles on his second visit to Singapore in May 1819. Pillai started a brick kiln, became Singapore's first building contractor and opened a shop for cotton piece goods. When he went bankrupt after the shop burned down in 1822, Raffles helped him restore his fortune.

Armenians were well-established in trade in Brunei and the Philippines, and an Armenian merchant, Aristarchus Moses, settled in Singapore in 1820. He was the first of a small but wealthy minority.

Raffles hoped Singapore would attract a large community of Arabs, who had played an important role in Southeast Asian trade for more than a thousand years. By the eighteenth century Arabs had begun to settle in various parts of Sumatra and Borneo,[32] and the first to arrive in Singapore in 1819 were two wealthy Palembang merchants, Syed Mohammed bin Harun Al-Junied and his nephew, Syed Omar bin Ali Al-Junied. They settled at Kampong Glam, where Syed Mohammed died a very rich man in 1824, and Omar lived on till 1852 as leader of the Arab community.

Apart from the East India Company officials, few European settlers came to Singapore during the earliest years, despite Calcutta turning a blind eye to the Company's normal ruling that private European residents needed licences to settle in its territories. Westerners were deterred by uncertainty as to whether Singapore would be retained as a permanent British possession and the consequent difficulties about buying land. Most of the earliest Europeans were former merchant navy men or agents of Calcutta firms. Scotsman Alexander Laurie Johnston, a former ship's owner/captain, who settled in July 1820 and established the firm of A.L. Johnston & Company, remained the doyen of the European merchants until his retirement from the East in 1841. Another Scot, Alexander Guthrie, founder of the oldest Singapore firm to survive into the twenty-first century, arrived from the Cape of Good Hope in January 1821. That same year, James Pearl, who was captain of the *Indiana* which first brought Raffles to Singapore and had subsequently made a good profit trading in and out of the port, decided to settle in Singapore. He bought up Chinese gambier plantations and built a fine country house on the hill that still bears his name. In 1822 John Purvis, a former partner of John Matheson in Canton, left China to found his own firm in Singapore.

Raffles ordered Farquhar to keep expenses to a minimum, and he had to administer the rapidly expanding settlement on a shoe-string budget, spending less on salaries in a year than Benkulen did in a month. Initially Farquhar had an Assistant Resident, but in 1820 Calcutta cut his establishment to one clerk, and by 1822 he was forced to employ two extra clerks at his own expense. The Resident had few means of raising revenue, since he was forbidden to levy trade dues and could not sell permanent land titles. In May 1820 he imposed small port clearance charges to cover the cost of the Master Attendant's establishment. Four months later, defying Raffles's instructions, he introduced a tax-farming system, auctioning monopoly rights to sell opium and *arrack* (Asian spirits), and to run gambling dens.

With this revenue, Farquhar embarked on a public works programme that was very ambitious in view of Singapore's precarious legal position but helped to boost confidence in her future. In January 1820 Calcutta had warned Farquhar not to encourage Asian immigration, since Singapore was still a temporary military post, and rumours that the Company might abandon the settlement led the sultan, the *temenggong*, and the *kapitan* to call on Farquhar to confirm that the British intended to stay and would defend them. Reassured by the subsequent flurry of public building, Chinese and European merchants began to seek land for godowns. This posed new problems, since Raffles had left no instructions about land grants, and Farquhar felt no permanent allocation could be made until the British title was settled. Moreover, he held the view that the East India Company was a mere tenant in Singapore and could not alienate the Malay chiefs' land by granting permanent titles to settlers. To complicate matters, shallow water and sandbanks made it impossible to land goods on East Beach, which Raffles had set aside as the European commercial quarter. The merchants complained it was not worth the expense of developing sites there, and Alexander Guthrie threatened to quit Singapore unless he was given more suitable land.

Farquhar referred the matter to Benkulen in April 1821 but received no reply until eleven months later, when Raffles prohibited erecting substantial buildings. When merchants insisted on putting up brick warehouses to protect their goods against fire, Farquhar gave Guthrie and others provisional grants of land on the firm north bank of the river but warned that they went there at their own risk and might have to move later.

In June 1820 Farquhar referred to Raffles a request by the sultan and *temenggong* for permission to levy a fee on property accumulated by Chinese when they left to return home to China. No reply had been received when, eight months later, Sultan Hussein arrested the *nakodah* of the first Amoy junk to arrive in Singapore and put him in the stocks, allegedly for not giving a sufficiently expensive present. Farquhar ordered the *nakodah's* release but was angry when a group of leading European merchants presented a letter of protest to Hussein, demanding an apology and a promise not to repeat such demands. Farquhar considered this protest "an improper, premature and very unnecessary interference", but the merchants argued there was such a thin line of demarcation between courtesy presents and trade dues that news of such demands and the ill treatment of *nakodah* might frighten away the Chinese junk trade. Once more Farquhar appealed in vain to Raffles for a definite ruling on presents and on fees.

These practical problems highlighted the legal ambiguity of the Malay chiefs' position. In making the initial bargain with Raffles, the *temenggong* was not only attracted by the immediate offer of money but envisaged a settlement patterned on earlier trade centres in the region, where a Malay hierarchy would preside over a cosmopolitan trading community, leasing land, judging lawsuits, and exacting dues. With his long experience of the region, Farquhar was prepared to accept this situation. He insisted the Malay chiefs should be accorded respect and recognized as lords of the soil. The Resident also admitted the judicial authority of the *temenggong* and sultan, and in place of the trade levies, which were the customary due of chiefs, from May 1820 he paid them an allowance out of the taxes to cover their assistance in police and judicial duties.

A pioneer town of rootless immigrants, early Singapore was notoriously lawless, and there was little money to provide a police force. In May 1820 Farquhar established the first regular force, headed by his son-in-law, Francis Bernard, as superintendent, with one constable, one jailer, one writer, one tindal, and eight peons, at a total monthly cost of 300 Spanish dollars. In 1821 the leading European and Asian merchants agreed to contribute $54 a month as a night-watch fund to provide for an extra constable and nine peons. The Chinese and Malay immigrants from Melaka were a peaceable community, who went unarmed, but the troublesome followers of the *temenggong* and the sultan preyed upon them "like tigers towards goats".[33] Stabbings and robberies in broad daylight were commonplace, and many people were murdered on the path to Kampong Glam.

⧜

For more than three years Singapore developed on her own under Farquhar's guidance. While Raffles welcomed the reports of rapid expansion, at that time the settlement played only a minor role in his ambitions. His loftier aspiration was to gather under his control all the Company's possessions in Southeast Asia – Penang, Province Wellesley, Singapore and Benkulen – and ultimately to become Governor-General of India and a peer of the realm. Bannerman's sudden death late in 1819 sent Raffles hurrying to Calcutta to push his claims but without success. While Hastings agreed in principle that it would be beneficial to put all the Company's eastern possessions under one authority, he deferred any such decision pending the settlement of the protracted Anglo-Dutch negotiations in London.

Raffles returned to Sumatra depressed and empty handed but soon threw off his dejection in an attempt to make Benkulen a model colony and the centre for new enterprise. Excited by travels in the remote interior, he dreamed of reviving the ancient glories of the Menangkabau Empire and simultaneously extending British influence throughout Sumatra. This was probably the most contented period of his life, experiencing years of domestic happiness, when, delighting in the company of an adoring wife and talented children, he could indulge his fascination in natural history and the romantic past in a new imperial dream.

The idyll was shattered by a series of cruel disasters. In six months, between July 1821 and January 1822, three of his four children, several relatives and close friends, all died in Benkulen, while Raffles and his wife fell seriously ill. Crushed, dispirited and numbed, his personal happiness destroyed, his career an apparent futile waste, Raffles abandoned his dreams for the resurrection of Sumatra. Prematurely aged, "a little old man, all yellow and shrivelled', as he described himself, he decided to turn his back on the accursed Benkulen and the East.

Before his retirement he arranged to pay a last visit to settle the administration of Singapore but, immediately on landing in October 1822, the bustle, cheerfulness and sense of purpose jolted Raffles out of his depression and gloom. Perhaps the greatest of Raffles's qualities was his resilience to misfortune and defeat, his ability to create new ideas out of shattered dreams and to snatch triumph out of apparent failure. Now he narrowed his horizons from reviving the ancient glories of Sumatra and Java to achieving perfection in this one small place. "It is here that I think I may have done some little good, and instead of frittering away the stock of zeal and means that may yet be left me in objects for which I may not be fitted. I am anxious to do all the good I can here, where experience has proved to me that my labours will not be thrown away." As his wife commented, "Sir Stamford's heart again expanded with the hope of happiness and rejoiced in the consciousness of possessing the power of diffusing civilization and blessings around him." Despite bouts of sickness and blinding headaches leaving him prostrate for weeks on end, it was Raffles's sense of mission and the imaginative and enlightened measures taken during his last eight months in Singapore which largely determined the future character of the settlement.

In June 1819 Raffles had written of Singapore, "It ... is a child of my own and I have made it what it is." Now this feeling of proud paternalism surged up again even more strongly. "I feel a new life and vigour [in seeing] this my almost only child", he confided to a friend in England on the day after he returned to Singapore, and he wrote to the Duchess of Somerset enthusiastically the following month, "Here all is life and activity; and it would be difficult to name a place on the face of the globe with brighter prospects or more present satisfaction."

Despite his delight with Singapore's progress, Raffles disapproved of many of Farquhar's pragmatic measures and was angry that some of his own instructions had not been carried out to the letter. He objected to Farquhar's allocation of land, although his own orders for land distribution were impractical. He considered Farquhar had paid too much deference to the sultan and *temenggong* and was shocked by Farquhar's support of legalized gambling and his lax attitude toward slavery. Raffles ignored the difficulties under which Farquhar had laboured: the shortage of staff and revenue, the difficulty of communications, and Raffles's own insistence that all matters, however trivial, should be channelled through Benkulen, although he himself often left letters unanswered for months on end. Raffles brushed aside Farquhar's considerable achievements, and their former friendship soured into mounting irritation. Farquhar had already angered Raffles by clinging to the post of Resident. Originally he intended to retire once the settlement was firmly established and he sent his resignation to Benkulen in October 1820. Raffles dispatched Captain Thomas Travers to succeed him, but Farquhar changed his mind, and after waiting several months for the handover, Travers finally quarrelled with the Resident and sailed for England.[34]

Even more galling was Farquhar's feud with Captain William Flint, Raffles's brother-in-law. Flint arrived in Singapore in April 1820, when Raffles appointed him Master Attendant in place of Farquhar's own son-in-law. Arrogant, overbearing, greedy and extravagant, Flint pushed his relationship with the Lieutenant-Governor to the limit. While Farquhar's staff comprised one clerk, Flint had a European assistant, two clerks, and several peons. The Master Attendant monopolized the hire of lighters to government and private individuals and pocketed the profit. Raffles insisted that Flint send his statistics direct to Benkulen, not through Farquhar, and when the Lieutenant-Governor returned to Singapore in 1822, he lodged for the first few months with Flint and took his part against Farquhar. He gave the Master Attendant more powers, including authority as magistrate over seamen and the right to collect anchorage and port clearance fees.

In Raffles's view Farquhar's administration was too traditional and old-fashioned. He had written in June 1819, "Our object is not territory but trade; a great commercial emporium and a fulcrum whence we may extend our influence politically as circumstances may hereafter require." He now set out to ensure Singapore's prosperity as a great port, to abolish slavery and injustice, to devise a way of government giving "the utmost possible freedom of trade and equal rights to all, with protection of property and person", and to make Singapore a beautiful and orderly city, the intellectual and educational centre of Southeast Asia.

Within a week of his return, Raffles set out to revise the layout of the town. The major modification concerned the commercial quarter. While Raffles was angry with Farquhar for allowing merchants to encroach on the government area, he had to admit that East Beach was unsuitable for commerce. Instead he decided to transfer the business sector across the Singapore River to the swampy southwestern bank. The Chinese settlers were moved further inland, and a hill was levelled to form Commercial Square (later renamed Raffles Place) using the earth to fill in the swamp to form Boat Quay. This area became the commercial heart of the city. The project was galling for Farquhar. It justified his arguments against the East Beach development, but the money saved through his frugal administration was used to finance Raffles's expensive reclamation scheme.

The other major change involved clearing the river for trade and removing the *temenggong* and his lawless followers – by then more than 600 strong – from the heart of the town to a 200-acre land reserve three miles to the west, along the coast between Tanjong Pagar and Telok Blangah.

The government retained land on the east bank of the Singapore River and Forbidden Hill as the official quarter and kept the southwestern tip at the river's mouth for a defence point. The Rochore plain east of the government quarter was reserved as a residential area for affluent Europeans and Asians. The Arabs were given land to the east of this zone, adjoining the 50-acre site at Kampong Glam allotted to Sultan Hussein, and the Bugis were moved further east beyond Kampong Glam. Since the Chinese were expected to form most of the future town dwellers, Raffles allocated to Chinatown the whole area west of the river adjoining the commercial quarter, to be divided among the various dialect groups, while the lower classes of Indians were allotted land further upriver.

In the urban area, houses had to be built in orderly straight roads of specified width, meeting at right angles, and all commercial buildings were to be constructed of masonry with tiled roofs. *Kapitan* were allocated larger plots of land than their countrymen, and well-to-do merchants were not compelled to live in the areas allocated to their community. Similarly in the commercial sector, big Asian and European shops, offices, and godowns adjoined one another. Naraina Pillai and Tan Che Sang were among the first to move their premises to Commercial Square. Prosperous Asians and Europeans were encouraged to live and trade side by side, thus founding the basis of Singapore's multiracial society where, from the start, the colour of men's money often counted for more than the colour of their skins.

Raffles built himself a wooden bungalow on Forbidden Hill (later renamed Government Hill and subsequently Fort Canning), partly to escape the oppressive heat of the plain below and partly in a death wish to be buried among the Malay rulers of old Singapura. In 1819 he had dispatched a European gardener from Benkulen to plant clove and nutmeg trees at the foot of the hill. These flourished, and Raffles now allocated 48 acres of adjoining land as a Botanic Garden. Working in collaboration with Dr. Nathaniel Wallich of the Calcutta Botanic Garden, who paid periodic visits to Singapore, Raffles hoped his experimental garden would provide the foundation for a prosperous agriculture.

In November 1822 Raffles appointed a committee consisting of one European merchant and two officials, who were to consult representatives of the Malay, Chinese, Bugis, Javanese, and Arab communities about the large-scale resettlement required by the revised town plan. Financial compensation and free land were offered to people who were forced to move from their houses and the old bazaar, but the upheaval encountered such resistance that the police had to be called in to evict residents by force and pull down their huts. The days of haphazard building were at an end. From these early times Singapore was a planned town, and the pattern of Raffles's Singapore remained in the heart of the city throughout colonial times.[35]

During all these months, relations between Raffles and Farquhar were strained to breaking point. Raffles humiliated

Farquhar by handing some of his duties over to junior officials, for instance putting the sale of land and collection of licence revenue in the hands of a twenty-year old writer, George Bonham. In January 1823 Raffles wrote to Calcutta declaring Farquhar to be incompetent, and at the end of April he summarily dismissed the Resident and took over the responsibilities himself. As a final insult, Farquhar only heard through unofficial channels a few days before his arrival that a new Resident, John Crawfurd,[36] had been appointed to succeed him.

Raffles's first priority was to prevent the sultan or the *temenggong* from putting any brake on the development of his settlement. Under the 1819 agreements the Malay chiefs had merely permitted the British to set up a post, and Farquhar, following Malay custom, believed that this did not confer ownership of land or the right to make laws. Whatever Raffles's original intentions in signing the 1819 treaties, Farquhar's interpretation no longer suited his more ambitious scheme. Raffles's professed admiration for the Malay people tended to pale when he was faced by actual flesh and blood individuals with their ambitions and foibles. He despised Hussein, distrusted the *temenggong*, and was not prepared to tolerate any obstruction of his plans. He attempted to reform their ways and offered to arrange shipments of goods from Calcutta for them to sell on commission, but they scorned the role of trader as beneath the dignity of Malay princes. They also rejected Raffles's offer to educate their sons in India at the Company's expense. After that Raffles gave up any attempt to turn the chiefs into enlightened partners in government. He paid their allowances promptly but steadily eased them out of public life. In December 1822 he commuted to a fixed monthly payment all their claims to a share in the revenue, and on the eve of his final departure in June 1823 he made an agreement to buy out their judicial powers and rights to land apart from the areas specially reserved for them.

The first of a series of administrative regulations that Raffles passed in his final weeks in Singapore dealt with the registry of land, which was to be sold on permanent lease by public auction. A second regulation concerned the port. It was common practice for new ports to offer incentives, and initially Raffles saw free trade as suitable bait to attract shipping and settlers to the new mart until the volume of commerce became worth taxing. On his return three years later he was so delighted with early Singapore's success, which he attributed to "the simple but almost magic result of that perfect freedom of trade, which it has been my good fortune to establish", that he decided to extend absolute freedom of trade permanently. When he finally left Singapore in June 1823, he assured the merchants "that no sinister, no sordid view, no considerations either of political importance or pecuniary advantage, should interfere with the broad and liberal principles on which the British interests have been established. Monopoly and exclusive privileges, against which public opinion has long raised its voice, are here unknown ... that Singapore will long and always remain a free port and that no taxes on trade or industry will be established to check its future rise and prosperity, I can have no doubt." This became the central tenet of the Singapore merchants' creed, to be defended with almost religious fervour for more than a hundred years.

A third regulation provided for the administration of justice. Raffles decided to apply indigenous Muslim laws in dealing with religious practice, marriage and inheritance among the Malay population, "where they shall not be contrary to reason, justice or humanity". But the general law of Singapore should be English law, modified "with due consideration to the usage and habits of the people", applied with mildness and common sense "and a patriarchal kindness and indulgent consideration for the prejudices of each tribe". Murder was the only capital offence, and compensation for the injured took precedence over punishment for the offender.

Raffles aimed to give an active role in government and legislation to the non-official European community and a measure of participation to Asians. He had already put this into practice by choosing a committee of European members and Asian representatives to help in laying out the town. Under the new judicial regulation, twelve responsible Europeans were chosen to serve as magistrates for a year. They were to assist in the Resident's court and also deal with petty crimes and minor civil cases in their own magistrates' court. The Resident was to seek their advice in drawing up laws and was obliged to refer to Calcutta any proposed regulations to which the magistrates objected. By giving the magistrates a share in government, Raffles hoped to avoid the friction between government and private European residents that was so common in small colonies without representative institutions.

Since he considered it was the government's duty to prevent crime and to reform rather than punish criminals, Raffles extended to Singapore the training schemes to turn convicts into useful settlers that he had adopted in Benkulu. Violence was to be discouraged by banning the carrying of weapons and prohibiting what he considered the heinous vices of gambling and cockfighting. Angry at finding that Farquhar had licensed gambling, in May 1823 Raffles closed all gambling dens and cockpits, as "disgraceful and repugnant to the British character and government". Heavy taxation was used to discourage supposedly lesser vices, such as drunkenness and opium smoking. While it was unrealistic to attempt to ban prostitution in a predominantly male immigrant society, his laws forbade men from living off the earnings of prostitutes.

Raffles shared the aversion of humanitarian and radical men of his generation to the practice of slavery, which he had abolished in Benkulu, but Farquhar had condoned slave dealing in Singapore as a local custom. Bugis traders, who were the main slave dealers of the region, frequently herded large numbers of slaves round the town on display. Others were imported in Malay boats from Sumatra, and there was a particularly brisk trade in young girls. Raffles was scandalized within days of returning to Singapore in October 1822, when Bugis traders sold fifty slaves near the Resident's house and offered a few as presents to Farquhar and himself.

Resolving to put an end to this traffic in human flesh, in May 1823 Raffles issued a regulation prohibiting the slave trade in Singapore. No one who had arrived after 29 January 1819 could be regarded as a slave, and the numerous Malay slave debtors were to work off their debts in a maximum period of five years. Raffles also attempted to control the semi-slavery of penniless Chinese immigrants, who pledged their labour to employers in return for payment of their passage money. He laid down that *nakodah* could demand no more than $20 for passage money, which had to be worked off in a maximum of two years, and such contracts were to be registered in the presence of a magistrate.

The principle of personal liberty was established and blatant slave dealing was checked from these early years, but it was more difficult to wipe out debt bondage, and the hidden slavery of immigrant labour persisted for decades. The interpretation of slavery was open to ambiguity, particularly in Malay society where everyone had obligations for service, although they might not be bought and sold for money. The Bugis continued to import slaves, ostensibly as debtors, selling them to Chinese middlemen, who paid off the debt and then consigned most of them to neighbouring territories.[37] As late as 1873 it was alleged in the Legislative Council that nearly all Arab households employed slaves, and at that time many Javanese and Boyanese gardeners and syces were virtual slaves, working off their debts to pilgrim shipmasters for passages to Mecca to perform the *haj*. The regulations on Chinese immigrant labour could not be enforced, and registration of contracts remained a dead letter until the Chinese Protectorate was established in the 1870s.

While in many ways Raffles was enlightened and ahead of his time, his puritanical zeal fathered harsh measures designed to root out corrupting vices. He ordered that gaming houses be confiscated and gaming-den keepers and gamblers be flogged. Despite his claim to an insight and understanding of the Malay character, Raffles was on occasion remarkably insensitive, as shown in his savage reaction in March 1823 when an Arab, Sayid Yasin, escaped from prison and ran amok, killing a police peon and wounding Farquhar. The Resident's son killed the attacker on the spot, but there was pandemonium among the panic-stricken Europeans, who at first suspected the *temenggong*'s men had perpetrated the outrage. Refusing the sultan's request to hand over the body, Raffles had the corpse carted round the town in a bullock cart and then hung up on display for a fortnight in an iron cage. The Muslim community watched in sullen fury at this desecration, and subsequently Sayid Yasin's grave at Tanjong Pagar became a holy shrine. The incident hung like a menacing shadow over Singapore for a long time, both European and Chinese merchants fearing Muslim retribution and conscious that the tiny garrison could give them little protection.

At the heart of Raffles's reform programme was his belief that "education must keep pace with commerce in order that its benefits may be ensured and its evils avoided". "Let us not be remembered as the tempest whose course was desolation, but as the gale of spring." It had long been his dream to revive the cultural heritage of the Malay world, which he considered had been degraded by Chinese, Arab and Dutch exploitation and by the influence of the Muslim "robber religion".[38] He wished to combine a reborn Hindu-Buddhist culture with the best in Christianity and modern Western scholarship for the intellectual enrichment of both Asians and Europeans, and in 1819 he had tried to interest William Wilberforce in creating a college in the Malay archipelago affiliated to Wilberforce's African Institution.

Singapore's geographic position, historical associations, and commercial prosperity marked her as the ideal centre "for the cultivation of Chinese and Malayan literature and for the moral and intellectual improvement of the archipelago and the surrounding countries", and, as his stay in Singapore drew to a close, Raffles was determined to found his Singapore Institution as "my last public act". He told his friend Wallich, "I trust in God this Institution may be the means of civilizing and bettering the condition of millions ... our field is India beyond the Ganges, including the Malayan Archipelago, Australia, China, Japan and the islands of the Pacific ocean." In April 1823 Raffles called a meeting to launch his scheme for the projected institution, which would instruct the Company's officials about the region, educate the sons of neighbouring rulers and chiefs, and produce a professional class of Asian teachers and government servants. He anticipated a great rush for education from all over Southeast Asia, particularly from the local aristocracy.

Without waiting to obtain approval from Calcutta, Raffles laid the foundation stone of the Singapore Institution three days before he left Singapore. Immediate provisions were made to appoint three Siamese, one Chinese and several Malay masters, with further plans for Javanese and Buginese teachers, when such could be found. Raffles led the way by contributing $2,000 to the school, and committing the East India Company to a payment of $4,000. Lady Raffles gave $500, the missionary, Robert Morrison, $1,200, and Raffles used his powers of charmed persuasion to press the sultan, the *temenggong* and Farquhar into parting with $1,000 each. Other officials and private residents followed suit, and soon subscriptions totalled more than $17,000. The East India Company considered the scheme premature but grudgingly allotted a maintenance grant of $300 a month.

A few days before Raffles's final departure the European and Asian merchants of Singapore presented him with an address praising his "comprehensive view ... and principles the operation of which has converted, in a period short beyond all example, a haunt of pirates into the abode of enterprise, security and opulence". Raffles was pleased with his work. Writing to Wallich in July 1823, he claimed, "The constitution which I have given to Singapore is certainly the purest and most liberal in India." And to another correspondent he explained. "I have had everything to new-mould from first to last – to introduce a system of energy, purity and encouragement ... to look for a century or two beforehand and provide for what Singapore may one day become."

It was characteristic of Raffles that he should plunge into the task of creating a society and looking ahead for a hundred years in a settlement whose very existence was still under dispute and in which he had no legitimate authority to frame laws. Nevertheless Raffles was sure that Singapore was already too successful for Britain to give up.

∾

After being ousted from office, Farquhar remained in Singapore for a few months as a private resident, and his final send-off in December 1823 has probably been unsurpassed in warmth and spontaneous enthusiasm in the history of the island. The Europeans contributed 3,000 rupees to buy him a present of silver plate, the Chinese gave him a gold cup, and the various communities presented addresses. Troops formed a guard of honour, the Resident, the military Commandant, nearly all the Europeans and hundreds of Asians came to the waterfront, and there was such a crush of people that it took Farquhar two hours to say his farewells. Hundreds of small *perahu* followed him out to his ship in the roads, their occupants singing and firing crackers. In Melaka he was warmly received by the Asian population and entertained by the Dutch Governor and officials, and on his final departure from Penang he was escorted by the Governor and given a salute of guns.

The Governor-General of India reproved Raffles for his harsh treatment of Farquhar but refused his plea for reinstatement. Bitterness against Raffles led him in later years to claim that he himself was responsible for the choice of Singapore, but this brought him little credit. Certainly Farquhar had long argued in favour of securing a base to command the southern end of the Straits of Melaka, and his acquaintance with the Malay chiefs and background knowledge of Riau-Johor politics were invaluable in the preliminary negotiations, but initially Farquhar had recommended the Karimuns. It is true that Raffles exaggerated claims that, through his study of Malay history and literature, he alone knew of the existence of Singapore. The island was familiar to contemporary sailors, traders and officials in Southeast Asia. Abraham Couperus, who surrendered wartime Melaka to the

British, suggested in 1808 that Singapore would be a superior site to Melaka as a future Dutch settlement. The British fleet had sailed past Singapore on its way to invade Java in 1811. The story of the British Captain Alexander Hamilton, who claimed that the Sultan of Johor offered him Singapore Island in 1703, appeared in William Milburn's *Oriental Commerce*, which was published in London in 1813.[39] Despite this, by visiting Calcutta, winning over the Governor-General and subsequently being prepared to exceed his orders, Raffles made it possible for the base to be secured. He above all appreciated the historical associations of Singapore, "once the great emporium of these seas, whose history is lost in the mists of antiquity" and had a far-seeing vision of the great city state it could become.

Raffles's treatment of Farquhar was perhaps the shabbiest episode in his career: the unfair repudiation of a friend, who had withstood all the difficulties and dangers in the first precarious years and nursed the settlement into the life and vigour that so inspired Raffles on his return in 1822. At the same time, Farquhar's conservative ideas stood in the way of Raffles's soaring ambitions for Singapore. At the very time when Raffles was stooping to his lowest in hounding and ousting the unfortunate Farquhar, he rose to the most idealistic high point in his career in drawing up his plans for the future of Singapore.

At the heart of the dispute between Raffles and Farquhar was a fundamental disagreement about the nature of the new settlement and the bargain that had been made with the Sultan Hussein and the *temenggong*. The 1819 treaties merely gave the East India Company the right to establish a trading station at Singapore. The Malay chiefs expected that, in accordance with custom, they still owned the land and were entitled to receive trade dues, to administer laws, and to exert rights over their subjects, which in some Western eyes was akin to slavery. Raffles was angry to find that Farquhar had respected this interpretation of the treaty obligations, which, whatever Raffles's own original intentions in February 1819, did not suit his wider ambitions in 1822.

On 7 June 1823, on the eve of his final departure from Singapore and in consultation with the incoming Resident, Dr. John Crawfurd, Raffles signed a fresh agreement with Sultan Hussein and the *temenggong* to buy out their rights and gain possession of the whole island. In return for monthly payments, the Malay chiefs gave up claims to port dues and monopolies and agreed that, apart from the lands personally allotted to them, "all land within the island of Singapore, and islands immediately adjacent, to be at the entire disposal of the British government".[40]

In view of Raffles's impending retirement, the Company decided to separate Singapore from Benkulen and make her a direct dependency of Calcutta, but on his final departure, Raffles left the new Resident a detailed Letter of Instructions on how the settlement should be administered. He had every confidence in Crawfurd, whom he considered to be "bold and fearless", "devoting his mind exclusively to objects in which my heart and soul are deeply interested". In November 1823 he wrote to Wallich, "Crawfurd has promised most solemnly to adhere to and uphold all my arrangements", but in this Raffles was to be disappointed.

Crawfurd had already acquired wide experience of Southeast Asia. Joining the East India Company's medical service in India in 1803 at the age of twenty, he was posted to Penang five years later, but his interests lay in languages, history and political administration rather than in medicine. Throughout the British occupation of Java he had held senior posts, and his three-volume *History of the Indian Archipelago*, which was published in 1820, established him as an authority on the region. Shortly afterwards he was sent on a diplomatic mission to Siam and Cochin-China, in the course of which he visited Singapore for the first time in January 1822 and was greatly impressed.

In contrast to Raffles, Crawfurd was a somewhat austere and forbidding character. Intolerant of criticism and "bent down by a love of the goods of this world", as Munshi Abdullah described him, he inspired little affection. His brusque impatience offended the Asian community, while Europeans considered him tight-fisted. But he was conscientious, painstaking, and canny, and he was familiar with Raffles's ways, which he regarded with a mixture of admiration and scepticism. In Java Crawfurd had on several occasions acted on his own initiative against the wishes of Raffles, who once admitted, "Two of a trade can never agree; and Crawfurd and I are perhaps running too much on the same parallel not now and then to be jostling each other." Crawfurd regarded Raffles's provisions for representative government, higher education and moral upliftment as visionary, Utopian, and premature, to be jettisoned in order to promote what he held to be Raffles's more sensible ideas, notably his commercial policy.

The first casualty was Raffles's illegal judicial system and the attempt to associate non-officials in government, which collapsed almost immediately. When the honorary magistrates used the wide powers authorized by Raffles to flog and banish gamblers and confiscate their property, Crawfurd annulled the proceedings. To Raffles's consternation, and overriding the magistrates' protests, in August 1823 the Resident licensed ten gaming houses in town and a cockpit in Kampong Bugis, arguing that the state should profit by gambling, since it was endemic among Chinese, Malays and Bugis and could not be eradicated.

Crawfurd appealed for a Charter of Justice to be granted to Singapore to put the administration of law on a proper footing. Meanwhile, he replaced the magistrates by a court of requests under an Assistant Resident, which dealt with petty civil cases, and he tried all other cases himself. He had no legal powers over Europeans, as the merchants well knew. Serious cases involving Britons could be referred to Calcutta, but this could be dangerous, as Farquhar had found to his cost when he sent to Calcutta a Captain Gillon who was accused of raping one of his passengers. Gillon was acquitted and successfully sued Farquhar for compensation. In practice the Resident's only legal remedy was to banish troublesome Britons, but this sanction never had to be invoked since the early British community was a law-abiding group, unlike their countrymen in other pioneer settlements.

Crawfurd was sceptical about Raffles's idealistic ambitions of cultural revival and the grandiose education programme that he was instructed to carry out. In 1826, the Resident urged Calcutta to concentrate on primary education and reported to the Directors, "The native inhabitants of Singapore have not yet attained that state of civilization and knowledge which would qualify them to derive advantage from the enlarged system of education held by the Singapore Institution." Calcutta gladly accepted Crawfurd's view about dispensing with higher education but failed to follow up on his proposals for primary schooling, with the result that education schemes at both levels lapsed, and Raffles's cherished ideal withered.

Raffles's other wishes were carried out with enthusiasm. Crawfurd continued the measures to suppress slavery. He obeyed the instructions on town planning and further whittled down the Malay chiefs' influence. Above all, he pursued Raffles's commercial policy with ardent devotion. Before he left, Raffles urged Crawfurd to practise economy and keep administrative costs down, "avoiding unnecessary expense rather than seeking revenue to cover it". Crawfurd found these orders congenial, promoting free trade and restraining government expenditure with more zeal than Raffles himself. Whereas Raffles was a late convert to the principle of free trade, Crawfurd had long been its staunch devotee. By pruning administrative expenses, he was able to abolish anchorage and other fees, making Singapore unique as a port that was free not only from tariffs but also from port charges.

Crawfurd edged out Raffles's and Farquhar's relatives. The Resident deprived Captain Flint of his office of magistrate and threw open to competition the Master Attendant's monopoly rights of wood, water and ballast for ships. He commandeered as an official Residency the house on the hill, which Raffles had built and subsequently given to his son-in-law. Flint continued as Master Attendant until his death in 1828, but his powers were gradually stripped away and he died in debt.

The period of Crawfurd's administration, which lasted from June 1823 to August 1826, was a time of vigorous upsurge in population, trade, and revenue. According to the first official census taken in January 1824, Singapore had nearly 11,000 inhabitants, of whom the Malays still formed the largest community, with the Chinese in second place. Third were the Bugis, and there were 756 Indians, 74 Europeans, 16 Armenians, and 15 Arabs. By that time there were 12 European firms, most of them agents for London or Calcutta houses. There was a steady trickle of European immigration, mostly young commercial assistants in their late teens, but also a few more mature men with wives and children. Nearly all were British, including a large Scottish contingent, later described as "a Scottish 'Mafia' with apparent nepotic tendencies",[41] but in December 1825 a former Portuguese naval surgeon, Dr. Jozé d'Almeida, arrived from Macau to set up a dispensary and subsequently became one of Singapore's leading merchants.

With the rise in population and trade, Crawfurd succeeded in extracting more revenue from the opium and *arrack* farms and sold licences for pawnbrokers and for the manufacture and sale of gunpowder. His major innovation, the revival of Farquhar's gambling farm, became the most profitable source of revenue. The revenue from tax farms rose from under $26,000 in 1823 to over $75,000 in 1825, of which nearly half came from gambling. By 1826 Singapore's revenue outstripped that of Penang.

Raffles's new town took shape under Crawfurd's direction. He enforced the standards laid down by Raffles for "beauty, regularity and cleanliness". Commercial Square was cleared and laid out, and a sound bridge was constructed across the river. The town streets were widened, levelled, and given English street signs, and coconut-oil street lighting first appeared in 1824. Land was allotted for religious buildings. The troops were moved from the town centre to a new cantonment on the northwestern outskirts at Sepoy Lines at the end of 1823.

A Dutch visitor, Colonel Nahuijs, who visited Singapore in June 1824 was grudgingly impressed but still rather bitter that the British had seized what he regarded as Dutch territory. He concluded that Singapore was not likely to become a great port or a threat to the Dutch, and considered that the dozen European firms were as much as Singapore could ever support. Nahuijs thought Raffles had made a fatal mistake in negotiating with the Malay chiefs, and in particular with the *temenggong* and his piratical "sea scum", instead of rooting them out.[42]

Despite the new agreement made by Raffles with the local chiefs in June 1823, the legal position remained ambiguous. The Advocate General of India considered the new arrangement to be an improvement on the original 1819 treaty, under which the Company was "little more than Tenants at Will of those Princes", with nothing resembling sovereignty or the right to make laws. Even the 1823 agreement was unsatisfactory, and he urged the need to obtain proper parliamentary endorsement for a new treaty.[43] Crawfurd was coming to the same conclusion. Never the most patient of men, he clashed with the chiefs on the interpretation of slavery and quarrelled over money. The *temenggong* demanded compensation in addition to the $3,000 that he had already been paid to move to Telok Blangah, while Sultan Hussein was deeply in debt to the Company and to private individuals. Declaring both the chiefs "utterly unfit for any useful employment", in January 1824 Crawfurd wrote at length to the Government of India, explaining his difficulties and seeking authorization to negotiate a new agreement that would prevent the chiefs from interfering in the local administration or drawing the Company into the political disputes of the Johor-Lingga Empire. The only remedy, he suggested, would be "the unequivocal cession of the island of Singapore in full sovereignty and property" in exchange for a down payment and a pension for life. In response, the Government of India admitted the shortcomings of the current "ill-defined nature of arrangements" and urged "the expediency and indeed the necessity" of immediate action to obtain sovereignty.[44]

These instructions reached Crawfurd in mid-May, but nearly three months of haggling ensued, mainly over whether the chiefs' proposed pension rights should be hereditary. A Treaty of Friendship and Alliance, which came to be commonly known as "Crawfurd's Treaty" was finally concluded on 2 August 1824, whereby the chiefs ceded to the East India Company and its heirs perpetual title to the island of Singapore and to all seas, straits and islands within ten geographical miles of her shores. This ensured control of both the Singapore and Johor Straits, and of the waters and myriad small islands immediately surrounding Singapore. The chiefs were permitted to reside on the land reserved for them in Singapore but were not to have any dealings abroad without the Company's consent. If they decided to withdraw from Singapore, the sultan would receive $20,000 compensation and the *temenggong* $15,000.[45] Crawfurd was disappointed that the chiefs did not take the compensation offered under his treaty and leave Singapore, but meanwhile the Resident had no qualms about making their lives uncomfortable. In September 1824 he freed twenty-seven female slaves, who had escaped from the sultan's palace complaining of ill-treatment, and a month later he drove a road to Kampong Bugis through Hussein's compound, smashing down his wall. These measures failed to dislodge him, and the chiefs' continued residence in Singapore was to embarrass the British administration.

When Crawfurd and the Malay chiefs signed the treaty in August 1824, none of them was aware that the protracted negotiations in London between the British and Dutch governments had concluded amicably some months earlier with the signing on 17 March 1824 of a Treaty of London "Respecting Territory and Commerce in the East Indies". To avoid any future friction, the signatories of the Anglo-Dutch Treaty sought a clear demarcation of territorial interests. The Dutch withdrew objections to the British occupation of Singapore, agreed to cede

Melaka to Britain and undertook not to create an establishment or make an agreement with any chief in the Malay Peninsula. In turn the British agreed to cede Benkulen to the Dutch and promised not to create an establishment or make an agreement with any chief in Sumatra or the islands south of Singapore. None of the plenipotentiaries who negotiated the Anglo-Dutch Treaty had any personal experience of the East, nor did they have any reliable charts or maps of the many hundreds of islands that constituted the Riau-Lingga archipelago. At one stage the Dutch proposed to draw a demarcation line through the Straits of Singapore, but this was rejected for fear that other European powers would suspect Britain and the Netherlands of trying to divide the region between them. In the interests of clarity, it was decided to specify the main islands by name, so that Britain undertook not to settle or make treaties "on the Carimon Isles, or on the Islands of Battam, Bintang, Lingin, or on any of the other Islands south of the Straights [sic] of Singapore".[46]

It was some months before the news filtered through to Singapore since, on the British side, many formalities and arrangements were required to put this treaty into effect. The first stage was to place Singapore and the ceded territories under the formal control of the East India Company, and the British Parliament passed an Act to this effect on 24 June 1824. On 4 August 1824, two days after Crawfurd and the Malay chiefs signed their treaty, the Directors dispatched copies of this Act and the Anglo-Dutch Treaty to Calcutta, together with detailed instructions about preparing the way for the complicated operations to transfer Benkulen and Melaka. The simpler situation in Singapore, where no change in administration was required, was dealt with in a single paragraph, "Article 12 [of the Anglo-Dutch Treaty], you will observe, puts an end to all questions between the British government and the Dutch as to the title of the British to Singapore. We have some reason to believe that the Harbour of Singapore is partly formed of one or more Islets lying very near to the main Island. In order to prevent any difficulty or dispute respecting these Islets, we authorise and desire you to take possession of any such Islets or Islands in the Straits of Singapore, at the same time as we enjoin your strict attention to the stipulation of the present Article respecting the Caraman [sic] Islands, and others lying *South* of these Straits."[47]

Crawfurd still knew nothing about this at the end of September 1824, when he first came to learn about the Anglo-Dutch Treaty by chance from seeing a copy in a Dutch official newspaper. Worried about the implications for the treaty that he had recently made with Sultan Hussein and the *temenggong*, he wrote to Calcutta immediately for clarification. Dutch acquiescence in the British occupation of Singapore had been anticipated, and the 10-mile territorial limit should not infringe the Anglo-Dutch Treaty, but the stipulation prohibiting Britain from making agreements with chiefs to the south was totally unexpected. As Crawfurd pointed out, it "virtually amounts to a dismemberment of the principality of Johore and must thus be productive of some embarrassment and confusion". The *temenggong* was put in a particularly anomalous position: since most of his domain lay to the south, the treaty would force him to choose between giving up the islands or moving to live there and severing all connection with the British.[48]

In March 1825 the Government of India gave warm approval to Crawfurd's treaty, agreeing that it conformed to the terms of the Anglo-Dutch Treaty, since the whole area ceded by the Malay chiefs lay north of the southern limits of the Singapore Straits. Calcutta made no comment about the repercussions on the Johor Empire.[49]

In view of their long relationship with Johor, the Dutch were more concerned with the empire's fate. In 1823 they had re-occupied Riau, forcibly seized the regalia from the late Sultan Mahmud's widow, and gave quasi-legitimacy to Abdul Rahman by having him formally installed as sultan in the presence of the Bugis under-king but without the *bendahara* or other senior officials. The Dutch government instructed their authorities in the Indies to explain the consequences of the Anglo-Dutch Treaty to Sultan Abdul Rahman (now styled Sultan of Lingga) and put the arrangement into effect. In April 1825 Batavia's envoy, Christiaan van Angelbeek, came to Singapore to clarify whether Crawfurd's Singapore treaty had any implications for the dismemberment of the old Johor Empire. After friendly conversations with Crawfurd, van Angelbeek reported that, far from infringing on the Anglo-Dutch Treaty, the Singapore treaty made the separation easier, since it amounted to a formal recognition of the claims of Hussein and the *temenggong* on the mainland. Van Angelbeek then pressed Sultan Abdul Rahman into writing to Hussein, as "Sultan of Singapore", granting him authority over mainland Johor and Pahang, and warning him to restrain the *temenggong* and the *bendahara* from getting involved in Sultan Abdul Rahman's domain in the islands. The so-called "Angelbeek Donation" did little to help Hussein, and the Anglo-Dutch Treaty dealt a near mortal blow to the *temenggong*. In reconciling the reluctant Sultan Abdul Rahman to relinquishing his mainland territories, the Dutch pointed out that he was losing nothing of consequence, since the *temenggong* had already ceded Singapore to the British, while the Treaty of London left the Sultan of Lingga in sole control of the rest of the Riau/Lingga islands. The *temenggong* had given away or been forced to sacrifice nearly all his patrimony, leaving a virtually uninhabited wilderness on the mainland. Temenggong Abdur Rahman died in 1825, apparently a ruined man.

Crawfurd saw for himself the desolation of the area when, on 2 August 1825, exactly a year after signing the Singapore treaty, he set off on a voyage round the island to confirm possession, in accordance with Calcutta's instructions. The party planted a flag and fired a 21-gun salute on Pulau Ubin at the northeastern end of the Johor Strait and sailed around to take possession of the Rabbit and Coney Islands, at the furthest southwestern point, with a further 21-gun salute. The voyage took nine days, during which, apart from a few woodcutters' huts on Pulau Ubin, they found no sign of habitation on either side of the Johor Strait. Outside of the town, most of Singapore was still unexplored jungle, and the *Singapore Chronicle* declared it would be easier to go to Calcutta

than cover the difficult terrain to Bukit Timah Hill, the highest
point and centre of the island.

❦

Singapore was fortunate in her three pioneer administrators:
Raffles, a man of extraordinary vision, but for whom Singapore
would never have existed, Farquhar, who by his energy, good
sense, and courage, nursed the infant settlement through its first
dangerous years, and Crawfurd, shrewd and sensible, with his
feet firmly on the ground, who converted into reality the more
practical of Raffles's dreams. These diverse characters set the
pattern of administration that was maintained throughout the
nineteenth century.

Farquhar played no further role in Singapore after he departed
in 1823, and Raffles died in July 1826. Crawfurd left in August
1826, and after undertaking a diplomatic mission to Burma, he
returned to England in 1830. He never revisited the East but
maintained his contacts with Singapore. For some years he tried
unsuccessfully to enter Parliament and spent the rest of his life
on the fringe of politics, battling against the East India Company,
first as an agent for the Calcutta merchants and later on behalf of
the Singapore trading community. From 1853 he devoted much
of his energies to advancing the cause of the Straits merchants
in London, composing petitions and memoranda for Parliament
and organizing deputations. In 1868, in the last year of his life,
when he was eighty-five years old, Crawfurd was made the first
president of the Straits Settlements Association, which was
formed to protect the new colony's interests. It was a fitting end
to his career.

Despite this long association, Crawfurd's name, like
Farquhar's, has faded almost into obscurity, and of Singapore's
pioneers only Raffles's fame and reputation have grown over the
years. In some ways, history has been unfair to Farquhar and
Crawfurd, who gave early Singapore the efficient administration
that Raffles could not supply. Despite his great imagination and

vision, Singapore was Raffles's only successful project, and this was largely because he had little hand in the actual running of the settlement. After the bold stroke of its founding, Raffles remained almost out of touch with the settlement during the first three formative years, when the port grew and prospered under Farquhar's careful administration. And after the whirlwind activity of Raffles's last stay, the actual implementation of his policies and negotiating the 1824 Treaty with the sultan and the *temenggong*, which secured its future, fell to the hard-headed Crawfurd. Raffles drew broad sweeping outlines, and it was left to other less imaginative but more practical and realistic men to fill in the details.

In the process, it was inevitable that they should shed some of Raffles's loftier dreams. The port quickly achieved a commercial success beyond Raffles's hopes, but his moral and educational policy soon crumbled, and Singapore developed into a highly materialistic society. While the merchants revered Raffles's memory and invoked his name as the high priest of free trade, many features of mid-nineteenth century Singapore would have saddened and disappointed her founder.

Despite this, Raffles's vision became an inspiration to intelligent and enterprising men, and he was a more influential force on later generations of empire builders than any other Briton connected with Singapore. Despite his lack of schooling and his long years of comparative isolation in the East as an employee of an old-fashioned monopolistic company, Raffles reflected the most advanced radical, intellectual, and humanitarian thinking of his day. The type of society he aspired to establish in Singapore was in many ways ahead of contemporary England or India. His horror of slavery and vision of the moral influence of government were in tune with Wilberforce and the Evangelicals. His enlightened penal system and concern for law were in line with Jeremy Bentham and the Utilitarians. In addition, in his final conversion to the cause of free trade, he established in Singapore a free port following the principles of Adam Smith and *laissez-faire* at a time when Britain was still a protectionist country.

2

"This Spirited and Splendid Little Colony"
1826–1867

In 1826 the East India Company united Singapore with Penang and Melaka to form the Presidency of the Straits Settlements, with Penang Governor Robert Fullerton as first Governor of the Straits Settlements. The merger put an end to Singapore's pioneering days: she came under Penang's executive and judicial control, and regular civil servants of the East India Company, with prior experience in Penang and Benkulen, brought her administration into line with the Company's practices. The Singapore establishment was enlarged. It was headed by a Resident Councillor with three Assistant Residents, but in the first four years Resident Councillors followed one another in rapid succession and none left a distinctive mark.[1]

The Royal Charter of Justice, which Crawfurd had requested, was granted to the Straits Settlements in 1826, giving Singapore her first judicial system and providing for citizens of standing to be appointed as justices of the peace or grand jurymen. At first the charter brought little improvement. The Recorder was supposed to travel on circuit from his Penang base and preside over a court in conjunction with the governor and senior councillor in each settlement in turn, but this machinery could not be put into operation because the Recorder, Sir John Claridge, refused to leave Penang following disputes about travelling arrangements and expenses. Fullerton was compelled to hold the first Singapore assizes himself in 1828, while Claridge was recalled to England the following year and dismissed.

The Straits Settlements Presidency was born with financial problems and doomed to an early death. The government could not extract enough revenue to support its overblown bureaucracy and elaborate judicial system. Fullerton's plans to raise land revenue failed, and London not only vetoed his proposals to bring Singapore into line with Penang's tariffs but instead compounded the financial problems by extending its free trade arrangements to Penang and Melaka. While Penang's deficit swelled, the Company faced an acute financial crisis in India, and in 1830 it swept away the expensive superstructure in the Straits Settlements. The presidency, the governor and his council were abolished, and the Settlements were reduced to the status of a Residency dependent on the Presidency of Bengal. The civil service was drastically reduced: senior posts were cut from nineteen to eight, only two of these tenable in Singapore, and the few officials who remained in their posts suffered big salary cuts.

The constitutional change created an immediate judicial crisis. Since no Recorder had arrived to replace Claridge and the offices and titles of governor and resident councillor had disappeared, Fullerton ruled that no one was entitled to administer justice under the terms of the existing charter. When he departed for England in 1830, he closed the courts and dismissed the judicial establishment. The Assistant Resident of Singapore opened a temporary court but hurriedly closed it again after being warned that he possessed no legal authority. Merchants in Singapore and Penang appealed to the British Parliament, but by then the Company had decided that Fullerton's interpretation was incorrect. The courts reopened in 1832, and a new Recorder arrived the following year. To meet the technical requirements of the judicial charter, the titles of governor and resident councillor were revived but in name only, without their former powers or status. For the remaining years of Indian rule, Governors were in practice mere Residents, and there was no council. In 1833 Singapore faced a further crisis when the East India Company lost its monopoly of the China trade, which the Straits Settlements had been acquired to protect. While the Company could not jettison what had become not only a costly but a useless burden, from this time on Calcutta pursued a negative policy in the Straits, trying to avoid expense and to insulate the settlements from problems in the Malay States by a rigid policy of non-intervention.

The skeleton civil service, which survived the 1830 cuts, remained almost unchanged until the end of Indian rule, despite the fact that between 1830 and 1867 Singapore's population quadrupled and her trade increased more than threefold. Consequently, officials could not cope with the growing complexity of administration. During that period, the Company's senior officials were usually respectable, intelligent men who carried out policy in an orthodox way. None stamped his personality so strongly on Singapore as the pioneers. There was no room in mid-nineteenth century Singapore for the flair and genius of a Raffles.

With few exceptions, government salaries remained static between 1830 and 1867, although the cost of living rose steeply. Even less favourable terms were offered to uncovenanted officials, who enlisted locally, and there was a good deal of resentment between them and the covenanted men recruited by the Company in England. Calcutta's obsession with collecting reports and statistics put a heavy burden on bureaucrats in Singapore, where there was no literate clerical class to support them. Officials had to correlate reports from the three settlements, compile narratives and statistics, and convert local figures into Indian weights and currencies. Frustration and futility, compounded by long service in an enervating climate, sapped efficiency and sense of purpose. Every case of sickness, transfer, or death among senior men caused major staffing difficulties, and Governor-General of India, Lord

Canning, acknowledged in 1859 that the shortcomings of the bureaucracy were "the greatest evil" in the Straits.

Officials had little time to become acquainted with local languages and customs. Schemes introduced by Fullerton to pay tuition fees and bonuses to officials who attained proficiency in Malay, Siamese, or Chinese were abolished in 1830. In the mid-nineteenth century, many officials were barely fluent in Malay, and none could speak Chinese. Chinese translations of new laws had to be made in Hong Kong, and the *Singapore Free Press* commented in 1857, "There is probably no other government in the world so incapable of addressing the people as that of the Straits."

The judicial establishment was also inadequate. From his base in Penang, the Recorder paid periodic visits to Singapore but left most of the judicial work to the Governor and Resident Councillor. Cases remained unheard for months, and the gaols were packed with men awaiting trial. Eventually in 1855, after long years of agitation, a new Charter of Justice was granted, which provided for two Recorders, one of whom was to administer Singapore and Melaka, but the Governor and Resident Councillor still retained their anomalous positions alongside the professional judge.

Already by 1826 Singapore was the most flourishing of the Straits Settlements, but Penang remained the seat of government for several years and the judicial headquarters until 1856. In practice, George Bonham, who acted as Governor from 1833 and became substantive Governor in 1836, spent most of his time in Singapore, but it was his successor, Governor William Butterworth, who formally established Singapore as the permanent capital.

❧

While officialdom struggled in drab frustration, private commerce flourished dramatically, and most of the important developments of this middle part of the nineteenth century were due to the initiative of Singapore's immigrant communities. The population expanded rapidly. Standing at less than 16,000 in 1827, it had nearly doubled to more than 30,000 by 1836, and in 1860 it numbered 81,000.

By 1830 the Chinese were the largest single community and by the end of Indian rule in 1867 they constituted 65 per cent of the population. Nearly all Chinese immigrants came from the provinces of Kwangtung and Fukien in southeastern China, and at this time comprised four major dialect groups: Hokkien, Teochew, Cantonese, and Hakka. The Hokkiens were the most numerous and dominated Singapore's commercial life from the beginning. Their main business rivals, the Teochews, were the second largest community. Cantonese generally came as agricultural labourers, tin miners, or artisans and included most of Singapore's carpenters, tailors, goldsmiths, and masons. Most Hakka immigrants passed through the port to the tin mines of the interior, but some settled in Singapore, mainly as labourers. There was some affinity among Hokkiens and Teochews in speech and customs, but a great gulf in dialect and character between the Cantonese and Hakkas.

Straits-born and some successful China-born immigrants settled down to permanent family life in Singapore, and several leading merchants became British subjects under a naturalization law passed in 1852, but most immigrants hoped to make enough money to return permanently to China after a few years. To this end they were prepared to work hard and live frugally, sending regular remittances of their savings to their families in China.

While the Malay community continued to grow, it soon lost its position of pre-dominance. Immigrants from Melaka, Sumatra and the Riau archipelago mingled unobtrusively with the existing Malay population and with Javanese, Boyanese, and others from the eastern islands. The *orang laut* disappeared as a separate community. Soon after the British arrival, the *temenggong* moved the Orang Kallang to the Pulai River in Johor, where most of them died in a smallpox epidemic.[2] The Orang Seletar continued their wandering existence undisturbed until the 1850s when the Johor Strait became more frequented. Some then drifted off to more peaceful creeks on the mainland, while the remainder became absorbed in the on-shore population. A large collection of Orang Gelam boats remained in the Singapore River until the late 1840s, attracting a shifting population of *orang laut* from the Riau-Lingga archipelago,[3] but the government dispersed this floating village because it obstructed port traffic and was rumoured to harbour pirates. From the middle of the century, the *orang laut* and their descendants merged into the Malay population.

By the 1860s, the Malays had fallen to third place in Singapore's population. Most were peaceful industrious immigrants, employed in humble occupations as boatmen, fishermen, woodcutters, or carpenters. Their one day of glory was the New Year's sports, when the Malays and *orang laut* in boats of their own design invariably triumphed over Europeans, Chinese, Bugis, and all other competitors.

Indians comprised less than 10 per cent of Singapore's inhabitants in 1845, but by 1860 they had become Singapore's second largest community, totalling some 13,000. Most came as traders or labourers, some as garrison troops or camp followers, and others as convicts. The majority was South Indian, but there were also Sikhs, Punjabis, Gujaratis, Bengalis, and a few rich Parsis. Most were young men, who skimped and saved to accumulate enough money to return home to settle. Very few Indian women came to Singapore until the 1860s, but some Indian Muslims married Malay girls and settled down, producing a class known as Jawi-Peranakan.

The Bugis were the only community that declined in actual numbers, shrinking to 900 by 1860 from a peak of 2,000 in the 1830s, when Bugis traders almost monopolized Singapore's trade with the eastern islands of the archipelago. The lifting of Dutch trade restrictions and the growing dominance of Western shipping in the archipelago trade lessened the Bugis' hold. The numbers of Bugis craft coming to Singapore dropped steadily, but the annual arrival of their fleet was still an impressive sight in the early years of the twentieth century.

Of the smaller minority groups, there were forty-four Armenian residents in 1836;[4] the first Baghdad Jew arrived in 1836, and the Arabs began to bring their womenfolk to settle in the 1830s. Arabs and Middle Eastern Jews only appeared in substantial numbers in the latter decades of the century. All three communities prospered, and the major Arab families in particular accumulated enormous wealth.

The European population expanded steadily but remained a tiny minority. In 1827 they numbered ninety-four, and in 1860 there were still fewer than 500 Europeans, barely half of whom were adult British men. Their influence was disproportionate to their numbers. Crawfurd had described the European minority in 1824 as "the life and spirit of the Settlement", without whom there would be "neither capital, enterprise, activity, confidence nor order",[5] and Britons continued to fill all upper and middle-grade official posts and provide most of the trading capital.

By the end of Indian rule, Singapore was a predominantly Chinese town, with sizeable Malay and Indian minorities and an upper crust composed of Europeans with a handful of wealthy Chinese, Arabs, Parsis, Indians, Armenians and Jews.

တ

The majority of immigrants were attracted to Singapore as a trading centre. While British and Indian commerce was controlled almost exclusively by European merchants, Singapore quickly became an important centre for Asian-dominated Indonesian, Siamese, Chinese, and Malayan trade. Her harbour presented a picturesque spectacle of exotic Asian craft, often hundreds at one time: Malay *perahu*, Chinese junks, and Bugis and Arab vessels.

In the days of sail, the trade winds determined the pattern of Singapore's life, which centred round two main trading periods: the junk and the Bugis seasons. Junks from China, Cochin-China, and Siam came with the northeast monsoon, which blows from November to March, and left with the southwest monsoon, which sets in during April. Most Chinese junks arrived in January and

February, which was a time of great bustle and excitement. Swarms of boats went out to escort in the first junk of the season. The town was crowded with employers jostling to hire new immigrants and shopkeepers coming to inspect the wares spread out on the decks.

Even during the East India Company's monopoly, Chinese junks had conducted a flourishing transshipment trade with Singapore, and after 1833 the port aspired to take over Canton's role as the focal point for Western trade with China. She enjoyed a short-lived boom when Canton was closed during the First Opium War, but the founding of Hong Kong in 1841, followed by the opening of five China treaty ports, dashed Singapore's hopes of cornering the China trade.

The main Bugis fleet, coming from Sulawesi via Bali, southern Borneo and other ports south of the equator, usually reached Singapore in September or October, leaving for home in November with the onset of the northwest monsoon in the southern tropics. The strange-looking Bugis *perahu* anchored as floating shops along the shore at Kampong Glam. In the 1830s about 200 Bugis craft came to Singapore every season, each manned by about thirty men. The influx of 6,000 such daring and quick-tempered men threatened the peace, and although the Bugis were forbidden to bring arms ashore, they were often involved in violent brawls, particularly with Chinese middlemen.

Singapore has always depended heavily upon Indonesian trade, for which she provides essential services. At the same time, her position as an entrepôt created an undercurrent of envy and resentment in Indonesia that goes back to Dutch colonial times. In the 1820s and 1830s Batavia imposed restrictions, surcharges, and heavy duties on goods transshipped at Singapore and excluded her from direct access to Dutch outposts in Sumatra, Borneo, Sulawesi and Timor, but Malay and Bugis *perahu* smuggled goods between Singapore and these ports. After the heaviest Dutch restrictions were lifted in 1841, Singapore's Indonesian trade expanded steadily.

By 1826 Singapore had supplanted Batavia as the entrepôt for Siamese trade with the archipelago, but this trade was dominated by Bangkok-based Siamese and Chinese junk masters. Singapore's European merchants only succeeded in breaking this monopoly when the Anglo-Siamese Bowring Treaty of 1855 opened Siam to British traders.

Chinese traders dominated Singapore's commerce with the east-coast Malay peninsular ports, selling opium and other supplies to colonies of Chinese miners and traders in exchange for gold, tin and rattan. Until the last quarter of the nineteenth century there was little trade along the west coast of the peninsula, which was almost uninhabited apart from Melaka and Penang.

American ships were at first formally excluded. Under an Anglo-American convention of 1815, Americans were permitted to trade with Indian presidency ports, including Penang, but no provision was made to extend this right to Singapore. Raffles dismissed Americans as "commercial interlopers" and gunrunners, but a few defied the ban until one American ship was seized and taken to Calcutta for trial on the grounds of illegal trading in 1825. After that, American ships anchored at Riau or at Bantam some 14 miles away to conduct their trade with Singapore. Eventually in 1840 the prohibition was formally lifted, after which Americans flocked to the port.[6]

By 1846 there were forty-three merchant houses: twenty were British, six Jewish, five Chinese, five Arab, two Armenian, two German, one Portuguese, one American, and one Parsi. Singapore's commercial system depended mainly on a combination of European capital and Chinese enterprise. Most European merchants imported goods on consignment, which they sold on commission, and they relied on Chinese middlemen to handle dealings with their own countrymen and with other Asian traders. Most Europeans lived comfortably and few were poor, but no Westerner at that time made a fortune that matched the most successful Chinese. Singapore's spectacular success as a port brought great profits for manufacturers in Britain, but for the individual European merchant, the fluctuating entrepôt trade in the mid-nineteenth century provided what the contemporary press described as "a long drudgery which men enter upon in their youth and leave in their old age".[7]

Some Chinese were adept at property dealing and short-term speculation, lacking capital themselves but obtaining goods from Europeans in exchange for promissory notes. This form of joint enterprise could be mutually profitable, but it also encouraged recklessness and wild ventures. Many European fingers were burned when middlemen either failed and could not repay their debts or absconded to China with their profits. On several occasions from the 1830s onwards European merchants agreed among themselves to restrict credit, but all such schemes broke down, because Westerners found the Chinese middleman indispensable, and the potential prizes were so tempting.

Steamships were rarely seen in Singapore during the first twenty years but began to frequent the port in the 1840s. Reliable marine charts and the "chain of light" provided by new lighthouses made it possible for steamers to sail safely day and night and to keep to a timetable. In 1845 the Peninsular and Oriental Steamship Company began monthly sailings to the Far East, and a regular steamship service was inaugurated between Singapore and Calcutta the following year. Initially P&O steamers plied between England and the Mediterranean, disembarking passengers and offloading freight at Alexandria to travel across the Isthmus by camel and pick up an ongoing P&O steamer at Suez. In 1855 the company expanded its schedule to provide a fortnightly service from Europe, and the Suez railway, which opened in 1858, provided greater comfort and safety to passengers and security for mail. It was so reliable that by the mid-1860s people complained if English mail took more than five weeks to reach Singapore. While sailing ships continued to carry the bulk of cargoes for another thirty years, the pattern of trade changed. Western square-rigged sailing ships invaded the archipelago trade, displacing Malay and Bugis craft, and by 1854 more than three-quarters of Singapore's trade was carried in square-rigged vessels.[8]

Commercial facilities and institutions came in the wake of trade expansion. The Singapore Chamber of Commerce was founded in 1837, the Oriental Bank was established in 1846, followed in 1855 by the Mercantile Bank of India and in 1859 by the Chartered Bank of India, Australia and China. The first telegraph was laid between Singapore and Batavia in 1859. The first dry dock was opened in 1859, and in 1864 the Tanjong Pagar Dock Company was formed.

The local press played an important role in boosting Singapore's fortunes in this era. Indeed newspapers were considered so crucial in publicizing the attractions of an up-and-coming port that Singapore acquired its first newspaper, the semi-official *Singapore Chronicle* or *Commercial Register* in 1824, more than twenty years before its first bank. The *Chronicle* was supplanted by two independent journals: the *Singapore Free Press and Mercantile Advertiser*, established in 1835, followed by the *Straits Times and Singapore Journal of Commerce* in 1845. As the titles imply, a large part of these journals was devoted to commercial and shipping intelligence, and they also carried official notices before 1858, when the first government gazette was published. Copies were distributed abroad, and both the *Free Press* and *Straits Times* issued "overland editions", which took advantage of the overland Suez route to Europe. Since it was customary for newspapers to relay information from other journals, and sometimes to re-print whole articles, the *Free Press* and the *Straits Times* reached a much wider audience than their tiny readership in Singapore.

The foundations for making Singapore a great modern international port were strengthened in this period, when for the first time the treacherous waters of the Straits were made safe for shipping by charting and lighting the marine highways. Much of this was due to the encouragement of Governor William Butterworth and to the work of John Turnbull Thomson, during his twelve years as government surveyor from 1841 to 1853. Thomson had already spent three years mapping Penang and Province Wellesley, when he was appointed government surveyor in Singapore at the age of twenty-one. Together with Captain Samuel Congalton, commander of the EIC steamship *Diana*, Thomson carried out the first detailed surveys of the Singapore Straits and subsequently charted the east coasts of Johor and Pahang. His greatest achievement was to construct the Horsburgh Lighthouse on the notorious Pedra Branca reef commanding the eastern approach to Singapore harbour, which was completed in 1851 after two years' arduous labour.[9] Raffles Lighthouse, on Coney Island, at the western entrance to the Singapore Strait was erected in 1855, but by that time Thomson had left Singapore, subsequently becoming the first Surveyor General of New Zealand.

Other problems persisted, often resulting from the shortage of revenue and lack of interest on the part of the East India Company. One major difficulty was the currency. The East India Company's rupee was the official currency but only appeared in statistical records, while the common currency in actual use in Southaast Asian trade was the Spanish silver dollar. This was supplemented by Dutch copper coins and copper tokens manufactured in England and imported into Singapore as a commercial venture by British merchants. While the Company disliked the circulation of a fluctuating foreign currency over which it had no control, Calcutta did not propose to abolish the dollar, but it wished to tidy up the system by also providing for a copper currency based on fractions of the rupee. The Singapore merchants wrongly assumed that an Act to this effect, passed by the Indian Legislative Council in 1855, was the first stage in trying to oust the dollar. As a result of their protests, the unpopular Act was withdrawn in 1857, and the currency question was not settled until colonial rule was established in 1867, when dollars and cents became the official currency.[10]

❦

Piracy had always been endemic in the region whenever there was no strong controlling power, and it remained a menace to

Singapore's trade throughout the period of Indian rule. The most dangerous and highly organized pirates were the Balanini from the Sulu archipelago and the Illanun from Mindanao, whose fleets of large, heavily armed boats made annual voyages to ravage the waters of the eastern archipelago and the Malay Peninsula and were not afraid to tackle Western square-rigged ships. Smaller Asian craft were plagued by local pirates, who were sometimes organized in expeditions, such as the Sultan of Lingga's followers or the Dyaks, Bajau, and Brunei Malays who raided the west coast of Borneo. Others were fishermen or small-scale traders, who pirated ships when opportunity arose: *orang laut* from the Riau-Lingga archipelago often attacked sailing boats as they lay helplessly becalmed in the Straits of Melaka and easily escaped into the labyrinth of shallow mangrove creeks that lined the shore of the southern part of the Malay Peninsula.[11]

In the early years pirates battened on the swarms of small Asian craft coming to the new port, and it was an open secret that they were receiving help from the *temenggong*. Legitimate trade was almost brought to a standstill along the east coast of the Malay Peninsula in the early 1830s. Singapore merchants were increasingly reluctant to entrust goods on credit for fear they would be lost to pirates, and in 1831 Bugis *nakodah* complained that unless the east coast pirates were suppressed, they would abandon trading from Singapore.[12] In the port itself, pirates, who traded openly in arms and loot in the town, attacked vessels within view of the seafront and waylaid passengers travelling on sampans to board ships in the roads. In 1832 and again in 1833, a group of Chinese merchants fitted out their own vigilante armed boats to patrol the waters just outside the harbour.

Since Singapore had no Admiralty jurisdiction, captured pirates had to be sent to Calcutta for trial, and it was common practice among ships' captains to inflict irregular but effective justice by throwing captured pirates overboard. Admiralty jurisdiction was eventually granted to the Straits Settlements in 1837 but was limited to attacks committed within territorial waters.

In 1835 Governor Samuel Bonham complained to Calcutta that piracy was threatening the Asian trade with "total annihilation", and in answer to a petition from the European merchants of Singapore, a royal naval sloop, HMS *Wolf*, was dispatched to the Straits to join the Company's steamer *Diana* in hunting down pirates. The *Diana* had already caused wonderment in Burma, as the first steamship used in warfare in Southeast Asia, and the two ships now brought terror to the pirates, who had never before encountered steamers. The Royal Navy carried out vigorous campaigns in the 1840s to eliminate pirates in the South China Sea, and the Illanun fleet made its last raiding expedition in 1850. For a few years the waters round Singapore were relatively safe, but in the early 1850s a new and more virulent menace surged up in the form of large-scale Chinese piracy, which the Ch'ing government was too weak to curb. They attacked large junks as well as smaller craft and killed Singapore's trade with Formosa and Cochin-China. Pirate attacks became so frequent that in 1854 it was alleged only half the Asian craft from the archipelago succeeded in reaching Singapore.[13] As the junk season began, empty but heavily armed junks carrying large crews left Singapore every day, obviously bent on piracy, but there was no legal authority to intercept them. Nor did the Straits government have the means to take action: its "lilliputian fleet" of three gunboats was supposed to provide both protection and official transport for all three Settlements.

In 1855 the Singapore merchants sent fruitless petitions to the Governor-General of India, the Royal Navy and both Houses of Parliament, pleading for naval protection and for legislation to permit the arrest of suspected pirates. The local newspapers reported cases of piracy in nearly every issue, and in 1866 the *Singapore Free Press* complained about Chinese pirates plundering ships "within the sound of our guns".[14]

By that time the heyday of piracy in Southeast Asian waters was coming to an end. Treaties signed between the Western powers and China in 1860 provided for co-operation to wipe out piracy, and the increasing importance of the China trade led to greater activity by the British navy in the Far East, with suppressing piracy in the China Sea and the Straits of Melaka as one of its priorities. The extension of Dutch power in Sumatra from 1858 onwards and the spread of British protection over the western Malay States after 1874 hastened the rapid decline of large-scale piracy.

Almost entirely dependent on a fickle entrepôt trade, Singapore's economy in the mid-nineteenth century was subject to violent fluctuations and to years of uncertainty and depression. Progress came in fits and starts. Merchants regarded booms as times of freak good fortune and bemoaned slumps heralding permanent ruin. They were constantly haunted by the fear that prosperity might wither as quickly as it had grown, if rival free ports appeared or if the Indian government undermined Singapore's free-port status.

In the early years Singapore traders complained that Dutch restrictions on Indonesian trade threatened their enterprise, but in the 1840s they switched to grumbling about the increasingly liberal Dutch trade policy, fearing that opening ports in the Netherlands East Indies to free trade would entice ships away from Singapore. When Makassar was declared a free port in 1847, many merchants predicted that Singapore's Bugis trade was doomed. Even new British ports were seen as potential rivals. The founding of Hong Kong and the opening of the China treaty ports to foreign trade after the First Opium War plunged Singapore merchants in gloom. They also feared their Borneo trade would be diverted to Kuching, which was acquired by James Brooke in 1841, and the colony of Labuan which was founded in 1846. "I think the trade of Singapore has reached its maximum: and that the town has attained to its highest point of importance and prosperity", merchant G.F. Davidson predicted in 1846.[15] Most contemporaries shared his pessimism, convinced that the settlement faced economic depression and possibly extinction.

Forebodings about competition melted away when the expansion of commerce with China and the Netherlands East Indies in fact boosted Singapore's trade. A record number of vessels came to Singapore during the official year 1851–52, and the trade figures induced the Calcutta newspaper, *The Friend of India*, to hail Singapore as "this spirited and splendid little colony, the most important of the outlying marts of Great Britain".[16] After the Bowring Treaty of 1855, Singapore quickly became an important centre for the Bangkok trade. By 1857 the value of trade was nearly double that of fifteen years earlier.

The boom faltered in the early 1860s with the extension of Dutch control in Sulawesi and the opening of further Chinese ports to Westerners at the end of the Second Opium War. In 1862 Governor Orfeur Cavenagh reported, "Singapore has ceased to be the great port of transshipment, either for native produce or European goods; vessels from England now pass through without breaking bulk whilst the native trade is naturally attracted to the nearest marts." The worst year of the slump in 1864 brought disaster to many firms, big and small, Asian and European. The most sensational was the bankruptcy of D'Almeida and Sons, one of the oldest and most respected of Singapore's business houses.

Despite this, the setback to Singapore's expansion was only temporary and Cavenagh's fears about her permanent eclipse proved unfounded. When she was handed over to the Colonial Office in 1867, Singapore was one of the most flourishing ports in the British Empire.

෨

In contrast to Singapore's commercial success, industrial progress was disappointing and the story of agriculture was one of almost unrelieved gloom. In part the problem was shortage of labour, which persisted throughout the nineteenth century. The Malays concentrated on fishing, wood cutting, and small-scale subsistence farming, and rarely went into trading or became hired labourers. The Bugis did not adapt to organized labour, while labourers from India emigrated to Penang rather than to Singapore. Chinese labourers were highly prized but preferred to work on their own account or for their own countrymen. Most European estates relied either on Javanese or on Boyanese from the island of Bawean off Java, who were reputed to be slow but steady workers. In 1860 there were 3,000 such immigrants in Singapore, but it was difficult to import Javanese and Boyanese labour on a regular basis. Many were pilgrims returning from Mecca, who pledged their labour to Singapore plantation owners in return for payment of their debts to the shipmaster.

Singapore's only industry of any note was sago manufacture. The technique of pearling sago was imported from Melaka or Siak into early Singapore, which quickly became the centre for producing high-quality sago for export to India and Europe. By 1849 there were fifteen Chinese and two European sago factories, but Westerners found it impossible to compete with the Chinese proprietors, who lived and worked in their factories alongside their workmen.[17]

The lush tropical jungle deceived early settlers into believing the island to be very fertile, and in 1836 a group of mainly European enthusiasts formed the Singapore Agricultural and Horticultural Society to experiment with crops. Nutmeg was the most popular, and in the middle of the century nutmeg growing was described as "a sort of mania in Singapore",[18] but disease struck the plantations and by the mid-1860s only one blight-stricken nutmeg plantation remained under cultivation. By that time the town was surrounded by sinister acres of dying nutmeg trees, their bark bleached white, and their branches overgrown with creepers.

Coconuts were the second favoured crop but grew only in the sandy coastal Katong area of southeastern Singapore and brought only a modest return on capital. Sugar planting proved disastrous and in 1848 bankrupted American Consul, Joseph Balestier, who was the most ambitious sugar planter. Coffee, cotton, cinnamon, cloves, and indigo, which were planted on a more cautious experimental scale, all ended in failure, and by the 1860s European estate-type agriculture had been defeated by soil deficiencies, plant diseases, pests, and the absence of seasonal change.[19]

Only the Chinese gambier and pepper plantations flourished. These crops complemented each other, since gambier waste provided an essential fertilizer for pepper, which was more profitable but quickly exhausted the soil. Gambier leaves required boiling soon after picking, and the virgin forests of Singapore Island furnished plenty of wood for the burners. There were about twenty gambier plantations in 1819 when the British arrived, some worked by Chinese and others by Malays, and the product was exported to China. In the 1830s British dyeing and tanning industries became the chief market for Singapore's gambier. Rising demand encouraged the opening of new plantations, and Chinese pushed north and west into the interior of the island.[20]

Gambier production reached its peak in the late 1840s, by which time there were 600 gambier and pepper plantations under cultivation, employing about 6,000 Chinese labourers, but fluctuating prices made it an uncertain form of agriculture. By the middle of the century many plantations had exhausted their soil, and farmers began to move to Johor. Nearly all planters borrowed their initial capital at stiff interest rates from town shopkeepers, in return for which they were obliged to buy food and supplies from their creditors and to sell them their gambier and pepper. This system tied farmers to creditors for years, and the established Singapore dealers continued to control the new enterprises in Johor.[21]

Not only declining productivity but the growing tiger menace scared gambier planters away. Tigers were first reported in 1831, when two Chinese were killed not far from town. As more plantations encroached on the virgin jungle, the danger became so acute that by the middle of the century Singapore was famous for her tigers, which were rumoured to be carrying off on average one victim a day. A tiger was even found in Orchard Road in 1846. At first estate owners tried to suppress stories of ravages by tigers for fear of deterring labour, but by the mid-1840s they gave up trying to disguise the truth. Creditors dared not visit their estates, and in 1859 one village near Bukit Timah was abandoned after tigers killed many of its inhabitants.

Tiger hunting became a favourite sport. The government offered rewards for killing tigers, and their flesh and skins commanded sufficiently high prices to induce two Eurasians to make tiger hunting a full-time living. In 1860 Governor Cavenagh sent parties of convicts to hunt tigers in the jungles. Gradually the menace faded as the island was opened up and developed, but a man was killed by a tiger at the seventh milestone on Thomson Road in 1890, two tigers were shot on Bukit Timah Road in 1896, and the last tiger was shot at Goodwood House in 1904.[22]

"Slash and burn" gambier and pepper cultivation was disastrous for Singapore. In his efforts to get rich quickly, the immigrant Chinese peasant, forsaking the intensive care with which he had cherished and replenished the soil in his homeland, raped the earth and deserted it. The soil was exhausted, the forest destroyed and the ground left open to the encroachment of coarse lallang grass. The gambier and pepper planter moved on "as the locust leaving a tract of desolation behind him". By 1867 much of the interior of Singapore Island was laid waste and abandoned. Only the superstitious believed Singapore's agriculture was doomed by the curse of Temasek's bloodstained history, but none could deny the stark curse put on her land by gambier and pepper planters five centuries later.

৯৩

By the early 1830s Singapore was known as "the Queen of the further East",[23] but her regal qualities lay in her great economic bustle, the natural beauty of her setting, and the fine houses and godowns of her prosperous merchants. The government had no money to build public buildings to match. Merchants' stores were used as government offices, and a private European house was rented as the courthouse. The Resident lived in the flimsy *attap*-roofed wooden bungalow that Raffles had built, a structure so frail that people looked up after a stormy night to see if it was still there. The botanical garden at the foot of Government Hill was overgrown by weeds, and the Singapore Institution on the beach was a half-finished shell, the first sight that greeted travellers entering the harbour. This imposing ruin gave the settlement an antique appearance belying its recent origin. Visitors were puzzled, but first impressions were correct: a contrast between the penury of government and the ruin of intellectual ambitions on the east bank, compared with the lusty pursuit of wealth across the river.

The Singapore River was the heart of the town, and up to the 1840s all shipping congregated at its mouth and along the crescent of Boat Quay. Merchants had their offices and godowns either on Boat Quay or Commercial Square, which then backed onto the sea. In the early days many Europeans lived above their offices, but by 1830 most had moved across to the east bank fronting the Esplanade and along the beach. Here, in the "Mayfair of Singapore", they built elegant houses in spacious compounds.

In the early 1830s much of the town area was still swamp, the main roads were causeways over the marsh, and whole districts were subject to frequent floods. Fire was a major hazard, and in 1830 a fire raged for three days in the centre of the town, burning down Philip Street and part of Market Street. There was no fire-fighting service, and the police acquired fire-engines only in 1846. Even these were not effective in combating a fire that destroyed a large part of Kampong Glam the following year.[24]

George Drumgold Coleman, a talented Irish architect, who was appointed Superintendent of Public Works in 1833, brought many improvements to the town and began making extensive use of convict labour. The first Indian convicts had been transferred from Benkulen in 1825, and Singapore became the major convict centre in the Straits, "the Sydney convict settlements of India". In view of the chronic shortage of labour, convicts carried out entire projects from quarrying stone, felling timber, and making bricks to constructing churches, government offices, and other public buildings.[25]

Coleman reclaimed land along the seafront towards Kampong Glam, drained marshes, constructed roads, and built many elegant private houses in a gracious Palladian style, which set the fashion for Singapore's delicate, graceful colonial architecture. Coleman retired in 1841 and died in Singapore three years later, leaving behind many impressive buildings, of which only a few survived into the twenty-first century. Most notable was the Armenian Church and a former private house that was to form the nucleus of the first Parliament Building. Coleman's own mansion, built in 1829 in the street still bearing his name, was leased to a Frenchman, who converted it into the London Hotel in 1831. The building housed a succession of hotels and boarding houses, but by the 1930s it had degenerated into a tenement slum, which was finally pulled down in 1969. Coleman's successor, Thomson, continued his work, building bridges, constructing roads, and mapping the town and its environs.

In the 1830s solid religious buildings began to replace the original flimsy makeshift structures. Coleman completed the Armenian Church in 1835 and the first St. Andrew's Church in 1836. The first Roman Catholic Church was built in 1833 and a second, which was later consecrated as the Cathedral of the Good Shepherd, was completed in 1846. The main Chinese temple was the Thian Hok Keong in Telok Ayer Street, then fronting the sea, which was finished about 1842 and became one of the sights of Singapore. Most of the materials, including the granite pillars, ornamental stonework and a statue of sea goddess Ma-Cho-Po, were imported from China at the expense of wealthy Hokkien junk owners. The first mosque was built in Kampong Glam in 1824, but the longest surviving and most attractive mosque was erected in 1846, also in Kampong Glam, by a prosperous Melaka lady, the mother-in-law of Arab merchant Syed Ahmed Alsagoff. The reconstruction of Indian temples reflected the burgeoning prosperity of the Indian community. The Siva Temple in Orchard Road was rebuilt as a solid structure in the early 1850s, the wood and *attap* Sri Mariamman Temple was replaced by a brick building in 1862, and rich *chettiar* built the imposing Subramaniam Temple in Tank Road in 1859.[26] The first Jewish synagogue opened in Synagogue Street in 1845.

By the middle of the century there were three reputable hotels. The London Hotel was the most fashionable, and in 1845 it moved to another splendid house, which was originally built by Coleman for a leading merchant, Edward Boustead. This occupied an imposing position on the Esplanade, the site of the twentieth century Supreme Court, and in 1865 the hotel was renamed the Hotel de l'Europe, predecessor of the later Cockpit Hotel. In the mid-1840s the majority of Chinese lived in the western district of the town, the Europeans predominated in the central area, and the eastern more rural district of Kampong Glam and its environs supported a mixed population of Malays, Bugis, Arabs and Javanese, with some Chinese. The western country districts were more sparsely peopled: more than half of the inhabitants there were Chinese planters, and the remainder were mainly Malays, centred on the *temenggong*'s settlement at Telok Blangah, and *orang laut* in the New Harbour area. This pattern of racial settlement persisted in Singapore up to the mid-twentieth century.[27]

The town area was still very small and surrounded by swamps. Chinese market gardeners grew fruit and vegetables along Orchard Road, which was a country lane lined with bamboo hedges and shrubbery, with trees meeting overhead for its whole length. In the late 1830s some wealthy Chinese and European merchants began to move to country houses, often surrounded by nutmeg plantations, on the town fringes. Some settled to the west along the coast adjoining Telok Blangah, such as William Wemys Kerr at Bukit Chermin, James Guthrie at St. James and Joaquim d'Almeida at Raeburn. Others moved eastward, notably Joseph Balestier, who planted sugar cane on the plain which came to bear his name, Thomas Dunman who grew coconuts at Katong, and Hoo Ah Kay (nicknamed "Whampoa") who built a mansion with a magnificent ornamental garden on Serangoon Road. Most Westerners preferred to move north towards Tanglin, where the roads were better and the approach to town was prettier. Dr. Thomas Oxley, the government surgeon and an ardent nutmeg planter, moved to Killiney in 1837, and was followed by Charles Carnie at Carnie's Hill (Cairnhill), Thomas Hewetson at Mount Elizabeth, and Dr. Mungo Johnston Martin at River Valley.

The interior of the island beyond these suburbs was still a mystery to Europeans despite the fact that the island was so small. Put off by the swampy coasts, the thick jungle terrain and apparently by sheer lack of curiosity, Westerners rarely ventured far beyond the town limits and left the interior to Asian, primarily Chinese, settlers. By 1840 roads extended to Bukit Timah and Serangoon, each about seven miles long. In 1843 a road was constructed to the top of Bukit Timah Hill, and the idea of building a miniature hill station was mooted but abandoned because of the fear of tigers. In 1845 the Bukit Timah road was extended through to the Johor Strait, giving access to the hitherto isolated plantations in the north of the island.

The Singapore River remained the heart of the business sector but became increasingly congested. Businessmen and military engineers complained that Raffles had made a mistake in siting the town on the river, where commerce was cramped and defence impossible. Keppel Harbour, then known as New Harbour, a fine, large, deep harbour that was sheltered and easy to defend, had been brought to Farquhar's notice in July 1819, but Raffles vetoed Farquhar's suggestions to develop it. Established firms were reluctant to move from Boat Quay until they were forced to do so by the advent of steamers, which needed deep water and coal supplies. The Peninsular and Oriental Steamship Company (P&O Company) was the first to establish itself at New Harbour in 1852. It was quickly followed by Jardines, the Borneo Company, and other big firms. Despite this, three-quarters of all shipping business in the 1860s was still done at Boat Quay in the heart of the town.[28]

Despite her lovely setting and orderly planning, many parts of Singapore in the mid-nineteenth century were still unsightly. The main streets frequently flooded at high tide and were lit by feeble coconut-oil lamps. The town was plagued by stray dogs, and dead ponies were left to rot on the beach. The city's refuse was thrown into the swamps, the roads were littered with garbage, and the Singapore grand jury complained at almost every session about pollution and stench. The problem was lack of money. Residents demanded more amenities but refused to pay higher property assessments, while Calcutta did not consider that lightly-taxed Singapore deserved further government subsidies. The Company refused to build a new bridge near the river mouth or to mend the two existing bridges, which could not cope with the increased traffic and fell into a dangerous state of disrepair. Traffic jams and reckless driving led to frequent accidents, many of them caused because the authorities could not enforce any rule about keeping to one side of the road.

༄

Despite the phenomenal growth of population and trade, throughout the period of Indian rule Singapore's merchants lived on their nerves, vulnerable to every slump in international commerce, and frequently at loggerheads with the Government of India and Straits officials. Haunted by a basic insecurity that drove them to an obstinate and sometimes hysterical defence of their privileges, they opposed all proposals to impose new taxes, which would have provided better port facilities, security and social amenities. For its part, the East India Company, which already subsidized Singapore's general revenue, refused to incur a greater deficit and lapsed into a neglectful parsimony.

The drastic economies of 1830 failed to make the Straits Settlements solvent, and the Singapore government could benefit only indirectly from increased prosperity and an expanding population in the form of excise revenue, licences, and property taxes. Until the last few years of the Indian regime, these were insufficient to cover administration costs, and the loss had to be made good by Calcutta.

The right to collect excise taxes was auctioned to private Chinese bidders, except in the case of the Indian-held toddy farm. Farming out excise taxes ensured the government a comparatively secure income at no cost. Direct excise collection was impracticable and, as Crawfurd said, "The government would be brought into a frequent and odious collision with the natives, and compelled to employ a vile, expensive and corrupt crew of native excise officers."[29] A few officials and private residents argued that a tax on vices officially encouraged moral corruption, but the majority of the ruling class had no such compunction and agreed with Governor Fullerton that "the vicious propensities of mankind are the fittest subjects of taxation".[30]

One vice was considered too morally heinous to tax, namely gambling. The gambling tax farm, started by Farquhar, banned by Raffles, and restored by Crawfurd in 1823, was in its time the most lucrative of all the Singapore revenue farms. But the temptation offered to immigrants to get rich quickly led to such misery, destitution, and crime that the grand jury demanded the prohibition of gambling. In 1829 it was declared illegal, and the gambling farm was never restored, despite many suggestions in later years that it would be a palatable means of balancing the revenue.

From time to time, other minor taxes were imposed on pork, toddy, and betel-nuts, while pawnbrokers and market stall holders paid licence fees, but the opium and *arrack* farms remained the main sources of revenue throughout the nineteenth century. As the Secretary of State for India commented in 1859, the revenue was "derived more from the vices than from the industry of the people". This fitted the self-righteous philosophy of Singapore's ruling class. The predominantly Scottish merchant group tended to be puritanical, stressing the spartan qualities of thrift and hard work. Many were kind, charitable, generous individuals, contributing handsomely to relieve distress or support worthy causes, but collectively their harsh *laissez-faire* cult and emphasis on the virtues of self-help and industry gave moral backing to callous practices.

In seeking to balance the budget, officials in Singapore and India made periodic proposals to tax trade, which the European mercantile community resisted indignantly. They argued that, apart from her geographical position, Singapore was blessed with few natural advantages, and her prosperity depended upon her liberal policy. Raffles had converted a temporary expedient to attract trade into a promise of permanent freedom from custom duties, which Crawfurd extended to include port charges. The principle of free trade was accepted by the East India Company's Board of Control in London in 1826 and thereafter defended zealously by the Singapore merchants. Free trade became a sacred cardinal principle and any threatened infringement was opposed vehemently as commercial heresy.

The merchants defeated suggestions made by Fullerton in 1829 to impose export duties and stamp dues and to tax aliens' exported capital. In 1836 they succeeded in obtaining a veto from the Company in London on port dues, which Calcutta had proposed to levy in order to finance anti-piracy measures in Singapore. The Singapore Chamber of Commerce was founded the following year to safeguard this freedom. Open to merchants of all races, its first committee included Europeans, Chinese, Eurasians and Arabs, and it became an important mouthpiece for the mercantile community in dealing with the Straits authorities.[31]

Since the government was compelled to guarantee freedom not only from trade tariffs but also from tonnage and port dues, wharfage and anchorage dues, port clearance fees and stamp duties, its revenue had no chance to share in commercial prosperity. Hampered by lack of money and shortage of officials, the lax administration provided a semblance of law and order that scarcely touched the lives of the inhabitants. This *laissez-faire* policy and the absence of taxes and restrictions benefited trade but led to deficiencies of government, particularly in the provision of security and social services. It also meant that the different communities retained and developed their own organizations, virtually outside the pale of official administration.

After the *kapitan* system was supplanted by the Charter of Justice in 1826, the government's control over the Asian population was tenuous. It enlisted the co-operation of influential members of different communities but gave them no formal functions. The result was an unsatisfactory compromise, with the authorities expecting community leaders to keep their own people in order but giving them no definite authority.

Most Indonesian and Arab immigrants settled in parts of the town still bearing their names, such as Kampong Jawa, Kampong Sumbawa, Bugis Street, and Arab Street. They adapted peaceably to their new environment without coming into much contact with the government.

For many years the Malay community lacked leadership and organization because Sultan Hussein did not possess the ability to profit from the sudden upward turn in his fortunes. The Company had recognized him as sultan to give a cloak of legality to their Singapore settlement, but he commanded no respect in the Malay world, which looked more to the sultans of Lingga as heirs to the Johor-Riau Empire. While the Anglo-Dutch Treaty of 1824 had dealt a blow to the already faltering empire, the formal installation of Hussein's half brother, despite being Dutch-sponsored, gave him some semblance of legitimacy. His successor as Sultan of Lingga was a young man of considerable ability, who was widely admired up to the time of his untimely death in 1841. By the early 1830s, exhibiting a Pickwickian syndrome, Hussein had become "so enormously stout that he appears to be continually on the point of suffocation ... and exists only in a torpid state".[32] Family scandals and mounting debts compelled him to move to Melaka, where he died in 1835. His fifteen-year-old son Ali returned to Singapore in 1840 and took possession of his father's property in Kampong Glam, but for many years the Straits government refused to acknowledge his claim to be sultan.

By the time Temenggong Abdur Rahman died in 1825, Raffles and Crawfurd had thwarted any ambitions that he may have harboured of turning Singapore into another Melaka, with a foreign trading community subservient to the Malay authorities.

The Crawfurd and Anglo-Dutch Treaties had deprived him of nearly all his patrimony, from which he would expect to derive his status, his income and the means to pay his retinue. No successor was appointed to the office of *temenggong* for nearly twenty years, and for some time confusion reigned in the Telok Blangah community. But during the 1830s the late *temenggong's* intelligent and enterprising younger son, Daing Ibrahim, who had been brought to Singapore in 1819 when he was eight years old, emerged as leader. Profiting from Hussein's disgrace and Ali's youth, he increased his prestige among his followers and neighbouring Malay chiefs. In 1841 the *bendahara* of Pahang formally installed Ibrahim as *temenggong* at Telok Blangah in the presence of Governor Bonham, and he immediately went to pay homage to the newly installed Sultan Mahmud of Lingga.

There were rich pickings to be had as Singapore's trade expanded, and at first Ibrahim's followers preyed on the swarms of small Asian craft that frequented the port. The *Singapore Free Press* alleged that, either with his connivance or at his becking, the *temenggong's* men were responsible for all the piracy in the immediate neighbourhood. The wily Ibrahim saw the value of cultivating the British governor's approval, and the vigorous campaign undertaken by the Straits authorities to suppress piracy induced him to restrain his subjects and assume the role of pirate hunter. This change of policy paid dividends, and at a glittering ceremony in 1846 Governor William Butterworth presented a sword to the *temenggong* in token of his vigilance in suppressing pirates. Many of the European merchants considered the occasion a mockery, but Ibrahim's decision to abandon piracy made the nearby waters around Singapore safe for small ships. It also changed the role of his entourage, whom the authorities had until then regarded as idle good-for-nothing mischief makers.

Seeking alternative sources of income, from the mid-1840s the *temenggong* turned his attention to exploiting the resources of mainland Johor. He established a profitable monopoly over the *gutta-percha* trade and licensed Chinese gambier and pepper planters to move from the island to open up Johore's southern river valleys. The development of New Harbour in the early 1850s made Ibrahim's property along the Telok Blangah waterfront very valuable, and by the middle of the century the *temenggong* was a wealthy man.

The Singapore authorities welcomed Ibrahim's conversion from pirate to businessman, and with their blessing he became influential in Singapore's commercial life. He struck up friendships with European merchants, particularly with his neighbour at Bukit Chermin, William Kerr, who became his business associate. After Kerr returned to England, his partners, William Paterson and Henry Simons, continued to act as the *temenggong*'s agents, and the firm of Paterson & Simons was the first European company in Singapore to extend its operations to Johor and taste the tempting fruits of the peninsular trade.

While the *temenggong* grew rich, the would-be sultan, Ali, was in a desperate financial plight, facing the threat of debtors' prison. Constantly bemoaning the insufficiency of his allowance but refusing to soil his hands with trade, Ali was unable to pay his diminishing band of followers, and his government pension was pledged to an Indian moneylender to pay the interest on his debts.

Merchants such as Kerr, Paterson and Simons hitched their fortunes to the *temenggong*'s rising star, but others, notably William Henry Read of A.L. Johnston & Co., tried to manipulate Ali's weakness to their own advantage. Alarmed by the intrigues among the European commercial community, Governor Butterworth attempted to stop this meddling in Johor politics. In 1855 he negotiated a treaty between Ali and Ibrahim, whereby Ali acknowledged Ibrahim as actual ruler of Johor but received a fixed allowance from the state revenue and acquired the long-coveted title of Sultan. It was an empty and meaningless honour. Ali's son was to lose the title, and the family sank into obscure poverty in Kampong Glam. The Johor treaty failed to settle the commercial intrigue, particularly between Johnstons and Paterson & Simons. The *temenggong* quarrelled with the Singapore authorities over leasing his land in New Harbour to private companies and over the alleged mistreatment of Chinese British subjects in Johor. The

British were startled to learn in the late 1850s that the *temenggong* was still appointing headmen on the islands in Singapore Harbour. When the Resident Councillor made a tour of inspection to set the record straight, he found one headman who did not know that the British had been ruling Singapore for the past 40 years and another who was aware of the British presence but did not see why this should affect his relationship with his traditional overlord.

The 1855 Johor Treaty, in which the British Governor officiated to allocate titles and territory, broke with Malay tradition. It angered Sultan Mahmud of Lingga and Bendahara Ali, who had installed Ibrahim in 1841 under the correct procedure as Sultan Mahmud's *temenggong*, but the *bendahara* was not present in 1855 and was not even informed about the ceremony. By that time Temenggong Ibrahim had decided there was more to gain from aligning with the British, and Butterworth's successor, Governor Sir Orfeur Cavenagh, established a cordial working relationship with Ibrahim's intelligent son, Abu Bakar, who succeeded him as *temenggong* in 1862. Christian-mission educated, Abu Bakar spoke good English, and co-operated with a series of governors to their mutual benefit. He transferred his headquarters to Tanjong Putri (the modern Johor Bahru) where he modelled his administration and legal system on the Straits Settlements, and in 1885 the British recognized Abu Bakar as Sultan of Johor.

The new Johor royal family kept residences in Singapore and remained prominent in the city's sporting and social life but played no political role. With the diversion of Telok Blangah's interest to the mainland and the decline of the Kampong Glam aristocracy into penury, no alternative leaders emerged to take their place at the head of the Malay community in Singapore.

Despite their numbers and their concentration in the urban area, the Indian community made comparatively little impact in this era. Nearly all were labourers, ferrymen, or petty tradesmen, who were divided in background, language, and religion. In the mid-nineteenth century there were seventeen Parsi, Tamil, and North Indian businessmen of standing in Singapore, but they were notable as individuals rather than community leaders. Indeed, the rich Parsis stood aloof from the Indian community, and the ruling class did not regard them as Indians.

ၜ

The Chinese facility to organize themselves and run their affairs independently was viewed with a mixture of approval and worry by the ruling community. Officials respected the Chinese as hardworking and self-reliant settlers but feared the clan feuds and secret societies that they brought with them. The vast majority of Chinese immigrants were hardy, resourceful pioneers from the coastal strip of East Kwangtung and South Fukien. In these hilly provinces, cut off from Central China by mountain ranges, a considerable part of the population was engaged in fishing, junk building and trade rather than agriculture, and ambitious young men were accustomed to emigrate in search of a living. These young emigrants, inured to frugal living and long hours of gruelling labour, were ideal pioneers in facing the hardships, dangers and deprivations of a new life in the Nanyang.[33]

Most Chinese immigrants to Singapore were illiterate youths who had never been outside their home villages, and when they moved to the bewildering new world of Singapore they sought out familiar organizations among their own people. Having no guidance from the Straits government and no contact with their own, they joined earlier settlers with the same family surname, coming from the same neighbourhood in China and speaking the same dialect. They adopted similar occupations, and later these district groups merged into wider dialect *pang* or guilds, which dealt not only with employment but covered broad social, religious and economic activities, such as offering mutual assistance and managing temples.[34] Some associations were formed by Chinese immigrants from Penang and Melaka. Records are fragmentary, but there was a Hakka Association in Singapore as early as 1823,[35] the Teochew community founded the Ngee Ann Kongsi about 1830, and the Hokkien Association of Singapore was established in 1839.

This family and regional loyalty helped Chinese immigrants to fit into the new society, but at the same time Fukien and Kwangtung were notorious for their bitter clan feuds. These provinces were also the major source of strength for the Triad, or Heaven and Earth Society, a political secret society dedicated to the overthrow of Manchu imperial rule in China. Political refugees probably formed societies in Melaka as early as the mid-seventeenth century, when the Manchus conquered China, but the main function of the secret societies overseas was to organize the coolie trade.[36] Until the passing of the Chinese Immigration Ordinance in 1880, the distribution of coolie immigrants was handled by brokers, who were senior secret-society members.[37] Triad branches were set up in the early days and by 1840 the Triad Society was said to have some 5,000–6,000 members in Singapore. Rival societies sprang up in the middle years of the century and accounted for much of the violence and crime that plagued the island at that time.

Despite this, the *hoey* political subversion was directed only against the Manchus, and they performed many useful social functions. They protected young immigrants, arranged their employment and admitted them to a brotherhood which provided a sense of belonging in a strange foreign land. They settled disputes among their own people, who found the official judicial system remote, complicated, and difficult to understand. But the secret societies' insistence on complete obedience and defending fellow brethren to the point of perjury impeded the British judicial system. Officials tried, without much success, to undermine the authority of the *hoey* tribunals and attract the Chinese into the British system by opening more magistrates' courts to deal speedily with petty crimes, firmly punishing any obvious perjury, and administering the law impartially to rich and poor. The Singapore authorities were loath to apply force against the societies. Governor Butterworth refused to support pleas from the Singapore grand jury to suppress the *hoey*, and he assured Calcutta in 1848, "I am of the opinion that the Chinese are the best and most peaceable colonists in the world."[38] Grand juries continued to plead for suppression and wanted to ban Chinese from jury service, for fear they might be secret-society members.

The secret societies sought to enrol all Chinese immigrants into their ranks and bitterly opposed the conversion of Chinese to Christianity, which constituted a threat to their own authority. In 1851 the *hoey* sent gangs to wipe out Christian converts on the plantations in the interior. It was rumoured that 500 Christians were slaughtered and nearly thirty agricultural settlements destroyed.

By the mid-1850s Chinese immigration had reached a new peak, as youths in their thousands defied the Manchu Empire's prohibition on emigration in order to escape land hunger and civil war. In the official year 1853–54 more than 13,000 Chinese immigrants arrived, many of them rebels and refugees from the civil war raging in southern China. Singapore Hokkiens supplied much of the money and leadership for the Short Daggers Rebellion, in which rebels seized temporary control of Amoy in 1853. Most of these rebels subsequently fled to Singapore where their arrival upset the balance of the existing societies. After weeks of tension, fighting broke out in the interior in 1854 and led to great bloodshed. There were reports of terrible atrocities, impaling and mutilation of men, women, and children, of whole villages wiped out, and rumours that hundreds of Chinese were massing on the outskirts to attack the town. Possibly about 400 Chinese were killed, many Chinese shops were looted, and after the fighting died down in the town, strife continued in the country areas for a week. But the disturbance was an internal dispute among the Chinese and not directed against the Straits government or the other communities.

The secret societies battened on the coolie trade and prostitution, which offered great scope for exploiting a floating population of predominantly young unattached men. Demands for labour led to gross abuses in the coolie traffic. Many youths were drugged, kidnapped or tricked by recruiting agents in China, and for most of them the voyage to Singapore was a nightmare. Confined to sweltering holds, hundreds died on the journey, and dead bodies were often thrown overboard in Singapore harbour. On one junk that arrived from Macau in 1863, only 120 of its 300 passengers were still alive.[39]

Immigrants were imprisoned in the hold until prospective employers paid off the passage money to the junk masters. Sick men, whom no one would hire, often died, but employers quickly snapped up the able-bodied. The immigrant worker, or *sinkheh*, was obliged to serve his employer for one year, during which he was housed, fed, clothed and given a small allowance. He was then free to find his own employment.

The British authorities used prominent Chinese merchants as go-betweens with the different dialect groups. Experience of European ways and an ability to speak Malay and sometimes a little English gave an initial advantage to the Baba Chinese, such as Chua Chong Long and Tan Che Sang, and subsequently to the Melaka-born Hokkiens, Tan Tock Seng and Tan Kim Seng. Tan Tock Seng was Singapore's first Asian justice of the peace. Tan Kim Seng, a third-generation Baba born in 1805, accumulated great wealth in property and trade in Singapore and at the time of his death in 1864 was reputed to be worth $2 million.

China-born immigrants, who had a reputation for great energy and acumen, soon began to challenge this Baba supremacy. Seah Eu Chin and Hoo Ah Kay were the two most prominent China-born immigrants in the mid-nineteenth century. Seah Eu Chin, a well-educated Teochew and son of a minor mandarin, settled in Singapore in 1830. He became a ship's chandler and invested in land, particularly in gambier and pepper planting. An early member of the Singapore Chamber of Commerce, a Justice of the Peace and one of the first Chinese to become a naturalized British subject, Seah was the Singapore government's trusted go-between with the Teochew community. He retired in Singapore in 1864, devoting the remaining nineteen years of his life to the study of Chinese literature.

The Cantonese Hoo Ah Kay, nicknamed "Whampoa" after his birthplace, was probably the wealthiest Chinese and certainly the best-known and most popular in European circles.[40] He also came to Singapore in 1830, at the age of fifteen, and remained there until his death in 1880. Having built up a flourishing ship's chandling business, he diversified his interests, opening a department store, a bakery, and an ice house, and speculating profitably in land. Whampoa rose to higher political office than any other Singapore Chinese in the nineteenth century, becoming the first Asian member of the Legislative Council in 1869 and an extraordinary member of the Executive Council a few years later.

The traditional pattern of leadership in mainland China, based on reverence for scholarship and the dominance of the mandarin class, was broken by immigration to Singapore. Wealth and material success, rather than learning, commanded respect, and rich Chinese acquired prestige in building hospitals, schools, poorhouses, and markets, and in sponsoring entertainment events.

Outwardly the wealthy Chinese merchants were co-operative with the Singapore authorities. Whampoa in particular cultivated the friendship of the British and was said to be "almost as much an Englishman as he is a Chinaman".[41] To some extent, the Chinese merchants leagued themselves with the ruling class against the rank and file of their own countrymen. Tan Kim Seng and Choa Chong Long entertained Europeans to dinners and balls, while Whampoa, who spoke excellent English, frequently invited European friends to his house and was particularly popular among British seafaring men. But however hospitable and cordial their behaviour towards the ruling community, even the most Westernized clung to their Chinese customs, traditions, and sense of values. They continued to wear Chinese dress, shave their heads, and wear pigtails. The private life of the well-to-do Chinese was a mystery to their closest European associates, who did not know whether they had any connections with Singapore's underworld. No respectable Chinese merchant would admit to membership of a secret society, but it was rumoured that Whampoa and other prominent Chinese were *hoey* leaders.

Despite its weakness, the government was not unduly alarmed, since it faced no serious challenge to its authority. The natural divisions in Singapore's mixed population were so deep that the authorities had no need to employ any conscious "divide and rule" policy. Chinese, Malays and Indians were separated in language, religion, customs, social organization and economic activity. Within the Chinese community there were wide divisions among the different dialect groups. While they brought their local and regional quarrels to Singapore, the Chinese showed no hostility to the colonial government, even when Britain was at war with China. In 1857 Lord Elgin, the British High Commissioner and Plenipotentiary, passing through Singapore with troops to fight in China, was astonished to receive an address from the leading Chinese merchants, expressing loyalty and appreciation of the advantages the Straits Chinese enjoyed under British rule.[42] The Chinese were seen as a potential danger "not from their sympathy with the country from which they sprang but from their want of sympathy with the country in which they have taken up their abode".[43] There were times of rumour and panic but no revolts.

Many merchants did not share the government's optimism. Europeans were apprehensive at being a tiny minority among thousands of Asians, and well-to-do merchants of all races looked with misgiving at the mass of poor, illiterate, half-starving rootless youths who came to make their fortune. They also began to appreciate that cheap convict labour had been recruited at the cost of flooding Singapore with dangerous criminals. In 1851 *The* Singapore Free Press lamented that the Straits Settlements were "the common sewer ... for all the scum and refuse of the populations of nearly the whole British possessions in the East",[44] and three years later declared, "We have in this small island the very dregs of the population of Southeastern Asia."[45]

In the early years, Indian convicts supplied Singapore with a steady supply of cheap labour for public works. Since there was insufficient revenue to provide guards for the large convict body, prisoners were allowed a great deal of freedom. This situation bred an enlightened system, in which they were supervised almost entirely by senior petty officers, who were themselves convicts and had been promoted for good behaviour. After a probationary period working in gangs on heavy manual labour, convicts were taught a skill to enable them to be useful during their confinement and to earn an honest living after their release. They learned brick making, weaving, tailoring, rope making, printing, carpentry, and even photography.

Born of financial necessity, this convict administration later became a matter of pride. Observers came from the Netherlands East Indies, Siam and Japan to study its applicability to their own society, and the prison was a tourist attraction in the 1860s. The emphasis was on training, reformation and useful employment rather than punishment. In convict administration mid-nineteenth century Singapore came nearer to advanced Benthamite thinking than anywhere else in the world.

Most convicts were Indians. Small numbers of Chinese convicts were transported from Hong Kong but with the help of the secret societies, they easily escaped to merge into the general population, and after many years of agitation, transportation of Chinese convicts was stopped in 1856.

The mass of the population was afraid of the Indian convicts. During the worst scare in 1853, when the first St. Andrew's Church was struck by lightning, rumours spread that the Governor had sent Indian convicts to collect human heads to pacify the spirits who were harming the church. Official proclamations failed to allay the panic, and leading Chinese merchants had to be called upon to restore calm among their people.

At first the European merchants welcomed convicts as an essential source of cheap labour, but by the middle of the century they worried about the violent under-currents in Singapore society and were alarmed at the large numbers of dangerous criminals, who included dacoits and thugs, coming from Calcutta.

Convict labour contributed much to Singapore, but the long-term effect on the character of the population is difficult to gauge. There was no provision before 1859 for repatriating convicts at the end of their sentence, and even after that date many released convicts remained as permanent settlers. Female convicts were in great demand as brides for Indian bachelors, and the government was so eager to rehabilitate them that even a murderess rarely had to spend more than two or three years in gaol.[46] Only a few former convicts were charged with subsequent crimes, but ex-convicts figured prominently among the turbulent Indo-Malay Jawi-Peranakan class, and the Hindu Dusserah and Muslim Muharram festivals, when convicts were given leave to stage street processions, were invariably times of unrest and violence.

The much-prized freedom of immigration contributed to Singapore's growth and success, but it brought a transitory population, consisting in the main of poverty-stricken young men. This made it difficult to maintain law and order, and for many decades Singapore had the air of a pioneering town: virile, bustling, and active but tending to be lawless and disorderly.

The sexes were evenly balanced among the Malays, Bugis, and Eurasians, but men outnumbered women by a large majority in the Chinese, European, and Indian communities. This problem was particularly serious among the Chinese, since the emigration of women from China was not only illegal but socially unacceptable. Wives and families sought temporary refuge with their husbands in Singapore in times of exceptional upheaval, such as the Amoy Rebellion in 1853, but even after China relaxed her emigration laws in 1859, it was many years before respectable women came to Singapore in any numbers. The only "Chinese" women were of mixed blood or young prostitutes imported by the secret societies.

The disparity between numbers of Chinese men and women was a major social problem. The ruling class wanted to promote Chinese female immigration on many counts: in order to encourage permanent settlement, to divert shifting, rootless youths from crime, to curb the secret societies' hold over prostitution, and to stem the drain to China of family remittances that could be used to develop Singapore.

In 1856 a group of European merchants offered to pay a bonus to Chinese who brought their wives to Singapore. Five years later Governor Cavenagh, in considering a scheme to legalize gambling, suggested using part of the proposed gaming licence money to subsidize Chinese female immigration in order to wean men from the gaming table to "the comforts of a home" and to build up a permanent resident labour force. None of these ideas bore fruit, and in the mid-1860s there was still only one "Chinese" woman to every fifteen men.

Weak government, lack of finance, secret society power, and a transitory population made early Singapore a violent place. The hundreds of Chinese who lived on the isolated pepper and gambier farms in the interior were beyond the writ of government, and the authorities did not pretend to exert any control in the country districts, but even the town was unsafe. The main danger came from gang robberies, which were reputed to be the work of Chinese secret societies. Gangs of up to 200 Chinese with blackened faces raided parts of the town almost every night in the early 1840s. Their chief targets were the Malay districts, but they sometimes attacked Indians and Europeans too, breaking into buildings, ransacking, and murdering. The whole town lived in fear, and the tiny police force prudently kept out of the way until the gangsters had gone.

In 1843 violent crime reached such a pitch that the English-speaking merchants held a protest meeting and persuaded the government to appoint Thomas Dunman, a young commercial assistant, as the first Superintendent of Police. A vigorous and sensible man, respected by European officials and merchants, Dunman also had useful contacts with the Chinese community. His initial difficulties were immense. The Netherlands East Indies authorities frequently shipped troublemakers to Singapore, and 3,000 Chinese immigrants arriving from Riau in 1846 included a number of deported secret society leaders, who instigated a wave of crime. This reached a climax with the ransacking of

Thomas Hewetson's plantation bungalow at Mount Elizabeth by a large gang of thieves, which led nervous householders in the neighbouring Claymore and Tanglin districts to appeal for protection. Dunman battled hard to produce an efficient force, but his material was unpromising. Police work was so arduous, dangerous, and poorly paid that the only recruits were unemployed men in desperate financial straits, many of them stranded sailors who became policemen as a temporary stopgap occupation. An underpaid, overworked force had no inducement to court danger with possible injury or death. It was more profitable for policemen to accept bribes from gambling house keepers and more prudent to keep away from violence.

Dunman struggled to improve the calibre of his policemen, fighting for better conditions and higher wages. He reduced their hours of work and taught them to read and write. Within a few years he managed to check gang robberies. He was promoted to become Singapore's first full-time Commissioner of Police in 1857 and within the limitations of his position achieved a striking improvement in the police in the last years of Indian rule. The force was still small, but its calibre and morale were greatly improved. The police began to be more effective in the country districts, and police posts were established along the coasts. The lack of money hampered police work but brought compensating advantages. Authority could not rest on brute force but on persuasion and co-operation, and by the time he retired in 1871 Dunman had laid the foundations for an efficient and humane force.

The police force and the government continued to fight an uphill battle in face of the great influx of immigrants. By the middle of the century Singapore was the focal point of Chinese immigration for the entire region. The 1854 riots alarmed the European community. They led to further demands for strengthening the police force, and to the European and Eurasian inhabitants forming the Singapore Volunteer Rifle Corps in July 1854, the first such body in Britain's possessions in the East. On occasion the authorities proposed checks on immigration to prevent the influx of criminals or sick paupers and to stem the evils of the coolie trade and the traffic in prostitutes, but the merchant community would tolerate no restrictions on immigrant labour. Free immigration was a cardinal principle, second only to the preservation of free trade.

⚬

The attitude towards external defence was initially very different. In the first half of the nineteenth century Singapore had no fears of being engulfed in an international war, and neither officials nor merchants showed much interest in providing for her defence. The Singapore merchants begrudged even the small amount spent on the modest Indian garrison.

Military and naval officers were more concerned about Singapore's defence needs, and in 1827 Captain Edward Lake of the Bengal Engineers was sent to advise the colony on fortifications. Realizing its potential strategic and commercial value, Lake incorporated New Harbour into his scheme of defence and also recommended constructing a line of batteries to protect the town from a sea attack. Nothing was done, except to begin erecting a battery at the entrance to the Singapore River, which fell victim to India's economy campaign and was left half-finished. In 1843 Captain Best of the Madras Engineers drew up an ambitious scheme to protect

New Harbour and to construct a chain of batteries along the coast with forts to accommodate 3,000 troops. These expensive suggestions were also ignored, and in the mid-1840s Sir Edward Belcher, captain of the survey ship H.M.S. *Samarang*, bemoaned the "utter want of defence".[47] Captain (later Admiral Sir) Henry Keppel surveyed New Harbour and reported its advantages to the Admiralty in 1848, but the British government eventually chose Hong Kong instead of Singapore as its Far East naval headquarters.

The Singapore merchants were rudely jolted out of their complacency by the outbreak of the Crimean War in 1854. Singapore's defenceless prosperity could make her an attractive target, and throughout the war the British community feared that a surprise naval attack or even an isolated Russian warship might blast the heart out of the town without warning. Tension persisted even when peace was signed because of the possibility of revolt on the part of her own lawless people.

After decades of inactivity, Calcutta suddenly launched into constructing elaborate fortifications in Singapore. Captain George Collyer of the Madras Engineers was sent in 1858, in response to an appeal by Governor Edmund Blundell for the construction of simple defence works and a place of refuge for the European population in the event of a local rebellion. Carried away by enthusiasm, Collyer planned a line of shore batteries and recommended constructing extensive fortifications on Government Hill overlooking the town and harbour, with an arsenal, workshops, commissariat, powder house and barracks. These, together with smaller forts on neighbouring hills and a refuge area to enclose the government buildings, courthouse, church and town hall, would turn the whole town into a quasi-military cantonment. Collyer also advised building forts on the islands commanding New Harbour and cutting a canal through to the Singapore River.[48]

These proposals appalled Blundell, who warned Calcutta that converting Singapore into "a great military fortress" might kill her trade. Collyer was ordered to modify his schemes, but he had already pulled down the old Government House and levelled the top of the hill to make way for Fort Canning, which was completed in 1860 and named after Governor-General of India Lord Charles Canning. A useless fortification, it might perhaps more appropriately be named Collyer's Folly. It could not provide refuge for the European population during internal riots because it had no independent water supply. Its guns could not protect the town against external attack because they were out of range of enemy ships and would merely destroy the town and shipping in the harbour. Indeed, one puzzled Dutch observer concluded erroneously that the guns were purposely fixed to destroy Chinatown in time of local trouble.

৯৯

Lack of revenue and the transient unbalanced nature of the population made it difficult to develop an education policy or provide social services. Raffles's dreams of Singapore as an educational centre soon faded, and she did not prove a magnet for learning in the way that she attracted trade. The East India Company showed no enthusiasm in educating its officials in the languages and customs of the region and withdrew its meagre maintenance grant in the 1830 economy campaign. Raffles's educational schemes were defeated not only by the Company's parsimony but also by the indifference of Singapore society. Until late in the nineteenth century there was little public demand for education. Immigrants came to make money, not to settle and raise families, and neighbouring rulers ignored invitations to educate their sons in Singapore.

In 1835 a group of European merchants raised funds to complete the Singapore Institution, which was to be renamed Raffles Institution in 1868. It comprised an upper English-medium school and a lower school, teaching partly in English and partly in vernacular languages, including Malay, Tamil, Bugis, Siamese and various Chinese dialects. The school committee was particularly keen to promote Malay education and employed five Malay teachers in 1838–39.

The upper school attracted resident European children, some Portuguese from Macau and the sons of affluent Chinese merchants. The standard was low, and most Asian children were withdrawn once they had learned enough English to find a job or deal with European customers. The lower school was a failure. Teachers were paid according to the number of pupils they could recruit, and, despite vigorous touting for students, Tamil, Bugis, Siamese, Malay, and most Chinese classes had to be closed down. By 1843 only one Hokkien group of twenty-five pupils remained.

The Singapore Institution and its sister school for girls continued as indifferent primary schools. Fees and subscriptions barely covered the costs, and the government would provide no money for repairs to the building, which by 1851 was in a dangerous state of dilapidation. The Christian missions showed only passing interest in early Singapore, where they were more influential in promoting printing than religion or education.[49] Protestant missionaries established temporary headquarters in Singapore, but had their eyes on the forbidden land of China. The London Missionary Society opened its first school in 1822 with twelve pupils learning Malay and English, and by 1829 the society had four schools. In 1834 the American Board of Commissioners of Foreign Missions made Singapore its base for China, and within three years the board had nineteen missionaries in Singapore and more than 300 Chinese pupils.

When China was opened to Christian missionaries after the First Opium War, the American and British Protestant missionary societies pulled up their Singapore roots and closed their schools, the Americans in 1842 and the London Missionary Society five years later.

The Roman Catholic community was torn by the rival claims of the Goa-based Portuguese mission and the Siam-based French mission, whose conflict was not settled until 1886. Meanwhile, Roman Catholic and Anglican education was left to private philanthropists and individual missionaries.

A French priest, Father Jean Marie Beurel, opened St. Joseph's Institution in 1852 and a sister school, the Convent of the Holy Infant Jesus, two years later. Beurel financed the schools from private subscriptions and his own personal fortune. When most of the missionaries moved to China, Reverend Benjamin Peach Keasberry remained behind and founded a school for Malay boys, which he financed largely by a printing press that he operated successfully for 30 years. Temenggong Ibrahim subsidized the school generously, enrolling his sons and those of his entourage. Sophia Cooke, a missionary from the Anglican Society for the Promotion of Female Education in the East, came to Singapore in 1853 and ran a school largely for orphaned girls and reformed prostitutes. After her death in Singapore in 1895, Miss Cooke's

School eventually became St. Margaret's, the oldest girls' school in Singapore to survive into the twenty-first century.

Apart from these individual efforts, in the middle years of the century, education in Singapore was in a parlous state, despite the East India Company's renewed interest in promoting education in its territories. A law passed in Calcutta in 1854, "the intellectual charter of India", sought to establish properly graded vernacular education from the primary stage to university level throughout the Company's territories. Singapore did not profit from this reform, which indeed proved a setback, since the Company agreed only to equal public contributions and fees. It matched the *temenggong*'s donations to Keasberry's school but reduced the official grant to the Singapore Institution and withdrew subsidies altogether from non-fee-paying charity schools, such as Father Beurel's.

The East India Company disapproved of Singapore pupils' preoccupation with acquiring basic English in order to secure jobs. They preferred children to become literate first in their own language, and successive governors tried to boost vernacular education in Singapore by providing free primary schooling in the Malay medium. The European merchants complained that it was unfair to enforce Indian educational policy on Singapore. While Malay was the indigenous vernacular, it was the language of a minority. The Chinese at that stage showed no interest in having Chinese-medium schools, and the European merchants, backed by the English-language press, argued without success that English should be promoted as the *lingua franca*.

For the remaining years of Indian rule, education remained in the doldrums. English-medium education was basic and reached only a tiny minority. There were no Chinese-medium schools and no opportunities to study Chinese apart from sporadic attempts to set up classes within the Singapore Institution. Despite the emphasis on providing free Malay education, the results were disappointing. The Koran schools were of low standard and did not equip Malay pupils to enter mainstream Singapore life. Keasberry's well-subsidized school had 52 boys on the roll in 1863, but half were usually absent.[50] In 1872 it was proposed to convert Keasberry's school into a Malay teachers' training college, but Keasberry died suddenly in 1875 and his school closed down. He was influential in educating the future Sultan of Johor, Abu Bakar, and training the first generation of Johor state officials but failed to lay a sound basis for Westernized modern Malay-medium education in Singapore. Despite this, the struggling educational establishments of the mid-nineteenth century survived and eventually blossomed to rank among Singapore's finest schools: Raffles Institution, St. Joseph's, St. Margaret's, Raffles Girls' School, and the Convent of the Holy Infant Jesus.

ॐ

In social welfare and education, Singapore fell below even the rudimentary standards expected of mid-nineteenth century governments, but it was impossible to counteract poverty, destitution or disease, or to provide the infrastructure for improved living and working conditions without putting some check on immigration.

There were no hospitals and virtually no medical services before the 1840s, apart from one or two government doctors and a few private practitioners. An apprentice scheme for Eurasian subordinate medical staff was started in 1823, but the small salaries and lack of prospects deterred recruits, and only two Singapore boys graduated under this scheme in the 1830s.[51]

Fortunately Singapore's climate proved to be exceptionally healthy, despite the constant damp heat, marsh and swamp, rotting vegetation, filth, and stench. Malaria and leprosy were uncommon, while cholera and smallpox were normally confined to the overcrowded slums. Cholera in particular was a social rather than a medical problem, arising from water pollution caused by filth and bad drainage, which the government had no money to remedy. Like most health hazards in Singapore, it was largely man-made.

The well-to-do, who included the Europeans, Jews, Armenians, Eurasians, Parsis, and rich Chinese, suffered mainly from over-indulgence in food and alcohol. Most European men counteracted this by dressing informally and taking vigorous physical exercise. It was customary to rise at dawn, take long early morning walks, and to ride or sail in the evening. The younger men played fives or cricket. Mercantile life was leisurely, except on mail days, and work rarely interfered with regular sport, since office hours normally ended by four o'clock. "We are the healthiest community in the East," the *Straits Times* claimed in 1861, "and attribute no small share of it to our activity and love of outdoor sports."[52] Singapore's early Christian burial grounds are perhaps the dullest in Asia because nearly all prominent Europeans lived to retire to Britain. Most of those buried in Singapore were visiting sailors, young women, and children.

Among the mass of the population, poverty, malnutrition, overcrowding and opium addiction took the heaviest toll. The annual influx of penniless Chinese and the fluctuations of demand for labour threw many immigrants onto the streets, along with destitute European seamen, who were often stranded in Singapore for months looking for work.

Initially, with the consent of the leading Chinese, the government levied a tax on the sale of pork to erect and maintain an *attap* shed to house sick paupers. However, in 1837 Calcutta prohibited this tax on an essential foodstuff, after which only chronic cases were admitted to the pauper shed. Both Chinese and European merchants began to feel ashamed that social services were so poor, and in 1844 Tan Tock Seng chaired a public meeting that appealed to the government to build a pauper hospital. The merchants objected to Governor Butterworth's proposals to prohibit the landing of diseased immigrants and to finance the hospital out of property assessments. A compromise was reached whereby most of the money came from private charity, supplemented by small property assessments, and the government supplied medical assistance, medicines, and a financial grant.

Tan Tock Seng presented $7,000 to build the pauper hospital, and the foundation stones for this and a European seamen's hospital were laid on adjoining sites at Pearl's Hill in 1844. While Tan Tock Seng's hospital was under construction, the position became desperate. In 1845 at least seventy Chinese beggars died from starvation, and four years later the Recorder, commenting on inquests where verdicts of death through starvation had been returned, said this was "a disgrace to a Christian community like Singapore".[53]

When the hospital opened in 1849 it only touched the surface of the problem. A grim place, it fronted a swamp that was used as the town's main rubbish dump. Paupers were brought in with ulcers, sores, and dropsy, many of them with limbs dropping off from gangrene. Not surprisingly, the mortality rate was high. In the official year 1852–53 one-third of the patients died, and in 1857 the hospital committee admitted, "No one will enter who can crawl and beg, unless compelled by the police."[54]

Much of this misery stemmed from drug addiction. Most Europeans regarded opium smoking as a bad habit, soothing and soporific, harmful only if taken to excess.

A private practitioner, Dr. Robert Little, and a few other Europeans campaigned to open the eyes of the government and the community at large to the medical and social evils of opium smoking.[55] Little estimated in 1848 that 20 per cent of the entire population and more than half the Chinese adults were opium addicts. Rich Chinese, who smoked high-quality opium, were not seriously harmed, but the poor smoked the refuse. Addicts were reduced to begging and living on rotten fish and decaying vegetables around the market, ending up in prison or the pauper hospital, or driven to suicide. Little tried in vain to persuade leading Chinese merchants to form a society to suppress opium addiction. The well-to-do Chinese found the opium revenue farm lucrative, other Asians made no protest, while European merchants were content to see taxes levied on opium rather than on virtuous commerce, property, or salaries. They dismissed Little as a crank, and the opium farm continued to be the mainstay of the revenue up to the twentieth century.[56]

The ruling class was embarrassed by the spectacle of destitute European sailors, but for many years the financial deadlock delayed extending to Singapore Indian legislation designed to protect seamen and their conditions of service, to supervise taverns, and to control prostitution. The plight of able-bodied unemployed sailors was acute, and there were so many destitute Australians, who arrived in charge of shipments of horses, that in 1863 Australian state governments warned men not to come to Singapore unless they had a definite promise of work.[57] The situation attracted many shady characters to Singapore to set up brothels and taverns where sailors were often given drugged liquor, robbed, and beaten up. In the early 1860s there were more than 200 disreputable taverns and so many foreign prostitutes that the *Straits Times* complained there were almost as many whores as respectable women among the European female population.[58] The situation improved somewhat after 1863, when Calcutta gave the Singapore authorities the legal right to close objectionable taverns, and many seedy underworld characters drifted away to happier hunting grounds.

❧

Singapore's social life underwent great changes during this period. Among the upper class, respect for material success blurred racial divisions. In the early days the small European society of Singapore was a friendly, hospitable community, where differences of wealth, colour, race, or age counted for little. They mixed freely with their Asian counterparts and were delighted to welcome strangers and visitors with news about Europe. Sailing ships took four months to reach Singapore from England, and even mail coming by the expensive, uncertain "overland' service, transshipped in Egypt and transported by camel across the Suez Isthmus, seldom arrived in less than two months. Britons could not afford the time or money to visit Europe and expected to spend their whole working lives in the East.

The affluent enjoyed a constant round of dances, suppers and sporting entertainment. A Billiards Club was formed in 1829, the first regatta was held in 1834, St. Andrew's Night was first celebrated in 1835, a fives club was set up in 1836, and the first cricket match was held in 1837. Snipe-shooting in the marshes skirting the town became a favourite sport in the 1830s. In 1840 the first tiger hunt was staged, and two years later the Singapore Sporting Club was founded to promote horse racing.

Changes came over Singapore in the mid-1840s, in her appearance, in commerce, and in social life. Visitors were impressed with the physical improvements but complained that much of the port's exotic charm and friendliness had gone.[59] Young midshipman Frank Marryat complained that nowadays "there is little hospitality and less gaiety".[60] This was largely the result of changing patterns of commerce with the advent of steamships. The steamship did not revolutionize trade overnight, and the bulk of cargoes continued to be carried in sailing ships for many years, but passenger-carrying steamships speeded up commercial activity and produced marked social changes in the British community. Some Britons could now afford to visit England periodically, and all of them could keep their links with "home" through comparatively up-to-date newspapers, regular letters, and new books. The old free and easy, uniquely Singaporean way of life gave way to a more formal society, which was staid, less adventurous, and reflected the values of the mid-Victorian British middle class.

The European community drew apart from Asians, while at the same time they did not open their doors so wholeheartedly to visitors from Europe, who were no longer such rare reminders of a far distant homeland. Steamers also brought greater pressure of office work, with merchants rushing to prepare documents for the mail. Visitors complained their compatriots were too busy making money to welcome strangers.

British governors and Asian and European merchants continued to hold multi-racial dinners, balls and celebrations, but much of this conviviality was superficial, and people tended increasingly to find relaxation among their own communities. Europeans sought entertainment of a Western type in amateur theatricals and formed their own clubs, such as the Cricket Club in 1852, the German Teutonia Club in 1856, the Tanglin Club in 1865 and the Swimming Club in 1866. Social life among Europeans became more sophisticated, snobbish, and exclusively Western. This alienation was apparent to some extent in commercial life, and in 1860 the Chinese withdrew from the Chamber of Commerce, leaving it with a predominantly European membership. At the mass level there was little mingling among the different communities, who were kept apart by deep differences in language, religion and customs. Even the New Year sports, in which all communities competed and which were for many years considered the best means to promote racial harmony, were described in 1865 as "a mercenary affair on the part of the natives and a somewhat absurd and tiresome spectacle to the European".[61]

There was a great gulf between the way of life of prosperous Asians and the mass of the population, but there was plenty of entertainment to temper the hardships. Troupes of strolling players performed frequent *wayang*, or theatrical entertainment, in the streets. Most of the numerous religious festivals were celebrated with processions and public festivities. At Chinese New Year, Whampoa opened his gardens to the public and the place became a fairground, with throngs of merry makers and hawkers. The gambling laws were lifted for a fortnight at Chinese New Year, and gambling and cockfighting took place all year long with the connivance of the police.

Singapore retained the air of a pioneer town, with a predominantly young adult male population primarily of shifting transients who did not regard Singapore as home. Despite the shortcomings of government, there were few signs of unrest among either the Asian or European inhabitants before the middle of the century. There was general contentment with the administration of Governor George Bonham, who had come to Singapore in September 1819 as a writer, and rose to be Assistant Resident, Resident Councillor, Acting Governor and finally Governor in 1836. Bonham provided a continuity of experience and influence dating from the early months of Singapore and was an approachable, gregarious, and cheerful bachelor, an excellent social mixer. There was no demand for formal organization when municipal problems could be settled at the governor's dinner table.

This cordial atmosphere changed with the arrival of Colonel William John Butterworth of the Madras army, who succeeded Bonham in 1843 and remained Governor of the Straits for twelve years. A newcomer to Singapore, the stiff and pompous Butterworth was nicknamed "Butterpot the Great" and was accompanied by a very grand wife. The Butterworths' arrival put an end to the friendly informality that had characterized Bonham's administration, and two years later the European merchants made their first demands for representation in municipal affairs and for more control over the police and property assessment. This led to bitter wrangles, to stormy scenes between the Governor and the grand jury, and to angry correspondence in the press. In 1847, with Butterworth's approval, Calcutta rescinded the rights of the Justices of the Peace to appoint and control the police force. All the non-official JPs resigned in protest, and for the next fifteen years men of standing refused to accept the office. In 1848 Bengal created a committee of officials and non-officials to administer the assessment in Singapore, but this first milestone in the development of municipal government aroused no public enthusiasm. Non-official members were appointed by the Governor, and the Singapore press dismissed the Municipal Committee as "a mere government bureau ... serving as a breakwater to protect the executive government from shocks".

Butterworth's early years as Governor coincided with the commercial depression of the 1840s, when some European merchants began to question whether Singapore would fare better as a Crown Colony rather than an appendage of the East India Company. Commercial bonds with Calcutta were weakening, while the growth of European trade and steamship communications made Singapore merchants look increasingly to London as their economic and political centre. By the middle of the century most British firms in Singapore were agency houses for London companies.

The proposal to convert Singapore into a Crown Colony had been talked about in Singapore for several years, but was now taken up as a practical issue by a young merchant, William Henry Read. Tiny in stature but dynamic and aggressive in manner, Read was born in Scotland in February 1819, within a few days of Singapore's foundation, and his fortunes were closely linked with the island throughout his long life. Arriving in 1841 to join the leading firm of A.L. Johnston & Company, he quickly became involved in public affairs and took part in the agitation for municipal representation. Read returned to England on leave in 1848 at the height of Singapore's commercial worries and of Butterworth's unpopularity. There he had lengthy discussions with John Crawfurd, who was fighting the cause of the Bengal merchants against the East India Company. By the time Read left Britain to return to Singapore in 1851, he and Crawfurd had decided to agitate for a complete break with India and the transfer of the Straits Settlements to the Colonial Office.

In England Crawfurd devoted his efforts to Singapore's interests, but Read arrived back in Singapore to find the situation unpromising for political agitation. Butterworth, learning from his mistakes, had set out with remarkable success to conciliate the merchant community, which was now riding high on a new wave of prosperity. The Governor had brought solid improvements to the town in roads, bridges and public buildings, and in September 1851 he took fifty guests on a picnic to witness the first light from Horsburgh Lighthouse, "this first Pharos of the eastern seas ... great lion of the Straits",[62] a masterpiece of modern technology. An 1850 visit by Lord Dalhousie, the Governor-General of

India, had left the Singapore merchants expecting a dramatic improvement in administration. Calling briefly at Singapore in the course of a convalescent voyage to China, Dalhousie was feted with enthusiasm. Europeans and Chinese alike vied for invitations to meet him, and "the whole settlement was drunk with loyalty".[63] Promising to give the Straits Settlements his personal attention, Dalhousie separated them from the Bengal Presidency in 1851 and put them under the direct charge of the Governor-General.

For the moment Singapore's merchants basked in the sunshine of commercial prosperity, but this euphoria could not last forever. Singapore was a thriving port, a triumph for the most advanced theories of free trade and *laissez-faire*, but ultimately she needed more modern and sophisticated administration, and prosperous European merchants became increasingly frustrated by the autocratic nature of the Company's governors and its inefficient bureaucracy. Businessmen resented exclusion from public affairs and sought a place in government that was more in keeping with their growing economic power.

The merchants complained that the East India Company neglected to provide the commercial amenities expected in a thriving international port. During the 1850s Calcutta brought in many measures to improve ports and shipping facilities in India. Singapore merchants complained loudly whenever Calcutta hesitated on financial grounds to extend the benefits of the new legislation to the Straits Settlements, but they were also adamant in refusing to pay charges to cover the costs of reforms. In 1852 battle was joined between the Singapore merchants and the Company over a levy made on all ships calling at Singapore to pay for part of the construction and maintenance of Horsburgh Lighthouse, but eventually the European merchants agreed to pay lighthouse fees provided Asian shipping was exempt. Adding to these frustrations, the Singapore merchants quickly became disillusioned with the constitutional reforms from which they had expected so much. Dalhousie's move to take the Straits Settlements under his own wing produced no tangible change, and the sole result of his visit was the Dalhousie obelisk, erected by the Singapore merchants in his honour, a suitably graceful and useless reminder of this pleasant but unproductive interlude.

The East India Company's charter was renewed in 1853, and a new Legislative Council with enlarged powers was set up in Calcutta the following year. While Singapore had no representative on this council, her merchants hoped it would be more energetic and enlightened in introducing reforms. In fact Singapore was to suffer more than any other Indian-administered territory from the council's policy of enforcing uniformity, and its vigorous centralization campaign eventually goaded the Singapore merchants to demand a break with India.

This storm could not be foreseen at the time of Butterworth's departure in 1855. His early quarrels with the mercantile community were long forgotten, and Butterworth retired in an aura of affection and respect. His successor, Edmund Blundell, was welcomed as a man with long experience of the East, where he had served for more than thirty years as Commissioner of Tenasserim, Resident Councillor of Melaka and subsequently Resident Councillor of Penang.

Blundell was worthy and conscientious, an excellent paternal administrator in the pioneer days, but he was obstinate and autocratic. Since the governor had no legislative council to strengthen his hand in dealing with Calcutta or to protect him against irresponsible opposition from the merchant community, in the 1850s the office required particular sensitivity and tact. Unfortunately Blundell did not possess these qualities. As Governor in the crucial years from 1855 to 1859, when the Indian Legislative Council was most energetic, he acted in defiance of popular opinion and encouraged Calcutta to pass unpopular legislation.

Blundell soon came into collision with the small active group of constitutional reformers. They objected most fiercely to his proposal that Calcutta should finance port improvements by levying modest port dues and fees for clearance documents. The Singapore merchants countered by suggesting that the Company raise the money by halving the governor's salary. In any event Calcutta withdrew the controversial proposal.

The vocal minority of European merchants set out to rally public opinion against Blundell and the Company's policy through the press, the grand jury, the Singapore Chamber of Commerce and public meetings. Despite the lack of representative institutions, the European mercantile community had plenty of opportunities for making their views known, since throughout the period of Indian rule Singapore enjoyed free speech and assembly, and press censorship was abolished in 1835.

There were no vernacular newspapers at this time, but Singapore's English-language press played a significant political role and provided an outlet for European public opinion in the absence of a legislative council. When the pioneer *Singapore Chronicle* was founded in 1824, the "Gagging Acts" still forbade criticism of the Company's policy and officials throughout Indian territories. While Crawfurd was Resident, the *Singapore Chronicle* remained a semi-official gazette, largely written by the Resident himself and designed to disseminate commercial information. Supervision was relaxed after Crawfurd's departure, but in 1827 Fullerton re-imposed close censorship and threatened to expel the editor when the *Singapore Chronicle* criticized official policy. Fullerton's successors were more tolerant, and in 1833 Calcutta agreed to exempt Straits editors from submitting proof sheets to the governor, so that censorship lapsed in Singapore two years before the "Gagging Acts" were formally repealed in India.[64]

The *Singapore Free Press* appeared in 1835 and quickly established a reputation as a reliable and moderate journal. Backed by private merchants and lawyers, it established an independent stance and soon ousted the *Singapore Chronicle*, which was forced to close down in 1837. The *Singapore Free Press* continued as a weekly paper until 1869, when it ceased publication for fifteen years but was revived in 1884. The *Straits Times* first appeared as a weekly in 1845, was published twice a week from 1847 and daily from 1858. Editors had to make ends meet by combining journalism with other jobs, and both Abraham Logan of the *Free*

Press and Robin Woods of the *Straits Times* were law agents and played prominent roles in public life.

Senior merchants could exert influence as Justices of the Peace or grand jurymen. At the close of each court session the grand jury presented a statement of comments and grievances, including matters that would normally have been the responsibility of a legislative council or elected municipal authority. Before Blundell's day, merchants regarded jury service as a tiresome duty, disrupting their business. In 1854 the European merchants petitioned for the grand jury to be abolished, but they changed their tune after 1855, when the grand jury became a rallying point for growing opposition to the government.[65] In the hands of a vocal opposition group, the public meeting developed into a regular means of agitating against official policy. In the mid-1850s the Indian Legislative Council's activities provoked the calling of many public meetings in Singapore at which petitions were drawn up to complain about alleged grievances, such as the failure to give adequate protection against piracy, the transportation of European convicts from India to Singapore, delays in passing judicial reforms, threats to the dollar, and proposals to impose port dues.

In 1855 the *Straits Times* urged the formation of a Reform League to agitate for radical changes in administration.[66] A motion seeking to throw off Indian rule was rejected at a public meeting, but a small group remained dedicated to breaking free from India. It was dominated by William Henry Read, Abraham Logan, Robin Woods, and Joaquim d'Almeida, a prominent merchant and son of Sir Jozé d'Almeida.

Discontent reached a peak in the crisis year of 1857. The year began with trouble over the implementation of tighter police regulations and municipal reforms, which provided for an elected majority on a reconstituted Municipal Committee with enlarged powers. The clumsy enforcement of this legislation provoked a strike among the Chinese and riots among the Indians. In February 1857, at a time when the British were fighting in China, a Chinese rebellion in Kuching, resulting in the murder of several of Rajah James Brooke's men, was misinterpreted by the nervous European merchants as part of a regional anti-British conspiracy that would engulf Singapore. Further fuel was added to this argument in March 1857 when disturbances broke out among the Penang Chinese over the new municipal laws. Blundell's low-key handling of these crises brought hostile criticism from European and Asian merchants, and in May 1857 the Singapore grand jury complained "at no period in the history of the settlement have the representations and remonstrances of the European community received so little attention at the hands of the local authorities".[67]

The first reports of the Indian Mutiny, reaching Singapore late in May 1857, brought nervous tension to a breaking point. There was in fact little reason to fear that the violence would extend to the Straits, as the garrison had troops from Madras, and the predominately South Indian population showed no signs of sympathy with the mutineers. Singapore was soon affected indirectly by the mutiny when Calcutta imposed a twelve-month press censorship throughout all Indian territories. Blundell took no steps to enforce this "Gagging Act" on the Singapore newspapers, but the press attacked the measure as further proof of Calcutta's refusal to recognize the special position of the Straits.[68]

In August 1857 rumours swept through Singapore of a planned uprising among the Indian convicts, who then numbered nearly 3,000. It was also learned that Calcutta intended to send dacoits and dangerous prisoners to Singapore to make room for mutineer prisoners in Calcutta's gaols. The general panic sent some families fleeing aboard ships in the harbour for safety and brought resentment against the Company's rule to a head. The European merchants called a public meeting, which resolved to support a petition sent to the British Parliament by the European merchants of Calcutta demanding the abolition of the East India Company. The Singapore merchants asked further that the Straits Settlements be separated from India and ruled directly from London.[69] Their object was to secure a local legislative council and participation in government. The petition claimed that Calcutta had treated the Straits Settlements as a part of continental India and persistently disregarded local wishes. It complained that the Indian Legislative Council gave no representation to the Straits, while the governor ruled as a despot with no council to advise or control him. To prove their general complaints, the petitioners recited specific grievances, such as alleged attempts to impose duties and tonnage dues and to standardize the rupee as the legal currency. They criticized the Company's reluctance to provide an adequate judicial establishment, its failure to wipe out piracy or build up British influence in the peninsula and the archipelago. They argued that Calcutta's policy towards the Chinese was weak, and concluded by dealing at length with the problem then uppermost in their minds: the danger and humiliation of using Singapore as a dumping ground for convicts.[70] While the petition was being prepared, mutineers and other dangerous prisoners arrived from Calcutta's maximum-security prisons. Singapore's open prison system was ill designed to cope with such an influx, and worried European merchants pleaded for transportation to Singapore to be discontinued altogether.

Singapore's petition began a process that, after ten years of confused negotiations, led to the transfer of the Straits Settlements to the Colonial Office in 1867. The petition came from Singapore alone. At a public meeting in Penang, only three people backed a motion to support Singapore's demands, and the overwhelming majority voted against adding to the Company's tribulations in its hour of danger.[71]

The House of Commons received the Singapore petition favourably and success seemed assured. The Singapore merchants had close links with Members of Parliament, chambers of commerce and other commercial bodies in England eager to support their cause. The more prosperous Singapore merchants visited England from time to time, and there was an influential group of former Straits officials and merchants who had returned to head their London offices.

India wanted to jettison the Straits Settlements but was unwilling to spend time unravelling the Straits' complicated accounts to the British Treasury's satisfaction. The Colonial

Office complained in 1860, "The India Office seem in the same breath to admit a deficit and claim a surplus."[72] The very enthusiasm of those who clamoured for the change also harmed the cause of transfer since Read, Crawfurd, other former Straits residents in London, and the Singapore Chamber of Commerce all produced optimistic but conflicting financial estimates, which only served to increase suspicion in the Treasury and the Colonial Office.

The British government was particularly worried about the potential defence costs. Collyer's complicated and expensive fortifications, which would require substantial and costly garrisons, were particularly unwelcome at a time when Britain was embarking on a policy to withdraw troops and military aid from her colonies. In 1862 the Secretary of State for the Colonies promised a select parliamentary committee that the British government would acquire dependencies in future only if they were no burden on the Exchequer.[73] Consequently the British Treasury broke off the negotiations. It was obvious that Singapore would be granted Crown Colony status only if her revenue could be increased to cover all her civil and military expenses, or if she could establish a claim to be of vital strategic and commercial importance to the British Empire.

Meanwhile the extinction of the East India Company in 1858 and the transfer of India to the direct rule of the British Crown made little impact in the Straits Settlements, which continued to be administered by Calcutta. In 1859 the unpopular Blundell was succeeded by Colonel Orfeur Cavenagh, the last and best-liked of all the Indian Governors. A warm-hearted, honest, and practical leader, firm but fair, Cavenagh consulted public opinion and paid heed to the press, the chamber of commerce, the grand jury and the Municipal Committee, winning not only respect but affection. He removed much of the friction between merchants and government and, within the severe constraints of finance and manpower, promoted considerable improvements in administration, public works, police, and prisons, and in the judicial field.

Cavenagh opened law courts in the country districts and backed Dunman in strengthening the police force. He made maximum use of convict labour to improve amenities. In 1860 Calcutta decided to stop transporting convicts to the Straits, but the last Indian convicts were not withdrawn until 1873, six years after Singapore became a Crown Colony, and in those last years the Straits authorities rushed through an ambitious programme of public works, many of which survived into the twenty-first century. Convict labour was used to build Fort Canning in 1860 and St. Andrew's Cathedral, which was completed in 1862. Convicts constructed roads and official buildings, including a town hall, a courthouse, which later formed the nucleus of the Empress Place government offices, a general hospital, a lunatic asylum, a new pauper hospital and Government House (later the Istana). Gas lighting replaced the feeble coconut-oil street lamps in 1864. The old wooden bridge linking North and South Bridge Roads was replaced by an iron bridge in 1862 and renamed Elgin Bridge. Land to the seaward side of Commercial Square was reclaimed between 1861 and 1864 to form Collyer Quay, which was protected by a sea wall. By 1866 it carried a complete line of buildings, "one of the sights of the Far East", many of which could still be seen a century later.

The town was beginning to look impressive. The prosperous commercial sector on the west bank faced the official quarter across the river, with the government offices, the Town Hall, the Singapore Institution, and St. Andrew's Cathedral set in well-kept green lawns. Fort Canning dominated the town, flanked by hills crowned with fine houses. The town was still small, extending scarcely more than a mile from the centre in any direction, but the rest of the island was accessible, with a network of roads, many villages and police stations along the coasts, and government rest houses at outlying Seletar and Changi. Singapore was one of the beauty spots of the East. "For forty-five years have the hands of man been busy accumulating wealth on its bosom and yet scarce a scar is visible."[74]

Cavenagh's popularity was strong enough to weather the storms of economic depression as well as Calcutta's campaign to impose a raft of taxes throughout its territories during the financial crisis caused by the Indian Mutiny. The Singapore merchants successfully warded off yet another attempt to levy port dues in 1862. They lost a hard-fought battle to avert an Indian Stamp Act, which was eventually forced through in 1863, but Calcutta withdrew a proposal to extend income tax to the Straits. In doing so, it stifled an interesting experiment at birth. Lacking the means to collect such a tax, Cavenagh proposed to grade the population in fifty-two classes according to their financial standing, levying a flat tax at each level and publishing the figures. Since Singaporeans identified status with wealth, he envisaged leading citizens would vie for position in the social scale and probably claim membership of a higher class carrying a heavier rate of tax than their actual income warranted. When Calcutta decided not to tax incomes in the Straits Settlements, Singapore lost the opportunity to put this novel psychological theory to the test and to determine whether the social-climbing ambitions of a *nouveau riche* society could be used for the painless extraction of revenue. When income tax was eventually introduced in 1947, it came in the conventional form of a secret and confidential tussle between reluctant citizens and a complicated bureaucratic machine.

During his beneficent regime Cavenagh enjoyed the support of the local press, the grand juries, the Municipal Committee, the chamber of commerce and the leading Chinese. He received unquestioning loyalty from his officials and warm respect from the general public. Grand juries gave up making presentments of grievances, and the Municipal Committee quietened down into discussing workaday improvements and trying to make ends meet. Cavenagh made the Indian regime more popular than it had ever been and stilled the aspirations for constitutional change.

Only a radical minority, comprising Read, Logan, Woods, and a few like-minded enthusiasts, kept the transfer issue alive, and with the help of their London friends, they persuaded the

British government to revive the negotiations. The Colonial Office would not accept their claim that Singapore was of vital strategic importance to the Empire, "at once the Gibraltar and the Constantinople of the East". The British government could be won over only by proof of financial solvency, and ironically this became possible when the proceeds from the new Stamp Act settled once and for all the apparently insoluble problem of how to balance revenue and civil expenditure.

At the end of 1863 the British government deputed Sir Hercules Robinson, Governor of Hong Kong, to report on the state of Singapore. His recommendations favoured a transfer to colonial rule, but negotiations dragged on over arguments about responsibility for military expenditure. London refused to take on any financial commitment to defend the Straits Settlements, but in 1866 the War Office suddenly took an interest in Singapore as an alternative base for part of the British forces stationed in Hong Kong, where the mortality rate among troops and families threatened to become a public scandal.

A bill was rushed through, and final arrangements for the takeover by the Colonial Office were made in such haste that the senior Indian officials found themselves compulsorily retired, since India refused to take them and the Colonial Office wanted their own men in charge. Cavenagh was also not officially informed that a Colonial Office appointee had been chosen to succeed him. Learning by chance from a private resident in Singapore that a new governor was already on his way from England, Cavenagh departed in high dudgeon. On 1 April 1867, the Indian administration came to an end, and the Straits Settlements became a Crown Colony.

3

High Noon of Empire
1867–1914

Thomas Carlyle's "happy the people whose annals are blank in history books", could well be applied to Singapore during the decades that followed the transfer to colonial rule. For almost three-quarters of a century, she enjoyed unbroken peace with orderly administration, and her steady expansion and prosperity were checked only temporarily by periodic international economic depressions.

Despite this outward calm, the character of Singapore society during these decades changed fundamentally. The conversion of the Straits Settlements into a Crown Colony was followed by four developments that did not revolutionize Singapore's role overnight but combined to accelerate and consolidate her growth in the last quarter of the nineteenth century: the opening of the Suez Canal in 1869, the extension of the European telegraph from India to Singapore in 1870, the steady conversion of cargo shipping to steam from the mid-1860s and the imposition of British protection in the Malay States, which began in 1874. Singapore ceased to be an isolated settlement, divorced from the hinterland, looking out to sea, living on her nerves and her wits in the uncertainties of international trade. She acquired permanent status as a major entrepôt on the leading East-West trade route, the focus for the trading wealth of the Malay Peninsula and the Netherlands East Indies and one of the most vital commercial points of the British Empire.

At the time of the transfer to colonial rule in 1867, the government in Singapore scarcely impinged on the life of the Asian population. An official commission reported in 1875, "We believe that the vast majority of Chinamen who come to work in these Settlements return to their country not knowing clearly whether there is a government in them or not." By 1914, while the inhabitants had not yet been assimilated into a specifically Singaporean society, the government had succeeded in bringing the whole community into its executive and judicial system, developing specialized departments of administration and making provisions for education, health and social welfare, which formed the foundations for the modern state. Many changes in the fabric of society were produced, not just in the legislative chamber but quietly and unobtrusively in government offices, law courts, schools, professional offices, and business houses, and among the organizations and associations of the immigrant communities.

༄

The first colonial governor, Sir Henry St. George Ord, formerly Governor of Bermuda, applied for the more challenging post in Singapore to act as a "new broom" in sweeping away the supposed inefficiency of Indian rule.[1] "Essentially a man of progress", *London and China Telegraph* described him in January 1867,[2] and as a military officer experienced in colonial administration, Ord seemed admirably fitted to govern the new colony.

Ord expected to find eager support for the new regime and for his spring-cleaning campaign. The deputations, letters, memorials and petitions, with which the minority of enthusiasts had bombarded the British government for the past ten years, deceived both Ord and the Colonial Office into believing that Singaporeans were unanimous in seeking change. The *Straits*

Times hailed the transfer as "the greatest political event which has occurred since the foundation of the settlement",[3] and the European mercantile community welcomed the provisions for formal consultation in the new constitutional arrangements. Yet there was a strong undercurrent of anxiety. Asian merchants had shown no interest in the movement. Few Europeans raised their voices in dissent while the transfer remained a remote possibility, but once it became a certainty many began to have doubts, fearing it might bring increased expense and higher taxation. Many of the grievances that had led the merchants to petition for separation from India in 1857 had since disappeared. The problems of piracy, commercial taxation, currency, and convicts had all been settled. Cavenagh's popular term of office had produced a golden sunset for the Indian regime, and the merchants were sorry to lose him.

In accordance with normal British Crown Colony practice, the governor was to rule with the help of executive and legislative councils. In 1867 the Executive Council consisted of the governor, the officer commanding the troops in the Straits and six senior officials. The Legislative Council comprised members of the Executive Council, together with the chief justice and four "unofficials" nominated by the governor.

The principle of the governor's executive supremacy, subject to the Colonial Office's ultimate control, remained intact up to the Second World War. The Executive Council met in private and constituted a type of Cabinet, but it was not responsible to the Legislative Council, whose debates were held in public and reported in the local press. The Legislative Council's advice was not binding on the governor, who initiated most legislation and had the power of assent or veto on all bills. Official members were obliged to support him, but unofficials were free to speak and vote as they pleased. The governor was instructed to pay deference to their views, particularly on questions of taxation and expenditure, and to report and explain to the Colonial Office any occasion when he overrode the unofficials' unanimous opinion. The success of the British colonial constitutional system depended on the willing co-operation of the governor and his council, and in practice a governor's full powers were rarely invoked. Some modifications were made over the years to broaden the basis of consultation. The numbers of unofficials and Asians were increased, with the first Asian, Whampoa, being appointed in 1869. By 1924 the Legislative Council comprised equal numbers of officials and unofficials, but the governor had the casting vote, so that final authority still rested with him and the Colonial Office.

∞

The Straits settlements colony comprised Singapore, Penang and Melaka, with additional entities attached from time to time for administrative convenience: the Dindings area of Perak was part of the colony from 1874 to 1934, Labuan from 1906 to 1946, the Cocos Keeling Islands from 1886 to 1955, and Christmas Island from 1900 to 1958.

Singapore was the centre of government, commerce and policy making. In principle, at least one unofficial legislative councillor was to come from each of the three Straits Settlements, but it was difficult in Penang and impossible in Melaka to find suitable people who could spare the time to serve. Of the four unofficials appointed in 1867, three came from Singapore. The government was so Singapore-dominated that Penang, which had not supported the movement for colonial rule in the first place, became increasingly resentful at the alleged neglect of her interests. In 1872 the Penang Chamber of Commerce petitioned to have its own legislative council or to become a separate crown colony, but quite quickly this ill-feeling gave way to a comfortable interdependence. In the later years of the century Penang prospered as a regional outlet for the rubber and tin industries in the Malay States, northern Sumatra and western Thailand and an important international port, but from time to time there were grumbles about having to play second fiddle and complaints about the proportion of the colony's revenue spent on Singapore.

☙

Even in Singapore the adjustment to colonial rule was painful.[4] After long years of opposition without responsibility, the radical minority was disappointed to find how little political power they were allowed, while the majority, who had not actively sought the transfer, looked back nostalgically to the old days whenever difficulties arose.

The transfer petition was granted as a concession by the British government after long prevarication, with no thought of strategic military or naval advantage and with no intention of introducing any radical change. Ord was merely instructed to rule efficiently and keep within his budget, but was given no authority to initiate any new policies in dealing with the Malay States or the Chinese secret societies. Those who had fought for the transfer were angry to find that the Colonial Office had no intention of taking a more active line than had Calcutta on these two problems, and Ord found himself in a frustrating position.

The new Governor was temperamentally unsuited for the delicate task of moulding Singapore into the colonial pattern. The situation called for patience and tact rather than energy and reforming zeal, but Ord's abrasive personality and autocratic disposition aggravated the irritations of the early colonial years. Within three months of his arrival, he warned the Colonial Office that critics of the new regime claimed the term "Crown Colony" was not suitable for the Straits Settlements,[5] to which the Colonial Office replied that "There is scarcely any colony under the English dominion in which the authority of the Crown and control of the home government is so indispensable as in the Straits Settlements."[6]

Governor Ord provoked considerable ill feeling in reorganizing the administration, stamping on carelessness and corruption, and demanding higher standards of efficiency.[7] His attack on nepotism and abuses of patronage, which had been accepted as normal practice before 1867, roused a fury of resentment. In his attempt to make the judiciary conform to normal colonial practice, Ord found himself in head-on collision with Chief Justice Sir Benson Maxwell, who had enjoyed personal independence and considerable rights of patronage as Recorder of Singapore under the Indian regime. Maxwell marshalled the unofficial members of the Legislative Council to support him in open conflict with the Governor, but the Colonial Office insisted on bringing the Straits judiciary into line with all other Crown Colonies by making the chief justice responsible to the governor in council. A Supreme Court Bill was passed to this effect in 1868.

Ord was accused of personal extravagance when he ordered a new government steamer and built a palatial Government House, which was later to become the President's Istana. The existing steamer was unseaworthy, and the governor of a thriving colony could not be expected to live in a rented house, as his predecessors had done for the past ten years, ever since the original governor's bungalow had been demolished to make way for Fort Canning. Both items of expenditure were justified, but unfortunately they were associated with the new Governor's personal comfort.

Ord's worst blunder was to question the revenue system, which he felt bore too heavily on the poor, letting affluent merchants escape lightly. The government's coffers were in a healthy state, but Ord incautiously told the Legislative Council at the end of 1867 that if further revenue were ever required, he proposed to raise it by direct taxation, adding that it would be undesirable to tax trade "except under the pressure of necessity which could hardly arise".[8] This intended reassurance had the opposite effect, and the idea that the sacred creed of free trade might be violated in any circumstances whatsoever unleashed the resentment which had been building up for months. The declared that the Governor had "thrown down the gauntlet to public opinion on a point that has never yet been questioned by any one at all conversant, even rudimentally, with the history of the Settlement and the circumstances of its commerce".

The former opposition group banded together once more. In January 1868 the ex-Straits residents who had fought for the transfer in England met in Boustead's London office and formed the Straits Settlements Association, "to guard against any legislation that might prejudicially affect the interests of the Straits Settlements, and in particular that might be calculated to check or interfere with their commercial prosperity as free ports of trade".[9] John Crawfurd was elected president, and local branches of the Association were formed in Singapore and Penang.

The Straits Settlements Association in London sent a memorandum to the Colonial Office in April 1869 claiming that the first two years of colonial administration had been "most disastrous to the colony". They objected that the Legislative Council was "a mere mockery, representing as it does, the will of the Governor alone; and that such a system is wrong in principle, demoralising and altogether objectionable".[10] This led to angry exchanges with the Governor, and to public protest meetings in Singapore under the chairmanship of Read, now the senior unofficial in the Legislative Council.

The Colonial Office was at first unaware of the Chinese immigrant problem that it had inherited, since the Indian regime had taken no steps to tackle the interrelated problems of secret societies, immigration, labour, coolie traffic, poverty, and prostitution. A commission of enquiry was appointed following secret society riots in Penang in 1867, and as a result of its findings a Dangerous Societies Suppression Ordinance was passed in 1869. Despite its name, this measure did not aim to suppress but merely to register associations. Societies were obliged to admit magistrates or police officers to meetings, and it became illegal to administer oaths or to recruit members by force.

The ordinance was ineffective, and the secret societies thrived on the growing coolie traffic as Chinese immigrants flooded into Singapore, attracted by the opportunities for work in the British Protected Malay States and the Netherlands East Indies. By the mid-1870s, the November–February junk season brought about 30,000 Chinese to Singapore each year. The immigrants included numbers of *samseng*, or professional thugs, attracted by the demand for fighting men in the Perak tin mines and other troubled areas. In 1872 it was said that the Singapore Ghee Hok society alone had 4,000 *samseng* at its command.

Many *sinkheh* were kept under guard on the coolie ships or locked up in filthy conditions in secret society depots ashore and then forcibly re-shipped to Sumatra and other places in Southeast Asia, where conditions were too deplorable to attract free labour. This practice of kidnapping was highly organized in the 1870s, sometimes entrapping even free immigrants who had paid their own passage.[11] On one occasion *samseng* marched a band of more than eighty *sinkheh* openly through the Singapore streets for shipment to Siak.

Rioting among the Chinese in Singapore in 1872 led to the appointment of a further official commission, which recommended the controversial steps of reviving the former *kapitan* system and curbing Chinese immigration. Leading Chinese, including Whampoa and Seah Eu Chin, petitioned the government to superintend coolie immigration and to prevent the forcible diversion of *sinkheh* away from Singapore, where "they know that in this fine country they will find a peaceful home, where the whole population are so prosperous that they sing for joy".

With this backing, Ord tried to make the first onslaught on the abuses of the coolie trade by means of a Chinese Coolie Immigration Bill, which he introduced in 1873. This modest bill proposed merely to register immigrants, not to enforce contracts or provide reception depots, but it provoked furious opposition from European merchants, legislative councillors, and the English-language press in defence of the treasured principle of free immigration, which was held to be the lifeblood of the Straits economy. The bill became law but was never implemented.

༺༺

Perhaps the most frustrating aspect of all Ord's work related to the Malay States, since he was secretly in sympathy with those who favoured positive action. Despite the official policy of non-interference, which the Colonial Office took over from India, in practice the Straits government was increasingly drawn into the affairs of the interior.

Rising demand in world markets stimulated the search for tin in Malaya from the middle of the century, and Chinese labourers poured into Perak, Sungei Ujong and Selangor. Mining operations were organized by Chinese entrepreneurs, often with financial backing from European merchants, who began to clamour for more protection for their capital and for the lives of the Chinese pioneers who braved the dangers and hardships of the interior.

The Singapore merchants' petition for transfer to colonial rule in 1857 was based mainly on domestic and constitutional issues, with policy in the Malay States only a minor grievance. By the end of Indian rule it had become a crucial concern, because these ten years had brought disaster to thousands of Chinese miners and severe setbacks to European and Chinese speculators. The rapid expansion of the tin trade and the influx of Chinese miners hastened the disintegration of traditional authority in Perak, Selangor and Negri Sembilan. After 1857 civil war in Pahang closed the Kuantan tin mines and cut off the valuable gold trade of the interior in which Singapore merchants were deeply involved. By 1867 the merchants had discovered to their cost that without official backing there could be no security. Conflicts between immigrant miners and Malay authorities and among rival Chinese societies brought bitter commercial rivalry to Singapore and the threat of bloodshed in Penang. Sooner or later political intervention was inevitable.

The Singapore merchants were disappointed to find that the Colonial Office did not intend to make Singapore the focus for extending British territorial power. In 1868 the Secretary of State instructed Ord that "The policy of Her Majesty's government in the Malayan peninsula is not one of intervention in native affairs", and "If merchants or others penetrate disturbed and semi-barbarous independent states ... they must not anticipate that the British government will intervene to enforce their contracts."[12] While Ord was in England on leave in 1871–72 he had long personal discussions with the Secretary of State, in which he pressed for a more active policy on the grounds that it was unrealistic for the British authorities to stand aloof and watch the rich trade of the hinterland disintegrate in the turmoil of Malay politics and secret society fighting. But the Colonial Office refused his request and Ord's hands remained tied.

In July 1873, with civil war raging in Perak and Selangor, the leading Chinese merchants of Singapore presented a formal petition seeking British intervention. Ord backed the appeal, and by that time the Colonial Office was beginning to feel that it might be necessary to strengthen British influence in the Malay States for fear other foreign powers might intervene. Ord's activities over the past seven years convinced them he was not the man to enforce such a policy. They had no confidence in his tact or judgement. Not realizing the strength of opposition that had already grown up before 1867 and refusing to admit Ord's argument that the majority had never wanted the transfer, they saw all the troubles of his regime as entirely of the Governor's own making.

❧

Shortly before his final departure from Singapore in 1873, Ord introduced a Criminal Procedure Bill that included a controversial clause abolishing the grand jury. Twenty years earlier the merchants themselves had agitated to get rid of the jury, but Ord's proposals provoked a violent outcry from the unofficial legislative councillors and from a public meeting, where Read alleged that the abolition of the grand jury would remove "the last check between arbitrary government and justice to the people".[13] The European merchants sent a telegram of protest to the Colonial Office and, with the exception of Whampoa, all the unofficials resigned. This important bill, which reconstituted the Supreme Court, provided for four puisne judges, and created a Court of Appeal, was passed in their absence and approved by the Colonial Office. The Secretary of State rejected a plea from European and Chinese merchants that the unofficials be reinstated and that future ordinances should not be put into force until approved by London. The Colonial Office objected to the principle that the unofficial minority should exert even a temporary veto on legislation.

The conflict highlighted the inherent problems of legislative councils and colonial constitutions. The Directors of the East India Company had opposed granting colonial-type institutions in India on the grounds that this would put power in the hands of expatriate unofficials, probably to the detriment of the indigenous population. This happened in Singapore and other Crown Colonies, where both European and Asian unofficial legislative councillors tended to represent hard commercial interests. Ord wrote scathingly to the Colonial Office in one of his last dispatches, "The mercantile community which constitutes the society of the place takes hardly any interest in anything beyond their own immediate business. Many of them openly avow that they come here solely to make money."

&

Despite Ord's personal unpopularity, he reorganized the administration efficiently, and his regime was a time of great material progress. The opening of the Suez Canal in 1869, coinciding with Singapore's fiftieth anniversary, brought an immediate boom and guaranteed Singapore's ongoing commercial viability. Trade figures jumped from just over £58 million in 1868 to nearly £90 million in 1873, and Ord retired from Singapore that autumn at a time of unprecedented prosperity. His successor, Sir Andrew Clarke, found the teething troubles of the new regime were over. Both the British government and the Singapore merchants looked to Clarke to smooth away friction, and the Colonial Office instructed him to investigate and report on the state of affairs in the west coast states of Malaya.

The new Governor was more in tune with the business community than Ord and more willing to "dance to the bagpipes of Singapore". Despite misgivings in the Colonial Office, Clarke immediately reinstated the unofficial legislative councillors. He also readily adopted the leading merchants' views favouring a more vigorous policy in the Malay States.

Clarke visited Perak where, exceeding the instructions given him in London, he made the Pangkor Engagement in January 1874. This provided for a British Resident to advise the Sultan, which paved the way for similar arrangements in Selangor and Sungei Ujong and began the process leading to British domination in these states. In view of the changed feeling then prevailing in London, Clarke's actions were not repudiated, and the way was open to develop the resources of the Protected Malay States, for which Singapore became the main port.

Clarke also succeeded in 1874 in winning the support of Chinese and European merchants for an ordinance to regulate passenger ships, which put the first modest check on some of the abuses of coolie travel.

≈

It has been said that "the course of running a Crown Colony, like love, rarely runs smoothly",[14] but for the moment administration ran more smoothly in Singapore than in most crown colonies. In January 1874 the *Straits Times* admitted, "It is very hard to be without a grievance, and we confess we are somewhat in this condition here at the present time."[15] The colony was set on a course of constitutional and political calm that lasted almost without interruption for nearly seventy years.

One of the main benefits brought by the transfer to colonial rule was a separate Straits Civil Service. After 1867 young men were recruited in England by the Colonial Office specifically for service in the Straits. From 1869 nominees had to sit for an examination and in 1882 the Straits Civil Service was thrown open to public competition. Young cadets were taught Malay on arrival in the colony, and from the 1880s those who were required to specialize in Chinese affairs were sent to learn Chinese dialects in Amoy, Swatow or Canton. Normally they served their whole career in the Straits, so that many officials exerted a stronger and more consistent influence on government policy through their long connection with Singapore than governors who came for relatively short spans of time.

Little happened on the surface of politics. Periodic trade fluctuations frayed political tempers, but not to the same extent as in the precarious pre-Suez days. The feeling of greater security induced more responsible, if still rather selfish, politics. The colony's military contribution was the most common source of discord, particularly when demands came at times of commercial depression.

In 1867 the British government did not admit that Singapore had any imperial strategic importance and insisted that defence costs were her own responsibility, apart from the support of the contingent of imperial troops transferred from Hong Kong on health grounds. The colony's contribution was fixed at £59,300 out of a total defence expenditure of £66,000, which was a heavier proportion than in most other colonies. There was not much to be seen for this expenditure. In 1869 Sir William Drummond Jervois, then Deputy Inspector-General of Fortifications and subsequently Governor of the Straits Settlements, reported that the existing fortifications in Singapore were useless, except possibly against a civil revolt. Four years later the general commanding the China station reported to the War Office that the forts at Singapore were "totally incapable of effective defence".[16]

With the opening of the Suez Canal and the use of the Straits of Melaka as the main route to the Far East, Singapore became an essential link in the chain of British ports and coaling stations, which stretched from Gibraltar, through Malta, Suez, Aden, Trincomalee and on to Hong Kong. Consequently in 1871 the British government agreed to assume part responsibility for Singapore's defence, to station a full-strength European regiment there and to pay 45 per cent of garrison costs. At the same time the War Office proposed to fortify Singapore against naval attack, offering to pay for the guns and armament but expecting the colony to meet construction costs. The Governor supported his Legislative Council's objections to this demand, but the Secretary of State refused to accept the principle that Singapore's defence was an imperial obligation and that the home government should bear the entire cost of erecting permanent defence works. Since there was no prospective enemy in sight and the Singapore merchants protested so hotly, the matter was left in abeyance.

∽

The Colonial Office began to prod the Straits authorities into taking more positive action to stem scandalous labour abuses. A commission appointed by Jervois, who became Governor of the Straits Settlements in 1875, reported the following year that "The government knows little or nothing of the Chinese, who are the industrial backbone of these Settlements; and the immense majority of them know still less of government." It recommended firmer control with more official protection for new immigrants, and its findings led in 1877 to the establishment of a Chinese Protectorate, with William Pickering as first Protector of Chinese.

Housed modestly in a Chinese shophouse in North Canal Road, the Protectorate marked a reversal of *laissez-faire* policy in favour of paternal, personal direct contact. Its foundation came at a time when Chinese immigration was rising to new peaks in response to demand for labour in the tin mines of the Protected Malay States. The numbers of Chinese immigrants increased from 34,000 in 1878 to 103,000 in 1888, and the Chinese population of Singapore rose threefold in the last thirty years of the century.

Pickering had worked in China for eight years before being appointed interpreter in Singapore in 1872. The first European official who could speak and read Chinese, he was appalled at the corruption of the court interpreters, and at the language used to describe the administration. Chinese translations of official government proclamations styled Europeans as "red-haired barbarians", judges as "devils", and police as "big dogs".

The Protector's first task was to tackle the abuses of the coolie trade. A Chinese Immigrants Ordinance and a Crimping Ordinance, which were passed in 1877, authorized him to license recruiting agents and board incoming ships. He was to discharge passengers who had already paid their passage and send the others to government depots, where employment contracts would be officially registered. Little opposition was offered to these sweeping new laws, since the revelations of cruelty and oppression practised on immigrants had touched the public conscience in the four years since Ord attempted to tackle the problem.

In the early days *hoey* agents often attempted to seize coolies from incoming ships and clashed with the Protector and his staff, but gradually these disorderly scenes petered out. A Labour Commission in 1890 confirmed that there were still considerable abuses in hiring coolie labour, but by the end of the century immigration supervision became an administrative routine, handled by cadets and subordinate officials.

The Protectorate made a great impact from the beginning, and with his strong personality, unique knowledge, and flair for practical administration, Pickering rapidly widened his authority from the protection of immigrants to general supervision of the Chinese community.

As a result of shocking disclosures about brutality and degradation in Singapore brothels, in the 1880s the Protectorate extended its activities to supervising Chinese women and girls.[17] The authorities did not seek to ban prostitution or to discourage the immigration of willing professional female prostitutes. Prohibition would have been unrealistic in Singapore, where in 1884 there were 60,000 Chinese men but only 6,600 Chinese women, of whom Pickering estimated that at least 2,000 were prostitutes. A ban would also have encouraged homosexual prostitution, which was supplied for many years by the importation of Hainanese boys. The Protectorate merely aimed to stop forced prostitution, since it was believed that 80 per cent of the young Chinese girls who came to Singapore in the late 1870s were sold to brothels.

In 1881 the Protectorate took over administration of the Contagious Diseases Ordinance, which had been passed in 1870 to provide for the registration of brothels. It also registered prostitutes and founded the Po Leung Kuk, or Office to protect virtue, which was administered with the advice of a committee of prominent Chinese. The Po Leung Kuk offered protection to girls who had been sold or unwillingly lured into prostitution. It did not seek to inhibit the activities of voluntary prostitutes, but initially roused great opposition from brothel keepers, and there were angry scenes at the Protectorate, with the brothel madams "throwing back their licence boards, dancing on the floors with wooden clogs and howling furiously". The Protectorate rescued many women from prostitution, but Pickering found European juries reluctant to convict in cases of alleged abduction, and complained:

> If in these trials they do as the Judge charges them to do – use the same common sense and judgement which they use in their ordinary business concerns – then it is no wonder the Chinese in the Straits are buying up all the land, building splendid houses and have the best carriages and horses, while the Europeans and Eurasians toil year after year in order to get a mere competency.[18]

The Protectorate also acquired the task of coping with the secret societies. In 1876 the Chinese leaders showed their power to organize their community in opposition to government measures during the "post office riots". Teochew merchants, who had hitherto monopolized the remittances sent by immigrants to their families in China, instigated this protest when a special post office was opened to handle such payments. They put up proclamations offering a reward for the heads of the new post office managers, and in ensuing riots the sub-post office was sacked. The police acted firmly, the riot was quelled, the merchants involved arrested, and the ringleader banished to China, after which the sub-post office was reopened.

In 1877 Pickering was appointed joint Registrar of Societies with Major Samuel Dunlop, the Inspector-General of Police. Pickering was confident that he could gradually bring the Chinese under government control by working through the *hoey*, converting the headmen into government agents and undermining their judicial power by making the Protectorate a more attractive arbitration centre. Gradually the Protectorate supplanted the societies in settling financial and domestic disputes.

As the societies lost their grip over immigration, labour and prostitution, they switched their interest to gambling. In 1886 an official commission of enquiry revealed widespread gambling abuses. It was common practice to rig gambling sessions where coolies on the point of returning to China were cheated of their life savings. Gambling was highly organized, the laws prohibiting it were blatantly flouted, and regular subscriptions were levied from gaming houses to buy police connivance.

The commission considered it impossible to suppress gambling but thought it immoral to resurrect the gaming farm. Pickering again urged strict measures, and this may have been the reason why a Teochew carpenter attacked him with an axe in the Protectorate office, leaving him seriously wounded.

By this stage the Straits Settlements were unique in still recognizing secret societies, which were banned in Hong Kong, the Protected Malay States and the Dutch colonies. Both Pickering and Dunlop agreed that it was time to begin a gradual elimination of the secret societies, but they were not prepared to accept the immediate abolition proposed by Governor Sir Cecil Clementi Smith.

An accomplished Chinese scholar, Clementi Smith had spent his career in the East. He joined the colonial service as a Hong Kong cadet in 1864, and with the exception of two years in Ceylon, he served from 1878 to 1893 in Singapore as Colonial Secretary, Acting Governor, and finally Governor. A forceful and efficient administrator, he resolved to get rid of the secret societies as they were "a standing menace to all good government and a great scandal to British administration", since "the government must be the paramount power, and it is not so in the eyes of many thousands of the Chinese in the Straits Settlements".

Pickering, Dunlop and the unofficial legislative councillors argued that total suppression would be precipitate, driving the societies underground, breaking the government's contact with society leaders and registered members without substituting any alternative control machinery.

With Colonial Office backing, Clementi Smith persisted with his policy, gradually winning public support. Dunlop and Pickering, who never fully recovered from his wounds, both retired in 1888, and the last opposition evaporated the following year when Clementi Smith created a Chinese Advisory Board to provide a formal link between the government and the Chinese community. A law to suppress dangerous societies and register harmless benevolent associations was passed in 1889 and brought into force in 1890 without any riots or disturbances. Six years later the Protector commented, "There exists at present no society which is in any way dangerous to the peace of the Colony."[19]

While the Societies Ordinance did not succeed in eliminating secret societies altogether, it broke the big *hoey* up into small bands of thugs, who continued to extort "protection money" from shops, gambling dens, opium dens, brothels, and hawkers, and fought among themselves for control of areas. In times of economic depression or political weakness the secret societies stepped up their criminal activities, and at certain periods they used political developments to resume an air of pseudo-respectability. But they were never able to reconstruct the large organizations or recover the widespread power that they wielded before 1890. Gang fights persisted, but the days of large-scale secret society riots that paralysed Singapore were over. The power of banishment was a particularly effective deterrent because the imperial Chinese government often arrested and sometimes executed deportees on their return to China.

The Societies Ordinance was an important landmark in the development of Singapore. It was rare for a governor to carry through legislation in the face of initial opposition from leading officials and unanimous objections from unofficials in the Legislative Council, but Clementi Smith's authority, tact, and long experience of the East enabled him to win over public opinion. He left Singapore in 1893 in an aura of great prestige, widely admired among all communities, and the Chinese petitioned for the extension of his period of office. With his departure the Protectorate entered a more prosaic phase, but Pickering had created and shaped it and laid down the traditions, which were maintained up to the Second World War. Long after his death, the Protectorate Office continued to be known among the Singapore Chinese as the Pi-ki-ling.

The establishment of the Chinese Protectorate and the ban on secret societies brought more law and order into Singapore society. This was helped by police reforms carried out in the 1880s following a commission of enquiry into the alleged inefficiency of the force. At that time most policemen were South Indians, with a few Boyanese and Malays because Whampoa, Seah Eu Chin and other leading Chinese had consistently resisted suggestions to recruit Chinese policemen for fear of secret society infiltration. As a compromise some Sikhs and a few European ex-army officers, inspectors, and constables were added to the force, a police training school was started in 1881, and a separate detective force established three years later. In 1904 a cadet system was started to recruit young Englishmen as police officers and give them specialist training.

❧

Singapore's trade rose dramatically in the last quarter of the nineteenth century. Despite many teething troubles in its early years, the opening of the Suez Canal was a significant milestone in Singapore's development. It hastened the decline of sailing ships because clippers could not use the canal, it enhanced Singapore's role as a coaling station for steamers, and it ensured her geographical supremacy since the Straits of Melaka supplanted the Sunda Straits as the major waterway from Europe to the Far East.

Singapore profited from the increase in European trade with Siam following the accession of King Chulalongkorn in 1868 and from the expansion of trade that came in the wake of colonization by other European powers in Southeast Asia in the last decades of the century. The French occupation of Indo-China, the extension of Spanish rule in the Philippines and in particular the liberalization of Dutch commercial policy made Singapore the focal point for trade in the Far East.

In Malaya, British influence spread quickly. After the first Resident of Perak was murdered in 1875, the British tightened their control and strengthened the Residents' authority in the Protected States. In 1888 a British Resident was established in Pahang and in the same year Sarawak, North Borneo and Brunei became British protectorates. In 1896 the Protected States of Selangor, Perak, Pahang and Negri Sembilan were formed into a federation, which encouraged investment in the Malay States, most of which came through Singapore.

The opening of the Suez Canal and the extension of European colonial rule in Southeast Asia coincided with a rapid expansion of the steamship in merchant shipping. This not only stimulated East-West trade and entrepôt commerce but gave an impetus to local commercial development throughout the region. As undisputed mistress of the seas, Britain held the key ports and controlled international shipping lanes, with Singapore as one of the most vital links in the chain.

Singapore's trade expanded eightfold in the period from 1873 to 1913 and shifted from the rather exotic wares of the early nineteenth century to the bulk movement of primary products, such as rubber and tin, copra and sugar, and to preliminary processing, such as tin smelting, rubber processing and pineapple canning.

The Malayan tin industry expanded rapidly with the extension of peace and order in the interior and in response to growing demands from the new American canning industry.[20] Smelting was Singapore's first modern industry. In 1890 the Straits Trading Company, backed mainly by local European capital, built a tin smelter on Pulau Brani. Ore was brought from the Malay States, later from Bangka and Billiton in the Netherlands East Indies, and by the early years of the twentieth century from Siam, Australia, Alaska and South Africa.[21]

In 1877 the first Brazilian rubber seeds were sent from England to the Botanic Gardens at Tanglin, which was developed in the 1860s as a public park and experimental station for new crops. The potential of rubber as an agricultural crop was ignored until the arrival of Henry Ridley as Director of the Botanic Gardens in 1888. By 1897 he had devised a method of tapping the tree without damaging the bark, and for years "Mad" Ridley pressed Malayan coffee planters to grow rubber. Rubber only came into its own in the early years of the twentieth century as a substitute crop when Brazilian competition ruined the Malayan coffee plantations.[22] The first rubber grown commercially in Singapore was on the Trafalgar Coconut Plantation at Ponggol about 1907.

The demands of the new motorcar industry for rubber tyres brought a boom. In nine years, from 1905 to 1914, Malayan rubber exports rose from 104 to 196,000 tons, which was more than half the total world supply, most of it exported through Singapore.

At first rubber from the big European estates was sent to London for sale, but in 1908 British firms in Singapore began to sell rubber locally, despite vociferous objections from London. In 1911 the Singapore Chamber of Commerce established a Rubber Association that organized sales in Singapore and made her an important international rubber market.

Oil became the third important commodity in Singapore's trade. At the end of the nineteenth century, Syme & Company constructed a tank depot on the offshore island of Pulau Bukum, since they were forbidden to store bulk oil in town. A few years later Dutch and British oil interests in the archipelago merged to form the Asiatic Petroleum Company, which later became the Shell Company, and by 1902 Bukum was the oil supply centre for the Far East.

Singapore now had a secure place in the pattern of world trade as a staple port, the entrepôt for Southeast Asian raw materials and Western manufactured goods, with an increasingly sophisticated infrastructure of commercial institutions and expertise. At the turn of the century most banking business was in the hands of three British banks: the Chartered Bank of India, Australia and China, the Hongkong and Shanghai Banking Corporation, and the Mercantile Bank of India. The first American bank opened an office in Singapore in 1902, the first Chinese bank, the Kwong Yik Bank, opened in 1903, and the first French bank opened in 1905.

The currency was stabilized for the first time. Hitherto the dollar had fluctuated, ranging in value from 4 shillings and 6 pence in 1874 to 1 shilling and 8½ pence in 1902. This caused commercial confusion, individual hardship, and perennial uncertainty in planning the government's budget. A new Straits dollar was introduced in 1903. The rate of exchange was fixed at 2 shillings and 4 pence in 1906 and remained at that level up to 1967.[23]

Communications were improving. The European telegraph was extended to Singapore in 1870, and during the 1880s telegraph communication built up with the Protected States. Singapore's first private telephone service was opened in 1879, and in 1882 it was taken over by the Oriental Telephone and Electric Company, which extended the service to Johor.

These economic changes put to rest the fears and uncertainties of Singapore's first half century. Recessions were only temporary setbacks. Singapore's superb geographical position, Britain's unchallenged naval supremacy, and the general growth of world trade guaranteed her increasing prosperity. Singapore merchants ceased to live on their nerves, although increased business brought new strains or, as the *Straits Times* complained in May 1872, "everlasting hurry and brain labour".[24]

By 1867 there were sixty European companies in Singapore, and in the last decades of the century European commercial houses expanded, some as general import and export businesses, others with special interests in rubber, tin, or shipping. Many long-established firms acquired a new prosperity, although the oldest, A.L. Johnston & Co., which continued under Read's personal management up to the 1880s, went out of business in 1892. Most of the others were more fortunate, such as Syme & Company founded in 1823, Boustead & Company and Maclaine, Fraser & Company, both formed in 1827, the German Behn Meyer & Company founded in 1840, the Borneo Company, which was established in Singapore in 1851, McAlister & Company founded in 1857, and Paterson, Simons & Company, which began trading under that name in 1859 but grew from a partnership first formed in 1828.

Most successful of all was the firm of Guthrie's, which was founded in 1821 by Alexander Guthrie and was the oldest company to survive into the twenty-first century.[25] Alexander's nephew, James Guthrie, took over the management from 1846 to 1876 and subsequently handed over to Thomas Scott, who was a partner for forty-five years. Guthrie's steadily extended its trading, banking and insurance interests in Singapore, while the retired partners, Alexander and James, looked after the company's interests in London. It first branched into the mainland in 1896, buying coffee estates but later turning to rubber, and it was one of the few firms in a position to profit from the early rubber boom. After the death of James Guthrie in 1900, followed by Thomas Scott two years later, the firm blossomed under the command of John Anderson. The son of a sea captain who had settled in Singapore, Anderson was educated at Raffles Institution and joined Guthrie's as a boy. By the early twentieth century he was undisputed leader of the Singapore business community and of the rubber industry. Anderson headed the Opium Commission in 1907 and was knighted in 1912. He kept control of Guthrie's until he retired in 1923 at the age of seventy-one.

Many new firms sprang up, such as Adamson, Gilfillan, which was established in 1867, and Straits Trading Company, which was formed in 1887 to smelt tin ore. The versatile Fraser & Neave partnership was formed by banker John Fraser and David

Neave, who bought up Keasberry's mission press, renaming it Fraser & Neave. In 1883 Fraser & Neave started Aerated Water Company, and John Fraser became involved in so many different enterprises that by the time he retired from Singapore in 1896 he was called the "Jolly Old Octopus". Fraser & Neave became a limited company in 1898 and later opened branches up-country, becoming one of the wealthiest organizations in Malaya.

Initially the Singapore business community was slow to realize the potential of steamships. The established companies, such as the Ben Line, founded in 1825 in the days of sail,[26] and the P&O Company, which was founded in 1837 and extended its services to Singapore in 1845,[27] stepped up their operations in the Far East. They were faced by a new competitor, the Ocean Steamship Company (the Blue Funnel Line), founded by Alfred and Philip Holt of Liverpool in 1865. Three years later the Holts gave the then unwanted Singapore agency to a struggling ship-chandling business, Mansfield & Company, which was headed by the far-seeing Walter Mansfield.[28] This began a flourishing partnership, which helped to make Singapore a centre of steamship communications, "the second doorway of the wide world's trade".[29] From the 1860s increasing numbers of Continental merchants and shippers settled in Singapore. French, Dutch, Italian and Scandinavian shipping lines established offices, and by the 1880s the German Norddeutscher Lloyd Company was strongly entrenched. The Germans in particular were vigorous competitors with the British firms, although British capital remained predominant. While the European sector's prosperity was substantial, it was obvious to the most casual observer that the greatest individual wealth lay in the hands of the Chinese. "England is by the uninformed supposed to own the island", Rudyard Kipling commented on first visiting Singapore.[30] Chinese business developed rapidly. Most early immigrants sent their savings back to China, but by the middle of the century some Chinese merchants began investing their accumulated capital in land and trade in the Straits Settlements. The Chinese often set up small family firms, and proprietors worked alongside their employees. From the beginning many Chinese family businesses in Singapore had close personal links with Melaka, and from the 1860s enterprising Chinese began extending their family and regional connections beyond the Straits Settlements. Tan Beng Swee opened a branch of Kim Seng & Company in Shanghai, and Tan Kim Ching set up rice mills in Siam and Saigon. These were the forerunners of the big family-dominated Nanyang commercial empires of the twentieth century, often centred in Singapore and holding sway over interests throughout the East.

In the 1880s enterprise in the peninsular states remained a Chinese preserve, largely because they exerted a stranglehold over the immigrant labour required for the tin mines, and European business activities were still largely confined to Singapore and Penang. In the last decade of the century, European firms extended traditional friendly contacts into more formal links with the Chinese in order to break into the peninsular economy.

The first such joint enterprise was the Straits Steamship Company, which was registered in Singapore in 1890 and founded by directors of Mansfield's together with three Chinese merchants, Tan Jiak Kim, Tan Keong Saik and Lee Cheng Yam. All three were members of former Melaka Baba families with interests in shipping and long connections with European companies. Tan Jiak Kim, grandson of Tan Kim Seng, took over Kim Seng & Company in 1884. Tan Keong Saik inherited the family business on the death of his uncle, Tan Choon Bock, in 1880. Lee Cheng Yam had founded Chin Joo & Company as a youth in 1858. The Straits Steamship Company dominated the Malayan coastal trade, and from the 1890s European firms began to branch out into the Malay States and acquire a tightening grip on the economy. Companies such as Guthrie's led the rush into rubber in the mid-1890s. European capital flooded into the tin mining and smelting industry. In 1912 the first tin dredge was brought into operation and by the 1930s the tin industry was Western dominated.[31] Westerners had the advantage of large-scale capital and joint stock companies. They succeeded in the tin industry by developing superior machinery and in the rubber industry by organizing the recruitment of cheap labour from southern India.

Singapore's port facilities failed to keep pace with the expansion of her trade. During the 1870s the volume of cargo handled and ships berthed in the port increased considerably, but the rough dirt track across the marshes was still the only link between New Harbour and the town. In the 1880s the government levelled the coastal hills to reclaim land from Telok Ayer Bay, the marshes were drained, and the former nutmeg plantations that lay between the harbour and the town began to give way to building.

In 1861 the Patent Slip and Dock Company was formed and later became the New Harbour Dock Company, largely controlled by Paterson & Simons. Under the leadership of Guthrie's and Tan Kim Ching, a rival Tanjong Pagar Dock Company was set up in 1864. Both companies faced several lean years in the trade doldrums of the 1860s, when there was insufficient work to warrant even one dock company, but business improved with the opening of the Suez Canal and the revival of world trade. The Tanjong Pagar Dock Company paid its first dividend in 1872. It built the Victoria Dock in 1878 and the Albert Dock in 1879, by which time the company employed about 2,500 men. By the end of the century, with the exception of the P&O Company (which had its own wharf), the Tanjong Pagar Dock Company had swallowed up all rivals: the Borneo Company's wharf, Jardine's wharf, and finally in 1899 the New Harbour Dock Company.

By 1903 Singapore was the world's seventh largest port in tonnage of shipping, but facilities were grossly inadequate, cramped, and congested. Services were expensive and subject to long delays. The quay, built at different times in sections, had an irregular face line that was difficult for large ships, and the wooden wharves were worm-eaten and dangerous. The four graving docks could only service small ships, which had to queue for repairs. There was no railway to the docks, since railway schemes mooted thirty years earlier had fallen victim to the clash of vested interests between Singapore companies and the government. The result was that in the early years of the twentieth century, all goods to and from the docks still had to be transported in bullock carts.

Large-scale modernization of Singapore's port facilities was needed to cope with the existing volume of traffic and to counter competition from Hong Kong and potential rivalry from Saigon and Javanese ports. In its anxiety to maintain dividends, the London board rejected improvement schemes put forward in 1904 by the local management of the Tanjong Pagar Dock Company, which would have cost the company $12 million. The government was forced to step in. In 1905 the Tanjong Pagar Dock Company was expropriated and transformed into a public-owned Tanjong Pagar Dock Board. During the next few years the port was modernized. The old wharves were replaced, new roads and godowns were built, modern machinery was installed, the recently reclaimed Telok Ayer Basin was developed, a wet dock was constructed, and electric power was introduced. In 1913 the Board was transformed into the Singapore Harbour Board. The graving dock, the second largest in the world, opened later that year, and the giant Empire Dock was finished in 1917.

The Singapore Harbour Board was a corporate statutory body and for many years the most important public utility in Singapore, with responsibility for its own public health, public works and fire brigade. Motor lorries replaced the bullock carts to transport goods between the docks and the town. In 1909 the peninsular railway was completed, linking Johor Bahru and Prai in Province Wellesley, and the Singapore railway was extended from the harbour to Kranji, opposite Johor Bahru.

The modernization of the port came just in time to cope with the rapid opening up of the interior and spiralling world demand for rubber and tin. By that time investment in the tin and rubber industries had become a flood, but the economic expansion highlighted political complications. British influence in Malaya had grown in a haphazard fashion, producing an untidy pattern of administration. The Straits Settlements was a motley collection of scattered communities, with Penang and Melaka limping rather reluctantly in the wake of the more powerful Singapore. British Residents in the Protected Malay States were responsible to the Governor of the Straits Settlements but in practice in the early years they pursued their activities with little control from Singapore. The federation of the Protected States in 1896 brought them more firmly into Singapore's orbit, although a proposal to include the Straits Settlements in the Federation was rejected.[32] The Governor of the Straits Settlements also became High Commissioner of the Federation, and at the senior level the civil services of the Straits Settlements and the former Protected States joined to form a united Malayan Civil Service. In practice the Federation's chief executive, the Resident-General, enjoyed considerable autonomy, and officials were rarely transferred between Singapore and the Malay States until the second decade of the twentieth century.

Federation satisfied neither the Sultans, who saw their powers whittled away, nor the Governor, who regarded the Resident-General in Kuala Lumpur as a rival rather than a subordinate. In 1909 the picture was complicated by the extension of British protection to the former Siamese states of Kelantan, Trengganu, Kedah and Perlis, whose rulers retained more powers than their counterparts in the Federation, and in 1914 a British Adviser was installed in the last remaining state, Johor. The constitutional confusion of "British Malaya" was compounded by commercial strains and competition, since Kuala Lumpur merchants continually resisted Singapore's domination of the Malay States' economy.

The Singapore authorities wished to streamline the complicated structure, and from time to time, particularly in periods of economic depression, they produced schemes of simplification. The first such attempt arose as a result of an international trade slump in 1908, at that time described as "the most serious financial and commercial depression in [the Colony's] history."[33] It hit Singapore at a time when the government had acquired big debts in taking over the Tanjong Pagar Dock Company and developing the port facilities. In 1909 the colony's expenditure exceeded revenue, but the Federation's revenue was expanding with the rising demand for tin and rubber. Many in Singapore wanted to amalgamate with the Federated Malay States on the grounds that Singapore deserved to share in the Federation's prosperity since she provided the defence and port facilities.

The Governor at that time was Sir John Anderson, not to be confused with his namesake and contemporary, who was the head of Guthrie's. Anderson, who held office from 1904 to 1911, had previously served in the Colonial Office in London for twenty-five years and had the complete confidence of the British government, but at first he was considered an outsider in Singapore. A lawyer by training, formal and serious, he seemed rather daunting, but he was an energetic and shrewd man, "an actor and not a talker",[34] and he came to be respected as one of the ablest of Malayan Governors.

Anderson wanted to draw the Malay States and Singapore closer but considered it was too early for complete union. To annex the Federated States would mean breaking faith with the Sultans and alarming the rulers of the northern states and of independent Johor. In 1909 Anderson created a Federal Council and the following year changed the Resident-General's title to Chief Secretary as a first step to reducing his status. Federation businessmen vigorously opposed the measure as the "thin end of the wedge by which the Colony will gradually get control of the revenues of these states". Bowing to their protests, Anderson agreed to leave financial control in the hands of the Federal Council, and the Chief Secretary retained powers as great as the former Resident-General. In this way, Anderson's intentions were defeated and his reforms made little difference.

Trade revived in 1911, and the years immediately leading up to the First World War were a time of unprecedented prosperity in Singapore. Commercial contentment and the outbreak of the war stilled discussions about political reorganization and produced a decade of constitutional calm.

༉

Singapore's rapidly expanding economy attracted ever-increasing numbers of immigrants in the last quarter of the nineteenth century. The population increased by more than 40 per cent in the decade 1871–81, and by 1911 Singapore had more than 185,000 inhabitants. By the end of the nineteenth century she was one of the most cosmopolitan cities in Asia: nearly three-quarters of the population were Chinese, but there were sizeable minorities of peninsular Malays, Sumatrans, Javanese, Bugis, Boyanese, Indians, Ceylonese, Arabs, Jews, Eurasians, and Europeans. The population was still predominantly male, and in the 1911 census men outnumbered women by eight to one.

The largest number of immigrants was Chinese, of whom 50,000 landed in 1880, 200,000 in 1900 and 250,000 in 1912. Most passed through to the Malay States or the Netherlands East Indies, but Singapore's Chinese community rose from 55,000 in 1871 to 87,000 in 1881 and nearly doubled in the next twenty years to 164,000.

The Malay population, coming from Sumatra and the peninsular states, also increased dramatically from less than 12,000 in 1860 to more than 22,000 in 1881, while the combined Javanese, Boyanese, and Bugis population more than doubled in the same period, rising from little over 4,000 to nearly 11,000.

The European population expanded but still numbered fewer than 3,000 in 1881. The Eurasians increased steadily and settled mainly in the Katong area. They were a mixed community, comprising people of Portuguese or Dutch extraction from Melaka and growing numbers of Anglo-Indians and Anglo-Chinese. Most spoke English as their mother tongue and found employment as clerks and subordinates in commercial or government offices.

A big influx of Middle Eastern Jews began in the 1870s, and by the turn of the century the prosperous Singapore Jewish community numbered about 400. The most prominent Jewish resident was Manasseh Meyer, who was born in India in 1846, and finished his education at St. Joseph's in Singapore. After some years in the family business in Calcutta and Rangoon, in 1873 he came back to found a branch in Singapore, which became the biggest import and export firm in the Indian trade. In the 1880s Manasseh Meyer bought land on a big scale, and in 1905 at his own expense he built the impressive synagogue that remained in use into the twenty-first century. Manasseh Meyer served as a municipal councillor from 1893 to 1900 and was belatedly knighted in 1929, shortly before his death.

The Indian community was the only one to decline in numbers, falling from nearly 13,000 in 1860, when Indians comprised the second largest group, to little over 12,000 twenty years later. Most Indian labourers sought work in the Malay States rather than in Singapore. Until 1903 Penang was the sole port of entry for assisted Indian immigrants into Malaya, and even after that Singapore took third place to Penang and Port Swettenham for Indian immigration. In the last years of the nineteenth century, an increasing number of commercial immigrants came to Singapore from India and Ceylon. Largely English-educated, they took up employment as teachers, journalists, traders, clerks, and shop assistants.

Indians also figured prominently in transport. Until the 1860s they held a virtual monopoly as river boatmen, dock coolies, and bullock cart drivers, and although others began to encroach on these activities in the later years of the century, Indians still predominated in transport, the harbour, and communications up to the Second World War.

Indians tended to concentrate in five districts in Singapore. The oldest, dating from the 1820s, was the west fringe of the business area around Chulia and Market Streets, where South Indian *chettiar*, moneychangers, small shopkeepers, boatmen, and quayside workers congregated. The second group, living in the High Street area, were mainly Sindhi, Gujarati, and Sikh cloth merchants. Other Gujarati and Muslim Indian textile and jewellery merchants operated in the Arab Street neighbourhood to the east, and a group of Tamil shopkeepers were on Serangoon Road, while Tamil, Telugu, and Malayalee labourers lived near the docks and railways.

The Indian community was very mixed and did not develop any strong local organizations or leadership. There was a gap between North and South Indians, while Muslims, Sikhs, Hindus, and the small Christian group all had their own mosques, temples, and churches. While some, particularly among the white-collared workers, settled permanently in Singapore, the majority planned to return home, and the Indian community was perhaps even more transitory than the Chinese in this period.

∽

In the last quarter of the nineteenth century Singapore was the economic and cultural centre of the Malayo-Muslim world in Southeast Asia, a focus for Indonesian immigration and for the peninsular and archipelago trade. She was a publication centre for Muslim religious writings, and Malay was one of the leading languages of the Islamic world.

Singapore became a staging post for Indonesian as well as Chinese labourers in the last decades of the century. Javanese, recruited by agents, or *orang tebunan*, pledged their labour against recovery of passage money in the same way as the Chinese did. Between 1886 and 1889, 21,000 Javanese labourers signed contracts with the Chinese Protectorate in Singapore.[35] And with the expansion of rubber planting from the last years of the century the numbers of immigrant Javanese agricultural labourers swelled.

With the advent of steamers, Singapore also became the centre for the Mecca pilgrim trade. By the end of the century most of the

7,000 Indonesians who made the pilgrimage each year left from Singapore. Many would-be pilgrims spent months, and sometimes years, in Singapore accumulating money for their journey to Mecca. Some never saved enough and stayed in Singapore permanently. Others stopped off to work there on their return journey in order to pay off debts incurred on the pilgrimage.

By 1901 the Malayo-Muslim population stood at more than 36,000, comprising some 23,000 peninsular Malays, over 12,000 from the Indonesian archipelago, about 1,000 Arabs, and 600 Jawi-Peranakans. The Arabs and Jawi-Peranakans, most Indonesian immigrants, and many Malays lived within the town limits, congregating in the areas set aside for their communities in Raffles's day: Kampong Glam and its environs, Telok Blangah, Kampong Malacca, and Kampong Bencoolen.

Malay and Indonesian immigrants assimilated quietly and unobtrusively. They adopted the Sumatran Malay *lingua franca*, adhered to the Muslim religion and customs, and married freely with the established Malay population. Of all the immigrant peoples, Indonesians kept the fewest links with their original homeland. Only a minority returned and few sent family remittances.

Some Indonesian and Malay immigrants became prosperous. The Buginese family, of which Haji Embok Suloh was in later years the most outstanding figure, owned substantial property in Singapore, together with pepper and gambier plantations in Borneo and Sumatra, and conducted trade in their own ships. The Sumatran Minangkabau were particularly successful as shopkeepers. Other immigrants became mosque officials, religious teachers, and petty traders. But the majority of Malays, whether local-born or immigrants, drifted into humble employment as watchmen, drivers, gardeners, domestic servants, or policemen.

By the end of the nineteenth century, steeply rising land values drove new Malay immigrants to seek cheaper land further from the city. Urban Malays found themselves submerged in a European-ruled Chinese city, and their commercial life wilted in face of Chinese competition. There was little opportunity for them to rise in society. Most were illiterate or educated only in the Malay vernacular schools, which were so elementary that up to 1894 they had not produced one clerk, interpreter or translator for government service.[36] Religion, language and ethnic affinity took on a new meaning in binding the Malay community together in the face of Western and Chinese pressures and the increasing complexity of urban life.

In the late nineteenth century Singapore was the centre of considerable political intrigue, with many peninsular chiefs coming to deal with officials, lawyers and businessmen. She also provided a refuge for chiefs who were dislodged by British intervention in the Malay States. Ex-Sultan Abdullah of Perak lived in Singapore from the time of his return from exile in the Seychelles in 1894 until his death in 1922. The Mantri of Larut, the Dato' Bandar of Sungei Ujong, Rajah Mahdi, and Rajah Mahmud of Selangor all retreated to live in retirement in Singapore. The descendants of Sultan Ali of Singapore still lived in Kampong Glam, and the new Sultans of Johor, Abu Bakar and his son Ibrahim, figured largely in Singapore social life. Abu Bakar gave up his Telok Blangah house and built a new European-style residence at Tyersall in fashionable Tanglin, where he associated mainly with Europeans and wealthy Chinese, "a man much petted and decorated by the British government for unswerving fidelity to British interests".[37] These colourful individuals were not the dominating influence in the Malayo-Muslim world of Singapore at the turn of the century. Leadership passed to new classes, notably to the largely English-educated Jawi-Peranakans, who were the most *au fait* with the colonial administration, and to wealthy Arabs who could compete with Chinese and Europeans in the economy.

For centuries Arabs had played a significant part in the archipelago as traders, teachers, and missionaries, but it was not until the last quarter of the nineteenth century that their numbers increased and they came to fill the vacuum in Muslim leadership in Singapore. Some Arab families, such as the Aljunieds, had been established in Southeast Asia long before the founding of Singapore, and Arab immigrants had married local Muslim women, since female emigration from the Hadramaut was forbidden. Despite their mixed blood, the Singapore Arabs kept close contacts with Arabia, often sending their sons to school there, observing Muslim custom strictly, seeking sons-in-law of pure Arab blood, using the Arabic language, wearing Arab dress, and adopting Arab titles, such as "sayyid" or "shaykh". At the turn of the century, when the Singapore Arabs reached the height of their influence among the Malayo-Muslim community, few of them knew any English. This was true even of the wealthy philanthropist, Syed Shaik Alkaff, who in 1909 built the Arcade, which in its day was the most outstanding commercial building in Singapore.

The Arab community was replenished in the late nineteenth century with fresh immigrants from the Hadramaut, who were often cultivated, devout, and learned men. Prominent Arabs were acknowledged in the last years of the century as respected leaders. The main families were very wealthy, controlling the Mecca pilgrim traffic and much of the inter-archipelago sailing-ship trade. Many owned tea, pepper, and gambier estates in nearby regions of the archipelago and in the later years of the century acquired large landed properties in Singapore, particularly in the Geylang and Serangoon areas. The three wealthiest families – the Alkaffs, the Alsagoffs, and the Aljunieds – were all active in charity work, endowing hospitals and schools, building mosques, and financing religious feasts and festivals.

At the turn of the century the ability of the small Jawi-Peranakan community to speak Malay and English gave them an entrée into Singapore's commercial world. Some flourished as shopkeepers, many were employed as clerks, interpreters, and schoolteachers, and a few, following Keasberry's tradition, took to journalism and printing. The *Jawi Peranakan*, which was the first Malay-language newspaper in Malaya or Indonesia, was published in 1876,[38] and from that time until the First World War Singapore was the centre for Malay journalism. In the first twenty years of the twentieth century she became the focal point of reformist

Muslim thought and literature in Southeast Asia. The Middle East Pan-Islamic reform movement appealed to Singapore's urban commercial Muslim community, and Singapore reformers challenged the traditional Islam practised by the aristocratic élite and the conservative *ulama* of the Malay States.

Arabs and Jawi-Peranakans began to adopt the European and Chinese practice of forming clubs and associations, notably the Persekutuan Islam Singapura, or Muslim Association of Singapore, which was founded about 1900. Most of these clubs were cultural, largely concerned with education, language, and Malay custom. They were patronized by the small middle class and well-to-do Arabs, Jawi-Peranakans, and educated Malays, who tended to look down upon the sports clubs favoured by the uneducated mass of Malays and Indonesians as a symbol of Malay backwardness.

જી

The Chinese population expanded rapidly in this period. By the outbreak of the First World War they constituted a little over three-quarters of Singapore's population and maintained that proportion throughout the twentieth century. In the 1880s the overwhelming majority was China-born, and at the 1881 census the Straits-born took fourth place after the immigrant Hokkien, Teochew, and Cantonese communities. Nevertheless the handful of Baba Chinese leaders commanded disproportionate influence through their contacts with the European official and commercial class.

In the 1860s a new generation of Singapore-born leaders emerged. Most were Hokkiens, notably Tan Tock Seng's son, Tan Kim Ching (1829–92); shipowner, opium and spirit tax farmer, and property magnate Cheang Hong Lim (1825–93); Tan Kim Seng's son, Tan Beng Swee (1825–84), and Beng Swee's own son, Tan Jiak Kim (1857–1917); Melaka-born compradore, labour contractor and landed proprietor Gan Eng Seng (1844–99); and importers and shipowners Tan Choon Bock (1824–80) and his nephew, Tan Keong Saik. Traditionally to the fore in trade and shipping, the Hokkiens strengthened their hold in banking, industry and sugar production in the late nineteenth century, and they were the largest and dominating element in the Chinese Chamber of Commerce, which was founded in 1906.

The Teochews remained the second most influential community, notably Perak-born Tan Seng Poh (1830–79), opium and spirit tax farmer and gunpowder magazine proprietor, and Seah Eu Chin's son, Seah Liang Seah (1850–1925). Already dominant in gambier and pepper production, the Teochews led the way in promoting new forms of export agriculture, in rubber production and pineapple canning, saw milling, rice milling, and fish distribution.

The majority of Cantonese in Singapore were artisans and labourers, but a prosperous minority made money, particularly in tin. The Hakkas, a smaller and poorer community, were overtaken in numbers in the early twentieth century by the Hainanese, or Hailams, who were at the bottom of the social and economic scale. Most Hainanese were sailors, domestic servants, or unskilled labourers, and they formed a particularly unsettled group because before 1918 Hainanese women were forbidden to emigrate and Hainanese rarely married outside of their own community.

Tan Kim Ching, Tan Beng Swee, Tan Jiak Kim, Cheang Hong Lim, and Seah Liang Seah all inherited considerable fortunes, but Gan Eng Seng rose from poverty on his own merit, starting as a clerk in Guthrie's warehouse.

The colonial government continued to seek the co-operation of the Straits Chinese leaders by appointing them to positions of authority as Justices of the Peace or members of the Legislative and Municipal Councils. After 1869 there was always a Chinese representative on the Legislative Council, and the first Chinese Municipal Commissioner, Tan Seng Poh, was appointed in 1870. Since an adequate command of English was essential to play an effective part in public life, such service attracted the most Westernized Straits Chinese. Tan Beng Swee refused a seat on the Legislative Council in 1882 because of his indifferent knowledge of the language, but his English-educated son, Tan

Jiak Kim, was appointed to the Legislative Council in 1889. The Chinese Advisory Board gave proportional representation to the five Chinese dialect groups: Hokkien, Teochew, Cantonese, Hakka, and Hainanese. As its name implied, the Board had the right to advise and it provided an airing ground for grievances, but had no executive authority. Clementi Smith toyed with the idea of making membership of the Board elective, but the small influential Straits Chinese group that was close to the British authorities consistently resisted the principle of election, not only for the Chinese Advisory Board but also for the Legislative Council and the Municipal Commission. They derived their influence from their close relationship with the colonial powers, not from authority within the Chinese community. Men like Tan Jiak Kim, who served as a nominated legislative councillor from 1889 to 1892 and again from 1902 to 1915 and was made a Companion of the Order of St. Michael and St. George in 1912, co-operated with the colonial authorities almost to the point of servility.

As in former days, the Singapore Chinese leaders aimed to increase their prestige through charitable works, financing schools, hospitals, roads, temples, gardens, and markets. They wielded influence through the different *pang*, or dialect group, associations: the Teochew Ngee Ann Kongsi, which had been formed about 1830 by Seah Eu Chin and continued to be dominated by the Seah family until after the First World War, the Hokkien Association, the Cantonese Kwong Siew Association, the Hakka Huichew Association, and the Hainanese Kheng Chiu Association. These were economic and benevolent social associations, which dealt with such matters as cemeteries, hospitals, schools, religious festivals, and social welfare. Early district-based associations joined together to form wider dialect groups or *pang*, which separated the Chinese population into largely self-contained communities. From their moment of arrival, new immigrants sought out fellow dialect speakers and continued to associate with them exclusively in their work, housing, religious worship, and entertainment, having little contact with other dialect groups. The various *pang* worshipped different deities in separate temples, laid their dead in different burial grounds, and attended different schools.[39]

🙨

Wealth remained the key to social standing among the Singapore Chinese until the emergence of a new university-trained professional class at the end of the nineteenth century. The first of this new breed, Lim Boon Keng, who studied medicine in Edinburgh, and Song Ong Siang, who studied law in London, were Singapore-born Hokkiens and recipients of Queen's scholarships, under a scheme established by Clementi Smith in 1889 to enable outstanding local students to proceed to British universities.

By the turn of the century, there was a warm and genuine feeling of mutual respect and co-operation between the Baba leaders and the British colonial authorities. It rested on confidence in the security and seemingly permanent strength of the British Empire, the prosperity of Singapore and the spread of Western education and professional activities among the Straits Chinese. In 1900 Tan Jiak Kim, Seah Liang Seah, Lim Boon Keng and Song Ong Siang formed the Straits Chinese British Association, which was designed to promote interest in the British Empire and loyalty to the Queen, to advance the welfare of Chinese British subjects in the colony, and to encourage higher education. Starting with 800 members, the Association came to include most Chinese professional leaders and legislative and municipal councillors. Many Baba Chinese began to value British citizenship not merely for the protection it offered in visiting China or travelling abroad but for its association with the British Empire. There were frequent displays of loyalty. Queen Victoria's golden jubilee was celebrated in 1887 with much warmth by all communities, and the Baba community presented a statue of the Queen, which was unveiled in the dining room of Government House.

British royal visitors, such as the Duke of Clarence who came in 1882, the Duke and Duchess of York in 1901 and the Duke of Connaught in 1905, were welcomed with enthusiasm in their drives round Chinatown, which were always a part of every visiting dignitary's itinerary. In 1901, as a result of an appeal by Song Ong Siang and Tan Jiak Kim, a Chinese company was created to serve alongside Europeans in the Volunteer Corps. Song Ong Siang and Lim Boon Keng went as members of the Volunteers to Edward VII's coronation, and Tan Jiak Kim represented the colony at the coronation of George V. British victories, such as the capture of Pretoria in 1900 and the end of the Boer War, were celebrated by mammoth Chinese processions. British crises, such as the First World War, roused the generosity of the Straits Chinese, who contributed large sums of money to the war effort.[40]

Increasing numbers of Straits Chinese adopted Western customs, took to European sports and pastimes and became Christians. In 1885 a Straits Chinese Recreation Club was founded, which offered facilities for tennis and billiards and later on for cricket and hockey, and in 1911 the Straits Chinese Football Association was formed. Christianity became a fashionable religion, and missionaries, who had previously found it hard to make headway among the Chinese community, won many converts in the later years of the century, particularly among Baba women. The Presbyterians, who were established in Singapore in 1856, and the Methodists, who set up their mission in 1885, were more successful than the Anglicans or Roman Catholics, since they had more women missionaries.[41]

Europeans came to think of the Straits Chinese as being a prosperous English-educated Westernized community, but in the late nineteenth century this was true only of the upper crust. The vast majority of the Straits Chinese were no more affluent, better educated, or oriented towards Britain than their immigrant China-born contemporaries.

The last years of the nineteenth century and first decade of the twentieth century were a time of confused loyalties among the Singapore Chinese, since they coincided with the upheaval of reform, reaction, and revolution in late imperial China. The leading Baba Chinese respected British power and sought

Westernized education as the key to a successful career in business or the professions. Yet those who had been most deeply immersed in the Western education system were most concerned to preserve the roots of their Chinese culture and to see China modernize. The founders of the Straits Chinese British Association were the keenest supporters in Singapore of China's Hundred Days' Reform Movement.

When Lim Boon Keng and Song Ong Siang returned from Britain to Singapore in 1893, they spearheaded the new group of Chinese professional men who attempted to extend Ch'ing reforms to Chinese schools in Singapore and challenge the apathy towards education, which had hitherto prevailed among the Singapore Chinese.

Up to that time, even the most Westernized Singapore Chinese had clung to traditional Chinese ways. Whampoa, probably the first to send his son to school in England, was horrified when the boy returned in 1847 shorn of his pigtail and professing to be a Presbyterian, and he sent him back to Canton to mend his ways. An English visitor to Singapore, meeting the legislative councillor Seah Liang Seah in 1889, was impressed by the fact that in habits and dress he was thoroughly Chinese, although he had never visited China, spoke perfect English and knew Europe well.[42] Despite the increasing Westernization of the leading Straits Chinese and their willing co-operation with the British colonial authorities, they also strengthened their ties with their Chinese background. The relaxation of China's emigration laws, combined with the protection of British citizenship, gave greater legal security to successful Singapore Chinese in visiting China. The journey by steamship was quicker, safer and more comfortable than by the sailing junks of the past. Even long-established Singapore Chinese revived family links, visited China frequently, often sent their sons to school in China, and sometimes retired there in old age. While the early Chinese settlers had often married local women, by the second half of the nineteenth century Baba Chinese preferred their daughters to marry pure-blooded immigrants and often sent their sons to seek wives in China. Those Chinese who were most exposed to contact with the European official and commercial community in Singapore put an increasing value on Chinese culture and customs. At the same time the Straits Chinese spoke Malay, or at least a Baba Malay patois. Lim Boon Keng and Tan Jiak Kim both addressed the inaugural meeting of the Straits Chinese British Association in 1900 in Malay, and Song Ong Siang produced the first romanized Malay newspaper, *Bintang Timor*, for the benefit of the Straits Chinese.

Lim Boon Keng typified the counter-pull of three different cultural loyalties, which threatened a "crisis of identity" among the rising younger generation of Singapore Chinese. A third-generation Baba born in Singapore in 1869, Lim was educated at Raffles Institution, became the first Chinese Queen's scholar, was a legislative councillor from 1895 to 1902, was founder member of the Straits Chinese British Association, was a member of the Chinese Advisory Board, and was the first to enrol in Britain's support in the Chinese Volunteer Company in 1901. Lim had a triple loyalty to Britain, China and Singapore and set out to modernize Chinese traditions along Western lines, discarding what he considered to be old-fashioned superstitions and practices but reviving and strengthening Confucian morality and confidence in Chinese culture. In 1897 he founded the Philomathic Society and that same year, together with Song Ong Siang, he published the first issue of the *Straits Chinese Magazine*.

Lim Boon Keng took up in Singapore the movement begun in China in 1898 to discard the pigtail and helped launch the first serious campaign against opium smoking. His main concern was education. He deplored the superficial schooling of most Straits Chinese boys, who attended English-medium schools and neglected their Chinese education. Some English-medium schools ran Chinese classes, but these were so poorly attended that the last to survive, which was held in Raffles Institution, closed down in 1894. There were more than fifty Chinese so-called "schools" in late nineteenth-century Singapore. Most were small classes, but a few public schools were endowed by wealthy Chinese merchants, such as the Chinese Free School, opened by Tan Kim Seng in 1854, and the Cheang Wan Seng School founded by Cheang Hong Lim in 1875. The Chinese schools taught in dialect, most of them in Hokkien, and along traditional Confucian lines, but the standard was so poor that in 1889 the editor of the *Lat Pau* suggested there was no point in keeping them open. They were designed to satisfy the philanthropic spirit of the wealthy merchants rather than to provide an up-to-date education.

Well-to-do Chinese merchants preferred to send their sons either to China or to the local English-medium schools. In 1893 Gan Eng Seng opened an Anglo-Chinese Free School, later renamed the Gan Eng Seng Free School, which aimed to provide bilingual education but eventually became an English-medium school.

Lim Boon Keng condemned "the absolute staleness of our education", the narrow concentration on English as a means to secure a job, breeding "neither patriotism nor piety, nor virtue nor wisdom". He deplored the divorce of the Singapore Chinese from their background, since "a people, like a tree severed from its roots, must wither away and degenerate". He urged Singapore Chinese to educate their children first in the Chinese tradition, which was designed "to ennoble man's mind and purify his character", but he also wanted a more modern, scientific curriculum, not merely the classics. The Baba reformers favoured Mandarin as a medium of instruction. Lim Boon Keng began teaching Mandarin to students in 1899, and classes were subsequently started at the Chinese Consulate and the Straits Chinese Recreation Club.

The Baba reform group also opened educational opportunities to Straits Chinese women, who by tradition were secluded and guarded from the age of puberty, prepared only for serving their husbands and mothers-in-law in marriages arranged by their parents. Most were illiterate or could at best read romanized Malay. They knew no English or Chinese, spoke Baba Malay, and took no part in activities outside their own households. As the Director of Public Instruction declared in 1906, "There is no more absolutely ignorant, prejudiced and superstitious class of people in the world than the Straits-born Chinese woman."[43] Lim Boon Keng started the first English-medium school for Chinese girls in 1899, with a curriculum that included Malay, music, sewing, cookery, and later Chinese. The first Chinese-medium girls' school, Chung Hua Girls' School, was opened in 1911. Straits Chinese women began to emerge from the isolation to which they had hitherto been condemned, and in 1913 a Chinese girl student enrolled in medical school.

In the early years of the twentieth century, the Ch'ing government began belatedly to encourage education among the Overseas Chinese in order to win their loyalty. In 1907 a special school for Overseas Chinese was opened in Nanking, which attracted many Singapore students. In addition, the Manchu government sent officials to raise money to found Chinese schools in the Nanyang, and the Chinese Consul-General helped to collect these funds and supervised education.

The reform movement in China itself had a strong impact on Singapore youths sent to school in China, notably on Khoo Seok Wan, son of a wealthy Singapore businessman. Khoo returned to Singapore in 1895 disgusted with the old-fashioned imperial Chinese government. With Lim Boon Keng, he encouraged setting up modern Chinese-medium schools in Singapore in the early years of the twentieth century.

As the main spokesman of the Baba reform group, Lim Boon Keng used his position in the Legislative Council to dispute some government measures more strongly than his predecessors had done, but with little success. The Baba reformers encountered resistance not only from the colonial authorities but also from Christian missionaries and from the more conservative elements in their own community. While they agreed with missionaries in attacking practices such as opium smoking or foot-binding in women, the reformers' concern to strengthen Confucian morality brought them into collision with some Christian teaching in the mission schools.

While some modern-minded Singapore Chinese began cutting off their queues from the early years of the century, conventional

Babas, such as Tan Jiak Kim, frowned upon the movement to discard the pigtail, and the practice was not generally adopted in Singapore until after the 1911 Revolution in China. The campaign to eradicate opium smoking received little support either from the government or, initially, from the Chinese Chamber of Commerce, some of whose leading members had a vested interest in the opium tax farm.

Despite these difficulties, the Baba reformers did succeed in gradually changing the attitudes of their community. Pigtails became a rarity after the second decade of the century, opium smoking came to be regarded as a disreputable habit, and the status of Chinese women and the standard of Chinese education improved.

ॐ

New Chinese immigrants arrived in large numbers in the early years of the twentieth century, their numbers fluctuating according to the state of prosperity in Malaya and harvest conditions in China. In 1907, 227,000 Chinese immigrants landed in Singapore, in 1909 numbers dropped to 152,000, but soared to a record figure of 270,000 in 1911, which was a year of flood and famine in southern China.

Hitherto the Ch'ing imperial government had not recognized or sought to establish contact with the Overseas Chinese, but Beijing policy changed in 1876, when she decided to set up consulates in the Nanyang, which aimed to harness loyalty to China by promoting interest in Chinese culture and education and by seeking financial support. The first Chinese Consulate was established in Singapore in 1877, with Whampoa as Honorary Consul, and the British authorities welcomed this appointment of a trusted Singapore Chinese.

After Whampoa's death in 1880, Tso Ping-lung (Tzu-hsing), an experienced Confucian career diplomat, was appointed Chinese Consul. During his ten years in the post Tso concentrated on strengthening cultural links with China. He was said to be behind the launching in 1881 of *Lat Pau*, Singapore's first Chinese newspaper. In 1882 Tso started the first Chinese literary club in Southeast Asia, the Hui Hsien She, or Society for the Meeting of Literary Excellence, and in 1888 he founded the Celestial Reasoning Association, which held debates in English about Chinese culture for Straits Chinese members who could not read Chinese. Tso also encouraged wealthy Chinese to found Chinese-medium schools and in 1884 started a medical dispensary for the poor.[44]

A major function of the Singapore Chinese Consulate was to raise money from the Overseas Chinese in Malaya and the Netherlands East Indies, and prominent Babas, such as Tan Beng Swee, frequently served on fund raising committees. The Straits authorities took no exception if the funds were for charitable purposes, such as the relief of flood and famine victims in China. They were less happy about some of the Consulate's other activities, notably when it published Beijing's appeal to the Nanyang Chinese during the Sino-French conflict in 1884 to poison all Frenchmen and scuttle French ships. But in general the charming Tso maintained an amicable relationship with the Straits authorities, co-operating in supplying information on secret societies and promoting the protection of women and girls. The Consulate's activities were neither political nor anti-British, but Tso Ping-lung began the process of changing the attitude of the Singapore Chinese towards Peking. In 1889 they officially celebrated the accession and marriage of Emperor Kuang-hsu and later welcomed the Chinese navy on a visit to Singapore. These were the first public expressions of loyalty to the Ch'ing, towards whom the Singapore Chinese had traditionally been at best apathetic and often openly hostile.

In the last decade of the century the Manchu Empire stepped up its demands on the loyalty of the Overseas Chinese, trying to harness their wealth and talents to serve China. Beijing embarked on this policy, which was to be continued in succession by Chinese royalist reformers, revolutionaries and later the Kuomintang for more than half a century. In Malaya it was to cause strains within the Chinese community, to create communal distrust and to embitter the relationship between the colonial government and the Chinese. In 1893 the Ch'ing government formally repealed the prohibition on emigration, which had been a dead letter in practice since 1860. Beijing actively encouraged emigration in order to ease the pressure of overpopulation and to raise financial help from Overseas Chinese for the mother country.

In 1891 the Singapore Consulate's status was raised to Consulate-General, with the appointment of Huang Tsun-hsien, an energetic Hakka diplomat, who had served for fourteen years in Tokyo, Washington and London. When Huang made Singapore the major centre for collecting funds from the Nanyang, the Straits authorities became alarmed about the consulate's influence and its campaign to extend fund raising on a large scale into the Protected Malay States. The British Foreign Office was contemplating means of having Huang removed, when he was recalled to China in 1894.

Huang brought the Chinese imperial government's prestige to its peak in Singapore, but this was shaken by Japan's victory in the Sino-Japanese War and the first stirrings of national discontent in China. Singapore Chinese were even more dismayed because in March 1894 they had feted the imperial navy, which surrendered to the Japanese only eleven months later. The humiliating peace dictated by Japan in 1895 was followed by the scramble for concessions by the Western powers and threats to the very existence of China. During the last years of the nineteenth century, the Singapore consulate put aside cultural activities and gave priority to raising money for investment in railways and other enterprises in China, which would keep out foreign capital. One method was by the sale of imperial titles and honours. A price list for such honours was published in 1889, and titles were sold in large numbers to Singapore Chinese up to the end of the Ch'ing Dynasty.[45]

The new Consul-General, Chang Pi-shih (also known as Chang Chen-hsuan or Thio Tiauw Siat), was not a professional diplomat but a wealthy Nanyang Chinese businessman. Born into a poor Hakka family, Chang emigrated from Kwangtung to Batavia at the age of seventeen. He moved to Penang in 1876, acquired control of the excise tax farms in Penang and Singapore, and built up widespread interests in tin mining, agriculture, trading and shipping in Malaya and the Netherlands East Indies. Chang set out to extract the maximum from the Nanyang Chinese. He sold Chinese titles and honours on such a scale that the Straits authorities persuaded London to offer British honours in competition. In 1898 Chang returned to China, where he became a prominent industrialist, but he continued his interest in the Nanyang and in 1904 was appointed Minister for Investigation of the Commercial Affairs of Southeast Asia.

As part of its policy, Beijing promoted the setting up of commercial organizations among the Overseas Chinese, and in 1906 the Consul-General and Shih Chu Ching, a Ch'ing official, founded the Singapore Chinese Chamber of Commerce. In 1909 Beijing asserted the principle of *jus sanguinis*, claiming as Chinese nationals all people of Chinese blood through the male line, regardless of where they were born or how long their ancestors had lived outside of China. The Chinese imperial government sought talent as well as money from the Overseas Chinese and wooed qualified men to return home to serve China in her "hour of need". A Melaka-born lawyer, Ng Ah Choy, became Chinese minister to Washington in 1896, and Penang-born Dr. Wu Lien-teh, the "plague fighter", went as a doctor to China in 1907.[46]

While the Consulate-General concentrated on economic and financial projects, its cultural activities were taken over by a group of Singapore Chinese who had studied abroad, either in China or in Britain. Most notable were Khoo Seok Wan, Song Ong Siang, Lim Boon Keng, and Lim's father-in-law, Huang Nai-shang, a wealthy newspaper editor.

The Hundred Days' Reform Movement, which was launched in China in 1898, with its emphasis on educational modernization, met with enthusiastic response from the reformers in Singapore. Khoo Seok Wan started a progressive newspaper, the *Thien Nan Shin Pao*, in 1898 in support of the Chinese reform policy, and after the Empress-Dowager crushed the short-lived movement in China, Singapore became a fertile field for exiled royalist reformers. In 1900, at his own expense, Khoo invited K'ang Yu-wei, the exiled reform leader, to come to Singapore. K'ang roused considerable support both among the well-educated China-born or Chinese-educated and among English-educated Babas, such as Lim Boon Keng and Tan Boon Liat. The new Chinese Consul-General Lo Tsung-yao asked Governor Sir Frank Swettenham to banish K'ang Yu-wei. Swettenham refused, although he would have been delighted to see K'ang leave and was worried by rumours that the Empress-Dowager was sending assassins to kill the former Chinese leader.

The revolutionary Dr. Sun Yat-sen came to Singapore in 1900 to try to make a bargain with K'ang Yu-wei,[47] but the latter refused to have anything to do with Sun, and the colonial authorities deported him. K'ang Yu-wei founded the Protect Emperor Party in Singapore early in 1900, but he moved to Penang shortly afterwards. By then Khoo Seok Wan and other supporters had become disillusioned with the former Chinese minister and his political cause, following the exposure of incompetence and corruption among the royalist reformers in the failed Hankow Uprising of 1900, to which Khoo Siok Wan had contributed considerable funds.[48]

The reform and revolutionary movements took different paths, and Singapore Chinese were forced to take sides, as the Ch'ing government, royalist reformers, and revolutionaries competed for their support and money. Most rich Singapore *towkay* favoured reform and contributed handsomely to support local educational institutions but were wary about financing revolutionary movements. While not wishing to alienate the potential future rulers of China, Singapore businessmen wanted some assurance of success before they parted with their money to back uprisings in China. The Singapore Chinese Chamber of Commerce was dominated by the royalist reformers and at this stage was a cohesive body, concentrating on raising funds to support the anti-opium campaign and finance schools.[49]

Despite Sun Yat-sen's speedy deportation, one of his revolutionary associates, Yu Lieh, came to Singapore in 1901, where he started workers' clubs, set up a clinic in Chinatown, built up a following among the poor, and attracted secret society members, who saw in the political revolutionary movement a chance to restore the respectability of their *hoey*. Yu also won the support of a few wealthy businessmen, including disillusioned former royalists Tan Chor-nam, Teo Eng-hock and his nephew, Lim Ngee-soon. In 1904 Lim contributed $50,000 to found the first revolutionary Nanyang Chinese newspaper in Singapore, the *Thoe Lam Jit Poh*, which aimed to appeal to all patriotic Chinese: workers and merchants, Straits-born and immigrant. Sun Yat-sen at that time was concentrating his political activities in Japan, where he founded the T'ung-meng Hui or Chinese Revolutionary League, forerunner of the Kuomintang. Too impatient and impetuous to devote himself to the careful building up of an organizational framework among the Overseas Chinese, Sun Yat-sen was impressed by Yu Lieh's efforts when he visited Singapore once more in 1906.[50] He decided to found a Singapore branch of the T'ung-meng Hui, which began with fifteen members and became the base for his movement in the Nanyang. Sun Yat-sen's revolutionaries worked through the new modern Chinese schools and other ostensibly innocent institutions, such as literary societies and Chinese Young Men's Christian Associations. The first was the YMCA of the Chinese Presbyterian Church, which stocked revolutionary literature and held lectures for young people, many of whom joined the T'ung-meng Hui.

Singapore was the planning centre for several Chinese risings in 1907 and 1908 but the failure of these risings, which coincided with a commercial depression in 1907–8, hit the T'ung-meng Hui in Singapore very hard. Ex-rebels, who flooded into Singapore after the risings failed, clashed with the reformists, became involved in crime, and discredited the revolutionary movement. The slump ruined Teo Eng-hock. Lim Ngee-soon survived to make a fortune in rubber but was reluctant to invest further in revolution. With a circulation of only thirty, the *Thoe Lam Jit*

Poh was forced to close, and its equipment was bought by the reformist *Union Times*.

Sun Yat-sen visited Singapore regularly in these years and continued to inspire loyalty among humbler supporters but found it increasingly difficult to raise money from the rich. In 1909 he moved his Nanyang headquarters to Penang, from whence he was deported the following year. Yu Lieh was arrested in 1909 and left Malaya on his release, after which his organization degenerated into gangsterism and was suppressed. The Singapore Chinese turned their backs on the revolutionary cause.

The atmosphere changed dramatically after the successful Wuchang uprising in 1911. In Singapore the Chinese went wild with excitement and joy and gave a tumultuous welcome to Sun Yat-sen when he passed through as a conquering hero *en route* to China. A joint committee of Hokkien and Cantonese leaders was formed under Tan Kah-kee and Lo Tsok-fu to collect funds for China, and young Singapore Chinese flocked to join the rebel army's ranks. Singapore money played an important role in the final revolution that brought Sun Yat-sen to power. Even the poorest contributed to the rebels' fund, and the culminating victory produced a wave of warm patriotism towards China. Young men enthusiastically cut off their queues and sometimes forcibly chopped off those of their more conservative countrymen, while the British, perturbed at the sudden upsurge of national pride, bemoaned "the mutinous tone of the lowest classes".[51]

Singapore Chinese basked in the praise bestowed by Sun Yat-sen on the Nanyang as "mother of the revolution", but few had contributed until the final stage. Sun Yat-sen seemed to look kindly upon Singapore in the hope of favours to come rather than gratitude for favours received. He had been bitterly disappointed at the lack of support in his early struggling days.

෧෬

The growing pressure exerted by China on the Overseas Chinese, enthusiasm for Chinese nationalism, and the spread of modern

Chinese education brought great changes to the Singapore Chinese community. In some ways they accentuated the differences between the leading Babas and the immigrant Chinese.[52] The English-educated Straits-born minority looked to the Straits Chinese British Association as their mouthpiece. Their leaders were merchants or successful professional men, lawyers, doctors and teachers. The Straits Chinese dominated the professions, were favoured for public office, and worked closely with the colonial authorities, concentrating on social and educational matters rather than politics. The rich China-oriented merchants, who banded together in the Singapore Chinese Chamber of Commerce, wielded great power in the Chinese community. Some were exceedingly wealthy, presiding over commercial empires that spread throughout the Nanyang, but often they had little formal education and a poor command of English. They neither sought, nor were sought after, for public office in the colony, and their interests lay in Chinese schools and philanthropic works and in politics in China.

Most outstanding of the China-born was Tan Kah-kee, who was born in the village of Jimei near Amoy in 1874, received little schooling and came to Singapore at the age of sixteen to work in his father's rice shop. He then set up his own rice store and a pineapple factory in 1904, extended his activities to rubber, rice milling, and shipping. By the time the First World War broke out Tan Kah Kee & Company was Singapore's premier Chinese firm, with interests in Malaya, Siam and China.[53] In the midst of riches Tan Kah-kee lived frugally and considered wealth an evil if not put to good use. He ploughed much of his profit into schools and colleges in Singapore and his native village, and in 1921 he founded Amoy University, which he financed almost single-handedly for sixteen years until it was taken over by the Nationalist Chinese government.

The interests and energies of the Straits-oriented and China-oriented diverged but did not necessarily clash at this time. The Straits Chinese British Association and the Singapore Chinese Chamber of Commerce were markedly different institutions but not exclusive in composition. Tan Kah-kee was a member of the Straits Chinese British Association, while Lim Boon Keng was a pioneer in Chinese education in Singapore and a founder member of the Singapore branch of the Kuomintang.

∽

Prosperity transformed the physical appearance of Singapore town in the last quarter of the nineteenth century. Cavenagh Bridge was opened in 1869, linking Commercial Square and the government quarter near the river mouth. It was the final major work carried out by Indian convicts and after they were withdrawn in 1873, official building became the responsibility of the Public Works Department. A general hospital was built in 1882, the Central Police Station in 1882, Coleman Bridge in 1886, and Raffles Museum and Library in 1887. The Esplanade was widened by reclaiming land from the sea to form Connaught Drive.

Successful Chinese businessmen built mansions in traditional mainland style. The first such house was built by Tan Seng Poh in Hill Street in 1869 and later became the Chinese consulate. The only one to survive into the twenty-first century was constructed by a wealthy Teochew, Tan Yeok Nee, about 1885 on Clemenceau Avenue. Philanthropic Chinese businessmen, such as Cheang Hong Lim, continued to provide amenities. In 1876 Cheang presented $3,000 to plant the park that still bears his name in crowded Chinatown, where open spaces were urgently needed.

Despite increasing congestion, the centre of the town retained some of the characteristics of more leisurely days, and horse sales continued to be held in Commercial Square until 1886. Business houses congregated in the Commercial Square/Collyer Quay area, and most big firms had offices along Collyer Quay where they could observe the coming and going of shipping through telescopes. It was not until the early years of the twentieth century that such observation became obsolete, and the telephone enabled firms to spread out from the traditional business centre.

In the later years of the nineteenth century, the narrow roads in the heart of the town were crowded with a motley assortment of bullock carts, private carriages, pony carts, public hack gharries, and rickshaws. The last were introduced in 1880 from Shanghai, followed in 1882 by the first "noiseless but deadly" bicycles. Battery Road was jammed with traffic all day, and there were no parking restrictions or regulations to force vehicles to use one side of the road. Rickshaws caused most accidents. Rickshaw pullers had to be licensed, but the vehicle owners bypassed the regulations and exploited the pullers, working them long hours and transferring licence badges indiscriminately. As the cheapest form of labour, inexperienced immigrants, newly arrived from villages in China and who had never seen heavy traffic, were often hired. As late as 1901 Singapore was paralysed by a rickshaw strike when the police attempted to enforce traffic rules to cut the accident rate, and the Governor had to summon the leading Chinese *towkay* to Government House and enlist their efforts in getting the men back to work.

Municipal expenditure rose from less than $63,000 in 1857 to more than $500,000 in 1886, but administrative reform was needed to cope with the rapid expansion of the town. Ord's proposal to abolish the elective committee of voluntary amateurs and absorb the Municipal Committee's work into the general government had been rejected by the Legislative Council as yet one more example of the Governor's authoritarianism, but eventually a Municipal Ordinance was passed in 1887. The town area was separated from the rural districts, which were left under direct government control. A full-time salaried Municipal President was appointed by the Governor, and the municipality's finances were separated from general revenue so that it could no longer treat the government as "a municipal milch cow".[54]

This measure was only a small step towards modernization, but within its limits the new Municipal Commission achieved a great deal. It drew up many schemes of improvement in the 1880s, including the provision of a professional fire brigade in 1888. It took over the existing waterworks, built a reservoir at

Thomson Road, and constructed the first filter beds in 1889. Most of this was the work of James MacRitchie, who held the post of municipal engineer for twelve years.

In the next decade municipal schemes were hard hit by a world slump, which triggered off a disastrous fall in the sterling value of the Straits dollar. This led to a sharp rise in the cost of imported raw materials and to a rigorous official economy campaign. Discontented municipal officials lost 20 per cent of the real value of their salaries through the depreciation of the dollar. Many resigned, and MacRitchie's death in 1895 robbed the municipality of one of its most far-seeing officers.

As the economy picked up in the late 1890s, the municipality revived its schemes. It enlarged Thomson Road Reservoir in 1904, and completed Pearl's Hill Reservoir in 1907 and the Kallang Extension River Scheme (later named Peirce Reservoir) in 1911. The Town Hall was renovated and reopened as the Victoria Memorial Hall in 1905, and the Victoria Theatre was finished in 1909. In 1900 the municipality took over the inefficient Gas Company. In 1906 it provided electric street lighting in the central area and arranged for electricity to be supplied to private consumers by the Singapore Tramway Company.

The Singapore Tramway Company, started in 1882, ran trams from New Harbour to Collyer Quay and east to Rochore. For the first twenty years it operated on steam but switched to electricity early in the twentieth century. The company found difficulty in competing with rickshaws, despite the fact that rickshaws were very uncomfortable and adopted rubber tyres only in 1904. Many people objected to the tramway, including one unofficial legislative councillor, who called trams the "modern car of Juggernaut" which would fill the hospitals with casualties. But the fast-spreading town needed efficient public transport.

∽

At the turn of the century, Singapore was a cosmopolitan city but largely an Anglo-Chinese preserve. The British rulers held a monopoly on official political power and provided protection, justice, and administration. To the visitor from Britain, Singapore was very English in appearance, "so flourishing and enlightened, so advanced and well-governed".[55] The heterogeneous society existed "in order and sanitation, living and thriving and trading, simply because of the presence of English law and under the protection of the British flag. Remove that piece of bunting from Government House, and all that it signified, and the whole community would go to pieces like a child's sandcastle when the tide rises. Its three supports are free trade, fair taxation and even handed justice."[56]

The mystique of British imperialism was at its height, and the death of Queen Victoria in 1901 plunged Singapore into silence "like a city struck with plague".[57] Britain's commercial and naval power seemed permanent and unshakeable, and Singapore's economy was largely dominated by Western firms, mostly based in Britain. These superficial impressions were deceptive. While most Europeans lived in comfort and some style as the agents and employees of Europe-based managements, the greatest individual wealth lay with a handful of Asians: Chinese, Jews, Indians, and Arabs.

For the affluent, life was becoming more pleasant. More people could afford carriages, and road improvements enabled them to live in spacious comfort in the suburbs. The first decade of the twentieth century saw the peak of horse-drawn vehicles, and this mobility encouraged more entertaining in private houses and parties that went on to later hours. The first motorcar was imported in 1896, but motor traffic remained a novelty for many years, and in 1908 only 214 people had driving licences.

Raffles Hotel opened in 1899, and social clubs provided a wide choice of entertainment for Europeans. The Yacht Club was formed in 1881, the Golf Club opened at the old racecourse in 1891, the new Swimming Club in 1894 and the Polo Club in 1899. Liveliest of all was the German Teutonia Club, the centre of European social life and of musical activity. In 1900 the Teutonia built a luxurious new clubhouse with a first-class restaurant, concert room, and sports facilities, which later became the nucleus of the Goodwood Park Hotel. There were plenty of opportunities for sport. Tennis became fashionable in the 1870s, association football came into vogue in 1889, and horse-riding parties on Sundays and early mornings were very popular. The first movie, depicting Queen Victoria's funeral, was shown in the Town Hall in July 1901.

Life in the tropics became even more comfortable with the first consignment of frozen meat, fresh butter, and fruit from Australia, which was imported by the Singapore Cold Storage Company in 1905.[58] Electric fans were installed in Government House in 1904, and after 1906 electric lighting and fans came to replace oil lamps and punkahs in private houses.

Well-to-do Asians also enjoyed a more pleasant and entertaining life. Rich Chinese merchants established their own social clubs, of which the Hokkien Ee Hoe Hean Club was the most prominent. The (Eurasian) Singapore Recreation Club was founded in 1883, the Straits Chinese (later Singapore Chinese) Recreation Club in 1885, and one wealthy Straits Chinese, Chia Keng Tye, had a tennis court at home.[59]

For the poor, life grew worse. In 1896 a commission of enquiry headed by Dr. Lim Boon Keng revealed a grim picture of mass living conditions. The mortality rate was higher than that of Hong Kong, Ceylon or India, ranging between 44 and 51 per 1,000 in the first years of the twentieth century. The senior army medical officer had warned in 1872 that "the town is a nursery for disease". Spectacular epidemics were surprisingly rare, but killing diseases, such as beriberi, tuberculosis, malaria, enteric fever, and dysentery, were endemic and were caused by poverty, overcrowding, malnutrition, and dirt. There was neither an adequate water supply nor a sewerage scheme, and night soil was collected for market gardens on a private basis. Tan Kim Seng had presented $13,000 in 1857 to provide a water supply, but this represented only a fraction of the sum needed for this costly amenity. Acrimonious discussions about how to raise the balance dragged on for years. In the end the works were completed in 1879 out of public funds, and most of Tan Kim Seng's gift was spent on an ornamental fountain, which was erected on the Esplanade. By the end of the century, the increase in population had again outstripped the water supply.

Government hospitals were substandard and official health services few. The mass of the population had no medical facilities or relied on a few charitable institutions founded by Chinese philanthropists, notably Tan Tock Seng's hospital and the Thong Chai Medical Institution, which was set up in Chinatown in 1867. Generously financed by Chinese merchants, notably by Gan Eng Seng, the dispensary was given free land by the government in 1892. It examined *sinseh*, who trained in China on traditional lines, and provided free treatment to poor people of all races. Both institutions were to survive into the twenty-first century, by which time the Tan Tock Seng Hospital was the second largest in Singapore. Medical facilities for the small but growing number of female immigrants developed very slowly and initially concentrated on treating venereal disease, which was prevalent among the large number of prostitutes. By 1884 Kandang Kerbau Hospital, which had been set up in the late 1850s, dealt solely with prostitutes. In the early twentieth century public concern about infant mortality led to opening a maternity wing at the General Hospital in 1908.[60] A cholera epidemic carried off 759 victims in 1905, and malaria was the main killer disease at the beginning of the twentieth century, accounting for 1,410 out of 9,440 deaths in 1909, but much ill health was attributed to opium addiction.

Lim Boon Keng and his partner, Dr. Yin Shut Chuan, launched a campaign to discourage opium smoking that attracted support from European missionaries, a few young Chinese who had been educated abroad and a handful of Baba merchants. The year 1906 was a watershed in the history of the opium trade, when the Philippines banned the trade outright, the governments of India and China agreed on a programme to reduce and eliminate the trade within ten years, and the British Parliament passed a resolution condemning the opium trade as "morally indefensible".[61] That same year the Chinese Consul-General founded a Singapore Anti-Opium Society with Tan Boo-liat as president, and an Opium Refuge was established in the Consulate, which was run by Yin Shut Chuan and Lim Boon Keng and financed by a group of Baba merchants.

At that time the opium excise still provided half of the colony's revenue, and the anti-opium movement encountered opposition from the tax farmers, from most Chinese and European merchants, and from the English-language press. The government was torn between financial and moral considerations, but at Colonial Office insistence it appointed a commission in 1907 to investigate the opium question. The commission advised that opium smoking was a fairly harmless, fashionable vice among the rich but the effects were more pernicious among the poor, who could only afford to smoke the dregs of used opium. It concluded that addiction was not widespread, except among rickshaw pullers, who rarely lived to be more than thirty-five or forty years old. Governor Sir John Anderson was prepared to prohibit the vice and to introduce income tax as an alternative source of revenue, but he had to withdraw this proposal in the face of bitter opposition. Unofficial legislative councillors and European and Asian businessmen protested against the proposed income tax and also argued that prohibiting opium smoking might deter immigration.

As a compromise, in 1910 the government took over the manufacture and sale of opium. A government factory at Pasir Panjang produced good-quality opium, and the authorities bought up and burned all opium refuse. This stemmed the worst abuses, but the sale of opium still contributed nearly half of Singapore's revenue up to the mid-1920s. By 1934 opium excise accounted for only one-quarter of the revenue and had been overtaken by duties on tobacco, petrol and alcohol. Opium could only be purchased under licence, and the aim was gradually to eliminate the vice, but the government continued to manufacture opium until the Second World War.

An official commission, which was appointed in 1909 to enquire into the high mortality rate and chronic slum conditions, led to a reorganization of the municipality. Governor Anderson wanted the government to take over full control, employing professional, technical executive officers and reducing the municipal board to a mere advisory body. A Municipal Ordinance of 1913 retained the Municipal Commission, but the governor was to nominate commissioners and have control of the municipal budget. Two European unofficial legislative councillors protested at dropping the elective principle, despite the fact that municipal elections had roused little interest for years and few voters turned out to cast their ballots, but Tan Jiak Kim, legislative councillor and a powerful voice in the Singapore Chinese Chamber of Commerce, declared that the Chinese community did not oppose the nomination of municipal councillors. The 1913 Ordinance remained in force, with minor amendments, up to the Second World War.

༄༅

Education did not keep pace with economic development. In 1870 the Woolley Committee reported to the Legislative Council that "the state of education in the Colony has been and is in a backward state". The committee suggested reorganizing all existing schools under a Director of Education, encouraging secular education, extending Malay and Chinese vernacular instruction, and improving the education of girls. These recommendations went further than the authorities were prepared to go at that time. In 1872 they appointed an Inspector of Schools, A.M. Skinner, but ignored the other proposals.

Like its Indian predecessor, the colonial administration acknowledged a special responsibility to provide free vernacular primary education in Malay as the indigenous language. There was no public demand, nor was it feasible, for the government to provide education in the diverse Indian languages and Chinese dialects spoken by the immigrant majority.

Malay education did not flourish despite the efforts of Christian missionaries and of Skinner, who held the post of Inspector of Schools in the Straits Settlements for thirty years. In 1876, the *temenggong* converted his Telok Blangah residence into a Malay college, with an ambitious programme to provide bilingual secondary education in Malay and English and to train Malay teachers, but the project was unsuccessful. Malay secondary education did not take root, and teacher training was transferred to peninsular colleges. Raffles Institution revived Malay classes in 1885 but abandoned them eight years later for lack of support. A Methodist missionary, Dr. W.G. Shellabear, tried to promote Christian education among the Malay community in the early 1890s, but he found that Muslim attitudes toward Christian teaching had hardened since Keasberry's day. Education among Malay boys reached a low ebb, and attempts to provide schooling for Malay girls were a total failure. After a select committee reported in 1893 on the inefficiency of Malay education in Singapore, many small schools were closed, but this led to no improvement in the quality of the remainder, which offered very elementary Malay instruction with no opportunity to learn English as a second language.

Chinese-medium education was left to the Chinese community. The government set up two Anglo-Tamil schools in 1873 and 1876, but these were converted into English schools because of lack of demand for schooling from the Tamil community. A similar fate overtook the Methodist Girls' School, which was created to cater to Tamil girls but soon became an English-medium school. By the end of the century no government-aided school offered any Tamil classes.

Before the twentieth century the Singapore authorities accepted no responsibility for providing English education but subsidized private English-medium schools, most of which were run by Christian missions. Despite the lack of official encouragement, the vocational benefit of English gave a boost to English-medium primary education in the later years of the century. The existing mission schools raised their standards, while

Raffles Institution blossomed under the headship of R.W. Hullett, who was principal from 1871 to 1906 and later became Inspector of Schools and Director of Public Instruction for the Straits Settlements.[62] New mission schools were opened: St. Andrew's in 1871 and St. Anthony's in 1879. The American Methodist Mission set up its base in Singapore in 1885, founding the Anglo-Chinese Boys' School in 1886 and the Methodist Girls' School in 1887. By 1915 it had seven schools in Singapore.

The only school that provided secondary education was Raffles Institution, which began post-primary classes in 1884. As Colonial Secretary and later as Governor in the 1880s, Clementi Smith tried to promote tertiary education but with little success. He was ahead of his time in his schemes for a technical college, a survey school, and a college for general education. Only a few well-to-do Chinese and Eurasians were interested. A medical school for training apothecaries opened in 1889 but closed the following year after only two students enrolled. Clementi Smith's one success was to found two annual Queen's Scholarships for the Straits Settlements in 1889, and in 1891 to introduce the Senior Cambridge examination, which was the basis for awarding these scholarships.

Clementi Smith's educational proposals were criticized at the time by the European community, and particularly by the *Singapore Free Press*, for ignoring the broader base of primary education, although the Queen's Scholarship scheme justified the thesis that the quickest and most effective way to raise general educational standards is to start at the top. Over the years Queen's scholars returned to Singapore as doctors, lawyers, and teachers. There was no outlet for their talents in government administration, where the senior ranks of the civil service were reserved for Britons of pure European descent, but they became leaders in the professions and served as legislative councillors, municipal councillors, and Justices of the Peace alongside the wealthy merchants. The English-educated professional Asian élite provided a new type of leadership and began a subtle Westernizing and modernizing of Singapore society, inculcating a respect for

Western education and professional success and opening the way for the Asian community to assimilate and accept Western medicine, the British judicial system, and European educational methods. It also became fashionable for prosperous Singapore parents to send to England at their own expense children who were not scholastically brilliant enough to win Queen's scholarships. The influence of the minority educated in England and of the growing numbers of children educated in the English medium in Singapore produced a gradual but significant revolution in the attitudes and character of Singaporeans.

By the beginning of the twentieth century, in addition to providing free Malay primary schooling, the Straits authorities were prepared to take more responsibility for English-medium education, although they continued to leave Chinese and Tamil education to private charities. A 1902 Education Code laid down the basis for official education policy for the next twenty years. For the first time the government provided English-medium primary schools. In 1903 it took over Raffles Institution, making it exclusively a secondary school, and in 1909 it founded an Education Board. Between 1904 and 1911 the number of places in English-medium schools doubled, and English education continued to progress steadily during the first two decades of the twentieth century.

Under pressure from the Straits Chinese, led by Tan Jiak Kim, the Singapore authorities agreed to establish and maintain a medical school, provided the petitioners could raise $71,000 towards the initial cost. To the surprise of officials, there was such enthusiasm for this project that a sum of $87,000 was raised almost overnight. The first class of twenty-three students enrolled in 1905, and the school was named the Edward VII Medical School in 1912. Initially staffed by part-time lecturers from government service and private practice, in 1920 it was upgraded to become the King Edward College of Medicine and acquired a full-time teaching staff. The college was built on the grounds of the new Outram General Hospital and was to form the first constituent part of the future University of Malaya.

The impetus in English-medium education, together with the rapid expansion of modern Chinese schools, produced a great change in Singapore society. It led to the emergence of an upper-level professional class and a literate middle class; it put new value on education as giving status in the community, and it began the slow process of emancipating women. English-medium education was a link between the upper classes. For the clever, it provided a path to professional eminence and a gateway to public life, and for many others it opened the way to clerical or commercial employment.

The overall effect was socially divisive, separating the English-educated from those taught in the vernacular, widening the gap between the different communities except at the highest level, accentuating racial, cultural and linguistic differences and the rift between rich and poor. Apart from the few exceptionally talented Malay students who were promoted to English-medium secondary schools, Malay and Tamil primary education was a dead end, offering no prospect for advancement in the framework of Singapore society. Chinese-medium education confined pupils largely to the Chinese sectors of Singapore's economy and society. While dialect divisions remained strong, increasingly the major gulf was between the Chinese- and English-educated.

$\backsim$

The spread of literacy and the growing awareness of international events stimulated the growth of the English press and gave birth to the first vernacular newspapers in the last quarter of the nineteenth century.

The *Singapore Free Press* was wound up in 1869, leaving the *Straits Times* as the only newspaper in Singapore, although a disastrous fire almost put an end to its existence. Its assets were sold for $40 at public auction, and John Cameron, the proprietor-editor, went bankrupt. He managed to revive the newspaper, but it continued to suffer financial difficulties. Cameron died in 1881, and in 1887 his widow appointed as editor a young Scottish professional journalist, Arnot Reid, who held the post for twelve years and succeeded for the first time in raising circulation above the 200 mark. After his retirement, a talented English journalist, Alexander William Still, was editor for eighteen years and made the *Straits Times* a great commercial success.

In 1887 the *Singapore Free Press* re-emerged under the able leadership of W.G. St. Clair, who edited the newspaper until 1916. Under Still and St. Clair, the rival newspapers attracted growing numbers of readers from the expanding English-educated community, with the *Singapore Free Press* appearing in the morning and the *Straits Times* in the afternoon.[63]

In contrast to the fortunes of the English press, most early vernacular newspapers had a difficult time. The *Jawi Peranakan*, which was owned by that community, first appeared in 1876 and survived for nearly twenty years. The newspaper was edited until 1888 by Mohammed Said bin Dada Mohyiddin, a Raffles Institution teacher of Malay and Indian Muslim stock. *The Jawi Peranakan* devoted much of its space to commercial information and was not critical of government policy. Its news was taken largely from the local English newspapers and also from the Egyptian and Arabic press. Its correspondence columns were lively, and the paper was concerned about the general backwardness of the Malay community and anxious to foster vernacular education and promote the Malay language.

Other Malay-language journals, such as the *Bintang Timor (Eastern Star)* and *Al-Imam (The Leader)*, were short-lived. The *Bintang Timor*, which was the only Malay-language journal then printed in romanized script, was brought out by Song Ong Siang for the Baba Chinese in 1894 but survived less than a year. *Al-Imam*, Singapore's first reformist journal, was launched in 1906, with the financial backing of Indonesian and Arab merchants. Its main sponsors, notably Mohammed Tahir bin Jalaluddin and Sayyid Shaykh bin Ahmad Al-Hadi, had extensive contacts with the Middle East modernist movement. Mohammed Tahir bin Jalaluddin, born in Menangkabau in 1869 and educated in Mecca, returned to Southeast Asia in 1899 as a teacher and scholar, living most of his life in Perak and Johor until his death in 1957. His close friend, Melaka-born Sayyid Shaykh bin Ahmad Al-Hadi, who was educated mainly in Riau, visited the Middle East several times, and from 1901 to 1909 he managed his father's Singapore office. A lively personality and a good writer, he helped to form study clubs and became prominent in Singapore's Malayo-Muslim society. *Al-Imam* was apolitical but aimed to raise the moral and material well-being of the Muslim population by reviving the purity and strength of Islam and modernizing Muslim education. *Al-Imam* survived barely two years, but it set the tone for other pan-Islamic Malay-language reformist journals, which appealed to religious teachers and the educated Muslim mercantile classes.

The Malay press came into its own and flourished for a quarter of a century under the inspiration of Mohammed Eunos bin Abdullah, "the father of Malay journalism". Born in Sumatra in 1876, the son of a wealthy Minangkabau merchant, Mohammed Eunos grew up in Kampong Glam and was educated at Raffles Institution. In 1907 the proprietor of the *Singapore Free Press* invited Mohammed Eunos to edit the *Utusan Melayu* as a Malay edition of the newspaper.

The *Utusan Melayu* was the first major national Malay newspaper and circulated throughout the Straits Settlements and the Malay States. Secular in outlook, it emphasized issues of interest to urban Malay readers. At first it was published three times a week, partly in Jawi and partly in romanized script for Baba Chinese readers. It became a daily newspaper in 1915, but the *Singapore Free Press* sold it three years later to a group of Indian businessmen, and it was forced to close down in 1922 after being crippled financially by damages awarded against it in a libel case.

Meanwhile in 1914 Mohammed Eunos bin Abdullah became editor of the *Lembaga Melayu*, the Malay version of a new English-language paper, the *Malaya Tribune*. Like the *Utusan Melayu*, the *Lembaga Melayu* was moderate and progressive in character: it appealed to urban middle class Malays, generally supporting the colonial regime but sometimes mildly critical of official policy towards the Malays.[64]

A *Singapore Eurasian Advocate*, started in 1888, lasted only three years, and a second English-language Eurasian newspaper appeared only briefly in 1900. A Tamil newspaper, *Singai Nesan*, was published in 1888 but had a small circulation.

The first Chinese newspaper, the *Lat Pau*, was founded in 1881 by See Ewe Lay, a fifth-generation Baba, whose grandfather came from Melaka to Singapore in the 1820s. See Ewe Lay was compradore of the Hongkong and Shanghai Bank and prominent in European commercial circles. He also had close connections with China and, like many of his generation, sought to strengthen the cultural bonds between the Singapore Chinese and their motherland. In 1900 the *Lat Pau*'s circulation still stood at under 500 and ran at a loss until the second decade of the twentieth century,[65] when the educated Chinese-reading public expanded.

Lat Pau was mainly concerned with commerce and offered no criticism of the colonial regime. It was a conservative newspaper, supporting Confucian values and opposing the breakdown of Chinese traditions, such as the queue-cutting campaign that divided the Singapore Chinese in the late 1890s. This gained it the support of many of the well-to-do, but its position was challenged by the reformist *Union Times*. In 1909 See Ewe Lay's nephew, See Tiong Wah, took over the *Lat Pau*. Like his uncle, See Tiong Wah was a Hongkong and Shanghai Bank compradore and a prominent public figure, a Justice of the Peace, municipal councillor, president of the Singapore Chinese Commercial Association, and head of the Hokkien Huay-kuan. He rescued the newspaper from debt, but it went into a decline after the chief writer's death in 1921 and was wound up in 1932.

By the 1880s possible threats to the *Pax Britannica* revived the debate about the colony's defences. The immediate worry was Russia's re-emergence as a naval power. In 1885, amid mounting fears of an Anglo-Russian war over Afghanistan, the Straits Settlements Association of London petitioned the Colonial

Office to provide for the defence of the Straits of Melaka and recommended that the colony should foot the bill for constructing defence works in Singapore if the War Office supplied the guns and equipment.

The Singapore merchants wanted protection not only for the harbour but also for the town, and in 1886 there was an outcry in the Legislative Council when Britain began erecting fortifications only for New Harbour and Blakang Mati Island (the modern Sentosa). The Colonial Office insisted that Britain did not intend to create "a naval fortress" in Singapore, but merely to protect the port area from casual small-scale attack, leaving Singapore's main defence to the Royal Navy.

In 1890 London demanded £60,000 towards the cost of barracks and other new military buildings and proposed to double the Straits Settlements' annual military contribution to £100,000. The Legislative Council agreed to the barracks, but the unofficials unanimously protested against the revised contribution, and the English-language press denounced Colonial Office demands as "imperial robbery". Public meetings were called and a petition to Parliament was drawn up, arguing that Singapore was now a vital imperial station.[66] Governor Clementi Smith supported the petition, warning the Colonial Office that the soured relationship "has tended to imperil good government", but London persisted in demanding full payment.

The trade depression that set in during 1891 and the fall in the value of silver forced the colony to draw on her reserves to meet the military contribution. This caused retrenchment in government departments, delays in executing public works and cheese-paring in education. In 1895, after bitter and long drawn-out arguments about military expenditure, the unofficial legislative councillors resigned, followed by the Justices of the Peace and the Chinese Advisory Board. The Legislative Council had to go into recess for some months. Eventually London agreed to a slightly reduced figure that would also include defence works, and this remained the basis of contributions until the 1920s, when London tried to increase the payment as a contribution towards the new naval base. Again Singapore resisted stoutly. The arguments raged throughout the 1920s and the forty-year battle was finally brought to an end in 1933, when the colony reluctantly agreed to pay $4 million a year, or 20 per cent of her revenue.

Singapore's case was weakened because she became a Crown Colony in 1867 at her own request on the condition that she financed her own military expenditure. Governors consistently fought on the colony's behalf against London on this issue but were forced to use the official majority to outvote unofficials, which was almost the only occasion on which this power was invoked. Britain's naval supremacy was threatened by the rivalry of France, who had united Indo-China under her control and in 1887 was discussing cutting a canal across the Isthmus of Kra. Even Japan was a potential rival. In February 1886 Governor Sir Frederick Weld wrote privately to a friend, "We have two Japanese ironclads of a very superior type built at Newcastle stopping here. Nothing in these parts could look at them. One of our naval men who went over them said either was worth all our fleet in these seas – which is made up of the greatest rubbish – put together, if it came to a fight."[67]

The troubled uncertainty of international relations in the mid 1880s led the Admiralty to investigate various ports with a view to creating a naval dockyard in the East. At one time Singapore was favoured, but negotiations over choosing a site and acquiring land dragged on until 1889, by which time the immediate crisis was over and the Admiralty had lost interest.

The proposal was revived in 1896 in face of deepening British anxiety over the implications of the new Franco-Russian alliance and fears of German economic rivalry and colonial ambitions. During the 1890s the theory of "the new navalism", which held that national strength depended on sea power and the key to naval power lay in heavy battleships, became an internationally accepted fashionable cult. Many nations, notably Germany, rushed to build up their navies.

The naval race and the growing challenge to her commercial supremacy revived the British government's interest in a Singapore naval base, but the very intensity of the new international rivalry eventually killed this scheme. It induced Britain to concentrate her fleet in home waters in face of the German naval threat and to seek protection for her overseas empire through alliances with other powers. In 1902 Britain made a defence pact with Japan, whose victory over Russia in the Russo-Japanese War three years later destroyed the long-standing Russian threat to British sea power in the East. The Anglo-French Entente of 1904 removed the dangers of French rivalry and gave Britain an ally to guard the Mediterranean Sea lane. Admiral Sir John Fisher, who became First Sea Lord in 1904, concentrated British naval strength in the North Sea, withdrew battleships from the East and the Mediterranean, closed down existing naval dockyards abroad and abandoned the Singapore scheme.

Britain's ability to mass her naval strength in home waters was of vital importance in her struggle with Germany in the First World War, but the long-term implications for Singapore were not generally appreciated. Contemporary Englishmen might claim with pride that "the port, phenomenal as its past progress has been, is only on the threshold of its career".[68] "All live at peace and prosper abundantly under the Union Jack, and the statue of Raffles looks down benignantly on a scene so much in harmony with the aspirations and policy of the original founder of the city."[69] Yet, behind this complacency lay the ominous truth that Britain needed French and Japanese friendship to guard her trade and help defend her Eastern Empire in the event of international war.

4

"The Clapham Junction of the Eastern Seas"[1]
1914–1941

Singapore stood on the sidelines while the First World War and the Chinese Revolution were played out, but these two events combined to change the course of her history. At the time the inter-war years seemed to be a period of undiminished imperial authority, with Singapore the pillar of the Eastern Empire and outside threats of dissent easily kept in check. In retrospect this era of comparative calm can be seen as a prelude to the cataclysm of 1942, which set in motion the political storms of the following years. It was a period when Singapore's future was determined largely by external events, by international alternating boom and depression, by developments in China and Japan, and by decisions in Tokyo, Washington and London.

When the First World War broke out in August 1914, German residents in Singapore were interned, German ships were seized, and German property was taken over. British residents had mixed feelings about this. In the early years of the twentieth century British merchants had viewed with some distaste and resentment the invasion of a new breed of aggressive young German businessmen, who differed from the suave German merchants of earlier days. German goods flooded the Singapore market, the German community expanded rapidly, and the opulent Teutonia Club overshadowed the nearby Tanglin Club, which was almost deserted and its building in a dangerous state of disrepair. The Germans were a hospitable and gregarious group, the life and soul of the Western community's social life. Consequently, at the outbreak of war, they were comfortably installed with their servants in the Teutonia Club, and A. Diehn, the senior German merchant and head of Behn Meyer & Company, was allowed into town to look after the firm's affairs.

In the early months of the war Singapore feared an attack by the German East Asiatic squadron in the form of the lone cruiser *Emden*, which raided Penang in October 1914, but the *Emden* sailed past Singapore, making no attempt to attack the now fortified harbour. Its destruction off the Cocos Islands in November 1914 put an end to any threat of German naval attack.

The turmoil and bloodshed of the European war seemed comfortably far away. To free men for active service, the Singapore garrison had been reduced to one Indian regiment, the 5th Bengal Light Infantry, together with a few British Artillery and Royal Engineers. The Singapore Volunteer Rifles had been wound up in 1904, but a new Singapore Volunteer Artillery, 450 strong, was formed in 1914.[2] Initially a party of Sikh Malay States Guides was posted from Perak to bolster Singapore's defence, but most were sent back to Taiping after Jagat Singh, a Sikh resident of Singapore, incited them into refusing to embark for active service overseas in December 1914. After the German naval threat had evaporated, the situation in Singapore seemed so quiet that in February 1915 the 5th Light Infantry was ordered to Hong Kong, but some of the sepoys mutinied on the eve of their departure. This uprising came as a shock to the placid calm of Singapore, which had always assumed that any danger would come from the sea and that a small garrison could cope with internal unrest. No provision had been made to defend Singapore against her own garrison.

Trouble had in fact been brewing for some time. Slack discipline, bickering among officers and poor leadership undermined the morale of the 5th, which consisted solely of Punjabi Muslims, who were bitter that the British were fighting Muslim Turkey. The soldiers came under the influence of Kassim Mansoor, a Gujarati Muslim coffee-shop owner, who lived near the Alexandra barracks. Kassim Mansoor's attempts to sow disaffection among Malay policemen, who formed a major part of the police force, were unsuccessful, but he made more headway with the Indian soldiers, and he was arrested in January 1915, after writing to the Turkish consul in Rangoon, petitioning Turkey to send a warship to Singapore to collect pro-Turkish Indian Muslim troops.

The Indian troops were put to guard the German military prisoners at Tanglin barracks. These included some of the *Emden*'s crew, led by Oberleutnant Julius Lauterbach, the *Emden*'s navigation officer. A fat, jovial ex-merchant navy skipper and old China hand, Lauterbach knew Singapore well and had been accorded almost a hero's welcome by his British captors when he arrived back in the port as a prisoner of war. The Germans struck up a cordial relationship with their Indian guards, and the enterprising Lauterbach fanned resentment against their British masters.

As their departure for Hong Kong approached, bitterness and suspicion spread among the Indian troops, with rumours that they were being taken not to Hong Kong but to fight in France or Turkey, or even that their ship was to be deliberately sunk. On 15 February Indian soldiers murdered some of their officers, seized the Alexandra barracks, released the German prisoners and then roamed the town in small groups, killing any Europeans they encountered.

With competent leadership, the Indian regiment, over 800 strong, could have had the town at their mercy, since they caught the authorities unawares in the middle of the Chinese New Year holiday. But after their initial success, their leaders did not know what to do. They appealed in vain to the Germans to lead them. Some of the German prisoners were already poised to escape through a tunnel that they had almost completed, and Lauterbach and Diehn with a few others took the opportunity to slip away by night. A number of them eventually got back to Germany, but most prisoners were less enterprising and remained in their camp.

Once alerted, the government shepherded European women and children from the suburbs to safety in town hotels or on ships in the harbour. The officer in charge of the troops acted quickly to marshal a motley collection of supporters: police, the Singapore Volunteer Artillery, British sappers, gunners and sailors, together with troops brought from Johor by the Sultan in person. Altogether there were about 500 men, only half of whom had military training. Nearly 400 civilian special constables were also recruited, together with the crews of Allied French, Japanese, and Russian ships, which rushed to Singapore to help.

Mopping-up operations took ten days. The mutineers dispersed to the west and north of the island, some fleeing to Johor where they were rounded up and sent back by the Sultan. After trials that lasted from February to May 1915, Kassim Mansoor was hanged, 41 mutineers, including two Indian officers, were shot, and a further 126 were imprisoned or transported. The executions were carried out in public at Outram Prison and were attended by thousands from all communities, including European dignitaries and their wives. The commanding officer of the 5th Light Infantry was dismissed, and the remnants of the regiment were sent to West Africa. The Singapore police were reorganized, European men were obliged to undergo military training, and for the remainder of the war Singapore was garrisoned by a small detachment of British troops supported by the Volunteers.

All Indian residents in Singapore were compelled to register, which caused considerable ill feeling among a basically loyal community. Other Singaporeans dismissed the mutiny as a ten-day wonder. In itself it achieved nothing. It revealed no concerted plot, leadership, or plan. It failed to rouse any support among the general population. The eastern part of the island was unaffected by the trouble and in Chinatown the New Year celebrations continued uninterrupted. But the incident contained a warning. Peace had been restored only with the help of Allied ships, and two of the four warships that came to British aid were Japanese cruisers. Almost half of the civilian special constables were Japanese. In time of international crisis Singapore's security rested heavily on Japanese friendship. Japanese observers, marvelling at this weak link in Britain's Empire and proud of Japanese intervention, hoped the experience might teach their arrogant allies to treat their Japanese saviours with more respect in future.[3] The First World War enabled the Japanese to expand their prestige and their commercial activities in Singapore,[4] but the full implication of the lesson of the Sepoy mutiny was to be driven home in Singapore on Chinese New Year's Day twenty-seven years later.

❧

Singapore's centenary in 1919 was a time of general rejoicing. The war was over, the world was returning to normal, and for the moment trade was booming. Wartime shortages stimulated a healthy demand for imported goods, particularly motorcars, which augured well for the rubber industry.

The euphoria was short-lived, and the post-war boom gave way to a recession in 1920. Rubber, which had fetched $1.15 a pound in February 1920, slumped to 30 cents by December. Tin, which had been $212 a picul in February, fell to $90 in December.

By 1922 Malaya was pulling out of the slump. Export quotas laid down under the Stevenson rubber restriction scheme, which was imposed that year, helped to maintain rubber prices. Firms, such as Guthrie's, which bought rubber land cheaply during the depression, started new planting schemes and diversified into oil palm. By 1923 the black times were over and demand for tin, rubber and petroleum was rising. The Johor Causeway linking

Singapore with the mainland by road and rail was opened in 1923, giving a new boost to Singapore's trade. Tin prices rose to a peak in 1926 and 1927. Immigration soared, and in 1927 the Chinese immigration figures achieved an all-time record of nearly 360,000.

Enormous fortunes were amassed almost overnight. Tan Kah-kee, who was at the peak of his business fortunes in the mid-1920s, claimed to have made $8 million in a single year in 1925, and there were other multimillionaires: Lee Kong Chian, born in Fukien in 1894, who began his career in Singapore as a schoolteacher, turned to business, married Tan Kah-kee's daughter, and formed his own Lee Rubber Company; Tay Koh Yat, born in Fukien in 1880, came to Singapore at the age of twenty-two and became the leading bus company magnate; Tan Lark Sye, born in Tan Kah-kee's village of Jimei in 1896, came to Singapore as a youth and became a leading rubber merchant and industrialist; Aw Boon Haw, one of Singapore's few prominent Hakka businessmen, was born in Rangoon in 1893 and made his fortune in patent medicine, earning the soubriquet of "Tiger Balm King".

In these boom years government spending increased rapidly, particularly in the hitherto neglected fields of policing, education and medical services. The Municipal Commission, whose works had been interrupted during the war, was enlarged and launched big improvement schemes to cope with Singapore's rising population and to repair past deficiencies.

In the years immediately preceding the outbreak of war the municipality had begun the attack on malaria-breeding mosquitoes, and from 1911 deaths from the disease fell steadily. In 1913 the first sewage pipes were laid, and the government began taking over night-soil collection. Infant mortality, which stood at 345 per 1,000 in 1910, began to decline after 1912 with the provision of home visiting by nurses.

The Middleton Isolation Hospital had been opened in 1913, and in the 1920s the government embarked on an ambitious programme to build hospitals, staffed largely by graduates of the King Edward College of Medicine. The new Outram General Hospital and the Trafalgar Home for lepers both opened in 1926, the Woodbridge Mental Hospital in 1927, and the Kandang Kerbau Maternity Hospital in 1928.

By the end of the First World War, the growing popularity of motorized transport presented both opportunities and problems. The change from horse-drawn to motorized fire engines in 1912 resulted in a dramatic improvement in tackling fires. Motor transport enabled people to move away from the crowded town centre, but private motor cars increased from 842 in 1915 to 3,506 in 1920 and caused acute congestion on the inadequate roads. Public transport facilities were poor; most people depended on trams and rickshaws, but Chinese-operated seven-seater "mosquito" buses came into vogue soon after the war. After the Singapore Tramway Company failed, the Singapore Traction Company, the first public motor-transport firm, was set up in 1925 to operate trolleybuses and omnibuses, while the small Chinese bus owners amalgamated to form two bus companies in 1935. The municipality resurfaced roads to cope with the heavier traffic, and a modern railway terminus opened at Tanjong Pagar in 1932.

Electric lighting was still a rarity outside the town centre in the early 1920s, but the first municipal power station was opened at St. James in 1927. The Pulai reservoir in Johor was brought into use to supply Singapore with water in 1929, and Seletar Reservoir was completed in 1940. A first attempt was made on slum clearance with the creation in 1927 of the Singapore Improvement Trust, a government-financed statutory body that worked in liaison with the municipality to provide public housing.

Many new public buildings were constructed, notably Fullerton Building, which included the General Post Office, in 1928, and the new Municipal Building (later City Hall) in 1929 on part of the site of the Hotel de l'Europe. An American visitor, returning to Singapore in 1929 after an eight-year absence, commented. "It is marvellous how you have progressed. Why, I hardly know the place."[5]

౽ଵ

The attitudes of the Singapore Chinese to the colonial authorities changed radically in the inter-war years. In the early years of the twentieth century most combined affection for their motherland and active sympathy for budding Chinese nationalism with passive loyalty to the colonial regime, but the initial exhilaration in Singapore when the Chinese Republic was founded gave way to disillusionment during the new regime's troubled early years.

During the First World War the Straits Chinese leaders pledged their support for Britain and marshalled the resources of their community. They called on Straits-born Chinese youths to volunteer for military service, campaigned to raise funds for the National War Loan, gave generous donations to purchase aeroplanes and other equipment, and supported a War Tax Bill to levy income tax, which the Legislative Council passed in 1917. The British put great store by these demonstrations of support, but they affected only a minority, even of the Straits Chinese. The basic feelings of most of the Singapore Chinese lay towards China, and the Chinese Republic's claims on Nanyang Chinese loyalty created mounting trouble for the Singapore authorities.

Sun Yat-sen's revolutionary T'ung Meng Hui was re-organized as the Kuomintang after the revolution and formed a branch in Singapore in 1912, with Lim Boon Keng and Lim Ngee Soon among the first office bearers. The party aimed to enlist the financial support of the Nanyang Chinese in rebuilding China's economy, but the movement soon ran into trouble because of rivalry between the "old" royalist-reformer Singapore Chinese Chamber of Commerce and the "new" KMT-controlled Chinese Merchants General Chamber of Commerce, which comprised less wealthy businessmen and shopkeepers.[6] President Yuan Shi-k'ai outlawed the parent Kuomintang when he seized power in China in 1913, and the Singapore branch of the Kuomintang formally dissolved the following year, by that time wilting under the strain of internal dissension and colonial government suspicion.

The Chinese business community in Singapore had shown its sympathy with China's cause on a number of occasions. In 1905 they boycotted American trade in protest against the United States Exclusion Act against Chinese immigration. Three years later they boycotted Japanese goods in support of imperial China's quarrel with Japan over the seizure of a ship, and in 1915 Japan's Twenty-One Demands against China provoked another boycott. These were peaceful protests, confined to the merchant group, but after 1919 the masses became caught up in China's politics, changing the whole character of Overseas Chinese involvement and their relationship with the Singapore authorities.

Young Hokkiens who had been prominent in the 4 May 1919 movement in China came to Singapore to rally support, provoking a mass demonstration that led to violence. Japanese shops, factories, workshops and houses were looted, and even the most desperately poor rickshaw pullers refused to carry Japanese passengers.[7] The colonial authorities acted firmly to repress the outburst, and looked with disapproval at the peaceful boycott organized by the Singapore Chinese Chamber of Commerce and the Chinese Consul-General in 1923 in protest against Japanese encroachments on Chinese territory.[8]

The Kuomintang's fortunes revived in the early 1920s when Sun Yat-sen succeeded in establishing a government in southern China and tried to put new life into the movement. The Kuomintang worked to bring Chinese schools in the Nanyang under its direction, sending teachers and textbooks from China, and in 1924 Sun Yat-sen established an Overseas Affairs Bureau to keep in close touch with the Nanyang.

Sun Yat-sen found a ready response among the Singapore Chinese, who contributed handsomely to establishing schools both in Singapore and China and invested large sums in Chinese industries. Tan Kah-kee in particular founded a number of schools in Fujian and contributed more than $4 million to build and maintain Amoy University, which was established in 1921, with Lim Boon Keng as its first president. At the peak of his fortune in the mid-1920s, Tan employed 10,000 workers in rubber planting and manufacturing, shipping, import and export businesses, canneries, sawmills, rice trading, newspapers, and property management, and was known as "the Henry Ford of Malaya".[9]

Interest in China's politics encouraged the growth of political clubs in Singapore and boosted the demand for Chinese-language newspapers, which became financially profitable for the first time: Tan Kah-kee's *Nanyang Siang Pau*, started in 1923, and the *Sin Chew Jit Poh*, founded in 1929 by Aw Boon Haw.

≈

The Singapore Chinese Chamber of Commerce played a strong role in fostering the sense of Chinese nationalism. Before the Second World War nearly all of the Chamber's leaders were China-born. While Chinese-educated multimillionaires, such as Tan Kah-kee, Aw Boon Haw, and Lee Kong Chian, had only limited pull with the colonial authorities, they were very influential among the immigrant Chinese.

Chinese-medium schools provided the main nursery for Chinese nationalism in Singapore, and patriotic Singapore Chinese often sent their children to China for secondary education, particularly to the Chi Nan School in Nanking. In 1919 Tan Kah-kee raised money to open the first Singapore middle school, the Nanyang Hua Chiao Middle School or Hua Chung, which taught boys up to pre-university level. The medium of instruction in the new schools was Mandarin or Kuo-yu, which was not the dialect of any Singapore group but was promoted by Manchus, royalists, revolutionaries and Kuomintang alike as a unifying factor in China.

The active participation of Chinese students and teachers in the violent anti-Japanese demonstration in 1919 awoke the

Straits authorities to the danger of political subversion in Chinese schools and forced them to abandon their traditional aloof policy towards Chinese education. In 1920 an Education Ordinance was passed which required the registration of all schools, teachers and managers, and gave the government powers to make regulations concerning the conduct of schools. Chinese schools objected strongly to this measure, organizing petitions and protest meetings. When government grants were offered to them for the first time in 1923, few applied for assistance, which entailed increased government supervision and an undertaking to teach in local Chinese dialects instead of Kuo-yu.

The authorities became more worried in the mid-1920s at the growth of radical left-wing politics among the Chinese, which for the first time expressed anti-British and anti-colonial sentiments. During the period from 1924 to 1927 when the Kuomintang and the communists leagued together to unify China, the communists came to dominate the left wing of the Kuomintang in Singapore. The origins of communism in Singapore are obscure. During World War I the colonial authorities deported a small group of Chinese vernacular teachers and journalists, who were preaching anarcho-communism, but the first agent of the Chinese Communist Party came to Singapore about 1922.[10] Fu Ta Ching, a Chinese Communist Party agent, arrived from Shanghai in 1925 to build up the movement, and that same year Tan Malaka, the chief Comintern agent in Southeast Asia, spent some months in Singapore, which was used as a base in plotting a communist insurrection in Indonesia. Communist teachers and professional cadres were most successful among young Hainanese pupils in Kuo-yu medium night schools, many of which had sprung up in the early 1920s, and in 1926 the communists formed the Nanyang General Labour Union.

The secret societies had recruited many Hainanese *sinkheh* to their ranks during the 1920–22 economic slump and battened on the left-wing political movement, which gave them a new lease of life. To counter this, the government passed a Societies Ordinance in 1924, stiffening the penalties against secret society gangsters, and it pressed more harshly on the Kuomintang as communist and *hoey* influence spread within it. Kuomintang branches were officially banned throughout Malaya in 1925, although a secret branch, dominated by the left wing, operated in Singapore. The authorities closed twelve troublesome Singapore schools in 1926, banished several teachers and students, and passed tougher legislation to tighten registration requirements.

At that time Singapore was known as the "Chicago of the East", the haven of gunmen and street gangs that carried out a reign of terror in Chinatown and the rural districts. A record number of murders was reported in 1927 and secret society fights were an everyday occurrence. The police force was ill-prepared to cope with violence and subversion on such a scale, despite recent reforms. A Special Branch was created in 1919 to deal specifically with political subversion, and a police depot was established in 1924 to step up recruitment and raise educational and physical standards, but the force was under strength and riddled with corruption. There were very few British police officers working in the field, and they were required to learn Malay rather than Chinese, although 90 per cent of criminal activity in Singapore involved Chinese people. The growing tendency of the ruling class to hold itself apart from Asians meant that the police leadership was remote from the realities of Singapore's underworld.

The Kuomintang's left-wing extremism began to alienate the Straits Chinese and many of the China-born. Violence erupted in March 1927 at a meeting held to commemorate the second anniversary of Sun Yat-sen's death. An official permit had been given to hold the event, which was attended by a huge crowd, including about 2,000 Hainanese, many of them school children. The demonstrators distributed anti-colonial pamphlets and protested when the organizers launched into anti-communist speeches. The Hainanese then set out for Kreta Ayer and refused to disperse when ordered by the police, who panicked and opened fire, killing six people. The official enquiry into this ill-managed affair opened the authorities' eyes to the extent of communist influence, particularly in schools. The government closed more night schools, banned some textbooks, and from that time exerted constant vigilance to suppress communism.

The movement received a setback throughout Southeast Asia later in 1927 when the Dutch put down a communist rising in Java, and the Kuomintang Nationalists broke away from the communists in China. After the failure of the Java revolt Tan Malaka, chief Comintern agent for Southeast Asia, decided that future hope for communism lay with the urban Chinese and tried to reorganize the Nanyang communist movement in Singapore. The party infiltrated schools and organized strikes, but these were broken by the police. The Nanyang General Labour Union was banned, and leading communists put in prison. In the late 1920s the fortunes of the Nanyang Communist Party were at a low ebb. Outlawed and harried by the Singapore police and the Chinese Protectorate, ordered by the Comintern to pursue a strict line of promoting proletarian revolution and to avoid collaboration with liberal or nationalist elements, the party was spurned by all but the poorest of Singapore Chinese.

In 1930 the communists attempted to remodel their organization in the Nanyang and established the Malayan Communist Party, which was to be centred on Singapore and responsible to the Far Eastern Bureau of the Comintern in Shanghai. Two front organizations, the Singapore Chinese Middle School Teachers' Federation and the Singapore Students' Federation, staged student strikes in the Chinese High School and Tiong Wah Girls' School.

The party's success was short-lived. In April 1931 a French Comintern agent, Joseph Ducroux, calling himself Serge Lefranc, came to Singapore to supervise the re-organization of the communist movement in Malaya. He was arrested and deported two months later, and his address book revealed the ramifications of the communist movement in the Far East. These disclosures led to fifteen further arrests and to the complete disruption of the Malayan Communist Party, which was almost wiped out by the early months of 1932.

Initially the Kuomintang profited from the communists' disarray. At the time of the split in 1927, most Singapore Chinese sided with the Kuomintang and were impressed with its northern expedition and reunification campaign in China. Once it had consolidated its position at home, the Kuomintang attempted to assert a more positive control over the Nanyang Chinese. A Nationality Law of 1929 restated the *jus sanguinis* principle established in the last years of the Manchu Empire, which claimed as Chinese nationals all persons of Chinese descent on the paternal side, no matter how long they or their ancestors had lived abroad. Demanding loyalty from all Nanyang Chinese associations, Nanjing issued new laws that same year covering the activities of chambers of commerce, and in 1932 it set up an Overseas Party Affairs Department. One of the Kuomintang's slogans was "Without Chinese education there can be no Overseas Chinese". In 1927 the Kuomintang established a bureau of education and drew up regulations to register overseas Chinese schools, to supervise their curriculum and to encourage Nanyang Chinese to go to China for higher education. In 1929 the Chinese Ministry of Education launched a five-year plan for overseas education, and the following year drew up a twenty-year plan to finance overseas education through local levies from wealthy individuals and organizations. Kuo-yu was to be the medium of instruction and was universally adopted in all Singapore Chinese schools by 1935.

During the late 1920s the Kuomintang's policy of demanding loyalty from the Overseas Chinese had evoked a positive and enthusiastic response in the Nanyang, and the party's overseas membership expanded rapidly. In Singapore it attracted the support of many prominent Chinese, and initially the Straits authorities took a lenient view of the Kuomintang and its anti-communist activities.

This situation changed at the end of 1929, with the arrival of Sir Cecil Clementi as Governor. The appointment looked ideal, since Clementi was proficient in Cantonese and Mandarin, and had long experience in working with Chinese communities. He had begun his colonial service in 1899 as a cadet in Hong Kong, where he rose to be Colonial Secretary and, after serving in British Guiana and Ceylon, Clementi returned to Hong Kong as Governor in 1925. With an outstanding reputation as an administrator and expert on China, he was welcomed in Singapore at a critical time when Malaya was facing the first brunt of the Great Depression. Clementi's period of office in Hong Kong had been turbulent because China's troubles had spilled over into the colony, and he arrived in Singapore with a deep distrust of the Kuomintang and a conviction that firm measures were needed to control sedition. The strong measures that Clementi took to counteract subversion and deal with economic distress were racially divisive and roused widespread opposition.[11]

In an attempt to suppress anti-colonial propaganda, which was mainly Chinese in origin, he censored the vernacular press, enforced the ban on the Kuomintang in Singapore, and prohibited fund raising for the party in China. The renewed ban came as a shock to many eminent Malayan Chinese supporters and roused a chorus of protest. As a compromise, the British government permitted Singapore Chinese to be members of the Chinese Kuomintang but refused to permit local branches to be established.

While many leading Baba Chinese were not sorry to see restrictions put on the Kuomintang, they were incensed at Clementi's other measures on education and immigration, which they took to be racially discriminatory and anti-Chinese. As an economy measure at the depth of the Great Depression in 1932, Clementi withdrew grants-in-aid from Chinese and Tamil vernacular schools, which meant that only Malay education was provided free and primary education in English was subsidized.

Immigration restrictions roused even greater opposition. An Immigration Restriction Ordinance had been drafted before the onset of the slump, with the object of improving labour standards and balancing the sex ratio of immigrant communities by restricting the inflow of unskilled male labourers. The bill encountered such opposition from employers and the Singapore Chamber of Commerce that it was held in abeyance, but it was brought into force in 1930, in the teeth of European commercial opposition, in order to cope with rising unemployment.[12] Quotas were imposed on unskilled male immigrants, and these were reduced in 1931 and further in 1932. The effect was dramatic. Chinese immigrant numbers dropped from 242,000 in 1930 to less than 28,000 in 1933, and the fall was most marked among adult males, against whom the legislation was primarily aimed. From 158,000 in 1930, their numbers fell to less than 14,000 in 1933.

In 1933 the Immigration Restriction Ordinance was replaced by an Aliens Ordinance, imposing quota restrictions and charging landing fees on aliens. In practice "aliens" meant Chinese, since the law did not affect Britons or Indians who were British subjects. Straits-born and immigrant Chinese united in opposing the social, racial, and political implications of the Aliens Bill, accusing the colonial government of abandoning its neutral policy in favour of active discrimination against the Chinese. The Chinese Chamber of Commerce protested, and the attack was led in the Legislative Council by Tan Cheng Lock, the scion of a Hokkien Baba family that had settled in Melaka in the eighteenth century, who complained that this was a poor reward for the services the Chinese had contributed to Malaya over many centuries. As he complained bitterly in the Legislative Council in October 1932:

> The government has no fixed and constructive policy to win over the Straits and other Malayan-born Chinese, who are subjects of the country, and foster and strengthen their spirit of patriotism and natural love for the country of their birth and adoption.... One is driven to the conclusion that the Bill is part and parcel of an anti-Chinese policy, probably with a political objective, based on distrust and fear, which the Chinese on the whole as a community have done nothing and have given absolutely no cause to merit.

The Secretary for Chinese Affairs admitted that immigration restrictions were partly designed to check political dissidence. The government policy created racial tensions, and the legislation of the Great Depression caused the Straits Chinese to question their future in Malaya.

~

In addition to curtailing immigration, the government repatriated large numbers of Chinese and Indians at public expense during the slump years. In 1931 emigrants outnumbered immigrants for the first time in Singapore's history, and the trend continued for the next two years. There was, however, some migration from the peninsula, particularly of unemployed Indian rubber plantation workers who drifted to Singapore.

The Depression hit Singapore particularly hard, as a staple port dependent on international trade and notably on the export of Malayan tin and rubber to the American market. Even before the slump, these vulnerable commodities suffered from overproduction. The Stevenson rubber restriction scheme was only partly successful and was abandoned in 1928 because the Netherlands East Indies refused to co-operate, while soaring tin prices in 1926 and 1927 had stimulated overproduction. The world economic crash converted these problems into a major crisis. The price of rubber fell from an average of 34 cents in 1929 to an all-time low of 4.95 cents in June 1932. Tin dropped to an average of $60 per picul in 1931. Singapore's revenue plummetted, while public expenditure reached a record high in 1931, partly because the authorities initially tried to stem unemployment by embarking on a public works programme. The following year the government slashed salaries, dismissed many officials, cut back on public works and health services, and at the same time increased taxation. It was a time of great hardship, and the island was a depressing place for all communities, for unemployed rubber planters and tin miners, who came south from the peninsula seeking work, for businessmen, shopkeepers, retrenched civil servants, commercial employees, and labourers.

§§

With the gradual revival of world confidence, Singapore recovered from the slump, helped by higher taxation rates and more effective output restriction schemes. In 1933 the budget balanced again. The first international tin-control scheme was introduced in 1931, and slowly the price of tin began to rise. Rubber restriction was more difficult to negotiate, but in 1934 an international agreement was eventually signed to regulate rubber exports and restricting new planting, and this remained in force until the outbreak of the Second World War.

The trade protection measures provoked bitter controversy. There were fierce objections in 1932 when the Colonial Office instructed colonies and protectorates to introduce imperial preference tariffs, and the Singapore Chamber of Commerce and Legislative Council stoutly resisted British demands for quotas to be imposed on foreign textiles. The measure, aimed primarily at cheap Japanese textiles, had to be forced through the Legislative Council in 1934 using the official majority. Thus the twin principles of free trade and free immigration both fell casualty to the Great Depression.

The slump also led to significant changes in Chinese business methods. Hitherto the Singapore Chinese had been slow to develop modern capital organization or banking, preferring to rely on regional associations and family links in a more personal form of trading. When European capital started to flood into the Malayan tin and rubber industries at the end of the nineteenth century, the Singapore Chinese used the compradore system to adapt to the new Western capitalism. The compradore was a go-between commission merchant who provided financial guarantees to Western organizations and personal credit to Chinese traders, receiving a salary from the European firm or bank that employed him and a commission from both sides. This worked smoothly and oiled the wheels of economic development and investment, but it made the Chinese subordinate to Western capital. The world slump taught them the danger of relying on European capital, particularly in primary production, and from that time enterprising Chinese turned to direct capital investment in secondary industries and to modern banking.[13] Hitherto Chinese banks had catered for particular *pang* – Hokkien, Teochew or Cantonese – but in 1932 three Hokkien banks amalgamated to form the Oversea Chinese Banking Corporation, the largest Chinese bank in Singapore.

Singapore did not regain the high pitch of prosperity that she had enjoyed in the late 1920s and continued to face many economic problems up to the outbreak of the Second World War. Her entrepôt trade suffered through imperial preference schemes and also from Dutch policy to develop rubber milling and grading in the Netherlands Indies. Singapore's trade was badly affected, but enterprising Singapore Chinese set up their own rubber factories in Sumatra and Dutch Borneo.

❦

The end of the slump and the return to normal conditions coincided with the arrival in 1934 of Sir Shenton Thomas as Governor. Clementi's departure was greeted with relief both by the Chinese, who had been alienated by his immigration and education policies, and by the European officials and unofficials, who found him an uncomfortable man to deal with. As the Inspector-General of Police admitted, Clementi was "far too clever for his advisers",[14] and in the words of a prominent Malayan Ceylonese journalist, he was "too much an intellectual for the average 'hail fellow, well met' and club back-slapping Malayans of those Days".[15]

According to the *Straits Times*, "What is needed is a man of pronounced administrative ability and a large measure of tact, who will … soothe feelings which have been sadly ruffled during the past three years."[16] Shenton Thomas was ideal for this role. Approachable and sympathetic, he soon struck up an easy relationship with the European community. He relieved unemployment by reviving schemes for public works, and in 1935 restored government grants to Chinese and Tamil vernacular schools.

On the surface, life in the late 1930s had never been so pleasant for the prosperous and the well-to-do. For the Western community, in particular, it was an era of gracious living in beautiful houses surrounded by green lawns and tended by plenty of servants, and the city centre and fashionable residential areas were meticulously kept.

The Singapore Cold Storage Company, which pioneered the processing and distribution of hygienic food supplies in Malaya, helped to make everyday living easier and healthier than ever before. In 1923 the company manufactured the first ice cream in Singapore; in 1926 it set up a pig farm, followed three years later by a dairy farm at Bukit Timah. In 1930 it began producing bread, and three years later set up a groceries department. Cold Storage brought in vegetables from Cameron Highlands, meat from New Zealand, fruit from South Africa and the United States, and groceries from Europe. In addition to fresh milk, fruit, vegetables, and tinned groceries, Singaporeans could also enjoy local-made beer. Malayan Breweries opened in 1932, and a German brewery was set up the following year.

Club life provided swimming, tennis, bridge, golf, and flying, and the wireless and cinema were added attractions. The first commercial wireless station was established in 1915, but wireless sets did not come into common use until the British Malayan Broadcasting Corporation set up its first commercial broadcasting station in Singapore in 1937.

The increasingly popular motorcar permitted the affluent to travel further afield for their pleasures and encouraged a different lifestyle. The golf club moved to a new and magnificent site at Bukit Timah in 1924, a second Island Club for golf opened nearby in 1927, the Singapore Flying Club was founded the same year; and in 1937 horse racing was transferred to the new Turf Club at Bukit Timah, the most beautiful racecourse in Asia. With the Hotel de l'Europe temporarily closed to make way for new public buildings in the 1930s, Raffles Hotel became the social centre for the European community, while the Seaview Hotel, which opened in the mid-1930s, became their favourite Sunday meeting place. The Swimming Club was very lively, and there was one open-air nightclub, the Coconut Grove at Pasir Panjang. Cocktail parties and elaborate dinners became the fashion. Entertainment was pleasant but restrained, and all hotels, restaurants, and clubs closed at midnight.

The wireless and the aeroplane speeded up contact with the outside world. The first aeroplane was flown by a Frenchman in Farrer Park in 1911, and in 1919 Captain Ross Smith landed at Farrer Park on his epic solo flight to win the first England to Australia air race. Singapore was a regular transit stop for many pioneer fliers, but was slow to develop her own aviation. In 1923 the British government decided to construct a seaplane base at Sembawang, near the proposed naval base, and a Royal Air Force base at Seletar. The Seletar aerodrome was completed in the late 1920s and at first served civil aircraft as well as the Royal Air Force, but regular air communications did not come until the 1930s.

Clementi told the Legislative Council in 1931 that Singapore would become "one of the largest and most important airports in the world". The first airmail was delivered from London that year, and in 1934 Imperial Airways and Qantas began weekly flights. A civil airport with a grass runway was opened at Kallang in 1937, and by the late 1930s there were daily flights from Singapore to Kuala Lumpur, Ipoh and Penang. Commercial flying was still a hazardous and novel form of passenger transport, but speedy postal and newspaper services brought Singapore into closer touch with world affairs.

Despite this, the Western community was still parochial in its attitudes. The atmosphere of spaciousness, serenity, and ease represented gracious living at its most superficial, and Singapore was said to be a place of "high living and low thinking".[17] The love of music and the excellent concerts that the city enjoyed at the turn of the century had gone, and in the inter-war years Singapore lacked cultural depth, as occasional visiting performers of the arts found to their cost. When the world's premier ballerina, the exquisite Anna Pavlova, gave a charity performance in 1922, she was excluded from the Town Hall by the Amateur Dramatic Society's rendering of Gilbert and Sullivan and forced to dance on the small stage of the Teutonia Club. After an over-enthusiastic Chinese stagehand emptied the contents of several waste-paper baskets over her during her snow dance, the enraged ballerina refused to dance a second performance.

The development of more complex administration, the expansion of schools and technical services, the growth of commerce and the new military bases brought in greater numbers of Europeans. Paradoxically, as elsewhere in colonial Southeast Asia, the influx of Westerners and the closer involvement of the government in everyday life inhibited social contact between rulers and ruled. It led to a widening chasm between Asians and the European minority, many of whom developed a swollen-headed "Singaporitis". The ruling class encouraged this aloofness in order to preserve the last vestiges of the mystique of superiority, which was rapidly being stripped away by exposure through the cinema, Western education, and the popular press.

Even the Christian religion did not draw Asians and Europeans together. While Europeans attended services at St. Andrew's Cathedral or the Roman Catholic Cathedral of the Good Shepherd, Chinese Roman Catholics went to the Sts. Peter and Paul Church, and Indians to the Church of Our Lady of Lourdes. The only social meeting places of Asians and Europeans were the three Shanghai-style entertainment parks or "worlds": the New World opened in 1923, the Great World in 1931, and the Happy World in 1935.

Most Europeans could lead lives oblivious to the poverty, slums and crime of the more crowded sectors of the city, and Singapore was a comfortable place also for the affluent Asian in the 1930s. Some of the benefits of the new amenities filtered through to the mass of the population, in the form of improved health facilities, cheap entertainment in the cinemas, amusement parks and traveling *wayangs*, and better law and order. But the poor still lived in squalor.[18] Rickets and malnutrition were common and the child mortality rate from beriberi was high.

Gang fights still occurred, but by the 1930s the police force was much more efficient. Telephones, motor vehicles and radio communications made police work easier, and by that time senior posts were filled by officers who had gone through the police cadet system. A large proportion of public funds was devoted to police training in the 1930s and, apart from the Supreme Court, which was completed in 1939, the most impressive public works put up in Singapore in that decade were police buildings. The police were vigilant in keeping secret society activity and subversion in check. The force was expanded to about 2,000 strong, and powers to banish troublemakers were used frequently, so that Singapore became a more peaceful and safe place for most of the population.

There was little blatant vice, and in the 1930s tourists in search of the lurid and picturesque were disappointed to find Singapore an outwardly staid and strait-laced port, which no longer lived up to its name of "Singalore". Opium dens were fast disappearing with the controls and restrictions on opium smoking, and brothels were illegal. Until the 1920s the notorious Malay Street red-light district was the haunt of prostitutes, many of them women of East European origin, whose careers brought them eastwards over the years with Singapore as the lowest point of degradation. In 1914 the sale of girls for prostitution was forbidden, and restrictions on brothel keepers were tightened during the 1920s. In 1927 the importation of girls for prostitution was stopped, and three years later brothels were closed after much argument, although prostitution remained legal. The law was only partially successful and tended to drive brothels underground, putting their inmates at the mercy of secret society gangsters. By the 1930s Malay Street had lost its custom to the more discreet Lavender Street, to the popular Japanese "hostesses" of Middle Road and the Japanese restaurant at Changi, or to the girls who plied their trade in the "rickshaw parade" at Dhoby Ghaut.

The buying and selling of children was common in Singapore in the 1930s, and the government tried, but with little success, to reform the *mui tsai* custom, whereby rich families "adopted" girls from poor homes. Such adoption could be beneficial, but the system was open to abuse, and *mui tsai* were often exploited as unpaid domestic servants and prostitutes. Laws passed in 1926 and 1933 that prohibited the purchase of *mui tsai* and the employment of servants under the age of ten were ineffective, since it was almost impossible to prove the age or the circumstances of acquiring *mui tsai*. The Colonial Office appointed a commission to investigate the *mui tsai* question in Malaya and Hong Kong. The commission's majority report was optimistic about the position in Singapore, but the government accepted the minority report, which claimed that the *mui tsai* system exploited young women. Legislation to abolish the practice and protect young girls was passed in 1939 but was not enforced because of the outbreak of war.[19]

Little was done to improve the legal status of women. A number of Straits Chinese leaders advocated marriage reform on Western lines, but most Chinese wanted to retain traditional practice. The Singapore government was wary of interfering in Chinese marriage customs, beyond making legal provision for concubines and their children on the father's death. A Chinese Marriage Committee, appointed by the colonial authorities in 1926, made no progress in face of divided opinion within the Chinese community. In 1940 a Civil Marriage Ordinance provided for the voluntary registration of monogamous marriages, but Chinese traditional marriages also continued to be recognized.

The authorities made some attempt to improve working conditions. Chinese indentured labour was abolished in 1914, and a series of labour ordinances passed in 1920, 1923 and 1930 provided more protection for workers. Chinese labourers were able to bring wage disputes to the Protectorate for settlement free of charge in the 1930s. But the colonial government did not favour the formation of Western-type trade unions, which failed to take root in Singapore before the Second World War. Nor did the nature of Singapore society lend itself to the growth of organized labour. Few Malays were engaged in enterprises involving large numbers of workers, although a Malay Seamen's Association was formed in 1916. Indians showed no interest in forming labour organizations before the abolition of their indentured labour system in 1938. The Chinese already had trade guilds and were the first to move towards modern labour organizations, but the identification of these early labour associations with Kuomintang and communist politics laid them open to government repression and inhibited the emergence of a genuine labour movement.

The Kuomintang encouraged the growth of trade unions in the Nanyang as a means to rally Chinese backing and tap workers' money, and the communists vied for Chinese working-class support. The South Seas General Labour Union was renamed the Malayan General Union in 1930, after the Malayan Communist Party was formed, and was affiliated to the Pan-Pacific Trade Union Secretariat, a branch of the Comintern. It attracted mainly unskilled workers, particularly Hainanese.

The Kuomintang/communist split in China, followed by the Great Depression and the destruction of the Malayan Communist Party in 1931–32, hit the infant trade union movement hard. But by the mid-1930s many Singapore workers were discontented, since wages and working conditions did not improve in step with the revival of the economy. Singapore experienced her first real labour trouble in 1936 when the communists tried to exploit this resentment. Singapore seamen made a bid to break the hold of licensed lodging houses over recruitment of sailors, and there were strikes among municipal and transport workers, pineapple factory employees, and building and construction workers.

The strikes were broken, and throughout the 1930s the colonial authorities were intent on keeping communist influence out of trade unions. The Special Branch of the police was often overzealous in branding genuine grievances as subversion, and employers took advantage of this situation. The Chinese Protectorate succeeded to some extent in tempering police repression and employers' exploitation, but its own popularity declined in the inter-war years because it was so much involved in enforcing restrictions, censoring the press and investigating political subversion.[20]

Shortly before the outbreak of war in Europe, Britain set out to extend its own type of labour legislation to her colonies. An Industrial Courts Bill and Trade Union Bill were passed in Singapore in 1940 and a Trade Disputes Ordinance in 1941. Neither employers nor workers showed enthusiasm for the measures, and no trade union was registered in Malaya under the 1940 Ordinance up to the outbreak of the Pacific War. In August 1941 the government outlawed strikes in essential industries and in public transport, and the Japanese invasion put an end to labour disputes.

☙❧

The expansion of the economy and employment opportunities increased demand for education. Government expenditure on education nearly doubled in the period from 1924 to 1932, although it still accounted for less than 6 per cent of the revenue. Most funds went into English-medium education, but this did not keep pace with demand, particularly from the Straits Chinese.

In 1917 the Straits Chinese British Association appealed for tertiary and technical education. It was decided to establish a College of Arts and Sciences to mark Singapore's centenary, and Raffles College was opened in 1928. The college awarded diplomas, and most of its graduates went into secondary school teaching or into subordinate official posts. Singapore's second government English-medium secondary school, Victoria School, opened in 1931. English-educated Singaporeans had no difficulty in finding jobs before the great slump, but the sudden shock of unemployment led them for the first time to criticize English education for being too bookish. In the 1930s more emphasis was put on practical and vocational training and on suiting the content of teaching to local needs. The first government trade school was set up in 1929, and in 1938 an official commission recommended expanding vocational and scientific education.

This commission, led by Sir William McLean, was appointed to investigate the state of higher education in Malaya. Many Straits Chinese and Indians wanted a university, but the Straits government and the British community in general thought the time was not ripe for such an institution. The McLean Commission concurred with this view.[21] The Medical College, to which a dental school had been added in 1937, enjoyed a high reputation in the East, but the commission considered that Raffles College was not up to international university standards, nor was it geared to meet local conditions. The commission recommended that Raffles College should establish departments of Chinese and Malay, with a view to expanding vernacular teaching in the schools, and it also proposed that a technical college be built adjoining Raffles College. These recommendations were not carried out, and the whole question of higher education was left in abeyance. The Methodist Mission contemplated setting up a tertiary Anglo-Chinese College and formed a council that included Tan Kah-kee and Tan Cheng Lock, but the scheme was shelved and the funds were eventually transferred to the Anglo-Chinese Boys' School.

By 1939 there were 72,000 children in school, of whom 38,000 studied in Chinese-medium schools, 27,000 in English schools, nearly 6,000 in Malay schools and 1,000 in Tamil schools.[22] Large numbers of children, particularly girls, did not attend school at all since all institutions, other than the government Malay schools, charged fees. Even Malay parents showed little interest in educating their daughters, and as late as 1916 there were barely 100 Malay girls in school in Singapore.

The Straits authorities provided four years of free primary vernacular schooling for Malay children, gave substantial subsidies to government and aided English-medium schools, and small financial grants to certain Chinese and Tamil schools.

Secondary education was supposed to be self-supporting. Scholarships at Raffles Institution and Victoria School were confined to very gifted pupils, and the scheme produced some prominent men, who invariably came from middle class and well-to-do families, but it provided few opportunities for the mass of schoolchildren.

The appointment of Richard Winstedt as Director of Education for the Colony and the Federated Malay States in 1916 gave a boost to Malay education. From 1919 provision was made for bright Malay children to transfer to and receive free tuition in English-medium schools, and from 1924 special remove classes gave intensive English instruction to such children. Neverthelesss considerable ability, effort, and parental backing were required to pass from the Malay primary to English secondary schools.

Malay-medium education was not geared to the needs of Singapore but was tied to the policy followed in the Malay States. Here Winstedt's aim was to avoid social dislocation and keep Malays contented in their traditional way of life by educating them to be better farmers and fishermen, with emphasis on practical arts, crafts, and gardening. Malay schools were no gateway to the commercial life of Singapore, and rudimentary vernacular education held most Malay children back from the mainstream of Singapore's development.

Tamil schooling in Singapore offered no outlets for pupils except to become unskilled labourers. When schools were first registered in 1920 there was only one Tamil vernacular school, which was run by the American Methodist Mission. A few others sprang up after 1923 when government grants were offered, and by 1941 there were eighteen Tamil schools registered in Singapore, run either by Tamil associations or Christian missions.

Chinese schools continued to stand aloof from the government as far as they could. Few accepted grants with the controls that these entailed. Despite attempts at government supervision, closing unsatisfactory schools and banishing troublesome teachers, the Chinese schools still brought in teachers and textbooks from China and oriented children towards their motherland. Wealthy Singapore Chinese businessmen contributed generously to Chinese schools, and despite friction with the government and rivalry between the Kuomintang and the communists, many Chinese schools made good progress in the 1930s, but they provided no avenue to government service or to the commercial world outside the Chinese sector. The vast majority of Chinese-educated children received only primary schooling and went into manual jobs.

Repeated, if half-hearted, attempts by the authorities to base education on vernacular teaching in the nineteenth century had all failed. Apart from some Chinese schools, vernacular education did not extend beyond the primary stage because it had no commercial value. In the first decades of the twentieth century the government followed the public demand in expanding English secondary education, which created a common but tenuous bond between the talented and ambitious élite of different racial groups but often cut them off from their cultural roots and separated them from the mass of their own community. This danger was beginning to be appreciated in the 1930s, and the McLean Commission advocated teaching vernaculars as second languages in English-medium schools. Nothing came of this before the Second World War, and the education system remained racially and socially divisive. It offered a promising career for the English-educated minority but condemned the mass of the vernacular-educated to unskilled work.

෴

While english-medium education was valued mainly as a means to a career, it inevitably imparted some Western ideas, attitudes, and ways of life. English and American films and sports, such as cricket and tennis, enjoyed great vogue. Among Singapore men, traditional dress gave way to European attire. Many younger Asian women also adopted Western fashions, and sleeveless frocks, high heels and cigarette cases became marks of sophistication among Straits Chinese girls in the 1930s.

The growth of an educated Asian middle class gave impetus to newspapers, both vernacular and English. The Penang *Straits Echo*, started in 1911, was the first English-language newspaper to cater for the Straits Chinese. A lively journal, it attracted devoted readership but circulated only in northern Malaya. Much more influential in Singapore was the *Malaya Tribune*, which began publication in 1914, with the support of Lim Boon Keng and a group of Eurasians, "to express the views and aspirations of the domiciled communities".

Whereas the two existing English-language newspapers were both European in outlook, the *Malaya Tribune* appealed to the English-speaking of all races. It filled a need and prospered despite opposition from the *Singapore Free Press* and the *Straits Times*. In 1937 the *Malaya Tribune* claimed a circulation of 13,000, far in excess of the *Straits Times*.[23] During the Depression the *Straits Times* circulation had fallen to 6,000, and it now responded to the competition by cutting its price to 5 cents to match the *Tribune*. The effect was instantaneous. By the late 1930s its sales rose to 15,000, and on the eve of the Second World War, the *Straits Times* claimed more Asian than European readers.

The expansion of Chinese education and increasing interest in affairs in China boosted the sale of Chinese newspapers. By 1935 Aw Boon Haw's *Sin Chew Jit Poh* had a readership of 30,000 in Malaya and Singapore, and Tan Kah-kee's *Nanyang Siang Pau* had nearly 10,000.

The character of the Malay press changed. Up to that time leading Malay newspapers had been linked to the English-language press, but the *Lembaga Melayu* closed down in 1931, and during the 1930s Singapore's Malay-language press was controlled by the Arab community. The Alsagoff family launched the *Warta Melayu*, which was published daily from 1930 to 1941 and initially edited by Onn bin Ja'afar. In 1934 Onn, with Arab financial backing, founded and edited *Lembaga Malaya*, which was published in Singapore until 1937, after which it moved to Johor Bahru.

In an attempt to shake free from Arab control, Malay journalists founded the *Utusan Melayu*, which was issued daily in Singapore from 1939 until the city fell to the Japanese. The first Malay-controlled newspaper, the *Utusan Melayu* was financed by widespread subscriptions raised from Malay peasants, taxi drivers, and other ordinary people, and edited by the distinguished Abdul Rahim Kajai. The Malay press matured during the 1930s, and a generation of professional Malay journalists came to the fore, but Malay newspapers devoted their interests to peninsular affairs, and the centre of Malay political and cultural life swung away from Singapore to Penang and the Malay States.

～

The steep rise in land values in the inter-war years bore perhaps most heavily upon the Malays, who wished to preserve a semi-rural way of life. They found themselves a neglected minority in an Anglo-Chinese city, but their immediate resentment was often directed towards wealthy Arab families who had bought up enormous tracts of land.

The Arab community reached the height of its prosperity in these years. Wealthy Arabs continued to finance charitable works and public amenities, such as the Japanese-style public gardens opened by the Alkaff family in 1929, but the new generation of Arabs often lived in European style and away from the mass of the Muslim community. Some of them, such as Syed Mohammed bin Omar Alsagoff, the leader of the Arab community in the 1920s, were educated in England.

The leadership of the Arabs and the Jawi-Peranakans, who had dominated the Malayo-Muslim community for fifty years, now came to be challenged by a new generation of Malays, many of them English-educated and influenced by Western secular ideas. Mohammed Eunos bin Abdullah was the most outstanding of this group. Prominent in Malay social welfare organizations and a member of the Muslim Advisory Board set up by the government during the First World War, Mohammed Eunos was appointed a Justice of the Peace and in 1922 became the first Malay municipal commissioner. He gathered about him a group of modern-minded educated Malays, notably Dr. Abdul Samad, the first Malay doctor, and Tengku Kadir, who belonged to the Kampong Glam royal family. They objected to the Persekutuan Islam Singapura (the Muslim Association of Singapore) as a rich man's club and founded a rival Muslim Institute to care for the needs of ordinary Malays.

Rivalry between these two associations came to a head when the colonial authorities decided to appoint another Asian representative to the Legislative Council in 1924. The Persekutuan Islam Singapura wanted a Muslim nominee, but the Muslim Institute wanted a Malay. The British preferred to choose on a racial rather than religious basis, and appointed Mohammed Eunos as the first Malay legislative councillor.

In order to give him support as the mouthpiece for the Malay community, in 1926 the Kesatuan Melayu Singapura or Singapore Malay Union was formed, with Mohammed Eunos as its first president.[24] It appealed specifically to Malays, and membership was confined to Malay people, indigenous to the peninsula and the archipelago, thus excluding Arabs and Indian Muslims. The Kesatuan Melayu Singapura's first concern was to provide for Malays who were forced to move to make way for the construction of the Kallang airport. In response to Mohammed Eunos's appeal in the Legislative Council in 1927, over 600 acres of land on the eastern outskirts of the city at Geylang Serai was set aside for Malay settlement, and in 1928 this was gazetted as Kampung Melayu, the first such designated Malay reserve in Singapore.

Kesatuan Melayu Singapura leaders were mainly English-educated Malay journalists, government officials and middle-class merchants, who differed greatly from the aristocratic Malay élite of the peninsular states. They pressed the Singapore authorities to improve the condition of the Malays, particularly in education opportunities, and Mohammed Eunos's campaign in the Legislative Council led to the opening of a trade school for Malays in 1929. When Mohammed Eunos died in 1934, Embok Suloh took his place on the Legislative Council and as president of the Kesatuan Melayu Singapura. Under his leadership, the party continued throughout the 1930s to co-operate with government, offering only mild criticism of official policies concerning the Malays and steering clear of more extreme Indonesian radicals.

The Kesatuan Melayu Singapura was the first political Malay association but could hardly be described as a nationalist party. It did not oppose British rule but was concerned to safeguard Malay interests in face of the rising political ambitions of the Straits Chinese. Kesatuan Melayu Singapura leaders were instrumental in establishing the new *Utusan Melayu*, which was not anti-British but often anti-Chinese and sometimes criticized the non-Malay Muslim community. Its chief concern was with Malay problems, particularly relating to education.

Politically the Kesatuan Melayu Singapura was important as the forerunner of the post-war United Malays National Organization. The Kesatuan Melayu Singapura stimulated the founding of similar Malay associations in the Malay States in the late 1930s, and at the second conference of the Malay associations held in Singapore in 1940, Onn bin Ja'afar expressed the conviction that the Malay associations would enable Malays to "regain the political and civil rights which have slipped from them". When Dato Onn succeeded in rousing Malay political feeling six years later, this was centred in peninsular Malaya, not Singapore.

Even if their work took them to the city as civil servants, clerks, drivers or labourers, Malays could preserve some of their traditional way of life in Singapore in the 1930s, living in peaceful surroundings in *kampong*-style houses in almost exclusively Malay districts, such as Kampong Melayu and Geylang Serai. Some small Malay communities were able to resist modernization almost entirely. As shipping and business interests took over Telok Blangah, many Malays moved along the coast to form a large enclave at Pasir Panjang, where they lived by fishing, making charcoal, and driving bullock carts in the harbour area. In the 1930s, when further construction of the Kallang airport displaced more Malays, they moved to a new settlement further west beyond Pasir Panjang, where they resumed a livelihood of fishing and growing fruit.

In the southern islands and at points along the north and east coasts of the island, Malay villages remained almost untouched by modern progress. When the development of the naval base, military installations and airfields forced villagers to move, they settled at other points on the coast to carry on their traditional occupations. Official educational policy encouraged Malays to cling to their accustomed way of life. With the growth of urban opportunities, the city's pull became stronger, but it was not yet irresistible.

༺༻

The English-educated Asian middle class grew rapidly in the inter-war years, and the proportion of Straits-born Singaporeans increased. In 1921 only a quarter of the Chinese were Straits-born. Ten years later the proportion had risen to 36 per cent, and the restrictive immigration policy in the 1930s reduced the inflow of the China-born. In 1933 adult male immigration was subject to a quota of 1,000 a month, and Chinese immigrants tended to remain in the Straits for fear that if they revisited China they might be unable to return to Singapore. Since no check was put on women immigrants until 1938, Chinese men had more opportunity to marry in Singapore than in previous times, and the birth rate among Straits Chinese in the mid-1930s was higher than among any other racial group.[25] Despite this, up to the Second World War, immigrant Chinese continued to outnumber the Straits-born, and the vast majority even of the Straits-born attended Chinese schools, if they received any education at all.

The growth of Chinese nationalism and of Kuo-yu education weakened, but did not destroy, traditional groupings along dialect or regional lines. It also fostered a distinction between the Chinese- and English-educated, which was accentuated by the growing fashion among well-to-do Singapore Chinese to send their sons either to Sun Yat-sen, Peking or Amoy universities in China, or to universities in Britain or the English-medium University of Hong Kong, where students from Singapore and Malaya almost equalled those from Hong Kong in the 1930s.[26] The politically minded Chinese-educated were absorbed with the problems of China and the Japanese threat. Anti-Japanese feeling had been growing in Singapore for many years. Chinese in Singapore boycotted Japanese goods when the Kuomintang clashed with the Japanese in Shantung in 1928 and when the Japanese invaded Manchuria in 1931.

At that time Kuomintang fortunes in Singapore were at low ebb, but they revived in face of Japan's invasion of Manchuria, followed in 1937 by the outbreak of the Sino-Japanese War. The Kuomintang's call for the Nanyang Chinese to raise money and send young volunteers to the mother country found a ready response from many influential Chinese in Singapore, particularly from Tan Kah-kee. Having spent a large part of his fortune on educational projects after the First World War, Tan Kah-kee went bankrupt during the Great Depression in 1933. After that time he left his son-in-law, Lee Kong Chian, to rebuild the family fortunes in the rubber and pineapple industries and in banking. Meanwhile, Tan devoted his energies to serving the cause of China and became the leading figure in the Nanyang Chinese National Salvation Movement. He was on friendly terms with Chinese Consul-General Kao Ling-pai, and with Chiang Kai-shek and other Kuomintang leaders in China.

In August 1937, one month after the outbreak of war in China, the dominant Hokkien group in the Chinese Chamber of Commerce formed the Singapore Chinese General Association for the Relief of Refugees in China, with Tan Kah-kee as president. In October 1937 he became head of the Singapore-based Malayan fund raising movement, and the Kuomintang sent former Consul-General Tiao Tso-chi'en to organize the sale of Chinese government subscription bonds among the Malayan Chinese.

They also sent agents to organize boycotts of Japanese goods with the help of local associations, such as the Chinese Chamber of Commerce, and enrolled secret societies in the patriotic cause.

The Singapore government became alarmed as anti-Japanese feeling grew. Chinese gave up patronizing Japanese shops, dentists, doctors and barbers. The boycott caused a dramatic fall in Japanese trade with Malaya, which dropped nearly 70 per cent in 1938. Chinese property owners evicted Japanese tenants, Chinese schools taught anti-Japanese propaganda, Chinese students stoned Japanese schoolchildren, and Chinese also picketed Chinese, Indian and Malay shops selling Japanese goods. Bands of youths, notably the Red Blood Brigade, intimidated Chinese traders who broke the boycott, damaging their shops, cutting off their ears, and sometimes murdering them. Japanese Consul-General Gunji Kiichi protested, and the colonial authorities prohibited anti-Japanese demonstrations, banned the import of anti-Japanese textbooks from China, and forbade the teaching of inflammatory propaganda and anti-Japanese songs in Chinese schools. They also prohibited the collection of funds for the war in China and were sceptical of Tan Kah-kee's assurances that the subscriptions were to help refugees and the bereaved.

The British were particularly worried about increasing communist infiltration in the National Salvation Movement. The communists had been thrown into disarray following the arrest of Serge Lefranc in 1931, and the constant vigilance of the police and the Chinese Protectorate, "the uncrowned kings of Malaya", had prevented the remnants of the Malayan Communist Party from exploiting the hardships of the Depression years. But the communists made a new start in 1934 with the arrival of an Annamese Comintern agent, Wong Kim Geok, alias Lai Teck, who became secretary-general of the Malayan Communist Party but from the beginning was probably a British double agent.

The Comintern Far East Bureau ordered the party first to gain control over labour, and communists played a big role in the strikes and labour disputes that broke out in 1936. In 1935 the Comintern had adopted a radical change in policy, abandoning its insistence on direct proletariat revolution in favour of allying with anti-imperial national struggles. The Malayan Communist Party could now exploit patriotic Chinese resistance to Japanese aggression. After the Chinese Communist Party formed a united front with the Kuomintang against Japan in December 1936, communists quickly infiltrated the Nanyang Chinese National Salvation Movement and changed the names of their organizations to give them a patriotic ring, so that the General Labour Union, for instance, became the Labouring Classes' Anti-Enemy-Backing-Up Society.

The outbreak of the Sino-Japanese War in 1937 gave the Malayan Communist Party the chance to widen its support. Although the party was illegal, it posed in the guise of the All-Malayan National Liberation movement. Between 1937 and 1941 the communists used anti-Japanese activities to extend their influence from impressionable students and disgruntled labourers to more prominent community leaders. The Malayan Communist Party formed a series of committees, some of which were secret bodies of hard core members while others, such as the Chinese National Liberation Vanguard Corps, were open organizations to which they attracted Tan Kah-kee and other patriotic leaders.

Anti-Japanese feeling intensified in Singapore as the Japanese swept into south-eastern China, seizing Amoy in May 1938 and bombing Canton, Swatow and Hainan. Demonstrations and protest meetings were broken up by the police. Parades and street meetings were banned, and the police raided a number of underground associations. Arrests and banishments in turn provoked more disturbances and unrest. The British authorities by then were deeply alarmed at the evidence of communist influence and secret society connections.

Supported by the Chinese Consul-General and by Lee Kong Chian, who was then chairman of the Chinese Chamber of Commerce, Tan Kah-kee stepped up contributions for China and put the collection on a systematic basis, making each dialect group responsible for raising funds from its own community. The object was to extract payment from all Singapore Chinese, including the Straits-born, ranging from a contribution of 1 per cent of a labourer's wages to large donations from the rich. This was supplemented by fund raising drama shows and flag days. At first the response from the immigrant Chinese was enthusiastic, but the demands came at a difficult time when rubber and tin prices were low. The Kuomintang put pressure on Tan Kah-kee to increase donations, and Chinese newspapers published the names of donors and also those of people who refused to contribute.

In October 1938 delegates from all the Nanyang countries attended a conference in Singapore, at which it was decided to co-ordinate patriotic efforts by creating a Nanyang Chinese Relief General Association. Tan Kah-kee was elected chairman, his *Nanyang Siang Pau* became the mouthpiece of the association, and the committee was dominated by Chinese from Malaya and Singapore. With thirty subcommittees in the Nanyang, the association had an active membership of over 20,000. It raised money, encouraged the purchase of Chinese government bonds, stimulated investment in industries in China and recruited youths to work on building the Burma Road.

The association was the nearest the Overseas Chinese came to a united movement, but it was soon undermined by clan and personal rivalries. Tan Kah-kee was the most prominent leader but Tan Ean Kiam, a Hokkien financier and managing director of the Oversea Chinese Bank, and Aw Boon Haw, who commanded support from the Cantonese as well as the Hakka *pang*, also vied for power. The predominantly Hokkien committee was at loggerheads with the Cantonese, and there was no Hakka representation. Aw Boon Haw organized fund raising independently through his *Sin Chew Jit Poh* and the Hakka Association. No prominent Baba served on the committee, and most Straits Chinese showed reluctance to contribute funds to the movement.

The Nanyang Chinese National Salvation Movement attained the height of its effectiveness in 1939 when the Nanyang Chinese closed ranks against Wang Ching-wei, who deserted Chiang Kai-shek in December 1938, came to terms with the Japanese, and set up a puppet government in Nanking. Wang tried to win the Nanyang Chinese over to his policy. He had long-established links with Malaya going back to the early years of the century before the Chinese Revolution, but Tan Kah-kee refused to support him and urged Chiang Kai-shek to continue fighting. The Singapore Chinese backed Tan Kah-kee's stand, and the *Nanyang Siang Pau*, the *Sin Chew Jit Poh* and other Chinese newspapers in Singapore condemned Wang Ching-wei as a traitor.

At that point the prestige of Chiang Kai-shek and the Kuomintang stood at its highest point with the Singapore Chinese, who appeared to have been brought together in united opposition to the Japanese. However, behind the banner of a united front, the Kuomintang and the communists were in reality competing for power, and these divisions eventually undermined the Nanyang Chinese Relief General Association.

In April 1939 the Malayan Communist Party called for an "All Races United Front to strive for a democratic system and oppose the Jap-Axis bloc". The party gained great prestige because of its vociferous opposition to the Japanese and by May 1940 claimed a membership of between 50,000 and 60,000.[27] It competed with the Kuomintang for the support of men such as Tan Kah-kee who had no bent towards socialism but were Chinese patriots.

The Kuomintang tried to strengthen its hold over the Overseas Chinese. In 1939 the Nationalist government opened an Overseas Chinese Investment Information Office, and early the following year sent General Wu T'ieh-ch'eng, Minister of Overseas Party Affairs, to try to step up Malayan investment in China's new industries. Following Wu's visit, an anti-Japanese youth organization, the San-Min-Chu-I Youth Corps, was established, and Chungking followed this up with further attempts to establish a tighter control over the Chinese National Salvation Movement in Malaya.

Profiting from the boom in the Malayan economy following the outbreak of the war in Europe, the Singapore Chinese increased their support for China's industries, but there was growing disillusionment with the Kuomintang. Tan Kah-kee was irritated by Chungking's interference in the Singapore movement and worried by reports of conditions in China. He decided to accept an invitation extended by Wu T'ieh-ch'eng to visit China and left Singapore for Chungking in March 1940. For the next nine months Tan travelled widely and was distressed at the conditions under which Nanyang volunteers were working on the Burma Road and shocked at the corruption of many of Chiang Kai-shek's supporters. In contrast, Tan was impressed by the spartan sense of discipline shown by Mao Tse-tung and his communist followers in Yenan.

By the time he returned to Singapore Tan Kah-kee was openly critical of the Kuomintang, and at the second congress of the Nanyang Chinese Relief General Association in Singapore in March 1941, he clashed with Consul-General Kao Ling-pai in bitter invective against the government's activities in China. Tan was re-elected chairman of the association, but the Kuomintang worked to discredit him, and this rift threatened to wreck the whole Nanyang Chinese National Salvation Movement.

The small minority of Baba "King's Chinese", who prided themselves on being British subjects, were not deeply involved in Chinese politics or committed to Kuomintang activities. They aspired, rather, to secure a larger share in Singapore's public life, and through the Straits Chinese British Association and their representatives on the Legislative Council, they agitated for better education opportunities and more political powers.

The Baba leaders consistently pressed for English-medium education. Their community had been largely instrumental in financing the Medical School in 1905 and Raffles College in 1928. In the 1930s they appealed for free primary English-medium education and more scholarships in English schools. Some wanted to see English as the *lingua franca* and campaigned to found a university.

With the steady expansion of English education, many Straits Chinese, Indians, and Eurasians became anglicized professionals and businessmen, and the most prominent were admitted to the Executive, Legislative and Municipal Councils and received British honours. But social barriers hardened. Although the Governor held multiracial receptions, there was little mixing in private homes. Interracial marriage was frowned upon, and Asians were barred from senior posts in the Malayan Civil Service and from membership of European social clubs.

This led to frustration, but as yet the irritations and resentments of the Straits Chinese were not channelled into any organized opposition. The colonial regime was snobbish, condescending, and somewhat contemptuous, but benign. While talented English-educated Asians had little prospect of political or bureaucratic careers, there were considerable material rewards to be gained in professional life and in business.

❧

On the eve of the Second World War, the Singapore government remained in many ways remote from the ordinary lives of the masses. Top-level administration was in the hands of a small group of officials in the Malayan Civil Service, which was confined to "natural-born British subjects of pure European descent on both sides", although British subjects of all races could apply for middle-ranking executive and technical posts. The Straits Medical Service was opened to Asians in 1932, but few Asian doctors rose above the bottom rungs of the service. Asians who had graduated from British universities could apply for posts in the Straits Civil Service, which was created in 1934, and the Straits Legal Service formed in 1937, but few were admitted. There was no provision for promotion to the Malayan Civil Service, since MCS officials were liable to be posted anywhere throughout "British Malaya", and the Malay rulers opposed the entry of non-Malay Asians to the civil service in their states.

Under the constitution,[28] which had not changed in principle since 1867, the governor worked in consultation with the upper strata of European unofficials and with a tiny section of the wealthy and professional English-speaking Asian community. The most popular, and often the most successful, governors were those who did not seek to rock the boat. In the words of Sir Laurence Guillemard, who was Governor from 1919 to 1927, "The main duty of the Governor must be to keep the colony in peace, prosperity and security."[29] While innovative and enterprising governors, such as Guillemard, stirred up opposition and difficulty, less gifted but genial governors often presided over periods of quiet construction.

The inefficient structure of British administration in Malaya came into question again during the inter-war years, and attempts to reform the constitution and make administration more effective were initiated by the two outstanding Governors of the period, Sir Laurence Guillemard and Sir Cecil Clementi.

Guillemard, who came with a brilliant record from the British Treasury, re-examined Anderson's proposals for strengthening the High Commissioner's authority over Kuala Lumpur and making administration more uniform between Singapore and the Malay States. In 1925 he proposed to abolish the post of Chief Secretary, to transfer some of Kuala Lumpur's powers to the separate state governments and to bring the states into more direct contact with the High Commissioner. Guillemard promised this would not mean any new centralization in Singapore, "no dark schemes of annexation or fusion with the Colony", but the proposals met with strong resistance from commercial interests in the Federation and were set aside in the prosperous years that followed.

In 1931, at a critical time in the Depression, Clementi announced plans to decentralize federal powers to the state governments. Clementi saw this as a prelude to uniting the whole peninsula into a Malayan League, which would lead to "the emergence of the brotherhood of Malay nations, each proudly guarding its historical individuality and autonomy but joining hands with the rest in enterprise that may be for the good of the

Malays of this peninsula as a whole and of the immigrants of other races who have made this country their home".

On paper, Clementi's scheme seemed sensible and tidy. The Malay sultans welcomed the prospect of greater local authority, and there was some support for the idea of creating a Malayan nation. In 1926 Tan Cheng Lock had declared in the Legislative Council that "the ultimate goal should be a united self-governing British Malaya with a Federal government and Parliament for the whole of it", and he had called for creating a "Malayan spirit and consciousness amongst its people to the complete elimination of racial or communal feeling".

This was a minority view, and the majority looked with suspicion upon the concept of a Malayan League. The Unfederated Malay States feared they would lose their individuality in a closer association. Federation businessmen once more baulked at being subjected to Singapore, while their Singapore counterparts dreaded the prospect of a Malayan common market with external tariffs, which would damage Singapore's treasured free trade entrepôt status. In 1931 Clementi appointed a committee, largely composed of Singapore businessmen, to investigate the possibilities of a Malayan customs union, but the committee reported unequivocally that such a union was "essentially opposed to the interests of the Colony and undesirable in any circumstances that can be foreseen". It claimed that "the interests of Singapore and Penang are largely extra-Malayan".

The Chinese in the Federation were afraid that, as a minority, their interests would be threatened in a united Malaya. The new constitutional proposals, coinciding with immigration restrictions, vernacular press censorship, the ban on the Kuomintang and cuts in government grants to Chinese schools, and compounded by the hardships of the Depression evoked unprecedented racial bitterness throughout Malaya and Singapore.

The British government sent Sir Samuel Wilson, Permanent Undersecretary of State for the Colonies, to investigate the position. In his report, published in 1933, Wilson advised that, while the unification of the country under one central government would be economically sound, the British were committed to preserving the individual states. "The maintenance of the position, authority and prestige of the Malay rulers must always be a cardinal point in British policy: and the encouragement of indirect rule will probably prove the greatest safeguard against the political submersion of the Malays which would result from the development of popular government on western lines."[30]

Wilson found that officials and commercial leaders in the Federation regarded the Chief Secretary as their champion against the High Commissioner and the Singapore authorities, but he recommended reducing the Chief Secretary's status and gradually devolving to the separate states the work of technical departments, such as agriculture, education, medical services, and public works.

The Colonial Office adopted Wilson's proposals, which were accepted generally in Malaya as a fair compromise, and the implementation proceeded smoothly in the hands of the conciliatory new Governor Sir Shenton Thomas. In 1935 the Chief Secretary was replaced by a Federal Secretary of somewhat lower status. Many functions devolved upon the individual states, while at the same time pan-Malayan departments were created, and other Singapore-based departmental directors acted as advisers for the Malay States. This gave Singapore more control over policy and encouraged more uniform administration, but the ambitious proposals for a political and economic union faded away. In later years many came to admit that Clementi was far-seeing in his vision of a united Malaya, but at the time neither the Federation, the Unfederated Malay States, nor the Straits Settlements was ready to make the necessary sacrifices. The result was to assuage regional and sectional fears and jealousies at the expense of leaving Malaya divided and disorganized.

⤳

Guillemard was able to make more headway in constitutional reform in the colony itself. In Singapore there was no demand for change before the 1920s, and the system of nomination and official majority rule was generally accepted. Indeed, commentators before the First World War had deemed it "a commendable feature of a place like Singapore that there is comparatively little self seeking in municipal and colonial politics".[31] Such matters were left to the heads of firms, and it was not deemed fitting for juniors to meddle.

Guillemard set out to increase participation. In 1921 he introduced the practice of allowing certain organizations to nominate municipal commissioners. The Singapore branch of the Straits Settlements Association nominated three, the Singapore and Chinese Chambers of Commerce two each, and the Straits Chinese British Association, the Eurasian Association, the Muslim Advisory Board and the Hindu Advisory Board one each.

In 1920 a select committee, which Guillemard had appointed to consider Legislative Council reform, recommended creating an unofficial majority, comprising seven Europeans and eight Asians, who together would outnumber the twelve official members, but giving the governor the power to suspend proceedings. The Straits Settlements (Singapore) Association welcomed this suggestion, but the Colonial Office refused to admit "a departure from the principle that responsibility and control must be in the same hands".[32] Guillemard introduced some modifications. From 1924 two unofficial members of the Legislative Council were nominated by the governor to sit on the Executive Council. The Legislative Council was enlarged to comprise twenty-six members, with equal numbers of unofficials and officials, the governor having the casting vote. The Penang and Singapore Chambers of Commerce were each permitted to nominate one unofficial, with the remainder nominated by the governor on a racial basis: five Europeans, including one each from Penang and Melaka, three Chinese British subjects, one Malay, one Indian and one Eurasian.

In 1930 the Straits Settlements (Singapore) Association proposed a similar equality of officials and unofficials in the Executive Council, and recommended that unofficial legislative councillors should be elected by a panel of British subjects of all races. There was little support for this suggestion, which the *Straits Times* labelled "a ludicrous scheme" and "crass folly".[33] In a community so divided by race, religion and language, with a large number of aliens, transients, and illiterates, it was argued that a governor was better able to reconcile justice for society than a "popularly" elected government, which would in practice represent the prosperous commercial class.

Initially interest in constitutional reform was confined to the Western community, the only politically vocal bodies being the Straits Settlements (Singapore) Association and the Association of British Malaya, which were both predominantly European in membership. The Association of British Malaya was formed in London in 1920 as a successor to the parent Straits Settlements Association, in order to extend activities to cover planting, mining, and commercial interests in the Malay States. The association invited the Singapore branch of the Straits Settlements Association to dissolve and transfer its members to the new organization, but the Singapore branch refused, insisting that it could look after Straits Settlements' interests itself.

The rivals quickly sank their differences in opposition to a Straits Settlements Income Tax Ordinance, which Guillemard introduced in 1921, and which C.W. Darbishire, president of the Association of British Malaya, said was "enough to make Sir Stamford Raffles turn in his grave".[34] Darbishire went on to attack Guillemard's alleged "squandermania" and extravagance on an official yacht and Government House servants, issues reminiscent of the opposition to Ord, which had given birth to the original Straits Settlements Association.

The unpopular income tax proposal was withdrawn, but the issue served to draw the two bodies together, and they maintained co-operation from that point. By 1927 the Straits Settlements (Singapore) Association had more than 700 members and was described as "rapidly becoming the most important unofficial body in the Straits Settlements".[35] At that time, however, the Straits Chinese British Association was beginning to assume the lead in political agitation, mild though this was. The most vocal spokesman was Tan Cheng Lock, who was born into a wealthy Baba family in Melaka in 1883, worked as a schoolmaster for six years and then went into the rubber industry, where he became director of several companies.[36] Tan Cheng Lock served as a municipal commissioner in Melaka from 1912 to 1922, as a legislative councillor from 1923 to 1934, and as an executive councillor from 1933 to 1935. He represented the colony at King George VI's coronation in 1937. In 1928 Tan Cheng Lock called in vain for an unofficial majority and direct popular representation in both Legislative and Executive Councils for all who had made their home in the Straits.[37] The Straits Chinese British Association pressed Clementi to increase Chinese representation on the Legislative and Executive councils but without success. Tan Cheng Lock continued the agitation throughout the 1930s, speaking forcefully in the Legislative Council against Clementi's discriminatory anti-Chinese legislation and addressing a memorial to Sir Samuel Wilson in 1932 entitled *Why the Chinese are Perturbed*.[38] Tan established contact with Arthur Creech-Jones, then a socialist backbencher, who had raised questions in Parliament about the Straits. They met at the House of Commons in June 1939, and Tan tried to arrange for regular communication with sympathetic Members of Parliament, who might press for constitutional, educational, and social reforms in Malaya.[39] The outbreak of the European War a few weeks after Tan's return to Malaya put an end to this dialogue.

Tan Cheng Lock represented only a minority view. Most Asians seemed content with the limited opportunities to participate in Singapore's public life, which had improved by the 1930s. All born in Singapore were automatically British subjects and eligible for appointment to the Executive, Legislative, or Municipal Councils or for admission to the Straits Settlements Medical, Legal, or Civil Services. They could serve on administrative boards, such as the Education Board, the Singapore Harbour Board, the Licensing Board, and hospital management committees. They could share in the work of racial and religious advisory boards, which were consulted by the government, or on the committees of the chambers of commerce. In practice the numbers of Asians in public life were very few. A small clique of wealthy businessmen dominated the chambers of commerce, and only a minority of the English-educated took any interest in official and quasi-official activities.

Apart from the clandestine Malayan Communist Party, there were no political parties in Singapore on the eve of the Second World War. Local apathy, the preoccupation of politically active Chinese with affairs in China, and the relative peace and prosperity of the immediate pre-war years were not conducive to the growth of political movements. Of the three semi-political organizations, the Kesatuan Melayu Singapura had no specific political programme, and the mildly liberal Straits Chinese British Association and Straits Settlements (Singapore) Association numbered only a few hundred members.

The constitution satisfied the limited objectives of colonial rule. The wealthy and well-educated had a voice in government that was usually heeded, although they had no ultimate control or power. The mass of the population was indifferent to government but not actively hostile. Singapore remained a collection of immigrant communities, with their culture, interests and loyalties rooted in foreign countries, their ultimate ambition often to return to the lands of their origin, whether it was Britain, India or China. Singaporeans were content to leave government in the hands of the colonial authorities, and on the whole this produced a tolerably efficient administration. One European unofficial legislative councillor in 1932 pictured "some future historian referring to the present era of the Straits Settlements as its 'golden age', when the art of governing was left to trained experts and the ordinary people were allowed to pursue their ordinary avocations unhampered by the virus of polities".

While command of the official majority was rarely used to overrule unofficials, the Legislative Council did not pretend to be democratic but was designed as an advisory body to air the views of various communities, to give the government a public platform and to test popular reaction to new legislation. The official and nominated character of the council made it appear more an organ of government than a guardian of public interest. The official majority crushed the council's vitality, meetings were poorly attended, proceedings were for the most part "formal, dull and brief",[40] where "a mumbled rigmarole is being carried on with very little relation to the realities of the life of the Straits".[41]

The late 1930s were a time of comfort and leisure for the upper and middle strata of Western and Asian Singapore society. Some of the benefits from improved public works and amenities permeated through to the mass of the population, but, as an acute young American observed in 1937, "The government of the Colony is run by a small group of insiders living a life the comforts and luxuries of which are rarely impaired by too close contact with the sordid poverty which has set its stamp on the great bulk of the population" ... and "it is still no exaggeration to say that it is a government run by and for those who have won through to power and wealth, and devil take the hindermost".[42] British colonial rule had lost the zest and vitality that characterized the early years of the century. It had become jaded, smug, and complacent, but it seemed as firmly rooted in Singapore as ever. "Imperialism appears always to be committed to perpetuating its own rule unless it is challenged by a force which makes it necessary or expedient for it to withdraw."[43]

5

War in the East
1941–1942

In the early hours of the morning of 8 December 1941, Japanese aircraft raided Singapore. Their main targets were the Seletar and Tengah airfields, but they also bombed Raffles Place in the heart of the town. The unsuspecting city was at rest, the streets and the ships in the harbour ablaze with light, and the headquarters of the civil air raid precautions organization unmanned. For the civilian population these bombs, and the newspaper headlines that greeted them next morning, were the first indications of war, beginning a train of disaster, which within seventy days forced the British to surrender Singapore to the Japanese army.

The origins of the debacle went back to the beginning of the century when, in her preoccupation with meeting the German naval threat in Europe, Britain had made an alliance with Japan to help safeguard her interests in the East. The extent of this dependence on the Japanese was highlighted by the sepoy mutiny in 1915, which threw the first doubts on Britain's ability to defend her Eastern Empire. After the First World War, the British government had re-examined its naval policy. In Europe the German naval threat had been destroyed, but in the East the balance of power was changing, since the extension of Japan's control over parts of China and former German Pacific islands transformed her into a rival and a potential enemy.

To deal with this changed situation, in 1919 Lord Jellicoe, the former British First Sea Lord, proposed the creation of a powerful imperial fleet, comprising British, Australian and New Zealand ships, to be stationed in the Far East. While this suggestion held appeal for Australasia, it found little favour in Britain, which, having just fought a "war to end all wars", had no appetite for costly defence projects overseas and was committed to ambitious expenditure on domestic reform. In August 1919 the British government adopted a "Ten Year Rule", by which policy was to be based on the assumption that the country would not be drawn into a major war for the next ten years. In deference to the United States, Britain allowed the Japanese alliance to lapse when it came up for renewal in 1921. In its place a Naval Limitation Treaty was signed at a conference in Washington in 1922 whereby Britain, the United States, Japan and France agreed to restrict the size of their navies and not to erect military or naval bases in the Pacific. In effect, Britain exchanged the definite commitment of an alliance with a country whose interests in the Pacific had hitherto been complementary to her own for a shadowy alignment with the United States.

Any threat in the Far East was to be met by sending contingents of the Royal Navy's home-based main fleet, but a local base was needed to offer repair and docking facilities. In June 1921 the British government formally approved the choice of Singapore, and in 1923 London voted £11 million to begin constructing the base, with supplementary contributions from the Malay States, Australia, New Zealand and Hong Kong. Rather than develop the crowded and vulnerable Keppel Harbour area, it was decided to site the naval base on the Johor Strait, with an airfield and sea-plane base at nearby Seletar. Initially it was estimated that a relief force could arrive in six weeks, and a small garrison and strong seaward defences were deemed adequate to hold off an attack for this period of time. The possibility of an assault from Johor was considered but seemed remote,[1] and the prospect of war in the East seemed so unlikely in the 1920s that the progress of the naval base was dictated not by strategic but by domestic considerations. The base was the Conservative Party's project, while the Labour Party opposed from the beginning what its leader, Ramsay MacDonald, dubbed "the wild and wanton escapade of Singapore", as a threat to international goodwill and a waste of precious resources.

Drainage schemes, which were needed to prepare the swampy mangrove area, were continued as a general health measure under MacDonald's short-lived Labour government, which came to power in Britain in 1924, and by the time the preliminary work was finished, the Conservatives were back in office. Construction proceeded slowly until 1929, when a new Labour government suspended all further work on the Singapore base in a bid towards international disarmament. Tokyo's growing aggressiveness put an end to these vacillations. In 1931 Japan occupied Manchuria and the following year resigned from the League of Nations. Work on the Singapore base was resumed and speeded up as the danger from Japan increased. In 1935 Japan withdrew from the London disarmament conference, in 1936 she terminated the Washington agreement and made an Anti-Comintern Pact with Germany, and in 1937 she invaded China.

Even more alarmed by the growing threat to peace in Europe posed by the aggressive policies of Nazi Germany and Mussolini's Italy, in 1937 a full review into imperial defence was carried out. During the initial planning stage of the Singapore base, a British general had expressed concern lest "we ourselves put a half way house and then – garrisoning it, as is our wont – make a present of it to the wrong people".[2] A strong but inadequately manned base conjured up in larger and more dangerous form the spectre that had made the Colonial Office so wary about accepting Singapore as a Crown Colony in 1867.

The strategy depended on a relief fleet being dispatched promptly, but as early as 1926 Australia had queried British assumptions about having sufficient ships to send to the East in time of war. The Chiefs of Staff warned the Imperial Conference in May 1937 that the Singapore base, without a fleet, was an inadequate deterrent, and Australia and New Zealand appealed for a peacetime fleet to be stationed in the Far East. Britain re-iterated her intention to concentrate naval strength in Europe and dispatch a fleet only if war broke out in the East. The assumption remained that the force could reach Singapore within forty-two days, despite warnings from Major-General William Dobbie, the General Officer Commanding Malaya, in March 1936 that this estimate was unrealistic.

In 1937 the British service commanders on the spot advised that the protection of the naval base was bound up with the defence of the whole Malay Peninsula. Dobbie, and his senior staff officer, Colonel Arthur Percival, visualized a wartime situation in which the British navy would not be able to reach Singapore in time and that the Japanese might attack down the Malay Peninsula. Percival drew up a plan from the Japanese viewpoint that bore an uncanny resemblance to the actual Japanese attack made four years later. His assessment was based on landings in the northeast of the peninsula, probably at Singgora, with subsidiary landings at Patani and Kota Bharu, and accepted that these would not only be feasible during the December/March northeast monsoon but might profit from the bad visibility common at that time. In July 1938 Dobbie argued that protecting the naval base involved holding the whole peninsula, strengthening air power in view of the increasing range capability of aircraft, and constructing defence works in northern Malaya and Johor. The War Office rejected the recommendations for military works. Airfields were constructed at Kota Bharu, Kuantan and in eastern Johor, but on sites that were chosen for operational purposes but difficult to defend.

Construction went ahead full speed in Singapore. In 1938 the King George VI dry dock was opened. It was capable of taking the largest vessels afloat, and the base was hailed by the *Sydney Morning Herald* as "The Gibraltar of the East … the gateway to the Orient … the bastion of British might".[3]

New airfields were constructed at Tengah and Sembawang, while virgin jungle was cleared and mangrove swamps were drained at Changi to provide heavy artillery and anti-aircraft defences covering the eastern approaches to the naval base. In 1938 barracks were completed at nearby Selarang to house a full battalion of infantry, so that by 1941 the naval base and its protective "Changi fortress" were complete. It inspired journalistic hyperbole, "a new, bigger and better Gibraltar, one of the most formidable concatenations of naval, military and strategic power ever put together anywhere".[4]

The Japanese occupied Canton in October 1938 and seized Hainan Island early in 1939, bringing their forces within closer striking distance of Singapore, but in March 1939 mounting tension in Europe forced the British government to extend its estimate for getting a relief force to Singapore from forty-two to seventy days. Britain and the United States grew closer in response to Japanese expansion but still aimed to maintain friendly relations with Japan. In Malaya there was general apathy and complacency among officials, British civilians, and the Asian population, and no improvement in co-operation between the armed services and civilian authorities or between the arms of the services.

When war broke out in Europe in September 1939, the time estimate for sending naval reinforcements to deal with any crisis in Singapore was extended from 70 to 180 days. Winston Churchill, then first Lord of the Admiralty, promised that the defence of Singapore, Australia and New Zealand would take precedence over the Mediterranean if the Eastern Empire was menaced. In the early months of the European war, the spread of the conflict to the Far East seemed unlikely, and London allocated Malaya the comfortable role of "a dollar arsenal", concentrating on production rather than defence. In 1939 Malaya produced nearly 40 per cent of the world's rubber and nearly 60 per cent of its tin, most of it for the American market. She came second only to Canada as the Commonwealth's biggest dollar earner. For civilians, the European war transformed Singapore into a centre of purposeful energy. The depressing restrictions on tin and rubber production of the 1930s were replaced by a drive for maximum output. Profit and patriotism lay in the same direction to produce a sense of virtuous activity. The only source of discontent among Singapore's mercantile community was the imposition of wartime income tax, which the Governor used his official majority to force through a grudging Legislative Council in February 1941.

The wars in China and Europe stimulated an appetite for news and boosted circulation of Singapore's English-language newspapers. The *Malaya Tribune*, with its predominantly Asian readership in mind, was a strong supporter of Nationalist China. The rival *Straits Times*, giving priority to Western business interests, tried to keep up morale and play down the disasters in the West. Both newspapers were hostile to the Japanese-owned English-language *Singapore Herald*, which started in April 1939. Under its lively and energetic managing editor, Tatsuki Fuji, the *Singapore Herald* set out to put the Japanese in the best light and in particular to counter the *Malaya Tribune's* pro-Chungking stand.

After Germany and Russia signed a non-aggression pact in August 1939, the Comintern instructed the Malayan Communist Party to foment labour trouble in order to impede the British war effort. In the early months of the European war, the Malayan General Labour Union organized a number of strikes in Singapore and staged an illegal mass rally on May Day 1940. The main communist support came from unskilled workers in Chinese firms, and the party failed to capture the key sectors of the labour movement: the railways and bus companies, the Harbour Board, municipality, and the naval base. The Singapore authorities acted swiftly to arrest and banish agitators and dissolve unions that engaged in subversive activities.

The colonial government was fully aware, probably through information supplied by Lai Teck, of the Malayan Communist Party's limitations and shifts in policy. The pro-Russian, anti-British stand was self-defeating, since it weakened the party's hold over anti-Japanese Chinese patriots. In September 1940 the Chinese Communist Party instructed the party in Malaya to stop all anti-British movements and consolidate the anti-Japanese front.[5] From that time, strikes in Singapore petered out.

The assumptions on which British imperial strategy in the Far East for the past twenty years had been based were shattered by the disasters in Europe in the summer of 1940: the collapse of France and Holland, the British retreat from Dunkirk, and Italy's entry into the war as an ally of Germany. Threatened with invasion, battling to preserve her Atlantic lifeline, Britain was now at war not only with Germany but with Italy and Vichy France, which had turned the Mediterranean into a hostile sea. There was no possibility of sparing an adequate fleet for the Far East. In August 1940 the Chiefs of Staff decided that defence could no longer be confined to Singapore Island but had to be extended to the whole peninsula, and that air power should become the primary defence, with increased army support. Meanwhile, very substantial land forces would be needed until sufficient aircraft could be supplied.

The situation in the Far East grew more menacing. In July 1940 the United States imposed the first economic sanctions to stem the flow of arms, iron, oil and other vital raw materials to Japan. This began a process that eventually forced Japan to choose between calling off her China campaign or seizing the main sources of war materials for herself. Japan occupied northern Indo-China in September, signed a ten-year pact with Germany and Italy and sent military missions to the Axis powers.

Public feeling became tense, with Singaporeans suspecting all Japanese residents of being spies. Tokyo had already ordered the return of the once flourishing group of Japanese prostitutes as degrading to their country's reputation, but about 4,000 Japanese remained: businessmen, journalists, dentists, photographers, barbers, and about 1,500 fishermen. The Special Branch of the police kept them under scrutiny, and several were arrested on charges of espionage in the first year of the European war, including Mamoru Shinozaki, press attache to the Japanese Consulate-General.

Retired Air Chief Marshal Sir Robert Brooke-Popham arrived in Singapore in November 1940 as Commander-in-Chief of land and air forces in the Far East, but with no powers over the navy, civil defence, or any aspect of civil administration. With no prospect of sending a relief fleet in time or bringing the air force up to the level required, the burden of defence now shifted to the army. Reinforcements of Indian and British infantry began arriving in the last weeks of the year, and in February 1941 the first troops of a newly raised Australian 8th Division landed, followed a few weeks later by a second Indian division. The number of Commonwealth troops stationed in Malaya trebled between June 1940 and April 1941, but many were inexperienced and they lacked supporting artillery and tanks. Brooke-Popham appealed for more aircraft, but in view of British losses at Dunkirk and new demands in the Middle East, Malaya's equipment needs could not be met.

The uneasiness of the summer months of 1940 gave way to a renewed complacency in Singapore, as army reinforcements continued to arrive, while the Anglo-American relationship grew warmer and the Japanese appeared to be bogged down in China. Social life among expatriate civilians and servicemen alike was relaxed and carefree. Far from the Spartan privations and the tense life-and-death struggles in Europe and the Middle East, Singapore was "a little spot of paradise",[6] where there was peace and plenty, no food rationing, no sense of urgency, or danger. Following Whitehall's instructions, the local government continued to give priority to rubber and tin production over the training of military volunteers or the construction of defence works. The War Office fixed wage rates unrealistically low, at less than half the market rate, so that it was impossible to attract labourers to build defence works, and there was no question of conscripting labour away from tin and rubber production.

"The majority of well-informed people do not believe that the Japanese in their present difficulties will branch out on fresh ventures", the *Singapore Free Press* declared in January 1941.[7] Most military men were confident that Japan's growing difficulties in

China and her fear of a Russian attack would dissuade her from ventures in Southeast Asia. Britain and the United States held secret talks in Washington in the early months of 1941 to discuss co-operation in the East. Britain would have liked some American ships to be stationed at Singapore, but the United States preferred to keep her Pacific fleet intact at Pearl Harbor. Both powers agreed that Europe was the area of first priority.

The German invasion of Russia in June 1941 put an end to Japan's fears of attack from the rear and gave her more freedom of action, but Churchill believed that Japan would agree to join her German ally in attacking Russia, rather than launch into a new type of tropical warfare in Southeast Asia, which would bring her into conflict not only with Britain and the Netherlands[8] but also with the United States. The outbreak of war between Germany and Russia dispelled the last vestiges of communist-inspired labour unrest in Singapore and brought communist and Kuomintang supporters together again. The Malayan Communist Party was illegal, but, with a central committee in Singapore and state committees on the mainland, it claimed some 5,000 members and 100,000 sympathizers.[9] The party dominated the Overseas Chinese Anti-Japanese Mobilization Committee and set up a Special Operations Executive in Singapore to train guerrillas in sabotage. The colonial authorities, anxious not to provoke Japan, continued to arrest Chinese communist sympathizers and to discourage anti-Japanese activities generally. They were particularly worried about the San-Min-Chu-I Youth Corps and the propaganda taught in Chinese schools, and the Nanyang Chinese National Salvation Movement continued to be an embarrassment to the authorities up to the outbreak of the Pacific War.

༄

The material comfort and plenty in Singapore seemed unreal and almost indecent to new arrivals, such as Arthur Percival, by now Vice-Chief of Imperial General Staff, who returned as General

Officer Commanding Malaya in May 1941, or Brigadier Ivan Simson, who was appointed Chief Engineer Malaya Command three months later. Fresh from organizing defences in beleaguered Britain, Simson in particular was appalled at the soft living among the troops in Singapore and the lack of attempts to organize the local population for their own defence.

Most European civilians were working hard and devoting much of their leisure time to civil defence duties, but the realities of war seemed remote. "There'll Always Be An England" was Singapore's theme song in 1941 and expressed the general feeling that Britain was battling for survival, with Singapore as a sympathetic, helpful but faraway onlooker. The ruling class had no wish to involve the Asian population in defence, doubting both their capabilities and their loyalties. There were few openings for Asians in the Volunteers and none in the British armed services, although the *Malaya Tribune* had called for conscription in May 1939.[10] It was assumed that the local population would panic at any hint of trouble, and that they would not be willing to suffer and die for an alien regime. In particular, the Singapore authorities clung to their pre-war suspicion about Kuomintang activities, despite a personal secret telegram to Shenton Thomas in February 1941 from the Secretary of State for the Colonies urging that, since Japan was now openly committed to the Axis, Singapore should reflect Whitehall's increased approval for Chiang Kai-shek.[11]

Japan's major concern was to finish the war in China and to secure the raw materials she needed for this purpose from Southeast Asia. Japanese talks with Dutch authorities in Batavia about oil supplies broke down in June 1941, and the next month the United States, followed by Britain and the Netherlands East Indies, froze Japanese assets, strangling her foreign trade and cutting off crucial oil supplies. Up to that point the Malayan authorities had applied trade restrictions sparingly in an attempt to appease Japan, but now Japan was suddenly deprived of her iron, bauxite and shipping interests in the peninsula.[12]

Tokyo forced Vichy France to provide bases in southern Indo-China, which gave Japan a naval base 750 miles from Singapore and airfields only 300 miles from northern Malaya. Percival appealed for reinforcements, but Churchill and the British Service Chiefs were not prepared to divert resources from the active Middle East sector to meet what was still only a potential threat. As Churchill later admitted, "In my mind the whole Japanese menace lay in a sinister twilight compared with our other needs."[13]

For the moment Singapore and Malaya were dangerously vulnerable to attack. They were short of planes and had no battleships, aircraft carriers, heavy cruisers, or submarines. Security depended on preserving peace with Japan or at least in postponing war until the spring of 1942, by which time it was envisaged that reinforcements could be sent to the East. But there was still little sense of urgency in Singapore, and Brooke-Popham continued to feed the British Cabinet with optimistic reports. On 1 October 1941 he assured London that "the last thing Japan wants at this juncture is a campaign to the South".

Despite informal co-operation with the Americans and the Dutch, no unified command was agreed, nor was any attempt made to streamline administration and consolidate British military command in Malaya. In September 1941 a British Cabinet minister, Duff Cooper, was sent to Singapore with vague terms of reference to enquire into the various forms of civil administration in the Allied countries of Southeast Asia and Australasia. To co-ordinate the complicated structure, he recommended appointing a Commissioner-General for the Far East, but this proposal was still under consideration in London when the Pacific War broke out.

The authorities remained reluctant to divert manpower to defence works or to take any action that might shake civilian morale and public confidence. Suggestions made by Simson in October 1941 to construct defences along the northern shores of Singapore Island with an outer defence around Johor Bahru were set aside. Proposals to build air raid shelters were rejected on the grounds that the water table was too high.

In October 1941 Percival called on Asians to come forward to serve with the Volunteers but gave no hint of urgency. That same month, Brooke-Popham declared publicly that Britain did not need American naval support, and assured a press conference early in December that the Japanese were too afraid of British power to attack Malaya.[14]

The Singapore authorities were still trying to preserve friendly relations with Japan. Representatives of the Japanese-owned *Singapore Herald* were admitted to press conferences and military demonstrations as late as September 1941. Japanese businessmen remained in large numbers until their business dried up as a result of the embargo, and an official evacuation ship repatriated about 600 of them early in October. Japanese Consul-General Tsurumi Ken was recalled later that month, but most of the Japanese photographers, barbers, and dentists remained, while the *Singapore Herald* and the Japanese-language *Singapore Nippo* continued to operate until the day war broke out.

The *Singapore Herald* declared as late as 6 December that "Peace can still be saved", a message which was welcomed by the British authorities as good for morale. Foreign correspondents and local journalists seethed at the official policy of suppressing any potentially disturbing information or opinions. "Malaya is in the drowsy languid interval between sleep and awakening," declared the Malaya Tribune in October 1941. "We in Malaya are metaphorically still in bed."

In the confused uncertainty of the summer and autumn of 1941, political considerations outweighed strategic ones, as Britain tried to balance Russian appeals for help against Australia's demands for a build-up of military strength in Malaya and Singapore. The Australians, the military men on the spot in Singapore, and the service chiefs in London all realized that air power was vital to cripple any invading force before it established a foothold. The Chiefs of Staff recommended sending aircraft and a fleet of four veteran battleships to the East, to be supplemented by two more ships in early 1942. Churchill, however, decided instead to send spare tanks and fighter planes to Russia, and to dispatch the *Prince of Wales*, accompanied by the veteran cruiser *Repulse* and an aircraft-carrier, to Singapore. The

Prime Minister was convinced that this fast and most modern of battleships, nicknamed "*HMS Unsinkable*" and pride of the British navy, would deter the Japanese into keeping the peace and that it would "exercise a vague general fear and menace all points at once".

Churchill took these decisions against the advice of all professional experts, including the First Sea Lord and Admiral Sir Tom Phillips, who was to be Commander-in-Chief of the Eastern fleet. The decisions had no strategic justification. The manoeuvrable modern Hurricane fighters, which would have been invaluable in Singapore, were of little use in the Russian campaign. The *Prince of Wales* had no deterrent impact on the Japanese, who had already decided that time had run out on their diplomatic wrangles and were preparing for war.

Early in 1941 Colonel Masanobu Tsuji, a veteran of the China campaign, was allocated a shoestring budget and put in charge of a small Southern Military Studies research group in Taiwan to investigate problems of jungle warfare. Tsuji was given a report drawn up by two senior Japanese army officers, who had visited Malaya in September 1940. They advised that any attack on Singapore would have to come from the north and reported that the British air force in Malaya was understrength and its planes obsolete.[15] Tsuji appreciated, as Percival and Dobbie had pointed out, that a frontal attack on Singapore was scarcely feasible but her back door stood open, and he realized that British propaganda was deluding only her own people.

Tsuji embarked on his task with enthusiasm and verve. The challenge was enormous, for the Japanese army had no experience of jungle warfare. Soldiers accustomed to cold weather fighting had to be trained to face tropical conditions, and the cavalry, which was used in China, would have to ride bicycles. The Japanese set up an espionage centre in Bangkok under Major Iwaichi Fujiwara, and in the three months before the outbreak of war, spies speaking fluent Malay, English, Cantonese, or Hokkien were sent to Singapore and Malaya to gather information and to stir up dissension among Indian troops in northern Malaya.

Japan's major long-term war plan was geared to attacking Russia, and it was only in September 1941 that the Japanese Cabinet decided to concentrate on a southward thrust, if negotiations to persuade the United States to lift economic sanctions were unsuccessful. In October 1941 the moderates in the Japanese Cabinet resigned, the aggressive General Hideki Tojo became Prime Minister, and early the following month the Japanese decision to attack was confirmed. Japan did not aspire to total victory but aimed to force a compromise peace on the United States and Britain in order to guarantee the resources needed to complete her war in China.

The 25th Japanese Army, which was hurriedly assembled for the invasion of Malaya, was put under the command of Lieutenant-General Tomoyuki Yamashita, who was Tojo's contemporary and rival and probably Japan's most able general. As head of the Japanese military mission, which had recently spent six months in Germany and Italy, he was impressed by the professionalism of the German army, if not by Hitler, whom he found to be "like a bank clerk when I had to talk with him face to face". On his return to Tokyo, Yamashita pressed for radical military reform, and in his Malayan campaign he put into practice much of what he had learned in Germany. A stickler for detail and precise planning, he had no time for those who valued spiritual fervour above material strength.

Yamashita was offered four divisions but decided to employ only three, knowing that this was the maximum force that could be fed and maintained as his supply lines became extended south. The 25th Army comprised the Imperial Guards, the seasoned 18th Division and the highly experienced crack 5th Division, which was one of the best in the Japanese army. Of an invasion force of 26,000 men, 17,300 combat troops would be immediately available, and Yamashita felt confident of victory, given adequate sea and air cover to make the initial landing. The able Lieutenant-General Sosaku Suzuki was Yamashita's chief of staff, while Tsuji became head of operations staff. With the exception of Takuma Nishimura, commander of the Imperial Guards, the leaders quickly responded to the impressive personality of Yamashita, who inspired respect among his officers and hero-worship among the rank and file. Even Tsuji, who was Tojo's protégé and in a sense belonged to a rival faction, acknowledged Yamashita as a man "who enforced upon all under his orders a military and moral discipline as rigorous as the autumn frost". The compliment was not returned: in his diary Yamashita commented on Tsuji, "this man is egotistical and wily. He is a sly dog and unworthy to serve the country. He is a manipulator to be carefully watched".[16]

Meanwhile, Duff Cooper, Brooke-Popham, and other British leaders were still convinced that Japan would attack Russia and would certainly not invade Malaya during the northeast monsoon. They were sure the Japanese were weary after long years of fighting in China, that their soldiers were inferior, and their aircraft obsolete.

Singaporeans were reassured by the sight of the *Prince of Wales* and *Repulse* as they sailed proudly up the Johor Strait to the naval base on 2 December 1941. Governor Brooke-Popham, Percival, Duff Cooper, the air force and naval commanders and many other dignitaries were there to greet them, and the base was "like Portsmouth in Navy Week".[17] In the words of Duff Cooper, the ships "conferred a sense of complete security".[18] But they had been forced to sail without their accompanying aircraft-carrier, which had run aground, and their only support craft were four small destroyers, two of them in poor shape. As a senior Australian officer commented, the fleet "went quickly from cream to skimmed milk".[19] Without protective air cover, the ships were too vulnerable in Singapore, and Phillips proposed to remove them to Manila.

By the end of the first week of December, the air was alive with expectancy in Singapore. Servicemen were recalled to duty, sailors were summoned back to their ships, and the naval base was blacked out. No similar precautions were taken in the town, and neither civil nor military authorities were prepared for the speed and intensity of Japan's onslaught, the quality of her aircraft, or the fighting mettle of her soldiers.

The Japanese appreciated that success depended on surprise to deal an immediate crippling blow against the United States' Pacific fleet and to establish a firm foothold on the Malay Peninsula. Within a few hours on the night of 7/8 December (Malayan time), the Japanese destroyed the American fleet in Pearl Harbor, invaded Hong Kong and the Philippines, landed troops in southern Thailand at Singgora, with ancillary landings at Patani and Kota Bharu, and dropped the first bombs on Singapore.

From the start the British lost the initiative. Prevarications in Whitehall made it impossible to launch a proposed "Matador" plan to enter southern Thailand and pre-empt any Japanese attack before it reached Malaya. The Thais put up virtually no resistance to the landing of Yamashita's main force, and within a few hours Japanese troops were established ashore at Singgora, Patani, and Kota Bharu. Admiral Phillips, faced with the necessity of removing his fleet from its exposed position in Singapore, decided to dash north to intercept any further Japanese invading forces. Without a supporting aircraft-carrier this was at best a risky undertaking, but it was not until the fleet was well under way that Phillips learned the Kota Bharu airfield was already in Japanese hands, and there would be no air support at all. Sighted by the Japanese, Phillips turned back but was too late to escape the Japanese air force's torpedo bombers. By the afternoon of 10 December, the two great ships were sunk, the Commander-in-Chief of the British Eastern fleet was dead, and the Japanese had control of the sea. No single incident did more to dash the defenders' morale and to exhilarate the Japanese.

Air superiority was crucial. In principle air power was the cornerstone of the British defence, but it was woefully inadequate. In the autumn of 1940 the Chiefs of Staff had agreed that 582 aircraft would be the optimum number but only expected to be able to provide 336. On the day of the invasion, Malaya had only 158 planes, of which 24 were obsolete Vildebeestes.[20] Within twenty-four hours the Japanese had mastery of the air; they had knocked out more than half the British aircraft operational in northern Malaya, and seized the inadequately protected British airfields in the north, which were invaluable to them in the ensuing campaign. British defence plans had depended on control of the air to repel attacks until the arrival of the fleet, with the army playing an ancillary role to hold the beaches, protect the airfields, and concentrate on the naval base and Singapore Island. In the first two days of the Malayan campaign the basis of this defence was destroyed. Air control was lost. The naval base was nearly empty. The army thenceforth had to bear the brunt of the campaign and to fight the whole length of the peninsula.

On the outbreak of war Duff Cooper was made Resident Minister for Far Eastern Affairs and formed a Far East War Council, which met daily and comprised the Governor, Percival, the naval and air force commanders and an Australian representative. Japanese newspapers were closed down, and all Japanese residents were arrested and subsequently sent to internment camps in India. As Commander-in-Chief Far East, Brooke-Popham issued an order of the day, declaring that Malaya was prepared and ready "to cripple the power of the enemy to endanger our ideals, our possessions and our peace", and to destroy the force of "a Japan drained for years by the exhausting claims of her wanton onslaught on China".

The battle for Singapore became a question of time, depending on whether Japanese troops could be held back in the peninsula until reinforcements reached Singapore. At the outbreak of war, Malaya had three full infantry divisions – one Australian and two Indian – but a large proportion of the troops were poorly trained and badly equipped. They had no tanks, few armoured cars, and few anti-tank or mobile anti-aircraft weapons. The Chiefs of Staff in London decided to divert to Singapore the 18th British Division, together with some anti-tank and anti-aircraft regiments, which were then *en route* to the Middle East, but a Far East fleet could not be assembled for several months, and there was little prospect of supplying much air support.

In a *kirimomi sakusen*, or driving charge, the Japanese swept down the Malay Peninsula, carried forward by audacious planning, good fortune, and the exhilaration bred by success. The main body of the force was composed of disciplined, hardy, and vigorous soldiers, who had fought together in the China campaign and were experienced in amphibious warfare. Yamashita used his mastery of the air and the coastal waters to conduct a dynamic technique of infiltration, and enveloping and outflanking that bewildered the defenders and compelled them to withdraw to avoid being cut off from the rear. Confined by the communications system of one trunk road and railway line, the British defence lacked mobility, and the Japanese could defeat them in detail. Without tanks and anti-tank guns or prepared lines of defence, the Commonwealth retreat was inevitable, and the Japanese drove relentlessly south. The Commonwealth commanders were at loggerheads. In particular Major-General Gordon Bennett, the fearless but irascible commander of the Australian Division, was critical of the retreat tactics employed by Major-General Lewis Heath, commander of the Indian troops in northern Malaya, and also disputed the disposition of Australian and Indian troops made by Percival in Johor.

Refugees streamed south into Singapore, and in an effort to maintain morale strict censorship was put on news of military disasters. Newspapers were forbidden to report the fall of Penang on 18 December, but it was soon common knowledge. Singaporeans were horrified to learn that Europeans had been evacuated from the island, leaving the local people to their fate, and at a tense press conference, community leaders demanded assurance from Brooke-Popham that there would be no such discrimination in Singapore.

On Christmas Day the Japanese began broadcasting propaganda from the Penang wireless station, and three days later dropped their first leaflets on Singapore. They urged Asians to rise against their European masters and to light up their homes in order to protect themselves from Japanese bombers. According to one observer, "the mutiny of 1915 lay like a shadow over the conversation",[21] making the authorities even more concerned to bolster confidence, preserve an air of normality and calm fears. The Governor refused to demand or even encourage the evacuation of foreign women and children, in order to avoid charges of racial bias. Apart from the American community, only a trickle of people departed, and ships left Singapore half empty throughout December 1941. The same routine prevailed in civil administration: officials continuing to bicker and be preoccupied with official memos, files, procedure, and a meticulous regard for petty legalities. This unwillingness to divulge accurate information and reluctance to harness the community to the war effort brought widespread criticism of the top leadership. The ageing Brooke-Popham was a hesitant speaker, lacking incisiveness, and he inspired no public confidence. Before the Pacific War broke out, it had been arranged that General Sir Henry Pownall would take over from Brooke-Popham, and Pownall's arrival on 23 December 1941 was hailed with enthusiasm and high expectations.

The strongest criticisms were levelled at the civil administrators, and in particular at Governor Sir Shenton Thomas, whom an American journalist described as "an uninformed individual ... a slave to Civil Service cliches, bromides and banalities ... he lives in a dream world".[22] Kindly and conscientious, Thomas had been chosen Governor eight years before to soothe ruffled feelings created by his predecessor and guide Malaya prudently out of the economic depression. In this task he had succeeded, and his relationship with his officials and with European and Asian civilians was cordial. But Thomas was not a man to lead or inspire the colony in an all-out war. The qualities of compromise and conciliation, the willingness to consult and if need be defer to the opinions of his officials, which had made him an effective and popular peacetime Governor, left him a weak, vacillating, and indecisive leader in a crisis. Thomas's aimless rambling broadcasts failed to create confidence and trust.

Criticism of the Governor extended to the Malayan Civil Service, described at the time as "a nineteenth century organization run by privileged mediocrities, trying to cope with a twentieth century crisis".[23] The Australian representative on the Far East War Council complained to his government that "in the Malayan civil service there seems to be too much of the old bureaucratic doctrine that action means to risk making blunders and inaction means safety".[24] The *Straits Times*, under the outspoken editorship of George Seabridge, thundered at the civil service throughout the Malayan campaign, and was largely instrumental in getting the Colonial Secretary replaced in late January.

The press and vocal elements of the public pinned their main hopes on Duff Cooper, who was decisive, energetic, and an impressive broadcaster – clear, straightforward, and not given to clichés. The *Straits Times* backed Cooper, calling on him to devise machinery to assume control in Singapore,[25] but his powers as Chairman of the Far East War Council were ill-defined. He proposed to appoint Brigadier Simson as Director-General of Civil Defence with plenary powers in Singapore and Johor, but the Governor limited Simson's scope. Thomas was also reluctant to accede to Cooper's proposals to proclaim martial law. Eventually, at the end of December, a modified form of martial law and a curfew were imposed, but the military authorities had limited powers, and Singapore never came under full martial rule even at the end.

Despite disillusionment with some of the military and civilian leaders, there was still in Singapore an air of unreal calm. The use of the word "fortress" convinced Singaporeans that their island was defended on all sides, although their eyes could tell them it was not. After the first night of the war there were few air raids on Singapore throughout the rest of December. On New Year's Day the *Straits Times* commented. "Terrible changes have taken place with a rapidity that still leaves us a little bewildered," but "We are not overwhelmed: we shall not be overwhelmed … we shall be rejoicing before 1943 comes round."

In a last-minute attempt to provide overall military leadership, Field Marshal Sir Archibald Wavell was appointed Supreme Commander in the Far East, over British, American, Australian, and Dutch forces. Wavell arrived in Singapore on 7 January 1942 but established his headquarters in Java, taking Pownall with him as Chief of Staff. The first result of Wavell's appointment was the recall to London of Duff Cooper, whose post became redundant with the creation of a Generalissimo. Cooper's transfer led to a public outcry. He had accomplished very little but seemed like a breath of fresh air, and the *Straits Times* appealed in vain for his retention as "the last bulwark against that minute paper mentality to which many of our present anxieties must be attributed".[26]

With Cooper's departure, the *Straits Times* called for the appointment of a military governor for Singapore to give overall direction and cut through red tape, but Wavell made no move to create such an office. Shenton Thomas instructed the Malayan Civil Service, "The day of minute papers has gone ... the day of letters and reports is over ... the essential thing is speed in action," but, as the *Straits Times* commented, "The announcement is about two and a half years too late."

By the time of Wavell's appointment, the Malayan campaign had reached a critical stage. On the day of his arrival in Singapore, the Japanese routed the 11th Indian Division and the Argyll and Sutherland Highlanders at Slim River. On 11 January they occupied Kuala Lumpur and five days later broke the Australian defences at the Muar River. This was the last defensive position on the peninsula, and Percival had warned Gordon Bennett, the Australian commander, that "if this position is lost, the battle of Singapore is lost".

On 19 January Wavell cabled Churchill to warn him that Singapore could probably not hold out once Johor was lost. Churchill was aghast. He had presumed the Japanese advance would be checked while they waited for the arrival of artillery to attack Singapore's fortifications and that this would give time for British reinforcements to take up their positions. For the first time he now realized that the northern shores of Singapore were not fortified. "Seaward batteries and naval base do not constitute a fortress, which is a completely encircled strong place", he protested.

Up to that time political leaders in Britain, ignorant of conditions in Singapore, were blinded by their own terminology. The legend of "fortress" Singapore's invincibility as "the Gibraltar of the East" had spread so wide that everyone except the Japanese planners and some of the British military commanders were lulled into a sense of security. As Churchill later commented, "The possibility of Singapore having no landward defences no more entered into my mind than that of a battleship being launched without a bottom."[27]

Churchill ordered that the "entire male population" be conscripted for defence works. "The most rigorous compulsion is to be used." "The whole island must be fought for until every single unit and every single strong-point has been separately destroyed: finally, the city of Singapore must be converted into a citadel and defended to the death. No surrender can be contemplated." "I want to make it absolutely clear that I expect every inch of ground to be defended, every scrap of material or defences to be blown to pieces to prevent capture by the enemy, and no question of surrender to be entertained until after protracted fighting among the ruins of Singapore city."

Churchill now feared that at best Commonwealth forces could only turn the inevitable Japanese capture of Singapore into a Pyrrhic victory, and he asked his Chiefs of Staff whether it would be better to cut losses and divert fresh reinforcements to defend Burma. The ultimate decision to prolong the fight was made on political rather than military grounds. It was dictated partly by feelings of responsibility to Singapore and Malaya, and of a need to match the ferocious defence of their homeland by Britain's Russian allies and the stout American and Filipino resistance in the Philippines. But Britain's prime consideration was her obligation to Australia, who considered Singapore to be the keystone of her own defence. On Christmas Day Churchill had promised Australian Prime Minister John Curtin that Singapore would be held "with the utmost tenacity". Reports that the British government was discussing abandoning Singapore provoked the Australian War Cabinet into holding an emergency meeting on 23 January, when Curtin cabled Churchill that any such withdrawal would be "an inexcusable betrayal" of his country. He complained, "We have acted and carried out our part of the bargain. We expect you not to frustrate the whole purpose by evacuation." There were bitter recriminations in the Far East War Council in Singapore when the Australian representative accused the British of regarding Singapore as having "nothing more than sentimental value" and deplored the prospect of the Australian 8th Division being cooped up and sacrificed in Singapore, while British reinforcements were diverted to Burma.

Fresh Commonwealth forces poured into Singapore. The 45th Indian Brigade landed at the beginning of January, 7,000 Indians of the 44th Brigade on 22 January, 3,000 Australians two days later, the main body of the 18th British Division on 29 January and its remaining battalions on 5 February. The Indians were semi-trained, and the Australians were raw recruits, many of them posted within a fortnight of enlisting. The British, who were diverted *en route* for the Middle East desert war, were fresh and fit but inexperienced, fed on a diet of contempt for their Japanese adversary on the ship and, in the words of one of them, "so much greener than the lushest grass around".[28]

Belated attempts were made to rally the local population to their own defence. About 8,000 civilians were already enrolled for voluntary service, nearly 2,000 of them forming the Singapore battalion of the Straits Settlements Volunteer Corps. Another 5,000 others were attached to auxiliary medical, fire, and air raid precaution organizations, and a further 1,000 were in the volunteer police reserve and local defence.

At the Governor's request Tan Kah-kee convened a meeting at the Singapore Chinese Chamber of Commerce, which formed a Singapore Chinese Mobilization Committee under his chairmanship, with a Volunteer Police force, which was headed by Tay Koh Yat, and a Labour section under Lim Bo Seng.[29] Members of the illegal Malayan Communist Party were welcomed as "loyal supporters of the British cause". Communist manifestos urging all-out war were printed in the three English-language newspapers, and political prisoners were released from gaol. Shenton Thomas had no qualms. "Post-war repercussions do not concern us in this emergency," he informed the Secretary of State.[30]

Thousands of Chinese flocked to help from all sectors of society, old and young, rich and poor. The Mobilization Council urged the government to arm a Chinese force, and demonstrators paraded the streets singing Chinese war songs and carrying placards saying, "Give us guns and we will fight". A Singapore Chinese Anti-Japanese Volunteer Battalion was formed, commonly known as Dalforce, since it was put under the command of Lieutenant-Colonel John Dalley of the Federated Malay States police force. With Hu Tie Jun as his deputy, Dalley set up his headquarters in a Chinese school and formed a motley collection of male and female students from schools and Raffles College, clerks, rickshaw pullers and dance hall hostesses into eight battalions of about 150 recruits each. Clad in blue uniforms with red triangles on their sleeves and yellow headbands, and equipped with elementary weapons – mostly shotguns, parangs and hand grenades – the volunteers were put through ten days' crash training. On 4 February they were posted to guard the Jurong Road, where they put up fierce resistance to the invaders and continued to do so even after Dalley formally disbanded the force on 13 February.[31]

The Mobilization Council met daily at the Chinese Protectorate and harnessed labour for manning essential services and constructing defences under Lim Bo Seng's leadership. A prominent Hokkien businessman and former student of Raffles Institution and Hong Kong University, Lim Bo Seng had taken such an active part in anti-Japanese activities before the war that the British had considered banishing him. At the Governor's request, he now formed a Chinese Liaison Committee for civil defence, with the help of the Malayan Communist Party, which claimed to control about seventy labour unions, including construction workers and dockers. Belatedly, on 29 January, the Legislative Council rushed through a measure to legalize the conscription of labour, and two days later the British government agreed to pay higher wages and compensation rates. By that time it was too late for the government either to attract or to impress labour because constant air raids in vital areas made work so dangerous, and Lim Bo Seng's committee was the only organization that could marshal workers. Even in this hour of peril old enmities still threatened the new-found unity of the Singapore Chinese. Chungking appealed to the British government to remove Tan Kah-kee as head of the Mobilization Council, but the Governor insisted that Tan was essential and he was not a communist.[32] While Tan Kah-kee was willing to assemble voluntary policemen and labourers, he opposed arming civilians to fight the Japanese, convinced that the British would give up and abandon them to terrible retribution. He blamed the British for obstructing the pre-war Nanyang Chinese Anti-Japanese Salvation Movement,[33] and when Dalforce was formed, Tan paid his employees' salaries, closed down his business, and on 3 February he fled Singapore.[34]

It was not until the second half of January that air raids on Singapore became intense. While the main targets were the airfields, which were Singapore's only hope of counter-attack, many bombs fell in the town, causing terrible casualties in the crowded streets. Often there would be three air raids in one night and as many more by day.

Despite the carnage, there was little panic among the local population, and the expatriate community, not crediting that danger was so near, tried to maintain a "normal" life. Evacuees only began to leave in large numbers in late January, priority being given to mothers and children. The elderly and childless had to wait, and exit permits were refused for European and Asian men of military age, who were all required to register for service. Banks were so crowded that clients could hardly get in the doors, and transport became difficult after cars and bicycles were requisitioned in the last week of January. Hotels, boarding houses, and private homes were crowded with refugees from up-country, and many restaurants and nightclubs closed down, but Raffles Hotel continued to hold its nightly dances, while the cinemas and the New World Cabaret remained open in the final days before the surrender.

On 27 January Wavell gave Percival permission to withdraw to the island when necessary but told him that Singapore must be held at all cost. On the last day of the month, the remaining 30,000 Commonwealth troops withdrew without casualty across the Causeway, marching in good order, with the ninety surviving Argyll and Sutherlanders and the bagpipes of the Gordon Highlanders bringing up the rear. With the help of Lim Bo Seng's Quarry Workers' Union, a 60-yard gap was then blown in the Causeway. It was a tense day, with the remnants of the Navy standing by to ferry survivors across to the island, but no Japanese planes came to molest the retreat.

It was twenty-four hours before the bewildered people of Singapore realized their island was beleaguered, but the censor still refused to allow correspondents to use the word "siege", and most civilians failed to appreciate the danger.

The troops who arrived back after seven weeks of continuous retreat and disaster, weary, hungry, dirty, and decimated, were appalled. All remaining bombers and most fighters had been withdrawn to Sumatra, since Tengah, Seletar and Sembawang airfields were under constant artillery fire from the mainland. The one fighter squadron of eight Hurricanes and six slow Brewster Buffaloes remaining at Kallang found it difficult to operate from the bomb-pitted runway. No defences had been prepared for the north coast of the island, and the exhausted soldiers retreating from the peninsular campaign had to set to work to construct the last-ditch defences themselves. Singapore's peacetime population of 550,000 had nearly doubled as refugees poured over from the mainland. Military leaders deplored this influx, which complicated defence and put great strain on supplies of food and water, but the civilian authorities refused to risk racial disharmony by barring entry to Asians while admitting the European minority.

Throughout eight days of brilliant weather the two armies faced each other across the Johor Strait, divided by less than a thousand yards of water, the Japanese massing for their final onslaught, the Commonwealth forces hurriedly preparing their defences. Yamashita installed his headquarters in the sultan's palace at Johor Bahru, from the heights of which he could survey Singapore Island, the naval base and Tengah airfield. Since Japanese reconnaissance aircraft could fly without hindrance over Singapore, it was difficult to construct defensive positions. Singapore's guns remained almost silent, partly to conserve ammunition and partly in an attempt even at this late stage to allay civilian alarm. No move was made to mine the Johor Strait, presumably in order not to harm soldiers escaping from the mainland or to impede Australian patrols that crossed the Strait at night to reconnoitre.

The central object of Singapore's defence plan, the protection of the naval base, was now shattered. With the opposite shore in enemy hands, the naval base was useless, and the remaining ships had gone. On the day on which the troops withdrew to the island, most European naval and civilian dockyard staff quit Singapore for Ceylon, leaving to the bewildered and battle-worn soldiers the disheartening task of destroying the base that had been their prime duty to protect. As Pownall noted in his diary, "the whole reason for building and defending Singapore, which has cost so many million pounds, has now gone.... So that is the end of a long, long story".[35]

Now the object was to hold Singapore Island as long as possible and inflict maximum damage on the Japanese, a contingency for which the defence plans had never provided. The permanent defences of Singapore were designed to protect the base and harbour from sea attack. There were fixed coastal defences at the Changi entrance to the naval base and the approaches to Keppel Harbour. For 20 miles from Changi along the south coast the beaches were strongly defended with pillboxes, anti-tank obstacles, barbed wire and land-mines, well-supported by anti-naval artillery. The whole northern shore lay naked and vulnerable to attack, and although the guns could be adapted to fire landwards, they were of little use, since they had only armour-piercing and no anti-personnel shells.

Government offices, shops and commercial houses continued to operate, but the city felt like "a ship without a rudder".[36] The defence of Singapore in this unexpected crisis depended upon dynamic leadership and adaptability, but neither the Governor nor the military commander were men to inspire a sense of urgency and strength in such an emergency. According to Pownall, Thomas needed "continual stirring up", and Percival was not the man to do it, since he had "the knowledge but not the personality to carry through a tough fight" and was himself "an uninspiring leader and rather gloomy".[37] As a colonial Governor, Thomas saw his first duty to the colony under his charge, not to military interests, and he opposed any rigid scorched earth policy. His main concern was to prevent panic, and he was probably the only individual in authority who genuinely believed that Singapore could hold out after Johor had been abandoned. He ordered expatriate and local officials alike to stay at their posts, forbidding any repetition of the demoralizing and unauthorized evacuation of Europeans that had taken place in Penang.

Arthur Percival, who assumed direct command of the Allied forces once they withdrew to the island, was also a man wholly unsuited for the role fate had suddenly thrust on him. A courageous, humane, and intelligent soldier of great integrity, he was "a brilliant blue-print general"[38] but not a born leader and field commander, and he was slow to adapt to changed circumstances. While he impressed many people who knew him well, Percival lacked public presence. Slight in build, he appeared shy and oversensitive, while his calm manner could easily be mistaken for apathy and weakness. In Yamashita's judgment, Percival was "a nice good man" but uninspiring: "he was good on paper but timid and hesitant in making command decisions".[39] Tired and exhausted after seven weeks of travelling to the front by day and working most of the night, Percival planned for a three-month siege but was convinced the battle was already lost.

Seeing the Japanese attack sweeping down the Malay Peninsula almost exactly with the same strength and in the same way he had predicted four years before, Percival seemed to be going through a nightmare already worked out to its conclusion and was mesmerized into accepting defeat. He saw all the locust years of wasted opportunities and unheeded warnings, when the War Office had neglected the advice of experts on the spot, including himself, and the Singapore Legislative Council had refused money for defences. Percival was all too conscious of the contradictions in his orders to fight to the finish while carrying out a scorched earth policy and systematic demolition. Late in January, when the War Office wanted assurances that everything of value would be destroyed, Percival protested, "You cannot fight and destroy simultaneously with 100 per cent efficiency in both."[40] Nor was it possible to evacuate useless mouths in preparation for a grim last battle, when only limited numbers could be taken to safety and no discrimination could be made between European and Asian without destroying morale.

It was said of Percival at the time that "he had a mind that saw the difficulties to any scheme before it saw the possibilities".[41] Possibilities there were. Singapore had adequate supplies of oil and ammunition, enough food to last six months, and, with rigid economies, the island could manage indefinitely on its water supplies. The defenders had a substantial numerical advantage, and while many of the Commonwealth troops were exhausted and shaken in morale after weeks of retreat, they had a short spell to reorganize and recoup their energies before the battle started afresh. There were also the Singapore Volunteers, the Malay Regiment, which had just been expanded to two battalions on the eve of war, and Dalforce, whose members had everything to lose in the case of failure and were prepared for all-out resistance. Wavell asked Singapore to hold out for one month until reinforcements came to save the day. An armoured brigade was due to arrive early in March, more ships were on their way, and fifty-one Hurricanes had been landed in crates, ready to be assembled.

Instead of an inferior ill-armed, poorly organized rabble, worn out by years of fighting in China, the Commonwealth forces faced a seasoned, disciplined adversary, equipped with up-to-date aircraft and weaponry. In this first encounter with a bewildering enemy, the initial misplaced contempt for the Japanese changed to a feeling of awe and to overrating their capabilities. If the former complacency had not given way to almost paralysing shock and defeatism, the defenders could have exploited many potential weaknesses among the attackers. While they were excellent field soldiers, traditionally the Japanese were not strong in staff work and supply. Divisions of command, obsession with seniority and personal honour encouraged inter-service jealousies, and a rigid devotion to timetables led to recriminations and sometimes to near panic in face of unexpected setbacks.

The success of the Malayan campaign had produced a sense of euphoria and a harmony that was unusual among the Japanese. The speed of the advance had enabled the leaders to push ahead without much interference from Tokyo or from the Southern Army headquarters in Saigon. Indeed Tsuji referred to an "unparalleled co-operation between Army, Navy and Air Force",[42] free from the wranglings and jealousies that plagued Japanese commands elsewhere.

From the early days of the campaign Yamashita was worried by the insubordination of Nishimura, the headstrong and temperamental commander of the Imperial Guards. Unlike the other contingents of the 25th Army, the Guards, though an élite force, had seen no action since the Russo-Japanese War in 1905 and had received no intensive battle training. Yamashita was furious when Field Marshal Count Terauchi, commanding the Southern Army, diverted most of the Japanese air force to bombing Sumatra before the final assault on Singapore was launched. This allowed the Commonwealth forces to retire to the island in good order instead of being pounded and destroyed before they reached the Causeway. With air mastery the Japanese could have played havoc with the convoys bringing in troop reinforcements to Singapore, but the only troopship to be sunk was the *Empress of Asia*, which was bombed in the approaches to the harbour on 5 February. Most of the troops escaped, but she took down with her the bulk of the equipment for the 18th British Division.

Japanese newspapers extolled Yamashita's successes, and by the time he reached the Johor Strait, "the Tiger of Malaya" was Japan's national hero. His success roused the jealousy and concern of Prime Minister Tojo and of Field Marshal Terauchi, his commanding officer. Yamashita tore up the instructions he received from the Southern Army for the attack on Singapore[43] and prepared his own plan, knowing he could expect little further co-operation from headquarters.

In Singapore the defenders had no inkling of these problems. In the headquarters at Fort Canning, or "Confusion Castle" as it was popularly known, there was dissension at all levels. At the War Council meetings, the Australians were at loggerheads with the British. Gordon Bennett was restive, urging counter-attack, and arguing in vain for the appointment of a military adviser to jolt the civilian administration into action.

On 4 February all civilians were evacuated from a belt one mile deep along the north coast, and two days later the demolition of the naval base began, smoke from its burning oil dumps darkening the sky across the whole island. To quieten alarm Percival held a press conference the next day, declaring "Today we stand beleaguered in our island fortress. Our task is to hold this fortress until help can come – as assuredly it will come. This we are determined to do." His words lacked conviction, and privately he knew that the troop reinforcements still being landed in Singapore were being sacrificed in vain.

∽∾

The Japanese had suffered heavy casualties in the peninsular campaign, but, against the advice of his supplies officer, Yamashita intended to attack Singapore before the exhausted Commonwealth troops regained their strength and acquired reinforcements. Since the British had no reconnaissance aircraft and no spies on the mainland, the initiative lay with the Japanese, who could choose their point and time of attack. They were running short of ammunition and food, their supply line was drying up, and they faced the formidable task of invading across the Straits against a numerically superior force. Since the Japanese had captured all of the British army's specially prepared maps of Singapore Island, they were better equipped with maps of the terrain than the defenders, and from reconnaissance they were aware that the Johor Strait and the opposite shore were not mined and that the defending troops were widely spread out. Speed and surprise would be crucial for a successful attack.

Any effective defence depended on preventing the Japanese from establishing a beachhead, and Percival decided to spread his troops along an extended front to guard all the beaches, keeping few troops in reserve, and thus tying himself down in a static defence. His largest force, the newly arrived 18th British Division, was stationed northeast of the Causeway, towards which a Japanese fleet was reported to be approaching, and the Japanese Imperial Guards made feint attacks, occupying Pulau Ubin and firing on Changi. In an ingenious plan, Yamashita reinforced this deception by sending empty convoys clattering eastwards, with lights on and making plenty of noise, but returning silently in darkness. He planned his real onslaught on the northwest, with the object of securing Tengah airfield and the dominant Bukit Timah heights.

An Australian patrol reported the massing of Japanese on the west side of the Johor end of the Causeway on the night of 7/8 February, but the speed and strength of the Japanese attack came as a surprise. Hiding in the jungle and rubber plantations until the last moment, the 5th and 18th Japanese Divisions assembled at the waterfront on the evening of 8 February. Using collapsible boats, brought down by rail and sea after the Singgora landings and where necessary linked together to carry field artillery weapons, thousands of Japanese troops landed silently in the darkness on the northwest coast, infiltrating the creeks and inlets until the defending Australian force found itself outflanked and enveloped on all sides. After hours of desperate and confused hand-to-hand fighting, the defenders had to draw back to a neck of land between the Kranji and Jurong Rivers, which had defensive possibilities but no prepared position apart from a half-dug anti-tank ditch.

By dawn the two Japanese Divisions were firmly established on the island with part of their artillery. By the end of the day Tengah airfield was in their hands, and Yamashita and his staff came across the Strait that night. The Imperial Guards were to force a landing at Kranji but this was almost disastrous, since Nishimura held his troops back and asked for the attack to be called off when the advance party was enveloped in burning oil flowing down the Mandai River. The oil had escaped by accident, but the Japanese feared the defenders might intentionally employ this tactic on a large scale. Yamashita was furious with Nishimura, the attack was resumed, and the Japanese gained control of the Singapore end of the Causeway. The defenders' demolition work was only partially effective, since the charge was inadequate to make a big enough breach to allow for low tide, and within four days Yamashita's engineers had the Causeway repaired and fully operational.

Once Japanese troops were firmly established on the island, the only hope for the defenders was to hold them along the Jurong-Kranji line, but this position was weakened when one commander misinterpreted as an immediate order a tentative plan issued by Percival outlining withdrawal to a proposed final battle defensive perimeter. On 10 February Churchill cabled Wavell insisting,

> There must at this stage be no thought of saving the troops or sparing the population. The battle must be fought to the bitter end at all costs .... Commanders and senior officers should die with their troops. The honour of the British Empire and of the British Army is at stake. I rely on you to show no mercy to weakness in any form ... the whole reputation of our country and our race is involved.[44]

Wavell, who visited Singapore for the last time on that day, urged Percival that there must be no surrender and recommended a determined counter-attack to hold the Kranji-Jurong line.

The ill-armed but determined members of Dalforce and other Chinese irregulars fought alongside the Commonwealth troops, many units fighting to the last man, but by the early hours of 11 February the line was broken and the Japanese were in command of Bukit Timah village. Yamashita was delighted to have breached this last defensive position, and Japanese aircraft dropped leaflets calling for surrender, but fierce resistance continued. The following day, Percival withdrew his troops to a final perimeter round the city stretching from Pasir Panjang to Kallang.

The last British planes flew off to Sumatra on 11 February, by which time Kallang aerodrome was under constant shelling. After that, the Japanese could watch everything undisturbed from an observation balloon, and the Penang wireless station poured out messages and propaganda to break morale. Within the town all was confusion and despair. About one million people were now crowded into a 3-mile radius from the waterfront, exposed to incessant bombing by day and shelling by night. There were no air-raid shelters and the dispersal camps on the outskirts of town were in enemy hands. The crowded tenements of Chinatown were death traps in air raids, and it is impossible to say how many civilians were killed in the last days of fighting. Some estimate the figure at 500, others as high as 2,000, a day. There were gruesome horrors, such as the destruction by fire of the wooden-hutted Indian Base Hospital at Tyersall when nearly all the 200 patients were burned to death. The regular hospitals were crowded, and hotels, schools, and clubs were taken over as emergency hospitals. Over all the pall of black smoke from the burning oil dumps rained down soot.

The army had not only to fight a last-ditch stand in the crowded city but to carry out a scorched earth policy at the same time. The Governor ordered the destruction of rubber stocks and the tin-smelting plant on Pulau Brani. To prevent any repetition of the invading army's drunken rampage through Chinese cities, he decreed the smashing of the massive stocks of alcohol, which Singapore held as supplier to the whole of Southeast Asia: some 1,500,000 bottles of spirits and 60,000 gallons of *samsu*. Thomas refused demands by the military to demolish small Chinese work-shops on which the livelihood of their owners depended, but he ordered the destruction of the stocks and machinery of British-owned engineering plants, often in the teeth of their owners' opposition. The wireless station was smashed and most of the currency burned, but destruction of the port facilities was hampered because the Harbour Board's key technicians had evacuated without notifying the government.

On 13 February, despite fierce and gallant resistance by the 1st Battalion of the Malay Regiment, the Japanese broke through the Gap on Pasir Panjang ridge. By afternoon the whole city lay within range of their artillery. No defensive position was left and the heavily populated town lay immediately behind the front line. All reservoirs were in Japanese hands. They did not turn the water off, knowing the problem they would face in getting it functioning again later, but the pipes in town were so damaged by bombing and shelling that most water was running to waste. By 14 February most areas of town, including hospitals, had no water. Without labour to clear the debris, bury the dead, or mend broken sewers, the town was filled with the stench of filth and death.

Percival appealed to Wavell for discretion to surrender to avoid the inevitable slaughter of the population, but Wavell cabled on 13 February, "You must continue to inflict maximum damage on enemy for as long as possible by house to house fighting if necessary." The following day, the Governor appealed to Percival to surrender and cabled the Colonial Office to warn how desperate the position was, but Wavell still insisted, "Your gallant stand is serving a purpose and must be continued to the limit of endurance."

Not only the Governor but all the military commanders argued the futility of going on, and, without informing Percival, Gordon

Bennett cabled the Australian Prime Minister, declaring he would surrender to avoid loss of life if the enemy entered the city. Still bound by his orders, Percival ordered resistance to continue, but arrangements were made to evacuate military nurses, vital staff officers, and technicians, who were allotted more than half of the 3,000 places aboard the few ships that remained in the harbour. The rest were taken up by civilians, mainly European women and children and Chinese, many of whom had been prominent in the anti-Japanese movement and active in the final defence of Singapore. For the first time there was a real scramble to escape, and many ugly scenes as army deserters struggled to seize places on the fleeing ships. Clifford Pier and the docks were in turmoil with Japanese planes strafing the evacuees, and the Japanese navy was waiting in the "Bomb Alley" of the Bangka Strait to intercept those who got away. Of the forty-four ships, all but four were sunk within two days of leaving Singapore, and nearly all the last-minute refugees were captured or killed.

While still urging Percival on, Wavell cabled Churchill on 14 February to tell him the situation was hopeless, and the Prime Minister gave permission for surrender when no useful purpose could be gained from continuing to fight. On the morning of Sunday, 15 February, Chinese New Year's Day, Percival held a final conference at Fort Canning. Petrol supplies and ammunition were almost exhausted. Makeshift hospitals in schools and clubs were crowded, and 10,000 patients were crammed into the 1,000-bed General Hospital. Parts of the city, including the civilian hospital, had been without water for twenty-four hours, and the danger of epidemic was imminent. Soldiers were deserting in the hundreds and roaming the streets. Thoroughfares were cluttered with overturned cars and trams, and traffic was snarled up bumper to bumper. Any counter-attack was out of the question.

All agreed on the need to capitulate in order to avert inevitable massacre, and Hugh Fraser, the Colonial Secretary, was sent to ask the Japanese to discuss peace terms. In view of the continued fierce resistance, Yamashita was astonished to hear the British wanted to parley and at first suspected a ruse.

Unbeknown to Percival, the Japanese general's own position was critical, and he could not afford to lose time. His ammunition was almost exhausted, his supply lines dried up, and he feared that the British would draw him into fierce house-to-house fighting, which could be disastrous for his smaller force. His senior officers were urging him to withdraw, but Yamashita had decided to overrule them. He planned to bluff by shooting off his dwindling supply of ammunition as if he had limitless stocks and launching an all-out attack on the town centre that night, with the object of splitting the defence in two and forcing defeat on the British before they could exploit his weakness.[45] Given the defenders' demoralized state, it is likely that Yamashita's bold plan to strike through the centre to the waterfront would have succeeded, unleashing an unrestrained soldiery on a defenceless civilian population.[46]

Suspicious and wary, Yamashita summoned Percival to come in person to the headquarters that he had established at the Ford factory in Bukit Timah. The adversaries began the interview by talking at cross purposes. Taking his surrender as assumed, Percival started discussing terms, while Yamashita kept thumping the table and demanding brusquely whether Percival was offering to surrender or not. Misinterpreting Yamashita's puzzlement, Percival thought the burly Japanese general with the glaring eyes was trying to humiliate him. After an hour of confused argument, Yamashita compelled Percival to accept surrender but acceded to the British commander's request that the Japanese army should not enter the city until the following morning. Yamashita thought Percival was a good man, who could be trusted, and, in view of his weak position, he was only too happy to agree to a peaceful handover that would avoid further bloodshed. A skeleton force of armed Commonwealth soldiers was to keep the peace until the Japanese took over, and all troops were commanded to remain at their posts to ensure an orderly surrender. A few made their escape after the ceasefire, including Gordon Bennett, who succeeded in reaching Australia but was subsequently officially reprimanded.

By mid-afternoon most guns were silent, and at 8.30 p.m. complete quiet came to the city. The night of the surrender was one of eerie but foreboding calm after the horrors of the past week's fighting. Victory brought a thrill of exhilaration to Japan and her allies. The previous year German military leaders had told Yamashita it would probably take five divisions eighteen months to conquer Singapore.[47] In fact the mission had been accomplished by three divisions in just over two months. For the British, the loss of Singapore was the blackest moment of the Second World War and, in the words of Winston Churchill, "the worst disaster and largest capitulation in British history".

The scapegoat was the unfortunate Percival, for whom Singapore was the end of a promising career. After more than three years of hardship and ill-treatment as a prisoner of war in Singapore, Japan, and Manchuria, Percival retired without recognition at the end of the war. His reputation remained under a cloud until his death in 1966, but he consistently refused to vindicate himself, seeking only to protect the reputation of the men who had served under him. Even Gordon Bennett, who clashed with Percival more strongly than most men, admitted that "the system was more to blame than the individual".[48]

At the time Wavell claimed that if Singapore could have held out for one more month, sufficient reinforcements could have been assembled to drive the Japanese back. Yamashita and Tsuji considered that if the British had held on for three more days, the Japanese would have been forced to call off their attack. Even if Percival had appreciated the weakness of the Japanese position, the price of further resistance would have been appalling. Amid ruins and carnage, a more ruthless, single-minded fire-eating military commander might have sent Singapore's name down in sacrificial glory in the annals of British military history. Thousands of Chinese were to die in the early days of the occupation, and death in battle would have been kinder for many British, Australian, and Indian troops than the terrible fate they later suffered in prison camps or on the notorious "death railway" in Thailand. But for most of the people of Singapore in February 1942, it was fortunate that she was not defended by such a commander. The Malayan campaign was the first encounter between Commonwealth troops and an enemy whose tactics were to defy larger forces of more experienced and better-equipped troops later in the war. As one of their commanders later said, "It was a case of British academics fighting Jap realists. They are not bloody marvels, but they are intensely practical and keen, and therefore aggressive and very, very fast."[49]

The defenders grossly underestimated their enemy, they made numerous tactical mistakes both on the mainland and in Singapore, and the long-term defence plans were thrown into the melting pot by unexpected disasters in the first two years of the Second World War. The seeds of the ultimate disaster were sown in pre-war days: in official parsimony and bickering, in lack of co-ordination between the services, creating a naval base without a navy, and airfields with virtually no aircraft or ground forces to protect them. "As a substitute for battleships (Britain) built the Naval Base at Singapore",[50] a base created to meet a set of circumstances that never existed. Ultimately it stemmed from the fact that "the military power of the British Empire was gravely over extended".[51] In terms of physical damage to the Allied war effort, the loss of Singapore was immense. It opened the way to the Japanese conquest of the Netherlands East Indies and her acquisition of vast resources of oil, rubber and tin, which would have been invaluable to the Allies. It did not lead, as the Australians had dreaded, to the invasion of the Australian mainland. As a naval base, Singapore was no more use to Japan than it had been to Britain, and Japanese naval superiority ended at the Battle of Midway in June 1942.

When the Japanese took Singapore, Tsuji claimed that "everything that Great Britain had built up here (since 1819) in the Far East had now been beaten to a stand-still".[52] Certainly, as the Japanese took over the city, the economy of Malaya upon which the British regime was founded lay symbolically in ruins before them: the rubber stocks smouldering, the tin-smelting works on Pulau Brani destroyed, and the Pulau Bukum oil on fire.

Tsuji was wrong in that the British returned to power in Singapore only three and a half years later. Physical disaster did not bring the imperial regime to an immediate end, but the events of the first six weeks of 1942 gave the lie to the basis of colonial rule. It undermined the old assumption of racial superiority and the belief that a colonial power could or should defend its subject people without calling on their co-operation. The ruling class was amazed at the inspired heroism of Dalforce and the Chinese irregulars, the tough fighting spirit of the Malay Regiment and the Asian contingents of the Straits Settlements Volunteer Corps, the spirited devotion of the auxiliary civilian voluntary workers, and the ordinary citizen's stoic fortitude in face of danger and death. They were ashamed of their previous doubts about the calibre of Singaporeans and the fact that they had to call on the help of people such as Tan Kah-kee and Lim Bo Seng, who had previously been an embarrassment to them. For a few brief days, racial distinctions and aloofness melted away. In the tragic saga of the Malayan military campaign, most of the actors were foreigners, with the local population until the last scene taking the role of bystanders and victims, but the final battle for Singapore showed of what stuff her people were made.

6

Syonan: Light of the South
1942–1945

The agony of battle was over; the ordeal of occupation was to follow. Singaporeans were numbed, hardly crediting what had happened. Up to the last minute they had believed British statements. For more than a century the security of Singapore in British hands had been taken for granted, but suddenly, in a few weeks, the hollowness of this seeming power had been exposed.

On the morning after the surrender, a small body of Japanese *kempei*, or military police, arrived to take control, but the main Japanese army was held back, and the final orderly surrender meant that the city was spared the horrors of indiscriminate slaughter, rape, and pillage at the hands of an unrestrained soldiery, which the northwestern districts of the island suffered. There was no repetition of the ugly incidents during the last days of fighting, when Japanese troops had rampaged through the British military hospital, bayoneting doctors, nurses, and patients.

Despite this, nearly all the Asian population kept indoors on the day after the surrender, and all shops were boarded up. Only the Singapore Cold Storage store remained open, operated by the manager and a handful of staff and doing a roaring trade, mainly among European customers.[1] Otherwise the Japanese found Singapore a "ghost town",[2] guarded by a small contingent of Indian and British troops, with only listless groups of dejected Commonwealth soldiers to be seen on the streets.

The next morning, 17 February, the European population, men, women and children, were assembled on the Padang, inspected, and questioned for hours. All British, Australian and allied European prisoners were to be interned at Changi, the civilians in Changi Gaol and the military prisoners, including British officers formerly attached to the Malay and Indian regiments, at nearby Selarang Barracks. The British and Australian troops set off in the early afternoon on their 14-mile journey, marching in orderly ranks and reaching their prison camp about midnight, with stragglers stumbling into the barracks in the early hours of the morning. The Asians, mainly Malays and Indians, who lined the route viewed this spectacle for the most part in bewildered silence, not with enthusiasm and delight as the Japanese expected. The European civilians were marched to Karikal Mahal in Katong, about five miles away. This was a compound with a central mansion and five identical family houses, which was the former residence of a wealthy Indian, known as "The Cattle King of Malaya", and his five wives. Early in March the internees set off on the long painful trail to Changi Prison, a few travelling by lorry but most of them trudging on foot.

On the night of the surrender the Malay regiment's surviving eight officers and 600 other ranks assembled on the Keppel Golf links, and on 17 February they were sent to join the 45,000 Indian troops at Farrer Park. Greeted as brother Asians, the Malays and Indians were urged to disown loyalty to the British Crown and transfer their allegiance to the Japanese emperor. Five Malay officers were executed when they refused, many of their men were arrested, and the rest were given permission to return home. The first batch of about 100 were loaded into lorries, ostensibly to be taken to the railway station, but were instead driven away to a mass execution. The remainder dispersed, either up-country or to join their families who had followed the troops to Singapore during the campaign and were lodged in the Kampong Glam *istana*. A few Malays subsequently joined the Japanese Volunteer Force, others slipped away to join the guerrillas on the mainland, and those who remained in Singapore were kept under close Kempeitai surveillance for the rest of the war.[3]

The Indian prisoners were urged to join an Indian National Army to fight the British for the independence of India. Despite the pressures put upon them, most regular professional soldiers of the Indian army remained steadfastly loyal to the British, the Gurkhas to a man resisting any inducement to change sides. Some were beaten, tortured and murdered, and those who refused were declared to have forfeited their prisoner-of-war status and imprisoned at Seletar. Many others considered such loyalty to former masters who had let them down was misplaced. Indian troops had taken the brunt of the fierce fighting in northern Malaya, and newly arrived reserves had been thrown untrained and ill-equipped into the Johor battle. About 20,000 volunteered to join the Indian National Army, either in the interests of self-preservation or because they saw this as a genuine opportunity to free India from British rule.

❧

Two days after the surrender the Japanese set up military headquarters at Raffles College, and their army vehicles streamed down Bukit Timah Road, all of them flying Japanese flags and their drivers blowing their horns. "The noise was fierce but cheerful, in fact there was a holiday spirit about the whole affair."[4] Yamashita did not intend to stage a triumphal parade but instead held a solemn commemoration service for the dead. He did not claim the conquest of Singapore as a brilliant achievement but "a bluff that worked",[5] and he saw the island merely as a staging post en route to the Netherlands East Indies and Australia.

Renamed Syonan, or Light of the South, Singapore was designated the capital of Japan's southern region. The first tasks were to repair the physical damage of the fighting, bury the dead, remove the wreckage and get municipal services working again. Within twenty-four hours the Japanese had cleared all patients from the General Hospital to accommodate their own wounded. Adult patients were sent home or moved to the Cricket Club, Victoria Hall, or the Singapore Club, children were transferred to the mental hospital, and babies were given away to anyone who would care for them. The Japanese acted swiftly to stop looting, firing into crowds of looters and executing individual offenders on the spot. Indians and Malays were usually released with a warning, but Chinese looters were summarily decapitated and their heads put on public display. Some found it prudent to make bonfires of their booty to forestall soldiers who went from house to house, making arrests when they found premises without an electricity supply but crammed with electrical appliances or expensive furniture.[6]

Waterworks, gas, electricity workers and municipal employees were ordered to report for duty a few days after the capitulation. Doctors were required to register, and private clinics and dispensaries reopened on 1 March. Prisoners of war were set to work clearing the debris. Water pipes were repaired, although it was six weeks before the supply was fully back to normal, and the air was dull with the smoke of oil dumps, which smouldered for more than a month.

The Japanese were eager to establish their information services quickly. Wireless-station staff were summoned to duty with other essential workers, and broadcasting started again in March, with programmes consisting largely of news and propaganda. All receiving sets were sealed to permit reception of medium wave transmission only, and it was strictly forbidden to listen to news from overseas.

A Malay newspaper, the *Berita Malai*, issued in both Jawi and romanized editions, appeared within two days of the surrender, and by the end of the week there were Indian, Chinese and English newspapers. The *Sin Chew Jit Poh* resumed publication as the *Syonan Jit Poh*, and the *Straits Times* became the *Syonan Times*.

Initially it was produced by former local staff, but in December 1942, on the anniversary of the outbreak of the Malayan campaign, the newspaper was re-named the *Syonan Shimbun*, issuing both Japanese and English editions. The English edition was edited by Tatsuki Fujii, former editor of the *Singapore Herald*, who returned in November 1942 as one of a group of Japanese internees released from Indian prison camps in exchange for British internees in other parts of the Far East.

∽

In view of her strategic and economic importance, the Japanese intended to keep Syonan as a permanent Japanese colony and recognized the need to win Chinese co-operation in rebuilding the economy. A secret policy agreement drawn up by the Japanese Army General Staff as early as March 1941 stressed the need for conciliation once hostile Kuomintang and communist elements had been removed. This policy was couched in vague terms, but the speed of Japanese victory brought their armies to Singapore before any precise plan of execution had been worked out. The manner in which Operation Clean Up was implemented by the men on the spot brought tragedy to the Singapore Chinese and left indelible hatred towards the Japanese conquerors.[7]

Conscious of his weak position and anxious to avoid any guerrilla attacks on his depleted forces, Yamashita, ordered an immediate rooting out of resistance elements. Tsuji was put in charge of the operation, and Major-General Saburo Kawamura, commander of the Syonan garrison, was instructed to carry out "severe punishment of hostile Chinese" in conjunction with Colonel Masyuki Oishi, head of the Syonan Kempeitai. Unlike the German civilian Gestapo, the Kempeitai was a military police force administered by the War Ministry. Specially trained in interrogation methods, its task was to crush all resistance to military rule, and it had powers to arrest and extract information from civilians and military alike. At that time there were only about 200 regular *kempei* in Singapore, but 1,000 auxiliaries were recruited from the army, mostly young, rough peasant soldiers, whose passions had been inflamed to fever pitch by the fierce resistance put up by Chinese irregulars in the battle for Singapore Island.

Oishi was ordered to act "in accordance with the letter and spirit of military law", but the instructions were not clear, and the result was a murderous *sook ching*, or purification through purge. In order to flush out their quarry, orders were given three days after the surrender, on Tsuji's authority, for all Chinese males between the ages of eighteen and fifty to report to registration "camps", bringing a week's rations with them. The *kempei* went from house to house driving out Chinese occupants at bayonet point, sometimes seizing women, children and old men too, and herding them into five major concentration areas. Here they were examined by the *kempei*, who, with the help of hooded informers, picked out those alleged to be anti-Japanese.

At the registration centres there was no order, method or organization. Most of the *kempei* were ignorant auxiliaries, who had no clear idea of what they were doing and spoke only Japanese. Some centres were comparatively efficient, sending away women, children and old people, separating those who had been actively involved in anti-Japanese activities and giving the others clearance to go home. Elsewhere, tens of thousands were kept for upwards of a week, crowded in the open without food, water or shelter, often kicked and slapped. The *kempei*, many of them rabidly anti-Chinese, condemned at will. In some areas they seized all Chinese schoolteachers and journalists, and all newcomers from China. Sometimes they arrested all Hainanese, since communism was so prevalent among this community, or men with tattoos, which might indicate membership of a secret society. Elsewhere they picked upon the well-dressed, those wearing spectacles, or signing their names in English, and sometimes even former domestic servants of European households. Those who passed the screening were given a paper with the word "Examined" in Chinese, or had square ink marks stamped on their arms or their shirts, which they tried to preserve for months afterwards.

The unfortunate were stamped with triangular marks and driven off. Some were taken to prison, but most were roped together and either taken out to sea in boats and dumped overboard off Blakang Mati Island (the modern Sentosa) or herded into the sea off Changi and machine-gunned to death. The major massacres were followed by a mopping-up operation in the eastern rural Siglap district, when hundreds more were executed. It is impossible to say how many Chinese died in the massacres during the first two weeks of the Occupation. The Japanese later admitted to killing 5,000, but the figure was probably closer to 25,000, and many Chinese put the total much higher. The massacres were kept secret, and the scale of the atrocity did not emerge until the war was over. Hardly any victims survived, but most families clung to the hope that their lost relatives had merely been conscripted and sent away as labourers.

After a fortnight the *sook ching* was suddenly called off, and by that time the Japanese had begun to appreciate that these methods were not only barbarous but ineffective. While thousands of ordinary people were slaughtered, many important men escaped the Japanese net. On the orders of Major-General Keishin Manaki, Yamashita's deputy, the mass screening was called off in favour of hunting out key individuals.

Some of these had already vanished. The remnants of Dalforce had slipped away up-country and taken to the jungle to form a guerrilla Malayan People's Anti-Japanese Army. Tan Kah-kee, prime target of the Japanese, had fled to Sumatra and thence to Java, where he lived in a modest bungalow under an assumed name throughout the war without being betrayed, despite the Japanese putting a price of one million Dutch guilders on his head and torturing associates to try to find out his whereabouts. Lee Kong Chian was in the United States and Aw Boon Haw in Hong Kong. Tay Koh Yat, a leading Kuomintang supporter, member of the China Relief Fund committee and head of the Mobilization Committee's Civil Defence, fled to Java and lived a hermit's existence, but his eldest son was caught and murdered by the Japanese. Lim Bo Seng escaped on a sampan three days before the surrender, but many of his family members were seized by the Kempeitai and never seen again. Lim Bo Seng made his way across Sumatra and thence to India, where he recruited men for the underground movement in Malaya.

Others remained and were arrested, including Tan Lark Sye, vice-chairman of the Chinese Chamber of Commerce, Yap Pheng Geck, commander of the Chinese company of the Singapore Volunteer Force, and Dr. Lim Boon Keng. The biggest prize was Lai Teck, secretary-general of the Malayan Communist Party. As an informer, Lai Teck had escaped arrest throughout the years before the Pacific War, when the British had been most active in suppressing the Malayan Communist Party, and he now agreed to collaborate secretly with the Japanese.

༄

The *sook ching* destroyed Japanese hopes of gaining the willing co-operation of Chinese Singaporeans. The Japanese were never welcomed as liberators in Singapore, as they were initially in some other colonial territories, but they had a splendid opportunity. Their victory inspired awe in a community that had always admired material success, and they had made the former British masters look "shaky and insipid".[8] While there was no nationalist movement in Singapore to exploit, the Japanese had the chance to strike a chord of sympathy in a divided and mixed community, united only in subjection to a British regime that had failed them. Many Chinese were already so alienated by the Chinese Protectorate that, shortly before the fall of Singapore, the Chinese Chamber of Commerce had petitioned the Governor to dismiss the Secretary of Chinese Affairs. Many Indians were stirred by the anti-British nationalist movement in India, the Malays were poor and felt neglected, and the Eurasians had no firm roots in any local community but had been barred from positions of power or social equality by the ruling colonial class.

The Japanese preached an exciting mission of Asian equality and co-operation in a Greater East Asia New Order, to comprise Japan, China, Manchuria and Southeast Asia. During the Malayan campaign, Tsuji had sought to impart a sense of mission to his troops. He printed 40,000 copies of a pamphlet entitled *Read this Alone – and the War can be Won*, for "front line soldiers, who were on fire with the high ideal of the emancipation of Asia". "We embark now upon that great mission which calls upon Japan, as the representative of all the peoples of the Far East, to deal a resolute and final blow to centuries of European aggression in these lands."[9]

It was declared Japanese policy to bring racial equality to former colonial territories. Five days after the surrender, Yamashita promised the people of Syonan, "We sweep away the arrogant and unrighteous British elements and share pain and rejoicing with all concerned people in a spirit of give and take." He declared Japan's intention to set up "the East Asia Co-Prosperity Sphere in which the New Order of justice has to be attained under the Great Spirit Cosmocracy, giving all content to the respective races and individuals according to their talents and faculties".[10] Condemning the British practice of divide and rule, the Japanese urged Asians to stand together in a universal brotherhood, or *hakko-ichiu*, respecting each other's religions, customs and languages.

Ten days after the fall of Singapore the *Syonan Times* declared, "It is our great duty and pride to place the life of the three million Malayans under the Great East Asia War State and to lead them in obedience to Nippon Military Commands under the aegis of the Empire of Nippon which is the strongest power and leader of East Asia."[11] The newspaper insisted two months later that "Nippon not only desires, but insists upon, interracial harmony in all territories within her sphere of influence.... The old system of administration in Malaya, with its careful fostered policies of preferential treatment to some and oppressive restrictions to others resulted in political pariahdom as the fate of all."[12] By the time these words were written, the Japanese had already squandered their initial assets of admiration, awe and respect.

"One of the first imperatives ... is the breaking down of the habit and custom left behind by the haughty and cunning British," the Japanese insisted. "Side by side ... must proceed the work of reviving Oriental culture based on moral and spiritual principles." It was easy to sweep away the externals of British power, although the Japanese needed to retain some British doctors, nurses, engineers and other specialist staff as a stopgap measure for a few months until their own people arrived. These internees were housed in the Maxwell Road Customs House. For the first twelve months the Bishop of Singapore lived on parole in the town, and in the early days the Reverend Hayter from St. Andrew's Cathedral was allowed out of internment camp to visit Christian patients in hospital.[13] The Director of the Botanic Gardens, his Assistant, and the Director of Fisheries were retained at the Gardens and the Museum throughout the Occupation. Himself an amateur biologist and Fellow of the Linnean Society of London, the Japanese Emperor ordered that museums, libraries and scientific collections in the occupied territories should be preserved. Professor Hidezo Tanakadate arrived from Saigon shortly after the surrender to secure the Raffles Museum's geological collections, and towards the end of 1942 the Science Council in Japan appointed Dr. Yata Haneda as Director of the Singapore Botanical Gardens and Professor Kwan Koribu as Director of the Museum. The Marquis Tokugawa, who was posted to Syonan as adviser to the head of the military government by virtue of his knowledge of Malaya and long-standing personal friendship with Sultan Ibrahim of Johor, became President of the Gardens and Museum. An expert on forestry, the marquis had headed Japan's delegation to the Pacific Science Conference in Java in 1929 and had travelled in the Malay Peninsula, Borneo and Sulawesi. The close and amicable co-operation between the interned British scientists and their distinguished captors attracted bitter recriminations and accusations of collaboration from other internees, but it meant that valuable pre-war books, archives and scientific papers were saved from destruction, and that fruitful scientific research continued throughout the war years.[14]

This positive achievement was a redeeming exception in the generally negative and destructive Japanese wartime administration,[15] and the comparatively comfortable lifestyle at the Gardens under Tokugawa's powerful and gracious protection was in stark contrast to the privations and brutalities suffered by other prisoners. The code of Bushido held it dishonourable for soldiers to surrender, and Japan had never ratified the 1929 Geneva Convention, which guaranteed the rights of prisoners of war to humane treatment. The Japanese did not hesitate to inflict brutal punishments, extract information by torture, punish groups for acts committed by individuals, and execute men who tried to escape. In theory civilian internees were entitled to better treatment, but in practice there was little difference in living conditions between the military and civilian camps at Changi.

At first European prisoners were left to organize themselves, since the Japanese were short of administrators, and military prisoners could move fairly freely over the eastern tip of the island. These early months were a time of divisions and recriminations, when men re-lived the disasters of the campaign and blamed their leaders. Bitterness rankled between the British and Australians and between officers and other ranks. Conditions in the prison hospital were dreadful. For many weeks it housed more than 2,000 patients and more than a quarter of these were buried at Changi by the autumn of 1942.

The soldiers resented Percival's insistence on regular drilling, but within two months some sense of orderliness and discipline had been restored. The Japanese commandeered groups of prisoners as outside work parties and by April 1942 had more than 8,000 at work, building a shrine and war memorial at Bukit Timah, repairing the docks and unloading

ships. Such assignments were popular since they meant bigger
rations, opportunities to barter or pilfer supplies, particularly
in unloading cargoes of food, and working pay, even if this only
amounted to 10 cents a day.

Security was tightened in August 1942. Four hundred senior
civilians and military prisoners, including Percival and Shenton
Thomas, were removed to Taiwan, and the Japanese put in their
own camp administration under Major-General Fukuye. In
September 1942 all military prisoners, numbering more than
15,000, were assembled on Selarang Square and ordered to
sign forms promising not to escape. Stubborn in their refusal,
the troops remained for three days without food or shelter, but
finally their officers ordered the declarations to be signed, after
the Japanese publicly executed four re-captured escapees.

This Selarang Square incident failed to break the troops' spirit
and in fact re-kindled among them a sense of unity and common
purpose. Trained to be disciplined, resourceful and self-reliant,
the military prisoners shared and developed a diversity of talents.
They planted vegetable gardens, kept chickens, and organized
camp workshops to produce soap, paper, tooth powder, brooms
and cooking utensils. By early 1943 a camp "university" had 120
teachers and more than 2,000 students, while a theatre group, a
camp magazine, and a talented Australian concert party provided
entertainment. At first prisoners were permitted to receive copies
of the *Syonan Times*, and after this was stopped they kept in touch
with the outside world through clandestine wireless sets, on
which they picked up news bulletins from London, New Delhi,
and the United States.

The Gurkhas, too, maintained a disciplined camp in true
regimental style, but conditions in the Indian camp at Seletar
were deplorable. These units had lost all their British officers,
many Indian officers had been executed or had joined the Indian
National Army, and there was constant friction and suspicion
between Hindus, Muslims and Sikhs. Discipline was lax even
among regular troops; morale was bad, and the incidence of
sickness and death was very high.

Escape was virtually impossible. Almost unique was the exploit of C.E. McCormac, a former Royal Air Force man, who organized the escape of a seventeen-man working party. With the connivance of a Portuguese Eurasian guard, they fled from Pasir Panjang and took a small boat from Kranji. Four survivors were picked up by a Dutch flying boat in the Straits of Melaka, and McCormac eventually reached Australia.[16]

During the first year conditions in the Changi prison camps were tolerable. Isoshi Asahi, the Controller of Enemy Civilians, who had served for eight years at the Japanese embassy in London, was a considerate man, and the only ill treatment came from the Sikh and Indian guards. The main hardship was shortage of food. The Japanese reduced rations in all prisoner-of-war and internee camps in October 1942, but their diet remained fairly constant, if meagre, throughout the twelve months that followed.

There was no contact between military and civilian prisoners, and little between the men's and women's sections in Changi Gaol. Civilian male prisoners were sometimes employed on working parties away from the gaol, but apart from two female doctors who worked on temporary assignment in town, women and children were confined to camp. Life in the women's camp was spartan and bleak, but they ran a school and for eighteen months issued a camp news-sheet.

❦

Given her strategic and economic importance, the Japanese intended to retain Syonan as a permanent Japanese colony. In March 1942 they set up a military administration, or *gunseikan-bu*, under Colonel Wataru Watanabe, and a new municipal government, or *tokubetsu-si*, with Shigeo Odate as mayor and a former Consul-General, Kaoru Toyota, as his deputy. In addition to normal municipal functions, the *tokubetsu-si* took over some former government departments, and its territorial responsibility extended to the Karimons and the Riau archipelago.

Odate, who was a first-rate administrator with high-level experience in civil government in occupied China, was given the honorary rank of general. Syonan was Japan's most important centre in the Nanyang but never had more than twenty senior Japanese civilian officials at any one time, and the civil and military authorities were constantly at odds. Sometimes Odate succeeded in overruling Watanabe by virtue of his rank and his personality, but in practice the *tokubetsu-si* was subordinate to the *gunseikan-bu*, which insisted on giving top priority to security and the needs of war.

The shortage of senior men compelled the *gunseikan-bu* to bring in low-ranking Japanese officials and also Taiwanese and Koreans, who had a reputation for being ruthless and cruel. The Taiwanese were particularly valuable as interpreters and *kempei* since they spoke the most commonly used Hokkien dialect, while the Koreans, who generally spoke neither Chinese nor English, were employed mainly as prison guards.

During the reign of terror in the first fortnight of the Occupation, the Chinese were paralysed with fright, and no one dared to come forward as spokesman. The more moderate Japanese wanted to reach an understanding, and the initiative appears to have been taken by Shinozaki, who was newly released from internment in Changi Gaol. He found a go-between in Lim Boon Keng, now an old man of seventy-two who had returned from Amoy to retire in Singapore five years earlier. With great reluctance, and reputedly feigning drunkenness to avoid being drawn into co-operation,[17] Lim Boon Keng was persuaded to form the Syonan Overseas Chinese Association, with himself as chairman and S.Q. Wong, a prominent Singapore-born Cantonese businessman and banker, as vice-chairman. Shinozaki persuaded the Kempeitai to acknowledge the Association and to release prominent Chinese leaders, such as Tan Lark Sye, to join it. About 250 well-known Chinese congregated for the inaugural meeting of the Syonan Overseas Chinese Association at the exclusive Hokkien Goh Loo Club, where the *gunseikan-bu* issued them with badges as Overseas Chinese liaison officers and they formed a peace maintenance committee.

Shinozaki later claimed that he started the Overseas Chinese Association in order to protect the Chinese community,[18] but Watanabe favoured taking a hard line and handed the Association over to Toru Takase, his tough civilian right-hand man.[19] With the help of Wee Twee Kim, a ruthless Taiwanese who had been a storekeeper for a Japanese firm in Singapore before the war, Takase used the Overseas Chinese Association to intimidate the Chinese and extract their wealth.

Tokyo expected local Japanese military authorities to raise their own revenue, and Watanabe decided to do this with a levy on the Malayan Chinese, which would achieve the twin objects of providing administrative expenses and making the Chinese atone for their past hostility. Day after day Takase summoned the Chinese leaders to military headquarters and bullied them with threats. Petrified, they pledged full support for the Japanese, and eventually were summoned before Watanabe, who ordered them to raise a $50 million "gift" within a month. An organizing committee was hastily formed under Tan Ean Kiam, managing director of the Oversea Chinese Bank, and Singapore's liability was fixed at $10 million, the remainder to be raised by Chinese in the peninsula.

Supplied by the Japanese with tax and property records so that no one could evade payment, the Chinese in Singapore decided to impose an 8 per cent levy on all individual properties worth more than $3,000 and 5 per cent on company assets. To raise such a sum was a Herculean task, since it represented a quarter of the total Malayan currency in circulation, and at the end of the month only one-third of the money had been collected. The Malayan Chinese leaders were summoned to Singapore, threatened with reprisals, and the deadline was extended for another month. Further failure resulted in another stormy meeting in Singapore, when the date was extended until June. When barely half of the $50 million had been collected by that time, the Chinese were permitted to raise the balance by loans repayable within a year from the Yokohama

Specie Bank, which had taken over the Chartered Bank's premises in Singapore.

Watanabe claimed the "gift" would stem inflation by taking surplus money out of circulation and was justified because the revenue was ploughed back into the country. But the demand and the intimidation used to enforce it, coming so soon after the massacres, left a burning hatred among the Singapore Chinese towards the Japanese regime.

ᗛᏉ

Indians, Eurasians and Malays were not sorry to see the Chinese squeezed but were afraid their turn would come next. The Japanese did indeed intend to make the various communities conform to the new state, but their attitude to the separate groups differed greatly.

Since they were not interested at that stage in fostering any budding Malay nationalism in Singapore, the Japanese tended, as the British had done, to leave the Malay community alone. For the young journalist Samad Ismail, a former assistant editor of the *Utusan Melayu*, his position as editor of *Berita Malai* provided scope to promote his anti-colonial views.

The Eurasians presented special problems. While they had never been accepted by Britons as equals, they had generally held themselves aloof from the Asian population. English-educated, Christian, usually speaking English as their mother tongue, Eurasians gravitated to middle-class white-collar jobs. The Japanese wanted to break down their privileged-underdog sense of semi-superiority, claiming "There are no 'superior' people in the New Order." Those with direct European antecedents were interned. The rest were assembled on the Padang early in March and harangued, "Until now you were spoiled in circumstances of individualism and liberalism. You were used to an easy going life of amusements," Eurasians were told, "the time for looking to personal and individual affairs is gone ...

the New Dawn has come over a new Great Asia", materialism was overthrown and Eurasians should "gain the spiritualism you have forgotten entirely".[20] They were commanded to consider themselves as Asians, to forget feelings of racial superiority, and to exchange clerical jobs for farming, shopkeeping, or other similar employment. A few responded to this challenge, but on the whole the Eurasians remained a distrusted unhappy community, ill at ease with the new regime. Many looked to the French Roman Catholic Bishop Devals as their leader or to the Eurasian Welfare Association, created by Shinozaki and headed by Dr. Charles Paglar.

Japanese policy towards the Asian Jewish community vacillated. All Jews were registered in mid-March, and several wealthy Jews were arrested and released after paying large sums of money, but eventually all Jewish residents were interned.

Orders were given to treat the Indian population with consideration as allies, but most Indian Muslims would have no truck with the Indian National Army and wished to set up an Indian Muslim Association to protect their minority group. The Japanese refused to allow this but at the end of 1943 approved setting up an Indian Welfare Association, under Dr. Nathan, to provide a link between the municipality and the Indian community. Many Sikhs and "free Indians" were employed as policemen, patrolmen in the docks, and as guards in the prison camps. Indians who refused to co-operate often suffered more from their countrymen in the Indian Independence League and the Indian National Army than from the Japanese.

‿

The municipality worked to restore normal conditions in everyday life. A few days after the capitulation, prices were officially pegged, and all refugees from up-country were ordered to return home, in order to relieve the strain on Singapore's resources. Dr. Kozo Ando, formerly in private practice in Singapore, became

Chief Medical Officer for the municipality. Instructions were issued to keep houses clean, to get rid of mosquitoes, and to attend to immunization against smallpox and cholera.

Shinozaki became Chief Education Officer and tried to reopen schools as quickly as possible. This was difficult because all European and some local teachers were interned, others had been killed, and most school buildings were occupied by the army. Despite this, some English, Malay and Indian schools reopened in April. The Japanese were more reluctant to reopen Chinese schools, but in June 1942 twenty-five Chinese schools also resumed teaching.

The first task for the schools was to organize a display to celebrate the Emperor's birthday at the end of April. Thousands of schoolchildren marched to the Padang carrying flags and singing the Japanese national anthem. Yamashita reviewed the parade and afterwards attended a gathering of about 400 community leaders at the Adelphi Hotel. This was Yamashita's first direct contact with Singaporeans, who regarded the Tiger of Malaya with awe and dread, but he assured them there was nothing to fear, now that they were all citizens of Japan.

Yamashita made a second public appearance two months later to receive the Chinese "gift". Sixty leading Chinese attended the ceremony, which was held in the former Singapore Chamber of Commerce in Fullerton Building. Despite the nerve-racking ordeal they had suffered, the Chinese were impressed with Yamashita, who spoke to them for over an hour about Japanese objectives and ambitions and concluded that, since the Japanese claimed descent from gods and the Europeans from monkeys, in any war between gods and monkeys, the gods must win.

This was Yamashita's last official appearance in Singapore. When Terauchi decided to transfer the Southern Army's headquarters from Saigon to Syonan, Yamashita was posted to Manchuria in July 1942. He hoped to visit Tokyo *en route* to present a report on the Malayan campaign to the Emperor but was ordered to proceed direct to Manchuria, where he remained far from any scene of operations until October 1944, when he was called to resist the American invasion of the Philippines. After a desperate and hopeless campaign Yamashita formally surrendered to the Americans in September 1945, ironically in the presence of Percival, who had recently been released. For both men the fall of Singapore was the beginning of tragedy, but Yamashita's end was the more dramatic. He was the first Japanese general to be tried by the Americans for war crimes and was convicted of committing atrocities in the Philippines over which he had virtually no control. U.S. President Truman rejected a minority recommendation for clemency, and Yamashita was hanged in February 1946 at an execution described at the time by two U.S. Supreme Court judges as a "judicial lynching".

❧

In the early months Japanese officials who advocated a policy of moderation towards the Chinese were regarded as soft and even unpatriotic by the military. In June 1942 Wee Twee Kim accused Shinozaki of treachery in helping the "enemy", and Mayor Odate sent him back to Japan to avoid arrest. After the Chinese "gift" was paid and the 25th Japanese Army departed, the feud between the military and Japanese civilians died down, and the fanatical pressure of the military authorities on the Chinese softened. Watanabe continued to demand firm measures, but Takase was sent back to Japan and Wee Twee Kim was dismissed.

In August 1942 Shinozaki returned to Singapore to become Chief Welfare Officer for the municipality, and the Overseas Chinese Association was transferred once more to his charge. For the rest of the Occupation, the Association acted as a go-between for the Chinese community and the Japanese authorities, even though it was rent with dissensions, particularly between the Straits-born and the China-born. The Straits Chinese, who had often been lukewarm in supporting China's cause against Japan before the Pacific War, blamed the China-born for bringing down Japanese reprisals on them. The deep involvement of the immigrant Chinese in pre-war anti-Japanese politics made them perhaps even more anxious to co-operate with the Japanese in order to save their lives. Lim Boon Keng could claim to speak for both communities, but he was not an effective leader in the mould of Tan Kah-kee, and many wrongly suspected that he had helped the Japanese create the Overseas Chinese Association specifically to milk the Chinese community's wealth.

While the Japanese promised not to discriminate against co-operative Chinese, in practice the Chinese of Singapore and Malaya were treated more harshly than their countrymen in any other part of Southeast Asia. In Singapore, they were always the first to be squeezed for money or arrested on suspicion of petty crimes. Many of their young women were seized for Japanese brothels, and their young men were sent away as labourers. Countless thousands suffered torture and death at the hands of the Kempeitai.

For the majority of Chinese, surviving meant adapting to the new regime. The Japanese found the Malayan Chinese puzzling, for they were "masters at pulling the line of least resistance".[21] They contributed to Japanese war funds, they gave presents, organized dinners and loyalty processions, but these were merely aimed to buy peace. Underneath there was bitter hostility. The long years of China's suffering at the hands of the Japanese, the brutality of the first fortnight of the Occupation, and the extraction of the "gift" confirmed Chinese hatred for the Japanese regime.

❧

The Japanese policy to sweep away the colonial economic superstructure and incorporate occupied territories into the Greater East Asia Co-Prosperity Sphere caused particular hardship in Singapore, where the regional entrepôt trade was closely geared to the international Western economy. The declared Japanese aim was to convert Syonan into a self-sufficient state, but in practice industry, communications, commerce and finance were harnessed to the war machine. Big Japanese firms, such as Mitsui and Mitsubishi, were given control of important branches of the Malayan economy: shipping, transport, rubber production, tin and iron mines, palm oil, and rice distribution. Subordinate trades and industries were handed over to Japanese or Taiwanese civilian traders, while non-Japanese needed special licences. From the middle of 1942 there was an influx of Japanese businessmen and *rikenyas*, or concession hunters, and restaurant, hotel, and geisha house proprietors.

The Japanese set up *kumiai*, or guild associations, to control the issue of essential materials that were in short supply. These monopolies were designed to supply the army's needs most effectively, but in practice the *kumiai* system produced a government-protected black market, controlled at the top by a handful of Japanese businessmen and operated by local entrepreneurs. Japanese restrictions challenged and sharpened the ingenuity of local Chinese businessmen, and as time went on they came to re-assume their former profitable and vital roles as middlemen. The economy became "a combination of Japanese officiousness with Chinese shrewdness, cunning and selfishness".[22] In many associations the Japanese were front men while Chinese businessmen were the real power behind them.

In the early months of the Occupation luxury goods were cheap as looters unloaded their booty to evade arrest, and wealthy Chinese sold their possessions to pay their share of the Japanese gift money. But the necessities of life were scarce. Singapore's artificial economy was heavily dependent on entrepôt trade and imported food.

Already by April 1942 the shops were nearly empty, householders were storing up supplies, and speculators were buying up stocks. The black market flourished, everything was "under the counter", and prices soared, with food costing two to three times as much as in up-country towns. In June 1943 the *Syonan Shimbun* declared that prices had risen to three times their pre-war level. Strict anti-profiteering regulations issued by the *gunseikan-bu* in August that year merely sent prices rocketing further since purchasers now had to pay risk money too.

The influx of Japanese military scrip to replace British currency put the country in the grip of chronic inflation and, once the fortunes of war turned against Japan, the value of paper money began to slide. Commonly known as "bananas" or "coconuts" because they bore the designs of those plants, the first notes were numbered but subsequent issues were not, and the poor quality made forgery easy.

Singapore became glutted with paper money whose face value was meaningless. Everyone knew that the Japanese currency would be useless after the war and quickly exchanged it for goods, sending the price of jewellery, property and other durables rocketing. At the beginning of 1944 the Japanese tried to stop trafficking in property by imposing crippling taxes on such transactions, but these were easy to evade and merely sent prices up further. By March 1945 shophouses that fetched $5,000 to $6,000 before the war were selling for $160,000 to $250,000. Town building sites fetched fifty or sixty times their pre-war prices, and the housing shortage was so acute that people paid up to $5,000 tea money for a cubicle and $40,000 to $60,000 for vacant possession of a house. Even bus tickets, cinema tickets and newspapers were sold at black market prices, and by June 1945 a bottle of Hennessy brandy cost $4,000 to $5,000.

This situation encouraged greed and speculation. Racketeers grew rich. Bribery and corruption flourished, and those who were squeezed in turn squeezed others. Businessmen could pass on their liabilities, "like a game in which the Ball of Inflation was quickly passed over to another as soon as it came to them".[23] Enterprising operators could make fortunes in quick deals, provided they swallowed their scruples, fraternized with Japanese officials, paid bribes and protection money, and contributed to the Japanese war chest. Money was easily made and easily spent because it was not worth saving. Despite shortages, the cafes, amusement parks, gambling establishments, and cinemas were crowded, mainly with Japanese, black marketeers and collaborators. Two of the three entertainment "worlds" reopened, largely for gambling, and Singapore sported an air of brash gaiety.

Some people refused to have anything to do with the regime, rejecting jobs under the Japanese, selling all their possessions, and living frugally, but the vast majority saw no virtue in letting their families starve, and they survived by giving and taking favours. Dealing on the black market was a necessity and therefore respectable. Sharp-witted practice became a virtue, and businessmen who had been ruined and then amassed new fortunes were held in general esteem.

Singapore's social world and sense of values turned topsy-turvy. It brought to the top a *nouveau riche* class of enterprising businessmen, racketeers, and gamblers. The Occupation offered profitable opportunities as middlemen to the former lower echelons of society: to hawkers, rickshaw pullers, and workers in restaurants, cinemas, and amusement parks, while labourers could demand higher wages or part payment in rice or cloth. Clerks, teachers, and other white-collar workers, who had formerly enjoyed a favoured position in Singapore, now became a depressed class, finding it very difficult to live on a fixed salary. Old people suffered perhaps most of all, since the Japanese refused to honour pensions. Rich men in Singapore had taken pride in showing their wealth, but now found it prudent to hide behind a cloak of poverty. Former car owners took to bicycles. Neckties, shoes and socks were discarded in favour of shorts, open-necked shirts, and rubber sandals.

In order to combat inflation and to divert funds to their war effort, the Japanese tried to mop up spare money in state lotteries, gambling, and savings campaigns. The first lottery was launched in Singapore in August 1943, while gambling was legalized at the end of that year for the first time in more than a century. Both measures were popular but did nothing to stem inflation. Savings drives were started in February 1944, and Singapore was in the middle of its fourth such drive when the war finished, while a government lottery was scheduled to be drawn in early September 1945. Singapore led the way in raising considerable sums of money for savings, amounting to $281,546,000 in 1944–45. The money was paid readily, since it was worth so little, but donors viewed these "savings" as a gift to purchase peace and quiet, rather than contributions to the Japanese war effort or sound nest eggs for their own futures.

The basic foodstuff, rice, became precious, because imports from Burma dried up and the Japanese hoarded stocks in preparation for further military campaigns. The Japanese encouraged Singaporeans to grow their own food; they organized gardening competitions, offered technical advice, granted loans to smallholders and incorporated vegetable gardening into the school curriculum. The response was so poor that in 1944 encouragement changed to intimidation. Non-co-operation in the self-sufficiency campaigns was regarded as sabotage. Government employees were forced to work on vegetable plots. People filled their front gardens with tapioca plants, which produced a lot of greenery without much effort, but by 1945, when the end of the war was in sight, even this show of home gardening was abandoned.

The Japanese were more successful in promoting substitute industries, which brought out the constructive inventiveness of Singaporeans. Most products were designed as alternatives for unobtainable imports: twine and rope were made from pineapple fibre; paper from bamboo, pineapple leaves and lallang; methylated spirit from tapioca; greases and lubricants from palm oil; motor fuel from rubber oil mixed with petrol. Ammunition was manufactured on a small scale, and in November 1942 the first Singapore-built steamship was launched. Many small soap factories sprang up and for a time Singapore exported soap to Thailand. Few of these substitutes were economical or survived the Occupation. The exception was the trishaw, a rickshaw pulled by a bicycle, which was adapted by Chinese mechanics to replace taxis and continued to be a popular and cheap mode of transport until it died out in the early 1970s.

While the wartime manufacturing campaign was superficial and ephemeral, it showed the ingenuity of Singaporeans and their innate capacity for future industrialization. The Chinese remained the backbone of Singapore's economy, and the strength of their traditional system of mutual co-operation and regional connections enabled them to survive and sometimes to prosper during the adversity of the Occupation.

❧

The preoccupation of Singaporeans with survival and material security contrasted with the Japanese call for spiritual revival and an end of Western colonial materialism. Five days after the surrender, Yamashita called on Singaporeans to adopt the Nippon spirit, or *Nippon-Seishin*, and work towards "moral unification".

One of Japan's declared aims was to instil Asian consciousness and pride. The press, radio and cinema were devoted to this purpose, and cinemas specialized in cultural and educational documentary films at cheap prices. The Emperor cult was stressed. The Emperor's birthday was declared a public holiday and everyone had to stand facing northeast to Tokyo, observing one minute's silence. Singapore clocks were put forward two hours to bring them into line with Tokyo time, and there was even talk of building a Singapore-Tokyo railway.

The Japanese considered, "The most profound of all means available to propaganda is education. This can be shaped and altered at will to suit the policy to be propagandized."[24] Initially schools were reopened to get children off the streets and provide teachers with employment. In Shinozaki's words, "I was just killing time."[25] By the middle of 1942 the Japanese were in a position to develop a more coherent education policy.[26] They concentrated on vocational and primary education, aiming to provide eight years' schooling, as in Japan. They rejected the former British emphasis on academic subjects in favour of character building, physical training, and vocational instruction.

The government wished to create a unified education system but in practice had to take over the different language schools inherited from the colonial regime, although all colonial, English, Chinese, or religious names were discarded. The Japanese took over the direct running of English, Malay, and Chinese schools and set up a few Indian "national" schools, most of which were staffed by unqualified teachers and were used mainly to disseminate propaganda about the Indian independence movement. Teaching in Malay was permitted in Malay schools since it was the indigenous language, but the Japanese encouraged the study of Nippon-go in other schools, particularly in Chinese-medium institutions. Watanabe wanted to ban the use of English in schools from the beginning, but Odate persuaded him this was impractical, and Japanese was introduced gradually as the medium of instruction.

All teachers were paid on the same scale, unlike in colonial times when teachers in English schools enjoyed higher salaries. All primary school fees and book charges were abolished in 1943. The declared aim of education was the "creation of a feeling of loyalty and the awakening of a national consciousness". All primary schools adopted a Japanese-style curriculum, each morning beginning with facing towards Japan and singing the Japanese national anthem and patriotic songs. Teachers were brought in from Japan and local teachers were required to learn Japanese. Free Japanese-language evening classes were organized, and Japanese instruction was given over the wireless. Teachers or government servants who learned Japanese received bonuses and those who showed exceptional promise were promoted and sent to Tokyo for further language training. Many teachers and students were keen to learn the language, and by 1944 classes in English and Chinese schools were often held in Japanese. The language was too different from the usual Singapore tongues to make it an effective medium of instruction, and much of the school day was taken up with physical drill, gardening, and singing. Many parents were reluctant to send their children to school, and classes were very small. There were never more than 7,000 children at school, and by 1945 the number had dwindled to a few hundred.[27]

The accent was on technical and vocational instruction. By March 1943 there were six technical schools in Singapore. The Medical College reopened in Tan Tock Seng Hospital in 1943 and re-admitted former students, but it moved to Melaka a few months later. Two teacher-training schools were opened in 1943. Even in technical institutions, the curriculum consisted of language training, indoctrination, and rudimentary crash courses designed to meet wartime needs. A six-month course at the Naval Construction and Engineering Centre devoted half the time to learning Japanese. Similarly, in the teachers' training colleges and the Leading Officials Training Institute, a great deal of time was taken up in studying the language, "Nippon spirit", military arts, and gardening.

Religious toleration was promised, but religious – and particularly Christian – organizations were kept under surveillance. Spies attended services, hymns were scrutinized, and sermons were prohibited.

In place of a Westernized intelligentsia, the Japanese wished to develop a small élite in their own image, confident of the superior virtues of their own society. Carefully selected students were sent to Japan to absorb Japanese ways, but of the 400 to 500 students brought from occupied territories to Japan for training during the war, only twelve came from Malaya or Singapore.[28]

Official propaganda urged "Asia for the Asiatics! Follow the leadership of Nippon and cast away every trace of Anglo-American influence!"[29] Raffles's statue was relegated to the museum, and English signboards were replaced by Japanese ones. People were encouraged to see Japanese films, but British and American movies remained popular until their showing was prohibited in November 1943. The object was to supersede English. "We regret that we are forced to use the language of the enemy.... It is a disgrace to use the language of people who exploited and suppressed us," declared the *Syonan Times* in September 1942. In January 1943 the Japanese threatened to prohibit the use of English in postal correspondence and telephone conversations. Japanese and Malay were the only official languages, but in practice it was impossible to abandon English even in official documents. In other occupied countries, the Japanese encouraged the local tongue alongside Japanese to replace European languages, but Singapore had no local *lingua franca*, and Japanese was a difficult alien language.

Singaporeans enjoyed some of the indoctrination, particularly Japanese films and music, but in general they were bored with constant repetitive propaganda and a concentrated fare of Japanese victories. All things Western were held up as soft and decadent in contrast to Japanese discipline, hardiness, and sense of sacrifice. The spectacle of half-starved, half-naked British and Australian prisoners performing manual labour was designed to contribute to this impression, but the campaign misfired because the Japanese were equally offensive to the dignity of local Singaporeans.

There were some honourable and respected military and civil Japanese officers, but the shortage of senior officials meant that most of those in authority in Singapore were men of inferior calibre. While the new Japanese masters preached a doctrine of Asian equality and of anti-materialistic, anti-Western sacrifice for Singaporeans, they themselves showed a predilection for big British and American cars, lording it in former colonial mansions, and enjoying tennis, golf, and horse racing. The two main department stores, Robinson's and Little's, were reserved exclusively for Japanese customers, and only Japanese could travel in certain lifts in office buildings. Syonan was a soft posting for Japanese, far from the rigours of the battlefront. Opportunities to make big fortunes attracted the more unscrupulous Japanese businessmen and adventurers, and *rikenya* became a new word for profiteer in Singaporeans' language. Administration was inefficient and corrupt, rules were evaded, and local businessmen took pride and pleasure in outwitting the Japanese. The result was general contempt for the Japanese and for the culture they extolled.

∿

Contempt was mixed with dread: the everyday fear of beatings and face slappings, the constant haunting terror of arrest, prison, torture, and death. The judicial system was subordinate to the military, and in April 1942 the Japanese set up a military court in the Supreme Court building to try political offences. Civil and criminal courts reopened the following month to try cases by the existing laws if these did not conflict with the military regime, but the old rights of *habeas corpus* were abolished. Cases were heard in public but were frequently settled by bribery behind the scenes.

The chief instrument employed to root out anti-Japanese elements was the Kempeitai, which had powers of life and death and employed secret agents and informers to denounce those suspected of disloyalty. Citizens found it prudent to get rid of all evidence of connection with the colonial regime and destroyed their English books, their sons' boy scout uniforms, and Western gramophone records. The English-educated, Christians, and affluent professional men were particularly vulnerable, often subject to blackmail at the hands of unscrupulous informers, and where possible they sought out a Japanese protector in case of trouble.

Many regular pre-war policemen had given up their jobs, and new recruits were often cruel and corrupt. The Special Branch of the police had virtually unlimited powers and was often as arbitrary and oppressive as the Kempeitai towards their own countrymen. The Japanese reverted to a system of collective security reminiscent of the pioneer *kapitan* days. In July 1942 all families were registered, householders were given a "peace living certificate", and were held responsible for their family's behaviour. Some were appointed as *sidang* with a wider remit, one-star *sidang* being accountable for a ward consisting of thirty households and answerable to district or two-star *sidang*. Each group of ten wards was placed under an auxiliary police assistant, and in May 1944 these were formed into an association, which arranged for every man between the ages of sixteen and forty-five to enlist for night patrols.

Not only the brutality but the haphazard and humourless uncertainty of Japanese administration left ordinary Singaporeans in a perpetual state of tension. Often people did not know why they were arrested or with what offence they were charged. Different branches of the Kempeitai appeared to vie with each other in hunting out suspects, and release from one Kempeitai centre did not guarantee freedom from arrest by another. Owning a radio, criticizing the Japanese, even grumbling about high prices, were political offences. One word from an informer could mean arrest, and some people were denounced to the Kempeitai out of sheer personal spite. No one dared speak up on behalf of the accused. Those arrested could be imprisoned without trial in terrible conditions, starved and often tortured, unless their families managed to purchase their release with bribes. The whole period of the Occupation was a time of rumour, fear and secrecy, suspicion and informing, when it was unsafe to voice any opinions at all. At best everyday life was dreary and lacking in purpose.[30] Singaporeans drifted from day to day, spending what they had earned, no longer being able to predict or plan for their own or their family's future.

The Japanese threw away their opportunities. Their initial aims could have attracted Singaporeans and, as a contemporary commented, "If Japan had less of *Seishin* and more of common sense, then her history and the history of East Asia would have been different."[31] Instead of Asian brotherhood, the Japanese brought cruelty and tyranny. In the words of one who suffered under the regime, "Undoubtedly her achievements were enviable, but Japan forgot to be humane."[32]

Their speedy military victory bolstered Japanese sense of racial superiority, and Japan was confident that Southeast Asian countries would admiringly follow her lead. Stress on sacrifice, willingness to die, devotion to the Emperor, and putting the state before the family and the individual inspired some grudging respect, but Japanese arrogance and excessive bragging about invincibility stood in stark contrast to the poor behaviour of many officials and military men and the inefficiency and unfairness of their administration.

The co-prosperity sphere translated into "co-poverty fear", economic hardship, drabness, and exploitation. The gross materialism and corruption of everyday life, which alone ensured survival, undermined the call for spiritual and moral upliftment. The monotonous dullness of Japanese propaganda made a mockery of the idealistic mission to free colonial peoples. While professing to work for Asian unity, the Japanese divided the population more deeply than the British had done, by the varied treatment meted out to the different communities.

Resistance was impossible in Singapore itself, but survivors of Dalforce escaped to the jungle on the mainland and formed the nucleus of a Malayan People's Anti-Japanese Army (MPAJA), which by the end of the Occupation had attracted several thousand followers. Attempts to bring in Malays and Indians were not successful, and the vast majority of recruits were Chinese. Many were merely anti-Japanese patriots, but the leaders were communists.

The guerrilla force lost its entire leadership at a meeting in Batu Caves, Selangor, in September 1942, when Lai Teck betrayed them to the Japanese and the eighteen most senior men were killed. Over the next year the MPAJA reorganized under younger men, notably Chin Peng (born Ong Boon Hua), who had joined the movement in 1940 at the age of fifteen but by the end of the Occupation was secretary of the Perak State Committee. In May 1943 British Force 136 agents, including Lim Bo Seng, arrived in Malaya to establish contact with the MPAJA. Lim fell into Japanese hands and died after torture a few months later without divulging any information, but an agreement was made between Force 136 and the MPAJA to co-operate in the liberation of Malaya.[33] The guerrillas were unable to carry out any significant sabotage during the Occupation for fear of Japanese reprisals against the civilian population, and had to bide their time until the opportunity came to confront their ultimate enemy: Western imperialism. Meanwhile they carried out party indoctrination among the force, and acquired experience in jungle living, together with weapons, money, and useful knowledge from and about their temporary British allies.

⚮

By 1943, as the tide turned against the Japanese, officials grew more nervous, harsh, and erratic in their administration. Shigeo Odate was promoted to Governor-General of Tokyo city in June 1943 and replaced by a lesser man, Kanichi Naito, who served as Mayor of Syonan until the end of the war. The mild Asahi was succeeded in 1943 as Controller of Enemy Civilians by a tougher American-educated Japanese, Sanemitsu Tominaga, who made life for the internees much harsher.

For military and civilian prisoners alike, these were years of overcrowding, disease, hunger, and malnutrition, which were all the more galling when the War Office subsequently proposed to deduct £500 from surviving officers' pay for "board and lodging" during the Occupation.[34] Food and medicines were scarce, and internees suffered from dysentery, sores, ulcers, skin diseases, beriberi, and diphtheria. Working parties toiled long hours at heavy manual work, and it was part of Japanese policy to humiliate Europeans by employing them as labourers in public view. Men were subject to beatings and slappings for trivial offences, living always in fear of snap Kempeitai inspections for possession of wireless sets or for suspected espionage. The worst such incident occurred in October 1943, when the Japanese suspected that civilian internees were involved in the sabotage of ships in the harbour. In fact this daring exploit, known as

Operation Jaywick, was carried out by six soldiers and sailors of an Anglo-Australian Special Z unit, who travelled in an old fishing boat and then used folding canoes to enter Singapore harbour by night. They attached limpet mines to ships in the roads and succeeded in sinking or putting out of action seven ships, including a big oil tanker. The mission slipped away and returned safely to Australia, leaving the Japanese convinced that this must be the work of British guerrillas from the mainland, acting on information supplied by civilians in town and the inmates of Changi Gaol.

The internees were not connected with this incident at all, but on 10 October 1943, the notorious "Double Tenth", the Kempeitai raided the gaol, carried out a thorough day-long search and arrested suspects. This was followed by more searches and arrests, and altogether fifty-seven internees were taken away by the Kempeitai, including the Anglican Bishop of Singapore, Hugh Fraser, the former Colonial Secretary, Robert Scott, the former Information Officer, and two women: Dr. Cicely Williams, head of the women's camp, and Freddy Bloom, editor of the women's camp newspaper. For the next five months suspects were kept in Kempeitai centres where they were crowded in tiny cells, men and women together, with no bedding, lights burning all night, no room to lie down, starved, subjected to repeated interrogation, beatings, and torture in a vain attempt to establish a link with the sabotage. One suspect was executed, fifteen internees, including Fraser, died as a result of torture, and others, including Robert Scott, were sentenced to long periods of imprisonment in the dreaded Outram Gaol.

While the interrogations revealed nothing about Operation Jaywick, they did bring evidence to light of contacts between the gaol and local civilians in town, involving passing messages, relaying news picked up on secret radios, and sometimes supplying food, money, and radio parts. This led to the arrest of about fifty Singaporeans on suspicion of complicity in the harbour sabotage. Among them was Eurasian Leslie Hoffman, a former journalist with the *Malaya Tribune* and outspoken pre-war critic of the Japanese, who was tortured and then condemned to rigorous imprisonment in Outram Gaol. After the Second World War Hoffman was to hold the post of editor-in-chief of the *Straits Times* for fourteen years. Particularly tragic was the ordeal of Elizabeth Choy Su-mei, formerly a teacher of English, and her husband, in peacetime a bookkeeper with a British firm, who were managing the Mental Hospital canteen. For more than six months Elizabeth Choy was imprisoned, the only woman crammed into a tiny cell with twenty male prisoners, forced to kneel all day, forbidden to talk, and subject to brutal beatings, electric shock, and water torture. Her husband was consigned to Outram Gaol and never fully recovered, but after the war Elizabeth Choy was awarded the OBE. She went on to play a prominent role in politics, education, and charitable work in Singapore until her death in 2006 at the age of ninety-five.[35] It was not until a second Anglo-Australian raiding party, Operation Rimau, was captured off Singapore in December 1944 that the Japanese learned the truth about the earlier raid.[36]

After the "Double Tenth", life became more rigorous for the civilian prisoners, but they were more fortunate than their military counterparts who were sent in their thousands to work in factories and mines in Japan or to build a rail link between Thailand and Burma. They fared better, too, than the thousands of Indian prisoners of war sent to work in New Guinea and other parts of the Netherlands East Indies.

In March 1943 the first batch of 600 military prisoners was dispatched up-country from Selarang. They were told they were moving to rest camps in the mountains but in fact were taken to build the Burma-Thailand Death Railway. Throughout 1943 more groups were sent to Thailand, Borneo, and Japan until eventually no fit men were left in Selarang. Late in 1943 the Japanese decided to build an airfield at Changi using prisoner-of-war labour to clear the ground, fill swamps and construct runways. In May 1944 civilian internees were moved from Changi Gaol to a former Royal Air Force camp at Sime Road, and all military prisoners were transferred into the gaol. Remnants of working parties were brought back from Thailand, with accounts of the dreadful conditions in which more than one-third of their number had perished. Eventually nearly 12,000 military prisoners were crowded into the gaol, which had been built to accommodate 600 men. Rations were cut in 1944 and again early in 1945, and inflation was so rampant that the prisoners' meagre wages would buy nothing on the black market. Sick men were expected to work alongside the fit in a feverish attempt to complete the aerodrome. Despite frequent beatings, the exhaustion of heavy work on starvation rations, and a constant tug of war between working hard enough to avoid beatings for malingering and going slow to impede the Japanese war effort, there was some sense of purpose in creating the airfield, which was completed in May 1945 and was strengthened and extended after the war to become a Royal Air Force station and later Changi International Airport.

ॐ

The Japanese demanded civilian labourers as well as military prisoners for the Burma-Thailand railway. It was simple to impress labour since workers had to register with the Labour Department and obtain passbooks in order to take up employment. The unemployed were the first to be rounded up to work for the military or be sent away as forced labourers.

In December 1943 the Military Administration formed compulsory labour service corps throughout Malaya. Every group of 150 men had to supply twenty workers between the ages of fifteen and forty-five, and the order was later extended to women. From December 1944 men of military age were forbidden to work as waiters, office peons, salesmen, cooks, tailors, hawkers, or in similar occupations, in which women had to take their place. Restaurants, cabarets and other non-essential establishments were closed down. Men were drafted into the military labour corps or defence.

Only about 600 of the civilian labourers for the Thai railway were recruited from Singapore. The first batch of 200 labourers, dispatched in May 1943, went voluntarily, attracted by the offer of high wages, and two more groups followed in the next few months. But by August, information about the dreadful working conditions on the railway trickled through to Singapore. As labour and welfare officer responsible for recruitment, Shinozaki claimed that he gained exemption for Syonan from further labour demands and satisfied military objections by sending only one further small group of unemployed vagrants.

❧

In August 1943, in face of the worsening food situation and rising discontent, the Japanese military administration began to tighten security and called for a drastic reduction of Syonan's population. Fearing this might be achieved by another and bigger massacre, Shinozaki promoted voluntary migration to open up agricultural settlements up-country.

The first venture was organized in conjunction with the Overseas Chinese Association. The Japanese promised that the new settlement would be self-governing and, until it was in production, the Syonan municipality would supply food. A group of leading Chinese toured Johor and chose a site at Endau. They collected $1 million for the project, sent out men to clear the jungle and recruited voluntary pioneers. By September 1944 there were 12,000 settlers in what Lim Boon Keng called "our Chinese Utopia". Despite attacks by guerrillas, the settlement fared quite well, production was moderately satisfactory, and the health record was good, but most Singaporeans were city dwellers with no taste for farming, and the Endau settlement was abandoned when the war ended.

A similar settlement organized by Singapore Eurasians and Chinese Roman Catholics at Bahau in Negri Sembilan was a disaster from start to finish. The site was unhealthy, the soil poor, and the settlers were mainly middle-class white-collar workers, unsuited to pioneering conditions. Many died at Bahau, including their leader, Bishop Devals, and the survivors returned to Syonan.

~~~

Despite increasing physical hardships, Singaporeans found some compensation in Japan's weakening position, since it induced Tokyo to allot Southeast Asians a larger say in running their own affairs, in order to give them a vested interest in supporting the Japanese regime against the return of colonial rule. Initially the Japanese had intended Malaya to form an integral part of their empire, as a federation of protected states with a Governor-General based in Singapore, which would remain a Japanese colony. But from mid-1943, when the Japanese were shifting to the defensive, their attitude changed. While making no promises of independence, they no longer referred to Malaya as Japanese territory and spoke instead of co-operation in building a "New Malai".

After Watanabe was succeeded in March 1943 by the more conciliatory Major-General Masuzo Fujimura, Japanese political control became gradually more liberal. Advisory Councils were established in the various Malayan states and towns. The Syonan Advisory Council, founded in December 1943, consisted of a Japanese chairman with six Chinese representatives, four Malays, three Indians, one Eurasian and one Arab. The Council had no power to initiate policy or discussion and it met only when the Mayor thought fit to summon it. In practice it did not advise but merely received instructions, which were mainly about supporting the war effort. In March 1944 an information and publicity committee was formed under the Mayor's chairmanship to report public opinion and to publicize government policy by means of lectures, pamphlets and broadcasts.

In a vain attempt to win more positive Chinese support, in 1944 Colonel Hiroshi Hamada, Secretary-General of the Malayan Military Administration, established an *epposho*, or reading club, for Chinese in Syonan, but it was not a success. The following year, in July 1945, the Japanese set up a *hodosho*, or Help and Guide the People Office, to receive complaints and suggestions from all Syonan communities, but this was also ineffective.

On the retreat and seeking to gain the co-operation of local inhabitants in what was expected to be a long drawn-out struggle against the Allies, in the last months of the Occupation the Japanese talked of giving autonomy to Malaya, but made only vague references to independence for Syonan. Tojo called Syonan the "key point for the construction of Dai Toa",[37] the centre where regional affairs were discussed and political decisions on neighbouring countries were made. Tojo met the Burmese leader, Ba Maw, in July 1943 in Syonan, which was the first headquarters of the Free India government, and the venue for preparatory conferences held in 1945 to debate plans for Indonesian independence. Syonan had no political prospects or aspirations of her own, nor did she have any local administrators or leaders of stature to demand the power and influence that nationalist leaders acquired in other countries in the later stages of the Occupation.

Syonan's only nationalist movement of importance was in support of Indian independence, a political issue that the Japanese began to exploit in 1941 before they launched their Malayan campaign. From his base in Bangkok, Major Iwaichi Fujiwara contacted Pritam Singh, an Indian Independence League organizer, and sent agents to stir up disaffection among the Indian troops in northern Malaya.

Fujiwara and Pritam Singh accompanied the invading Japanese armies and won the support of Captain Mohan Singh, a regular officer of the British Indian army, who formed a detachment of Indian troops to fight alongside the invaders. Japanese troops were ordered to deal softly with Indians, not to antagonize them, or take reprisals. During the Malayan campaign they tried to induce Indian soldiers to change sides, often sending Indian prisoners back to their units with invitations to surrender. About 200 Indians took part in the Japanese decoy operation at Pulau Ubin before the invasion of Singapore, and they joined in the battle on the island.[38]

Fujiwara, Mohan Singh, and Pritam Singh addressed the assembly of Indian troops at Farrer Park following the surrender and persuaded half of them to join an Indian National Army under Mohan Singh's leadership to fight alongside the Japanese for the liberation of India. Pritam Singh organized branches of the Indian Independence League throughout Malaya, with a headquarters in Syonan, and a prominent Singapore lawyer, S.C. Goho, as first president. Fujiwara, Mohan Singh, Goho, Pritam Singh, and other Indian Independence League and Indian National Army delegates set off for a meeting in Tokyo in March 1942, but Pritam Singh was killed when his plane crashed.

Two months later Rash Behari Bose, head of the parent Indian Independence League, arrived in Singapore from Japan. Born in 1886, Rash Behari Bose had fled from India to Japan in 1915 after plotting an abortive mutiny. He founded the Indian Independence League in Tokyo in 1921, married a Japanese, and became a Japanese citizen in 1923.[39] From Syonan, Rash Behari Bose broadcast to urge Indians all over the region to join the movement, and in June 1942 the Japanese organized an Indian Independence League conference in Bangkok, which resolved to end British control in India by force.

The appeal roused considerable response, particularly from Sikhs and Hindus, but the first Indian National Army was a failure. The Japanese were reluctant to create an effective military force, preferring to divide it into small units attached to the Japanese army. Mohan Singh, who was a well-meaning patriot and at first viewed the Japanese as liberators of his country, soon came to realize that the Indian National Army was designed merely to be an instrument of propaganda.

The Indian community was divided in itself. Many Indian Muslims feared the movement would mean the subjection of their community to the Hindu majority. Even supporters and members of the Indian National Army began to criticize the soft living of Mohan Singh and other leaders, who resided in luxury at Mount Pleasant and moved about Singapore freely, frequently consorting with Japanese in hotels and restaurants. Their easy life was in stark contrast to their followers' spartan existence, provoking false rumours that Mohan Singh was using the movement to advance his personal ambitions and line his own pocket, and even that he had engineered Pritam Singh's death.[40]

In December 1942 the Japanese put Mohan Singh under house arrest, and the first Indian National Army was disbanded. It was reorganized first under Lieutenant-Colonel Bhonsale and subsequently under Lieutenant-Colonel Gilani, who had been Mohan Singh's second in command, but the army flagged. Attempts by Rash Behari Bose to keep the Indian Independence movement alive met with little enthusiasm because, after all his years in exile, he seemed more Japanese than Indian and was regarded as Tokyo's puppet.

The situation changed dramatically with the arrival in Singapore in July 1943 of a new dynamic leader, Subhas Chandra Bose, formerly the President of the Congress in India who had resigned at the beginning of the war in Europe, when the other Congress Party leaders refused to make a bid to seize independence through force. After Subhas Chandra Bose formed a militant Forward Bloc, the British put him under house arrest, but he escaped to Germany, whence he was smuggled by submarine to Singapore.

Rash Behari Bose, who was old and suffering from tuberculosis, willingly handed over leadership to Subhas Chandra Bose. The vibrant Netaji, or Leader, as he came to be known, stirred the Indian community and brought new life and force into the independence movement. At a mammoth meeting at the Cathay Building in July 1943, the great crowd listened spellbound and roared their approval. Shortly afterwards the

Indian National Army paraded on the Padang before Premier Tojo, the community leaders of Syonan, and about 20,000 spectators. Subhas Chandra Bose described Singapore as "the graveyard of the British empire",[41] and he set out to marshal the efforts of all Indians throughout the Far East to oust the British from India. He toured the Japanese-occupied countries, raising recruits and money, and at another meeting at the Cathay Cinema in Singapore in October 1943, he proclaimed the formation of the Azad Hind, or provisional government of Free India, and formally declared war on Britain and the United States.

Not only former Indian National Army members, but also many civilians and prisoners of war, who would have nothing to do with Mohan Singh's first army, now rushed to join the new Indian National Army and the Indian Independence League. Indians came from all over the East to enlist in Singapore. Tamil and Malayalee labourers joined in their thousands, girls and boys were organized in a "children's army", some young men were sent as cadets to Tokyo, and about 600 women joined a parallel women's movement, the Ranee of Jhansi Regiment, led by a Madras-born doctor, Lakshmi Swaminathan. Recruits were required to recite a Daily Prayer, which started with pledges of loyalty to Azad Hind and to Netaji Subhas Chandra Bose. Affluent families contributed gold and jewellery, and rich Indian businessmen donated large sums of money. Muslims were less enthusiastic, but most of them contributed, partly out of fear of reprisals and partly because membership of the Indian Independence League conferred some degree of immunity from Kempeitai oppression. Unemployed Indians were swept into the army, sometimes press-ganged by the Kempeitai.

By the end of 1943 the Indian National Army had two divisions. The first units, ill-equipped, ill-trained but high in spirit, were sent to fight in Burma, and in January 1944 Subhas Chandra Bose moved his Azad Hind government headquarters to Rangoon. In the months that followed, excitement reached fever pitch in Singapore, with the other communities resenting Indian collaboration with the Japanese but half envious of their evident enthusiasm and sense of purpose. Throughout February, March and April 1944 news of successes in Burma filled the Singapore newspapers. When Indian National Army units reached the border and raised their flag on Indian soil, new recruits and former fence sitters rushed to enlist, and Indian businessmen contributed enthusiastically to the cause. Indians in Singapore waited to celebrate the expected fall of Imphal, but the success stories and newspaper reports dried up. For weeks there was silence about Burma, but eventually stragglers came back to Singapore with news that the Japanese were being pushed back, and that the Indian National Army was breaking up with large-scale desertions.

Subhas Chandra Bose did not lose heart. He returned to Singapore in May 1945, set up his headquarters at Katong, and tried to revive support for the cause. But his movement never regained strength. Young men did not wish to risk their lives or businessmen their capital in a doomed venture. When Subhas Chandra Bose was killed in an air crash in Taiwan in August 1945, the Indian Independence League held a formal service for him in Singapore, but there was no public demonstration and little show of mourning.

ॐ

Despite a strict prohibition on press reports of Japanese reverses, news of defeats eventually began to filter through the thick Japanese propaganda screen. In November 1944 the American air force carried out its first raid on Singapore harbour. From that time Allied planes were frequently seen, but they restricted bombing, not wanting to damage installations that would be useful to them later. They preferred to neutralize Singapore by mining her waters and disrupting rail and sea communications.[42]

The Japanese retreat was welcomed with anticipation tinged with uncertainty and foreboding. Singaporeans feared that the liberation would be grimmer and bloodier than the initial defeat.

The Japanese conscripted the local population and concentrated prisoners-of-war working parties to construct defences, which they intended to hold to the death. Prisoners of war and internees feared they would be slaughtered in a last-ditch stand, and rumours went round among the local population that all English-educated Singaporeans and those suspected of sympathy with Britain were on blacklists, to be murdered if the British attacked Singapore. Singaporeans were convinced that the Japanese intended to fight to the last man and to eliminate any civilians who refused to co-operate.

Everyday living became almost unbearable. Even prisoners brought back from slaving to build the Burma-Thailand railway were shocked at the listless hunger and despair of the population. There were long queues for rice. Essential services, such as water, gas, and electricity, were breaking down as machinery wore out and could not be replaced. Bare of equipment and drugs, hospitals could not cope with the spread of beriberi, fevers, and other diseases that were rife in the Occupation. Even those in full-time employment had to supplement their incomes to pay soaring black market prices for food and medicines. Many people were dying of malnutrition, and most pathetic of all were Javanese workers, of whom the Japanese brought in about 10,000 as forced labourers and turned them loose on the streets like pariah dogs to die when they were no longer fit for work.

Prisoners of war and civilian internees were at their lowest ebb, and many died in the last dreadful months of the Occupation, when rations dwindled to starvation point. Early in 1945 the Japanese marshalled nearly 6,000 prisoners into work parties to construct defence works in Singapore and Johor, and from May 1945 intensive military exercises were held on the Padang for civilians, including women workers. It was obvious that the Japanese, unlike the British, intended to enrol Singaporeans as active participants, not merely spectators, in the battle for the recovery of Singapore. News of the end of the European war in May 1945 and the re-capture of Rangoon trickled through to Singapore and was celebrated secretly. By July 1945 Allied planes were seen overhead nearly every day, and the liberation of Singapore was only a question of time.

Japanese rule finished quietly in Singapore, which was spared the horrors of a battle for re-occupation. Initial reports about the explosion of atom bombs, the destruction of Japanese cities, and the parley for peace were kept secret among senior Japanese military officers, and the abrupt end of hostilities came as an unexpected shock even to most Japanese officials in Syonan.

Prisoners at Changi Gaol heard on their secret wireless sets about Japan's surrender on 15 August, but the Japanese made no public announcement until two days later. The prisoners in camp were then informed of the surrender, and Shinozaki made a public statement, not mentioning unconditional surrender but merely declaring that the Emperor had decided to end the war. Fearing the reaction of the Japanese soldiers, he warned Singaporeans not to hoist Union Jacks or celebrate openly. The announcement led immediately to a scramble to get rid of Japanese currency, and for a few days prices rocketed, cafes trebled their prices, and rickshaw pullers doubled their fares.

On 21 August the Singapore press formally announced the Japanese surrender for the first time. The Syonan Overseas Chinese Association and pro-Japanese organizations disbanded themselves, many policemen, officials, and rich collaborators quietly slipped away, and Taiwanese, who could pass for local Hokkien Chinese, faded into the general population. For a few days there was sudden deflation as Japanese organizations unloaded their hoarded commodities at giveaway prices, and Japanese employers stepped up rations of rice and cloth in a last-minute bid for popularity. Japanese signs were pulled down and Rising Sun flags were destroyed, while enterprising tailors started making Allied flags.

The Japanese prepared an internment camp at Jurong, to which most of them retreated with their belongings, leaving only a few officers to hand over to the incoming British administration. Three weeks of anxious waiting followed, since General Douglas MacArthur, Supreme Commander for Allied Powers, ordered that other Allied military forces should not land or re-occupy territory until the Japanese had formally surrendered to him.

Work parties were brought back to Changi and within a few days there were 12,000 military prisoners in the gaol. British aircraft dropped leaflets to tell them to remain there, and at the end of the month doctors and stores were dropped by parachute into the camp. The Governor had been taken away, the Colonial Secretary was dead, and, unlike their counterparts in Hong Kong, former officials, who were numbed and dazed rather than exhilarated, made no attempt to resume control but stayed as instructed in the Sime Road internment camp. Since guerrilla resistance had been confined to the jungles of Malaya, Singapore did not experience on the same scale the up-country bloodbaths, kangaroo trials, racial bitterness, and retribution at the hands of the Malayan People's Anti-Japanese Army in the interregnum between Japan's collapse and the British return. Instead, the island was gripped by a "Whispering Terror" during these jittery weeks.[43] Gangs of Chinese youths in trams and lorries carrying communist flags sought out collaborators. "People's trials" were held in the Geylang district and some collaborators, including Wee Twee Kim, were executed. Some Sikh watchmen and Malay policemen were killed, but most hid away. Former Indian National Army troops lived in terror in their camp at Bidadari and many fled.

The *Syonan Shimbun* appealed for calm, but the administration had broken down, the currency was worthless and there was widespread looting. Most Singaporeans waited impatiently for the British to return, afraid to celebrate openly for fear Japanese soldiers might take retribution. At last, on 5 September, British warships arrived and Commonwealth troops landed to a tumultuous welcome. The 3-mile route from the Empire Dock to the Cathay Building was lined with cheering crowds, waving British, American, Russian, and Kuomintang flags. A week later, on 12 September, amid the jeers of the assembled crowd, five Japanese generals and two admirals led the delegation that climbed the steps of the municipal building to surrender formally to Admiral Lord Louis Mountbatten, Supreme Allied Commander in Southeast Asia.

The same Union Jack used in 1942 at the time of the British surrender, and had been hidden since then in Changi Gaol, was raised over the city by Lady Thomas, who had spent the war years in the women's internment camp. The flag was a symbol of the old regime. The myth of Japanese invincibility was shattered. "Singapore is British Again! Our Day of Liberation!" proclaimed the *Straits Times* in its first post-war issue on 7 September.

Commonwealth troops returned in 1945 to a different Singapore and a changed Southeast Asia. As Tsuji put it, the statue of Raffles, which the British restored to Empress Place with great ceremony a few months later, had somehow faded in colour. "The halo of victory must shine on the Union Jack, but today there remains little vestige of its glory of former times." The regime was welcomed back with genuine relief because it was benign, its weaknesses were sins of omission, its memory was not marred by cruelty, or dragooning the population. Nevertheless, the only ultimate justification for a colonial power was its ability to protect, and in this the British colonial regime had been tried and found wanting. The old unquestioning trust in British protection had been shattered forever.

For the moment, the return of the British meant the end of a nightmare. Another ten troubled years were to pass before a new generation of leaders emerged, who had experienced the shock of the surrender and occupation and the exhilaration of the post-war winds of change, and who were to challenge the British right to rule.

7

The Aftermath of War
1945–1955

To suggest that the British returned to Malaya "to find the entire population caught up in a vast social, political and cultural uprising"[1] but determined to re-impose the old regime is misleading on both counts. While the colonial authority's days were numbered, the immediate concern of the vast majority of the local population was to get back to the normal pattern of everyday life: to find work, decent accommodation, schooling, and enough to eat. Rice, not politics, was Singaporeans' first priority in September 1945. And, so far from reverting to "business as usual", the British arrived back with a radical new plan for political re-organization, which was to turn Malaya topsy-turvy and provoke an ethnic backlash of a most old-fashioned kind.

The Colonial Office had begun drawing up schemes for the future in the months immediately following the collapse of British power in Malaya.[2] The most pressing concern was to silence American criticism and forestall any demands from Washington and Chungking for the permanent dismantling of British colonial rule in Southeast Asia. For some years London officials had looked uneasily at the growing anachronism of "British Malaya", with its collection of protectorates and its "reactionary Governor and his

Council of quaint notables".[3] In particular, Edward Gent, the Assistant Permanent Under-Secretary in the Colonial Office, who had accompanied Sir Samuel Wilson on his visit to Malaya in 1932, saw the dramatic break in colonial rule as an opportunity to put a unified political structure in place of the pre-war fragmentation. This would ensure administrative efficiency and military security, and would facilitate the British government's declared policy to encourage self-government.[4]

An initial proposal to group the Malay States, Straits Settlements, North Borneo, Sarawak, and Brunei into a union, with Singapore as "the natural centre of trade and communications"[5] was abandoned as premature. Instead Gent drew up alternative plans to break up the Straits Settlements, merge the former four Federated and five Unfederated Malay States, Penang and Melaka into a Malayan Union, leaving Singapore as a separate entity and the base for a governor-general, who would co-ordinate policy in British territories throughout the region.[6]

Singapore was excluded in order not to jeopardize the complicated negotiations for establishing the Malayan Union, which already presented immense problems in persuading the Malay sultans to surrender sovereignty and incorporating immigrant communities in a common citizenship. There were many reasons why trying to include Singapore would threaten difficulties: a history of jealousy and distrust in past relations with the peninsula and her incompatibility as a free port, an imperial strategic base, and a predominantly Chinese city.[7] In any event the island was expected to remain under military rule for a considerable time after liberation, as the Southeast Asia logistics centre for Allied operations against Japan, while the rest of Malaya would probably revert fairly quickly to civil rule.

The War Cabinet approved the constitutional scheme in principle in May 1944, and detailed planning for the post-liberation administration of civil affairs was handed over to a Malayan Planning Unit. Established in July 1943, this small unit of half a dozen officials comprised Ralph Hone, legal expert and former Attorney General of Uganda, and senior Malayan

Civil Service officials, such as Patrick MacKerron, who had escaped internment by being outside the country at the time of capitulation.

Advice was sought from those with experience of Malaya, but most favoured a federation rather than a unitary state and were averse to separating Singapore. In a sharp exchange with Gent, Sidney Caine, then Economic Adviser to the Colonial Office and subsequently the first Vice-Chancellor of the University of Malaya, suggested waiting to see what local people wanted before foisting a ready-made plan on them. Since Singapore and peninsular Malaya were economically interdependent, separating the island would be like cutting London out of Britain. Provided some facilities were retained to protect Singapore's entrepôt trade, Caine argued that a union would offer economic and administrative advantages and encourage the growth of a Malayan national consciousness. "We have everything to gain by blurring and not by sharpening the distinctions between one race and another in the peninsula."[8] Gent brushed this aside along with other unwelcome advice from Malayans who had taken refuge in India. These included Tan Cheng Lock, his son, Tan Siew Sin, and two pre-war Singapore municipal councilors: John Laycock, a prominent British lawyer, and Tan Chin Tuan, co-managing director of the Oversea Chinese Banking Corporation. A Malayan Association of India was formed in December 1942, but, after some months of wrangling with the Europeans, in September 1943 most of the Chinese members formed their own Overseas Chinese Association, with Tan Cheng Lock as president, Tan Chin Tuan as vice-president and Tan Siew Sin as secretary. In November 1943 Tan Cheng Lock sent a long memorandum to the Colonial Office, appealing for a union or federation of the Straits Settlements with all the Malay States, and for equal rights and representation for all who made Malaya their home. The Colonial Office welcomed the moderate tone of the memorandum but was not swayed by Tan's arguments about keeping the integrity of the Straits Settlements. They thanked him, referred vaguely to closer liaison in the future, then filed the booklet away and ignored it.[9]

A further memorandum from India, submitted by John Laycock and Tan Chin Tuan, together with Tunku Abu Bakar of the Johor royal house and Oliver Holt, a British Singapore businessman, objected to any shift of the political centre from Singapore to Kuala Lumpur as "opposed both to geography and good sense", but the Colonial Office waved this opinion aside too, with the comment that it "offered nothing to help to guide our thought in formulating future policy".[10] A proposal from the Association of British Malaya in London for a federation to include the Straits Settlements also received short shrift.

The British government was making its plans in the dark, with hardly any knowledge of what was going on in Malaya. After the war in Europe came to an end, the Allies planned to retake Singapore as a first priority, and to use the island as a support base for ten army divisions, of which two would be actually maintained in Malaya.[11] They hoped to capture Singapore early in 1946 but doubted whether all the troops diverted from Europe would be fully operational in the Far East until the summer of that year, after which they expected many months of hard fighting before Japan was finally defeated. During this time the British intended to test "the temper of the people" and their reaction to the constitutional proposals. Details for Operation Tide-race, the plan to recapture Singapore, were still being finalized in Rangoon in mid-August 1945, when Japan capitulated. This sudden and unexpected end of the Pacific War threw all political schemes out of gear. Ten days later, on 25 August 1945, before the British had completed preparations to land their forces, the Malayan Communist Party's central executive published a liberal eight-point manifesto, with its major declared aim, "To establish a democratic government in Malaya with an electorate drawn from all races of each state and the anti-Japanese army". Chin Peng later accused Lai Teck of treachery in throwing away a golden opportunity to strike before imperial forces re-occupied the country, but, whatever the secretary-general's motive, this co-operative "soft line" declaration was not entirely welcome to Lord Louis Mountbatten, the Supreme Allied Commander. Relief that the potentially dangerous communist-dominated guerrilla army was not going to make trouble was mixed with embarrassment that the communists "have rather stolen our thunder and that we have lost that element of surprise for our progressive policy which would politically have been so valuable".[12] On paper the manifesto resembled the Colonial Office's own plan so closely that London feared their long-deliberated schemes might appear to have been dictated and forced upon them by the Malayan Communist Party.

Abandoning hopes of a long period of consultation, the British government dispatched an emissary, Sir Harold MacMichael, to renegotiate treaties with the sultans. At the same time the Secretary of State for the Colonies announced the new policy to Parliament immediately after it re-assembled from the summer recess in October 1945, and set out detailed proposals in a White Paper issued in January 1946. He stressed that Singapore had ties with the mainland, but union should not be forced. "Union must grow, if grow it will, and a premature decision to force into one entity communities with such widely different interests might cause friction and might cast a shadow over the whole future of the area."

Retired governors and senior Malayan officials protested the proposed separation and demanded a meeting at the Colonial Office. Sir Shenton Thomas, who had himself drawn up a detailed proposal for re-organizing Malaya while he was in internment, considered the scheme with two separate governors and an overall governor-general as "overloaded and extravagant in conception". "The Governor of Singapore will not have enough to do." Thomas's protests carried no weight with the Colonial Office,[13] neither was it swayed by Sir Cecil Clementi's argument that to exclude Singapore was to "cut the heart out of Malaya".[14]

◈

Once the war cabinet had agreed to separate Singapore, little thought was given to its future, while the Colonial Office concentrated on the complicated peninsular problems. After a long period of military administration the island was expected to become "a sort of District of Columbia", the headquarters of the British Governor-General for Southeast Asia, with its own local government.[15] The Colonial Office memorandum on "Constitutional Reconstruction in the Far East" drawn up in July 1943 was vague as to whether Singapore should even be a colony proper or be treated merely as an enlarged municipality.[16]

Nothing had been decided when the British landed in September 1945. For the moment the island became the headquarters of the British Military Administration under Supreme Allied Commander Lord Mountbatten, who had overall political and administrative control throughout Southeast Asia. Mountbatten delegated civil government to Sir Ralph Hone, Chief Civil Affairs Officer for Malaya, with Patrick McKerron as Deputy Chief Civil Affairs Officer in Singapore.

British Military Administration officials took charge of civil affairs immediately, and a programme was launched to send expatriate internees home on recuperative leave as quickly as practical. This applied not only to government employees but to commercial employees, planters, miners, and others. Plans to restrict the English-language press to one official *Malayan Times* news-sheet were thwarted by the enterprise of the *Straits Times* journalists. Local staff, who had saved the machinery and newsprint from looting on the day of liberation, together with their Western colleagues, who came straight from internment camp to join them, defied orders to stop printing. Within twenty-four hours they produced and distributed free copies of the first post-war edition of the *Straits Times*. Mountbatten was so impressed that he told the *Straits Times* to carry on, and the official *Malayan Times* was abandoned.[17]

Both Mckerron and Hone recommended merging the former central and local authorities into one Island Council,[18] but the Colonial Office decided to play safe or, in their own words, to keep "well tried and successful organs of government"; the unwieldy hierarchy of Executive, Legislative, Municipal Councils and Rural Board that had served the former Straits Settlements would remain, but there would be greater opportunities for representation.

Meanwhile, in November 1945 Hone presided over the opening session of a Singapore Advisory Council, comprising seventeen nominated members, including Tan Chin Tuan, Lee Kong Chian and former guerrilla leader Wu Tian Wang, chairman of the Malayan Communist Party's Singapore Town Committee. The first meeting was amicable and constructive, but the Council became increasingly critical of the slow pace of reconstruction, the trade restrictions, shortages, and hardships.[19]

Singaporeans had welcomed the British forces back as liberators, but hopes of a quick recovery soon faded, and honeymoon bliss turned sour. As the official British history of the period admits, "While propagandists contrasted Allied 'liberation' with enemy 'occupation', the distinction between the two processes was not always so clear to those who were being 'liberated'."[20]

Peace did not bring an end to hunger and want. Food was in short supply, shipping was disorganized and neighbouring rice-producing countries had no surplus to export. Prices of essential commodities soon soared to ten times the pre-war level, and regulations to control the price of rice, fish and vegetables could not be enforced. The *Singapore Annual Report for 1946* lamented "the false hopes, the disappointments, the occasional reliefs, and above all, the nightmare expectations of what might happen next month, after scraping the cupboard bare of all supplies".[21]

The railway and docks had been damaged by Allied bombing. Six major wrecks choked the harbour, 70 per cent of godown accommodation had been destroyed and not a single crane was in working order. More than half the Harbour Board's machinery was destroyed or missing, and all the pre-war tugs and dredgers had vanished.

The town was dirty, neglected, and dilapidated – the roads full of potholes – while water, electricity, gas, and telephone services were run down. Overcrowding, poverty and disease were chronic. The enormous sums demanded for accommodation during the Occupation had forced thousands to become squatters, putting up unsanitary shacks without any amenities. The death rate in 1945 was twice the pre-war level, and hospitals were bare of equipment or medicines, often even lacking furniture or bedding.

One of the most urgent problems was to restore law and order. The incoming administration found the police force "nothing more than an ill-clad, badly equipped and poorly disciplined rabble", "undernourished, dirty, driven to corruption through necessity, and untrained".[22] The police were so hated and despised as tools of Japanese oppression and cruelty that in the first weeks after the liberation, police stations had to be barred and guarded for fear of reprisals.

Permeating the whole of society was the Occupation's worst legacy, the corruption of public and private integrity: flourishing gambling dens and brothels, both legalized by the Japanese, the resurgence of opium smoking, universal profiteering, and bribery. Perhaps most insidious of all was the selfish cynicism and contempt for the old virtues of honesty, hard work, and thrift in favour of quick profits and easy spending. Too often profiteers and former collaborators prospered, while many loyal government employees were subject to humiliating investigations before being reinstated in their former posts. The restored British administration often leaned on men who had been useful to the colonial regime in the past and equally adaptable to the Japanese: the professional survivors who had grown rich and influential during the Occupation.

The senior British Military Administration officials were honest men of high calibre, but minor officials were often not so scrupulous, and the opportunities for black-market enterprise, which had attracted the worst sort of Japanese during the Occupation, now brought in the most corrupt Westerners. "We Chinese never realized that there were Europeans like them," a senior Malayan Civil Service official was told.[23] The British Military Administration requisitioned private property arbitrarily and grossly mismanaged the distribution of rice. Its financial inefficiency and scandalous corruption were criticized openly in the Advisory Council and the "BMA" was commonly referred to as the "Black Market Administration".[24] In its seven months it destroyed the goodwill that existed at the time of the liberation and brought British prestige in Singapore to an even lower point than in February 1942.[25]

At least the fear and brutality of the Occupation had gone, and despite disappointments, inefficiencies, and corruption, the British Military Administration made some positive achievements. Top priority was given to restoring public utilities, water, electricity and gas supplies. The Royal Navy transferred the port to civilian control within eight weeks, law courts reopened, collaborators and undesirables were weeded out of the police force, and a new police recruiting campaign was launched.

The administration came to grips quickly with the most pressing demands for education, and within three weeks reopened fourteen Malay and fourteen English schools. Despite lack of equipment and neglected buildings, teachers set to with enthusiasm and vigour on the task of rehabilitation, trying not only to satisfy the great hunger for education but also distributing food and other supplies and coping with many problems of social distress. The Chinese also rushed to reopen their schools, and by the end of 1945, sixty-six Chinese, thirty-seven English, and twenty-one Malay schools were in operation. In addition to the normal intake, a generation of overage children who had received no schooling during the Occupation had to be absorbed, and by

March 1946 62,000 children were in school. It took a little longer to revive higher education, but the Medical College took back former students in June 1946, and, together with Raffles College, admitted the first new intake in October that year.

The main key to recovery lay in resurrecting the ruined Malayan economy, but the military bureaucracy was not well-suited to do this. The intention was to restore free private enterprise as quickly as possible and not to interfere with Singapore's free port status, but initially the Military Administration selected seven leading industrial, transport, and mining companies, six based in Singapore and the seventh in Selangor, giving them priority in importing supplies and getting staff released from military service.[26] Very few other foreign-owned companies managed to reopen before the early months of 1946, and Asian businessmen, who had sought refuge overseas, found it difficult to secure passages to return. Companies had lost many of their staff, and virtually all their records had been looted, while buildings were requisitioned by the military or were in disrepair.

A war crimes commission was established to investigate atrocities, and in October 1945 a special court was established to try such cases. *Kempei*, prison guards, and other Japanese accused of committing atrocities were put in Changi Gaol to await trial, but the rest of the Japanese community, almost 7,000 strong, were held in the camp at Jurong. Japanese military prisoners were brought in later from the surrounding countries and about 12,000 were employed as labourers for the next two years.

Indian National Army men and Indian Independence League supporters were screened. Most were exonerated, but many former regular soldiers were discharged from the British army, and the officers were sent to stand trial in Delhi. Indian troops pulled down the monument that the Indian National Army had erected on the Esplanade, and the Japanese shrine and war memorial were blown up.

There was loud public demand to punish collaborators, and many arrests were made, including the Eurasian and Indian community leaders, Charles Paglar and S.C. Goho and *Berita Malai* editor, Samad Ismail. The cases against all three were dropped in March 1946, but Paglar's trial roused considerable passions among the British community. Many regarded collaboration by Eurasians as special treachery, but Shinozaki, who had been released and employed by the British field security service as a translator and interpreter, spoke in Paglar's defence. Most accusations took the form of complaints against informers and blackmailers. The court often found it difficult to weigh evidence and distinguish spite from genuine grievances, and, in their concern to heal wounds, the British administration came to condone collaboration where no physical brutality was proved. Lai Teck, the most notorious of all the collaborators, gave himself up to the British, with whom he co-operated in secret for the next two years, unbeknown to his former comrades in the Malayan People's Anti-Japanese Army, while remaining secretary-general of the Malayan Communist Party.

The first war crimes case, which opened in Singapore in January 1946, dealt with allegations of cruel treatment of Indian prisoners of war, who had been consigned as forced labourers to the Netherlands East Indies. This was followed in March 1946 by the "Double Tenth Trial", in which twenty-one members of the Singapore Kempeitai, including its then chief, Lieutenant-Colonel Sumida Haruzo, were accused of the torture and murder of internees and civilians in the reign of terror that began at Changi Gaol on 10 October 1943. The crimes were specific, the survivors' testimony was overwhelming, the perpetrators were well-known to their victims, and the trial resulted in the conviction of fourteen of the accused, of whom eight, including Sumida Haruzo, were executed, and the other six imprisoned.

The outcome of the *sook ching* trial was very different. The trial, which was the last of its kind, opened in Victoria Memorial Hall in March 1947, and the accused included Major-General Kawamura and Colonel Oishi. Tay Koh Yat, whose eldest son had disappeared in the *sook ching*, headed a Singapore Chinese Massacre Appeal Committee, and wealthy Chinese contributed generously in time and money to collect testimony. Evidence of individual culpability was inconclusive. Of the chief people allegedly responsible, Yamashita had already been executed, Tsuji had disappeared, and others had been killed during the war. Hardly any victims survived to act as witnesses to specific crimes, and those who carried out the actual killing were small fry, who could not be identified or had perished in the war. While there were strong indications that Tsuji had deliberately set targets to massacre up to 50,000 Chinese,[27] the exact origin and interpretation of the instructions were ambiguous.[28] Kawamura and Oishi were condemned to death and five others to life imprisonment, but the Chinese community was incensed at the leniency of a verdict so disproportionate to the enormity of the crime. The Massacre Appeal Committee petitioned the Governor to review the sentences, but in vain. There was insufficient concrete evidence of specific crimes, committed by known individuals against particular victims, which would hold up in court and warrant more convictions. To the Chinese it seemed that the British were only interested in securing justice for crimes committed against a handful of their own people and cared little for the much greater brutality inflicted on countless thousands of Chinese.

Many years later, in March 1962, building work uncovered mass graves in Siglap, which bore out the rumours of wartime massacres in that district. The discovery unleashed a torrent of emotion among the Chinese community, with the Singapore Chinese Chamber of Commerce and the Chinese newspapers renewing the call for Japan to pay blood money to the bereaved families to appease the souls of their hungry ghosts. Coming at a dangerously critical moment in Singapore politics, Lee Kuan Yew feared the left wing would exploit the clamour as a divisive racial issue. In the keynote speech at a mass rally held in August 1963, he insisted this was an atrocity against all the people of Singapore. In October 1965, soon after independence, Japan finally agreed to pay a blood debt to the Singapore government. The urns containing bones of thousands of corpses were buried beneath a Civilian War Memorial with four pillars to represent the four main communities, supposedly united in common suffering.[29]

❧

At the time of the liberation, the communists were hailed as great heroes of the day. The communist-dominated Malayan People's Anti-Japanese Army had gained prestige both among the masses and many middle-class Chinese by being identified as anti-Japanese patriots. Committed for the time being to a soft-line approach, the Malayan Communist Party agreed for the time being to disband its military arm and to work towards its goal by political subversion.

The Malayan People's Anti-Japanese Army was formally disbanded in January 1946 at a moving final parade on the Padang in Singapore, when Mountbatten presented medals to the resistance leaders, including the guerrilla commander, Chin Peng. Arms and ammunition were surrendered, but the Party had secretly retained substantial stocks of weapons and formed an ex-servicemen's association to keep the organization together.

Singapore's post-war political climate was ideal for cultivating communist influence. A man of liberal views, Mountbatten was eager to encourage the free expression of political opinions, and as a reward for wartime co-operation the British felt obliged for the first time to recognize the Malayan Communist Party as legal. Wu Tian Wang's appointment to the Advisory Board enabled him to make political capital by taking a public stand against the corruption of the administration.

The Malayan Communist Party's small Singapore Town Committee operated through several front organizations, the most important being the General Labour Union, by means of which the party sought to consolidate a mass following among Singapore's workers. Here the communists had a virgin field to plough. The Japanese had stamped out labour unrest, and there were no existing trade unions, while the liberal labour legislation passed just before the war permitted people who were not connected with the trade to share in the management of unions and placed few restrictions on the use of union funds.

Immediately after the surrender, the General Labour Union set up its headquarters in Singapore with branches in other Malayan towns and promised to campaign for better working conditions, shorter hours, and the creation of an All-Malayan Working Class United Front. The glamour and prestige that the Malayan Communist Party had acquired during the war, combined with genuine grievances arising from the immediate post-war dislocation, unemployment, inflation, and shortages, enabled the General Labour Union to build up its membership quickly.

A successful strike by 7,000 dockers to obtain higher wages in October 1945 was soon followed by strikes among Singapore Traction Company employees, hospital staff, firemen, and even cabaret girls. Not wanting to use force against organized labour, Mountbatten pleaded for disputes to be settled by amicable negotiation without intimidation. The increasingly aggressive tactics of the General Labour Union led to a tougher official line and the use of Japanese prisoners of war to replace strikers, which in turn generated further labour trouble.

The source of discontent was genuine enough. There was widespread unemployment, food was scarce, and the cost of living was rising steeply. In December 1945 a reduction of the rice ration to 3 *kati* (600 grams) a week provoked a mass demonstration of 6,000 workers who assembled on the Padang to demand bigger rations and higher wages, after which the authorities banned meetings and processions except under licence.

By the end of 1945 the Singapore General Labour Union included more than sixty trade unions, and it staged a two-day general strike in January 1946, after the British Military Administration jailed Soon Khwong, its secretary-general, on charges of intimidation and extortion. Altogether 173,000 strikers stopped work, and transport came to a halt. When the government gave way and released Soon Khwong, the communists were convinced that the British Military Administration was too weak to take action against them.

In February 1946 all the unions incorporated in the General Labour Unions of Singapore and Malaya formed a Pan-Malayan Federation of Trade Unions, with two constituent parts: one on the mainland and the other registered as the Singapore Federation of Trade Unions. Both were dominated by the Malayan Communist Party and affiliated to the World Federation of Trade Unions. The Pan-Malayan Federation of Trade Unions, which claimed a membership of 450,000, was formally inaugurated on 15 February 1946, the anniversary of the British defeat in Singapore, when the Malayan Communist Party applied to hold a procession ostensibly to lament this "day of mourning". The British Military Administration refused a permit and on the eve of the planned procession arrested twenty-seven leading communists, ten of whom were subsequently banished without trial. After this setback the communists gave up direct action in favour of quietly extending their hold over the trade union movement and supporting other radical groups in seeking constitutional change.

∽

The period of military administration came to an end in April 1946, when the Malayan Union was enforced on the mainland, and Singapore reverted to civil administration as a Crown Colony, under the governorship of Sir Franklin Gimson.

The British Labour government agreed with some reluctance to accept the wartime Cabinet's decision to dissolve the Straits Settlements.[30] Singapore in fact preserved many links with the Malayan Union: currency, higher education, immigration, income tax, civil aviation, posts, and telegraphs were to be administered on a pan-Malayan basis. As the British government declared, "It is no part of the policy of His Majesty's government to preclude or prejudice in any way the fusion of Singapore and the Malayan

Union in a wider union at a later date should it be considered that such a course was desirable."[31]

Britain's post-war constitutional proposals had taken Malaya by surprise. The war had weakened colonial authority without creating a positive nationalist movement to replace it, and the country lacked political organizations to respond immediately to the proposed change. Most Singaporeans showed little interest, but vocal minorities objected to the separation of Singapore from various viewpoints. The Malayan Communist Party saw it as a threat to its projected united Malayan Republic. The Kesatuan Melayu Singapura did not want to raise barriers between peninsular and Singapore Malays. The Chinese Chamber of Commerce objected to cutting off Singapore as "the centre of Malayan economy, politics and culture".[32]

The Malayan Union proposal provoked the formation of Singapore's first indigenous political party, the multiracial Malayan Democratic Union, which supported the idea of a Malayan Union, but insisted Singapore should be included too. The party's manifesto, issued in December 1945, was a moderate document, proposing to work towards self-government by extending representation in the Legislative Council and liberalizing citizenship requirements, with the eventual aim of making Singapore part of a self-governing Malaya within the British Commonwealth. The party called for social and education reforms: an expanded housing programme, integrated schools where different language streams would study under one roof, a local university, and democratic trade unions. It was a lone voice in welcoming the introduction of income tax to finance social improvements.

Philip Hoalim, the party's chairman and chief financier, was a well-known lawyer who was born in British Guiana but had practised in Singapore for the past sixteen years,[33] and most members were English-educated, middle class, often university-trained professional men of moderate political views, who believed in uniting to work for an independent united Malaya. But from the start effective leadership lay in the hands of left-wing radicals, such as Cambridge-educated lawyers, Lim Kean Chye and John Eber, who founded the party, and Eu Chooi Yip, journalist and former Raffles College economics graduate, who was the paid secretary. Wu Tian Wang also gave strong support, and by 1948 the Malayan Democratic Union had become a Malayan Communist Party front organization.

Meanwhile, in peninsular Malaya, the Malayan Union scheme provoked passionate opposition and the formation of the United Malays National Organization (UMNO), which came into being in Kuala Lumpur in March 1946 on the eve of the inauguration of the new form of government. UMNO boycotted the Malayan Union ceremony, claiming that the transfer of sovereignty over the Malay States was invalid since the sultans had been forced to sign away their rights, and that the proposed citizenship laws offering equal political status to immigrant communities were unfair to the Malays. This spirited opposition and the widespread and vociferous support that UMNO aroused among the Malays at all levels of society came as a shock to the British, who entered into confidential consultations with UMNO leaders and the Malay sultans to draw up revised proposals. These were based on a federation of the peninsular states and settlements, with stricter citizenship requirements, more safeguards for Malays and their sultans, and elective representation postponed to an unspecified date.[34] The only feature of the Malayan Union that survived was the separation of Singapore, on which the Malay leaders insisted on the grounds that, if Singapore were incorporated in the Malayan federation, the Chinese would outnumber the Malays.

The upsurge of Malay nationalism sparked off a countermovement, particularly in Singapore. The communists, denouncing the new constitutional proposals as "the cloven hoof of British Imperialism", called a mass rally of 20,000 people at Farrer Park in September 1946 to demand self-government for Malaya and equality for all who made their home there. In October 1946 the Malayan Democratic Union asked the government to appoint a committee representing all parties and communities to discuss new constitutional proposals. The disparate opposition groups decided to form a united front, and in December 1946 they created a Pan-Malayan Council of Joint Action, with the veteran Straits Chinese leader, Tan Cheng Lock, as chairman. The body comprised the Malayan Democratic Union, the Malayan Indian Congress, the Singapore Women's Federation, the Singapore Clerical Union, the General Labour Union, the Straits Chinese British Association, the Singapore Indian Chamber of Commerce, the Singapore Tamils Association, and various communal, commercial, women's, and youth organizations.[35] While the Malayan Communist Party was not officially a member, it was the dominant force behind the scenes and was represented by a number of front organizations, notably the Malayan People's Anti-Japanese Ex-Service Comrades' Association.

The British refused to recognize the Pan-Malayan Council of Joint Action's claim to be consulted as the representative of domiciled non-Malay opinion and insisted on negotiating only with UMNO leaders and the Malay rulers. In April 1947 the Pan-Malayan Council of Joint Action made a formal alliance with the Pusat Tenaga Ra'ayat (People's United Front or PUTERA) formed by the left-wing Malay Nationalist Party, which opposed the conservative, aristocrat-dominated UMNO and aimed to merge Malaya in a union with Indonesia.

John Eber, as secretary-general of the now renamed All-Malaya Council of Joint Action, drew up a counter scheme in the form of *The People's Constitutional Proposals for Malaya*.[36] This demanded the inclusion of Singapore in a federated Malaya, with an executive council responsible to a legislative assembly elected by all adults domiciled in Malaya, but with certain safeguards to ensure the predominance of Malays in the assembly during a transitional fifteen-year phase.

The All-Malaya Council of Joint Action organized mass rallies and in October 1947 obtained the support of Chinese Chambers of Commerce throughout Singapore and Malaya for a nation-wide *hartal*, or economic boycott. This marked the high-water mark of opposition unity and was supported with enthusiasm by the immigrant communities, although it kindled little response among the English-educated. It aroused passionate Malay hostility, and the British bowed to the Malay leaders' view that communal differences were too deep to create an immediate self-governing state with racial equality. They accepted the UMNO proposal for the gradual assimilation of immigrants into a Malay state that would work towards independence under British guidance. On this basis the Malayan Union gave way to a Federation of Malaya in February 1948 while Singapore remained a separate Crown Colony.

The polyglot All-Malaya Council of Joint Action-PUTERA alliance disintegrated rapidly. While the Associated Chinese Chambers of Commerce opposed the separation of Singapore and restrictive citizenship clauses, they had no liking for the radical *People's Constitutional Proposals*, nor did they relish any communist connection. They refused to respond to Tan Cheng Lock's call for a second *hartal* in January 1948 and turned their backs on the movement. In March 1948 the Malayan Communist Party withdrew its support, and, deprived of financial backing and mass support, the All-Malaya Council of Joint Action fell apart.

Singapore was left to follow her separate course and work out her own constitutional problems, although events in the Federation were soon to have a powerful impact upon the colony.

∾

For the present, most Singaporeans were preoccupied with the hardships of everyday living. Food was still desperately short, and in May 1947 the weekly rice ration fell to 1½ *kati* a head, equivalent to the lowest level during the Occupation. Singaporeans had to revert to eating tapioca, and there were queues for bread, tinned milk, and other foodstuffs. Malnutrition and tuberculosis were rife, and wages did not keep pace with rising prices. Some employers issued workers with free or cheap rice supplies, and the government set up people's restaurants in 1947 to provide meals at controlled prices, but these measures went only a small way in alleviating the general misery. Secret societies flourished and violence reached such a pitch that the pre-war Societies Ordinance, which was held in abeyance in the immediate post-war period, was reinstated in April 1947.

The Malayan Communist Party set out to exploit the widespread discontent for its own political ends in a renewed bid to capture the labour movement. In 1946 and 1947 the General Labour Union organized strikes in the Harbour Board, public transport, fire and postal services, hospitals, and many private firms, both European and Chinese. Some stoppages involved thousands of workers and dragged on for weeks at a time. Most strikes succeeded in gaining higher wage awards, which gave the Malayan Communist Party great *kudos* and attracted more workers to its unions.

Those who were reluctant were forced to join. The Singapore Federation of Trade Unions formed a Singapore Workers' Protection Corps, consisting largely of secret society gangsters and former Malayan People's Anti-Japanese Army members, who broke up or intimidated non-communist unions. By the beginning of 1947 the Singapore Federation of Trade Unions claimed to control three-quarters of the entire organized labour force and aimed to dominate the port, the municipality, public works and transport. The combination of determined leadership, successful strikes and intimidation gave the communists a stranglehold over labour, which would be difficult to break, unless democratic unions could take root and living conditions improved.

In an effort to build up a legitimate democratic trade union movement in Malaya, in December 1945 the British government had appointed John Brazier as Industrial Relations Adviser to the British Military Administration and subsequently Pan-Malayan Trade Union Adviser. A former National Union of Railwaymen organizer, "Battling Jack" Brazier was an energetic and determined opponent of both communism and imperialism, and was anxious to create non-political unions. His position was extremely difficult. Employers resented him, the colonial government gave him only lukewarm support, and he found workers reluctant to become involved, caught between fear of communist intimidation on the one hand and government repression on the other. Nevertheless, from March 1947 the colonial authorities began to register a number of non-political unions under the 1940 Trade Union Ordinance, which enabled closer official supervision over finance and membership and forbade the use of funds for political purposes.

At the same time the standard of living began to improve at last as a worldwide demand for rubber and tin hastened Singapore's recovery. Despite quotas, currency restrictions, and strikes, by 1947 the volume of trade was considerably heavier than before the war, and in 1948 Malayan rubber production exceeded even the wartime 1940 peak. Trade expansion, more effective enforcement of rationing and price controls, and abundant harvests in 1948 brought an end to the worst shortages and hardships. By 1949 social services were restored at least to pre-war levels, while infant mortality and general death rates were the lowest on record.[37]

The steadily improving economic position undermined the effectiveness of communist agitation, which up to that point had played with considerable success on genuine grievances among workers. By the end of 1947 many Singapore workers were disillusioned with the Malayan Communist Party's use of trade unions to promote political ends instead of fighting for better conditions. A mission sent out from Britain early in 1948 to investigate the state of trade unions revealed how the communists used strikes for purely political purposes. They "call strikes but pay no strike pay … frame demands but carry out no negotiations … while pushing forward union leaders whom they interfere with and often intimidate".[38] When the communists embarked on a programme of defiance that had little to do with wages or conditions of labour, workers became less willing to take strike action or to contribute to union funds, and strikes staged by the Singapore Federation of Trade Unions in the latter months of 1947 petered out ineffectively.

༄

After the separation of Singapore in 1946, the colonial authorities aimed to work gradually towards internal self-government and to build up a feeling of common loyalty towards Singapore as a permanent home. The inhabitants were still cosmopolitan and mixed, comprising approximately 78 per cent Chinese, 12 per cent Malays and Indonesians, 7 per cent Indians, and 3 per cent Eurasians, Europeans, and other small minorities.[39] The immigration restrictions introduced in the 1930s, followed by the dislocation of war, had changed the character and outlook of the population, which was less transitory and more balanced, with a higher proportion of women, children, and old people. Male adults had comprised half the population in 1931 but only one-third in 1947.

The Chinese in particular were more settled. At the 1931 census only 38 per cent of Singapore Chinese were Straits-born, but by 1947 the proportion was 60 per cent and by the mid-1950s had increased to 70 per cent. According to a 1947 social survey, more than half of the China-born immigrants had neither re-visited China nor sent remittances to families there, so that link with the motherland was more tenuous than was generally supposed.[40]

The Indians kept stronger personal ties with their land of origin. It continued to be common practice for Indian men to come to work in Singapore on their own, and the proportion of women was smaller than among any of the other communities. The majority of Indians sent money to families in India and travelled frequently between India and Singapore.

Between 1947 and 1957 Singapore's Indian population increased rapidly. Two-thirds were migrants from the Federation of Malaya, who were attracted by higher salaries and better opportunities of employment in Singapore or who wished to escape the dangers and hardships of the communist Emergency. There was also an influx of northern Indians, particularly Sikhs and Sindhis, who emigrated to Singapore in

1947 and 1948 during the unrest that followed independence and partition in India. In addition many Malayalees came from Kerala in the immediate post-war years. Some were employed as building workers, but most were clerks and shopkeepers, often finding employment in or round the mushrooming British military installations.

While most Indians, Pakistanis and Ceylonese still looked with pride to their homelands and many continued to return there to marry, to educate their children, or to retire, increasing numbers settled down permanently in Singapore. From the late 1950s, when immigration restrictions were tightened, the stream of Indian immigrants dwindled to a trickle of professionals and wealthy businessmen and their families.[41]

&

For the first two years after liberation, the Governor of Singapore ruled with the help of an Advisory Council consisting entirely of officials and nominated unofficials. Gimson started by appointing six unofficials, later increasing the number to eleven, so that for the first time unofficials outnumbered officials and Asians outnumbered Europeans. The Advisory Council remained a consultative body, but the only occasion on which Gimson exercised his right to force measures through was on the question of income tax. Attempts to impose income tax in 1860, 1910, and 1921 had been strenuously resisted, and the tax had hitherto only been levied in time of war. Only the Malayan Democratic Union supported the Income Tax Ordinance, which the Governor enacted by decree in November 1947 in the face of opposition from the unofficial advisory councillors, both the International and Chinese Chambers of Commerce, and the Singapore Association, successor to the Straits Settlements (Singapore) Association.

The 1947 census, which revealed an unexpectedly large proportion of local-born Singaporeans, strengthened arguments in favour of promoting political responsibility and self-government.

The colonial authorities, in co-operation with the Advisory Council, planned to transfer power to Singaporeans in stages by developing the existing executive and legislative bodies and widening representation.

As a first step a new constitution, to be implemented after elections scheduled to be held in March 1948, created an Executive Council with an official majority and a Legislative Council with nine officials and thirteen unofficials, of whom four would be nominated by the Governor, and three chosen by the chambers of commerce, although some members of the Advisory Council criticized this special commercial representation as "repugnant to all ideas of democracy".[42] The remaining six legislative councilors were to be elected by adult British subjects who had been resident in Singapore for at least one year before the election.

The Colonial Office had expected councillors to be elected by racial communities, but the Malayan Democratic Union opposed this vigorously and the Advisory Council insisted unanimously that legislative councillors should represent geo-graphical constituencies. The Governor retained powers over reserved subjects and could veto the Legislative Council's proceedings. He still remained subject only to the ultimate control of the Secretary of State for the Colonies in London. The Singapore constitution was more liberal than the constitutions of the Malayan Union and the subsequent Federation of Malaya, which made no provision for elected legislative councillors. The constitutional reforms did not satisfy the Malayan Democratic Union's militant radicals, who decided to boycott the election and staged mass protest rallies at Farrer Park.

This left the field clear for the Singapore Progressive Party, which had been established in August 1947 with a view to contesting the 1948 election. Founded by lawyers C.C. Tan, John Laycock, and N.A. Mallal, its leaders came from the Straits Chinese British Association or Singapore Association and belonged to the class of commercial and professional men who had traditionally been associated with the colonial regime. Laycock and the Pakistan-born Mallal had served as municipal councillors in the 1930s, and C.C. Tan, the party's first chairman, was an unofficial member of the post-war Advisory Council. The Progressives were willing to co-operate with the British to promote steady constitutional reform by gradually extending the numbers of elected councillors and eventually creating a Cabinet of ministers responsible to a legislative assembly. Unlike the Malayan Communist Party and the Malayan Democratic Union, they were a specifically Singapore party, which aimed to establish self-government within the island before merging with Malaya. Membership was open only to British and British protected subjects and about three-quarters of the membership came from the middle or upper middle income class.[43]

The Progressives were the only party to fight the 1948 election and won half of the six elected seats, the remaining three falling to independents. All the successful candidates were lawyers, three of them Indian, one Chinese, one European, and one Malay.

The prominence of the Indian minority in Singapore politics was a unique feature of the immediate post-war years. Indians enjoyed a favoured position since active participation in politics was confined to British subjects, but they also showed more eagerness than other communities to take advantage of their opportunities. Only 23,000 voters registered out of a potential electorate of more than 200,000. Of these more than 10,000 were Indians, and eight of the fifteen candidates were Indian.

The enthusiasm of Indians arose partly from concern about their future place as a minority in a self-governing Singapore, but it also reflected a natural predilection for national and industrial politics and an upsurge of confidence at India's achievement of independence in 1947. This gave status and a sense of pride to the Indian community and a pre-eminence in Singapore politics, which they never achieved before or since. No successful Indian contestant stood for communal interests, and the 1948 election revealed a refreshing freedom from racial friction. In October 1948 Governor Gimson commented with satisfaction, "Communalism as known in other countries has never carried any weight in Singapore, and I am confident that it never will, as no truly democratic system can ever be founded otherwise." The British also planned to expand the Municipal Commission's authority, and make it more democratic as training for self-government. The pre-war administration, in which all members of the Municipal Commission and Rural Board were officials or the Governor's nominees, was restored in 1946 as an interim measure, while a committee appointed under John Laycock drew up a more liberal scheme. This provided for two-thirds of the municipal commissioners to be elected by British subjects or British-protected persons possessing certain property and residential qualifications. At the first municipal election, held in 1949, the Progressive Party triumphed, winning thirteen of the eighteen elective seats, but there was little public interest and, of a potential electorate of 100,000, fewer than 10 per cent registered.

∽∾

By the time the new legislative council assembled in 1948, Singapore seemed poised for steady if unspectacular constitutional and social reform.

The Malayan Communist Party was rent by internal discord and scandal. In March 1947 the party was left reeling from shock when Lai Teck disappeared with the party funds amid rumours that he was a double agent. He was eventually tracked down and murdered in Bangkok. The new communist leader, Chin Peng, favoured militant action to make up for the party's failure to exploit labour unrest and the constitutional debate, which ended in February 1948 with the establishment of the Federation of Malaya. The party's decision to adopt a new policy of mass struggle against British imperialism may have been influenced by a communist international meeting held in Calcutta in February 1948, which two of its members attended. Lawrence Sharkey, the Australian communist leader, spent a fortnight in Singapore on his return from Calcutta to Australia, and may possibly at that time have pressed for a revolt in Malaya.

The first trial of strength came in February 1948 after the Singapore Harbour Board began to employ dockers directly instead of working through contractors. This benefited workers but threatened the hold that the Malayan Communist Party exerted over contract labour. The communist-controlled Singapore Harbour Board Labour Union staged a strike, but this collapsed within forty-eight hours and convinced many workers that the communists were not working for their interests. The strike led to the arrest of union leaders and the discovery of documents relating to the illegal communist Singapore Workers Protection Corps, which the authorities broke up. The Singapore Federation of Trade Unions then attempted unsuccessfully to launch a general strike. It also planned a May Day rally, hoping to marshal 100,000 participants, but the government banned the procession, the leaders called it off, and May Day 1948 proved to be the first crime-free day Singapore had enjoyed for years.

It was obvious that the Malayan Communist Party had lost its hold over the labour movement and that urban revolution in Singapore had no chance of success. In May 1948 the majority of leading communists left Singapore for the Federation, the former Malayan People's Anti-Japanese Army was revived, and acts of violence in May and June 1948 led to the declaration of a state of emergency in the Federation, which was to last for twelve years. A week later the Emergency regulations were extended to Singapore, putting restrictions on meetings, associations, and strikes, and permitting the detention of individuals without trial. All radical political groups were suspect, since they had been associated with the Malayan Communist Party in campaigning for the constitutional future of Malaya and Singapore. The Malayan Communist Party was proscribed, many Malay Nationalist Party leaders were arrested, and the Malayan Democratic Union dissolved itself. The Singapore Federation of Trade Unions had already disbanded on the eve of the outbreak of the rising up-country, and when police raided its offices they found the premises deserted and all its papers gone.

While armed conflict was confined to the peninsula, the Emergency had a profound impact on Singapore, distorting its political development. In the early years the Emergency regulations were rigorously applied: the police Special Branch clamped down on anything that smacked of political subversion, and hundreds of arrests were made. Former organizations were made illegal and driven underground, and it was difficult for new ones to emerge.

❧

The immediate side effect of crippling left-wing political movements in Singapore was to leave the stage to conservative politicians, who were willing to co-operate amicably with the colonial authorities in working for gradual constitutional reform and modest social change while preserving the economic status quo. The Singapore Progressive Party was at the forefront of formal politics for the next seven years.

A rival Singapore Labour Party was formed shortly after the 1948 election by three English-educated Indian trade union leaders: M.A. Majid, president of the Singapore Seamen's Union, together with Indian-born M.P.D. Nair and Ceylon-born Peter Williams, who were leaders of the Army Civil Services Union. They also recruited an English schoolmaster, Francis Thomas, who had worked in Singapore as a teacher for fourteen years, and legislative councillor Lim Yew Hock as president. A third-generation Straits Chinese, born in Singapore in 1914, Lim Yew Hock was a former clerk, who rose to become full-time secretary-general of the Singapore Clerical and Administrative Workers Union and was nominated by the Governor in 1948 to represent the interests of labour in the Legislative Council. Lim subsequently became a founder member of the Singapore Trade Union Congress.

Modelled on the British Labour Party, the Singapore Labour Party sought to break communist influence in the labour movement by furthering the practical interests of workers, bettering their conditions and redistributing wealth more fairly. It aimed to achieve self-government for Singapore by 1954, followed by full independence through merger with the Federation, to produce a "socialist society in Malaya" in which the rubber and tin industries would be nationalized. Like all other Singapore parties, the Singapore Labour Party was multiracial in its leadership and membership but was drawn from a lower income group than the Progressives. Most of its leaders were English-educated, many of them immigrant Indians, and a few had university training, but the majority were trade unionists and clerks. Discipline was slack: the party had little financial backing and was weakened by personal jealousies and clashing ambitions. The moderate Lim Yew Hock and the Fabian Francis Thomas were soon at loggerheads with Peter Williams's more radical wing. Personal squabbles and quarrels over nominations for municipal elections in 1951 split the party into factions. By 1952 Williams had gained control and expelled Lim Yew Hock, but the party splintered in confusion, leaving the Progressives a clear field in Legislative Council and municipal politics. Both the colonial authorities and the Progressives recognized the need for a new approach to social welfare and education if Singapore was to become a settled, self-governing society.

Attitudes in Europe towards the role of governments changed greatly after the Second World War, when citizens came to demand more active official involvement in providing social services and improving living standards at home and in the colonies. Pioneer Colonial Welfare and Development legislation, which had been passed in 1929, was very modest in scope but introduced the principle of responsibility. The Attlee Labour government's moderate Fabian socialist policy found a ready response among English-educated Singaporeans, although employers – and sometimes the colonial authorities on the spot – were less enthusiastic.

Before the Second World War social welfare in Singapore was left to charities, which sometimes received government grants, but in June 1946 a Social Welfare Department was established. Initially this dealt with exceptional post-war hardships through people's restaurants, children's feeding centres, and a citizens' advice bureau, which was set up to help refugees and displaced persons. As conditions returned to normal, the department's work expanded to provide more permanent services.

In 1947 it carried out a survey of living conditions, which revealed an appalling state of misery and chronic overcrowding. By that time Singapore's population had increased from 560,000 in 1931 to 941,000 and was rising fast. Most were packed into the inner city area, where the majority of households lived in one room or cubicle, and a quarter of unskilled worker families had even less space.[44] Some had no permanent living space at all. It was customary for shop assistants to sleep on the floor after shops had closed. In crowded Chinatown the same shelves could be hired out to so-called "spacemen": overnight to day labourers and during the day to night-shift workers.

A housing committee reported in 1948, "The disease from which Singapore is suffering is Gigantism. A chaotic and unwieldy megapolis has been created ... by haphazard and unplanned growth."[45] Barely one-third of the urban population was housed satisfactorily, and the situation was getting worse: the population was expanding so fast that the Singapore Improvement Trust's building programme could only accommodate the equivalent of just one-third of the annual increase. The Trust could not begin to eliminate slums or to clear the thousands of miserable squatter huts. Jolted by these shocking revelations, in 1948 the government increased loans to the Singapore Improvement Trust, launched an interim plan to house 36,000 people and proposed a master plan to create satellite towns. The Progressives suggested establishing a Housing Trust, which foreshadowed the later Housing and Development Board.

The post-war colonial government also accepted greater responsibility for education. Not only did it need to make up for schooling that had been interrupted by the Occupation, it also needed to expand facilities to meet the increasing demands and different requirements of a more settled society with growing numbers of children, and to inculcate a sense of common citizenship in preparation for self-government.

In the immediate pre-war years, critics had voiced concern that English-medium teaching was cutting Singaporeans off from their cultural roots.[46] In 1946, when the Director of Education proposed to expand vernacular primary education, confining English primary schools to native English speakers, the unofficials in the Advisory Council objected on the grounds that English was the only common language. C.C. Tan argued that English-medium primary education should be available to any children whose parents so wished.[47]

In deference to these views, a Ten-Year Programme launched in 1947 provided for six years of primary education in any of the four main languages, in accordance with parents' choice. The government continued to finance Malay schools and to subsidize Tamil and Chinese schools that met its standards, but most resources were poured into expanding English-medium schooling, for which there was great demand, since it offered the best prospects for secondary and tertiary education and for profitable employment. By 1957 attendance in English-medium schools had risen to four times the pre-war 1941 figure. The colonial government, regarding English schools as "hitherto the nursery for the more Malayan minded of our youth", was content to plough more and more funds into English-medium education, to the neglect of Chinese and other vernacular schools.

While the emphasis at that stage was on expanding primary education, the localization of the civil service and modernization of society offered increased opportunities for a well-educated élite. In 1949 the King Edward College of Medicine merged with Raffles College to form an independent English-medium University of Malaya,[48] which was initially based in Singapore but also served the Federation of Malaya and the British Borneo territories. This was followed the next year by opening a Singapore teachers' training college.

Modest advances were made in improving social services. In 1949 a Young Persons Ordinance consolidated and extended laws to protect young people, enforcing the pre-war legislation against the *mui tsai* system, setting up a juvenile court, a probation service, and approved schools. In the same year a ten-year medical plan was launched to expand health services and hospital facilities, and a five-year social welfare plan was adopted. Social benefits were paid to the old, unfit, blind, crippled, and widows with dependent children. In 1954 the Progressives put through a Central Provident Fund bill, which was implemented by the next government in May 1955. The objective was to provide retirement benefits for workers, the vast majority of whom were not covered by an employers' scheme. A Retirement Benefits Commission appointed by the colonial government recommended a state pension, but both the Employers Federation and the Singapore Trade Union Congress preferred a compulsory savings scheme funded by contributions by employers and employees. The decision to opt for the seemingly more popular self-financing Central Provident Fund scheme had important long-term repercussions, which were far more fundamental than was appreciated at the time, since the alternative tax-funded state pension would have committed Singapore to an expensive welfare state.[49]

The expansion of education and other social services was financed partly through proceeds from the new income tax and partly from revenue arising from the economic boom generated by the Korean War. The year 1951 was a record trading year, when the price of rubber rose to almost $2 a pound and tin to five times its pre-war level.

⚮

Constitutional reform proceeded slowly. In 1951 the colonial authorities increased the number of elected seats in the

Legislative Council to nine and allowed the unofficial legislative councillors to elect two of their number to serve on the Executive Council. Governor Gimson described this as "a new political experiment", when for the first time there would be an equal number of unofficials and officials on the Executive Council, although the Governor retained his casting vote and his reserve powers over currency, banking, trade dues, treaties, defence, and racial or religious privilege.

At the 1951 election, the Progressive Party won six of the nine elected seats. Elizabeth Choy failed to win a seat but was appointed as a nominated member, becoming the first woman to serve on the Legislative Council. The Progressives continued to dominate the council for the next four years. At first they were content with the leisurely pace of constitutional advance, but developments in the Federation of Malaya quickened their interest in speeding the advance to more effective self-government in Singapore. In 1951 Tunku Abdul Rahman, the new president of UMNO, took up the cry of "Merdeka!" or "Freedom!" for the Federation, and a Member system was introduced in Kuala Lumpur, giving Members ministerial responsibility for certain government functions.

In 1953 the Progressives set a ten-year target date for achieving self-government in Singapore, to be followed by full independence through merger with the Federation. In the meantime they advocated introducing a predominantly elected Legislative Council, with a Member system along the lines of the Federation. The colonial authorities welcomed these suggestions, and indeed Governor Sir John Nicoll prodded the Progressive Party into drawing up definite plans for responsible government. The Progressives were seen as a reliable group, in whose hands the transition to stable self-government could be made in an orderly, peaceful fashion, without upsetting the economy. Fearing that public apathy was the main obstacle to the development of democratic government and admitting "the present constitution has fallen considerably short of Chinese aspirations",[50] the British were convinced that enthusiasm could be stimulated by offering more challenging opportunities in both central and local government.

Accordingly, in 1953 Sir George Rendel was appointed to head a commission to review the constitution of the colony, including the relationship between the central and municipal government. The Rendel Commission included the Attorney-General and the president of the City Council, together with Chinese, Malay, and Indian representatives nominated by the unofficial members of the Legislative Council, and a European unofficial nominated by the Governor. It set out to devise a "complete political and constitutional structure designed to enable Singapore to develop as a self-contained and autonomous unit in any larger organization with which it may ultimately become associated".[51]

While it was not in its terms of reference to consider closer association with the Federation, the Rendel Commission considered the two territories so linked in geography, economy, politics, and defence that "it makes it difficult to visualize any permanent solution of either problem which does not take account of the other". It wished to ensure that its recommendations would not impede the ultimate closer association of Singapore with the Federation of Malaya as a basis for gaining full independence.

In the meantime the object was to encourage political awareness and responsibility by putting effective control over domestic policy into the hands of a predominantly elected government, a "genuinely responsible body with real power and authority", which would provide a sound base for further constitutional development. The commission recommended keeping local government separate in the hands of a new island-wide, wholly elected "City and Island Council". For the central government it proposed a single-chamber Legislative Assembly of thirty-two members, consisting of twenty-five elected councillors, three *ex officio* ministers and four nominated unofficials. The chambers of commerce were to lose their special voting privileges. Voters would be registered automatically and according to geographical constituencies, not racial communities.

Turning to the Executive Council, the commission suggested this be replaced by a council of nine ministers, three to be appointed by the Governor and the remaining six recommended by the leader of the strongest party in the Legislative Assembly, who would enjoy many of the functions of a Prime Minister. The council of ministers, acting like a Cabinet with collective responsibility, would have authority over all matters except external affairs, internal security, and defence. Elected Assemblymen would gain control over commerce, industry, labour, immigration, social welfare, education, housing, communications, public, works and health, leaving the three crucial ministries in the hands of the Financial Secretary, the Attorney-General and a Chief Secretary, successor to the former Colonial Secretary. The commission resisted the Singapore Chinese Chamber of Commerce's appeal for multilingualism and recommended that English be retained as the sole official language.

The British government accepted the Rendel central government proposals and arranged to hold elections to implement the new constitution in 1955, leaving the final decision of re-organizing the local authorities to the incoming government.

∽

The armed communist revolt in Malaya ultimately failed, but it distorted the development of nationalism in both the Federation and Singapore by destroying the former radical parties and pan-Malayan political movements.

Enforcing Emergency regulations, banning political meetings except during election times, imprisoning troublemakers and proscribing left-wing parties gave Singapore a few years of superficial peace, when the colonial government worked quietly towards a more liberal and representative administration, and the minority of Singaporeans in the political limelight concentrated on trying to secure some form of ministerial powers and more elected seats in the legislature. There was an air of unreality about this scenario. For the majority of Singaporeans, the Legislative Council's business, all conducted in English in gentlemanly debate, had nothing whatsoever to do with their lives and their problems.

In clamping down on subversion, the Emergency regulations in effect suppressed nearly all political activity outside of the Legislative Council, and the colonial authorities were misled by its placid moderation. Traditionally the British relied on this body to keep them informed about public opinion, but at this time its members were out of touch with the mass of the population. In particular, the Chinese unofficials were exclusively English-educated, upper-class Straits Chinese and closer in outlook to the ruling class than to the majority of their own countrymen. The British visualized Legislative and Municipal Councils gradually becoming more elective and Asian-dominated and steadily taking over more responsibility for Singapore's affairs. Far from being a liberal training ground for democracy and a stepping stone to independence, the Legislative Council instead could be a barrier to progress. The restriction of voting rights to British subjects and insistence on English as the sole official language made the Legislative and Municipal Councils the preserve of Europeans and of English-educated, Western-oriented, well-to-do professional and commercial men, whose interests and thinking were in line with the ruling community. In the first post-war decade the sole occasion on which the unofficial legislators clashed with the government was over the imposition of income tax.

The political institutions of the first post-war decade were remote from the real issues: they did not stimulate mass interest in politics and failed to keep the government in touch with the trends of the time. Indeed the support of unofficials for government policy blinded the authorities to the social discontent simmering just under the surface.

The four nominated unofficial legislative councillors, sometimes known as "the Queen's Party", were regarded as colonial puppets, and the three representatives of the chambers of commerce were criticized by labour leaders as the voice of commercial capitalism. The elected members were no more representative than the appointed ones. At its peak, the Progressive Party had a membership of approximately 4,000, was supported by substantial donations from wealthy individual backers and remained a stable fairly homogeneous group, with continuous leadership. But the Progressives had little contact with the working class, nor did they seek mass support. Full membership was open only to British and British-protected subjects, and three-quarters of the members came from the middle and upper income groups. Conservative in their economic policy, the Progressives wanted to give equal opportunities to local and foreign-financed industrial enterprises. They wished to keep political control in the hands of the English-speaking and to support a leisurely programme of constitutional reform and gradual Malayanization of the civil service. The Chinese masses regarded them as collaborators, supporting the colonial government's unpopular policies on education, language, immigration, citizenship, and national service.

To the Chinese-educated and a minority of English-educated radicals, the activities of the Legislative Council were unreal and irrelevant, and the genuine political issues of the time lay in the world outside the council chamber.

လ

It was impossible for left-wing politics to flourish overtly in Singapore during the early years of the Malayan Emergency. The atmosphere of fear and uncertainty inhibited freedom of speech, stifled debate and deterred students, intellectuals, and trade unionists from taking an active part in public life. Repression masked a whole range of political feeling. On the extreme left were sworn-in members of the now illegal Malayan Communist Party, who were dedicated to harnessing the masses for the overthrow of the colonial regime by force, destruction of the capitalist economy, and creation of a Marxist-Leninist state. Others were strongly anti-colonial and favoured radical social and economic reform and redistributing wealth but were opposed to violence. Many resented the inequalities and injustices of the colonial economy and were primarily concerned to secure a better deal for the working class. Others wanted to establish their own more liberal society, free from foreign rule. And for a large number, their political attitudes had not yet crystallized but they were deprived of the normal outlets for discussion and expression.

While the Malayan Communist Party concentrated its major efforts on the mainland struggle, the Singapore Town Committee continued to operate secretly, taking its orders from the party's South Malaya Politburo in northern Johor. In 1949 it created a Workers' Protection Corps and an Anti-British League, including a Singapore Students' Anti-British League with cells in Chinese middle schools and the new University of Malaya. The Workers' Protection Corps carried out sporadic acts of intimidation, including a bomb attack on the Governor in Happy World, which injured him slightly. The Anti-British League was a clandestine organization, which attracted a variety of anti-colonial radicals. A testing and training ground for selecting suitable comrades to join the Malayan Communist Party, it attracted likely recruits by a mixture of seductive ideology, helpfulness in providing money and jobs, and incrimination in undertaking risky errands, such as carrying illegal weapons, ammunition or subversive literature.[52]

The Malayan Democratic Union had collapsed, but former members continued to uphold the party's ideas and keep in contact. Indeed some of them lived under the same roof. Since accommodation was scarce and expensive, it was commonly shared, and this brought together a collection of left-wing radicals, including former Malayan Democratic Party stalwarts, who lived in or frequented a ramshackle, rambling house, fittingly the former headquarters of Subhas Chandra Bose. These included Eu Chooi Yip, Lim Kean Siew, teacher P.V. Sharma, John Eber, C.V. Devan Nair, Samad Ismail, and Sinnathamby Rajaratnam. Born in Ceylon in 1915 but brought up in Malaya since infancy, Rajaratnam had studied at Raffles Institution and then went to London to read law but was trapped in England during the war and took up journalism to support himself. Later Rajaratnam was to become one of the inner circle of PAP Cabinet ministers, but at that stage he was writing fiery anti-colonial editorials in the *Malaya Tribune*, and from 1950 for the *Singapore Standard*.

The police was vigilant in hunting down suspected subversives. Under a new School Registration Ordinance, which gave them increased powers to search and close suspected schools, they closed two leading middle schools for a few weeks in 1950, dismissed some teachers and expelled a large number of students. In December 1950 the police succeeded in rounding up most of the Singapore Town Committee and shortly afterwards arrested thirty-three English-speaking radicals, including John Eber, Devan Nair, Sharma, Samad Ismail, and two University of Malaya students, James Puthucheary and Dollah Majid. A few managed to escape arrest, notably Eu Chooi Yip, who sought refuge in Riau, Lim Kean Siew, who eventually reached Beijing, and a younger Anti-British League journalist, Fang Chuan Pi, later to become known as the Plen, who managed to remain undercover in Singapore. Altogether about 1,200 Singaporeans were arrested under the Emergency regulations in the period from 1948 to 1953, and the Anti-British League was virtually broken up.

The Communist Party failed to exploit the one opportunity for fomenting trouble that presented itself at this time: the Hertogh riots of December 1950. Maria Hertogh was a thirteen-year old Dutch Eurasian girl who had lost contact with her interned parents during the Japanese Occupation and she was brought up by a Muslim family. The custody battle between the natural parents and the foster family roused considerable passion among Malay, Indonesian, and Indian Muslims in Singapore. The judge's decision to send the girl back to the Netherlands, coupled with irresponsible pictures in the English-language press showing her praying in a convent, sparked off violence, which was stoked up by the vernacular Malay press. The Commissioner of Police allowed the situation to get out of hand, and in two days of rioting, Europeans and Eurasians were attacked indiscriminately. Eighteen people were killed, 173 were injured,

72 vehicles were burned, and 199 damaged. The Chinese secret societies were quick to take advantage of the trouble, but the Malayan Communist Party was caught by surprise. By the time it intervened to call on all races in Singapore to unite against British rule, law and order had been restored.[53]

∽≈

The draconian suppression of perceived subversion jammed the lid dangerously tight on a seething cauldron of genuine grievances and injustices, involving language, education, and culture, which was complicated further by the impact of events in the surrounding region and particularly in China.

The communist victory in China in 1949 hardened the colonial power's attitude towards the involvement of Singaporeans in China's politics and reopened rifts between the Kuomintang and communist supporters among the Chinese-educated in Singapore. Both parties by that time were proscribed in Singapore, since the Malayan Communist Party was outlawed when the Malayan Emergency was declared, and the Kuomintang failed to register in 1949, but the conflict of loyalties persisted in the background. Tay Koh Yat, director of the anti-communist newspaper, the *Chung Hsing Jit Pao*, led the pro-Kuomintang faction, but Tan Kah-kee saw the Chinese Communist Party as the saviours of China and came out publicly in support of their cause.

Most Singapore Chinese, whatever their political feelings, were stirred by the Chinese Communist Party's triumph in their motherland, putting an end to long years of civil war. This did not necessarily imply sympathy with the Malayan Communist Party or its plans for establishing a republic in Malaya, but the British, hard-pressed by the mainly Chinese communist guerrilla army in the Federation, feared Beijing would stir up the Malayan Chinese against the colonial authorities.

At first it appeared that the new People's Republic of China intended to take over the Kuomintang policy of harnessing the loyalties of the Nanyang Chinese. In 1949 Beijing created an

Overseas Chinese Affairs Commission and asked Nanyang Chinese organizations, schools and newspapers to establish links with the commission. Former Overseas Chinese were elected to represent the interests of the Nanyang Chinese on the National People's Council. Beijing began broadcasts to the Overseas Chinese in 1949 and started the China News Service for their benefit three years later. It declared an interest in supporting Chinese education overseas, encouraged Nanyang Chinese to maintain contact with and send remittances to their relatives in China, invited them to send their children for education in China, and appealed for qualified doctors, engineers and teachers to go back to help rebuild the motherland.

The Singapore authorities regarded this policy as a threat to their attempts to build up a sense of common civic loyalty in Singapore and a menace to the physical security of Singapore and Malaya. They clamped down on contacts between Beijing and the Singapore Chinese and in 1950 passed a law that prohibited visitors to China returning to Singapore. When Tan Kah-kee visited China in 1950 to supervise the rehabilitation of the educational institutions he had sponsored, which had fallen into disarray during the years of civil war, the British authorities refused to re-admit him. He never set foot in Singapore again, and in 1957 he renounced the British citizenship he had acquired forty years earlier. The Chinese Communist Party gave Tan Kah-kee a party post, but this was a token of esteem for an ageing patriot rather than a position of power. He continued to live in Fujian province, travelling to Beijing for occasional meetings, and died in his home village in 1961.

The traditional leaders of the Chinese-educated resented the colonial government's harshness towards what they considered to be Chinese patriotism. The Singapore Chinese Chamber of Commerce, which had been the most influential spokesman for the Chinese community before the war, was still considered in 1950 to be the "premier society of the Chinese in Singapore",[54] with 2,000 individual members and more than sixty associations representing a further 10,000.

The Chamber's confidence increased with the emergence of China as a big power, and many of its leaders, such as Lee Kong Chian and Tan Lark Sye, made enormous fortunes during the Korean War boom. Yet they felt excluded from the local political scene and nervous about their future in a self-governing Singapore or an independent Malaya. They resented paying taxes to support measures that detracted from what they conceived to be the interests of the China-born, particularly an English-medium education system, which was seen to hit at the roots of their own language and culture.

Confining participation in politics to Straits-born or naturalized British subjects who were literate in English excluded the mass of immigrant and vernacular-educated Singaporeans, who constituted about half the adult population in the immediate post-war years. In 1946 the Chinese Chamber of Commerce began agitating for multilingualism in the Legislative and Municipal Councils and for Chinese to be admitted as an official language. From 1951 it campaigned for two years for long-term China-born residents to be enfranchised under the Rendel Constitution. The colonial authorities refused to waive naturalization requirements, and in this they had the support of the Progressive Party and the Straits Chinese British Association.

The Chamber was incensed at the Immigration Bill passed in 1950 to restrict travel to China. While the legislation was designed primarily to bar entry to those with communist sympathies, it affected the whole Chinese community.

For the traditional Chinese, the most alarming aspect of colonial policy was its threat to Chinese-medium education. The Singapore Chinese were concerned about a new education policy launched in the Federation in 1952, which concentrated on English and Malay schooling. They feared that the authorities were also bent on burying Chinese education in Singapore: in devoting the greater part of finances to the English-medium schools, it appeared that the colonial government was content to see Chinese education atrophy and die.

Chinese schools showed no desire to integrate with any national unified system and continued to be run by independent management committees, but despite the large grants that the Chinese Nationalist government had given to rehabilitate Singapore's Chinese schools in the immediate post-war years, they could not match the facilities in the government-aided English schools. Chinese schools were overcrowded; their teachers were often untrained and were paid only about one-third the salary of their counterparts in English-medium schools. Belatedly the government was forced to pay more attention to the problem. Under the terms of a White Paper published in December 1953, grants were offered to Chinese schools provided they were efficiently managed and gave bilingual instruction in Chinese and English. Nevertheless the declining standards in Chinese schools and greater opportunities offered by English education continued to attract increasing numbers of children into English-medium schools, where in 1954, for the first time, the new intake was greater than into the Chinese schools. Most Chinese-educated pupils finished school at the primary level to take up unskilled or semi-skilled jobs. There were only nine Chinese middle schools in Singapore and no opportunities for Chinese-medium tertiary education. Large numbers of young Chinese flocked to the People's Republic for further education, often leaving protesting parents behind on the quayside in tears. Beijing at that time welcomed Overseas Chinese students, giving them privileges and subsidies, waiving minimum educational qualifications, and opening special schools to provide intensive language instruction and political indoctrination. In 1954 the steady stream of young Singapore Chinese going off to seek their new Mecca swelled to a flood, but it was a one-way exodus because the immigration laws prohibited their return to the colony.

Tan Lark Sye, president of the Singapore Chinese Chamber of Commerce, in 1953 bemoaned that English education resulted in "increasing taxes, laying traps, turning out fools and wasting public funds".[55] His proposal to open a Chinese-medium university in

Singapore as a centre for the whole region met with enthusiastic response from rich and poor Chinese alike. Millionaires contributed handsome donations, with Tan Lark Sye himself giving $5 million, the Hokkien *huay-kuan* presented a magnificent site at Jurong, while taxi and trishaw drivers sacrificed one day's earnings, amounting to $20,000. Coming from the same village as Tan Kah-kee, Tan Lark Sye had arrived in Singapore a penniless youth with only three years' primary schooling and insufficient qualifications to be a clerk. He rose from being a labourer in Tan Kah-kee's rubber factory to become a rubber magnate and one of the richest tycoons in Singapore. He was passionate to promote Chinese-medium education and provide the opportunities of which he had been deprived.[56]

∾

Students from Malaya and Singapore found a more congenial atmosphere for talking politics in Britain, where a new breed of Singaporean politicians began to emerge. The overnight collapse of a seemingly unshakeable colonial regime in 1942 and the ingenuity required to survive the hard years that followed provided the nursery that bred a crop of remarkable political leaders among the English-educated middle class, who had formerly accepted without question the colonial society and their own semi-privileged position within it.

In 1949 six students formed a Malayan Forum discussion circle in London, which included future Malaysian Prime Minister, Abdul Razak, and was chaired by Goh Keng Swee. Born in Melaka in 1918, Goh had graduated from Raffles College with an economics diploma, served in the Singapore Volunteer Corps, and went to London after the Second World War to further his studies. On returning to Singapore in 1950, Goh handed over the chairmanship of the Malayan Forum to another Malayan-born Raffles College graduate, physiologist Toh Chin Chye, who was born in Batu Gajah in 1926. For the next three years Toh was assiduous in fostering the Forum, producing its *Merdeka* newsletter, and bringing together politically minded students from Malaya and Singapore. These informal discussions built up support for the Malayan independence movement, and the Singapore students resolved to work for the colony's independence as part of a united Malaya within the Commonwealth, in which there would be racial equality and a fair distribution of wealth.

The Malayan Forum met in London, where most of the postgraduates were studying, and many of them living in the university's Malaya Hall residence. They were also in contact with Lee Kuan Yew, who was reading law at Cambridge. Lee was a fourth-generation Straits Chinese, whose great-grandfather arrived as a penniless immigrant and made sufficient money to return to China and buy an official rank, leaving his wife and children in Singapore. Lee Kuan Yew was born in 1923 into a comfortable middle-class background. Educated at Raffles Institution, he was a Raffles College freshman when Singapore fell to the Japanese.

Returning to Singapore in August 1950, after achieving distinction in his law examination, Lee quickly made a reputation as a quick-thinking and effective courtroom lawyer. He joined a leading law firm, Ong and Laycock, and campaigned for John Laycock and the Progressives in the 1951 Legislative Council election. But Lee was impatient with the slow pace of the Straits Chinese politicians and realized that the future belonged not to the "Queen's Chinese" but to those who could command wider support.

Steadily Lee built up his contacts and influence. Since Ong and Laycock were legal advisers to the *Utusan Melayu*, Lee was sent to see Samad Ismail, one of the ten internees on St. John's Island, and this encounter provided him with one of his earliest windows into Singapore's radical politics. Samad introduced Lee to fellow internee C.V. Devan Nair of the Singapore Teachers' Union, through whom he was to meet left-wing extremist Chinese student leaders and University of Malaya undergraduates.

Lee went on to become legal adviser to a number of trade unions, first of all among English-speaking government employees. In May 1952 he represented the Postal and Telecommunications Workers' Union during a postmen's dispute, which was the first public workers' strike to be launched in Singapore since the outbreak of the Emergency. This peaceful stoppage, lasting two weeks, ended in an agreement to pay higher wages and established Lee as a champion of the underdog. It also brought him into contact with Rajaratnam, who argued the postmen's cause in the *Singapore Standard*.

Union work also brought Lee Kuan Yew in touch with senior local officials who were bitter against continuing racial discrimination in the public service. In 1946 the British government had adopted the principle of localization throughout the colonial service.[57] From 1948 local officials were admitted to administrative grades in the Malayan Civil Service, and in 1950 a public services commission was set up to handle local recruitment when the first students graduated from the University of Malaya. Asian officials were recruited in growing numbers but quickly became dissatisfied at the disparity between themselves and foreigners in conditions of service and promotion prospects. In practice the public services commission dealt only with junior administrative posts, and London continued to control senior civil service appointments, without any date being set for Malayanization. Expatriate officials saw the civil service as a body of administrators aloof from politics and visualized Malayanization as a gradual process, by which local men would rise through the service and take over as expatriates retired. Local officers took a contrary view, considering political reforms were meaningless unless Singaporeans also gained control of the bureaucracy.

Discontent came to a head in 1952 over a government decision to pay special family allowances to European officials, and Lee supported Goh Keng Swee and Kenny M. Byrne, a Malayan-born, Oxford-educated Eurasian official who had served as a magistrate during the Occupation, in forming a

Council of Joint Action. To oppose the scheme the council marshalled representatives from twenty-one government unions, including a Local Senior Officers' Association that Byrne formed two years previously. It organized a mass demonstration that forced the authorities to increase allowances to low-paid local employees, and it converted the question of Malayanization into a major political issue.

৵৹

By 1953 the atmosphere of intense political repression began to lift. As the Federation government gained the upper hand against the communist insurgents up-country, tension slackened in Singapore too. Detainees were released. Some left Singapore: John Eber went to Britain and Sharma returned to India. James Puthucheary and Dollah Majid returned to the university and became founder members of a University of Malaya Socialist Club.

The Malayan Communist Party took advantage of this easing of repression to revive the united front policy in 1954, and it set out to infiltrate open organizations, notably Chinese schools and labour unions. The Anti-British League quickly expanded, numbering more than 2,000 members by 1954. The Malayan Communist Party saw great future opportunities in the Rendel Constitution, the emergence of new political parties, the proposal for a Chinese-medium university, and the revival of trade union activity. Meanwhile they played upon the genuine grievances of students and workers.

The frustration of intelligent and ambitious Chinese school students combined with intense pride in communist achievements in China to feed pro-Chinese and anti-colonial feeling. Chinese middle school graduates were not qualified to gain access to the English-medium University of Malaya or to English-speaking universities overseas. Nor were there any openings for the vernacular-educated in government and quasi-government organizations in Singapore. A number of senior schoolboys were young men in their early twenties, since secondary schools were closed during the Occupation and many overage pupils were admitted in the immediate post-war years. These youths and their teachers had good reason to be bitter against the colonial government. They admired the new Beijing regime and eagerly absorbed contraband books and communist propaganda from China. Although Chi Nan College in Shanghai had granted scholarships to past generations of Chinese students from Malaya, taking up tertiary studies in the People's Republic of China was daunting because it meant leaving home forever. Most outstanding among these young men were two Chinese High School graduates and former Singapore Students' Anti-British League cell leaders: Lim Chin Siong,[58] who was born in Singapore in 1933 but brought up from infancy in Johor, and Malayan-born Fong Swee Suan who was two years his senior. Lim had returned to Singapore in 1949 to attend Catholic High School, and the following year had transferred to the Chinese High School, where he and Fong had been involved in organizing class boycotts that had resulted in the police raiding the school. Fong Swee Suan left school after narrowly escaping arrest, and Lim Chin Siong was expelled in 1952. They took low-paid jobs, Fong Swee Suan as a bus conductor and Lim Chin Siong as a part-time teacher, while devoting most of their energies to helping to build up left-wing support.

The government's decision to enrol 2,500 youths for part-time national service provoked mass student protest demonstrations in May 1954. Police broke up the demonstrations, and many students were arrested. This stirred up further demonstrations to demand their release, and nearly all students refused to register for national service. Lee Kuan Yew acted as supporting counsel to prominent English Queen's Counsel D.N. Pritt in defending the students arrested during the riots and also in a second case that was brought against the editorial board of the University of Malaya Socialist Club's publication *Fajar* (Dawn), who were charged with publishing an allegedly subversive editorial but were acquitted.[59] These two trials caused a public furore and enhanced Lee's reputation as a left-wing lawyer.

In an attempt to counter the growing unrest in Chinese schools, in September 1954 the government passed a School Registration Amendment Ordinance, extending its powers to close schools on grounds of subversion. This was coupled with the offer of a $12 million grant to Chinese schools, which would match the financial aid given to English schools. The offer had strings attached. While leaving the management committees to conduct everyday affairs in the schools, the government proposed to appoint a nine-man board, consisting of three officials and six Chinese representatives, which would allocate grants and supervise discipline, curriculum and textbooks, with the Governor having the final say. The Chinese Chamber of Commerce protested that the board should be appointed and run entirely by Chinese, and the new offer failed to satisfy the student population. Chinese school committees, which were often dominated by rich businessmen of Kuomintang sympathies, found it increasingly difficult to enforce discipline among the unruly, overage students, and communist cells in the schools intimidated principals and teachers. Students protested against the government having any say in the content and method of teaching. Negotiations broke down, three-quarters of the Chinese schools, including the leading middle schools, refused to accept aid, and communist student leaders set up a Singapore Chinese Middle School Students' Union, which the government refused to register.

By mid-1954 communist leaders began to draw students into supporting labour disputes. The labour movement was ripe for communist infiltration. In principle official policy aimed to suppress only communist-dominated unions and wanted to build up a democratic trade union movement as part of the battle against communism. In practice its vigilance over trade union activities after the outbreak of the Malayan Emergency stunted the growth of legitimate unions, since workers were afraid to become involved and risk police persecution.

Legislation amended in 1948 required trade union leaders to have three years' employment in the industry they represented and to restrict federations of unions to allied occupations. This excluded professional political agitators from leadership and automatically dissolved the Pan-Malayan Federation of Trade Unions. In the months that followed the outbreak of the Emergency, trade union membership slumped and most unions disappeared.

From 1949 the government encouraged the formation of a Singapore Trade Union Congress. After much dissension this was eventually set up in 1951 and within a year claimed a membership of 23,000. These were mainly English-speaking, white-collar clerical workers, and most of the leaders were Indians, since the Congress failed to attract the mass of Chinese-speaking manual workers. The Congress' organization was inefficient, its finances shaky, it had difficulty in collecting dues since it offered little benefit to its members, and it soon splintered into factions. The government's failure to stimulate democratic trade unionism was compounded by the short-sightedness of many Singapore employers, who exploited the labour movement's disarray in order to keep wages low, despite rising profits during the Korean War boom. This played into communist hands. The Singapore Trade Union Congress was discredited, its leadership rent by the same personal dissensions that had split the Singapore Labour Party with which it was closely associated, and by 1953 the body was almost dormant. It had done nothing to better the lot of its worker members. In 1954 the unemployment rate was higher than it had been at the time of the 1947 social survey, and most working-class families still lived in appalling conditions.[60]

The mass of Chinese blamed their troubles on the colonial regime and resented the privileged position of the English-educated. The new generation of militant young student leaders set out to harness the labour movement to the anti-imperialist cause. In May 1954 Lim Chin Siong became secretary-general of a recently formed Singapore Factory and Shop Workers' Union. Despite his youth, his slight boyish appearance, and "humble, sometimes innocent"[61] demeanour, Lim was a dedicated radical and a charismatic orator who could charm and sway mass audiences with his eloquence both in his native Hokkien and in Mandarin.

The Singapore Factory and Shop Workers' Union was efficiently administered by a hierarchy of committees, and it employed similar tactics to those used to good effect by the General Labour Union in the immediate post-war years, building up support by successful strikes that brought concrete benefits for the strikers. A number of small-scale stoppages in 1954 gained the first improvements for workers in many years, and the first big strike was organized in the Paya Lebar Bus Company in February 1955. From that point the Singapore Factory and Shop Workers' Union launched a series of strikes, which extracted higher wages and better conditions and attracted thousands of recruits. Membership soared from 375 in April 1954 to nearly 30,000 by the end of 1955, by which time the organization included thirty industrial unions.

While the majority of members were Chinese, the union's twelve-man executive committee included both Chinese- and English-educated militants: Fong Swee Suan, secretary of the Singapore Bus Workers' Union; Devan Nair, adviser to the Singapore Traction Company Employees' Union; Jamit Singh, secretary of the Harbour Board Staff Association, and Sandrasegaram (Sidney) Woodhull, secretary of the Naval Base Labour Union. For the first time Chinese- and English-educated radicals, many of them Indian, linked together student and labour politics into a militant anti-colonial movement, which ran counter to the designs for steady constitutional reform planned by the British and the Progressives. Radical Singaporeans had no wish to see an independent Singapore with a colonial-type economy, which would be ruled in the interests of the traditional English-educated élite.

ভ

The publication of the Rendel report in February 1954 and the prospect of elections to establish a measure of self-government the following year stimulated a flurry of discussions and negotiations to form new parties and alliances.

By this stage the Singapore Labour Party existed in name only. In July 1954 Lim Yew Hock and Francis Thomas drew former socialists together to form a Labour

Front under the leadership of David Marshall, a prominent lawyer. Marshall, then forty-seven years old, was a member of the small but notable Jewish community, although he did not belong to one of its richer families. He qualified as a lawyer in England in the mid-1930s, fought with the Singapore Volunteers during the Japanese invasion and was subsequently sent as a prisoner of war to work in the coal mines of Hokkaido. By the early 1950s he had built up a reputation as an outstanding criminal defence lawyer. A man of warm human sympathies, a powerful speaker, and persuasive courtroom advocate, Marshall was a passionate defender of the underdog. His admiration for the British legal system and concern with the dignity and freedom of the individual made him in many ways European in outlook and perhaps for that reason all the more bitter at what he considered to be the degradation and humiliation of colonial rule. An outspoken critic of British colonialism before the war, he was invited to join the Malayan Democratic Union but was repelled by the communist-style intemperate abuse of the party's language. Later, in 1954, he refused to defend the University of Malaya Socialist Club editorial team, saying they were masquerading as socialists but using *Fajar* to publish communist propaganda.[62] Meanwhile he joined the Progressives but resigned because the party was content to move so gradually towards independence. In 1954 he accepted the invitation to head the new Labour Front.

Meanwhile other aspiring politicians had been gathering at weekends in Lee Kuan Yew's basement dining room, including Toh Chin Chye on his return from London in 1953. Toh was disappointed that many former members of the Malayan Forum had lost interest in politics and that, apart from the Socialist Club enthusiasts, most University of Malaya students preferred to concentrate on promoting their careers and taking up the attractive offers of graduate employment that were opening up for the English-educated élite. Lee Kuan Yew was more impressed with the dedication of young Chinese-educated men, such as Lim Chin Siong.

The Labour Front leaders approached Lee Kuan Yew, but negotiations were fruitless since Lee saw more advantage in alliance with the extreme militant radicals. The illegal Malayan Communist Party welcomed the possibility of using the English-educated left wing as a front political party to exploit the new constitution in preparation for eventual armed struggle, and Lee Kuan Yew's group, now fully alive to the force and discontent of the Chinese-educated masses, realized that an alliance with such men, dangerous though it might be, offered the only path to political success. The future belonged to politicians who could command the allegiance of the Chinese-educated masses.

When they were released from St. John's Island, Samad Ismail and Devan Nair joined the basement circle, and by now the group was growing so large that it was infringing the Emergency regulations limiting political gatherings. Toh Chin Chye suggested the answer was to register as a political party, and the People's Action Party was born.[63] With Lee Kuan Yew as secretary-general, Toh Chin Chye as chairman, and a committee comprising trade unionists and Chinese- and English-educated radicals, the party was inaugurated in October 1954 in Victoria Memorial Hall. The gathering of more than 1,500 people was the largest meeting held in Singapore since the Emergency regulations were introduced in 1948, but it was orderly and rather staid. Samad Ismail and Fong Swee Suan were among its founding members, but not Lim Chin Siong. The presence of Tunku Abdul Rahman, head of UMNO, and Sir Tan Cheng Lock, now leader of the Malayan Chinese Association, underlined the new party's intention to look beyond parochial Singapore affairs to a wider Malayan horizon. The party pledged to agitate in the coming elections for immediate independence in union with the Federation, repeal of the Emergency regulations, a common Malayan citizenship, Malayanization of the entire civil service, free compulsory education, the encouragement of local industry, the amendment of trade union legislation, and a workers' charter.

The wealthy China-born business community was slower to appreciate the new political opportunities that the Rendel Constitution offered to the Chinese-educated, but shortly before the 1955 election an influential section of the Chinese Chamber of Commerce formed a Democratic Party. It had little organization but strong financial backing, notably from Tan Lark Sye. The party pledged to foster Chinese education and culture, to make Chinese an official language and to obtain liberal citizenship terms for the China-born. Despite its name, the new party was conservative in its economic outlook, and it was popularly dubbed "The Millionaires' Party".

The battle lines were drawn for the electoral contest that was to open a new era in Singapore's development.

8

The Road to Merdeka
1955–1965

The Rendel constitution was designed to stimulate an appetite for self-government among seemingly reluctant Singaporeans. The colonial authorities had spent ten years prodding life into a movement towards political maturity with little apparent sign of success, but the 1955 election marked a lusty, vociferous political awakening. It heralded years of vigorous constitutional struggle when new nationalist leaders emerged and issues that were of real concern to the mass of Singaporeans were brought into the political arena.

The election held in April 1955 to implement the new constitution was the first lively political contest in Singapore's history, and the temporary easing of Emergency restrictions increased election fever. This spirited competition did not come from the biggest and ostensibly strongest contestants, the Progressive and Democratic parties, which both fielded large teams of candidates and aspired to win outright control of the Assembly. Regarding each other as the only serious competitors, they appealed to the traditional middle classes, made little attempt to woo the masses, ignored the left-wing parties, and clashed in no less than eighteen constituencies.

Despite the fact that neither the People's Action Party nor the Labour Front aspired to win office, it was the new parties of the left that stirred the mass of the population. The PAP considered that "to form a government under the Rendel constitution was to work with our hands tied behind our backs",[1] nor was it strong enough to make a successful bid for power. The party's extreme left wing favoured boycotting the election and concentrating on direct action, but the moderates prevailed, and the party decided to field a token four candidates. They campaigned intensively, attracting mass rallies, including large numbers of Chinese voters who had shown no interest in previous elections.

The Labour Front fielded seventeen candidates and aimed to be a strong opposition party in the new Legislative Assembly. The party campaigned for immediate independence within a merged Singapore/Malaya and promised to Malayanize the public administration within four years, extend Singapore citizenship to the 220,000 China-born inhabitants, abolish the Emergency regulations and introduce multi-lingualism in the legislature. In a stirring and emotional election manifesto, "I Believe", Marshall denounced colonialism as exploitation and promised "dynamic socialism" to counter "the creeping paralysis of communism". Bringing the flamboyant histrionics of his courtroom technique to excite large audiences, Marshall made ever more extravagant election promises, warning of "the near-erupting volcano of impatient youth thirsting for independence".[2]

The election results were a shock to the victors, the losers, and the British alike. David Marshall's Labour Front emerged the strongest single party with ten seats, and the PAP won three of the four seats it contested. The Progressives won only four seats and the Democratic Party two. Apart from Lim Yew Hock, no former legislative councillor won a seat in the new Assembly. Some who had previously been nominated or chosen by the chambers of commerce had preferred not to face the hurly-burly of an election. Others were discredited because of their association with the old regime and close co-operation with the colonial authorities. C.C. Tan, John Laycock, and Nasir Mallal all lost their seats.

The right-wing parties were rejected partly because they split the moderate conservative vote between them but mainly because they had failed to appreciate the changed character of the electorate. Automatic registration of voters had increased the electorate from 76,000 to more than 300,000, of whom the majority were working-class Chinese. The left-wing parties appealed for the new voters' support, whereas the Progressives offered only a continuation of the unpopular, pro-colonial conservative policies of the past. The Democratic Party championed Chinese culture, language, education and citizenship but its strident chauvinism attracted little enthusiasm among middle-class Straits Chinese, while the capitalist economic policy of the Millionaires' Party was indistinguishable from that of its Progressive rivals and drove the mass of Chinese towards the more radical Labour Front and the PAP.

The 1955 election was the funeral of conservative politics and ended the days when the Chinese Chamber of Commerce could exert direct political power. The following year the Progressives merged with the Democratic Party to form a Liberal Socialist Party, but this inappropriately named organization attracted no popular support and was decisively trounced in the next general election. The future belonged to politicians of the left who aimed to seize self-government as quickly as possible and to build up mass support against colonial rule.

∽

Marshall's labour front formed a government with the support of the three Alliance[3] members, the *ex officio* members and two nominated unofficials, who together formed a motley group of eighteen in an Assembly of thirty-two. From the start the minority government's position was precarious, but the opposition was also divided, comprising six Liberal Socialists, three PAP members, including Lee Kuan Yew and Lim Chin Siong, three independents, and two nominated unofficials.

A left-wing minority government, facing a partly conservative, partly extreme left-wing opposition, was a situation that no one had envisaged. The British government had expected that the familiar Progressive Party figures of the old Legislative Council would fill the new Assembly's front ranks. It had hoped that a strong Progressive Party, stimulated by a small radical opposition, would guide Singapore in a peaceful and orderly transition to internal self-government, leaving economic and defence interests undisturbed. This did not happen.

The Rendel Constitution created a Cabinet that was responsible to the Assembly but did not define the powers or place of the Chief Minister, and David Marshall found himself suddenly thrust into titular power without much substance. New to politics and parliamentary practice, he was temperamentally unsuited to the task of minority government leader, which required special qualities of restraint and diplomacy. Denied his more natural role as opposition leader, Marshall lacked the strong majority needed to carry out his ambitious election promises, and he was forced to compete with the PAP opposition for the left-wing position. From the beginning Lee Kuan Yew denounced the Rendel Constitution, "We say this Constitution is colonialism in disguise." Marshall also felt it was a mere sop to nationalist aspirations, and he was put into the difficult position of having to operate a constitution that he despised. At the same time the PAP opposition goaded Marshall to fulfil his election promises to repeal the Emergency regulations and demand immediate self-government, so that from the first Marshall was driven into demanding ever more powers.

To make this complicated situation work required a mutual sympathy and political subtlety on the part of both the Governor and the new Chief Minister, which neither possessed. Elsewhere in the Empire the British were quick to acknowledge strong nationalist leaders, as they did in the Federation of Malaya, where elections in July 1955 also produced unexpected results. Winning all but one seat, Tunku Abdul Rahman's Alliance party was swept to power with such an overwhelming mandate that London agreed to speed the process towards independence, and the Federation soon overtook Singapore's hitherto more liberal constitutional status to become a fully independent state in 1957.

The British response to the new political situation in Singapore was very different. The minority government lacked firm foundations, and Governor Sir John Nicoll made it plain that Marshall's victory did not give him a clear mandate. The Rendel Constitution laid down that the Governor must consult his Chief Minister but did not specify that he must act on his advice. The somewhat stiff and unimaginative Nicoll attempted to treat Chief Minister Marshall as a figurehead, for a time even refusing to allot him a room, until Marshall threatened to set up his desk under a tree in front of the secretariat. Since it was customary for colonial governors to write in red ink, the petulant Marshall retorted by using green, a practice that he continued into later life. Nicoll had anticipated that the leader of the House would only be Minister of Commerce and Industry, but Marshall, who was not a man to be browbeaten, insisted on making the office of Chief Minister a full-time appointment and created a separate Ministry of Commerce and Industry.

Marshall's victory also created unexpected difficulties for the PAP moderates, who were forced to keep to the left in order to be more radical than the government, giving a fillip to the extremist element in the party. From the start the PAP was anti-imperialist and socialist but divided into two wings, the moderates under Lee Kuan Yew and the extreme left under Lim Chin Siong. The alliance of communist and non-communist was a particularly hazardous game in Singapore in the mid-1950s. While Lee Kuan Yew was the party's most vocal member in the eyes of the English-educated community, during the early years Lim Chin Siong and the militant wing were the real force in the PAP, commanding the support of left-wing students, organized labour and the mass of Chinese.[4] From the start the moderates had no illusions about this. In fighting the 1955 election Lee Kuan Yew's group received no help at all from students and Chinese-speaking unions, in stark contrast to their enthusiastic campaigning on behalf of Lim Chin Siong and Devan Nair. To Lee it was obvious, "We were a united front of convenience".[5] Despite this Lee used his influence to secure the appointment of several of his left-wing clients to crucial trade union paid secretary posts, including former University of Malaya Socialist Club members Jamit Singh with the Singapore Harbour Board Union and Sandra Woodhull with the Naval Base Union. The Malayan Communist Party appeared to have bright prospects of turning the infant PAP into a second Malayan Democratic Union.

The days of leisurely, gentlemanly political debate were over and the verbal duels of the two leading political rivals, Marshall and Lee Kuan Yew, electrified the legislative chamber and brought crowds to its previously empty public benches. Both powerful speakers and strong personalities, the two men shared some features in common. They belonged to the English-educated middle class but were members of two minority groups, the Jews and Hakkas, which were both noted for their toughness, enterprise, and resilience. They were newcomers to Parliament but enjoyed the turmoil of the hustings, the cut and thrust of parliamentary debate. Both were English-trained Middle Temple lawyers, who sought to work through British constitutional methods to create a non-communist Singapore as part of a wider independent Malaya.

Here the resemblance ended. They differed fundamentally in their principles, style and methods. While Marshall loved the limelight of political life, he was not adept at treading the corridors of power. Impetuous, impatient, and quick-tempered, he wore his heart on his sleeve and met problems head on, disdaining compromise as deceit. Lee was both a man of vision and a careful schemer, unsentimental, cold, and calculating in his analysis. To Marshall the rights and liberties of individuals, human justice, dignity, equality, and protection for the underprivileged took first priority. Lee Kuan Yew put society before the individual and was impatient with those whom he took to be weaklings or fools. Marshall made no secret of his antipathy towards the Malayan Communist Party and wanted no dealings with the extreme left wing, relying for popular support on the non-communist Singapore Trade Union Congress. He tried to bridge the gap between his middle-class English-educated background and that of the ordinary population by "meet the people" sessions, in which he held open house in person to discuss individuals' problems. Lee Kuan Yew, on the other hand, considered that the only means of acquiring mass support among the Chinese-educated majority was to work in alliance with left-wing leaders among the trade union movement and Chinese middle schools. As he said in 1955, "Any man in Singapore who wants to carry the Chinese-speaking people with him cannot afford to be anti-Communist."

❧

Marshall felt deeply about the political and social ills of the time and was eager to come to grips with the vital problems that had been largely swept under the carpet during the post-war years: vernacular education, language, citizenship, and Malayanization. The extremists were quick to take advantage of the new government's weakness to exploit these issues, while the moderate elements of the PAP were equally anxious to see these problems dealt with speedily in order to take the fire and power out of the left wing of their own party.

The outcome was a stormy and acrimonious battle, which paradoxically produced solid and lasting benefits, but at the time Singapore appeared to be descending into chaos. Lim Chin Siong and extremist leaders ignored constitutional methods and launched the student and labour movements into a joint direct militant campaign of obstruction and violence. On the eve of the election nearly 10,000 Chinese middle school students staged a strike and boycotted classes, demanding the registration of the

Singapore Chinese Middle School Students' Union. Organized by a dedicated minority, Chinese school students campaigned *en masse* for the PAP during the election and continued afterwards to support riots and labour strikes. In May 1955 students joined workers in escalating a strike at the Hock Lee Bus Company into a violent demonstration, which led to a night of terror and death.[6] Ignoring the Governor's advice, Marshall refused to call in troops to restore order, and the strike resulted in triumph for the Singapore Bus Workers' Union and its Singapore Factory and Shop Workers' Union allies.

The Labour Front government arrested some students and threatened to close schools involved in the trouble unless they expelled student ringleaders and restored discipline. Two thousand students then barricaded themselves in Chung Cheng High School, demanding the release of their leaders and repeal of restrictive school legislation, while the Singapore Factory and Shop Workers' Union threatened to call a general strike in their support.

The Chief Minister refused to take stern measures, because he genuinely sympathized with the Chinese students' cause and attributed blame to colonial education policy, "Our son is as one who is ill. This is not the time for the whip and the knife," he insisted. Marshall reopened the schools and appointed an all-party committee to examine the Chinese education problem. This committee ultimately produced a long-term compromise policy, but at the time Marshall's move was interpreted as weakness, and jubilant students held a big victory parade at Chung Cheng High School.

Marshall also agreed to register the Singapore Chinese Middle School Students' Union, provided it kept out of politics. The Malayan Communist Party ordered the students to accept this offer but had no intention of honouring the conditions. At the union's inaugural meeting, it attacked the Public Security Ordinance and supported strike action by the Singapore Traction Company. The Singapore Chinese Middle School Students' Union was efficiently organized by an executive committee, with branch committees in each middle school, sub-committees and cells at form level, and a membership of nearly 10,000. The union became the dominant power in the Chinese schools, physically attacking teachers who did not conform to its revolutionary views, and school managements found themselves powerless to enforce discipline.

During May and June 1955 labour trouble mounted, fomented by the militants. Membership of the Singapore Factory and Shop Workers' Union expanded dramatically, and in June the extremist labour leaders tried to escalate a Harbour Board dispute into a general strike. The Labour Front government forestalled this by arresting five leaders, including Fong Swee Suan, but the incident revealed the intentions and the power of the Malayan Communist Party to manipulate trade unions for political ends, and Marshall accused the PAP Legislative Assemblymen of "an open effort to substitute mob government for government by the people's elected representatives". Of nearly 300 strikes in 1955 only one-third involved claims for better wages and conditions, while the rest were sympathy strikes or demands for the release of imprisoned trade union officials.

The new government had taken off to a troubled start, and the weakness of Marshall's minority position forced him to be all the more bellicose in his dealings with the colonial authorities. The British deplored what they considered to be Marshall's excessively soft handling of riots, while the Chief Minister's lack of political guile and his underlying sympathy with dissident workers and students made his relationship with Government House more difficult. The Emergency regulations were a particular bone of contention. Marshall was pledged to repeal the draconian legislation, which offended his respect for individual liberty, yet he needed to retain the restrictions if public order was to be maintained. In order to enable Marshall to fulfil his election promise, Nicoll invited the Chief Minister to repeal the Emergency regulations, whereupon the Governor would re-impose them, a step that would give Marshall *kudos*, throw all the blame on the colonial authorities and yet preserve the colony's peace and order. Marshall dismissed this compromise as a piece of political chicanery.

In order not to be outdone by the extremist opposition, Marshall sought more power and in July 1955 he demanded the appointment of four assistant ministers. When Governor Sir Robert Black refused, Marshall threatened to resign unless Singapore was given immediate self-government, claiming that the issue was "whether the Governor governs or we govern". In view of his turbulent few months in office, the demand seemed preposterous, but the British feared Marshall's departure would open the way to a more radical and irresponsible government. The Colonial Office ruled that the Governor should henceforth act on the Chief Minister's advice, and it agreed to hold constitutional talks at the end of the Assembly's first year, instead of allowing it to run its full term. Despite his difficulties and inexperience, Marshall had accomplished a great deal. He had forced the British to respect his interpretation of the Chief Minister's role, he had succeeded in appointing additional ministers, and he had brought the British to the conference table. He had also taken steps to deal with fundamental grievances. Marshall had appointed an all-party committee to investigate Chinese education and a Malayanization Committee under the chairmanship of a distinguished doctor, B.R. Sreenivasan. His government passed a Labour Ordinance in December 1955 to restrict hours of labour, and it drew up proposals for a single Singapore citizenship. While the Colonial Office and the Governor found Marshall a cross to bear, he aroused their grudging respect.

༄༅

The Colonial Office approached the constitutional talks in London in April 1956 with caution. "We do not intend that Singapore should become an outpost of Communist China, and, in fact, a colony of Peking," the Secretary of State warned, and he rejected Marshall's contradictory view that "*merdeka* will rally the majority of the people against Communism". Marshall demanded full internal self-government by April 1957, leaving foreign policy and external defence in Britain's hands but allowing Singapore a veto on defence and the right to be consulted on foreign affairs.

The British government was prepared to grant a great deal: a fully elected Assembly, the removal of *ex officio* members, special Singapore citizenship, and local control of trade and commerce. But it insisted on a defence council on which Britain and Singapore should have equal representation, with a casting vote in the hands of a British High Commissioner. The Colonial Office promised to use this power only in an emergency but refused to agree to Marshall's demand to abolish the casting vote, and the talks broke down on this point.

The Singapore delegation was divided about whether to accept London's offer, but Marshall had made a pre-commitment, leaving no room for bargaining. He refused to compromise and returned to Singapore empty-handed to face bitter press criticism and hostile debate in the Legislative Assembly.[7] He had staked his pledge on getting internal self-government and resigned in June 1956. This was a personal decision, not forced upon him by his colleagues, and it caused no rift in the Labour Front. His place was taken by Deputy Chief Minister and Minister for Labour Lim Yew Hock, who retained Marshall's entire Cabinet and continued to rely on the co-operation of the Labour Front and Alliance parties.

Lim Yew Hock's position was far from strong. The Labour Front had been hastily put together to fight the 1955 election, at which time it was merely a collection of some 300 to 400 individuals. After coming to power it began to build up its organization and by the end of 1955, on paper at least, the party had some 5,500 members. The troubles and dissensions of the first year in office put immense strains on its fragile structure. Two Labour Front Assemblymen went over to the opposition as independents, so that by September 1956 Lim Yew Hock could command the support of only eleven of the twenty-five elected members. He depended on the opposition remaining divided.

This weak government soon faced a new crisis in the Chinese middle schools. The committee on Chinese education issued its report in February 1956, condemning the divisive colonial educational policy and recommending equal treatment for all schools and all four leading languages and cultures.[8] The committee concluded that the best hope for creating a harmonious multiracial Singapore lay in breaking down exclusive educational streams and encouraging young people of different racial groups to mix. To this end, the committee urged bilingual primary education, with a common syllabus, common textbooks, equal grants, equal pay for teachers and equal opportunities for school leavers from all language streams to enter government service.[9] It also recommended banning students from active politics, and the government's decision to implement the report brought it into head-on conflict with communist aspirations and with radical Chinese students and teachers.

As part of a general campaign to counter subversion, in September 1956 the Lim Yew Hock government dissolved seven communist-front organizations, including the Singapore Chinese Middle Schools Students' Union, closed two Chinese schools and expelled 142 middle school pupils, some of them "professional students" in their mid-twenties. Five thousand students, organized by Lim Chin Siong and left-wing leaders, then staged a protest sit-in at six Chinese schools. When neither teachers nor parents could dislodge the students, the police drove them out with tear gas, whereupon they formed processions that resulted in rioting in many parts of the city. Fifteen people were killed, more than 100 were injured, and for two days Singapore was under curfew, while police and troops were rushed from the Federation to help quell the disturbances. Documents found in a police raid on the headquarters of the Singapore Factory and Shop Workers' Union proved the implication of labour leaders in the student demonstrations. As a result, the union was dissolved in October 1956, and extremists, including Lim Chin Siong and James Puthucheary, were arrested.[10]

This determined action strengthened Lim Yew Hock's position when he led a second all-party delegation to London in March 1957 to renew discussions about self-government. The Colonial Office responded more sympathetically to the quiet conciliatory style of this self-effacing, unassuming, pliable man of smiles than it had to Marshall's explosive rhetoric. The 1957 negotiations were also easier because the Federation of Malaya was about to become independent. The Colonial Office proposed to create a seven-member Internal Security Council on which Britain and Singapore would have equal representation, while the Federation would appoint the seventh representative. This satisfied Singapore's pride and her aspirations towards merger, while putting the casting vote in the hands of the Federation, which shared Britain's concern to curb subversion in Singapore. Otherwise the Singapore delegation accepted constitutional terms similar to those that Marshall had refused the previous year.[11]

When the offer came to be debated in the Legislative Assembly, Marshall criticized the delegation, and in particular Lee Kuan Yew, for accepting what he dubbed the "fraud constitution" that they had rejected under his leadership. Following this challenge both Marshall and Lee Kuan Yew resigned from the Assembly. Lee immediately fought and won a by-election in defence of this issue, but Marshall retired temporarily from the political arena.

A majority in the Assembly agreed to accept the British offer, and a third all-party mission was to go to London in 1958 to settle final terms for the new constitution.

The prospect of a self-governing Singapore in which Britain and the conservative Federation held control over internal security provoked the communists into new forms of militancy. Left-wing student activity shifted from the middle schools to the new Nanyang University, which admitted the first students in 1956, while the campus was still under construction. When building work was completed, the university formally opened in March 1958 amid great enthusiasm and a monumental traffic jam.

It was said that 2,000 guests were invited to the ceremony but 100,000 came. The 12-mile narrow winding country lane out to Jurong was littered with broken-down, overheated vehicles, and an important official function due to be held in the city that evening had to be cancelled when the Governor, the Chief Justice and other dignitaries were still stranded at the university in the early hours of the morning. No one could be left in any doubt about the passionate emotions unleashed among large swathes of the Singapore Chinese, radical and conservative, old and young, rich and poor.

This exuberance was not matched by efficient management or by devotion to academic learning. As chairman of the Nanyang University Council, Tan Lark Sye treated the university as his personal fief. Together with fellow wealthy, but often ill-educated, benefactors, he made unwise appointments, and the ineffective administration confronted a restive student body, which was more interested in political protest than study. Very quickly the new university became a hotbed of trouble, since former members of the banned Singapore Chinese Middle School Students' Union set up the Nanyang University Students' Union and organized acts of protest and violence.

At the same time the Malayan Communist Party set out to revive its strength in the trade unions, to infiltrate the Singapore Trade Union Congress, and to seize complete control of the PAP. Despite the arrest of trade union agitators and the dissolution of the powerful Singapore Factory and Shop Workers' Union, by mid-1957 the communists had built up a new central union. They tried to dominate Labour Day celebrations in May 1957, subsequently organized mass rallies under the guise of picnics and extended their influence in the PAP through the party's cultural and education committee. The left-wing leaders then set out to oust the moderates from the party's central executive committee.[12]

The extremists had not stood for election to the party's central executive committee at the first anniversary party conference in 1955. At the 1956 annual conference the left wing gained only four of the twelve seats, although Lim Chin Siong won the highest individual number of votes. The third annual conference in August 1957 witnessed an all-out battle for control of the party between the moderates and the extremists, who objected to the terms of self-government accepted by Lee Kuan Yew as a member of the all-party mission to London, to the proposed Internal Security Council and to the principle of seeking independence through merger with the Federation. When the extremists succeeded in winning half of the seats, the future of the moderates appeared precarious, and Toh Chin Chye and Lee Kuan Yew stood down from the leadership.

In face of the widespread communist threat, the Lim Yew Hock government stepped in to arrest thirty-five active communists, including five members of the newly elected PAP central executive committee and eleven PAP branch officials, together with trade union leaders, students and journalists. Lim Yew Hock's object was to purge extremist influence from the student and labour movements, including the Singapore Trade Union Congress, which was the basis of his own party's power. The arrests also crippled extremist power in the PAP and gave the moderates the opportunity to regain mastery of the party. This dramatic change of fortune was so propitious for Lee Kuan Yew and his associates that many, including his radical colleagues, felt that he had been privy to the intentions of Lim Yew Hock and the colonial authorities. In order to consolidate their hold over the party, the moderates extended the executive committee's term of office to two years and created a cadre system, by which the PAP was divided into four categories of members, of whom only full cadres could vote for the central executive committee. Cadres had to be literate Singapore citizens over twenty-one years of age, which automatically excluded most students and many China-born working-class members, who were the most enthusiastic supporters of the communist wing.

While the majority of PAP members continued to be Chinese-educated, cadre membership had to be approved by the central executive committee, which thus entrenched the supremacy of the English-educated moderate leaders.

The moderates continued outwardly to support their left-wing colleagues and to agitate for the release of their imprisoned associates, thus cultivating popularity with the masses and creating suspicions among the expatriate and many among the Singaporean middle classes. At the same time, despite the outspoken anti-colonialism of the English-educated PAP leaders and their acrimonious opposition to the Labour Front government, Lee Kuan Yew was able to play a strong role in the Legislative Assembly. As a member of the all-party committee appointed by Marshall to deal with the problem of education and of the teams that went to London to seek self-government, he took a constructive part in the developments of the 1955–59 period without being identified with the ruling regime.

❧

The British government was pleased with the general performance of the Lim Yew Hock government in countering subversion, and the independence granted to the Federation of Malaya in August 1957 was a further stabilizing factor. The Singapore Legislative Assembly sent its greetings. "We of Singapore look forward to that day when our strength will be added to your strength and our separation will be ended."

Steady progress was made on the crucial issues of Malayanization, citizenship, and education. In December 1956, after some heated debate, the Legislative Assembly accepted the Malayanization Committee's majority report, which advocated the localization within two years of all general administrative posts in the public service and the remaining professional posts within four years. The following year a Public Services Commission with full executive powers was set up, and Malayanization proceeded rapidly.

The citizenship controversy was settled by a Citizenship Ordinance in 1957, which offered Singapore citizenship to all residents born in Singapore or the Federation and to British citizens with two years' residence and offered naturalization to all those who had lived for ten years in the colony and were prepared to swear loyalty to Singapore. This enfranchised the majority of the 220,000 alien-born Chinese.

In December 1957 an Education Ordinance based upon the all-party committee's recommendations gave parity in principle to the four main language streams, and this continued to be the foundation for Singapore's educational policy for the next thirty years. Reforms undertaken since 1955, when the Department of Education was converted into a ministry, were already beginning to take effect. The ministry had opened ninety-six new primary schools and eleven secondary schools. It established technical and commercial schools, initiated an energetic programme of adult education, established training courses for Malay and Tamil teachers, and opened a polytechnic in 1958.[13]

When the third all-party constitutional mission went to London in April 1958, the situation looked much brighter and the terms of the new constitution were quickly agreed. The British Parliament passed a State of Singapore Act in August 1958, which provided for converting the colony into a "state" with control over all domestic affairs, including finance.[14] A fifty-one member Legislative Assembly, elected on the basis of adult suffrage by all Singapore citizens, could conduct its debates in English, Malay, Mandarin, or Tamil. The Prime Minister would select his Cabinet, and after a short interim period a local Yang di-Pertuan Negara, or chief of state, would be chosen. Internal security would be in the hands of the Internal Security Council, comprising representatives from Singapore, Britain, and the Federation.[15] While the British government retained control of foreign affairs and external defence, it could only suspend the constitution and assume full powers of government through its High Commissioner in the event of a dire emergency. The only controversial point was the British insistence that known subversives should be excluded from the first elections, scheduled to be held in May 1959 to bring the new constitution into force, which meant banning the political internees in Changi Gaol from standing as candidates.

လ

Meanwhile, in Singapore, the centre of interest shifted from the Legislative Assembly to the hitherto quiet, stately, rather dull City Hall. The British attached great importance on local government as a training ground for democracy and extended its scope in the post-war years. Singapore acquired city status in 1951 and, during the following four years, three commissions reported on local government. The first was a one-man commission in the person of Dr. L.C. Hill, a local government expert from Britain, who was appointed in 1951. Hill recommended increasing the powers of the city council by making it fully elected by universal adult suffrage and transferring to it government and quasi-government functions, such as public health, communications, and housing. He also suggested expanding the responsibilities of rural district councils in order to involve the whole adult population in local government as training for political freedom.[16]

The Rendel Commission also considered local government within the framework of its constitutional proposals and recommended streamlining local functions into one island-wide City and Island Council. Marshall feared such a body would rival the Legislative Assembly, and in 1955 he appointed another committee under Percy McNeice, the Municipal President, to plan separate city and district councils along the lines of the Hill Report.[17]

As a result new local government legislation came into force in July 1957. The Singapore Improvement Trust and Singapore Harbour Board retained their independent status, and the City Council's powers remained largely the same, while the Rural District Councils continued to be "no more than glorified rural district advisory committees".[18] But the composition of the City Council and its electorate changed radically. The council became an entirely elected body of thirty-two members, one of whom would be chosen as mayor. Candidates who were literate in any of the four main languages were eligible to stand, and all four languages were to be permitted in council debates. All adults were automatically registered as voters, subject to certain residence qualifications, and in this way the vote was extended to about half a million new voters who were not British subjects.

The City Council elections held in December 1957 roused interest and fire for the first time. The Liberal Socialists, who had dominated the old council, retained only seven seats. Victory went to new men, in particular the PAP candidates, who promised in their election campaigns to fight corruption and re-organize the council to serve the people. Despite the arrest of its most radical leaders a few months earlier, the PAP won thirteen of the fourteen seats it contested to become the largest party in the new council.

Ong Eng Guan, a Johor-born, Australian-trained accountant, founder member, and treasurer of the PAP, was elected mayor. Rabidly anti-colonialist but not a communist, Ong was a favourite with the Chinese masses. He had already shown a taste for adventurous methods when, as a member of Lee Kuan Yew's "basement" group, he proposed to settle Toh Chin Chye's worries about infringing the restrictions on numbers by burying the minutes in Lee's garden.[19] Unorthodox and unpredictable, Mayor Ong disdained to be a "ceremonial figurehead attending cocktail parties" and converted the council into what he rightly described as "the most controversial Municipal Council in the world".[20] Ong appointed and dismissed staff at will, forced resignations, and issued instructions without reference to the council, which he harangued for hours on end concerning the alleged wrongs of colonialism. Stormy, abusive meetings raged all day and long into the night. Derided at the time as "a Chinese carnival for baiting the British and cuddling the hawkers",[21] they played to crowded public galleries, packed with sometimes shirtless labourers who had never set foot in the council chamber before. At length the other parties rallied together to stop Ong's activities, objecting to his attempt to create a special mayor's fund, which they alleged was being used for political purposes, accusing him of dismissing staff on political grounds, and using his powers, particularly in the granting of hawkers' licences, to gain political influence.

In March 1959 the government took over part of the City Council's functions; the next month Ong Eng Guan and the other PAP councillors resigned, and the Lim Yew Hock government appointed a commission of enquiry to investigate alleged irregularities in the working of the council.

∾

The PAP set out to make a bid for power in the general elections scheduled to implement the new constitution. In March 1958 Fang Chuan Pi, who had spent the last eight years since the debacle of the Singapore Town Committee living in hiding, had sought a secret meeting with Lee Kuan Yew. Still a young man in his late twenties, Fang was given plenipotentiary power by the Malayan Communist Party – and hence nicknamed "The Plen" – to patch up the bruised relationship between the two wings of the PAP, and to impress on the moderates that the communists could still command powerful influence behind the scene, despite the setbacks of the past few years. It was the first of several meetings in which communist support for the PAP was offered, on the understanding that, once in office, the PAP would let the communists operate freely. The encounters appear to have consolidated mutual incomprehension, leaving Lee Kuan Yew overestimating the strength of the extreme left wing, and the communists overconfident of their would-be ally's leftist sympathies.

After drawing up a comprehensive political, economic and social programme, in February 1959 the PAP launched a pre-election campaign of weekly mass rallies to publicize the party's policy. At the first meeting they charged the Labour Front with receiving political funds from the United States government, which Education Minister Chew Swee Kee was alleged to have converted to his own use. Lee Kuan Yew called for the immediate resignation of the entire Lim Yew Hock government "in view of public disgust and loss of public confidence in the government". Francis Thomas, the Minister of Communications and Works, who disapproved of Lim Yew Hock's methods and his willingness if need be to use underworld support to smash the PAP, resigned from the government and backed Lee Kuan Yew's demand for a commission of enquiry. The Labour Front had fallen apart. Lim Yew Hock organized a new Singapore People's Alliance Party to fight the coming election, but this was merely a new name for the old Labour Front leadership with a few Liberal Socialist allies.

The unsavoury disclosures, rumours and allegations that came to light at the enquiry hearings held in the weeks immediately before the May 1959 general election discredited the existing regime. By contrast PAP candidates, dressed in white as a symbol of incorruptibility, offered the electorate a constructive programme of economic and social reform. Claiming to be "a party founded on principle, not opportunism",[22] PAP leaders promised "honest and efficient government", which would tackle the problems of education, labour, trade unions, social security, housing, rural development, health, and the status of women. They pledged to work towards gaining independence by uniting Singapore with the Federation of Malaya. Their primary aim was to "infuse into our multi-racial society the spirit of belonging to a nation", and the second priority was to transform Singapore from a trading to an industrial society, "to obtain for the general masses of the people a happy, full and secure livelihood".[23] Big commercial companies had fears and doubts, but the electorate was impressed. The PAP contested all fifty-one constituencies and swept the polls to secure forty-three seats. Of the remaining eight seats, four went to the Singapore People's Alliance, three to UMNO-MCA Alliance candidates and one to an independent. For the first time, Singapore had a fully elected government with a strong working majority.[24]

After 1959 the former leaders ceased to play a dominant role in Singapore politics. Lim Yew Hock returned to the new Assembly with diminished prestige, and David Marshall, who had used trade union support to form a new Workers' Party, was defeated at the polls. Unable to create a strong disciplined political organization to harness grassroots support, the Labour Front petered out in dissensions, accusations, and ignominy, which clouded the substantial achievements of the past four years. In the words of Francis Thomas, the Marshall government "gave a tremendous psychological boost to the people".[25] The Labour Front won full internal self-government within the lifetime of the Rendel Assembly, it created a special Singapore citizenship, drew up a programme for swift Malayanization of the public services, and established the principle of official multilingualism. It inaugurated an education policy that averted an immediate dangerous crisis and gave long-term equality in principle to the four main language streams. It also kept the path to merger open by maintaining a harmonious relationship with Kuala Lumpur.

The Labour Front governments also acted as a safety valve in tackling basic issues that threatened the future of Singapore, because by 1955 the colonial government was dangerously out of touch with the mass of Singaporeans. An official described the Singapore Special Branch in 1956 as "unquestionably the world's greatest authorities on Communism in Asia",[26] but the heavy handed repression tended to blind the colonial authorities and to delude them into being too quick to interpret real grievances as subversion.

For all its faults, and despite the irresponsibility of Ong Eng Guan's tenure of office at City Hall, the Labour Front handed over the machinery of government intact and unimpaired, providing the foundation for the later success of the more disciplined, hard-headed, calculating, and practical People's Action Party.

The PAP Government

The PAP's clear victory at the polls struck chill in the hearts of most conservatives, businessmen and property owners, especially expatriates, who regarded the election as the prelude to irresponsible and vindictive government and ultimately to communism. Up to that time the party's activities had on the surface been almost entirely disruptive, and Lee Kuan Yew's group had given open encouragement to the extravagant demands of the extremist wing. The storms in the Legislative Assembly, the pandemonium at City Hall, the anti-capitalist tirades, strikes, and demonstrations that had troubled Singapore in the past four years had already undermined the confidence of businessmen. The intensity of the PAP's election campaign and the party's record of extremism and inciting workers against employers frightened the professional and commercial community. European clubs prepared to be closed down, the price of property slumped, there was a flight of capital, the *Straits Times* newspaper and many foreign firms moved their headquarters to Kuala Lumpur, and a general air of gloom and foreboding in business circles augured badly for the future economic health of Singapore.

The immediate aftermath of the election increased these fears. Lee Kuan Yew refused to take office until PAP detainees were released, and he gave several of them posts in his government. The new regime launched an attack on Western culture and pressed heavily on the hitherto privileged English-educated middle class. Six thousand civil servants suffered a cut in allowances and were drafted into carrying out "voluntary" manual work on Sundays. Western films and magazines, which were held to have a corrupting influence or to belittle Asian culture, were banned. Liberal terms for British subjects to obtain Singapore citizenship were withdrawn. Even Raffles's statue almost fell victim to the wave of anti-Westernism.

In reality the situation was less unsettled than it appeared. Some of Singapore's most critical problems, such as education, language and citizenship, were already well on the way to solution. Widespread fears of retribution against capitalism and colonialism were unfounded. Despite their fiery election speeches and appeals to mass emotionalism, the exuberance of the election obscured what the party's English-speaking leaders really stood for. After the 1958 constitutional talks in London, Lee Kuan

Yew had satisfied the Colonial Office that he could form a moderate government and contain the disruptive elements in his party. During the 1955 and 1959 Assembly elections and the municipal election campaign of 1957, the PAP moderates ranted against colonialism and promised socialism, but they preached social welfare, not ideological Marxist-Leninism. In 1959, while emphasizing self-reliance, they acknowledged that foreign capital was essential for building up the economy. They planned radical changes in Singapore society, but, as Lee Kuan Yew promised in a broadcast speech at the time of assuming office, this was to be "a social revolution by peaceful means".

The need to retain the support of the Chinese-educated masses and to keep to the left of the Labour Front government had driven Lee Kuan Yew to cultivate an extremist public image that was at variance with his long-term political thinking. Few in Singapore at that time were aware of the Fabian views he had urged as a student in favour of a mildly socialist non-communist state, with independence to be achieved through constitutional means within the framework of the Commonwealth. Nor was it generally appreciated how the moderates within the PAP had used the opportunities of the past few years to win control of the party's central machinery.

Lee Kuan Yew manipulated his grasp of English constitutional practice with great skill to strengthen his leadership, and he exploited this advantage over his left-wing allies. Realizing the suicidal mistake made by the Malayan Democratic Union in boycotting the 1948 election, he had prevailed over Lim Chin Siong, Devan Nair, and other left-wing advocates of direct action in insisting the PAP should secure a foothold in the 1955 Assembly. It was the PAP moderates who came to power in June 1959, and, before their extremist colleagues were released from prison, Lee Kuan Yew organized the re-election of the existing central executive committee for a further two-year period. When Lim Chin Siong and three other ex-detainees were appointed as political secretaries in the new government, they were put in ministries where they could exert little power and were not given cadre membership of the party.

The new Cabinet presented an imposing display of talent. The inner corps comprised Lee Kuan Yew, Toh Chin Chye, Goh Keng Swee, and S. Rajaratnam, whose ability to act as a team despite personal differences proved a major source of strength. Their abilities were complementary: Toh Chin Chye a dedicated party chairman, Goh Keng Swee a practical economist, and Rajaratnam an imaginative thinker and capable journalist. All three were very able men, but they were willing to leave the limelight and the leadership to Lee Kuan Yew, the most impressive public personality among the party's English-speaking group. A compelling orator, fluent, direct, and analytical, Lee possessed the power to impress not only English-educated Singaporeans but also foreign men of affairs and international intellectuals. He appreciated the importance of being able to speak directly to people in their own language and at their own level. The limitations of his own typically Straits Chinese background, English-educated, speaking a smattering of dialect, and bazaar Malay but illiterate in Chinese, was forcibly brought home to him by the spectacle of Lim Chin Siong's magnetic command over mass audiences. Lee put to good use his own facility for mastering foreign languages, which had started with training as a Japanese interpreter during the Occupation. Over the years he became fluent in Malay, Mandarin, and Hokkien.

All the PAP leaders were pragmatists, and they attracted men of similar ilk to their ranks: economists, bankers, architects, and town planners. The party took pride in rejecting not merely communism but ideologies in general, in the belief that people wanted good government in the solid shape of jobs, housing, schools, and healthcare.

The former Governor, Sir William Goode, who acted as Yang di-Pertuan Negara for the first six months, worked in close co-operation with the new government, helping by his sympathetic personality and unobtrusive tact to achieve a smooth transfer of power. In December 1959 he was succeeded by Yusof bin Ishak, former chairman of the Public Services Commission. Born in Perak in 1910, the son of a government official, Yusof completed his schooling at Raffles Institution. An above-average student and keen sportsman, he became a journalist and in 1938 he founded the new *Utusan Melayu*. A simple-living, hardworking, disciplined, rather shy man, Yusof exemplified the radical, modern-minded Muslim. He stood for multiracialism and secular modernization and urged Malays to improve their condition through education and their own efforts, rather than seeking special privileges and protection.

When the office of governor was abolished, the leading British authority became a Commissioner for the United Kingdom, who combined the office with that of Commissioner-General for the United Kingdom in Southeast Asia. The British Commissioner remained in the background but had considerable potential powers, being entitled to see the agenda of Cabinet meetings, together with all Cabinet papers. He was also Chairman of the Internal Security Council, with the ultimate right in time of emergency to suspend the constitution and assume charge of the government.

కొ

In a statement of policy read by the Yang di-Pertuan Negara in opening the first session of the new Legislative Assembly, the government pledged "to end colonialism and establish an independent, democratic, non-Communist, socialist Malaya", declaring "The future of Singapore lies ultimately in re-uniting with the Federation of Malaya as a state in an independent country."

From the start the PAP was divided on union with Malaya. Finance Minister Goh Keng Swee's economic programme aimed to achieve a common market with the Federation and to encourage industrialization in conjunction with private, and if need be foreign, capital. The left wing was alarmed at the prospect of a capitalist economy and merger with the anti-communist Federation. In office it was more difficult to keep extremists in check without losing the mass support behind them than it had been in opposition, and the new government was soon threatened with disaster when its leaders sought to establish economic stability and ease the way for union with Malaya. The PAP pledged to achieve merger within its four-year term of office. The British government also looked forward to an ultimate reunion of the two territories, and the Governor of Singapore, in opening the second session of the former Legislative Assembly in August 1956, had said, "The government will continue to foster and strengthen those links so that ultimately the narrow gap will be bridged bringing about the fusion of the two territories in a single united nation."

While the "narrow gap" was small in physical terms across the Johor Strait, it was psychologically broad and was widening. Since their separation in 1946, divergent constitutional development and education policies had driven Singapore and the Federation further apart. Initially Tunku Abdul Rahman was willing to consider incorporating Singapore into a confederation as a single state unit, but this was unacceptable to Singapore leaders, and discussions between Marshall and Tunku Abdul Rahman in December 1955 had produced no agreement. By the time the Federation achieved independence in 1957, Singapore was rent by political strife, and the Malayan Prime Minister was no longer prepared to envisage merger on any terms.

The tumultuous election campaign and the PAP victory in 1959 intensified the resistance of the essentially right-wing conservative Alliance in Kuala Lumpur to the idea of union, but the new Singapore government rejected any suggestions that it should seek a separate independence. A Malayan nation was, in the words of Rajaratnam, "a historical necessity".[27] "Nobody in his senses believes that Singapore alone, in isolation, can be independent," an official publication stated in 1960.[28] "Without this economic base (the Federation), Singapore would not survive," declared Lee Kuan Yew. "Whatever we do," commented

Goh Keng Swee, "major changes in our economy are only possible if Singapore and the Federation are integrated as one economy. The political reason for merger has a strong economic basis."

The new government realized "we must also resolve the ... fears which make the Malay majority in the Federation not want the Chinese majority in Singapore".[29] When the party was first formed in 1954, the PAP created a Malay Affairs Bureau under the direction of *Utusan Melayu* journalist Othman Wok.[30] Initially the PAP hoped to reach an understanding with the Singapore UMNO similar to the alliance between UMNO and the MCA in the Federation. It proposed a link in the city council in 1957 but was rebuffed by the Singapore UMNO on instructions from Kuala Lumpur. As a result, a number of radical Singapore Malays resigned from UMNO to join the PAP, which devoted increasing attention to Malay problems.

In 1956 the PAP moderates advocated a unified education system to draw the Federation and Singapore together. The 1958 constitution acknowledged the Malays as the indigenous people, and the new government appointed Yusof bin Ishak as the first local Yang di-Pertuan Negara. It recognized Malay as the national language and promised to improve the condition and prospects of Singapore Malays through education and social development. A Malay Education Advisory Committee was set up in 1959, the first Malay secondary school was opened the following year, and free secondary and university education was offered to suitably qualified Singapore Malay citizens, together with liberal bursaries and allowances. More schools and community centres were established in Malay areas, and in 1960 a new Malay settlement was set up at Sembawang, with its own board of management, school, community centre, and mosque.

Despite this policy of conciliation, talks held with Federation leaders in 1960 to discuss the possibilities of a pan-Malayan common market bore no fruit, and the PAP government found it impossible to woo Kuala Lumpur and satisfy its own extremists at the same time. While the PAP moderates regarded the Internal Security Council as the first constitutional link with Malaya, to the radicals it was a symbol of colonialism and oppression. The left wing criticized the government for accepting Malay as the national language and making Chinese schools conform to the policy laid down by the Labour Front regime.

The PAP leaders sought merger as a matter of urgency not only to achieve political independence but also to guarantee Singapore's economic survival. During the 1950s the British and nearly all Singapore politicians were preoccupied with political issues, but Singapore's economic problems were equally pressing. In 1959 Singapore was still largely dependent on international entrepôt commerce and servicing Malayan staple commodities, and on income from British military bases. But the Singapore population was growing rapidly, with one of the highest rates of growth in the world and more than half the population under the age of twenty-one. With the reluctant support of the Municipal Council, a group of middle-class Chinese and Western women established a Family Planning Association in 1949, but even the poorest of Singaporeans continued to regard children as a social and economic asset. Already many unskilled and semi-skilled workers were unemployed, and the traditional colonial economy was not geared to meet increasing demands for jobs or to satisfy rising expectations in the provision of education, health, and other social services. There was a crying need to re-house the population. A start was made in building the first satellite town at Queenstown, under a master plan drawn up in 1958, but otherwise little was done to remedy the housing shortage during the Labour Front's tenure of office, when priority was given to the problems of self-government, education policy, citizenship and Malayanization.

While Singapore was one of the world's leading ports, with well-developed facilities in banking, insurance, and other commercial services, in 1955 the International Bank for Reconstruction and Development feared that economic expansion would not keep pace with her growing population, the pressure on social services, and demands for employment.[31] In the next few years, as Lee Kuan Yew later admitted, the PAP opposition used the trade unions as "a banner behind which we challenged the whole system", and labour unrest threatened to bring the economy to the point of collapse. A pan-Malayan common market seemed a remote dream.

Before the 1959 election Goh Keng Swee had called for industrialization as the key to rapid economic growth, which would mop up unemployment and finance social reform. Goh's careful programme had gone almost unnoticed during the frenzied polemics of the hustings, and the subsequent PAP victory scared away the foreign and local investors on which his plans depended.

The immediate problem was to achieve financial stability and confidence, and strong government was needed to introduce a planned economy, to take firm action to curb population growth, and to discipline workers. Despite its landslide victory, the PAP was not a united party, and its election victory brought immediate internal strains between the moderates, who wanted to woo the Federation and capitalists in order to boost the economy, and the extremists, who wanted to establish a socialist independent state and destroy capitalism. Political storm clouds gathered in the first two years of the new government, and uncertainty and labour unrest deterred the investment needed to industrialize.

The PAP moderates wanted to convert the trade unions into partners of the establishment, but such a transformation was unwelcome to many trade unionists. Lee Kuan Yew had declared in 1959 that "a PAP government is a government on the workers' side",[32] and he promised them a fair share of increased wealth in the form of better wages and good working conditions. He warned against letting a tussle between labour and capital damage the economy. The objective was to secure "industrial peace with justice", through collective bargaining without strikes. An Industrial Relations Ordinance was enacted in 1960 providing for conciliation, arbitration, and settling disputes by collective bargaining. The following month an industrial arbitration court was set up whose decisions were binding in law. Trade unionists resisted government attempts to legislate for a National Trades Union Congress, which would unify the labour movement, co-operate closely with the government, and have sole authority for calling strikes. The government then withdrew its bill and tried to control the unions by withholding and withdrawing registration. This led to internal dissensions within the party, which were reflected in public bickering and weakened confidence in the political stability needed to lay the foundations for a sound economy.

Resistance to the idea of merger with Malaya came not only from the labour unions but from their radical student allies, now centred in Nanyang University (Nantah), where the Nanyang University Students' Union and Guild of Nanyang University Graduates revived the political agitation of the banned Singapore Chinese Middle Schools Students' Union. The extreme left wing dominated the Students' Union's executive committee and controlled its journals, which published a great deal of propaganda material from the People's Republic of China and items relating to workers and peasants. Nantah students also had grievances of their own following the publication in July 1959 of a damning report on the university by the independent Prescott Commission. Scathing in its criticism of the whole administration, staff morale, curriculum, standards, and running of the new university, the Commission refused to recommend that its degrees be recognized. This was a devastating blow to students, since it meant their degrees would not qualify them for graduate employment or further study. Tan Lark Sye was reduced to tears and, after a few months of bitter recriminations and an equally negative report by a second commission that was appointed to look into the university's affairs, in May 1960 he resigned as chairman of the university council. The PAP government was alarmed too, since the prospect of hundreds of frustrated Nantah graduates with unacceptable qualifications being thrown on the labour market threatened to revive the explosive position of 1955 in even more severe form. As a compromise solution the government decided to admit Nantah graduates to executive posts in the civil service on a probationary basis and to consider promotion to the administrative grade dependent on individual performance. This concession failed to satisfy the student body and fuelled their already bitter discontent and political radicalism.

஠

The first open quarrel within the PAP came not with the left wing but with the maverick Ong Eng Guan. Ong's standing in the party and his popularity with the masses had not suffered as a result of the commission of enquiry into the proceedings of the city council, which was adjourned when heated allegations and arguments among witnesses and counsel threatened to prejudice the 1959 election. The commission was never reconvened, and controversy ended in July 1959 when the PAP absorbed the city council into the central government. For good or ill the days of municipal democracy were over, and the merging of local and central authority that Governor Ord had first proposed ninety years earlier was pushed through by the PAP government within a few weeks of taking office.

Most City Council functions were transferred to a Ministry of National Development, which also directed economic planning and supervised the Harbour Board and a Housing Board, which was created in 1960 to take over and expand the functions of the Singapore Improvement Trust. Despite Ong Eng Guan's unsettling and unorthodox record as Mayor, he was given this key ministry and was also appointed as one of the three Singapore members on the influential Internal Security Council. The assignment soon led to a clash of personalities and principles. Ong resented the rising star of Lee Kuan Yew as a threat to his own ambitions, while the party executive feared Ong's appeal to Chinese chauvinism would jeopardize their policy to court Kuala Lumpur and build up the economy. Moreover, Ong used the same disruptive techniques to run his ministry that he had brought to his office of Mayor, with the result that industrialization was at a standstill and housing construction fell below even the level of previous years. Within a few months Ong's powers were clipped when local government and the Harbour Board were removed from his portfolio. Ong then decided to challenge the party executive. In June 1960 he formally charged the leaders with creating an undemocratic party structure and failing to advance with sufficient speed towards independence and socialism. He found little support within the party and was opposed by both the moderates and the pro-communists. The party executive charged him with raising the issue to cover up his own ambitions and maladministration. He was dismissed from his ministry and expelled from the party, the first victim of the authoritarian discipline that he himself had helped to create.

Ong resigned from the Legislative Assembly, and a sordid and vindictive squabble ensued in which the executive sought to discredit him on personal moral grounds. This did not diminish his charismatic appeal among his former constituents at Hong Lim, where he fought a by-election to regain his seat in April 1961. Using his personal popularity to exploit Chinese chauvinism and anti-colonialism, Ong demanded immediate and unconditional independence from Britain. He won a landslide victory, despite communist support for the government's candidate, and in June 1961 he formed a rival United People's Party.

The Hong Lim by-election was crucial. It threatened to topple the government, but this very danger led to the salvation of the PAP ruling group. Hitherto Tunku Abdul Rahman had aimed to keep the Federation clear from the turbulent politics of Singapore. Now, in view of the possible fall of the Singapore government to more extreme left-wing leaders, the Tunku feared that Singapore might achieve independence as a communist state, potentially a "second Cuba"[33] and a danger to Malaya's security. Despite the immense difficulties of establishing a successful merger, the Malayan Prime Minister came to the reluctant conclusion that the dangers of a hostile, independent and communist-controlled Singapore were even more frightening. In a luncheon speech to the Foreign Correspondents' Association in Singapore in May 1961, Tunku Abdul Rahman tentatively suggested that "sooner or later" Malaya, Singapore and the Borneo territories should work for closer "political and economic co-operation". This informal and unexpected suggestion received a delighted official welcome from the Singapore government but caused consternation among the PAP's left wing and precipitated an open confrontation between the moderates and extremists. The left wing dreaded the prospect of Singapore coming under the control of the anti-communist government in Kuala Lumpur and instead wanted independence for a separate Singapore, in which they were confident they would have the upper hand.

Conflict between the PAP party executive and its left wing was bound to come, and by this stage the ruling group wanted to rid themselves of this "albatross round our necks".[34] They were relieved to fight the inevitable battle on the issue of merger, on which it was difficult for the opposition to whip up popular emotions. "Merger was the perfect issue on which to break," Lee Kuan Yew recorded in his memoirs.[35] Yet the ensuing struggle almost resulted in annihilating the PAP.

The test came as a result of a by-election in the Anson constituency in July 1961, when Lim Chin Siong, together with other left-wing PAP Assemblymen, party officials and trade union leaders, withheld support from the government's candidate and backed his opponent, David Marshall, now chairman of the Workers' Party. Marshall, who won by a small majority, stood for immediate independence, the abolition of the Internal Security Council and the evacuation by Britain of her military bases in Singapore. Lim Chin Siong's group supported these demands and in addition protested against the proposed merger with Malaya, calling for "internal democracy in the PAP" and the release of all political detainees.

Meanwhile James Puthucheary, with Lim Chin Siong, Sandra Woodhull and Fong Swee Suan, sought an urgent interview with Lord Selkirk, the British Commissioner-General, at his residence at Eden Hall. Suspecting that Lee Kuan Yew had long been collaborating with the British, they wished to assure themselves that Britain would not suspend the constitution if the Prime Minister was voted out of office and they themselves came to power. In accordance with his open-door policy, Lord Selkirk received the four dissident PAP members and stressed that the constitution was a free one, which they should respect.[36]

The British intended to keep to the constitutional arrangements and timetable that had been laid down, but the "Eden Hall tea party", coming at such a dangerous moment for Lee Kuan Yew, drove him to fury. He labelled it as a sinister British plot to encourage the communists into licence in order to force Lee either to smash the left wing for them or to resign and give the British the excuse to step in and suspend the constitution. The opposition derided Lee's allegations as "a fairy tale of British lions and communist bears", but he used it to whip up popular support and risked demanding a vote of confidence from the Legislative Assembly.

During the debate in the legislature, which raged all night, the extremists denounced the proposed merger as an imperialist plot. When the final division came, twenty-seven Assemblymen voted for the government but twenty-four, including thirteen of the PAP's left wing, either abstained or voted against the motion of confidence. The PAP rebel Assemblymen, who included five parliamentary secretaries, then proceeded to form an opposition Barisan Sosialis, or Socialist Front, with Lim Chin Siong as secretary-general, but they continued to sit in the Assembly as representatives of their constituencies.

Outside of the Assembly, the PAP executive's position in the party was even more precarious. While the moderates had controlled the central executive committee since 1957, the communists continued to consolidate their strength at the second level of leadership and at the base of the party structure. When the split came in July 1961, most key figures in the party's branches defected to the Barisan, and at the lower level the PAP's organization was almost crippled. Within a few hours thirty-five of the fifty-one branch committees resigned and nineteen of the twenty-three paid organizing secretaries defected. Many branches disappeared completely, including Lee Kuan Yew's own branch at Tanjong Pagar, Toh Chin Chye's at Rochore, and Rajaratnam's at Kampong Glam, where the defectors even took away the fixtures and fittings.[37] Others were almost destroyed. Eleven were left with fewer than twenty-five members each and one had only ten. The PAP lost most of its active party workers and a great mass of supporters, including many who were not pro-communist but thought the party was doomed and scrambled to leave the apparently sinking ship. Large numbers of cadres quit, and only 20 per cent of the party's former members paid their subscriptions in 1962.[38]

The Barisan Sosialis started with a great deal of strength at the grassroots level and controlled the Work Brigade, the People's Association, and most other secondary political associations formerly attached to the PAP. It also had strong support outside of the party organization among Nanyang University students and graduates and among trade unionists. At the time of the split, the Barisan controlled two-thirds of organized labour, and forty-three unions publicly pledged to back the new party.

$\wp$

This dangerous time proved to be the turning point in the fortunes of Lee Kuan Yew and the PAP. The domestic crisis impelled the Singapore government to continue its negotiations for merger with a vigour born of near-desperation. Tunku Abdul Rahman feared that a simple merger of Singapore and Malaya would give too much power to Singapore and to the Chinese, who would be the largest single community, comprising 43 per cent of the total population compared with 41 per cent Malays. He decided therefore to promote a wider partnership, based on a federation of Malaya, Singapore and the three British Borneo territories.

The principle of merger was approved at a regional conference of the Commonwealth Parliamentary Association held in Singapore in July 1961 with representatives from Malaya, Singapore, North Borneo, Brunei, and Sarawak, and formal agreement in principle was announced after the Prime Ministers of Singapore and Malaya conferred the following month. By

November 1961 it was agreed that Singapore should be a special state with greater autonomy than the other units in the proposed federation, but Singapore citizens would not automatically become Malaysian citizens, since the terms for obtaining citizenship were more stringent for immigrant communities in Malaya. Singapore would have a smaller representation in the federal government than her population would otherwise warrant, but would be able to retain her own executive state government. Britain agreed to these merger terms, provided she retained control of the Singapore military bases.

The Barisan Sosialis opposed the government's approach to merger, criticizing in particular the restrictive citizenship stipulations. The communists wanted to see Singapore as part of a united Malayan republic but not of a conservative Federation including the Borneo territories, which was designed by Tunku Abdul Rahman to prevent, not to facilitate, a communist takeover in Singapore. In a series of broadcasts Lee Kuan Yew set out to enlist popular support for the proposed merger, portraying the Barisan as a communist organization, intent upon sabotaging the whole scheme. The government decided to submit the question to a popular referendum, presenting three alternative forms of merger, but without offering the choice of voting against the union.

The different elements in Singapore, Kuala Lumpur, and the Borneo territories that opposed the merger began to make common cause. Some Barisan Sosialis members attended a meeting of the Indonesian Communist Party in December 1961, at which a resolution was passed condemning the Malaysia proposal, and in January 1962 a conference was held in Kuala Lumpur, at which the (Malayan) Socialist Front, Barisan Sosialis, Sarawak United People's Party, and Brunei Parti Rakyat combined to oppose the project. Subsequently the Barisan Sosialis, supported by David Marshall's Workers' Party and Ong Eng Guan's United People's Party, sent a mission of nineteen Assemblymen to appeal to the United Nations committee on colonialism against the form of the proposed merger, but in July

1962 Lee Kuan Yew went to New York and successfully defended the issue.[39] He then proceeded to London to join the British and Malayans in working out final details.

The campaign leading up to the Singapore referendum in September 1962 was as heated as a general election, since the government's survival depended on the issue. Seventy-one per cent of the electorate voted in favour of the government's proposals, but 25 per cent showed their disapproval by returning blank or spoiled ballots. The PAP's troubles were far from over, because by that time it had lost its parliamentary majority with the defection of a PAP Assemblywoman to the Barisan in July 1962. Henceforth the government had to rely upon Lim Yew Hock and the Alliance representatives, who supported the PAP on the merger issue but on nothing else. The position was so precarious that it dared not hold a by-election to fill a vacancy in the Assembly arising from the death of a government minister, since the seat would almost certainly have fallen to the Barisan.

෫෨

The summer of 1961 marked another important turning point in Singapore's development, when crucial decisions were made concerning the direction of Singapore's economy, which had far-reaching political consequences and were to have a profound impact in determining the future character of the state.

At the PAP government's request, a United Nations Technical Assistance team visited Singapore in 1960 to advise on the prospects for industrialization. Headed by a distinguished Dutch economist, Dr. Albert Winsemius, who had played a major role in Holland's economic revival after the Second World War, the mission spent two months in Singapore and became increasingly gloomy about this "poor little market in a dark corner of Asia", plagued by strikes and political turmoil. Nevertheless Winsemius was impressed with the potential of the people. The team produced a four-year plan, launched in June 1961, which laid stress on economic development and industrial growth with the government participating directly and providing background services.[40]

In August 1961 an Economic Development Board was set up under the chairmanship of Hon Sui Sen,[41] a very able and experienced civil servant. Work began on building an industrial estate on nearly 4,000 acres of former swamp and wasteland at Jurong.[42] Giving priority to mopping up unemployment, the first stage of the economic programme concentrated on labour intensive, low value industries, such as textiles, which required little skill or capital outlay, and investors in pioneer industries were wooed with tax concessions and temporary protective import tariffs.

The economic plan's success, Winsemius insisted, depended on restoring the trust of foreign investors, getting rid of the communists, and cultivating a common Malayan market. Lee Kuan Yew's government had no problem in implementing Winsemius's first recommendation – saving Raffles's statue as a token gesture to reassure the Western community – nor with promoting merger with the Federation of Malaya, but the prospects for defeating the communists looked bleak at that time of acute crisis.

The security situation eased after February 1963 when the Internal Security Council ordered the detention under the first stage of Operation Cold Store of more than 100 left-wing political, trade union and student leaders who opposed the formation of Malaysia and were suspected of involvement with A.M. Azahari,[43] the socialist leader of the Brunei Parti Rakyat. After winning all the elected seats in the Brunei Legislative Council, Azahari's party had opposed the idea of Brunei joining the proposed Federation of Malaysia, demanded independence, and in 1962 staged a revolt against Sultan Omar, which was put down by Malaysian, British and Commonwealth forces. Azahari found asylum in Jakarta, which became the focus for anti-Malaysia, communist, and other left-wing groups throughout the region. The Singaporeans detained under Operation Cold Store included Lim Chin Siong, half of the Barisan Sosialis's central executive committee, and sympathizers who were close to the party, notably journalist Said Zahari. Born in Singapore in 1929, Said Zahari succeeded Yusof bin Ishak as editor of the Kuala Lumpur-based *Utusan Melayu* in 1959, and two years later led a three-month strike to oppose UMNO taking control of the newspaper. After visiting Singapore, he was banned from re-entering the Federation. The Barisan Sosialis tried to recruit Said Zahari, hoping to use his unique combination of far-left views and influence in the Malay community to broaden the party's appeal, and he edited the party's publication, *Rakyat*. On 1 February 1963 he was elected to lead the Beijing-oriented, anti-Malaysia Partai Rakyat Singapura and prepared to leave next day to attend a conference of Afro-Asian journalists in Jakarta. In the early hours of the morning he was arrested and was to spend the next seventeen years under detention.[44]

The Operation Cold Store arrests provoked protest riots, which led to further arrests, mainly of second-echelon Barisan leaders. This was a severe blow to the Barisan. Once again the PAP's rivals had been removed at a dangerous time in circumstances in which the responsibility could be laid at the doors of others, this time the British and Malayans.

Lee Kuan Yew gained considerable personal success in negotiating the final terms for the Malaysia merger, which were very favourable to Singapore. Under the Malaysia Agreement, which was concluded in July 1963, Singapore, Sarawak and North Borneo (Sabah) were federated with the existing states of Malaya to form Malaysia.[45] Foreign affairs, defence and internal security were controlled by the central government, but Singapore was given considerable powers over finance, labour and education. She was allotted just fifteen seats in the new 127-member federal legislature but was to retain her own executive government and Assembly, with her own Yang di-Pertuan Negara and separate Public Services Commission. The Singapore government was to be responsible for executive administration and day-to-day policies, and payment to the central government was limited to 40 per cent of her income from taxes, which amounted to 27 per cent of her total revenue.

The Federation of Malaysia was scheduled to come into being on 31 August 1963,[46] but Tunku Abdul Rahman deferred implementing the agreement until mid-September because of objections from President Sukarno of Indonesia, who denounced the Malaysian concept as a "neo-colonialist plot" and a menace to his dream of uniting the Malay world. To counter his complaints, Tunku Abdul Rahman arranged for a United Nations survey, which confirmed that the people of the Borneo territories favoured the merger, but Sukarno launched an armed confrontation (Konfrontasi) against the new state, which lasted for nearly three years.

Lee Kuan Yew declared Singapore's freedom unilaterally on 31 August 1963, the date originally set for the coming into being of the new federation, so that the island enjoyed an anomalous fifteen days of full independence before becoming part of Malaysia. During that transitional period the PAP government called a snap election. Once union with Malaya was achieved, the basis for co-operation with the Alliance Assemblymen disappeared. Hitherto the government had relied on their support to ward off left-wing attacks, but now it needed a fresh mandate to renew its power.

Three major parties contested the September 1963 election: the PAP, the Barisan Sosialis and a new Singapore Alliance, which consisted of the remnants of Lim Yew Hock's Singapore People's Alliance together with the Singapore branches of UMNO, the Malayan Chinese Association, and the Malayan Indian Congress.

The result of the contest hung in doubt. Despite the arrest of so many of its key officials, party activists, and trade union and student supporters, the Barisan Sosialis still had considerable mass appeal among workers and students, particularly at Nanyang University. It also had influential backing from Chinese community leaders and the wealthy businessmen who had funded Nantah and Chinese schools, notably Tan Lark Sye. The Chinese-educated felt that the fruits of self-government had fallen to the English-educated, while they continued to be excluded from influence and suffered discrimination.[47] Despite the fact that official education policy now gave Chinese schools similar grants-in-aid to English schools, Chinese teachers enjoyed the same salaries and conditions, and Chinese school leavers were admitted to government service, very few Nantah graduates were promoted to the administrative grade of the civil service, and Chinese schools resented being drawn into the state system. Chinese schoolchildren boycotted examinations in December 1961 in protest against attempts to unify curricula and examinations.

The government proposed measures to raise Nanyang University's standards and open it to students of all races. The university and its sponsors objected to the erosion of its exclusively Chinese character, and in August 1963 the Chinese Chamber of Commerce called for more money to be spent on Chinese education to stem the falling enrolment in Chinese schools. This ran counter to the PAP's policy of creating a unified educational system, which many Chinese community leaders regarded as sabotaging Chinese education and culture. The left wing continued to exploit the issue of Chinese education. Nanyang University students and guild of graduates supported the Barisan's election campaign, with the encouragement of Tan Lark Sye who himself contributed substantial funds.

While the PAP no longer enjoyed the broad mass support it commanded at the time of the 1959 general election, the party's position was stronger than it had been in its darkest hours two years before. Since the debacle in 1961, a vigorous attempt had been made to revive its organization and recruit new members, particularly among the Malay and Indian communities. Many leading opponents were in gaol, including the charismatic Lim Chin Siong. There were also more positive reasons for the party's improved fortunes. It had achieved its main political goal in successfully negotiating merger with the Federation and winning independence from colonial rule within the time limit promised in 1959. As the ruling party, it held the initiative. For a long time, the government had intended to hold an election immediately after Malaysia came into being and planned its strategy accordingly. From the early months of 1963, Lee Kuan Yew took advantage of his position as Prime Minister to carry out extensive personal tours in all constituencies, particularly in the rural areas where the left wing had built up strong support in the mid-1950s. By this time Lee had polished his own language skills and could speak directly to the people.

Local community centres were developed as channels of communication under the direction of a People's Association, which was formed as an independent statutory body in 1960 under the Prime Minister's chairmanship. The 1952 Hill Report on local government had recognized that "community centres should be the nursery of citizenship", whereas "central government is anonymous, it is impersonal, to most people it is nothing more than an idea".[48] In a very different way from that envisaged by Hill, community centres were to become one of the most important instruments of government and consolidation of PAP power. In 1959 there were only twenty-four community centres, but during the next four years the PAP built more than a hundred new ones, providing a social meeting place, recreation facilities, literacy classes, wireless, and later television. The government controlled both broadcasting and television, which began a pilot service early in 1963.

After Ong Eng Guan's supersession, the PAP turned its back on doctrinaire socialism and embarked on a vigorous pragmatic programme of economic expansion and social reform. A first priority was to channel substantial funds into constructing public housing. Lim Kim San,[49] one of the few successful businessmen to support the PAP in its early days, was appointed first chairman of the new Housing and Development Board and, under his dynamic direction, the Board built as many housing units and shops in its first three years as the Singapore Improvement Trust had constructed in the whole of its thirty-two years' existence.

Starting with new housing, slum clearance and resettlement, in 1962 the Board widened its scope to include urban development and re-development.

A Public Utilities Board was established in 1963 to take over the water, electricity and gas functions of the former City Council. Health facilities were improved. A mass X-ray campaign was launched in 1960 to combat tuberculosis, which was then the main killing disease. School health services were expanded, more maternal and child welfare clinics were set up, and better sanitation and immunization were provided, particularly in outlying villages.

Expenditure on education rose from $600,000 in 1960 to $10,000,000 in 1963, and the school population increased over the same period from 290,000 to 430,000. The PAP pledged to provide universal free primary schooling as the first educational priority, and soon after taking office it embarked on a crash school-building programme and stepped up the recruiting and training of teachers. The number of students at the teachers' training college doubled from 2,500 in 1959 to 5,000 in 1965. The principle of bilingualism and parity of the four language streams laid down in 1956 was promoted vigorously. In 1960 the first integrated schools were opened, where pupils could study in different language media but mingle socially under the same roof, and eighty-four such schools were built in the next seven years.

The PAP fulfilled an election promise to enhance the status of women by passing a Women's Charter in 1961, which required marriages to be registered, prohibited polygamy, except among Muslims, and made divorce illegal other than by court order.[50] It had taken a hard battle to reach this milestone, and the proposal was stoutly resisted by many, even within the ranks of the PAP. Success was due mainly to the efforts of Chan Choy Siong,[51] a formidable champion of women's rights, with the support of Kenny Byrne. Women had hitherto played little part in political life. The first two women took their place as legislative councillors in 1951: Elizabeth Choy, who was appointed as a Nominated Member after failing to win election, and Mrs. Vilasini Menon, who won a seat as an independent. A Singapore Council of Women, which was formed the following year, with Elizabeth Choy as president and a largely upper-class, English-educated membership, argued the case for ending polygamy. But the young Chan Choy Siong and her PAP Women's League brought fire to the campaign. Born into a poor family in Singapore in 1934 but better educated than most of her Chinese female contemporaries, Chan attended Chinese Girls High School and was fluent in Mandarin. She threw herself into politics, became a PAP City Councillor in 1957 at the age of twenty-three, served on the party's central executive committee from 1957 until 1963, ran programmes for women and children, and formed women's committees in PAP branches. In 1956 she created the PAP's Women's League, which organized mass rallies, and she persuaded the party to set up a Women's Affairs Bureau and to include "One Man, One Wife" in its 1959 election campaign slogans. PAP diehards were reluctantly won over, since the women's vote was vital. Chan herself gained a seat in the 1959 Legislative Assembly elections, and continued as a PAP MP after independence until she retired from politics in 1970.

Vigorous measures were taken to combat crime. Full use was made of the Emergency regulations to arrest secret society members and keep others under supervision. Kidnapping gangs were broken up, and in 1963 the number of secret society incidents dropped to less than half the monthly average of 1959.

By 1963 the government claimed to have the "most advanced and enlightened labour legislation" in Southeast Asia, but the path to industrial peace was not easy. When the Barisan Sosialis splintered from the PAP in July 1961, the trade union movement also split into factions. Since pro-communists dominated the secretariat of the Singapore Trade Union Congress, the government de-registered this body and encouraged the formation of an alternative National Trades Union Congress. The left wing formed a rival Singapore Association of Trade Unions, but many of its leaders were arrested in Operation Cold Store in February 1963.

The PAP's social and economic activities were beginning to bear fruit by the time Singapore went to the polls in September 1963. The four-year development plan was ahead of schedule,[52] the housing programme had surpassed the target set, and considerable strides had been made in education. The first few years of self-government had brought material benefits to large numbers of people. The party had begun to build a broad base for industrialization and a better livelihood, and had advanced some way in redistributing national income through extended social services, housing, education, and health facilities. It had improved the status of women and brought relative peace to industrial relations.

Despite this, the PAP was afraid that the Singapore Alliance would split the moderate vote in the general election, allowing the Barisan to win outright control of the Assembly. While it fought the election on the basis of its record as evidence of its effective economic and social policies, at the same time the PAP exploited every means within the law to defeat its opponents. The government called the election in the minimum permissible time, excluded imprisoned Barisan leaders from standing by requiring candidates to present their papers in person, restricted meetings, froze funds of hostile trade unions, and withdrew the registration of seven Barisan-dominated trade unions.[53]

Feelings ran high and the outcome of the polls appeared to hang in the balance, but, to the surprise of Barisan and PAP supporters alike, the ruling party gained a clear victory in the election, winning thirty-seven of the fifty-one seats. The Barisan won thirteen, and the remaining seat fell to Ong Eng Guan, sole victor of the United People's Party. The biggest upset of the election was the total defeat of the Alliance. Other familiar figures also disappeared from the Assembly, notably Lim Yew Hock, who did not contest the election, and David Marshall, who was heavily defeated at the polls. When the new Assembly met in September 1963, Lee Kuan Yew was the sole survivor of the 1955 Legislative Assembly.

The ruling party's success resulted partly from clever manipulation in pushing constitutional practice to the limit of the letter of the law. It also owed much to the Westminster-style system of "first past the post" one-member constituencies, which gave the PAP nearly 73 per cent of the seats, despite winning less than 47 per cent of the vote, with its majority slumping dramatically in most constituencies. The Barisan's 35 per cent share of the vote gave it only 13 seats.

There was also a more solid basis for the party's victory: it offered the best hope of orderly government to the business and professional community and had already begun to provide tangible social and economic benefits to the middle and a large part of the working class. Many former right-wing and moderate opponents now backed the PAP as the best guarantee for stability, law, and order. The left wing stood in disarray, still commanding the sympathies of a large part of the population, but disunited and with many of its leaders imprisoned or expelled.

The 1963 general election marked the first swing away from the left and was a turning point in Singapore politics. It gave the ruling party a clear mandate and, with the support of the central government in Kuala Lumpur, the PAP moderates used this new power and confidence to come down heavily on both Chinese chauvinism and communism. One of its first actions was to revoke Tan Lark Sye's citizenship. The Malaysian government moved quickly to order the arrest of Nantah students and graduates following clashes with the police, boycotting of classes and protest marches. After its defeat at the polls, the Barisan reverted to the direct action tactics that its leaders traditionally preferred. After calling abortive strikes in October 1963, the Barisan-dominated Singapore Association of Trade Unions was de-registered, and its leaders, including three Barisan Assemblymen, were arrested. The government also dissolved Barisan-dominated rural associations and hawkers' organizations, withdrew the registration of more Barisan-controlled trade unions and encouraged employers to dismiss Barisan trade union cadres.

The result was that within a few weeks of the formal inauguration of Malaysia, the political situation in Singapore was more firmly controlled than at any time since 1955. The determined clamping down on student protest continued. In 1964 representatives of Chinese schools, both the universities, and two colleges of further education formed a Students' National Action Front to demonstrate against a proposal to introduce suitability certificates. Continuing restiveness in Nanyang University led to the issue of a White Paper on *Communism in Nanyang University* in June 1964, followed by the sacking of twenty-one non-academic staff and expulsion of more than 100 students in July and a further 130 in November 1964, and the appointment of a Curriculum Review Committee under Wang Gungwu.

❦

On his return to power in September 1963 and against the new background of confidence, Lee Kuan Yew looked forward to turning Singapore into the "New York of Malaysia, the industrial base of an affluent and just society". He announced his government's first task would be to establish harmony with the central Malaysian government. The relationship was far from happy. The months leading up to the final Malaysia Agreement had been a time of acrimonious haggling over finance, taxation and trade, and for a time it appeared negotiations had reached an impasse because Singapore was driving too hard a bargain.

The terms eventually hammered out in July 1963 were favourable to Singapore, allowing her to retain 60 per cent of her revenues, together with control over labour and education, and the agreement included provision for a common market, which Singapore sought more eagerly than the Federation. Both Malaya and Singapore wanted an expanded domestic market for their new industries. However, Singapore was unwilling to abandon her free port status, while the Federation did not want to lower her tariff walls to the competition of Singapore industry, which benefited from tax-free raw materials. Malayan Finance

Minister Tan Siew Sin argued that a free port was incompatible with a common market and Singapore must choose one or the other. Singapore succeeded in getting a provision written into the Malaysia Agreement for a progressive common market to be introduced over the next twelve years, causing the least possible upset to Singapore's entrepôt trade.[54]

In securing these advantages Singapore lost goodwill in Kuala Lumpur, and the wounds in the relationship failed to heal. Despite the clash of economic and financial interests, it appeared in September 1963 that the two territories' immediate political interests coincided, because both governments wanted to hold in check the extreme left wing in Singapore. Paradoxically, it was political conflict that embittered their relations and helped within two years to bring the brief unhappy marriage to stormy divorce.

The PAP government's unilateral declaration of independence and its decision to stage an immediate election before Malaysia formally came into being irritated the central government, and Tunku Abdul Rahman visited Singapore to express in person his pained shock at the electorate's rejection of the UMNO-Alliance candidates. The Tunku attributed this to "a few traitors" in the Singapore Malay community, but support for the PAP was spreading among Singapore Malays, since at this point the party seemed more effective in advancing their interests than the Singapore UMNO. The government had promoted the Malay language and education, and it had achieved a union with Malaya from which the Singapore Malays expected great benefits. After the breakaway of the Chinese left wing in 1961, Malay membership of the PAP had expanded. Othman Wok became a PAP Assemblyman in the 1963 election, was appointed Minister of Social Affairs the following month and held that office for fourteen years, subsequently becoming Singapore's ambassador to Indonesia.

Lee Kuan Yew wished the PAP to work in alliance with UMNO in the central government. The PAP regarded the formation of Malaysia as the launching point for creating a socialist society and saw the conservative Malayan Chinese Association as a major obstacle in achieving this goal. In May 1963 Tan Siew Sin, federal Finance Minister and president of the Malayan Chinese Association, had declared that his party had "a duty to perform in Singapore. It is Singapore's only hope for future stability and progress."[55] The PAP resisted this proposed intrusion into Singapore politics and aimed eventually to supplant the Malayan Chinese Association as the second partner in the central Alliance. On the eve of the Singapore election in September 1963, when PAP candidates were opposing UMNO men, Lee Kuan Yew claimed "It is my belief that the Tunku and Tun Abdul Razak will work with us – not today or next month, but in years to come. We calculate in terms of decades, not in terms of elections."[56]

At that time the Prime Minister of Singapore declared the PAP would not contest the federal general election in 1964, and for some months the Singapore government continued to woo federal UMNO leaders, but the Singapore UMNO, backed by Kuala Lumpur, set out to consolidate its strength in opposition to the PAP.

The PAP then changed its tactics and decided to bring forward its plans for taking an active role in Malaysian politics. In March 1964, on the eve of the federal election, Deputy Prime Minister Toh Chin Chye announced the PAP would field a token team to show that the party was "a force to be reckoned with in five years" and could thus be a worthy partner for UMNO. The PAP's immediate fear was that the radical Chinese urban population in Malaya might turn away from the Malayan Chinese Association – now renamed Malaysian Chinese Association – and be driven into the arms of the communist-influenced Socialist Front. The Socialist Front, which had opposed the formation of Malaysia from the start, now joined forces with radical Malays, who looked to ultimate union with Indonesia. This anti-Malaysia front was reminiscent of the ill-assorted alliance of left-wing extremists and Malay-Indonesian nationalists who had opposed Malayan Union nearly twenty years earlier, and to the PAP it appeared to threaten the whole basis of the new federation.

The PAP based their election stand on support for Malaysia. They put themselves forward as a non-communal party, but they did not challenge the privileged position of the Malays, and they recognized Malay as the national language. They declared they were not fighting the central government nor UMNO but only the Malaysian Chinese Association. Lee Kuan Yew claimed, "A vote for the MCA is a vote for continued inactivity, complacence and decadence ... there must be a jolt in the leadership of the government."

The PAP leaders threw themselves with enthusiasm into administering just such a jolt, and the month-long election campaign generated enormous excitement. In all the major towns up and down the country huge crowds attended the PAP rallies, particularly those addressed by Lee Kuan Yew, who felt confident that the party had effectively put its message across.

The central government interpreted Singapore's intervention into federal politics as a breach of faith. At his opening election rally Tunku Abdul Rahman declared his solidarity with the Malaysian Chinese Association, repudiating the proffered alliance with the PAP. "We don't want them," he declared.[57]

The party's campaign was disastrous. Despite their non-communal stand, PAP candidates appeared as the spectre of potential Chinese Singapore dominance. The only successful candidate of the nine fielded by the PAP was C.V. Devan Nair, the Indian leftist union leader and former detainee, who had remained loyal to the PAP in the 1961 split. Nair won only a slender majority in a constituency previously held by an independent, not in a Malaysian Chinese Association stronghold. His lone voice was to be ineffective in the Malaysian Parliament, and his pre-occupation with peninsular politics in the next few years was to be a major factor in stunting the growth of the National Trades Union Congress in Singapore.

Hastily undertaken, with inadequate preparation and no election organization or local branches on the mainland, the PAP's ill-judged plunge into federal politics showed an impatience that was characteristic of its leadership. In reviewing its first year in office in Singapore in 1960, a PAP publication had admitted to "minor mistakes of haste, born out of impatience to put the world right ... errors not of the rashness of the policy to be implemented but of the intemperate haste in not preparing and carrying the people".[58] Similarly in 1964 Singapore's rulers believed that racialism could best be eliminated by vigorously attacking the economic and social inequalities that affected all ethnic communities. The Alliance leaders, on the other hand, were convinced that racial distrust could only be soothed away by gradually learning to live together. "Young men ... want to rush things," complained the Tunku. "Why rush? ... why not take time to make a strong nation?"[59]

The election bid was not merely an error of tactics. The socialist leaders of Singapore were out of tune with the conservatism and communalism of federal politics, and in the 1964 election they entered an unfamiliar arena. The electoral tussle highlighted the incompatibility and lack of understanding between the two territories, which had threatened the incorporation of Singapore into Malaysia from the beginning. To bring together the essentially urban, commercial, and industrial society of Singapore with the largely rural Federation of Malaya was a most difficult undertaking, given even the most favourable circumstances. The basic economic needs of the two societies were so fundamentally different that they were bound to clash over priorities and direction.

More fundamental still were the racial divisions. Constitutional development and nationalism had followed diverse paths in Malaya and Singapore. Malaya's *merdeka* in 1957 had been won by an alliance of the Westernized élite of the three major ethnic communities, which recognized the need to satisfy Malay cultural aspirations and improve the lot of the disadvantaged peasantry, if long-lasting racial harmony was to be achieved. Distrust and resentment against the immigrant communities, and particularly the Chinese, ran deep among the Malay population. Their suspicions of Chinese loyalty remained as strong as ever, despite Beijing's attempts to spell out a new doctrine, which repudiated the Kuomintang's *jus sanguinis* principle and urged Overseas Chinese either to take up local citizenship or steer clear of local politics. The Emergency, which had only recently come to an end, had been deeply divisive, since nearly all the communist terrorists had been Chinese. Despite the fact that the mass of the Chinese population was poor, Malays saw the prosperous Chinese middle class as excluding them from their rightful share in the country's wealth. The PAP's attempt to divert politics from communalism towards socio-economic questions that affected all communities was interpreted as a threat to Malay privileges, and it aroused the very communal passions that the PAP aimed to allay.

Singapore's premature rush into federal politics was fatal to the unity of Malaysia. It drove the UMNO/MCA partners closer together, created suspicions about the personal ambitions of Singapore leaders, particularly Lee Kuan Yew, and set the relationship between Singapore and the central government on a downhill track, along which it continued to slide with increasing momentum. Not surprisingly, in throwing down the gauntlet to the MCA, the PAP earned the implacable hostility of its president, Tan Siew Sin. Confident that the election gave the MCA an overwhelming mandate to speak for the Malayan Chinese, Tan accused the PAP of stirring up passions that endangered the racial harmony the Alliance had achieved. From the start Tan had been convinced that Singapore had secured too generous a financial deal and was unwilling to contribute its fair share. The stage was set for a drawn-out battle with Goh Keng Swee, who resisted Tan's policies as deliberately designed to put Singapore down, obstructing its progress, careless of its interests, and sometimes devised out of sheer spite.

Singaporeans began to resent the strains and irritations that merger in Malaysia involved.[60] Confrontation with Indonesia damaged trade and brought physical violence. Between September 1963 and May 1965 saboteurs exploded a number of bombs in Singapore, and Indonesian gunboats seized many Singapore fishing craft. Industrialization progressed at a snail's pace, and it was difficult to attract manufacturers to the Jurong industrial estate, which acquired the nickname "Goh's Folly".[61] Singapore's traditional Chinese firms and British agency houses, which still dominated the economic scene, were not geared to spearhead industrialization, and foreign capitalists held back. Despite tax incentives, most were wary of investing in a small island with unstable politics and a tiny domestic market. Some textile manufacturers from Hong Kong and Taiwan found in Singapore a means of bypassing quota restrictions on imports of textiles into the United Kingdom, but their activities merely soured Singapore's relations with Britain without providing substantial employment, let alone laying a healthy foundation for an industrial Singapore. Hopes that merger would solve many of these problems gave way to complaints that Kuala Lumpur treated Singapore unfairly in granting pioneer status certificates and sharing textile export quotas, and the feeling grew among the business community that the price for membership of Malaysia was too high.

There was even greater disappointment among Singapore Malays, who had expected to receive the same preferential quotas in employment opportunities, promotions and licences that applied in the Federation. At the time of merger, the PAP government promised to encourage Malay as the national language and to safeguard Malay "political, educational, religious, economic and cultural interests". Apart from offering financial benefits in education to give Malay children the chance to better themselves, Singapore did not intend to adopt the federal system of privileges.

As discontent mounted, the Singapore UMNO, which had re-organized after the debacle of the 1963 election, found a ready response among the Malay community, and in June 1964 it asked for legislation to help the Malays. Lee Kuan Yew proposed a meeting with Malay representatives, but in the meantime Singapore UMNO called a convention with delegates from 150 bodies. At this gathering in early July, Secretary-General Dato Syed Ja'afar Albar and other ultra UMNO leaders from Kuala

Lumpur played upon the fears and grievances of the Singapore Malays to stir up feelings against alleged discrimination. A Singapore Malay National Action Committee was formed to demand special rights, and the Malay press waged a strident campaign against the PAP, the *Utusan Melayu* accusing Lee Kuan Yew of trying to suppress Muslims and turning Singapore into another Israel. Special abuse was hurled at Malay PAP Assemblymen, particularly Minister for Social Affairs, Othman Wok, who were denounced as traitors to Islam. Representatives from a hundred Malay political, religious, educational, cultural, and literary organizations met with the Prime Minister a few days later, but Lee Kuan Yew refused to extend special concessions beyond the field of education.

Emotions reached fever pitch at the celebration of the Prophet Mohammed's birthday in late July. Clashes between Malays and Chinese during a Muslim procession in the Geylang district quickly spread to rioting in other areas. The whole island was put under curfew and the trouble continued for more than a week, during which twenty-three people were killed and many hundreds injured. Early in September communal violence broke out again, this time complicated by Indonesian provocation and coinciding with a few parachute landings by Indonesian armed forces on the mainland. Again law and order were restored within a week, but the atmosphere remained heavy with foreboding and fear.

The riots came as a deep shock. In 1949 the colonial government had dismissed problems of race in Singapore with the remark, "There are no social problems of race or cultural relations of any magnitude. All races live and work harmoniously together."[62] Singapore had prided herself on her racial tolerance, which now seemed threatened for the first time in her history.

Appalled by the communal strife, Lee Kuan Yew and Tunku Abdul Rahman made an agreement in September 1964 to avoid sensitive issues for two years, but it was an uneasy truce. The following month a Malaysian minister, Mohammad Khir Johari, declared that the Singapore Alliance aimed to win the next election in Singapore, and Toh Chin Chye retorted that the PAP should be reorganized to "get at Malaya".[63] In late November 1964 Goh Keng Swee crossed swords with Tan Siew Sin in the federal parliamentary debate over Budget proposals to introduce turnover and payroll taxes, which would be particularly burdensome for Singapore businesses. Tan warned that ultimately Singapore's contribution to federal funds would be raised from 40 per cent to 60 per cent.

In mid-December 1964 the Tunku met Lee Kuan Yew in Kuala Lumpur, and for the first time the two leaders mooted the possibility of a looser constitutional arrangement that would leave defence and foreign affairs under the control of the central government. The talks continued in January but faltered on the question of whether Singapore should be represented in the federal Parliament. Malaysia's Commonwealth partners frowned on any re-organization that could weaken defence capabilities. The British government pressed the Tunku not to loosen ties while Indonesian Konfrontasi continued, and in March 1965 Lee embarked on a tour of several weeks in New Zealand and Australia at the invitation of their governments, with the objective of stiffening his resolve to maintain the status quo.

Meanwhile UMNO and the *Utusan Melayu* kept up a barrage of criticism and abuse. Syed Ja'afar Albar, whom Lee later called "a rabble rouser" and "the hatchet man of the UMNO leaders hostile to Singapore",[64] accused Lee of causing the Singapore riots and of being a communist agent, out to "destroy Malaysia and pit Malays and Chinese against each other". Lee began libel proceedings against Albar and the *Utusan Melayu*, and rather belatedly the federal government appointed a commission of enquiry into the riots. Hearings began in April 1965 but behind closed doors.

After its setback in the 1964 federal election, the PAP had declared it would continue the policy of "multi-racialism and Malaysian nationalism, offering a democratic socialist way to a more equal and just society – appealing to Malay and non-Malay have-nots to raise educational and living standards". When the four separate Alliance parties in peninsular Malaya, Singapore,

Sabah, and Sarawak merged in April 1965 to form a Malaysian National Alliance Party, the PAP set out to draw together the radical parties of the various Malaysian territories to form a united opposition.

On 8 May 1965 delegations from the PAP and four opposition parties from the peninsula and Sarawak met in Singapore under the chairmanship of Toh Chin Chye to form a Malaysian Solidarity Convention. Under the slogan "a democratic Malaysian Malaysia", the Convention called for communal politics to be replaced by affiliation on the basis of "common political ideologies and common social and economic aspirations". The Malaysian Solidarity Convention claimed to be non-communal and committed to improving the lot of the disadvantaged of all races, but it attracted mainly non-Malays and particularly the Chinese, since the equality it sought implied the ultimate withdrawal of Malay privileges.

The Convention was the brainchild of Toh Chin Chye and Rajaratnam, but Lee Kuan Yew was the focal point of hatred among the UMNO extremists, who saw the Malaysian Solidarity Convention as a naked attempt by Lee to marshal Sarawak and Sabah against Kuala Lumpur and seize power for himself. However much Lee might claim to be a non-communal exponent of secular modernization, to conservative Malays he personified what they most feared in the Chinese: aggressive ambition and a threat to their religion and culture.

Lee himself did nothing to soften this impression in his frequent abrasive appearances on television, which quickly became the most compelling channel of political communication in homes and community centres. In May 1965 the Malaysian Minister of Information and Broadcasting threatened to take over radio and television services in Singapore if they discredited the central government, and Kuala Lumpur protested when the Singapore Ministry of Culture distributed its *Malaysian Mirror* to schools. Lee Kuan Yew declared this was necessary since "Every day dreadful poison is being poured out [in the Malay press] about the PAP being communalistic and anti-Malay."[65]

Tunku Abdul Rahman became increasingly incensed by the speeches made by the PAP leaders. He was also sensitive to the impact Singapore leaders were making abroad and to criticism of the central Malaysian government in the foreign press. During Lee's extensive foreign travels he was indeed making friends in high places, most notably among Malaysia's Commonwealth defence partners. While he was in Europe in September 1964, Lee gave a striking performance speaking at the British Labour Parliamentary Association dinner, and he later described a private talk with Harold Wilson on that occasion as "one of the most important meetings of my life".[66] The Prime Minister-in-waiting was in high spirits in the run-up to the Labour Party's almost certain victory in the forthcoming British general election, and Wilson's friendship and support were to be vital in the troubled times that followed. Lee consolidated his international reputation with the excellent impression he made on his tours in Australia and New Zealand in the spring of 1965. Rather than strengthening the cement binding Singapore into Malaysia, these indications of approval emboldened the Singapore Prime Minister to adopt a more belligerent tone. In May 1965 he declared, "If we must make trouble, let us have it now instead of waiting for another five or ten years."[67]

Passions reached a crescendo when the federal Parliament convened in late May. Dr. Mahathir Mohamed, then an UMNO backbencher, launched a tirade against the PAP, accusing the party of being "pro-communist and positively anti-Malay". Lee Kuan Yew gave an electric performance in what was to be his final speech in the Malaysian Parliament, speaking for an hour without notes in fluent Malay to lash out against the central government's policy. Tan Siew Sin, denouncing Lee Kuan Yew as "the greatest disruptive force in the entire history of Malaysia and Malaya", declared co-operation was impossible while Lee remained Prime Minister, and an editorial in the *Straits Times* labelled Lee "reckless".[68] UMNO extremists demanded the arrest of Lee and other PAP ministers, UMNO Youth burned an effigy of the Singapore Prime Minister and marched through the streets with banners proclaiming (in Malay), "Arrest Lee Kuan Yew! Crush Lee Kuan Yew!" When Lord Head, the British High Commissioner urged reconciliation, Tunku Abdul Rahman replied that "he did not trust [Lee] a yard and was completely disillusioned about him". Lee in turn was in a defiant mood, eager to confront a Malay-dominated Malaysia and prepared for arrest. Head told London, "We are now confronted with a serious crisis", and the British government warned Tunku Abdul Rahman against removing the Singapore Prime Minister by force.[69]

A few days later on 6 June 1965, enthusiastic delegates from all over Malaysia packed the National Theatre in Singapore for the first meeting of the Malaysia Solidarity Convention, which was chaired by Toh Chin Chye. Lee Kuan Yew delivered the closing speech, which was broadcast on Radio Singapore and widely reported in the press, rousing further outcries in Kuala Lumpur.

Saddened and anxious, Tunku Abdul Rahman left in mid-June to attend a Commonwealth Prime Ministers' Conference in London, where he fell ill and was admitted to hospital. Meanwhile in Kuala Lumpur, on 29 June Abdul Razak met Lee in what the Singapore Prime Minister later described as "a most uncomfortable two hours [with] ... no meeting of minds."[70] Faced with Razak's report of this meeting and with Special Branch warnings about possible riots, the Tunku from his hospital bed feared the situation was slipping from his control: compromise with Lee Kuan Yew seemed impossible, and he was losing his grasp over the extremists in his own party. To remove the PAP government by force or arrest its leaders was impractical and would be resisted by the British and Australians. Drawing up a balance sheet of pros and cons, separation seemed to be the only solution, and the Tunku asked Abdul Razak to sound out senior Cabinet colleagues' views about cutting Singapore out "in order to save the rest of the body from gangrene".[71]

The weeks that followed were filled with wild rumours of arrests and assassinations, and the crisis became more acute with the Tunku's prolonged absence. Behind the scenes a handful of senior politicians were engaged in secret talks and shuttle diplomacy. In mid-July Abdul Razak met Goh Keng Swee and broached the possibility of loosening the tie. By then Goh was convinced that Singapore's economy could only flourish if it was completely free of control from Kuala Lumpur. After consulting Lee Kuan Yew, Lim Kim San and E.W. (Eddie) Barker, Singapore's Minister for Law, Goh was authorized to return on 20 July for further discussions with Abdul Razak and Dr. Ismail bin Dato Abdul Rahman, the Malaysian Minister for External Affairs. They agreed on separation provided it was done quickly before the PAP government became too deeply committed to the Malaysian Solidarity Convention, that the preparations be kept secret, the announcement be made in concert, and the agreement be presented as a *fait accompli* when the federal Parliament re-assembled on 9 August, with all the legal formalities to be completed on that same day.

In Singapore only a tiny group was privy to this intent. After months of vituperative wrangling in full public glare, the actual arrangements for the split were made by a handful of conspirators in complete secrecy. Not only were civil servants and secretaries kept in the dark, but even some senior PAP Cabinet colleagues, notably Toh Chin Chye and Rajaratnam, the founders and enthusiastic promoters of the Malaysian Solidarity Convention. No word was to leak out to the Commonwealth defence partners.

Without the help of his law officers and secretaries, Eddie Barker had to look up precedents in the University of Singapore law library and draft the constitutional amendments himself. While this was being done, the Singapore inner circle remained on tenterhooks that the plan would collapse. The Tunku was still in London, and Abdul Razak, who was by nature cautious and indecisive, continued to prevaricate. In late July he toured Singapore's southern islands and spoke out about the PAP dragging its feet on rural development, while Tan Siew Sin accused the Bank of China of financing subversion and proposed to close its Singapore branch, which was crucial to many small local businesses and to the island's substantial food trade with China.

At the end of July Lee Kuan Yew left Singapore for his annual family holiday in the Cameron Highlands. On 3 August Goh Keng Swee and Abdul Razak met in Kuala Lumpur and agreed to a tight schedule. The Tunku was due to arrive back from London the following day, Goh and Barker would produce the draft documents in Kuala Lumpur on 6 August, any amendments would be agreed on 7 August, the final documents would be signed on 8 August, and the separation would be announced and put into effect on 9 August.

Amidst the public clamour, it took considerable ingenuity and subterfuge to rush through this secret timetable. On his return the Tunku assured a press conference that he intended to meet with Lee Kuan Yew, but the decision had already been taken. Goh Keng Swee telephoned Lee in Cameron Highlands, resorting to speaking in halting Mandarin in order to throw the operator off the scent. The next morning Lee met Goh and Barker in Kuala Lumpur and approved the draft documents, which Goh and Barker then presented to Razak, Ismail, and the federal Attorney-General. Amendments were agreed, but, without the help of support staff, the final typing took until after midnight. Despite the late hour Lee telephoned Toh Chin Chye and Rajaratnam to come from Singapore, contacting them separately to avoid rousing public suspicion or risking collusion between them if they travelled together.

On reaching Kuala Lumpur early next morning, Toh was distraught to hear the news, and Rajaratnam arriving soon afterwards was also deeply upset. They argued for hours with Lee and Goh Keng Swee but could not be persuaded to sign. In a bid to prevent a Cabinet split, Lee called on the Malaysian Prime Minister and proposed reverting to the less radical confederation plan, but the Tunku had made up his mind. When the two Singapore ministers still resisted, Lee called on the Malaysian Prime Minister once more and urged him to talk to them. The Tunku refused, but he agreed to write a note to Toh advising him to assent, since there was no other way out. Eventually Toh and Rajaratnam gave way, but with the greatest reluctance.

To avoid publicity, Lee Kuan Yew flew to Singapore in a Royal Malaysian Air Force plane on Sunday 8 August to secure the signatures of the remaining PAP ministers. For those born in the Federation the news was particularly shocking, and Ong Pang Boon was dumbfounded, but they all signed. One set of documents was then sent to Kuala Lumpur, while the second was given to Stanley Stewart, the head of the Singapore civil service, who locked the government printer and his staff in the printing office until the special gazette and the proclamation of independence were ready to be issued the next morning. Encoded messages of explanation were prepared for dispatch to the British, Australian, and New Zealand Prime Ministers.

Singapore permanent secretaries and Assemblymen, consular heads, and journalists were alerted to gather for a briefing on the morning of 9 August. The proclamation was read on Radio Singapore at 10 a.m., declaring the island's independence and assuming full sovereignty over her territory.[72] At precisely the same moment the Tunku announced the separation to a stunned federal Parliament in Kuala Lumpur. By nightfall all three readings of the legislation had been completed in both Houses of Parliament, and the Yang di-Pertuan Agong gave the royal assent.

Meanwhile at noon in Singapore Lee held an emotional press conference, which had to be interrupted for 20 minutes when he broke down in tears. Later the Singapore Prime Minister attributed his "moment of anguish" to a sense of guilt at letting down the Malaysian Solidarity Convention and described facing the Convention's three leaders the next day as "one of the most painful meetings of my life".[73]

The local press was caught completely by surprise. Only the previous day the *Sunday Times* had welcomed the Tunku's return, in the hope that this would put an end to the "noisy war of words".[74] The special issue of the *Singapore Gazette* containing the separation agreement and supporting documents was handed out shortly before 10 a.m. to the assembled journalists, but they were forbidden to leave or to make telephone calls before the appointed hour.[75]

Malaysia's Commonwealth defence partners had been worried for many months about the worsening relations between Kuala Lumpur and Singapore, and in early June the British High Commissioner sent a gloomy message to Whitehall about possible riots. The actual separation announcement caused consternation and a flurry of diplomatic activity. Only ten days earlier Lee Kuan Yew had met Lord Head while passing through Kuala Lumpur *en route* to the Cameron Highlands but had given no hint of what was planned. Learning what was afoot only hours before the announcement was to be made, the British High Commissioner burst into the Tunku's late night dinner party in a state of agitation in a vain attempt to prevent the break.[76]

In Britain Prime Minister Harold Wilson was on holiday in the Scilly Isles and the Secretary of State for Commonwealth Relations was away in West Africa, but on 10 August Wilson sent an understanding note to Lee Kuan Yew extending recognition to the new state. Australia, New Zealand and the United States also gave immediate recognition to the independence of Singapore, which became a member of the Commonwealth and on 20 September was admitted to the United Nations, with Malaysia's Dr. Ismail acting as one of the new republic's three sponsors.

9

The New Nation
1965–1990

Unaware of what had been going on behind the scenes, Singaporeans were dumbfounded to find independence suddenly thrust upon them. The PAP leadership – and indeed responsible politicians of all parties – had consistently repudiated any suggestion that the island should seek a separate independence. The official memorandum submitted to the United Nations Committee on Colonialism in 1962 had insisted, "Singapore ... is dependent on the Federation of Malaysia for its water supply, its trade and its survival. It is not viable by itself."[1] Less than two months before the break, Lee Kuan Yew had declared, "The question of secession is out. Any change must be a step forward and not backward."[2] Now Singapore was alone, and the impossible had to be achieved. She must survive.

Most Singaporeans were shaken but not necessarily dismayed. Many were relieved to be spared further bouts of the communal stress that caused the racial riots of 1964, rising to a crescendo of hysteria in the middle of 1965, and some businessmen welcomed liberation from Kuala Lumpur's taxation policy with unconcealed glee.

There were no public protests or demonstrations, the island remained calm, and the Cabinet maintained an outward appearance of unity despite inner strains. Goh Keng Swee was probably alone in his conviction that Singapore must cut loose in order to determine its own economic destiny. While Lee Kuan Yew had reluctantly come to agree that divorce was inevitable, and the passionate energy with which he waged the battle had contributed much to the final break, nevertheless the separation from Malaysia was a bitter political blow. For his senior colleagues, the rift meant personal anguish of a different order. Lee was a Singaporean, but the majority of his ministers came from up-country, and Singapore-born Othman bin Wok was sad to see prospects dashed for uniting fellow Malay communities on both sides of the Causeway. As its founder and chairman, Toh Chin Chye suffered deep remorse about betraying the Malaysian Solidarity Convention. He later claimed that of all the PAP Cabinet, only he and Rajaratnam "really believed in Malaysia",[3] and he resented the subterfuge that had excluded them from the deliberations and then kept them apart on the final journey to Kuala Lumpur. Given time, Toh believed the Convention would have won fellow Malaysians over to its philosophy.

Personality and individual antipathies played a large part in forcing the break: the abrasive Lee Kuan Yew, passionate Syed Ja'afar Albar, severe unbending Tan Siew Sin, vacillating Abdul Razak. There were plenty of recriminations: Goh Keng Swee holding Tan Siew Sin's lack of sympathy for Singapore's economic welfare responsible; Tan accusing the Singapore leaders of greed; Tunku Abdul Rahman resenting Lee Kuan Yew's impatient ambitions; Lee accusing Syed Ja'afar Albar of deliberate incitement to religious strife. At the same time long-standing personal contacts and friendships across the Causeway softened the blow of the break and its repercussions: contacts forged at school, college or overseas, and notably the friendship between Goh Keng Swee and Abdul Razak at Raffles College and their co-operation in founding the Malayan Forum in London.

In view of their anxiety about Malaysia breaking up during Konfrontasi and the manner in which they had been hoodwinked, Commonwealth defence partners accepted the deed with surprisingly good grace. Lee Kuan Yew proved correct in his calculation that paradoxically the Konfrontasi crisis was a safe time to provoke a split, secure in the knowledge that the very danger would guarantee allies rallying in support. The excellent impression Lee had made on his foreign tours and the skill with which he had cultivated contacts overseas meant that international sympathies tended to favour Singapore, which was perceived as a small underdog, bullied and threatened by alleged Malay extremism. In particular Harold Wilson held Lee Kuan Yew's tribute to him as having "saved my life" to be almost literally true.[4] Foreign politicians were understanding to the point of indulgence towards a clever and articulate leader, whom they admired as standing for the modern approach favoured in the West.

A shocked Australian press lamented the split as a boost to President Sukarno and Konfrontasi, the London newspapers saw it as a calamity for British policy in Southeast Asia, while the Soviet news agency, Tass, relished the prospect of the imminent break up of "this neo-colonialist offspring". The local English-language press, which had been desperately urging unity and was critical of Lee Kuan Yew's defiance up to the moment of separation, now played a constructive role in steadying nerves and healing wounds. The *Straits Times* insisted the situation had not "deteriorated nearly as much as friends now fear and enemies hope",[5] and within a week readers were presented with a detailed straightforward account based on interviews with some of the leading players to show the endgame had been a negotiated agreement, not a panic decision.[6]

At first the PAP government spoke of Malaysia as "one people in two countries" and contemplated Singapore eventually being re-admitted to the Federation.[7] Malay remained the national language, the new national anthem was sung in Malay, and her Muslim Yang di-Pertuan Negara, Yusof bin Ishak, became the republic's first President.

Few Malaysian leaders took a sanguine view of re-unification. In his speech to the Federal Parliament announcing the separation in August 1965, Tunku Abdul Rahman spoke of "shattered dreams" and declared, "In diversity I am convinced we can find unity, or, in ordinary everyday parlance, absence will make the hearts grow fonder", but privately he expected that, after failing on its own, a chastened Singapore would seek to return to the fold on the central government's terms.

The separation agreement provided for co-operation in economic questions, defence and foreign policy, but the early months put new strains on the relationship.[8] The two governments set out to produce competitive rather than cooperative economies, while quotas, duties and retaliatory tariffs caused distress among manufacturers who had set up industries with an eye to a unified domestic market. Kuala Lumpur was incensed when Singapore revived a limited barter trade with Indonesia and in retaliation threatened to divert her rubber and palm oil exports to Port Kelang (the former Port Swettenham). Singapore challenged Malaysia's right to station troops on the island and, to Tunku Abdul Rahman's annoyance, withdrew unilaterally from the joint defence council and combined operations committee. Meanwhile, immigration controls at both ends of the Causeway caused considerable hardship to people who had hitherto moved freely between the mainland and the island. The political and personal abuse that had soured relationships during the union persisted, although in a lower key. Lee Kuan Yew spoke of Malaysia as "a medieval feudal society",[9] while UMNO still singled out PAP Malay leaders for special attack as disloyal to their race, "like peas who have lost their pod".[10]

Talk of re-unification faded as confidence grew in Singapore's viability, and PAP leaders cultivated a sense of separate nationhood, so that within a few years most Singaporeans came to accept their independent status as inevitable. Unlikely myths sprang up concerning Singapore's brief involvement in Malaysia. Some alleged the merger was a deliberate PAP tactic to get rid of the left-wing opposition and then seize total independence.

Others saw it as an anti-Chinese plot devised by Britain and Kuala Lumpur, a "curiously quixotic, drawing-room plan".[11]

At the time of Singapore's separation the PAP government enjoyed a strong position at home. However painful at the time, the merger had helped to avert the apparently unavoidable political chaos that the island faced in 1961, and few Singaporeans held the PAP leadership to blame for the separation from Malaysia, which was viewed as "unanticipated independence"[12] rather than expulsion. There was no open Cabinet split or any move to change the leadership, and the party gained many new recruits in the later months of 1965. Even in July 1965, during the hectic weeks leading up to the separation, the PAP's strength was demonstrated when Ong Eng Guan resigned from the Assembly, and the PAP carried his seat by a large majority in a straight by-election fight with the Barisan. This was the same Hong Lim constituency where the PAP's defeat four years before had driven Tunku Abdul Rahman into proposing the merger.

୨୦

The spotlight in 1965 was on the political crisis, but the most vital immediate problem was the economy. Despite the efforts of the past few years, Singapore was still heavily dependent on entrepôt trade. In the early stages industrialization had concentrated on mopping up unemployment in labour-intensive industries and on import-substitution to cater for the proposed Malaysian common market. Prospects for such a market were now receding, and Singapore's traditional role as the financial, banking, and shipping centre for the peninsula was threatened as Malaysia sought to bypass her port and raise tariff walls against her manufactures in order to protect her own economic programmes. Rapid industrialization geared to export markets was essential to meet the new situation.

In mid September 1965 Albert Winsemius was invited back, and from then until his retirement in 1984, he was the chief economic adviser to the Singapore government, visiting the republic two or three times a year. At that point Singapore's position was perilous but challenging. Winsemius found Singapore keen to give priority to economic development and willing to follow his advice to the letter. Working in close co-operation, the Dutch economist and successive Finance Ministers Lim Kim San, Goh Keng Swee and, Hon Sui Sen were the architects of what came to be hailed as Singapore's "economic miracle". The concentration on the economy accounts in large measure for the vigour with which the PAP came to discipline the labour force, for its zealous enforcement of internal security laws to suppress political instability, and for its relentless opposition to politicians whose alternative policies threatened to detract from the single-minded pursuit of economic efficiency.

Winsemius's prescription for economic development flew in the face of the methods then fashionable among aspiring Third World countries, which put up protective shields of tariffs and quotas and kept the giant multinational corporations (MNCs) at arm's length. No such protection was to be offered to inefficient industries in Singapore or later to her national airline, and the republic invited the MNCs to bring their capital, their technology, and their skills. Winsemius himself was responsible for attracting the big oil companies, Shell and Esso, and persuading the Dutch giant Philips to set up manufacturing in Singapore. Learning from the MNCs, Singapore was able to upgrade workers' skills. Already an important international port with substantial commercial institutions, Singapore expanded to become a financial centre and major hub for international traffic, with one of the world's largest container ports and a fine airport. At the time of independence more than 70 per cent of foreign investment in Singapore had been British, but the republic set out to publicize its economic attractions more widely and offer further incentives to local and foreign capital, in order to diversify the pattern of trade and investment.[13] Within a generation the Singapore economy was to shift from entrepôt to broad-based manufacturing, oil refining, financing, and servicing.

๛

Already shaken by the arrest of key figures by the central Malaysian government, the Barisan Sosialis weakened still further and split the party's rank and file by repudiating Singapore's independence as spurious. The party claimed the new republic was a neo-colonial state, tied to Britain by a defence treaty, its economy dominated by foreign capitalists and its freedom trammelled by the Internal Security laws. The five remaining Barisan Assemblymen who had escaped arrest in the past few years boycotted the new republic's Parliament when it met for the first time in December 1965 and formally resigned their seats ten months later. Reverting to its preferred direct action, the Barisan attempted once again to use student discontent as a political weapon. The party supported student protests and boycotts that greeted the publication in December 1965 of the Wang Gungwu Curriculum Review report. This recommended concentrating on courses designed to produce graduates to administer the public services and promote the new nation's commerce and industry. More students were arrested, and government moves to exclude student agitators in future by insisting on suitability certificates as a requirement of university admission provoked fresh outbursts of violence in Nanyang University, restiveness in Ngee Ann College, and protests in the University of Singapore. The government stifled a Students National Action Front formed in November 1966, expelling nearly 200 students from Nanyang University and Ngee Ann College, banishing those who were not citizens, and imprisoning Barisan Sosialis instigators of the student troubles.

The Barisan was in no position to take effective militant action. At home arrests and de-registration of unions had destroyed its control over organized labour. Overseas, links with the communist Malayan National Liberation League in Jakarta were shattered in September 1965 with the annihilation of the Indonesian Communist Party.

Nor could the party expect support from communist China, which maintained a low profile in Southeast Asia. While Beijing valued remittances and investments from the Nanyang, the actions of Overseas Chinese would-be followers had often been an impediment to friendly foreign relations. From 1954 Beijing had officially encouraged Overseas Chinese to identify with their host countries and had assured David Marshall when he visited China the following year that Singapore Chinese, including the China-born, could take up the new Singapore citizenship. Overseas Chinese students often carried militant action much further than Beijing intended, and China had found herself blamed for the violent 1956 student demonstrations in Singapore. Students from overseas proved an embarrassing strain on the Chinese educational system, and by the late 1950s only those of above-average calibre were welcomed. Singapore students who had previously flocked to China became disillusioned, while the opening of Nanyang University offered them opportunities to acquire Chinese-medium higher education at home.

The Singapore government continued to be suspicious of the People's Republic, and briefly in 1967 during the Cultural Revolution it appeared that Beijing would stir up Overseas Chinese. In practice the quiet disengagement continued. The policy of trying to bind the Overseas Chinese to China, which had been consistently followed since the 1890s by royalists, reformers, revolutionaries, and the Kuomintang, was unobtrusively laid to rest.[14]

By the time Singapore's first parliament met in December 1965, the PAP leaders had recovered from the shock of separation and launched an ambitious policy for the new city state. Only minor changes were made in the machinery of government, notably the appointment of a non-executive President as head of state. Otherwise the state constitution was retained, with power in the hands of the Prime Minister and Cabinet, who were responsible to a single-chamber Parliament – the former

Legislative Assembly – which was elected by adult suffrage for a maximum five-year term.[15]

The new state retained the national anthem, flag, and crest unveiled in December 1959, when the Yang di-Pertuan Negara was installed in place of the British governor. These were still appropriate to Singapore's new status: the red and white flag symbolized universal brotherhood and purity, with a white crescent moon standing for a rising young nation and five stars representing democracy, peace, progress, justice, and equality. The state crest incorporated the same theme, flanked on one side by the Singapore lion and on the other by a tiger, denoting the island's long links with the Malay Peninsula. To inculcate a specific loyalty to the republic, Foreign Minister S. Rajaratnam devised a Singapore Pledge, which was approved by the Cabinet in August 1966 and has been recited at school assemblies and National Day ceremonies ever since: "We, the citizens of Singapore, pledge ourselves as one united people, regardless of race, language or religion, to build a democratic society based on justice and equality, so as to achieve happiness, prosperity and progress for our nation."

National cohesion was to be based on a multiracial, multilingual secular society. Addressing Parliament in December 1965, Lee Kuan Yew stressed, "We have a vested interest in multi-racialism and a secular state, for the antithesis of multi-racialism and the antithesis of secularism hold perils of enormous magnitude." The campaign to achieve merger with the Federation of Malaysia had precluded building an exclusively Singaporean identity, and the creation of a feeling of nationhood in a mixed immigrant society posed special problems. Singapore could not adopt the course favoured by most new countries, which promoted the culture of an indigenous majority, since this would have fostered Chinese chauvinism. Instead of trying to suppress ethnic differences, official policy lauded the richness of cultural diversity but sought to superimpose on this a special Singaporean identity and sense of values. As Rajaratnam explained to the United Nations General Assembly in 1965, "If we of the present generation can steadfastly stick to this policy for the next thirty years, then we would have succeeded in creating a Singaporean of a unique kind. He would be a man rooted in the cultures of four great civilizations but not belonging exclusively to any of them."

Despite divisions in language, colour, religion, and culture, the island state was small and compact. Every community centre had its wireless and television set, and the government-operated Singapore Broadcasting System was harnessed to the task of nation building. The government sought to inculcate discipline and dedication, to build a "rugged society" in which spartan puritanism would toughen moral fibre, and to wipe out corruption in high politics and in everyday administration. While in principle all the major languages, religions, and cultures received equal recognition, Singaporeans were expected to accept the general political, economic, and social ethos of modern Singapore, with its strongly traditional Chinese flavour: insistence on discipline, hard work, competition, self-reliance, respect for worldly success, and desire for material gain. Some communities were more adaptable than others in conforming to these ideas.

❦

Singapore was fortunate in that the years immediately following independence were a time of international economic buoyancy when the new republic was able to make impressive advances in industrialization, in providing employment and in raising the standard of living. Indonesian trade improved with the end of Konfrontasi in June 1966, and growing American involvement in the Vietnam War boosted Singapore's role as a supplies centre. Even the Seven Days' War in the Middle East in 1967, leading to the closure of the Suez Canal on which modern Singapore's fortunes had largely been built, had a silver lining in boosting demand for her ship-repair facilities. The increasing volume of trade with Japan and the United States also reduced dependence on the canal, and improvements in steamer design cut the time required for the alternative Cape of Good Hope route.

This growing confidence received a blow in January 1968, when Britain suddenly announced she would withdraw from her Singapore bases within three years, posing a serious threat not only to Singapore's security but also to her economy. At the time of separation, defence was guaranteed by the Anglo-Malaysian Defence Pact, and as late as 1967 British policy was to reduce the bases in gentle stages. In the months that followed, mounting economic troubles convinced the British government that it could no longer afford to guarantee protection east of Suez and to rush through the withdrawal.

In view of Lord Curzon's gloomy prediction early in the century that the loss of India would herald the end of British imperialism, it is perhaps surprising that this policy change did not come sooner. Faced with near-bankruptcy after the Second World War, in 1947 the Labour government proposed a radical reduction in defence spending overseas over the next few years, which would have meant abandoning the Singapore bases. Meeting stout resistance from the Foreign Office and the service chiefs, who saw the Far East and the Singapore base as vital to imperial defence, the plan was overtaken by the Malayan Emergency and was set aside with the outbreak of the Korean War in 1950.[16]

Instead of gradual disengagement in Southeast Asia, a new east of Suez policy evolved in which Malaya and Singapore became increasingly important in Whitehall's defence planning. British politicians and the defence chiefs of staff were agreed that Britain still had a crucial role to play in the volatile and vulnerable region in defending her remaining colonial territories, in co-operating with Australia and New Zealand in Commonwealth defence, and as a major anti-communist power in the Cold War.[17] Malaya itself was a dollar fortress for the sterling area, accounting in the 1950s for almost one-third of the Empire/Commonwealth's dollar earnings. Under an ANZAM[18] arrangement, in 1953 Britain, Australia, and New Zealand agreed to set up a joint Commonwealth Strategic Reserve. In the following year Britain joined the United States, Australia, New Zealand, Thailand, the Philippines, and Pakistan in forming the South East Asia Treaty Organisation (SEATO), which was envisaged as a regional equivalent to the North Atlantic Treaty Organization (NATO) in providing collective security.

In the wake of the 1956 Suez disaster, the new Prime Minister Harold Macmillan and his forceful Defence Secretary, Duncan Sandys, set out to re-appraise strategy over the next five years, with the object of maintaining Britain's role as a global power while reducing demands on manpower and money.[19] The plan was to share the defence burden as part of regional groupings, such as NATO, SEATO, or ANZAM, and to reduce conventional forces by developing an alternative nuclear deterrent and phasing out national service in favour of a smaller professional army. The ultimate objective was to run down fixed bases overseas and rely on a UK-based, rapidly mobile Strategic Reserve force, which could be sent to tackle problems wherever they occurred and support United Nations operations. For the present Sandys' defence plans specified maintaining British naval strength east of Suez at its existing level, and keeping a "balanced, all-purpose fleet of appreciable strength" in Singapore[20] to meet Britain's commitments to Malaya, SEATO, and Commonwealth partners. When an Anglo-Malayan Defence Agreement (AMDA) came into force in October 1957, soon after Malaya became independent, the Singapore base became even more vital for Britain, as the only means through which her troops in Malaya could be deployed to SEATO, which Kuala Lumpur refused to join.

Over the next few years British forces in Germany were substantially reduced, and national service was finally phased out in 1962. Despite the cuts in manpower, overall British defence expenditure grew to finance the modernization of the navy, the expansion of air facilities, and to meet the rising expectations of the volunteer regular servicemen who replaced national service conscripts. Almost half of the substantial overseas budget in 1960–61 was spent on service and civilian personnel in the form of higher wages and improved health, housing, education, social, and recreational facilities.[21] A big proportion of this expenditure was in Singapore, the main base in the Far East, and seen as vital for the deployment of all three armed services over the next five to ten years.[22]

The first nuclear-powered naval vessel completed trials in December 1962, ships were to be supplied with the most advanced equipment, and the Ministry of Defence declared, "In the entire sea area east of Suez across the Indian Ocean the Royal Navy plays the leading role in safeguarding the trade and commerce of the free world."[23] An air base was constructed at Gan in the Maldives and brought into full operation in 1961. Britain poured in expenditure on defence installations on an unprecedented scale in Singapore in the early 1960s. This enabled the speedy deployment of forces to crush the Brunei rebellion in December 1962, participation in a mammoth SEATO maritime exercise, and a display of daunting force to counter Indonesian Konfrontasi from 1963.

With the Ministry of Defence unified as "a single swift-moving, flexible, almost infinitely adaptable instrument of defence policy", Whitehall's goal was to concentrate on creating a UK-based Strategic Reserve force. By early 1964 nearly half its naval personnel were serving east of Suez, large and increasing numbers of British and Gurkha soldiers were on duty in Borneo, and the British government had promised to maintain the Far East bases "for as long as circumstances in these areas, and the vital interests of our friends and allies, demand".[24]

This complacency was shaken when Harold Wilson's Labour government came to power in October 1964 and was immediately faced by the grim reality of a stagnant economy and alarming balance-of-payments deficit. Nevertheless, both the Prime Minister and Defence Secretary Denis Healey were strongly in favour of keeping defence commitments in the Far East. In November 1964, soon after taking office, Wilson told his Cabinet that he regarded maintaining Britain's role in the East as "an article of faith",[25] and a few months later he warned that any proposal to withdraw British forces from east of Suez would be "the surest recipe for a nuclear holocaust".

In presenting its first defence report to Parliament in February 1965, the new regime warned that it had inherited defence forces "seriously overstretched and in some respects dangerously under-equipped". For the past dozen years of Conservative government, it complained, "There has been no real attempt to match political commitments to military resources, still less to relate the resources made available for defence to the economic circumstances of the nation."[26] Declaring "defence must be the servant of foreign policy, not its master", Wilson's government stressed the first priority for the next decade was to defend Britain and support NATO, while it needed to scale down military tasks further afield and relieve the strain. By far the largest British forces outside Europe were in the Far East, fulfilling commitments to Malaysia and SEATO. The leaders of both parties had fully supported the enterprise in defence of Malaysia against Indonesian Konfrontasi, and the new government felt it would be irresponsible to abandon the bases while they were still needed to promote peace in an unstable region: "Our presence in these bases, our Commonwealth ties, and the mobility of our forces, permit us to make a contribution towards peace-keeping in vast areas of the world when no other country is able to assume the same responsibility."[27]

The annual review in February 1966 still insisted Britain should maintain a "substantial and constructive role in keeping the peace" in the Far East, which posed the most likely threat to the Commonwealth in the next decade, and her bases would remain as long as Singapore and Malaysia were happy to accept them. There was concern to obtain value for money in the form of "modern, flexible and effective forces"[28] and steadily prune the proportion of GNP devoted to defence in stages over the next few years.[29] Priority was given to helping friends and allies build up their own forces: "to foster developments which will enable the local peoples to live at peace without the presence of external forces", so that Britain could eventually withdraw from fixed bases in the Middle and Far East and supply forces from the United Kingdom in a crisis.[30]

The twelve-year Malayan Emergency, followed so soon by the three-year Konfrontasi, contributed to Britain's financial woes. Fifty thousand British troops were involved in Konfrontasi, which increased Far East Command's expenditure from £70 million in 1964 to £250 million in 1966.[31] The prospects for making savings looked promising with the end of the conflict in 1966, and within months nearly all British troops had been withdrawn from Borneo.[32] But there was growing impatience among the Labour party rank and file, which was traditionally opposed to heavy defence spending, and the party's annual conference in October 1966 called for the Far East bases to be closed.[33]

With the situation in maritime Southeast Asia calmer than for many years past, in April 1967 the British Cabinet drew up a timetable to cut the Far East Command in half by 1970/71 and to start withdrawing gradually from the bases from 1973, completing the process by 1977. Healey informed Singapore of this intention to pull out in stages. While there was no imminent crisis, Lee Kuan Yew visited London in June 1967 and again in October to ask that the process be slowed and for British combat troops to remain until 1975,[34] in order to give Singapore time to develop her own defence capability.

At the time of independence, Singapore's armed forces consisted of two infantry battalions, the first created in 1956 and the second in 1962, together with one partially mobilized volunteer infantry battalion, a volunteer artillery regiment, an armoured car squadron, some engineers and signals, in all comprising some 50 officers and 1,000 men. A small volunteer unit that had operated with the Malayan Auxiliary Air Force during the Emergency had been disbanded in 1960. On merger in Malaysia, a few patrol boats that belonged to the former Straits Settlements Royal Naval Volunteer Reserve had been put under the Royal Malayan Navy, which was based at Woodlands, adjoining the Naval Base.

Immediately after separation a Ministry of the Interior and Defence (MINDEF) was created and put under Goh Keng Swee, who remained in charge for the next two crucial years.

Reluctant to incur large defence expenditure, Lee Kuan Yew favoured having a volunteer territorial-type army and continuing to rely on AMDA, but he bowed to Goh's counter-argument for a substantial independent force, based on universal male conscription, with a strong regular officer cadre.[35] Accordingly, in November 1965 MINDEF laid down plans for a small regular army supported by a large force of national servicemen. A big recruitment drive was launched in February 1966, and the two regular infantry regiments were amalgamated with the Singapore Volunteers to form the first Singapore Infantry Brigade.[36] A Singapore Armed Forces Training Institute opened at Jurong in 1966, and, under legislation passed in March 1967, National Service required most male Singapore citizens to undergo a period of military training at the age of eighteen, after which they were put on the reserve.

While national service was primarily designed to create and maintain a substantial defence force at minimum cost, it was also seen as a valuable tool in forging national unity. The infant republic looked to Israel as the model: a small country surrounded by hostile neighbours, which had developed methods to overcome immensely superior enemies in war, and in which compulsory military service in a citizens' force, followed by long-term reserve obligations, had also helped to meld disparate groups into a common national identity. An Israeli mission was invited at the end of 1965, Israeli advisers were appointed to train the Singapore army, and they remained in Singapore until April 1974, exerting a strong influence.

Meanwhile the British economy continued to flounder, and in November 1967 a stark balance-of-payments crisis forced a drastic devaluation of sterling. Even at that stage Defence Minister Healey assured Singapore that this would not interfere with the programme for steady withdrawal, but the British Chiefs of Staff now insisted that commitments must be cut in line with resources, and this forced a fundamental change of policy. Wilson and Healey – and for many years the Chiefs of Staff too – had tried to stave off change and reconcile incompatible aims to maintain a strong east of Suez policy but reduce expenditure. It has been said that, "Wilson in particular seemed emotionally rather than analytically determined to keep the flag flying in the Far East even with less money."[37]

After all the assurances and attempts to resist change, the eventual facing up to reality created an even greater shock. In mid-January 1968, without consulting those affected, the British government suddenly announced to Parliament the urgent need to review the whole range of public spending in order to make radical savings, which would include evacuating all British forces from Malaysia and the Singapore bases by April 1971.[38]

The defence review, which was announced the following month, made gloomy reading. With responsibility concentrated in Europe and the North Atlantic, there was to be a swingeing cut in the 1969/70 overseas defence budget and further economies in the next few years: reducing manpower, phasing out the carrier force, slashing the rate of new naval construction, running down the Brigade of Gurkhas, cancelling orders for aircraft, and accelerating the pull-out from Malaysia and Singapore.[39] Crucially, irrespective of whether Malaysia and Singapore were threatened, there would no longer be provision for a special capability force for the Far East in the proposed Strategic Reserve.[40]

Whereas the 1966 White Paper had been a balanced scheme, the decision in January 1968 was dictated purely by Britain's domestic financial plight, and it created grave and unexpected problems for Singapore's security and economy. The British bases accounted for 20 per cent of Singapore's gross national product, employed 25,000 local people and indirectly provided a livelihood to thousands more. Despite Singapore's efforts to industrialize and to diversify her economy, there seemed little chance of absorbing the expected large-scale unemployment with its consequent threat to political stability.

In the first surge of angry panic Singapore leaders contemplated withdrawing from the sterling area and taking retaliatory action against British shipping, insurance, and banking interests, but soon came to realize this would damage Singapore more than

Britain. When Malaysia, Australia and New Zealand could not be persuaded to press the British government to delay the pullout, Lee Kuan Yew flew to London, where he argued his case forcibly and effectively in private talks with British ministers and business leaders, and before the British public on television.[41] British economic interests, such as the Confederation of British Industry, added their voices, and the Conservative Party indicated it would reverse the Far East pullout if it came to power. Wilson and Healey were genuinely sympathetic, conscious of the grave problems their abrupt policy change brought to the young republic and to Lee Kuan Yew, for whom they had great personal admiration. Anxious to be as helpful as circumstances allowed, the British Cabinet postponed the plans for final withdrawal until November 1971, and in May 1968 agreed to a generous aid package. This included a £50 million soft loan of which 25 per cent was an outright gift, retraining redundant employees, helping to create an air defence system, and handing over the bases with assets intact, which were estimated to be worth about £19 million.

The Singapore government wasted no more time on recriminations but set out to exploit this valuable bequest to the full and turn the Ministry of Defence's extravagance of the past few years to its own advantage. Since the British military occupied more than one-tenth of the total area of the island, including some of its most favoured locations, Singapore inherited large tracts of prime land, together with substantial buildings, schools, hospitals, sports complexes and other amenities. It also acquired virtually all the technical installations, including the magnificently equipped naval dockyard, most of which was transferred by the end of 1968 and became the foundation for a new shipbuilding industry and a ready-made base for an oil search boom. Hon Sui Sen,[42] who had played a major role in the successful development of industry in Jurong, established a Bases Economic Conversion Department to develop the commercial potential of the new assets, and by April 1970 most land, facilities and equipment were handed over.[43]

❧

Always adept in turning adversities into opportunities, the PAP leaders used the crisis to draw Singaporeans closer together in even greater effort to build up the economy and defences in the two years that remained before the British departure.

The ruling party went to the polls in April 1968 to seek a new mandate. The result was a foregone conclusion, and there was no need for the political manoeuvrings that had helped to ensure victory in the 1963 election. Impressed by their leaders' effective reaction to the crisis, most Singaporeans saw them as best capable of bringing them out of the current dangers. Opposition parties were disorganized, and many of their leaders were in gaol. The Barisan Sosialis boycotted the election, and the Workers' Party put up only two candidates. In all but seven of the fifty-eight parliamentary constituencies, PAP nominees were returned unopposed, and the party won every seat with more than 84 per cent of the vote.

This solid backing from an electorate prepared for sacrifice in face of the obvious crisis made it possible to enact what would otherwise have seemed a draconian reform of working practices. At the first Parliament in December 1965, the government had declared "The excesses of irresponsible trade unions ... are luxuries which we can no longer afford",[44] and the new laws passed in August 1968 were designed to discipline the work force, curb strikes, increase productivity, and provide an attractive climate for investors. The legislation permitted longer working hours, reduced holidays, restricted overtime and bonus payments, and curtailed white-collar workers' fringe benefits. Compensating benefits for the mass of workers were in the form of sick leave, retrenchment payments, and increased employers' contributions to the Central Provident Fund.[45] Faced with a grim alternative, the trade unions grudgingly accepted the necessity for the tough new laws, and the year 1969 was the first strike-free year since the PAP came to power. In 1971 a National Wages Council was set up, comprising government, trade union, and employers' representatives, to formulate guidelines on wage policy, pre-empt industrial action, and transform confrontation into co-operation.

In order to promote export-oriented industrialization, Singapore intensified its courtship of both foreign and local investment and expertise. In July 1968 the Economic Development Board was re-organized and development financing operations were transferred to a Development Bank of Singapore, headed by Hon Sui Sen, which provided long-term financing to manufacturing industries and took a sizeable minority equity in new industries in partnership with private capital. Six months later an International Trading Company (Intraco) was set up, jointly owned by the government, the Development Bank of Singapore, and private capital, with the initial task of dealing with countries whose international trade was state controlled.

Singapore grew rapidly as a financial centre and capital market. In 1968 she was made the headquarters of the Asia Dollar Market, and in 1969 she became a gold market, quickly outstripping Hong Kong and Beirut.

The government planned to make Singapore Asia's second biggest shipping, ship-repairing and shipbuilding centre after Japan. In 1966 the republic set up its own register of local ships. Two years later foreign ships were offered tax-free registration, creating the first Asian "flag of convenience", and Singapore launched her own national Neptune Orient Line. In 1972 a National Shippers' Council was created to break the monopoly held by the Far Eastern Freight Conference, which dated back to 1897 and was dominated by the old European, mainly British, shipping lines.[46] The shipbuilding and ship-repairing business almost doubled between 1966 and 1968. In 1969 Singapore became the busiest port in the Commonwealth, and the completion of her container complex in 1972 made her the transshipment centre for Southeast Asia. By 1975 she claimed to be the third port in the world after Rotterdam and New York, although she was later overtaken by Hong Kong.

Hitherto cautious foreign investors began to pour into Singapore. In 1968 Jurong was placed under a Jurong Town Corporation, and by the end of 1970 the former "Goh's Folly" boasted 264 factories employing 32,000 workers in production, with more than 100 others under construction.

Dependence on Britain declined with the influx of capital from other countries: from Western Europe, Japan, Hong Kong, Taiwan, Malaysia, and Australia, but above all from the United States. In 1972 America supplied nearly half of the new foreign capital invested, and the next year she became, after Malaysia, Singapore's second trading partner. By 1972 one-quarter of Singapore's manufacturing companies were foreign or joint-venture firms, accounting for nearly 70 per cent in value of the republic's industrial production and 83 per cent of her direct exports, and employing more than half of her labour force. Multinational organizations, mostly of American origin, were welcomed as an effective means of expanding the economy, since they also provided technical expertise, management and export outlets.

The quest for oil in neighbouring Indonesia brought an influx of capital, equipment and expertise to Singapore, as the natural centre for support operations. By 1970 petroleum was the leading export industry, accounting for nearly 40 per cent of the republic's total manufactured products, and in 1973 Singapore claimed to be the third largest oil-refining centre in the world after Houston and Rotterdam. At that time thirty major oil exploration companies were located in Singapore, together with more than a dozen consulting concerns, diving companies, and construction and specialist engineers.[47]

A worldwide boom in shipbuilding and repairing, demand for supplies for the escalating Vietnam War, the recovery of the Indonesian economy, and off-shore oil exploration in Southeast Asia enabled Singapore to make notable economic gains. A World Bank team reported: "In 1968 Singapore entered a new phase of accelerated growth with boom conditions in private investment, a decline in unemployment, buoyancy of government revenues, the emergence of an over-all surplus of savings over investments, and a significant build-up of external reserves." During the

1960s Singapore managed to diversify and expand her economy. Her gross domestic product expanded by a compound annual rate of over 9 per cent, her annual rate of increase in industrial production was more than 20 per cent, and the number of factories more than trebled.

❧

While most Singaporeans focused their attention at the time of the April 1968 election on the economic hardships threatened by the precipitate British withdrawal, the government's immediate concern was the impact on national security. Relations with Malaysia were frosty. British ministers, who visited the Far East to consult the two governments, found it difficult to agree with adjustments to the Anglo-Malaysian Defence Agreement in view of Kuala Lumpur's resentment at the aggressive Israeli influence in Singapore. The republic had few forces of her own, and hitherto had devoted only a small part of her resources to defence, but spending tripled following the election victory and within six months had risen to 10 per cent of gross national product.[48] With the need to create her own air force and navy, the republic established an Air Force Command in April and a Maritime Command in December 1968. The Royal Air Force supplied training and handed over Seletar Air Base in April 1969. The thriving economy made it comparatively easy to divert energies and resources to defence, which by 1971 was to absorb one-quarter of the budget. The challenge also provided a chance to unite the new nation in patriotic effort, and there was no opposition to national service.

Singapore had come a long way in preparing herself for the closure of the bases, when, in June 1970, a general election in Britain brought the Conservatives back to power. The new government declared its determination to restore security to high national priority, make good "the damage of successive defence reviews", resume "a proper share" of responsibility for preserving world peace and stability, uphold treaty obligations and support SEATO.[49] Despite these bold words, the policy of withdrawal was delayed but not reversed. The Tories did not want to shed all responsibility for the region and, to replace AMDA, Britain made a Five-Power Defence Agreement with Malaysia, Singapore, Australia, and New Zealand, which came into effect in November 1971.[50]

Modest numbers of British, Australian, and New Zealand troops, supported by air and naval contingents, were designed as a show of confidence and to provide technical backup to the defence capabilities of Singapore and Malaysia. The Agreement provided for a Commonwealth presence but without real responsibility and substituted a nebulous provision for consultation and discussion in place of a definite commitment to military aid should a crisis arise. Its effectiveness was never put to the test, and at best Singapore leaders regarded the arrangement as offering a breathing space to build up the republic's defences. Australia pulled out her ground troops in 1973. A Labour government returned to power in Britain in March 1974 and embarked on further cuts: the last British naval units and helicopters left in 1975 and the last British soldiers early the next year. By the end of March 1976 British withdrawal from Singapore was complete,[51] and SEATO was wound up the following year. The last vestiges of the colonial era had disappeared.

Britain's ambitious defence policy in Southeast Asia had contributed to her economic plight, but the bases had played a valuable role in stabilizing the region and bringing Singapore and Malaysia safely through the Emergency and Konfrontasi. In addition, the extravagance of the final years left the new republic a dowry, which it exploited to the full.

The psychological legacy was perhaps equally valuable and was used by the PAP leaders to drive home a lesson that Singaporeans must always stand on their own feet and never rely on outside help. This became a staple of the national ethos. At the time, the shock announcement of the accelerated British withdrawal acted as an immediate stimulant, enhancing the sense of solidarity, instilling discipline, and energizing the population to tackle the problems of survival.

Singapore celebrated her 150th anniversary in February 1969 in an atmosphere of buoyant optimism and festivity. She could claim many solid achievements, which had seemed remote and unattainable at the time of separation only four years earlier, and she came virtually unscathed through the severe racial conflicts that struck Kuala Lumpur and other parts of peninsular Malaysia in May 1969.

By the end of the decade Singapore had achieved a state of nearly full employment, with labour shortages in some categories. Despite the retrenchment of 17,000 civilian employees by the British armed services, there was such a demand for labour that in 1971 immigration laws were relaxed to give work permits to non-citizens, and by the following year immigrant workers would constitute 12 per cent of the labour force.

According to the 1970 World Bank and International Monetary Fund report, the young republic exuded "a general atmosphere of ebullience and optimism", and "It is this proper sense of urgency which makes Singapore such an exciting place to live in and which, tempered as it is with humanity and concern for the well-being of the individual citizen, lies at the heart of Singapore's outstandingly successful development and achievements."

In a week of brilliant weather in January 1971 Singapore played host to the biennial Commonwealth Heads of Government Meeting. As Chairman, Lee Kuan Yew displayed unusual tact and this, coupled with the republic's general euphoria of confidence and prosperity, did much to soothe the passions and arguments of an otherwise unproductive conference. Singapore symbolized the pride of independence within the Commonwealth, a beautiful, thriving city-state that had risen in little over a century and a half to be one of the world's great ports and a fast-developing modern nation. A disciplined society showing little political, labour, or student unrest was unusual anywhere in the world in 1971 and was in marked contrast to Singapore's own turbulence of a few years earlier.

When the once dreaded day of the final mass troop withdrawals arrived in November 1971, Singapore's *New Nation* newspaper carried the headline: "The British pull out causes scarcely a ripple".[52]

☙

Education was seen as the most important long-term means to inculcate national values and build a united, stable, and prosperous state. During its first nine years in power the PAP government devoted almost one-third of the budget to education. In 1959 the party had insisted that "education must serve a purpose" and be tailored to suit society,[53] and after 1965 the education system was adapted to mould a nation.[54] The path was fraught with difficulties: training the work force for maximum economic productivity would be a mammoth task in itself, but, beyond the practicalities, education in Singapore was a deeply emotional and divisive issue, with far-reaching social and political complications. Malay, the language of Malaysia and the enveloping Malayo-Muslim region, was still the official language, but in Singapore the Malays were a minority. Mandarin, the medium of modern Chinese education, was the mother dialect of very few Singapore Chinese and had long been associated with conflicting external loyalties and left-wing subversion. English, the dominant language of global modernization and international commerce, was stigmatized as the language of former colonial masters and the Westernized élite.

In principle the policy of equal treatment for all four language streams, which was laid down in 1956, still held good, but schools were brought more closely into the national system, and greater importance was given to multilingualism, to scientific and technical studies, and to physical fitness training.

Universal free primary education was already available by the time of independence, and a Five-Year Plan for the 1966–70 period concentrated on secondary and tertiary education. Following the recommendations of the Lim Tay Boh Commission,[55] from

1966 the teaching of a second language became compulsory in secondary schools, and this policy was vigorously promoted by Education Minister Ong Pang Boon,[56] who had himself received both Chinese- and English-medium education.

More secondary school pupils were diverted into technical and vocational schooling, while at the university level, emphasis shifted to training engineers, scientists, and business managers. Parents were exhorted to send their children to government schools, which would instil the national ethos and ensure they were trained in the skills and professions the state deemed necessary. Private foreign schools were closed to most Singapore citizens, and from 1971 heavy financial penalties were imposed on parents sending boys abroad, mainly to prevent the evasion of national service obligations. This was only partially effective. Many affluent parents continued to send their sons to boarding schools and universities overseas, and there was no restriction on daughters.

British and Chinese traditions both set store on formal examinations, and the ideal of meritocracy appealed to a competitive society, which admired success. It offered attractive opportunities for able young people whatever their social or ethnic background, while gearing vocational education to economic demands guaranteed employment for the mass of Singaporeans. The object was to develop every child's useful capabilities to the full. High-calibre students from both English- and Chinese-medium schools were creamed off for intensive pre-university training, and in 1969 a National Junior College was set up for this purpose, the first of a number of well-equipped junior colleges. The system offered tempting rewards but put great strains on talented youngsters and pushed the weak and less intelligent to the wall. Successful people from poor families were admired as role models, but increasingly "equality" of opportunity favoured the children of ambitious professional and middle-class parents.

Despite the improved facilities and extra resources put into Malay, Chinese and Tamil schools, career openings in government service, the professions and commerce favoured those with a good command of English. By 1968 more than 300,000 pupils attended English-medium schools compared with only 135,000 in Chinese schools, and enrolment in Malay and Tamil primary schools plummetted.

The drift towards English schooling was not at this stage the result of deliberate official policy. Initially the government resisted pressure for universal English-medium education, notably from Malay spokesmen who argued that teaching in the vernacular held back their community as it had done in colonial times. Attitudes had changed since 1951, when official policies to gradually extend the teaching of English in Singapore Malay schools had met with resistance. In 1970 the Singapore Malay Teachers' Union formally appealed for a national system of education based on English as the main language of instruction, but at that time such a measure posed political problems: suspicion from Indonesia and Malaysia, and hostility from those Singapore Chinese who wanted to maintain traditional Chinese education.

Paradoxically Chinese education, which was so vigorous in times of discrimination under colonial rule, withered when it was incorporated on equal terms into a national system. Politicians and education leaders stressed that, while English was needed for modern technology and commerce, study of the mother tongue would provide basic values, without which Singaporeans would be "completely deculturized and lost".[57] Government leaders made no secret of their conviction that the Chinese-educated tended to be more disciplined, more resilient in misfortune, and more willing to make personal sacrifices for the common good. The Prime Minister and a number of other prominent English-educated leaders sent their own children to Chinese schools, claiming that these provided better character training. Other forward-looking parents, who could not provide the same facilities for learning English at home, preferred to opt for English-medium schooling.

Chinese schools were no longer a dead end, as they had been in the 1950s. Their pupils now learned English as a second language and had the chance to continue their studies at Nanyang University, although Nantah graduates found greater difficulty than their English-educated peers in securing employment in commerce or industry. Even within government service, where in 1970 they constituted nearly 40 per cent of the executive civil service, few gained promotion to the administrative grade.

The persisting decline in Chinese-school enrolment caused particular concern to the Chinese Chamber of Commerce and to Chinese-language newspaper publishers, who saw their potential readership dwindling. In May 1971 bitter press criticism alleging intentional official neglect of Chinese education and culture led to the arrest under the Internal Security Act of the three leading members of the *Nanyang Siang Pau* editorial staff, on the grounds of conducting "a deliberate campaign to stir up Chinese racial emotions".

Over the years, attitudes to the Chinese language changed. Mandarin came to be seen as a means to break down dialect barriers and later as a useful commercial tool. In 1979, with enthusiastic backing from the Chinese press and the Singapore Chinese Chamber of Commerce, the government launched a Mandarin-promotion campaign, urging everyone, including government clerks, hawkers, bus conductors, and taxi drivers, to use Mandarin instead of dialects. As the People's Republic of China opened up from the early 1980s, a command of Mandarin gave Singaporeans an advantage over Westerners and Cantonese-speaking Hong Kong Chinese in business dealings.

By that time it was evident that bilingual education was too arduous for many young Singaporeans and even threatened to turn Singapore into what Lee Kuan Yew had described as a hybrid "calypso society" with no language or distinctive culture of its own. In 1979 Deputy Prime Minister Goh Keng Swee also took on the task of Education Minister and initiated the New Education System, which divided children into mono-lingual or bilingual streams at the age of nine, and classified them again at the age of twelve into normal, express, or advanced streams. While this policy was designed to lessen the burden on weak students, in practice it exerted even greater pressures to surmount these repeated hurdles, and after a few years it had to be modified.

Meanwhile the universities and colleges became politically quiet and even docile. In the years immediately following independence the government set out to bring the hitherto independent English-medium University of Singapore under its control. Anxious lest the revolt of youth that was sweeping through universities in the Western world would spread to Singapore, the political leaders voiced heavy criticism of liberal Western academic staff and wanted to divert students from fashionable disciplines, such as sociology, into studies considered "more relevant" to nation building. Lee Kuan Yew intervened personally to harangue the entire student body, and Toh Chin Chye was appointed vice-chancellor. For many staff and students it was a painful process. Proposals to vet all higher-education applicants and admit only those who were granted suitability certificates provoke outcry from both universities and from Ngee Ann College. Nevertheless University of Singapore student leaders were broadly supportive of the modernizing, pragmatic administration and the booming economy that offered so much to English-educated graduates. When they did seek the chance to dissent on some aspects, the government discouraged such debate, and the student body did not contest the issue strongly, realizing that dissident views might jeopardize careers in a small society where the government controlled most of the patronage. A moderate University Democratic Socialist Club was established in 1964 to challenge the more radical pro-Barisan University of Singapore Socialist Club, which went into decline and was struck off the register of societies in 1971.

During the 1974–75 recession, Tan Wah Piow, president of the University of Singapore Students Union, was arrested after staging a protest against the deportation of Malaysian and Hong Kong students. While this was a pale shadow of the 1950s protests, Tan made a forceful impression at his trial. Convicted and jailed for a year on the charge of inciting workers to riot, he later went into hiding and fled into exile in London. In 1975 the government re-constituted the University of Singapore Students Union so that the officers would not be directly elected by students and the university administration would control union funds. This marked the end of student activism at the University of Singapore.

In 1980 the two universities were merged to become one National University of Singapore. This was the culmination of many years in which official policies and independent developments drew the English and Chinese streams together. As early as 1960, in an effort to diffuse the political heat, the University of Singapore started admitting Chinese middle school graduates, and from that same year the government began giving scholarships for talented Chinese-medium school graduates to study in universities abroad. Meanwhile the pool for recruiting undergraduates to Chinese-medium education shrank. During its first decade, despite – or perhaps because of – its lively politics, Nanyang University attracted bright students not only from Chinese schools in Singapore but also from Malaysia and Indonesia. The numbers of Singapore pupils entering Chinese-medium schools dropped dramatically from nearly 46 per cent in 1959 to less than 11 per cent in 1977, while at the same time education policies in Malaysia and Indonesia discouraged their students from going to Singapore. Inevitably academic standards at Nanyang University declined further, and its future as a Chinese-medium university looked precarious. In 1975 the government induced Nantah to start gradually introducing English as the medium of instruction, joint courses were started with the University of Singapore in 1977, followed by full merger three years later.

After all the high hopes and emotional enthusiasm that had greeted the birth of Nantah, its demise saddened those who regarded Chinese education, in the words of Dr. Lim Boon Keng long ago, as a system "to ennoble man's mind and purify his character". The dream of creating a centre of excellence for Chinese education and culture that would be a beacon for the whole region was over. Yet at the same time the fears that Nanyang University would divert loyalties towards the People's Republic of China were also laid to rest. Unlike earlier generations who had sought higher education in their ancestors' motherland, Nantah students were more oriented towards Singapore as their home.

English had long been the language of government administration and was increasingly accepted as the language of development and modernization. In 1971 it became the recognized language of the armed forces, and in 1987 it was officially adopted as a first language of schools. By that time Singapore was prepared to promote English as the common unifying language, with no reservations about its colonial origins. Ironically the policy adopted in 1956, to give equal official weight to all four languages and provide bilingual education for all Singapore children, resulted in English emerging as Singapore's major language.

❧

Meanwhile the island was physically transformed. On the recommendations of a series of United Nations missions, an ambitious state and city project was drawn up in 1967. A Land Acquisition Act, passed in 1966, gave sweeping powers to purchase private land for public purposes, superseding earlier more restrictive colonial legislation that had limited earlier master plans. Under the new law compensation would be paid, but at a low valuation, and, if the offer was contested, the property would be taken but the seller would not be paid until the appeal had made its way through the courts.

This measure was crucial for the development of the island over the next thirty years. It gave the authorities a free hand in urban clearance and renewal, in the building of new towns, industrial estates, housing, and transport systems. The government embarked on large-scale drainage schemes to alleviate flooding and giant reclamation projects, which extended along the entire east coast from the Singapore River to Changi and to the west from Pasir Panjang, incorporating the off-shore southern islands into the rapidly expanding industrial complex at Jurong.

The population was dispersed from the crowded central areas where it had hitherto been concentrated. The old city centre remained the financial and administrative hub, but elsewhere, comprehensive urban renewal schemes transformed decaying districts into modern steel and concrete skyscrapers, high-rise flats, hotels and offices. Wholesale bulldozing demolished most of Chinatown, and Malay *kampong* areas disappeared as their occupants were moved to resettlement estates. Slums, squatter shanties and semi-rural *kampong* gave way to new townships of modern housing estates with their own shopping centres, schools, markets, clinics, and recreational facilities. The first new town, Queenstown, was completed in the mid-1960s; a second, bigger town at Toa Payoh was finished by 1973, followed by new towns at Bedok and Telok Blangah, after which the emphasis shifted to the northern part of the island and the creation of the even larger new town at Woodlands.

In 1964 a homeownership scheme was launched to sell flats at heavily subsidized prices to citizens with low incomes. Ownership was encouraged to give a vested interest in national stability while at the same time releasing capital for further development, and from 1968 buyers were permitted to finance the purchase from their Central Provident Fund savings. Whereas only 9 per cent of the population lived in public housing in 1960, when the Housing Development Board was created, by 1975 this figure had risen to 42 per cent, and the Board began to construct higher-quality housing for middle-class Singaporeans who found difficulty in meeting the rising cost of private property. By the end of the decade nearly 70 per cent of Singaporeans occupied public housing, and in the last years of the twentieth century this peaked at almost 90 per cent.

Even in colonial times Singaporeans had been responsive to measures designed to better their health and material well-being, and an independent government had no inhibitions about disciplining its citizens for their own good. A far-reaching Environmental Health Act, passed in 1968, was rigorously implemented to curb pollution, enforce cleanliness, and demand beauty in physical surroundings. "Clean, green and beautiful" was the watchword of the day.

Public utilities expanded to cater for the growing population, the needs of industry, and the new housing estates. Extensions to the Seletar Reservoir were finished in 1969 to help cope with the demand for water, which doubled between 1966 and 1971. By the early 1970s nearly 95 per cent of the population had a piped water supply, and by 1980 the whole island was linked to the main sewerage system.

Health standards rose dramatically as a result of improvements in the general environment and in public housing. By the 1970s infant mortality and life expectancy rates compared favourably with most developed countries. Smallpox, cholera, diphtheria, and polio virtually disappeared as a result of comprehensive vaccination and immunization programmes, whilst tuberculosis lost its traditional place as the main killer to the "diseases of civilization" – cancer and heart disease.

Physical education was vigorously promoted in schools, as a means both to improve the health of the rising generation and help build up a robust national defence force. The British had imparted some of their enthusiasm for sports to affluent Singaporeans, particularly among Eurasians and Indians.[58] In colonial times few Singaporeans could afford to play golf, cricket, and tennis, but after independence such sports became fashionable among the rising middle class. At a more popular level, from 1966 an annual *Pesta Sukan*, or Festival of Sport, was organized in conjunction with National Day celebrations, and a mammoth international sports complex, which opened at the old Kallang airport in 1973, enabled Singapore to play host that year to the Southeast Asia Games.

By the early 1980s Singapore had solved many of the physical problems plaguing large modern cities, but in the course of this dynamic redevelopment, much of the old Singapore was being swept away. With the rising cost of private property, mansions and rambling bungalows set in spacious compounds and gardens were replaced by luxury apartment blocks, and the former Asian and colonial European styles of architecture, which had given Singapore its distinctive character, gave way to modern anonymity in both public and private buildings. The new towns and clean public housing, which provided a healthier and more comfortable lifestyle to the masses than the crowded shacks and slums of the past, held little appeal for the tourist, who missed the picturesque spectacle of other people's poverty. In 1986 the Urban Redevelopment Authority designed six conservation zones to restore the exotic East image of the old Chinatown, Kampong Glam, and Little India and to preserve part of Singapore's colonial heritage. Even the notorious transvestite haunt Bugis Street was rebuilt, and a preservation order for at least another century was put on Raffles Hotel. The Singapore River, which was little more than an open sewer in the early 1980s, was cleaned up, the godowns lining its banks were restored, and the area became the heart of vibrant outdoor café nightlife.

In later years displacement was to cause distress, but in the initial stages the energetic programme of uprooting, renewal and modernization met with general popular enthusiasm. There were no regrets at demolishing overcrowded slums, and the land used for new construction was often dreary scrub and wasteland, much of it the disastrous legacy of early nineteenth century gambier and pepper farming. The main problem was adjusting to unfamiliar neighbours. In accordance with official policy to avoid creating ghettos, break down the ethnic separation of the past and build a multi-ethnic society, the occupants of every apartment block were mixed, flats being allotted in line with the proportions of ethnic communities in the population as a whole.

Effective control over land, which was a very scarce commodity, was essential to Singapore's speedy development. The Land Acquisition Act gave the authorities a free hand to carry out ambitious plans to construct new towns quickly and cheaply, and to build mass housing, which could be rented and subsequently sold to citizens at subsidized prices. This prevented land speculation, helped to keep inflation and wage demands in check, and gave the worker-houseowner a stake in the economy.[59]

ϒʕ

As a small island with stringent immigration restrictions, Singapore was largely protected from the influx of rural migrants and the lumpenproletariat problems that faced most primate cities in the developing world. But the very high birth rate threatened to jeopardize PAP promises to raise living standards and conjured up the spectre of mass unemployment, with all the political, economic, and social ills that would entail.

By the late 1950s the annual rate of increase had spiralled to 4.4 per cent. It then dipped slightly, as a result of the efforts of the Singapore Family Planning Association over the past decade. A voluntary enterprise, run by English-educated upper middle class Asian and expatriate European women, the Association's aim was purely philanthropic: to lessen the burden on the poor by helping married women to space out births and limit the size of their families. The Association faced considerable – largely male – prejudice, and it could offer assistance only to those who chose to approach its clinics.

While acknowledging the Association's modest success,[60] the government wanted stronger measures, and in 1966 it created a Singapore Family Planning and Population Board, which supplanted the Singapore Family Planning Association. The object was no longer to dispense individual charity in a gentle and voluntary fashion but to slash the birth rate in the interest of society as a whole, and the full weight of official authority was thrown behind the new statutory board's campaign.

In 1972 a two-child family policy was promoted, backed by an array of inducements and penalties. Abortion laws were liberalized, and considerable pressure was put on women to be sterilized or abort third babies. Tax concessions and priorities in government housing formerly given to large families were withdrawn, hospital fees for third and subsequent confinements were raised, and school admissions discriminated in favour of first and second children. The draconian policies brought considerable personal distress to individual families and unease among some doctors and the Roman Catholic Church, but the principle of curbing population growth was accepted as a national necessity. Determined and vigorous official action, combined with new medical techniques and applied to a broadly receptive citizenry in a small island, achieved dramatic results. Indeed the policy was to prove too effective, since by the mid-1980s the birth rate fell below replacement level.

☙

Firmly rejecting the concept of a welfare state on the Western model, Singapore concentrated on policies that would enable a self-reliant citizenry to improve their standard of living through their own skills and efforts. The government saw its role as providing the opportunity to acquire decent housing, a good education, and worthwhile employment. The self-financing Central Provident Fund was widened to help home purchase and medical treatment as well as retirement, but schemes for state-financed old-age pensions and unemployment benefits, which had been mooted in the immediate post-war years, were set aside.

This left little compassion for the handicapped, the weak, and the less gifted, and the amount paid out in public assistance declined after 1965. Within a decade the numbers receiving welfare subsidies dropped dramatically from more than 22,000 in 1966 to fewer than 7,000 in 1976, excluding all but the near-destitute. The policy was to enable people to improve their lot and promote family responsibility, with even the old encouraged to do casual work.[61] Public health and hospital services, which had been provided free to the needy, were subject to small charges, except in maternity and child-welfare clinics and in the treatment of socially dangerous diseases, such as tuberculosis. Care of the handicapped, the infirm, and the aged poor was left almost entirely to the family or to voluntary charitable agencies. By the early 1970s more than ninety such bodies belonged to the Singapore Council of Social Service, which received government subvention but relied mainly on private contributions.

֎

The immediate post-independence years were perhaps the most dynamic in Singapore's history,[62] inspiring admiration in many Western countries, who saw the tiny republic living on its wits, seeking a way out of its artificial and precarious position and overcoming apparently insuperable obstacles, while more developed societies floundered in indecisiveness. Lee Kuan Yew emerged as a respected champion of his nation and a significant international figure. As a result the island state and its leadership quickly acquired a reputation out of proportion to the country's size or importance.

Singapore's remarkable rise was purchased at a price. Political stability, economic prosperity, and budding national identity had been achieved by compromising some of the PAP's early principles: democracy, socialism, and close amity with her neighbours.

The leaders' dexterity in exploiting good fortune and turning setbacks into opportunities, which had won them the early battles, gave them a stranglehold on power in more stable times. The PAP leadership had been quick to recognize this potential danger. At the end of its first year of office in 1960, an official publication had commented that, while a government must restrict the rights of individuals in the interests of the common good, "if it does so to a point where it becomes in fact a totalitarian society, the purpose of the restriction has been negated".

In December 1965, shortly after the separation from Malaysia, Lee Kuan Yew declared in Parliament that Singapore had inherited a tendency for too great a concentration of executive power and needed "to liberalize the constitution and make the weight of executive authority less inhibitive to the legislature and to the judiciary". No such changes took place.

The British-model constitution vested strong powers in the Singapore Parliament, which were further increased by the absence of a second chamber, the elimination of separate local authorities in 1959 and the voluntary abdication of the only effective opposition party, the Barisan Sosialis, in 1965. A constitutional commission, appointed in 1966 to recommend safeguards against racially discriminatory legislation, reported unanimously that communalism was a negligible danger but there was a need to protect the rights of individuals where the ruling party had a near monopoly of power. The commission recommended appointing an independent Ombudsman to deal with faults and abuses in administration, and creating an advisory council of state, meeting in public and comprising eminent citizens with no political affiliations. It recommended too that fundamental constitutional provisions should be altered only by a two-thirds parliamentary majority, confirmed by a further two-thirds majority of the whole electorate in a referendum.[63]

These new constitutional proposals provoked little public or press comment.[64] The government rejected the suggestion for a referendum but agreed to the safeguard of a two-thirds parliamentary majority in making changes to the constitution. They approved the principle of an Ombudsman but postponed appointing such an officer. A Presidential Council was created in 1970,[65] but it met in private and its founder members included serving Cabinet ministers, notably Lee Kuan Yew, Goh Keng Swee and S. Rajaratnam, together with former leading politicians, such as C.C. Tan, David Marshall, and Francis Thomas Marshall. Marshall resigned after seven months, objecting to the limited nature of the council's functions, the secrecy of its proceedings, and the inclusion of active politicians, Cabinet ministers, and permanent secretaries in its membership. In 1973, it was reduced to a smaller Presidential Council for Minority Rights, whose functions were confined to drawing attention to measures that discriminated against particular communities after a bill's final reading.

The early years of independence laid the foundations and established the pattern for PAP government. The sudden separation from Malaysia, followed so soon by Britain's abandonment of the bases, shocked Singaporeans into relying on strong leadership to guide them through the crises and readily accepting radical, and often uncomfortable, policies relating to labour, national service, education, and family limitation. Singapore was not a one-party state, but for the first sixteen years after independence, the party held every seat in Parliament. The republic continued to hold elections based on universal adult citizen suffrage at regular intervals, conducting its parliamentary business openly and meticulously according to the British parliamentary practice from which it derived. Backbenchers were encouraged to take on the role of a "loyal opposition" in debating official policy, but such parliamentary debates were mere academic discussions. Backbenchers could not hope to alter official policy except in minor detail, and Parliament became even more staid than the former colonial Legislative Council. It also became a male preserve. Chan Choy Siong, the ardent champion for women's rights, who had battled to bring in the Women's Charter, was the only female Member of Parliament to survive the 1968 general election, and after she retired in 1970, women disappeared from Parliament for the next fourteen years.

Singaporeans showed little concern over growing PAP power in the immediate post-independence years. They were quick to respond to practical programmes and to discard customs that inhibited economic growth, but they left initiative to the politicians and were content to follow their energetic and dedicated leadership. The main impetus for construction and development planning came from the Cabinet and senior civil servants, not the professions, the universities, the press, or other institutions. Lee Kuan Yew claimed with some justification that independent Singapore was built on the ability, drive, and dedication of about 150 individuals. Most of the population accepted PAP leadership since it was effective, but the government's intense activity tended to deaden the sense of involvement on the part of the community as a whole. Singaporeans fell into the habit of following directions, while the ruling group, conscious of the efforts they had put into building the state, became impatient of criticism.

Western liberals looked somewhat askance at Singapore-style democracy, but in the words of Rajaratnam, "The people are more interested in what is good government than in having an opposition." Singapore followed a trend common to most countries of Southeast Asia in the 1970s in preferring "guided" to misguided democracy and subordinating politics to economic development and administrative efficiency.[66]

The Cabinet was an able and vigorous team. The need for cohesion in the struggles of the 1950s and early 1960s forged a remarkable solidarity of PAP leadership in later years, preserving a united outward front despite personal differences. Preferring pragmatism to ideology, they brought a variety of skills in the law, the economy, business, public administration, academia, journalism, and town planning to the practical problems of the time. In their way of life they avoided ostentation, and neither the Prime Minister nor his colleagues sought to glorify their reputations by the erection of statues and monuments or the naming of buildings and roads.

With a monopoly of patronage and authority, the party could co-opt or neutralize potential dissenters. After the debacle of 1961 the leaders took care not to let power accumulate in the hands of locally elected branch committees. Instead, the central executive committee appointed the branch committees, with the local MP as chairman. By 1965 the PAP had already established channels of control and communication within the party and outside, which were further developed in the years that followed. Government leaders toured constituencies frequently, making speeches and attending social gatherings, and MPs held regular meet-the-people sessions on the lines started by David Marshall in 1955. The government tried to keep its fingers on the pulse of popular opinion through PAP branch committees, the People's

Association and citizens' consultative committees. In contrast to the 1950s, when none of the English-educated ruling group could communicate adequately with the masses, by the 1970s Lee Kuan Yew in particular had mastered language skills to establish direct contact with the people who were the strength of their party.

The People's Association, with the Prime Minister as chairman of its management board, administered 180 community centres, nearly 400 kindergartens and other amenities. All People's Association kindergarten teachers had to be PAP members, so that a popular service was combined with indoctrination.[67] The community centres had government-trained organizers and provided social and recreational facilities, particularly for young people.

Citizens' consultative committees were set up in each electoral district early in 1965, and, within each constituency, *kampong* and streets had their own committees. In theory the citizens' consultative committees were independent of party organization, but inevitably these government-nominated committees became organs of the PAP, a means of supporting the party and attracting new blood to its ranks. Citizens' consultative committees and community centres served as listening-posts and provided opportunities for the party leadership to explain official policy, but most of the communication was downward. They were sounding boards for public opinion, not vehicles for criticism or opposition. In one sense the absence of formal parliamentary opposition freed government ministers from the inhibiting need to tailor their public utterances to political tactics. This suited the analytical intellectual tastes of the party's leaders, who explained government policy and sometimes admitted mistakes with a candour rarely seen in countries with greater freedom of press and speech, but this did not imply any bending to public opinion.

❧

Broadcasting and television were under direct official control, and soon after independence the government declared its intention to use these means "to continue to inculcate national attitudes and political understanding".[68] Newspapers were commercially owned but were required to renew their licences every year under the Emergency regulations dating back to 1948. The PAP had already clashed with the *Straits Times* and the International Press Institute at the time of the 1959 general election, and its relationship with the local and international press continued to be rocky. The government insisted it wanted a responsible and constructive local press, free from sectarian or other interests that could threaten the nation's security, racial harmony or well-being, and it was particularly suspicious of foreign elements with hidden agendas acquiring a foothold in the Singapore press, which might be used for political purposes.

At the beginning of 1971, in addition to the *Straits Times*, which had its headquarters in Kuala Lumpur but was the largest circulating English-language newspaper in Singapore, there were three local-based newcomers: the *New Nation*, the *Eastern Sun* and the *Singapore Herald*. The *Nanyang Siang Pau* and the smaller *Sin Chew Jit Poh*, both family-owned, continued to be the most influential Chinese-language dailies. The Jawi *Utusan Melayu* had recently been banned on the grounds of inciting racial passions, leaving one romanized Malay daily, *Berita Harian*, which was published by the *Straits Times*. There were also three Indian vernacular newspapers, which catered for a small Tamil readership.

Chinese-language newspapers in Singapore were increasingly concerned about the falling numbers of entrants into Chinese-medium schools and the potential damaging effect on circulation. In May 1971 bitter press criticism of the alleged neglect of Chinese education led to the arrest under the Internal Security Act of the three leading members of the *Nanyang Siang Pau*'s editorial staff, including a member of the owner-family, on the grounds that they were conducting "a deliberate campaign to stir up Chinese racial emotions". Soon afterwards, government accusations that communist money from Hong Kong was behind the *Eastern Sun* led to the resignation of its senior staff, and the newspaper closed down. Within a few days, the government attacked the *Singapore Herald*, on evidence supplied from abroad that foreign money was being put in to control the newspaper. The *Herald*, which had shown some spirited criticism of government policies during its ten months' existence, tried to fight back but had to give up the struggle when its licence was withdrawn and the senior expatriate executives were expelled. Coming under fire for these actions at the International Press Institute assembly in Helsinki soon afterwards, Lee Kuan Yew countered that while "the mass media can create a mood in which people become keen to acquire the knowledge, skills and discipline of advanced countries ... freedom of the press, freedom of the mass media, must be subordinated to the overriding needs of the integrity of Singapore, and to the primacy of purpose of an elected government".[69]

The action taken against the press, and particularly the fate of the *Singapore Herald*, caused an unwonted flurry of excitement and popular criticism, but it was short-lived. There was little opposition to a Newspaper and Printing Presses Act, which was passed in September 1974 after quite a long period of consultation. The new law prohibited Singapore newspapers accepting funds from foreign governments and organizations and from individuals who were not Singapore citizens. Newspapers could only be published by public newspaper companies whose directors must be Singapore citizens. Furthermore, approval of the Minister of Culture was needed for the issue of management shares, which could only be held by Singapore citizens or companies and carried enhanced voting rights. Not only did the Act prevent foreign manipulation and keep newspapers in the hands of Singapore citizens, it gave the government the power to prevent subversives gaining control of management shares and dealt a blow to traditional family dominance of the Chinese press. The *coup de grace* came in an amendment to the legislation in 1977, which forbade individuals or families from holding more than 3 per cent of ordinary shares.

A.C. (Bill) Simmons, the chairman of the *Straits Times*, was pessimistic about future prospects for a free press but felt public apathy was largely to blame. "Development of a mature, responsible press in Singapore is as much a responsibility of the public and the government ... as that of newspapermen.... 'No comment' is not always the best policy", the newspaper urged readers in November 1972.[70] A few months later Simmons observed sadly to his London manager, "What is happening to the Press is only a reflection of the pressure that is on the public generally in Singapore ... there is no organized protest and very few people seem really concerned."[71]

❧

The voices of labour leaders and students, who had traditionally led the opposition in Singapore politics, were muffled. After the disintegration of the communist-controlled Singapore Association of Trade Unions in 1964 and the arrest of militant leaders, the organized labour movement ceased to be an important political force. In its place the PAP formed the National Trades Union Congress, with which it continued to have a close relationship. The first secretary-general, C.V. Devan Nair, was made President of the republic in 1981; the second, Lim Chee Onn, was, for a time, a Cabinet minister; and his successor, Ong Teng Cheong, who was a government minister and chairman of the PAP's central executive committee at the time of his appointment to the National Trades Union Congress, went on to become a Deputy Prime Minister and finally President of the republic.[72]

The labour legislation of 1968 set the tone for co-operation. Devan Nair returned from Malaysia to Singapore in 1969 and set out to find a new role for the trade unions in partnership with the government. "A modern Singapore with an old-fashioned trade union movement is an intolerable contradiction," he insisted, pressing for "active acceptance" of government measures. With official encouragement, the National Trades Union Congress entered the world of co-operatives, insurance, and business.[73]

There was no fire in the new-style unionism, and membership shrank, mainly because the National Wages Council took over many of the unions' functions, and its benefits applied to union and non-union labour alike. The decline was hastened by the scandal surrounding the secretary-general of the two largest unions who, after being charged with criminal breach of trust in 1979, jumped bail and disappeared. Experiments to create house unions on the Japanese model in the early 1980s flopped. By 1986 union membership had plummeted to only 16 per cent of the work force, and there was little contact with the international labour movement.

❧

As the safety valves for institutionalized criticism closed, some Singaporeans became more concerned about the nature of the regime. The PAP's sweeping victory in the 1968 election was a genuine expression of popular confidence and trust. At the same time it marked a potentially dangerous voluntary abdication of authority by the electorate into the hands of one political group, threatening the isolation of government and encouraging an arrogance of power. The following year saw the beginning of dissent in the form of public protests, opposition from the Bar Council, and in particular from David Marshall, when the government abolished trial by jury for capital offences in favour of trial by a panel of two judges.

The action taken against the Chinese and English press in 1971 came as a shock, and the brief burst of public support for the *Singapore Herald*'s fight revealed an undercurrent of liberal sympathy with the *Herald*'s implied criticism of the over-disciplined regimentation in Singapore society, which alarmed the government.[74]

The swift pace of modernization inevitably brought stress. Urban renewal uprooted families, disrupted jobs and imposed unfamiliar ways of life. In particular, many Malays, who constituted the largest minority community, found difficulty adjusting to the national mould. The rapid expansion of the economy and major schemes for urban renewal and re-housing compelled many *kampong* dwellers to move into new apartment blocks. The island-wide clearance of *kampong* was yet to come, and in the early years mainly older dilapidated districts were affected. Those involved found difficulty in moving from a semi-rural existence to urban living in high rise flats alongside non-Malay neighbours. At the same time, earlier concessions and incentives were gradually withdrawn. While Malay was officially the national language, in practice English became the common tongue. Special educational bursaries for Malays were awarded more sparingly and were restricted to students of proved merit. Some Malays adapted readily to the new situation, taking jobs in factories and offices, welcoming the convenience of modern apartments, and sending their children to English-medium schools, but for the broad mass adjustment was painful. Feeling that their community was neglected now that Singapore no longer needed to court favour in Kuala Lumpur, many branded the Malay PAP MPs as traitors, and no political organization remained to channel the community's dissatisfaction.

∽

As the general election of 1972 approached, there were murmurings of discontent among the Malay minority, English-educated intellectuals, Chinese-educated conservatives, and workers. The PAP's strength and successes made it difficult for the old opposition parties to compete or for effective new ones to emerge. Opposition parties offered only negative or outmoded platforms with no credible alternative to the ruling regime.

Of fifteen legally registered political parties, all claiming to represent "democratic socialism", five opposition parties entered the fray.[75] Only the Barisan had any following, but the party was divided, with most of its rank and file opposed to taking part in the election, and it was weakened by the continued imprisonment of many of its leaders and by long years in the political wilderness, cut off from power and patronage. Dr. Lee Siew Choh did not command the support accorded to the fiery early leaders, who by this time had withdrawn from Singapore's politics. James Puthucheary, Sandra Woodhull, and Fong Swee Suan had moved to Kuala Lumpur after their release from prison. Lim Chin Siong was freed in 1969 and immediately left for England. He was still only thirty-six years old but was a broken and disillusioned man, repudiated as a traitor by the Barisan.

Once again the ruling party won all the seats, but only eight were uncontested and nearly one-third of the votes went against the PAP. The government stepped in swiftly to analyse the protest vote. They set out to remove some sources of discontent, delaying some Malay resettlement plans and raising the wages of some low-paid workers, but at the same time, they became tougher in suppressing political opposition. Alleging foreign backing and interference, the PAP insisted on parties opening their accounts to inspection, and the Barisan Sosialis was crippled by a heavy fine imposed in a libel action.

৯৯

Democracy was the first casualty of the PAP's successes and socialism the second. In order to convert herself into an industrial society, Singapore shed her radical image to court nervous foreign capital and reassure reluctant local capitalists. This meant not only achieving political stability but modifying socialist principles, both in state planning and in the ownership of economic wealth. In 1960 the PAP leadership had said, "We have clearly stated that we stand for an independent, democratic, non-Communist, socialist Malaya. We have never stated that we stand for an independent, democratic, non-Communist, socialist *Singapore* ... because we realize that a socialist Singapore is an economic impossibility."[76] After independence, doctrinaire socialism was expediently abandoned in favour of a more pragmatic approach.

The Singapore government did not intend to nationalize the means of production. As Lee Kuan Yew stated in 1969, "In an underdeveloped situation where you have no managerial or technological class, the state ownership of all basic industries simply does not make sense." The Singapore government believed that capital and skills could best be built up by private entrepreneurs but was prepared to take extensive ownership in commercial enterprises through shareholding and representation on boards of directors. By 1974 it had direct or indirect participation in 124 firms, including vital industries, such as iron and steel, shipbuilding and shipping, and it supplied "seed capital" where private investors were hesitant. The Development Bank of Singapore helped finance projects, such as hotels, real estate, oil refining, publishing, sugar refining, and insurance, with the twin aims of bringing profit to the state and expertise to the workers, but the authorities refused to use public money to bolster ailing or uneconomic activities.

Spectacular progress was achieved in the first eight years after independence, and external trade expanded at more than 15 per cent per annum. The republic could now offer political stability and a disciplined work force, rather than cheap labour and tax holidays, as the main attractions to investors. Moving on from the first labour-intensive stage, Singapore began to break away from her "sweat shop" image and encourage more sophisticated industries, which would develop workers' technical skills and raise their standards of living.

In 1974 Singapore faced the biggest economic threat since separation, when Arab oil producers decided to restrict oil exports and raise prices, sparking off a worldwide recession. Heavily dependent on crude oil imports from the Middle East, Singapore's manufacturing industry was severely hit. Growth slowed in 1974, foreign investment declined sharply, and the following year the economy registered near zero growth. On the tenth anniversary of independence in August 1975, National Day was celebrated in a sober mood. Yet Singapore weathered the recession better than most countries, without wage cuts, high unemployment, or great social strain. The service sector was not so badly affected as manufacturing, and increased spending on public works, especially housing and communications, mopped up unemployment while improving the infrastructure for the future.

In 1976 the economy recovered momentum and foreign investment picked up. By 1977 per capita income had trebled since independence, and for the first time the International Monetary Fund mooted promoting Singapore out of the category of developing countries that qualified to receive international aid. Malaysia, the United States, and Japan were Singapore's main trading partners, accounting in 1978 for 40 per cent of Singapore's exports, but she still had important traditional markets in Britain and Western Europe, was seeking new opportunities in the Third World and was forging links with China and Vietnam.

Entering a new economic phase in the late 1970s, a "second industrial revolution" was launched, which aimed to move from labour-intensive industries to more advanced technology, and to create a new Japanese-style work ethic based on teamwork between management and workers. In 1979 a Skills Development Fund was set up to retrain workers, with the aim of phasing out lower-wage industries completely by the end of the 1980s.

The next few years witnessed a further upsurge in the economy and in the standard of living. Since the government had encouraged a type of dynamic economy that was increasingly vulnerable in the modern world, it needed to remain highly competitive, predicating constant expansion and ever greater sophistication in industrial production and finance. The old leaders continued to show their customary resilience and adaptability in reacting to the world recession and regional political changes, but they found it more difficult to galvanize the new generation into urgent response to crises, in the main because Singaporeans had come to take for granted that their leaders would find solutions.

Strong leadership produced a disciplined society at the expense of independent initiative. The result, as Goh Keng Swee complained as early as 1970, was "We have in Singapore intellectual conformity in place of intellectual inquisitiveness and the sum total is a depressing climate of intellectual sterility."

☙

Singapore's brand of "socialist democracy" was difficult to reconcile with the Western concept of this term. The state did not aim to own the means of production nor to establish a welfare state, but the government initiated planning, supervised economic development, and aimed to distribute the fruits of prosperity more widely by using taxation to finance benefits in education, housing, and public health. Goh Keng Swee declared, "The government has to be the planner and the mobilizer of the economic effort, but the free enterprise system, correctly nurtured and adroitly handled, can serve as a powerful and versatile instrument of economic growth."[77] In 1977 Goh explained that the government intended to create new industries either on its own or in partnership with the private sector, but not to nationalize existing industry, which would not create new employment, wealth or income, but only transfer it.[78] The need to attract outside capital, to offer a secure haven to the industrialist, and yet furnish a good living for the mass of the people produced a mixed economy akin to paternal capitalism.

Foreign capital, expertise, and technology were vital to achieve rapid growth, build up exports, and keep ahead in technology. Yet Singapore's success in attracting foreign investors laid her open to the charge that she was a neo-colonialist economic dependency.[79]

Rapid expansion accentuated the disparities of wealth that the PAP had once pledged to abolish. By the early 1970s Singapore's per capita income was second in Asia only to Japan, but a disproportionate share fell to a small multimillionaire group and to the professional and business classes. Managerial skills were at a premium, making well-paid appointments the prerogative of the highly educated minority. Profits from the booming economy went into the pockets of business tycoons, while workers bore the main brunt of economic sacrifice. The line between haves and have-nots was almost as clearly marked as it had been in colonial times. Between 1959 and the early 1970s the wages of low-paid workers increased by only about 5 per cent, whereas executive-grade salaries doubled or trebled.

While Singapore's open economy was vulnerable to international fluctuations over which she had no control, at the same time competition with her larger neighbours kept her alert, adaptable, and ready to upgrade her services in extending and modernizing port and airport facilities, ship repairing, and manufacturing facilities for the off-shore oil industry. The very advantages that Singapore enjoyed in her contacts with developed economies – her sound educational system, high standard of English, and opportunities for overseas training for her people – meant that qualified personnel might be lured abroad by higher material incentives unless terms at home were attractive. To remain competitive she needed to expand the economic cake before attempting to divide it up fairly. As Lee Kuan Yew said in 1970, "We are developing painfully, unequally, often unjustly."

‿

The young republic's immediate aim was to forge a sense of distinct nationality and build up military security, but her long-term interests lay in international peace and regional harmony. She was too small to defend herself effectively except in alliance with other powers, nor could she afford to divert too many resources to defence. Dependent on peace and goodwill to preserve her international commerce, the new nation needed to find a role in Southeast Asia acceptable to her neighbours, and seek a fair portion of an expanding Southeast Asian prosperity, rather than the lion's share of a static regional economy.

At the time of independence Singapore was still under British military protection, her economy was largely geared to Britain, and she was tied to colonial apronstrings longer than any other country in Southeast Asia. In the early 1970s these strings were rudely severed, and she had to establish her regional status as a member of the Association of Southeast Asian Nations (ASEAN), the smallest state in size and population and the odd man out ethnically and culturally. The republic needed to win recognition and to establish friendly relations and trading links with all countries, regardless of ideology. Soon after independence Deputy Prime Minister Toh Chin Chye and Foreign Minister Rajaratnam embarked on extensive travels, in Africa and Eastern Europe, signing trade agreements, explaining the facts of separation, and seeking to ward off possible criticism by the anti-colonial bloc in the United Nations about retaining the British military bases.

These efforts were largely successful, but Singapore's relationship with other Southeast Asian powers in this period was not so happy. The initial stress on the unique qualities that distinguished the republic created an abrasive, arrogant image. PAP leaders cultivated a style of plain speech that Singaporeans liked and many in the First World found refreshing, but which grated and jarred when it was used to criticize and denigrate neighbours. Cocksure and proud of her own rapid achievements, the young republic was impatient with other nations' difficulties, prone to offer unsought advice, and slow to appreciate that methods that worked well in her own small community could not be transplanted to other countries with more complex, if perhaps less stark, problems.

Throughout her history, the profits made by Singapore in providing the servicing infrastructure for developing the natural resources of neighbouring areas had been a source of resentment. In modern times this acquired bitter racial undertones. While Malaysia and Indonesia tried to diversify the internal control of their own economies, the Chinese in both countries continued to play a dominant commercial role. Singapore remained the nerve centre for a major part of the Chinese-controlled commerce of Southeast Asia, so that her prosperity was a source of political embarrassment and isolation in the region. The political leadership in Indonesia and Malaysia looked upon Singapore as an economic parasite. Indonesia set out to attract major oil-servicing investment and build up her own rubber milling industry, while Malaysia began to break the formal economic links that had survived the political separation.

During Konfrontasi Singapore had said many harsh things about Indonesia, at one point likening her ambitions to those of Japan in the 1930s and accusing Jakarta of "grooming itself for the role of protector in Southeast Asia".[80] Singapore's insistence in 1968 on executing two Indonesian marines who had been responsible for a bomb outrage during Konfrontasi, despite President Suharto's personal pleas for clemency, sparked off anti-Singapore violence in Jakarta, during which the Singapore ambassador had to flee for his life. Even in the short term this friction hurt Singapore's real interests, since it was estimated that probably one-fifth of Indonesia's trade passed through Singapore, although the trade figures were kept a jealously guarded secret to cover up extensive smuggling.

Britain's military rundown forced Singapore and Malaysia to draw closer together, and a thaw in the Cold War dictated fundamental policy reappraisals. The admission of the People's Republic of China to the United Nations in 1971, the lessening antipathy between China and the United States, the *rapprochement* between Washington and Moscow, America's withdrawal from Vietnam at the end of 1972 and the fall of Indo-China to communist rule in 1975 all combined to change the premises upon which international relations had rested since the end of the Second World War.

In the new climate Singapore feared that small powers might be trampled underfoot. During the 1950s and 1960s, while the Afro-Asian anti-colonial group was a force to be reckoned with in the United Nations and presented something akin to a united Third World front, the big powers paid court and looked for its support in the East/West Cold War. In the early 1970s, as the great powers reverted to policies based on traditional national interests, the fragile Afro-Asian group disintegrated, and small nations lost their bargaining power. The prospect of international peace did not mean the end of local wars and in some ways made them more likely.[81] When President Nyerere of Tanzania, at the Commonwealth Heads of Government Meeting held in Ottawa in 1973, quoted an African proverb that it was the grass that was hurt when elephants fight, Lee Kuan Yew countered grimly that "when elephants flirt the grass also suffers. And when they make love, it is disastrous".

For the countries of Southeast Asia, the best option was to set their own neighbourhood in order, cultivating national prosperity and contentment while building up regional co-operation and persuading friendly big powers to guarantee their integrity.

The path to regional co-operation was not easy. At her own insistence, Singapore was a founder member of ASEAN, which was formed in 1967.[82] While Thai Foreign Minister Thanat Khoman had originally thought in terms of a four-nation association, comprising Indonesia, Malaysia, Thailand, and the Philippines, Rajaratnam urged that Singapore should be included too.[83] In the early years ASEAN remained a collection of disunited states, competitive rather than complementary in their economies and threatened by internal tensions.

While seeking friendship and active support from powerful countries, Singapore wanted to repair damaged relationships and forge closer links with her neighbours. In a world of changed priorities, where Southeast Asian cohesion was an important factor, Singapore recognized Indonesia as the natural leader of the region. Despite the failure of political merger, Malaysia remained Singapore's major trading partner, the defence of the two countries was inseparable, and a close working relationship was necessary.

As a first step, the Malaysian and Singapore leaders began to patch up their differences. In 1970 Goh Keng Swee gave tax incentives to encourage Singaporeans to invest in the Malaysian and Indonesian economies. In 1972, making his first visit to Kuala Lumpur since separation, Lee Kuan Yew promised co-operation in cordial talks with Tun Abdul Razak, who was now the Malaysian Prime Minister. The following year Abdul Razak returned the visit in a spirit of warmth and harmony. Paradoxically the relationship between the two countries improved when the last formal links were broken: their joint airline in 1972 and common currency arrangements, rubber and stock exchanges, and banking associations in 1973. These had all become sources of friction, and, at the time, Malaysian Finance Minister Tan Siew Sin compared the two territories to "Siamese twins whose future growth would be threatened unless they were separated". Singapore and Malaysia continued to maintain close co-operation in matters of mutual concern: combating communist subversion and illicit trading in narcotic drugs, and protecting the Straits of Melaka.

In 1973 Lee Kuan Yew visited Indonesia for the first time in thirteen years. It was an unexpected success. After a solemn ceremony at the graves of the two marines whom Singapore had executed five years earlier, Lee and President Suharto held friendly talks, and the two leaders issued a cordial joint communiqué. Both realized the need for firm friendship and regional solidarity to safeguard themselves as small fry in a dangerous sea. The Indonesian president reciprocated in a friendly visit the following year.

The three nations recognized their interdependence in checking subversion and, whatever their feelings towards the PAP, the Indonesian and Malaysian leaders realized that the present regime constituted the surest safeguard against a communist Singapore. The republic shed the Israeli military advisers, whose presence had alarmed Indonesia as much as Malaysia, and played down her image as the Israel of Southeast Asia: "a far-fetched analogy", as Goh Keng Swee called this in December 1972.[84]

While ASEAN members agreed on the need for closer co-operation, they differed in their view of the region's international role. In 1972 ASEAN supported a proposal put forward by Tun Abdul Razak that Southeast Asia should be a "zone of peace, freedom and neutrality", but Singapore put little trust in such aspirations and preferred solid big power support for the region.

The 1974 international oil crisis, followed by the unexpectedly swift collapse of Indo-China to the communists in the spring of 1975, drew the ASEAN countries closer together, with Singapore now leading the way in promoting the concept of regional solidarity. A summit meeting held in Bali in February 1976 produced a Declaration of ASEAN Concord, which was confirmed at a Kuala Lumpur summit in 1978. ASEAN initiated dialogues with so-called Third Countries, namely Australia, Canada, the European Economic Community, Japan, New Zealand, and the United States, which aimed to establish "a symbiotic relationship" on equal terms. They were followed by the signing of an ASEAN-EEC co-operation agreement in 1980.

While Singapore sought friendship with all countries, her leaders had little patience with the so-called non-aligned movement. Attending the fifth non-aligned summit meeting in Colombo in 1976, Rajaratnam presented a statement from Lee Kuan Yew querying whether the movement was truly non-aligned and arguing that they must live with the different economic and political systems of their many members and not support movements to establish Marxist states.[85] Singapore objected to doctrinaire pro-communist attitudes and the condemnation of foreign military bases and multinational companies. At that time Singapore's foreign-owned oil refinery installations were the world's fourth biggest, providing employment for 15,000 workers, with spin-off benefits for another 50,000. In particular, Singapore gave short shrift to an offer from Laos to help Singapore, Malaysia, Indonesia, and Thailand to fight for "genuine independence". Over the years Singapore continued to appeal for the movement to return to its original stance.[86]

The fall of the countries of Indo-China to communist rule shook Southeast Asian confidence in the United States as its protector and led each country to reassess its relationship with China and the Soviet Union. In 1974 Malaysia had been the first Southeast Asian country to establish diplomatic relations with China. Now the Philippines and Thailand also began talks with Beijing, Singapore sent goodwill and trade missions in 1975, and Lee Kuan Yew paid a state visit to the People's Republic the following year. Anxious to play down Singapore's Chinese majority, the Prime Minister reiterated that his would be the last ASEAN country to establish formal diplomatic ties. At the same time he fostered trade links with the People's Republic, and in 1985 a branch of the Xinhua (New China) News Agency was established in Singapore. Concurrently Singapore continued to maintain friendly contact with Taiwan and to use its facilities to train its own forces.

∽

After the communist victories in Indo-China in 1975, the extreme left wing re-grouped to attempt a resurgence in Singapore and Malaysia, but the two governments collaborated to arrest leading cadres of the Malayan National Liberation Front, the militant satellite of the Malayan Communist Party. Increasingly out of sympathy with radical politics, the PAP resigned from the Socialist International in September 1976.

Six opposition parties and two independents contested a general election that the government called in December 1976, but once more the PAP won all the seats with 72 per cent of the vote. The most notable parliamentary recruit was 35-year-old Goh Chok Tong, managing director of the national shipping line, who was eventually to succeed Lee Kuan Yew as Prime Minister. The election campaign also marked the less successful debut of a quiet independent, Chiam See Tong, who lost to senior PAP stalwart, Lim Kim San, in a creditable fight but later won through on a third attempt to become Singapore's longest serving opposition MP.

By the late 1970s prosperity, political stability and the PAP's unchallenged position combined to encourage a somewhat more relaxed atmosphere. Some political prisoners were released, including a few who had been arrested in Operation Cold Store in February 1963, notably journalist Said Zahari, and Dr. Lim Hock Siew, founder member of the PAP and later the Barisan Sosialis. After being detained for more than fifteen years without trial under the Internal Security Act, both men were granted conditional freedom to live on separate off-shore islands in November 1978 and finally released the following year.

While most citizens were content with their lot and their greatly improved standard of living, independent-minded Singaporeans were discouraged from taking an active part in public life by the harsh treatment meted out to opposition parliamentary candidates and critics and the spectacle of political prisoners held in gaol without trial long after they had ceased to constitute a danger to society. The Prime Minister cited finding the next generation of leaders as Singapore's most important single political problem, but keeping the electorate on such a tight rein inhibited opportunities for new ideas and thought to grow. New leaders would not emerge from the hustings but be recruited and groomed for office. The PAP central executive committee selected the party's parliamentary candidates for their intellectual calibre, moral fibre, and conformity to party discipline. While the rank and file of the party continued to be largely primary-school educated, the political leaders recruited likely successors from the professional class: intelligent, well-educated, and experienced in their own field, but untried, since the majority had never had to face hard battles at the hustings or make personal sacrifices to achieve good fortune.

The Prime Minister and most of his colleagues were only in their mid-fifties, but Lee Kuan Yew wished to start preparing for handover to the next generation by appointing promising recruits to responsible office. All three new senior ministers of state were university-educated technocrats in their thirties: economist Goh Chok Tong, banker Tony Tan Keng Yam, and architect Ong Teng Cheong. A former civil servant, Goh Chok Tong became managing director of Neptune Orient Lines at the age of thirty-two. Entering Parliament in 1976, he was appointed Senior Minister of State for Finance the following year and Minister of Trade and Industry in 1979. Ong Teng Cheong trained in Australia and England to be an architect and town planner before becoming an MP at the 1972 election at the age of thirty-six. He was appointed Minister of Communications in 1978. Scientist Dr. Tony Tan was an academic before taking up a successful career in banking, becoming general manager of the Oversea-Chinese Banking Corporation in 1978. He entered Parliament at a by-election in 1979, at the age of thirty-nine, and became Minister of Education a year later. At a party conference on the eve of the December 1980 general election, the young leaders shared the stage with the old guard, and Lee Kuan Yew described this as a watershed in PAP history with "the graduating class coming into their own after tutelage in the wings".

Seven opposition parties contested the 1980 parliamentary election, but the ruling party achieved another landslide victory, winning all seats for the fourth successive election and capturing nearly 78 per cent of the votes.

∞

The 1980 election victory was the high-water mark of the party's power and self-confidence, and in 1981 the economy recorded its best growth rate in eight years. The republic was also acquiring a sense of nationhood, and the 1980 census showed that more than 78 per cent of the population was Singapore-born.

This complacency was shaken in 1981 when, at his sixth attempt, J.B. Jeyaretnam, secretary-general of the opposition Workers' Party, won a parliamentary by-election, polling 52 per cent of the vote. Jeyaretnam's triumph was a shock to the ruling PAP, which had enjoyed a monopoly of parliamentary power for thirteen years. PAP leaders saw themselves in a Confucian light as benevolent rulers: fathers and teachers of their people, offering wise and good government. While they tolerated other parties and organized regular elections, these polls were seen as an outlet for expressing grievances, not for electing opposition members. The PAP could see no need for confrontational politics. In a speech in February 1982, Rajaratnam said, "The role of an opposition is to ensure bad government", and the PAP feared Jeyaretnam's election was the first step on the road to Singapore's ruin.

It led to a reappraisal of the political situation and further developments in party structure. The PAP had ceased to be a mass party after the 1961 upheaval, when the cadre system was introduced, whereby the leadership chose the cadres, who in turn elected the leaders. In 1982 power was further consolidated in the hands of the fourteen-member central executive, and the PAP redefined itself as a national movement, not a mere political party.

At that time the party had about 9,000 ordinary members, but the leadership had lost touch with the rank and file, and Lee Kuan Yew and his ministers embarked on energetic tours of constituencies to explain PAP policies. They set out to upgrade public housing and give a greater political role to the residents' committees, which were launched in 1977 but did little more than carry out informal housing estate management.

Meanwhile the government placed even greater emphasis on the need for political stability and increased its vigilance towards both the domestic and foreign press. The PAP leadership was irritated by the extent of coverage in the *Straits Times* given to opposition politics in the 1980 election campaign and blamed the newspaper in part for its 1981 by-election setback. PAP politicians, and Lee Kuan Yew in particular, involved themselves a great deal in the affairs of the local press in the 1980s: appointing a retired senior civil servant, S R Nathan, as chairman of the *Straits Times* in 1982; trying to promote a second English-language paper, the *Singapore Monitor*, which survived only three years after a very long gestation period; directing a major restructuring of the three big Chinese- and English-language newspaper groups, which culminated in 1984 in their merger to form Singapore Press Holdings. This giant conglomerate gathered into its fold all the English-, Chinese-, and Malay-language newspapers, and acted as distributor for the one Tamil-language newspaper to survive into the 1980s. Singapore Press Holdings remained a public commercial company, and, despite the flurry of official activity in restructuring, there was little interference in editorial policy. While the local press reached an understanding with government, relations between the latter and the foreign press were very different.

The press had no need to join battle at all on what became the most explosive issue of the mid-1980s: the so-called "Great Marriage Debate". The vigorous promotion of the family limitation policy was so effective that by the mid-1980s the birth rate fell below replacement level. In particular there was a steep fall-off in the number of well-educated women who married and had children. In his National Day review in August 1983 Lee Kuan Yew expressed concern about the deterioration in quality of the population if women graduates failed to pass on their supposedly superior genes. In the face of some scepticism, the government offered incentives, organized matchmaking occasions, encouraged graduate mothers to have a double quota of four children, and offered them priority in school admissions. The press was circumspect in its editorial comment on this eugenics issue, the *Straits Times* calling for more research and leaving its readers to fill its columns. The Great Marriage Debate roused more passion and mainly hostile protest than any topic since the proposals to introduce an income tax in the 1940s. Singaporeans were certainly not apathetic about issues that directly concerned them.

By 1986 the birth rate dropped to a historic low of 1.44. This indicated that within three generations the population would shrink to half its then size of 2.5 million,[87] which would be insufficient to provide an adequate labour or defence force. In the immediate future it threatened a new imbalance in the population with a rapidly increasing proportion of old people to support, and uneven growth among ethnic communities, the Malays and Indians having stable birth rates while the Chinese rate at 1.26 was possibly the lowest in the world.

In 1987 Deputy Prime Minister Goh Chok Tong officially announced the end of the two-child policy. Penalties were replaced by incentives, including housing benefits, tax rebates, priority school admission, medical benefits, and child care subsidies, which aimed at encouraging a return to three-child or even four-child families, particularly among the more prosperous and better educated groups. The new towns were designed to provide employment, housing, health and recreational amenities, and transport to cater for a predicted population of three million in the 1990s, which was expected to stabilize at about four million in the twenty-first century.

Caring for the aged was to be left to the individual family, but official policy over thirty years of building small flats for nuclear families meant that by 1980 nearly four-fifths of families comprised only parents and children. The government wanted a return to the three-generation traditional Chinese family. It preached Confucian virtues of supporting aged parents, and offered material benefits, such as inheritance tax concessions and housing benefits to those who took in their parents to live. Nevertheless the Prime Minister declared himself "saddened that Confucianist morality and custom will now require legislation before filial obligations are honoured".[88]

$$\backsim$$

In 1984 Singapore celebrated the twenty-fifth anniversary of internal self-government and of PAP rule, but many who took the relatively high standard of living for granted were becoming less tolerant of the more arbitrary aspects of PAP policies. At the general election in December that year, thirty PAP candidates were returned unopposed, but the party's share of the total votes declined sharply to about 64 per cent. Jeyaretnam improved his position against a carefully selected PAP candidate, and the ruling party lost a second seat to Chiam See Tong, now secretary-general of a liberal Singapore Democratic Party. This setback caused disproportionate consternation among the PAP leadership. Two opposition members in Parliament posed no threat to the government, and Jeyaretnam eventually lost his seat in 1986, following his conviction for false declarations about his party's accounts. This also disbarred him from contesting any election for five years. There was still no viable alternative to the PAP, but the period of the party's unchallenged dominance was over.

Lee Kuan Yew's first reaction to the December 1984 election was "If … it continued this way then the one-man-one-vote system must lead to our decline, if not our disintegration". Goh Chok Tong, newly appointed as First Deputy Prime Minister, talked of the danger of the democratic system, which produced such a reduced vote for the PAP despite the excellent economic performance in the period since the last general election, with the highest ever rate of Housing Development Board flat construction and unprecedented rises in incomes.[89]

The government began to consider appointing an "intelligent political opposition": MPs who would accept the basic structure of multiracialism, non-communism and "the realities of Singapore's position". Legislation was passed providing that if fewer than three opposition candidates were successful at the polls, "non-constituency" seats with restricted voting rights could be offered to opposition parties to make up the number. This quest for a tame opposition proved elusive when a National Solidarity Party candidate who had narrowly missed victory at the polls declined the government's invitation to take up a seat as a founder member of the "intelligent opposition".

The old guard were giving way to the new generation, some more willingly than others. A disgruntled Toh Chin Chye left the Ministry of Health in 1981 and retreated to the backbenches. Goh Keng Swee retired from politics in 1984, and only three PAP veterans remained when Lee Kuan Yew appointed his new Cabinet in January 1985. The 1984 election also brought Lee Kuan Yew's elder son to the forefront of political life. After a brilliant academic record at Cambridge University, Lee Hsien Loong joined the army, becoming a brigadier-general and second-in-command of the armed forces in 1984 at the age of thirty-two. Entering Parliament that same year, he was appointed a junior minister in 1985 and Minister of Trade and Industry in 1986, becoming head of the PAP's newly created youth wing later that year. Fluent in English, Chinese, and Malay, Lee was an impressive speaker with considerable charisma. He had also inherited some of his father's arrogance and shared the elder Lee's predilection for meeting sensitive issues head on and his mistrust of the free world press. The 1984 election also saw the reappearance of women MPs after an absence of fourteen years.

The following months brought some political shocks, notably the resignation of President C.V. Devan Nair in March 1985 and the suicide in late 1986 of a government minister while under investigation for corruption. Devan Nair had been appointed President of the republic in 1981 following the death of the second President, Dr. Benjamin Sheares. At that time he was one of the most trusted members of the old guard. A left-winger, former member of the Anti-British League and imprisoned by the colonial authorities for two lengthy periods in the 1950s, Devan Nair had stood by the PAP moderates in the 1961 crisis, won through to the Malaysian Parliament in the 1960s as the sole PAP (DAP) member, and subsequently reorganized the Singapore trade union movement. His forced resignation from the presidency on charges of alcoholism was a shock to the public and to the government's reputation.

$\backsim$

Lee Kuan Yew began to leave daily administration in the hands of the new generation of leaders, with Goh Chok Tong as First Deputy Prime Minister. The replacement of the old guard was designed to bring young men forward and inject fresh energy and dynamism into coping with new political and economic problems. But the effects were to enhance Lee Kuan Yew's own position and to remove the restraining influence of his former peers. Goh Keng Swee in particular had successfully adopted a contrary stand on a number of issues, such as separation from Malaysia, the organization of the armed forces, and education. Now Lee was in undisputed authority over his own protégés, who were on probation. Far from retiring to the background, the release from everyday executive functions freed the Prime Minister for even more energetic direction of policy and for engagement in public debate.

Lee became increasingly authoritarian and intolerant of opposition, directing in person a campaign against Jeyaretnam and later against other critics of government. While Lee frequently talked of retiring, he showed no inclination to relax his hold on the essentials of policy or to risk having the results of twenty years' effort squandered by a younger generation untempered by hard apprenticeship. As he declared in August 1988, "Even from my sick-bed, even if you are going to lower me into the grave, and I feel something is wrong, I will get up."

Meanwhile in 1985 the economy was caught in a downturn. In that year the country's gross domestic product declined in real terms and per capita incomes fell for the first time since independence. This came as a blow to Singaporeans who had come to take economic growth for granted. Manufacturing, oil refining and property development were all badly hit, and the National Wages Council was instructed to freeze increases for the next two years. For the first time the Stock Exchange was closed for three days in December 1985 when a major Singapore-based conglomerate, Pan-Electric Industries, went into receivership. Economic problems continued into 1986, with prospects of unemployment and the local dollar coming under pressure on foreign exchange markets. The government announced its intention to streamline the civil service. Business and property taxes, defence expenditure, and employers' contributions to the Central Provident Fund were all substantially reduced. This latter form of savings had been one of the foundations of the economy, and only a few months earlier it had been described by Lee Kuan Yew as "the nest-egg of last resort".

The recession proved to be less protracted than expected, and by late 1986 the economy started an upswing. Nevertheless the comparatively brief setback led to a re-appraisal of the premises on which the Singapore economy rested. The younger leaders in particular pressed for loosening state regulation, and a report of a committee headed by Lee Hsien Loong, which was released in March 1987, recommended "robust privatization".

ॐ

Coming so soon after the disappointing fall in PAP support at the 1984 election, the economic crisis made the leadership even more determined to strengthen its control, and this led to discord with the local and international press, the Law Society, the Roman Catholic Church, and the U.S. State Department. An Undesirable Publications Act dating from 1967 already authorized the outright ban on publications from abroad that were considered morally objectionable or designed to stir up political, religious, or ethnic trouble. In May 1986 a Newspaper and Printing Presses (Amendment) Bill was introduced, which proposed a lesser penalty of imposing quotas on the circulation of foreign journals deemed to be unfairly trying to influence Singapore's domestic politics, "indulging in slanted, distorted or partisan reporting", or refusing to publish government replies to press criticism. Copies would be available in libraries and could be photocopied, the object being to hit sales and advertising revenues without being accused of restricting freedom of information. Local opposition to these proposals included a press statement by the Singapore Law Society, signed by its president, Francis Seow, objecting that the amendments would impede the flow of ideas and arguing that foreign journalists should be able to comment freely.

The Law Society and its president were engaged in a battle of their own with the authorities over a Legal Profession (Amendment) Bill, which included proposals to disqualify Law Society members guilty of professional misconduct from holding council office, and to forbid the society from commenting on impending legislation unless requested by the Minister for Law.

After joining the Singapore Legal Service in 1956, Seow quickly made his mark as an ambitious, engaging, and able young lawyer. Awarded the Public Administration (Gold) Medal and appointed Solicitor General, he was a rising star with an apparently glittering future, when he decided in 1970 to leave government service and take up private practice. Seow was suspended for twelve months in 1973 for making a false declaration, but in 1986 he was elected president of the Law Society and announced "plans for a more assertive and caring bar". In September 1986 the Law Society met to discuss the Legal Profession (Amendment) Bill and voted to ask the government to withdraw it. An angry Lee Kuan Yew retorted, "It's my job to stop politicking in professional bodies", and challenged his lawyer critics either to form their own political party or to join the Workers' Party. The bill became law in October 1986, automatically disqualifying Seow from retaining the presidency because of his temporary suspension in 1973. The legislation also effectively banished the Law Society from the political arena.

The Newspaper and Printing Presses (Amendment) Act was also passed in 1986 and was invoked on a number of occasions against *The Asian Wall Street Journal, The Far Eastern Economic Review, Time and Newsweek,* creating a furore that extended to the U.S. State Department. *The Asian Wall Street Journal* widened condemnation of this "banana republic action" to cover a whole range of Singapore policies, including even the Great Marriage Debate, which in the *Journal*'s view risked the country "shrinking to an island backwater". The Singapore government published all the documents in a pamphlet entitled "The Right to be Heard", which Lee Hsien Loong defended before the World Congress of Newspaper Publishers in Helsinki in May 1987. In 1990 a further amendment to the Newspaper and Printing Presses Act, which was aimed primarily at U.S. and Hong Kong-based journals, required all publications that dealt with current events in Southeast Asia but whose "contents and editorial policy were determined outside Singapore" to obtain an annual licence, which would stipulate the number of copies admitted for sale.

By that time Singapore had become embroiled in what came to be known as the "Marxist conspiracy". After being used sparingly for many years, the Internal Security Act was again invoked in May and June 1987, when Operation Spectrum was launched to arrest twenty-two suspected activists who were accused of participating in a "Marxist network". These detainees were a varied group of Roman Catholic priests and church social workers, Workers' Party supporters, lawyers, and members of an avant-garde theatre group. The alleged mastermind was Tan Wah Piow, living in exile in London and working in conjunction with Vincent Cheng, the executive secretary of the Roman Catholic Church's Justice and Peace Commission in Singapore.

Like many young seminarians of his generation, Vincent Cheng had given up training for the priesthood in Penang to serve instead as a lay church worker in the community. At that time the Roman Catholic Church all over the world was turning away from doctrine towards practical work with the poor, the disadvantaged, and the oppressed. Sometimes this was expressed in the revolutionary Marxist Liberation Theology, which was sweeping through South America and the Philippines, or the non-Marxist but still radical form of the Christian Student Movement, the Young Christian Workers Movement, Industrial Evangelism, and Community Organization. In 1972 Cheng was sent to the Philippines on a Student Christian Movement leadership course, followed by some years of study and work in Southeast Asia, during which he was caught up in Industrial Evangelism and its campaign to redress injustice and poverty. In 1982 Cheng came to Singapore, where he worked for the Geylang Catholic Centre before being put in charge of the Justice and Peace Commission three years later.

Under the approving eye of Archbishop Gregory Yong, organizations such as the Young Christian Workers Movement, the East Asia Christian Conference, and the Geylang Catholic Centre were very active in Singapore at that time. The republic offered a fertile field for Industrial Evangelical work among those whom the "economic miracle" had left behind, those who had lost their jobs in the mid-1980s recession, and particularly the large numbers of unskilled and semi-skilled migrant workers who did not enjoy the same conditions and protection as citizens. The Geylang Catholic Centre received help and advice from locally based Australian and French priests and from a team of sympathetic local lawyers, including Teo Soh Lung, a Law Society council member and Workers' Party supporter, who gave their services free to defend Malaysian labourers and Filipino maids.

As secretary of the Justice and Peace Commission, Vincent Cheng set out to co-ordinate these activities and hold study groups into redressing the plight of the poor, the oppressed, and the unemployed: ending the exploitation of migrant workers, securing a guaranteed minimum wage and better working conditions, and criticizing discriminatory measures, such as the priority given to the children of graduate mothers, streaming in schools, the special programme for gifted children, the family limitation policy, and abortion.

At this point the authorities stepped in, first arresting Cheng and church workers, then widening the net in a second round of arrests. They alleged that a Marxist plot had been nurtured in Tan Wah Piow's London study group, influenced by revolutionary Liberation Theology, and extending its tentacles to involve church workers, lawyers, and other suspected subversives in Singapore.

Not wishing to bring the Church into conflict with the government, Archbishop Gregory withdrew his support and posted overseas the four priests who were the guiding light behind the Young Christian Workers movement. Most of the Operation Spectrum detainees were released quickly. The majority were interested only in charity work. Others were unlikely subversives: Tharman Shanmugaratnam, a future PAP Cabinet minister, was held for questioning for nearly a week about his attendance at Tan Wah Piow's study group meetings during his undergraduate days in England. A few were re-arrested for a short time in 1988 after alleging they had been forced to make confessions and abused during their earlier detention, but the last two prisoners, Vincent Cheng and Teo Soh Lung, were released in 1990.

The alleged Marxist conspiracy and the Liberation Theology menace turned out to be myths, but the episode did reveal a strong undercurrent of dissatisfaction with some of the ruling party's basic policies, which attracted these disparate elements.

At the time of independence the PAP had hoped the Christian churches would help nation building by providing moral fibre and encouraging sacrifice for the good of society. But the Church in many respects was out of sympathy with the road to nationhood that the PAP had chosen, with its emphasis on tough self-reliant meritocracy, material achievement, entrepreneurship and profit-making. The Roman Catholic Church had long been unhappy with the official efforts to limit population growth and facilitate abortion. Church workers' efforts to improve conditions for migrant labour also ran counter to the official policy to upgrade citizens' skills and living standards while relegating unskilled and semi-skilled jobs to cheap, readily-expendable immigrants, for whom there was no long-term commitment. A co-operative work force, prepared to work long hours for fair but modest pay, was the PAP recipe for attracting investors and employers, and the party's answer to unemployment was to tighten belts and learn new skills, not to expect handouts. Inequality was seen as unavoidable in the interest of nurturing, rewarding, and retaining talent for the good of the state as a whole.

Not only the church workers' activities but their methods drew official disapproval: holding meetings and encouraging aggrieved workers or flat dwellers to combine together to demand their rights; getting involved with outsiders, particularly foreigners; and straying into the field of politics along lines akin to the Workers' Party programme. Determined that the government should set the agenda and that there should be no "politicking" in the Church, a Maintenance of Religious Harmony Act was passed, forbidding leaders and followers of religious groups from engaging in politics.

❧

Despite the 1987 international stock market crash, by mid-1988 Singapore's economy was once more on the upswing, bringing a sense of relief amounting almost to euphoria. Taking advantage of this optimistic spirit, in August 1988 the government decided to call a general election, fifteen months ahead of time, and to campaign under the slogan of "More Good Years".

In preparation for this election, thirty-nine constituencies were merged in blocs of three to form thirteen Group Representation Constituencies, to be contested by teams of three, of which one candidate was to be drawn from an ethnic minority group. Members of Parliament would also double as town councillors in the management of the new towns. Lee Kuan Yew described this as a means to give the electorate more responsibility in local government, and to make the PAP more multiracial by running a mixed team of candidates. The scheme was also seen as a device to exclude maverick candidates and to make it more difficult for smaller parties to assemble a team.

If this was the PAP's intention, their leaders were in for a shock, when the Workers' Party came very close to winning the new Eunos Group Representation Constituency. Jeyaretnam was still disqualified from standing, but his party mustered the required team of three to contest Eunos, comprising a Malay candidate and two surprising newcomers: Lee Siew Choh and Francis Seow. When the Barisan Sosialis was dissolved, Lee Siew Choh and the remaining members moved to the Workers' Party. Francis Seow had been arrested in May 1988 under the Internal Security Act for allegedly conspiring with a representative of a foreign power to interfere in Singapore's domestic affairs, and the U.S. embassy official involved was expelled for "meddling in Singapore politics". After being held for questioning for seventy-two days, Seow was released and joined the Workers' Party.

The most spirited opposition campaigning in twenty years generated enormous public excitement in Eunos, and the Workers' Party team lost the group constituency by a very narrow margin. It made only a slight dent in the ruling party's percentage of the overall vote. On this occasion the PAP was returned unopposed in only eleven out of eighty-one constituencies, with eight parties and four independents contesting the remaining seats, but once again the party lost only one seat to Chiam See Tong. Nevertheless it was a morale-shaking experience and created the prospect of two formidable opposition figures qualifying to fill both vacant non-constituency seats. In fact Francis Seow was never able to take up his parliamentary seat: charged with tax evasion, he fled to live in exile in the United States.

In the last few years Singapore's economy had bounced back from the recession. Lee Kuan Yew had won his battles to keep the Law Society and the Church out of politics, to neutralize the local political opposition and to restrain the foreign press. This had been achieved at the cost of alienating the Western – and particularly the American – press into long-standing hostility and establishing articulate critics in exile.

After the 1988 election the last of Lee Kuan Yew's old guard colleagues retired from the political scene: founder PAP member S. Rajaratnam and lawyer E.W. (Eddie) Barker, who had entered Parliament in 1963, was returned unopposed in five subsequent elections, and had headed the Ministry of Law ever since independence. The programme of "self-renewal" was complete. It had been achieved quietly and without a public quarrel, but some ministers felt they had been removed too soon and were doubtful of the calibre of their untried successors.

In November 1990 Lee handed over the premiership to Goh Chok Tong, with Lee Hsien Loong and Ong Teng Cheong as Deputy Prime Ministers.

10

The New Guard
1990–2005

L ee Kuan Yew held power as Prime Minister for more than thirty years, beginning in 1959 when the colony acquired internal self-government. During those three decades the island was physically transformed. The political violence, mass unemployment, poverty, homelessness, and illiteracy of the mid-century were all but forgotten, together with the riots and rancour that marred the brief unhappy union within Malaysia, the shock of separation, the stark problems of the early years of independence, and the crisis threatened by the British military pull-out. By 1990 Singapore was a modern, stable city state with a thriving economy and one of the highest living standards in Asia.

As his former colleagues dropped out of active politics, Lee had become more authoritative, the sole surviving dominant figure. Yet his decision to give up the premiership brought no dramatic break in the way Singapore was governed, nor was it intended to do so. For the time being he retained his powerful post as secretary-general of the PAP, and he remained in the Cabinet with no intention of treating his new role as ceremonial. While he stayed in the background, spending much of his time on overseas visits, Lee kept a watchful eye as Senior Minister over his colleagues' proceedings and from time to time made public pronouncements on the performance of the new Prime Minister and other Cabinet ministers along the lines of a headmaster issuing progress reports about his senior prefects. Nevertheless the spirit of change was in the air as Singapore approached the last decade of the millennium. The republic had survived the early dangers to prosper greatly in its first two decades, but now a better educated and affluent citizenry aspired to a more sophisticated lifestyle beyond the preoccupation with economic growth.

The new guard had already undertaken a great deal of preparatory work to set the country on a new course. In March 1990 proposals to change the nature of the Presidency were revived. First mooted in the early 1980s, the idea that future holders of the office would have greater powers and be directly chosen by the electorate met with such hostility that it was put to one side. The suspicion that Lee Kuan Yew might be redesigning the post for himself became a key issue during the 1988 general election, but the change was finally agreed in October 1990 with no dissentient voice, and the constitution was duly amended in January 1991. The new-style president was to be elected for a six-year term, with a duty to safeguard the state's large financial reserves and the right to veto senior civil service and judicial appointments. Eligibility was restricted to those who had served as Cabinet ministers, chief justices, top civil servants or heads of large companies. The first election would be held to choose a successor when President Wee Kim Wee finished his term of office in 1993.

Cautious steps were taken to create a parliamentary "opposition". In addition to the existing Non-Constituency Members of Parliament (NCMP), who were appointed to make up the numbers if fewer than three opposition candidates were returned in a general election, in April 1990 legislation was passed to permit the appointment of up to six Nominated Members of Parliament (NMP), who would hold office for two years but be eligible for reappointment. Individuals of proven ability in their fields, but with no political affiliation, they were expected to raise the level of debate by offering independent comment and constructive criticism. Nominated members were only excluded from voting on financial or constitutional legislation, and they were permitted to introduce private members' bills, which could be more freely debated than government measures. Chiam See Tong objected that appointing nominated members detracted from the authority of an elected Parliament, but they were there to stay. In 1997 their number was increased to nine.

The republic celebrated its twenty-fifth anniversary of independence in August 1990 in an aura of well-being with the slogan "one people, one nation, one Singapore", and the electorate looked to the new team to continue the PAP's efficient administration but in a more liberal way. In an interview with *The International Herald Tribune* a fortnight before he took over as Prime Minister in November 1990, Goh looked forward to a more gracious Singapore and wider political participation.[1] And at his swearing in ceremony, he declared, "I ... call on my fellow citizens to join me, to run the next lap together".

By the end of 1990 all political detainees had been released from prison, although a few were still subject to strict constraints, being compelled to live on off-shore islands and only allowed to receive a limited number of visitors. In February 1991 the ban on visiting the republic was lifted on nine former left-wing dissidents, including James and Dominic Puthucheary, Sandra Woodhull, Fong Swee Suan, and Samad Ismail, of whom all except Samad Ismail had been barred from crossing the Causeway for nearly twenty years.

The most pressing need in the eyes of the new guard was to draw the nation together. Rajaratnam's dream of achieving truly multiracial nationhood in one generation after independence was far from being realized, and in some ways modernization had widened the ethnic divide. Lee Kuan Yew admitted publicly that Singapore was not yet ready to accept an Indian as Prime Minister when he stepped down. For many Malays economic development had undermined their entire traditional way of life, while the issues of language and education still troubled the Chinese majority.

The Malays suffered the greatest disruption from the physical redevelopment of the island after independence. Whereas other ethnic groups were largely concentrated in the urban area in colonial times, the Malays were more widely scattered. Many lived in fishing villages on the off-shore islands and along the coasts. Others were small farmers, while large numbers found employment and settled near the British military bases. Even those who worked in town managed to preserve their semi-rural lifestyles, many in areas specifically reserved for Malays. The first Malay Reserved Settlement, Kampung Melayu Jalan Eunos, which was gazetted in 1928 following agitation by the Kesatuan Melayu Singapura when land was being cleared to make way for Kallang airport, expanded over the years to a peak of some 1,300 houses. After the Second World War more reserved settlements were gazetted: in 1957 Kampung Melayu West Coast at Pasir Panjang; in 1959 Kampung Melayu Ayer Gemuroh, which had grown up after the RAF opened the Changi air base; and finally in 1962 Kampung Petempatan Melayu Sembawang, near the British military airfields and naval base in the north of the island.

The Land Acquisition Act and the Concept Plan for island-wide redevelopment changed all this, and over the next twenty years the *kampong* were systematically demolished. The massive slum clearance in the 1960s concentrated on the urban areas and was in general well-received by Chinese and Indians. For some Malays too it meant upgrading from rundown, dilapidated shanties into flats with modern amenities, although it brought them alongside unfamiliar neighbours and often made it difficult to pursue their normal livelihoods.[2] Others lived in flourishing *kampong* communities, enjoying a peaceful village way of life in well-kept houses with gardens, chickens, and fruit trees. They were swept into the anonymity of high-rise flats not to give them a better standard of living but because their land was required for other purposes. The policy was particularly unpopular when the clearance was extended to gazetted Malay Reserved Settlements.

In Kampung Melayu Jalan Eunos, the register of new occupants was closed in 1966, some inhabitants were moved over the years to make way for new roads, and in 1981 the last remaining houses were demolished to construct a housing estate. In the mid-1970s Kampung Melayu West Coast was cleared by the Housing and Development Board, and Kampung Melayu Ayer Gemuroh made way for Changi International Airport. Finally Kampung Petempatan Melayu Sembawang was demolished by the Jurong Town Corporation in the 1980s.[3] Traditional *kampong* were virtually obliterated, because they occupied a disproportionate amount of scarce land, encouraged communal ghettos that impeded multiracial nation building, and represented a lifestyle that was considered old fashioned and out of place in modern Singapore. The clearances caused deep distress, and it would be some time before many former *kampong* dwellers – particularly among the older generation – became reconciled to the upheaval and transformation in their lives.

Among the majority Chinese community, many were upset by the growing dominance of the English language. The 1990 census showed the number of households using English as their main language had doubled over the past ten years. The attitude of government leaders towards the Chinese language was also changing. Since its inception in 1978, the official Speak Mandarin campaign had succeeded in gradually reducing the use of dialects, but Mandarin itself began to be threatened by the rapidly expanding use of English, which became the medium of instruction in schools from 1987 and was seen as the agent of modernization. Meanwhile commercial links with China were built up through the 1980s, Singapore established full diplomatic relations with the People's Republic in October 1990, and Lee Kuan Yew immediately embarked on his first visit to Beijing. With the opening up of China, Mandarin was increasingly seen as a language of business opportunity and was no longer associated with subversion. The annual Speak Mandarin exercise in late 1990 shifted the usual emphasis away from dialect speakers to target the English-educated Chinese, urging them to improve their Mandarin in order not to lose contact with their traditional roots.

In October 1988 Goh Chok Tong, then First Deputy Prime Minister, had suggested a national ideology of guiding principles, similar to the Rukunegara in Malaysia or the Pancasila in Indonesia, and a parliamentary committee chaired by Lee Hsien Loong was appointed to deliberate on this. Lee attributed difficulties to rapid Westernization, which had produced impressive economic growth but eroded traditional values: "Singapore's problem is how to be cosmopolitan, but yet not rootless ... our problem is to retain our roots and identity".[4]

After two years of discussion, a White Paper on "Shared Values" was presented in January 1991, generating heated debate both in and outside Parliament among English-educated liberals, such as Chiam See Tong, who saw it as "thought control", and among minority communities who were uneasy about the Confucian emphasis. With a few amendments, a national ideology was agreed, based on five common values: nation before community and society above self; the family as the basic unit of society; community support and respect for the individual; consensus not conflict; racial and religious harmony. The inclusion of belief in God as a sixth value was rejected as inconsistent with a secular society.

The following month the government published a short book entitled *The Next Lap*,[5] which set out its priorities for the next stage of Singapore's development. This publication was also the fruit of long deliberations. In 1988 Goh had issued a discussion green paper, "Action for Change". Advisory councils were appointed to consider various aspects of social, cultural, and recreational activity, and their findings, together with the recommendations of other recent reports, were reviewed by a Long Term National Development Committee and co-ordinated as *The Next Lap*. Over the next twenty to thirty years the overall aim was to involve all citizens in making Singapore "more prosperous, gracious and interesting". There was to be "continuity and change": continuity in building on the sound foundations laid down by the first generation of leaders and maintaining strong economic growth, "Singaporeans will have to work hard, work smart, and work together". Continuity too as a "rugged society", helping the unfortunate to stand on their own feet: "we must avoid the pitfalls of the welfare state", but "our objective is to be both a cultured and a rugged society", to make Singapore an attractive place to live. Giving priority to people as "our most precious resource", the target was to increase the population to four million in the twenty-first century by encouraging larger families, attracting talented immigrants, and discouraging emigration. The share of gross national product devoted to education was to rise from 3 per cent to 4 per cent, and an Edusave fund was launched to help with the payment of school fees.

Censorship was gradually relaxed. George Yeo Yong Boon,[6] Acting Minister for Information and the Arts, set up a committee to review the legislation relating to censorship in the arts and cinema. Chaired by diplomat and law professor Tommy Koh,[7] Chairman of the National Heritage Board and enthusiastic patron of the arts, the committee was broadly representative and included writer and lawyer Philip Jeyaretnam, son of Workers' Party leader, J.B. Jeyaretnam. As a result of its deliberations, the laws were relaxed, less puritanical standards were applied to imported books and magazines, and soon even the racy *Cosmopolitan* was back in Singapore bookshops.

As National Day approached in August 1991, Goh Chok Tong was beginning to win the cautious approval of even the international press, and Lee Kuan Yew rather grudgingly admitted that his successor had "done better than I expected". Hong Kong's *South China Morning Post* commented that after eight months in office Goh looked far more relaxed and was much more affable and freer in discussion with the media than his predecessor.[8] In his National Day television address, the Prime Minister put "people bonding" as his main objective. While paying tribute to Lee Kuan Yew's achievements, Goh insisted he would "walk his own way", and he outlined an ambitious programme for improving education, housing, and health.

The government's five-year term was not due to expire until 1993, but the auspices looked promising, and in August 1991 Goh called a snap general election to seek a mandate for his proposed more open-style administration. When Jeyaretnam accused the PAP of deliberately bringing the election forward in order to exclude him, Goh pledged to give the Workers' Party leader an opportunity to fight a by-election when his time ban expired. Adopting an ingenious scheme proposed by Chiam See Tong, the opposition parties agreed among themselves to contest only forty of the eighty-one parliamentary seats, thus conceding an overall PAP victory at the outset but offering the electorate free rein to choose a strong opposition. The tactic dented the PAP's majority; the party's share of the vote slipped to 61 per cent, with three seats falling to Chiam's Singapore Democratic Party and a fourth to Low Thia Khiang,[9] assistant secretary-general of the Workers' Party. The PAP's parliamentary supremacy remained unassailable, but Goh was disappointed. Before the election he had threatened to revert to a more authoritarian style if he did not receive popular support, and he now declared he would continue the consultation policy but move rather more slowly to an open political system.

By the end of the following year the Prime Minister had acquired much stronger personal authority. The economy continued to grow, and many of the benefits of prosperity were passed on to all levels of society in the form of tax rebates for the better-off and in programmes to upgrade Housing and Development Board flats, to top up citizens' Medisave accounts, and to offer bursaries for bright students from low-income families. Early in December 1992, with Lee Kuan Yew's support, Goh was elected unanimously to succeed Lee as secretary-general of the PAP. Later that month the Prime Minister's team won a large majority in the promised by-election, which he staged in his own four-member group representation constituency, where Jeyaretnam's party was unable to muster the required large team. Meanwhile in November 1992 it was announced that both Deputy Prime Ministers were suffering from cancer. This was low-grade in the case of Ong Teng Cheong, and Lee Hsien Loong gained remission after relinquishing office for only a few months, but Goh's victories in party and parliamentary elections and his two deputies' health problems put him in a stronger personal position than at any time since he became Prime Minister. Lee Kuan Yew made no secret of the fact that initially Goh was the Cabinet's preferred candidate and not his own first choice of successor, but now the days of rather diffident probation came to an end, and Goh could act with greater confidence.

From 1987 onwards the economy recorded very high annual growth rates, and these were scarcely affected even by the first Gulf War, which drove the republic's main trading partner, the United States, into recession. From the late 1980s Singapore ceased to be a net importer of capital and began to run up consistent budget surpluses. By 1990 the republic had accumulated substantial foreign exchange reserves and was ready to take its economy in a new direction. Ever since it came to power, the PAP had pursued a vigorous economic interventionist policy, involving the state directly or indirectly in enterprises through the Economic Development Board, and using the Central Provident Fund as a means to control inflation and obtain cheap finance. In the 1960s the first priority was to mop up unemployment in low-grade industries, in the 1970s the emphasis shifted to diversification and upgrading skills, and at the end of that decade the republic had embarked on a "Second Industrial Revolution" involving higher technology. "Singapore Inc.", as the republic was dubbed on account of its state-financed and managed enterprises, had been very successful in attracting trade and investment. Now it needed to invest surplus capital. In 1989 support was given to boost small and medium local enterprises, but the Government of Singapore Investment Corporation, which managed the foreign reserves, looked for opportunities to invest abroad and to make Singapore a significant player in the regional and global economy. The republic aimed to become the hub of the Johor-Riau-Singapore Growth Triangle; it gave warm support to the ASEAN Free Trade Area proposal, which was mooted at the 1992 Singapore summit meeting, and it sought investment opportunities in Europe and other overseas economies. In 1994 the republic pledged strong backing for the newly established Asian Infrastructure Fund, with substantial investment in burgeoning Asian economies, notably the People's Republic of China, India, and Vietnam.

❧

An increasingly sophisticated and prosperous electorate grumbled about the constrictions of the "nanny state", and the first presidential election, which was held in 1993, generated considerable popular enthusiasm. Former Deputy Prime Minister Ong Teng Cheong[10] was nominated by the National Trades Union Congress and supported by the PAP, but more than 41 per cent went in protest votes to the somewhat reluctant rival contestant, a former accountant-general with no political associations. Ong himself was an approachable, well-liked figure, a hard-working constituency MP and Cabinet minister, who was equally at ease with Mandarin, Hokkien, and English. After attending Chinese High School, he qualified as an architect and urban planner at Adelaide and Liverpool Universities, and played an important role in the construction of Changi International Airport and the Mass Rapid Transit, which opened in 1981 and 1987, respectively.[11] He went on to be a popular and independent-minded president, but at the time of the election Ong was seen as the PAP's man.

Nominated MPs took advantage of their right to present private bills, which provided more scope for lively discussion than official legislation. The first such bill, a Maintenance of Parents Bill, which was introduced by Professor Walter Woon[12] in 1995, gave destitute parents over the age of 60 the right to claim maintenance from their children. The proposal sparked off spirited debate in both Parliament and the press. Some were shocked – confident that the depth of natural filial devotion in their society would make such a law superfluous – but they were sorely disillusioned when dozens of neglected parents brought cases to court. A bill introduced by NMP Dr. Kanwaljit Soin[13] to combat domestic violence against women also provoked excited argument, but it was rejected by Parliament and replaced in 1996 by a broader government measure to revise the Women's Charter and widen its provisions to protect families in case of violence or divorce.

While Nominated Members of Parliament, who had been chosen to participate in politics, enjoyed a fair degree of latitude, the same tolerance was not extended to independent academics, writers, and other armchair commentators. In November 1994 a respected local author, Catherine Lim, published a mildly critical analysis in the *Straits Times*, comparing the difference in style of government between Lee Kuan Yew and the new Prime Minister. This drew a sharp public reprimand that Lim should either join a political party or make her remarks to the Feedback Unit rather than publish views that threatened to undermine the Prime Minister's authority. Goh insisted that would-be objectors should enter the political arena themselves and meanwhile should respect those in authority who had been chosen by the electorate and were responsible to them. The PAP claimed that the elected government alone had the right to decide the limits of consultation: the so-called out-of-bounds markers, beyond which those who were not prepared to mount the hustings themselves were not entitled to venture.

This severe reaction caused surprise at the time, but perhaps should not have been unexpected. In introducing the Nominated Members scheme in 1989, Goh had explained this was designed "to further strengthen our political system by offering Singapore more opportunity for political participation and to evolve a more consensual style of government where alternative views are heard and constructive dissent accommodated". In looking forward to more political participation, Goh had told *The International Herald Tribune* just before taking office, "it has to be channeled to meaningful participation, with the focus on real issues and on solutions to problems", while the role of the press was "to report, not participate … not indulge their own view of what Singapore should be".[14] Over the last few years the government had steadily built up an array of means to gather and disseminate information, and hear and defuse discontent through the Feedback Unit, town councils and government parliamentary committees. These were intended to provide the forums where "alternative views [could be] heard and constructive dissent accommodated", while citizens would contribute "meaningful participation" in municipal activity. The PAP ideal was government by consensus, less charitably described by others as a "national ideology to exclude confrontational politics".[15]

The local press had come to accept the PAP interpretation of its role and did not see itself as a Fourth Estate: it did not claim the right to attack elected politicians or set the national agenda. Different criteria were applied to overseas journals that circulated in Singapore on the grounds that, unlike their local counterparts, foreign journalists did not have to live with the consequences of their irresponsibility. When invited to speak to the American Society of Newspaper Editors in April 1988, Lee described the media in the United States as "invigilator, adversary, and inquisitor of the administration".[16] He was determined that neither the Western nor the local press should assume any such role in Singapore. After several quiet years, in 1994 the Newspaper and Printing Presses Act was again invoked, and punitive damages were awarded against *The International Herald Tribune* and the American author of articles that it had published, not specifically naming Singapore but implying that its government leaned on a compliant judiciary to suppress opposition by bankrupting rival politicians. The incident served to consolidate the image of Singapore as an authoritarian state in the U.S. liberal media.

In general Singaporeans sought a greater say in voicing their opinions but showed little appetite for entering the political arena themselves. The PAP's success in producing stability and prosperity offered easier ways of earning a good living than facing the hurly-burly of politics or conforming to the discipline and hard work involved in being a minister or even a parliamentary backbencher. Few came forward except by government invitation. The party was at once demanding and critical. It set high standards in recruiting young parliamentary candidates with ministerial potential and in appointing Cabinet ministers who had attained distinction elsewhere in the public service or private spheres. Some incentives were offered: young MPs were encouraged to combine political duties with a business or professional career, and in 1994, despite considerable public criticism, ministerial salaries were raised to a level comparable with private sector high fliers. Yet, while selection for office was viewed as an honour and a patriotic duty, it carried the risk of public humiliation in the event of failure.

Following the sound maxim to "co-opt the rebellious by awarding them management responsibility", the government neutralized some potential dissenters by recruiting able but independent-minded citizens to public service outside of mainstream politics: some to head institutions in Singapore and others to serve as envoys overseas. The republic's diplomatic corps included a fair share of outspoken critics, such as David Marshall, who made the transition from opposition politics to serve as Singapore's ambassador to France from 1978 to 1993, law professor Tommy Koh[17] and Chan Heng Chee,[18] professor of political science and Singapore's ambassador to the United States.

Those who chose the path of outright confrontation faced a bleak fate. Opposition politicians no longer feared being arrested and imprisoned without trial: the Internal Security Act remained in place, but had not been invoked for some years, and in 1998 the final restrictions were lifted from the last and longest-serving detainee, former Barisan Sosialis MP Chia Thye Poh, who had been arrested in 1966. After severing his links with the Barisan, Lim Chin Siong was released in 1969 in order to further his studies in Britain, where he lived for the next ten years, before returning to Singapore, where he died in 1996. A number of prominent left-wing opponents who had fled into exile were allowed back in the latter years of the century. Eu Chooi

Yip, who had taken sanctuary in China, was permitted to return at Goh Keng Swee's request in 1989,[19] and P.V. Sharma soon afterwards. Goh was also instrumental in getting approval for the Plen's son, a qualified engineer, to settle in Singapore in 1990. The Plen himself angled for readmission and met Lee Kuan Yew in Beijing in 1995, but they could not agree to the terms.[20] The PAP continued to give no quarter to individuals whose opposition was deemed to be dangerous or potentially damaging to the state. They were usually treated with derision and contempt and liable to be pursued relentlessly through the courts for financial shortcomings or sued for libel on account of remarks that would commonly be tolerated in the West as the customary cut and thrust of robust democratic electioneering.

❧

In January 1997 the government called a general election, adopting the slogan "Singapore 21: Make it our best home". Against the background of a buoyant economy, Goh claimed a record of six years' achievement and presented a detailed programme to carry the republic forward into the next century, promising further stability, economic growth, and rising living standards. To help put this into effect he introduced a team of twenty-four new parliamentary candidates: carefully selected and well-qualified professionals from a mixture of ethnic backgrounds, all of whom had risen on their own merit.

The character of the opposition parties had changed since the 1991 general election. Jeyaretnam was once more in full command of the Workers' Party, Chiam See Tong headed a new party, and the Singapore Democratic Party had moved sharply to the left under energetic young leadership. Fresh from completing his doctoral studies in the United States, neuropsychologist Chee Soon Juan took up a post at the National University of Singapore, and was one of the Singapore Democratic Party's team that unsuccessfully contested the by-election in Goh Chok Tong's constituency in December 1992. Soon afterwards Chee was dismissed from his university lectureship on the grounds of misusing departmental funds. He staged a protest hunger strike and made accusations against his head of department, who sued for libel and won substantial damages. It was the beginning of a rocky career in politics. As a counter to "The Next Lap", in 1994 Chee published *Dare to Change*, which alleged that, in achieving the PAP's material success, "freedom, justice and the spirit of Singaporeans has been ruthlessly quashed" and they now faced "the political gargoyle of authoritarianism".[21] Dedicated to "all those political detainees who struggled for democracy and all the Singaporeans who long for openness, humanness [sic] and justice for our nation", *Dare to Change* called for "a tolerant and vibrant pluralism" where, in place of "an over-powering state-elite with a subjugated mass", "the masses must be strong and courageous in its [sic] participation of the nation's politics". Chee threw down the gauntlet on almost every aspect of PAP policy from the "shared values" concept and promoting Mandarin over dialects to the Internal Security legislation, labour laws, attitudes to women, tax incentives for graduate mothers, high ministerial salaries, and encouraging MNCs. Instead he called for individualism, abolishing the Internal Security legislation, freeing the media, and redistributing wealth to help the old and the poor.

Despite the Singapore Democratic Party's substantial success in winning three seats in the 1991 general election, the organization was already troubled by internal disputes before Chee Soon Juan arrived on the scene. Alleging there was little to show for Chiam See Tong's ten years of gentle tactics, Chee was elected secretary-general in his place. *Dare to Change* was accepted as the Singapore Democratic Party's policy, and the party prepared to take a more aggressive stance. After a good deal of wrangling and infighting, Chiam See Tong was expelled and formed a new Singapore People's Party, which aimed to continue his moderate liberal policy, seeking to relax the Internal Security legislation and calling for a "caring and civic society in which people could enter politics without fear".

Once more the PAP candidates were returned unopposed in more than half of the elective parliamentary seats,[22] so that the party was again assured of victory, but the battle for the remainder was strenuously fought. Determined to stem the steady erosion in its share of the votes, which the party had suffered in the last three general elections, the PAP regarded this contest as a watershed. Several single member constituencies were merged into group representation constituencies, and some group representation constituencies were increased from four candidates to five or six, which made it even more difficult for smaller parties to field teams. The PAP decided to put local issues at the heart of the campaign: it pointed to the improvements in everyday life that had already been made by the municipal councils and by the ongoing programme to upgrade Housing and Development Board flats. For the first time Goh proposed to give priority in community services and refurbishing housing to those constituencies – and probably to those specific wards within constituencies – that supported the government candidates. This innovation was bitterly denounced by the opposition parties as unfair.

It was the racial issue that provided the most heat in the campaign. The ruling party was alarmed by the enthusiasm that the Workers' Party was rousing in Cheng San – by then a five-member group representation constituency – and in particular by the emotional response of Chinese-educated voters to Workers' Party team member Tang Liang Hong. A well-known lawyer, sixty-two years of age, Tang was a newcomer to politics, although he had at one time been considered for appointment as a Nominated Member of Parliament. Educated at both Nanyang and the University of Singapore, he was passionately concerned about promoting the Chinese language and Confucianism. A former chairman of the Nanyang Academy of Fine Arts, Tang had served on the management boards of several Chinese schools, and was worried that the Chinese language was losing ground to English in Singapore. In his election campaign, Tang alleged neglect and discrimination. Accusing Tang of inflaming racial discord, the Prime Minister and Lee Kuan Yew personally entered the fray. The PAP succeeded in retaining the constituency, but the Workers' Party polled 45 per cent of the votes.

Overall the PAP gained the best results since the 1984 general election, winning back two seats and increasing its share of the vote. Low Thia Khiang retained his seat for the Workers' Party, and Chiam See Tong was returned for a fourth term but as leader of the Singapore People's Party, but Chee Soon Juan's Singapore Democratic Party was routed. As the loser with the highest score, Jeyaretnam was admitted as a Non-Constituency Member of Parliament, since only two opposition candidates had been elected.[23]

Despite the victory, the government was badly shaken by the serious challenge in a large group representation constituency, and the acrimonious campaign spawned bitter court disputes. The Prime Minister and Lee Kuan Yew were awarded punitive damages for defamation against Tang Liang Hong, who fled to settle in Australia, refused to pay, and was declared bankrupt. The PAP leaders also won heavy damages and costs against Jeyaretnam. The following year Jeyaretnam was sued by members of a Tamil Language Committee and incurred further heavy defamatory damages, as a result of which he was declared bankrupt, lost his parliamentary seat, and was barred from contesting the next election. Finally, in May 2001 at the age of seventy-six, Jeyaretnam gave up the post of secretary-general, which he had held for the past thirty years, handed over leadership of the battered Workers' Party to Low Thia Khiang, and retired from politics, a ruined man. It was a sad end for a politician of honest conviction, who had sacrificed a secure career and suffered so much personal and financial distress in order to fight for what he believed to be a democratic, fair, and just society. Lee Kuan Yew dismissed him as "a poseur, always seeking publicity, good or bad",[24] but it was probably obstinacy that contributed to Jeyaretnam's undoing because he was too rigid in his total condemnation of the PAP. In the words of David Marshall, himself an outspoken critic of many aspects of the regime but prepared to admire the ruling party's considerable achievements, "If the Archangel Gabriel himself came down from heaven and sat on the PAP benches, Jeyaretnam would complain that the glare was too bright and his wings were taking up too much room".

The 1997 general election and its aftermath left the political opposition in disarray. No fewer than twenty-two opposition parties were registered in 1998, but thirteen of these were dormant, and the others rarely held meetings. The Singapore Democratic Party continued to be beset by trouble: in 1999 Chee Soon Juan was convicted of holding an unlicensed public meeting and was imprisoned briefly when he refused to pay the fine. From the beginning the PAP had treated Chee with contempt as a brash youth and denigrated his personal integrity. Despite his enthusiasm and his ambitious debut, Chee's strident style alienated the electorate: his party failed to win a single seat under his leadership and lost the gains that his predecessor had made.

Appealing for unity to heal the wounds, Goh launched a widespread consultation exercise to plan for the new millennium. In Parliament the Prime Minister talked of encouraging civil society "to harness the talent and energies of its people and to build a cohesive and vibrant nation". Civil society associations, which had thrived in early colonial times, had suffered a mauling during the Malayan Emergency and the transition to independence[25] and were inhibited by the Societies Ordinance. The original Societies Ordinance of 1890, which was designed to check Chinese secret societies, required associations to register, and gave the government power to dissolve them. The Ordinance was re-introduced after the Second World War, when all societies were required to re-register. It was extensively used to control or ban radical political, labour, and student associations during the Malayan Emergency, and was retained after independence.

In some instances, such as the Singapore Family Planning Association, a non-government organization's function was taken over and run by the state. Others were prodded into existence by the government itself, notably Mendaki (Council on Education for

Muslim Children), which was formed in 1982 in response to Lee Kuan Yew's call to community leaders to tackle the problem of low academic achievement among young Malays. The government supplied premises, and PAP Malay MPs joined representatives of Malay social and cultural groups on the council. But in general organizations outside of government control were regarded with suspicion by the PAP and received short shrift if their activities encroached on official policy.

Civil society was at a low ebb, but the Great Marriage Debate inspired the creation in 1985 of what was to become one of the most influential non-government organizations: the Association of Women for Action and Research (AWARE). The controversy awakened professional women in particular to the limitations of the 1961 Women's Charter and spurred them on to protect what had been gained and to get rid of remaining discrimination. The Women's Charter had concentrated on establishing legal equality, chiefly by abolishing polygamy except among Muslims. The appeal by middle-class, English-educated women for the practice to be outlawed had come up against a stout wall of male resistance, and the Charter was the fruit of determined efforts by Chan Choy Siong and fellow members of the Women's League, which represented the interests of Chinese working-class women. In view of the importance of the women's vote in the 1959 election, the PAP adopted the Charter as part of its platform, despite considerable hostility within the ranks of the party. Four women won seats in the 1959 Assembly, but after the resignation in 1970 of Chan Choy Siong, the last of these pioneer MPs, Parliament remained an exclusively masculine preserve for the next fourteen years. Despite Lee Kuan Yew's personal admiration for his remarkable mother and clever wife, neither the Prime Minister nor the rest of the PAP leadership showed any interest in recruiting women into politics.

While the Women's Charter was not seen at that time as the first step in a systematic campaign to extend women's rights, in general the lot of Singapore's women improved in the years that followed, irrespective of ethnic or social background, and they enjoyed an enviable position compared with their sisters in most other countries. Released from the burden of raising large families, women were encouraged to play full and active parts in contributing to the nation's progress. Albert Winsemius acknowledged that female workers were crucial in developing the labour-intensive textile industry, which constituted the first stage of his industrialization plan. Working-class women benefited from regular wages, better living conditions in the Housing and Development Board flats, and wider opportunities for their children's schooling. Well-educated middle-class women with access to reliable domestic help profited even more. The career woman was respected and encouraged by tax incentives. Exempt from the obligations of their male counterparts to undertake national military service, ambitious women enjoyed a head start in employment and seniority, quietly establishing themselves in the middle and senior ranks of professional and commercial life. Shocked by Lee Kuan Yew's proposals to encourage female graduates to marry and have more children, which threatened to relegate them to the traditional role of wife and mother, in 1984 a small group of enthusiasts organized a seminar on "Women's Choices, Women's Lives" and went on to form AWARE. The association promoted research, supported legislative reform, ran educational programmes, and offered direct help and advice, with the ultimate object of securing equality for women.[26] At times it steered a difficult course, uncertain of the political boundaries and impinging on the government's population and social policies. Nevertheless it played a constructive role in securing or influencing reform, and Dr. Kanwaljit Soin, the president of AWARE, became the first female Nominated Member of Parliament in 1992.

ॐ

Official planning for the future received a rude jolt in mid-1997, when after a decade of unbroken growth and prosperity, Singapore was swept into the regional economic crisis, which started in Thailand and quickly spread to the whole of Southeast Asia. This came as a terrible shock: only the previous year the Organization for Economic Co-operation and Development (OECD) had raised Singapore to the rank of a "more advanced developing country".[27]

Manufacturing, construction, and commercial sectors were all hit, tax revenue fell, and by the end of 1998 the economy was formally in recession. The government introduced stringent measures at all levels, slashing salaries of ministers and senior civil servants, scaling down Housing and Development Board upgrading schemes, reducing business costs by cutting wages, and halving employers' Central Provident Fund contributions to deter them from dismissing workers. Some grants were made to the elderly and the very poor, but the government refused to accept Workers' Party proposals for widespread welfare measures to ease the pain. Instead it insisted on stepping up investment in the economic infrastructure and in education, retraining programmes, and upgrading skills, with an eye to coming out of the crisis in a stronger position to face the future.

The refusal to consider spending any of its large reserves on relieving the widespread distress brought the government into conflict with President Ong Teng Cheong, who announced in June 1999, on nearing the end of his term, that he did not intend to seek re-election. Ong complained about restrictions to his rights of veto, and obstruction in obtaining details about the reserves. This was the first occasion on which the scope of the new-style president's authority was put to the test. The Prime Minister insisted that the president was largely a ceremonial figure: a safeguard of last resort, whose powers were confined to ensuring that no future irresponsible government could squander the reserves or make unsuitable appointments. In July 1999 Parliament agreed on new rules to define the relationship between the executive and the presidency. Since there were no other candidates with the required qualifications, S R Nathan,[28] former civil servant and latterly ambassador-at-large, became president the following month without an election being held.

By that time signs of a mild economic recovery encouraged the republic to look forward more hopefully to the new millennium. In May 1999 Parliament debated at length an official publication entitled *Singapore 21: Together We Make the Difference*, which was the fruit of a wide-ranging consultation exercise over the past two years. This envisaged a three-way partnership between public and private sectors and all citizens to forge a truly multiracial society, in which each community would have its own distinctive identity but overlap into a central Singaporean character, with equal opportunities for all and sharing English as the common language.

At National Day in August 1999 Goh envisaged Singapore as "a world class renaissance city", boasting not only an outstanding economy but excellence in education, the arts, and sport. Participation and consultation were cited among the main objectives, with the republic becoming "a nation of ideas". In September 2000 an outdoor Speakers' Corner was designated, where any citizen could speak freely, provided that he or she kept within the law, respected racial and religious sensitivities, and avoided slander.

As the century drew to a close, the main difficulties were seen as an ageing population and a shortage of graduates and skills. The tribunal established in 1996 to implement Walter Woon's Maintenance of Parents law was welcomed as a means of relieving pressure on healthcare and other social services by enforcing family responsibility for older relatives, and in 1998 the retirement age was raised from sixty to sixty-two. The population target was raised to five million by the middle of the twenty-first century, but this was going to be difficult to achieve. Despite measures to encourage marriage and child bearing, the rate of natural increase was still falling. Further incentives were given in the form of bonuses for second and third children. Immigration laws were relaxed to attract foreign talent and labour, and by the end of the century one-quarter of the population were non-citizens. After a two-year freeze, substantial pay rises were awarded to senior civil servants and ministers as part of a strategy to deter professionals from emigrating and encourage skilled Singaporeans to return. These provoked angry protests from workers, since the cuts in employers' Central Provident Fund contributions had only partially been restored. The gap was widening between First World salaries and Third World wages. There were still many unemployed among the unskilled and a persistent minority of the very poor.

❧

Disappointingly the fragile recovery faltered and the economy relapsed into recession in the wake of the global slowdown that occurred when the information technology bubble burst. Then came the shock of the Al-Qaeda attack on the World Trade Center in New York on 11 September 2001. Singapore immediately declared support for the American effort to create a worldwide alliance against terror but was convinced that terrorism would not be defeated primarily by military force but by settling the causes of Muslim extremism, and urged that Third World and Muslim countries should participate.

In order to secure a mandate to counter terrorism and to tackle the continuing recession, the government decided to bring forward the general election, which was not required by law until August of the following year. This was a risky manoeuvre, since in the past general elections had been called when the economy was doing well. The gamble paid off. A record fifty-five seats were uncontested, and in November 2001 the PAP secured eighty-two of the eighty-four seats, with a greatly increased majority of 75 per cent of the popular vote. Low Thia Khiang and Chiam See Tong retained their seats, but with reduced majorities, and Chee Soon Juan's Singapore Democratic Party suffered another defeat.

Goh announced he would remain in office to see the recession through but intended to hand over before the next general election, by which time the new generation of leaders would be in place. Meanwhile he pressed on with his policy of involving citizens in local issues and encouraging them to look after their own communities. In November 2001 the island was divided into five districts under mayors, who were also MPs and equivalent in rank to junior ministers, and nine Community Development Councils were created to administer local social services, welfare, health, and sports. In Parliament the government relaxed its rules to permit PAP backbenchers to speak and vote freely except on matters of national importance, such as security, the constitution, or the budget.

While the atmosphere in Singapore had remained calm after the 9/11 attacks, and individual Muslims were not harassed, the republic feared it was vulnerable as a capitalist enclave in a Third World region and a predominantly Chinese island in a Muslim sea. A national security secretariat was created, and in December 2001 fifteen suspected terrorists were arrested, of whom thirteen were imprisoned under the Internal Security Act. They were believed to be members of Jemaah Islamiah, part of a larger network covering Malaysia and Indonesia that planned to create a Java-based Muslim state embracing the Malay Peninsula, Indonesia, and the southern Philippines. The organization was alleged to be linked to Al-Qaeda, and some of its members were trained in Afghanistan and under orders from Indonesian militants. The arrests foiled an elaborate Jemaah Islamiah plot against targets in Singapore with simultaneous attacks on American embassies in Kuala Lumpur and Jakarta.

The crisis revived the long-going concern about the state of Singapore Malays. The government recognized that the community as a whole still lagged behind in prosperity, and in many ways they were isolated and held back from the mainstream of progress by the special arrangements that had been designed to benefit them, such as exemption from military service, the waiver of tertiary education fees, and concessions made for Islamic religious schools, or *madrasah*. But bringing such practices into line with other Singaporeans was far from popular. From 1985 national service had been extended to all males, including Malays, and in 1990 the automatic remission of higher education fees for all Malays was replaced by grants to help only poor students.

Education was the chief stumbling block. Mendaki had produced modest improvement, which speeded up after the formation in 1991 of an Association of Muslim Professionals. A voluntary association, independent of government, the Association aimed "to play a leading and active role in the development and long-term transformation of Malay/Muslim Singaporeans into a dynamic community", and successful Muslim professionals helped with family welfare, upgrading work skills and improving children's education. A Malay middle class grew rapidly in the last decade of the century, with increasing numbers of Malays going on to tertiary education and entering the professions, but the *madrasahs* lagged behind. Government proposals in 1999 to set minimum standards for all schools had led to heated exchanges with the Association of Muslim Professionals, but the tension eased after the Prime Minister and Senior Minister met large gatherings of Muslim community leaders. A compromise was reached, and Malay MPs drew up a blueprint for progress.

The authorities were shocked to find that those arrested in December 2001 did not in fact come from the poorer, marginalized, *madrasah*-educated section of Malay society. With one exception, all were middle-class Singapore citizens, who had been educated in secular national schools, and none had been closely involved with mosque activities. In face of this setback to the government's multiracial policies, Goh Chok Tong, Lee Hsien Loong, and other senior ministers organized a closed meeting of some 1,700 community leaders to discuss the impact of the arrests and to stress the need for even greater cohesion. Muslim leaders expressed their strong support, and in January 2002 new grassroots Inter-racial Confidence Circles were established in each constituency.

In a second wave in September 2002, a further twenty-one Singaporeans were arrested, of whom eighteen were detained and the other three put under restriction orders. Unlike the earlier group, these were all blue-collar workers, foot soldiers of the movement. The arrests disrupted the Jemaah Islamiah network in Singapore, but the regional threat remained strong. In October 2002 Goh proposed a draft Code on Religious Harmony to another large gathering of community leaders, and in January 2003 Parliament debated a White Paper on Jemaah Islamiah and its international links. The three opposition MPs joined in the unanimous support for the government's proposals to tighten security and extend intelligence gathering, while at the same time strengthening social solidarity and religious harmony, and encouraging the Muslim community to curb extremism in religious education.

∽

With unemployment in December 2001 standing at its highest level for fifteen years, equally robust measures were needed to tackle the problem of the economy. In order to increase every citizen's stake in the country, "new Singapore shares" were issued to all, with generous allotments made to the poor.

An Economic Review Committee was appointed under Lee Hsien Loong, with seven sub-committees chaired by businessmen and politicians. Charged with proposing long-term restructuring to cope with the prospect of increased competition from China and northeastern Asia, in April 2002 the committee recommended that the government gradually relinquish state-owned enterprises to the private sector and only remain involved in strategic areas, such as the Port of Singapore. The committee also supported a major revision of taxation and employment to liberalize the labour market and create jobs.

The recession continued to deepen into the longest and worst since independence, and Singapore's economy suffered further in the aftermath of the Al-Qaeda terrorist attack in Bali in October 2002. Early the next year many port employees were declared redundant, and civil service salaries were again cut, particularly at the senior levels. The economy was further hit by the outbreak of the Iraq war in March 2003 and by a serious outbreak of Severe

Acute Respiratory Syndrome (SARS), which deterred tourism and led to drastic retrenchments at Singapore Airlines.

On a more positive note, bilateral Free Trade Agreements were signed with Japan, New Zealand and Australia, culminating in August 2003, after years of difficult negotiations, in an agreement with the United States, which was the most prized of all. At the same time, in order to reduce over-dependence on Western economies, commerce was developed with China, Taiwan and Hong Kong, and in 2002 for the first time trade with those countries overtook that with the United States.

$\wp$

From the beginning the small infant republic had seen ASEAN as vital to her security and economic well-being. Singapore had been an enthusiastic founder member in 1967, and welcomed the admission of Brunei in 1984 and Vietnam, Myanmar, Laos, and Cambodia in the 1990s. The international terrorist threat and the economic crisis made it even more imperative to maintain cordial relations and promote regional peace and economic co-operation. Anxious to restore trade and investment in Southeast Asia, in 2002 Singapore proposed hastening the introduction of the proposed ASEAN Free Trade Area, welcomed drawing China, Japan, the European Union, and the United States into a closer relationship with ASEAN, and warmly endorsed a Joint Declaration for Co-operation to Combat Terrorism, which was agreed with the United States at the ASEAN meeting in Brunei in 2002. Goh Chok Tong even floated the idea of forging closer regional political and military links along the lines of the European Union.

In general Singapore's relations with fellow ASEAN countries were harmonious, and the abrasive nationalism of the early post-independence years had matured into a more sensitive appreciation of her neighbours' problems. In 1995 Manila broke off diplomatic relations for almost a year in protest at the execution in Singapore of a Filipino maid convicted of murder, but this was exceptional.

The need for political stability, economic prosperity and countering terrorism made it particularly important to bury past hostilities and maintain friendly terms with her nearest neighbours, Indonesia and Malaysia, and in the 1990s Singapore sought closer integration with the Indonesian and Malaysian economies. The republic worked closely with the regime of President Suharto of Indonesia up to his resignation in 1998, and the less cordial relationship with his immediate successors did not impede a long term agreement over a West Natunas natural gas pipeline, which was opened in a joint ceremony by Goh Chok Tong and the Indonesian president in 2001. The two countries drew closer in their concern to suppress Jemaah Islamiah, which was credited with plotting the unsuccessful attack in Singapore in December 2001 and subsequent atrocities in Bali and Jakarta.

Malaysia and Singapore signed a bilateral Defence Co-operation Pact in 1995 and finally agreed on the boundary of their territorial waters after fifteen years' negotiation. There were still tensions below the surface: conflicting interpretations about Malayan Railway land in Singapore; derogatory remarks about Johor by Lee Kuan Yew, provoking protests by UMNO and in the Malay press in Kuala Lumpur, and the publication in 1998 of the first volume of Lee's outspoken memoirs, which reopened old wounds about the unhappy break in 1965. The two Prime Ministers and their senior officials gradually smoothed relations. An informal visit by the Senior Minister Lee in August 2000 – his first to Kuala Lumpur in ten years – was an unexpected success, and the second volume of his memoirs, which was published the following month, was warmly received in Malaysia. Lee Kuan Yew and Prime Minister Mahathir met in Kuala Lumpur in August 2001 and agreed in principle to an amicable settlement of all differences between the two countries, leaving the details to be worked out by the officials, but these caused practical difficulties. Apart from a contested claim to sovereignty over the lighthouse island of Pedra Branca, which was to be referred to the International Court of Justice at the Hague, Singapore wanted to include all other issues in one overall agreement, whereas Malaysia insisted on settling the dispute about water first. Agreements signed in 1961 and 1962, whereby Kuala Lumpur undertook to supply raw water to Singapore and receive treated water in return, were due to remain in force until 2011 and 2061, respectively. Malaysia's wish to revise the terms ahead of schedule generated heated public comment on both sides of the Causeway. Meanwhile the republic set out to reduce its dependence on Malaysian water by constructing a desalination plant, two new freshwater reservoirs and two recycling plants. The recycled "new water" was deemed fit for both industrial and domestic use, and thousands of bottles were distributed to the public on National Day in August 2002.

Northeast Asia's expanding economy, and particularly China's spectacular development, presented not only competition but also new opportunities. Singapore continued to cultivate friendly relations with the People's Republic and to encourage investment, joint ventures and commercial links. Goh Chok Tong and the Chinese president exchanged official visits and agreed to set up a high level joint council to explore areas for co-operation. Beijing offered Singapore military training facilities on Hainan Island as an alternative to those she had for many years enjoyed in Taiwan.

Laying to rest the dispute between the People's Republic and Taiwan was vital to the continued stability and prosperity of the whole region. Singapore hosted the first Taiwan-China talks in 1993 in the hope that an agreement could be reached on the basis of a peaceful "one-country two-systems" reunification, but a proposed second round of negotiations in 1999 was abandoned when the Taiwanese President Lee Teng-hui declared that relations with the People's Republic must be on a "state to state" level. Tension escalated further in 2000 after the election of a new president, Chen Shui-bian, at the head of a pro-independence party. Lee Kuan Yew was courteously received when he paid a private visit to Taiwan in October 2001 for the first time in six years, but his advice to accept what he considered to be the favourable terms for reunification then being offered by the

People's Republic was not welcomed. The dispute continued to cast a shadow over the region.

While Singapore sought to reduce its dependence on Western economies, maintaining good relations with the United States continued to be crucial. The republic had distanced itself from the Clinton regime's hostile stance towards China, and relations were cool after Singapore insisted on flogging a young American convicted of vandalism in the mid-1990s. But the government's efforts to mitigate the regional economic crisis in the last years of the century drew praise from the usually critical American press, and in view of its support after the 9/11 attacks, Washington designated Singapore a "friendly foreign country".

∾

Singapore society was changing as the republic entered the new century. Tertiary education had expanded rapidly after the merging of the University of Singapore and Nanyang University to form the National University of Singapore in 1980. The following year a Nanyang Technological Institute was established on the former Nantah campus, and ten years later it joined with the National Institute of Education to become the Nanyang Technological University. Singapore Management University was opened in 2000 and a fifth polytechnic began in 2003. The emphasis was on subjects that would promote modernization and prosperity: science and technology, mathematics, engineering, economics and business management, and languages. While both the government and private sector continued the practice of sending talented graduates overseas for further education, more emphasis was placed on upgrading the quality of tertiary institutions in Singapore. Formal links were forged with prestigious overseas universities for joint degree programmes, a multiplicity of research centres were set up within local institutions to attract overseas as well as Singaporean postgraduates, and Singapore aspired to become the "Boston of the East".

The swelling ranks of ambitious, well-educated, widely travelled professionals were growing restive within the constraints of out-of-bounds markers. A number of civil society bodies began to emerge, such as the Association of Muslim Professionals and similar organizations set up by other communities to help their weak students: a Singapore Indian Development Association in 1991 and a Chinese Development Assistance Council the following year. New associations came into being, such as the Nature Society,[29] and Roundtable, a discussion group of young professionals who sought a review of the Societies, Internal Security, and Public Entertainment Acts. There were signs of wary tolerance of civil society by the authorities, as seen in the acceptance of the Association of Muslim Professionals, despite the fact that its activities overlapped those of the government-sponsored Mendaki. The Nature Society's concern for conservation was sometimes at odds with official development policy, such as its objections to recreational facilities being promoted in the Sungei Buloh bird sanctuary, but in 2004 Dr. Geh Min,[30] who was very active in environmental work and the first woman president of the Nature Society, was chosen to be a Nominated MP.

Dr. Geh Min was among a growing number of prominent women at the turn of the century, by which time the position of women in Parliament, in the workplace and in the home had shown a marked advance. Three women had entered Parliament at the 1984 general election, and the numbers increased at each subsequent contest, although the female electorate was still under-represented in the first decade of the twenty-first century, and no woman had yet reached the highest Cabinet offices. After the 2006 election there were twenty women MPs: seventeen elected PAP members (including two ministers of state and one district mayor), two Nominated MPs and one opposition Non-Constituency MP. Of the three 1984 pioneers, the longest-serving was Yu-Foo Yee Shoon, who was still in Parliament in 2006 as Minister of State for Community Development, Youth and Sport. A second 1984 recruit, Aline Wong,[31] served for seventeen years as an MP, and became a senior minister of state, working on issues concerning women, children, the family, and health. Founder member and chairman of the women's wing of the PAP for sixteen years, she was later appointed chairman of the Housing and Development Board. The most senior political office attained by a woman was held briefly by Dr. Seet Ai Mee, who became an MP at the 1988 election, was appointed Acting Minister for Community Development and Sport for two months in 1991 but retired from politics after losing her seat in the general election later that year. Several women served as Nominated MPs, and as chairmen of parliamentary committees. A few became diplomats, notably Professor Chan Heng Chee, who was appointed Singapore's permanent representative at the UN in 1989 and ambassador to the United States in 1996. In Singapore women came increasingly to the fore in the civil service, business, the professions, and academia. There was a steady erosion of discriminatory practices: restrictive quotas for women medical students were abolished in 2003, joint status for men and women as heads of households was recognized in 2004, and medical benefits for male and female civil servants were equalized in 2005. Women tended to be particularly concerned with health, family, and welfare issues, which was sometimes out of keeping with the PAP's hard-line stance.

The Goh regime's ideal civic society was "a kind of apolitical activism",[32] which would complement but not encroach on official activities, keeping well clear of out-of-bounds territory, and taking responsibility for worthy charitable or cultural activities. In January 2000 Lee Hsien Loong told the Singapore 21 Forum that constructive criticism was acceptable if it was designed to help the government but not if the intention was to attack or overthrow it. Over time the out-of-bounds markers would gradually be rolled back, but meanwhile the authorities would determine when and how this would be done.

Probably the greatest agent for change was the rapid expansion of the Internet, which was one of the most powerful tools for modernization and success in globalization and yet posed the most likely challenge to the existing political order.

Always keen to promote the latest technology, the government had enthusiastically embraced computerization, drawing up a series of plans: a National Computerization Plan (1981–85); followed in 1992 by an IT 2000 master plan, which visualized linking up the whole of Singapore into an "intelligent island"; and an Infocomm 21 master plan for the new century. The Internet gave rise to a new type of what has been called "contentious journalism".[33] The government could manage the mainstream media, either directly through state-ownership of broadcasting and television or indirectly by licensing the press, but the Internet did not require a production licence. Singapore was among the first countries that tried to draw up rules in an attempt to extend accountability not just locally but to the World Wide Web: in 1996 regulations were laid down requiring Internet providers who supplied material with political or religious content relating to Singapore to register with the Singapore Broadcasting Authority. A Parliamentary Elections Act restricted the use of the Web for campaigning to registered political parties, and the May 2006 general election was the first in which the Internet played a role. It had little impact on the result, and once again the PAP won eighty-two of the eighty-four seats. But Chiam See Tong and Low Thia Khiang increased their majorities, and early the following year a "new media" committee was established to devise means to counter the influence of anti-government blogs. Control was likely to be virtually impossible in an open society where the Internet was so widely used and encouraged.

❧

In another seamless transfer of authority, in August 2004 Goh stepped down in favour of his deputy, Lee Hsien Loong, while he himself became Senior Minister and Lee Kuan Yew was styled Minister Mentor. Initially seen by a sceptical public as a stopgap arrangement to provide a decent interval before the younger Lee assumed his father's mantle, Goh's premiership lasted for nearly fourteen years. To begin with, the new leader was in an uncomfortable position, knowing that he was not his predecessor's nominee and living with the prospect of being overshadowed by the younger Lee. Steadily this "quiet problem-solver" earned respect, and throughout his premiership the triumvirate worked closely together in a smooth and constructive partnership. While Goh exercised calm authority, Lee Kuan Yew assumed the role of international statesman and father figure, and Lee Hsien Loong, gradually shedding the impatient arrogance of his youth, was seemingly content to curb his ambition and serve out his long political apprenticeship as heir-presumptive. Goh has been described as "the ideal leader for the times",[34] coming at a time when the old guard had brought Singapore through danger to great material wealth, and the country was ready for a new style. Dubbed in his early days at state-owned Neptune Orient as "the young managing director of Singapore Incorporated", Goh applied his commercial and administrative skills to the business of government.

Under his tutelage the republic came close to resembling a very successful commercial company. Parliamentary elections were akin to annual general meetings, where the chairman reported on the firm's activities and reviewed its past achievements and future plans, and shareholders had the opportunity to ask questions before reappointing the directors and endorsing their policies. The board of directors was responsible for recruiting and training new talent, headhunting senior management and arranging an orderly succession of executive authority, and for paying out a dividend to citizen/shareholders from the company's profits. While general elections were not expected to change government or official policy, they were a useful barometer in gauging the degree of popular approval and indicating sources of discontent. Political opponents might be dispatched without mercy, but action was taken to deal with the grievances they exposed: reviewing the condition of the low-paid Chinese workers who responded to Tang Liang Hong in the 1997 contest; setting up the Speaker's Corner in September 2000 following Chee's attack on the Public Entertainment Law's restrictions on free speech; pruning ministers' pay in May 2003, a few months after Jeyaretnam complained of unequal sacrifice when unemployment was at its peak.

Disappointed when the more open political system that Goh had initially promised became subject to stricter controls, the desire for the public to be given more of a say in politics grew stronger, but there was no call for fundamental change. Despite the widespread hardship, Singapore came through the recession in better shape than any of the other countries in Southeast Asia, and confidence revived. During Goh's years in office the republic had suffered and survived the worst economic recession since independence and thwarted the most dangerous terrorist plot. The determination in tackling these crises, avoiding easy options but insisting on sacrifice for the future good, gained the electorate's approval and earned the respect of foreign observers. At home citizens were prepared to follow the government's lead, despite the hardships. Anti-terrorism measures commanded unanimous support, domestic opposition politics subsided, while erstwhile liberal critics overseas grudgingly admired the republic's vigorous response to its economic woes and security threat and stopped denouncing the Internal Security Act so confidently when their own countries began to adopt protective measures.

༄

When Singapore celebrated its fortieth anniversary of independence in August 2005, it could look back on four decades of remarkable achievement. The seemingly unviable infant republic had not only survived but blossomed into one of the world's wealthiest and most stable nations. Domestic peace had not been marred by any ethnic or religious violence. An energetic executive and efficient civil service governed the state with minimal corruption. The physical transformation of the island was spectacular, with large areas of land reclaimed from the sea, an array of new towns, well-kept housing estates, and an efficient public transport system. No longer dependent on entrepôt trade, Singapore's well-balanced economy was now based on a mix of manufacturing, construction, and service sectors. Twenty-first century Singapore was an important financial centre and a leading international communications hub, with one of the largest container ports in the world and an impressive airport. Enjoying one of the highest standards of living in Asia, the great majority of its people were decently housed and educated. The republic had shed its image as an irritant, "a poisonous prawn", or a parasite battening on its neighbours, to become a co-operative regional player and a force for peace in the world beyond. Helped by the growing experience of a talented diplomatic corps, the "little red dot"[35] punched well above its weight on the international scene.

The population was estimated to number about 4.4 million in 2005, of whom nearly one in five were temporary foreign workers. Of the permanent population, the proportions of the three largest communities had stayed fairly constant since independence: approximately 75 per cent Chinese, 14 per cent Malays and 8 per cent Indian. The remaining 3 per cent comprised Eurasians and a mixture of very small minorities: fluency in English and experience in administration and commerce gave an advantage to the Eurasians, who tended to be middle-class, official, professional, and commercial people in colonial times, but many of the once prominent Armenian, Arab, and Jewish communities emigrated in the early days of independence to countries where they felt more at home.

While differences in race, colour, and religion were of diminishing importance, and loyalty to ancestral homelands overseas had weakened, intermarriage between the different Asian communities was still relatively uncommon, and although the policy of mixing different racial groups in public housing and integrated schools appeared to cause little friction, neighbours of different ethnic background still tended to keep themselves aloof.

The demands of the expanding economy, combined with the low birth rate, accounted for the very large proportion of foreigners, who in 2005 constituted nearly 18 per cent of the total population and almost 30 per cent of the work force. By the early 1980s rapid industrialization and the drive to upgrade workers' skills led to labour shortages and rising wages, which threatened to make Singapore uncompetitive. The government was forced to reverse its family limitation policy and to relax immigration restrictions. From 1987 the inflow of low-skilled and unskilled labour was kept in check by a system of passes and levies on employers. Most low-skilled immigrant workers came from the Philippines, Thailand, or the Indian subcontinent and were employed in manufacturing, construction, and domestic service. The growing sophistication of the Singapore economy also created the need to recruit highly qualified foreign talent, and from the mid-1990s the government devised elaborate arrangements to attract and retain overseas expertise. These ranged from recruitment incentives and housing advantages to favourable terms for acquiring permanent residence status or citizenship. Special efforts were made to attract wealthy businessmen and professional people from Hong Kong in the years leading up to the territory's rendition to China in 1997. By the early twenty-first century immigrants were admitted at all levels, from top-flight experts, managers, and skilled workers, who numbered about 90,000 in 2005, through to unskilled and semi-skilled labourers. Whereas the talented and skilled were welcomed wholeheartedly as desirable residents and potential future Singaporean citizens, the unskilled were tolerated reluctantly as a necessary source of low-paid labour.

At the turn of the century Singapore was a vigorous and healthy but materialistic and not particularly caring society, despite government attempts to instil moral values by promoting religious instruction, and especially Confucianism, in schools. The political leadership spurned the Western welfare state concept and commended the virtues of private philanthropy, filial piety, social discipline and family strength, the duty of children to support their aged parents, and of families caring for their disadvantaged relatives. The state provided the infrastructure of employment, education, a healthy environment, and housing to enable citizens to pull themselves out of poverty by their own efforts, but it felt little obligation to help the handicapped and none at all to support any able-bodied unemployed.

Some groups were left behind in the general rise in prosperity. The plight of neglected immigrant workers – particularly foreign maids – was a major concern to the church workers involved in the "Marxist conspiracy" in the late 1980s. Strict work permit controls prevented abuses of illegal trafficking, but immigrant workers suffered from low wages and inadequate protection from exploitation at the hands of irresponsible employers. The problem of the impoverished elderly citizen was likely to become even more challenging. In principle the Central Provident Fund and Medisave ensured a comfortable retirement and covered medical expenses in old age. Workers were compelled to save substantially throughout their working lives, with employees paying about one-third of their wages into their Central Provident Fund account and employers also making contributions. In practice the sum available on retirement was likely to be substantially reduced, since Central Provident Fund savings could be used to purchase a Housing and Development Board flat, and employers' contributions were cut in times of economic recession. With a life expectancy in 2005 exceeding seventy-nine years for men and eighty-four for women, longevity and inflation added to the complications, making the prospect bleak for men and worse for women, who earned lower wages and were more likely to have breaks in employment because of family responsibilities. Those over sixty-five years of age constituted more than 8 per cent of the population by 2005, and the proportion was set to grow. At one stage Lee Kuan Yew had suggested limiting the ability of the elderly to seek their own interests by giving an extra vote to married working parents between the ages of thirty-five and sixty. A less quaint proposal – but one that would confront the anti-welfare state orthodoxy – was put forward in 2006 by former Nominated MP Dr. Kanwaljit Soin, by then a director of the UK-based HelpAge International, calling for state-funded pensions to be granted to all Singapore citizens over the age of sixty-five.

༘

By the end of the twentieth century, 85 per cent of the land in Singapore was owned by the state, compared with 44 per cent when the PAP first came to power. This comprised Crown land inherited from the colonial government and the British armed forces, coastal reclamation, and land taken over from the private sector under the 1966 Land Acquisition Act. In 2007 that law was amended so that henceforth the full market price would be paid for requisitioned land. By then the major redevelopment schemes had been completed. The Land Acquisition Act had achieved its purpose, facilitating the swift and radical transformation of the island at reasonable cost without causing inflation or land speculation. By the turn of the century the demand for Housing and Development flats had fallen, and the proportion of the population accommodated in public housing began to decline as more people could afford to move up the social ladder and buy private property.

༘

Problems and anomalies remained. Some were endemic: the constrictions of size, a dearth of natural resources, and a shortage of land and water supplies. Others were akin to those of First World countries: an ageing population, a declining birth rate, and a growing gap between rich and poor. A global city state meant constant striving for ever greater growth and exposure to the vagaries of the international economy. Singapore faced also the particular challenge of how to consolidate its sense of national identity and reconcile the form of government with the changing character and rising expectations of the population.

Early twenty-first century Singapore was a nation of incongruities. It was a state with no natural resources but considerable sovereign wealth. The island was already one of the most densely peopled territories in the world, but, in order to maintain the phenomenal economic progress, the republic set an official population target of 5 million and meanwhile relied on temporary immigrant labour to supply almost a third of the work force. The state encouraged citizens to embrace the latest information technology, to upgrade skills, and achieve ever higher standards of education, but at the same time tried to keep them under disciplined control.

In transparency, consultation, and curbing corruption, Singapore fulfilled many of the standards expected of a liberal democracy, and general elections based on universal adult suffrage were held at regular intervals. Despite adopting the rules and practices of its Westminster parent in parliamentary and election procedures, the republic developed its own unique form of parliamentary guided democracy. The "first-past-the-post" system, which in its native habitat was supposed to produce effective government in contests between two fairly equal parties, produced a virtual monopoly of power when transposed to Singapore, where one party invariably won at least 60 per cent of the contested votes and was unopposed in most constituencies.

The government opened many channels of communication, invited discussion, explained its policies, and over the years became more willing to listen to grass-roots opinion, but decisions continued to come from above. The greater freedom of expression given to PAP backbenchers encouraged more lively parliamentary debate but had little impact on changing policy, while political leaders pulled back nervously, declaring out-of-bounds markers in the face of even moderate dissent from the public. According to the official argument, only elected politicians were entitled to set the agenda, since they alone had won a mandate from the electors and were responsible to them. But in some general elections, nearly 40 per cent of the votes were cast against the government, and so many seats were uncontested that a large part of the electorate had no opportunity to vote at all, in effect being disenfranchised, sometimes for years on end. Furthermore, those who did support the PAP did not necessarily agree with each and every aspect of the party's policies.

Parliamentary elections in Singapore were described in the early 1990s as "a stunted political expression",[36] and they continued to move further away from the Westminster model in spirit if not in form. Goh Chok Tong was pleased with the result of linking upgrading public housing to voting support, which was first used in 1997. It certainly secured votes, but the practice distorted the results in several ways: it induced electors to vote in the hope of their own personal gain; it infringed on the principle that MPs had a duty to represent the interests of all constituents, whether they were supporters or not; and it deprived the government of what had once been a useful indication of public opinion. Other means were devised to keep in contact with the electorate and gather information, which became a continuous process and was not confined to election time.

While following the West in her capitalist economy and concern with technology and modernization, the republic rejected competitive politics, individualism, and the concept of the welfare state. The political system drew strong criticism from Western liberals and was sometimes seen as a systematic power-hungry quest for central state control.[37] In many respects it suited the pragmatic nature of Singaporeans and grew naturally out of their Asian and colonial traditions. The electorate and the local press shared an Asian distaste for confrontational or abusive politics, and were prepared to accept authority and show respect towards leaders as long as they were ruling effectively and for the common good. During the heyday of the British colonial era, the constitution of governor, executive, and legislative councils provided a strong, paternal administration, and it was commonly said that the population was quite content to leave their colonial masters to "repair the roads and fix the drains", while they busied themselves making money and looking after family interests. In modern times the electorate was generally prepared to leave the government to take the initiative. There was much grumbling about wanting a greater say in decision-making but little sign of desire for radical change and certainly none for upsetting efficiency and material well-being.

Some topics roused passionate interest from time to time, such as the proposal to levy income tax in 1947, the Great Marriage Debate in 1984, and decriminalizing homosexuality in 2007. But in general Singaporean liberals held back from active engagement in politics, partly deterred by the sort of bitter personal invective that poisoned the 1997 general election campaign, the financial and legal risks, and fears of damaging their careers. It also looked seemingly impossible to dislodge the entrenched party machine, with its hold over power and patronage. Opposition politicians were still divided, only representing the voice of dissent not that of alternative leadership. No party offered a credible alternative or aspired to govern the country. Chiam See Tong's scheme for opposition parties to agree to leave the majority of seats uncontested in order to encourage voters to choose a strong opposition was an admission that the electorate had no wish to vote the ruling party out of office. The government's considerable achievements were generally respected even by its most vocal opponents, who criticized the PAP's style of administration rather than its policies.

Singaporeans were held on a firm rein from their school days through to adult life, with the drive for excellence and perfection in education, in living environment, in workers' skills, and even in culture and manners. The remarkable economic, political, and social evolution induced a feeling of self-confidence in the younger generation that tended to obscure the scale of their leaders' achievements. Memories of hardships and dangers faded, so that some Singaporeans, and especially the young, began to question the restrictions and discipline that irked in easier times. Foreign observers, who often had little appreciation of past events, criticized the authoritarianism of the regime and sometimes belittled its success.

At the same time, Singapore's vulnerability and the dangers of the recent past weighed perhaps too heavily with the old leadership, making them over-fearful for the future and trapped in their own experience of history. Singapore was no longer a collection of divided transient immigrant communities, but a settled prosperous, literate, largely home-owning society, no longer ripe for communism. Communism itself was a waning danger, with Russian and Chinese leaders putting their national interests before any international ideological crusades.

Tight discipline and harsh treatment of individuals seemed out of date in a more relaxed era and could be counterproductive. The prolonged detention of a few left-wing dissidents, long after they could have any subversive influence, and the hounding of individual political opponents who were no real danger seemed spiteful and elevated them to the status of martyrs. The insistence on carrying out sentences passed on convicted foreign nationals – whether Indonesian saboteurs, a Filipina murderess or a teenage American vandal – despite pleas for clemency from their heads of state put the principle of punishing the guilty above cultivating international goodwill. The heavy penalties imposed on overseas journals for alleged interference by publishing irritating articles about Singapore's internal affairs contributed to building up an exaggerated picture of the regime as being far more oppressive than it was in reality for the great majority of Singaporeans. The American dominance of the Internet reflected the critical attitude towards the PAP regime, which had built up in the long-running battle with the Western media.

While they were no longer likely to be subverted by left-wing extremism or the foreign press, Singaporeans remained wary of getting involved in public life. The government called for citizens to take responsibility and participate more positively in local practical affairs. This was designed to keep citizens busily and usefully engaged away from central politics, in contrast to late colonial times when local government was seen as a training ground for self-government and eventual – if far distant – independence. The authorities were keen to promote *gotong-royong*, the spirit of community self-help, to undertake useful charitable welfare, which the state was unwilling to manage or finance, but they were anxious to keep such activities within their purview, and it remained difficult for independent civil society to flourish. It was safer and simpler for citizens to steer clear of any activity that could be construed as controversial, and the deeply ingrained habit of leaving initiative to officialdom developed into apathy.

Intellectuals and academics indulged a certain nostalgia for the lively politics of the mid-twentieth century and for those dedicated and idealistic individuals who were beguiled by radical ideologies and often crushed in struggling for lost causes of culture and language,[38] but for most people the excitement had gone out of domestic politics, the initial flurry of enthusiasm about Speaker's Corner soon died down, and it seemed there were no great issues left to fight. The battles against colonialism, communism, and mass poverty had been won, leaving the majority with no desire for fundamental change.

The PAP did not accept the Westminster concept of a "loyal opposition" that supported the broad national interest even if it attacked the ruling party's policies and sought to take office itself. The confrontational party politics of contemporary Westminster democracy were seen as inefficient at best and often destructive. The nineteenth century English philosopher John Stuart Mill had doubted whether democracy based on universal suffrage could work, since there was no guarantee that the masses would choose leaders who were more intelligent and virtuous than themselves. By the early twenty-first century Western democracies had lost respect for their politicians and subjected them to ridicule. Party rivalry meant short-term politics, with sights set no further than winning the next election and meanwhile constantly pandering to the whims of the electorate. Increasingly Westminster democracy surrounded itself with focus groups, unelected "special advisers" and unaccountable quangos, and found it difficult to devise ways of protecting its citizens without infringing on the personal freedoms that were the foundation of liberal democracy.

In contrast to this the PAP ideal was government by consensus, where rival political parties would be replaced by a single national movement, with respect accorded to wise political leaders and hard-working, incorruptible officials, and all would collaborate in a harmonious partnership of the public and private sectors and the citizenry. Society was more important than individual freedom, and there was no compunction about locking away those who were considered a danger to the community as a whole. Lee Kuan Yew once told Chatham House (the Royal Institute of International Affairs) that, if he did not have to trouble about elections, he could govern people in their own interests,[39] and virtual one-party PAP government had indeed achieved impressive results in Singapore. Confident of maintaining control into the foreseeable future, the government was able to take a long view, to identify future trends, and develop appropriate policies and legislation after wide-ranging study and consultation. Parliamentary committees heard expert opinion and invited citizens to offer suggestions and if necessary "constructive criticism" for improving official policies.

Yet harmony and conformity had their downside. In 2000 Cherian George described "a political sphere that is sterile in both senses of the word – not just antiseptically clean, but devoid of vibrant life".[40] It was a danger the PAP leaders had seen in the early days, and echoed the phrase Goh Keng Swee had used thirty years earlier to complain of "a depressing climate of intellectual sterility" in Singapore.[41]

༄

Lee Hsien Loong's succession marked a crucial stage in the policy of "self-renewal" on which his father had embarked three decades earlier. Anxious to provide for the continued efficient running of the state and to avoid an ageing leadership clinging to power beyond their prime, Lee Kuan Yew had resolved on a systematic process of recruiting young talent to Parliament and choosing men who had been outstandingly successful in their fields to take over ministries. There were murmurings among the old guard against being superseded by untried political novices, and party chairman Toh Chin Chye in particular objected strongly to Lee's strategy, arguing that it was premature and demoralizing to retire the first generation, and that the leaders of the future should fight their own way up the political ladder as the PAP pioneers had done. Lee was ruthless in his determination to push his policy through, and after the 1980 general election he dropped Toh from his Cabinet to stop disaffection spreading among his colleagues.[42] It was a brutal severance. Stalwart organizer of the Malayan Forum, founder member of the PAP and chairman since the party's inception,[43] a Cabinet minister from the time the party first came to power in 1959 and for many years Deputy Prime Minister, Toh had been Lee's vital supporter throughout the many crises in resisting the left-wing radicals, and he was genuinely enthusiastic about the merger with Malaysia. Despite being sorely tried by the break with Kuala Lumpur and the way in which it was done, Toh had remained a loyal Cabinet minister throughout the first fifteen years of independence. Now consigned to the backbenches, he stayed on in Parliament for a further unhappy two terms, finally retiring from politics in 1988.

Over the next two decades the policy of rejuvenation and self-renewal proceeded steadily. By 1988 the last of the old guard retired, to be replaced by the specially recruited second generation of leaders: Goh Chok Tong, Lee Hsien Loong and their contemporaries. At each general election many PAP MPs stood down, and new teams of carefully chosen and groomed candidates were presented. Despite standing to one side as Senior Minister, as the new century dawned Lee remained even more prominently in the picture. Old foes were dead, in exile abroad, or living out their last days quietly in Singapore. Many old friends and allies had also faded from the scene. Goh Keng Swee and Toh Chin Chye lived on in the shadows, long departed from public life, and others had died: Eddie Barker in 2001, Ong Teng Cheong in 2002, former presidents Devan Nair (in Canada) and Wee Kim Wee in 2005, Rajaratnam and Lim Kim San in 2006.

By the first decade of the twenty-first century, Cabinet, Parliament and party combined to exert powerful central control. Lee Kuan Yew remained as Senior Minister and later became

Minister Mentor in a Cabinet composed entirely of his protégés. Parliamentary candidates were selected by the leadership, not by the local party branches, MPs were the government's rather than the people's representatives, and in the party itself the leadership chose the cadres. The political establishment was in effect recreating itself in its own image. Lee Kuan Yew was fulfilling his promise to rise from the grave to set things right. He had created a unique legacy: a structure so strong that it was designed to survive the passing of the architect.

The rapid expansion of tertiary education and rising expectations among the prosperous professional class were creating pressure for more liberal politics, which would undoubtedly grow. The ever-widening contact with the international scene encouraged a more sophisticated élite to resent the constraints of a firmly directed, tightly disciplined society and seek a relaxed and less conformist atmosphere more in keeping with the standards of the twenty-first century. The old security legislation and the long incarceration of political prisoners without trial no longer seemed appropriate for an aspiring First World state. Helped by the expanding influence of women in public life, attitudes were softening towards those unfortunate citizens – and particularly the increasing numbers of the elderly poor – who for no fault of their own did not share in the general rising living standards. There was concern too about the growing disparity between rich and poor, and the feeling that it was becoming more difficult for the disadvantaged to improve their lot. Those who attained merit received very generous rewards, but it was more difficult in modern times for the disadvantaged to gain access to the ladder.

Pressures to relax political life would come up against the deeply entrenched system. Not only was the state organization strong but, as homeowners and holders of Singapore shares, most of the citizenry had a direct stake in preserving the security, stability, and prosperity of the current regime.

Probably neither Western liberal democracy nor Confucian paternalism would be appropriate to meet the challenges of the twenty-first century, but an acceptable "third way" was conceivable. While the public showed little sympathy for Chee Soon Juan's proposals for radical change, there were calls for more consultation. There was no strong demand for a fully fledged welfare state, but only for relaxing the official "fair share, not welfare" slogan to include those who used in times past to be known as "the deserving poor". There was no widespread call to redistribute wealth, provided meritocracy was based on a truly level playing field of opportunity. On the other side, Lee Hsien Loong acknowledged that out-of-bounds markers were not forever embedded in stone and would in time be moved. There was room for compromise on loosening the reins.

The long-term impact of self-renewal is more difficult to assess. The succession of Lee Hsien Loong inevitably brought murmurs about nepotism, but the younger Lee was a man of undoubted commitment and proven ability. More pertinent than the continuity of family was the continuity of mindset, since Lee Hsien Loong was clearly in awe of his remarkable father and in tune with his philosophy. Lee Kuan Yew, as Prime Minister, had started as "the first among equals" in a Cabinet of remarkable individuals, with quite different personalities, abilities, and priorities, who came together and combined their various talents to create the republic. The Prime Ministers of the future could be leaders of like-minded protégés drawn from a self-perpetuating ruling class. While the initial stage of the self-renewal policy was marked by considerable achievement and the state made great strides under the second generation of very able leaders, the question remained whether the policies of the second half of the twentieth century, however brilliantly successful, would be appropriate to cope with the new world of the twenty-first century – the Internet revolution, globalization, international terrorism, and unknown problems to come – or whether a new age will ultimately require an independent challenge and a fresh approach from outside the system.

∽

The ability to adapt to changing circumstances has been a recurring theme throughout Singapore's history and will determine its future. At times in her past Singapore was faced with the prospect of danger and sometimes of extinction. Yet on each occasion the prophets of doom were confounded. According to astrologers, the combination of stars under which modern Singapore was established spelt her lasting good fortune. Throughout her history she was saved by the intelligent and vigorous exploitation of opportunity and by a constant need for delicate balancing and quick wittedness, which continued to serve her well in modern times. Born a precarious outpost of the East India Company, she survived the Company's abolition to be accepted grudgingly as an unwanted crown colony, which blossomed into one of the most important and prosperous ports in the British Empire. She outlived the dissolution of that empire to become, very briefly, the potential New York of the Malaysian Federation, before suffering amputation to be left a seemingly unviable separate nation. The republic's independent existence defied the accepted concepts of twentieth century politics and economics, yet she not only survived but prospered spectacularly.

Singapore entered the new millennium still a place of anomalies: a blend of Confucius and Adam Smith, an authoritarian constitutional democracy, a meritocracy where individual achievement and self-reliance were balanced against obligations to society and the family, a dynamic economy and significant global player, and dedicated to modernization and growth yet seeking to preserve traditional values. Often described by its leaders as an "artificial" or "unnatural" nation, whose only natural resource is its people and their skills, modern Singapore is a city state that can never relax in its adaptability to change.

Notes

Introduction to the First Edition

1. R.O. Winstedt, *Malaya and its History* (London, 1948), p. 61.

Introduction

1. S. Rajaratnam, "The Uses and Abuses of the Past", a paper given at a seminar on Adaptive Re-use: Integrating Traditional Areas into the Modern Urban Fabric, held at the Shangri-La Hotel, Singapore, 28 April 1984, *Speeches*, VIII, 2 (March–April 1984), p. 5.
2. Ibid., p. 6.
3. S. Jayakumar, Minister of State (Law and Home Affairs), "Awareness of our History must be promoted", 21 July 1983, *Speeches*, I, 2 (July–August 1983), p. 62.
4. S. Rajaratnam, Second Deputy Prime Minister (Foreign Affairs), "Life-and-Death Struggle with Communists in 1950s–60s", 18 June 1984, S*peeches*, VIII, 3 (May–June 1984), p. 8.
5. Tay Eng Soon, Minister of State for Education, "The 1950s – Singapore's Tumultuous Years", 18 June 1984, *Speeches*, VIII, 3 (May–June 1984), p. 51.
6. Brig. Gen Lee Hsien Loong (Acting Minister for Trade and Industry), speech in San Francisco, 2 July 1986, *Speeches*, X, 4 (July–August 1986), p. 53.
7. S. Dhanabalan, Minister for Foreign Affairs & Minister for Culture, "Windows into Singapore's Past", 26 May 1984, *Speeches*, VIII, 3 (May–June 1984), p. 33.

8. Ong Pang Boon, "It is necessary to preserve our history", August 1981, *Speeches*, V, 3 (September 1981), pp. 47–48.

9. George Yong-Boon Yeo, Minister for Information and the Arts, 21 August 1993, *Speeches*, XVII, 4 (July–August 1993), p. 58.

10. Examined in detail in Albert Lau, "Nation Building and the Singapore Story", in Wang Gungwu (ed.), *Nation Building: Five Southeast Asian Histories* (Singapore, 2005), pp. 221–50.

11. *Straits Times* (hereafter *ST*), 9 February 1992.

12. K. Hack and K. Blackburn, *Did Singapore Have to Fall? Churchill and the Impregnable Fortress* (London, 2004), p. 179.

13. Goh Chok Tong, Prime Minister, opening the exhibition on 7 July 1998, *Speeches*, XXII, 4 (July–August 1998), p. 2.

14. C.A. Trocki and M.D. Barr (eds.), *Paths Not Taken: Political Pluralism in Postwar Singapore* (Singapore, 2008).

15. For instance, M.H. Murfett, J.N. Miksic, B.P. Farrell and Chiang Ming Shun, *Between Two Oceans: A Military History of Singapore from First Settlement to Final British Withdrawal* (Oxford, 1999); and J.N. Miksic and Cheryl-Ann Low Mei Gek (eds.), *Early Singapore 1300–1819: Evidence in Maps, Text and Artefacts* (Singapore, 2004).

16. Tan Tai Yong, in Aileen Lau and Laura Lau (eds.), *Maritime Heritage of Singapore* (Singapore, 2005), p. xiii.

17. C. Wake, "Raffles and the Rajas: The Founding of Singapore in Malayan and British Colonial History", *JMBRAS*, XLVIII, 1 (1975), pp. 47–73; Ernest C.T. Chew "Who was Singapore's Real Founder?", *Heritage Asia*, III, 1 (Penang, 2005), pp. 20–23.

18. K.J. Leonard, *Wei Yuan and China's Rediscovery of the Maritime World* (Cambridge, MA, 1984).

19. Quoted in ibid., p. 100.

20. Quoted in ibid., p. 135.

21. Yen Ching-hwang, *A Social History of the Chinese in Singapore and Malaya 1800–1911* (Singapore, 1986) had useful information about the early years but a much fuller description about the later nineteenth century.

22. C. Wake, "Raffles and the Rajas: The Founding of Singapore in Malayan and British Colonial History", p. 73.

23. J.F. Warren, *Rickshaw Coolie: A People's History of Singapore (1880–1940)* (Singapore, 1986); J.F. Warren, *Ah Ku and Karayuki-san: Prostitution in Singapore, 1870–1940* (Singapore, 1993).

24. C. Bayly and T.N. Harper, *Forgotten Armies: The Fall of British Asia, 1941–1945* (London, 2004).

25. D.L. Kenley, *New Culture in a New World: The May Fourth Movement and the Chinese Diaspora in Singapore, 1919–1932* (New York, 2003).

26. Yong Ching Fatt and R.B. McKenna, *The Kuomintang Movement in British Malaya, 1912–1949* (Singapore, 1990); Yong Ching Fatt, *Chinese Leadership and Power in Colonial Singapore* (Singapore, 1992); A.H.C. Ward, R.W. Chu and J. Salaff (eds. and trans.), *The Memoirs of Tan Kah Kee* (Singapore, 1994).

27. B.P. Farrell, *The Defence and Fall of Singapore 1940–42* (Stroud, UK, 2005); K. Hack and K. Blackburn, *Did Singapore Have to Fall? Churchill and the Impregnable Fortress* (London and New York, 2004).

28. B.P. Farrell and S. Hunter (eds.), *Sixty Years On: The Fall of Singapore Revisited* (Singapore, 2002).

29. Yoji Akashi, "General Yamashita Tomoyuki: Commander of the 25th Army", in Farrell and Hunter (eds.), *Sixty Years On*, pp. 185–207.

30. Henry Pownall to Churchill, Comments 2 January 1949, Churchill Papers (Churchill Archives, Churchill College, University of Cambridge), CHUR 4/258, pp. 29–30.

31. Louis Allen, *Singapore 1941–1942* (London, 1977; revised edition, London, 1993).

32. Notably the works of Paul H. Kratoska, and in particular his *The Japanese Occupation of Malaya* (London, 1998).

33. K. Blackburn, "Memory of the Sook Ching Massacre and the Creation of the Civilian War Memorial of Singapore", *JMBRAS, LXXIII*, 2 (2000), pp. 71–90.

34. C. Bayly and T.N. Harper, *Forgotten Armies: The Fall of British Asia, 1941–1945* (London, 2004); and *Forgotten Wars: The End of Britain's Asian Empire* (London, 2007).

35. Chin Peng, *My Side of History* (Singapore, 2000).

36. D. Bloodworth, *The Tiger and the Trojan Horse* (Singapore, 1986; 2nd edition 2005).

37. For example C.A. Trocki, *Singapore: Wealth, Power and the Culture of Control* (London & New York, 2006); and the works of Garry Rodan.

38. Lily Zubaidah Rahim, *The Singapore Dilemma: The Political and Educational Marginality of the Malay Community* (Kuala Lumpur, 1998).

39. Ernest C.T. Chew and Edwin Lee (eds.), *A History of Singapore* (Singapore, 1991).

40. Melanie Chew, *Leaders of Singapore* (Singapore, 1996).

41. Barr and Trocki (eds.), *Paths Not Taken*.

42. M.H. Murfett, J.N. Miksic, B.P. Farrell, and Chiang Ming Shun, *Between Two Oceans*.

43. Albert Lau, "The National Past and the Writing of the History of Singapore", in Ban Kah Choon, Anne Pakir and Tong Chee Kiong (eds.), *Imagining Singapore* (Singapore 1992; 2nd edition 1994), p. 64.

44. R. Worthington, *Governance in Singapore* (London & New York, 2003).

1 The New Settlement, 1819–1826

1. J. Miksic and Cheryl Ann Low Mei Gek (eds.), *Early Singapore 1300s–1819: Evidence in Maps, Text and Artefacts* (Singapore, 2004).

2. P. Wheatley, *The Golden Khersonese* (Kuala Lumpur, 1961), p. 152.

3. Hsu Yun-ts'iao, "Notes on Malay Peninsula in Ancient Voyages", *JSSS*, V, 2 (1948), pp. 1–16; Hsu Yun-ts'iao, "The Historical Position of Singapore", in K.G. Tregonning (ed.),

Papers on Malayan History (Singapore, 1962); Hsu Yun-ts'iao, "Singapore in the Remote Past", *JMBRAS*, XLV, 1 (1973), pp. 6–9. Of K'ang T'ai's *The Book of the Native Customs of Funan*, describing his embassy to that country about ad 231, only fragments survive in Sung texts.

4. G.R. Tibbetts, "The Malay Peninsula as known to the Arab Geographers", *Malayan Journal of Tropical Geography*, IX (Singapore, 1956), pp. 40–42; B.F. Colless, "The Ancient History of Singapore", *JSEAH*, X, 1 (1969), pp. 5–7.

5. Ibn Said, quoted in O.W. Wolters, *The Fall of Srivijaya in Malay History* (Ithaca, 1970), p. 11.

6. W.W. Rockhill, "Notes on the Relations and Trade of China with the Eastern Archipelago and the Coast of the Indian Ocean during the Fourteenth Century, Part II", *T'oung Pao*, XVI (Leiden, 1915), pp. 61–159, gives translated excerpts from Wang Ta-Yuan, *Tao-I Chih-lioh* (*Description of the Barbarians of the Isles*) (1349).

7. Derek Heng Thiam Soon, "Economic Networks between the Malay Region and the Hinterlands of Quanzhou and Guangzhou", in Miksic and Low (eds.), *Early Singapore*, pp. 73–86.

8. J. Miksic, "14th-century Singapore: A Port of Trade", in Miksic and Low (eds.), *Early Singapore*, pp. 41–54.

9. A. Cortesao (ed. and trans.), *The Suma Oriental of Tomé Pires*, 2 vols. (London, 1944), II, pp. 231–32.

10. Kwa Chong Guan, in Miksic and Low (eds.), *Early Singapore*, p. 86.

11. P. Borschberg, in Miksic and Low (eds.), *Early Singapore*, p. 107.

12. The two kingdoms were united at this time.

13. P. Borschberg, "Mapping Singapore and Southeast Asia", in Aileen Lau and Laura Lau (eds.), *Maritime Heritage of Singapore* (Singapore, 2005), pp. 43–46.

14. T. Barnard, in Miksic and Low (eds.), *Early Singapore*, pp. 118–23.

15. C. Trocki, *Prince of Pirates* (Singapore, 1979), p. 43, and map on p. 46.

16. P. Borschberg, "The Straits of Singapore" in Irene Lim (ed.) *Sketching the Straits* (Singapore, 2004), pp. 37–44; Kwa Chong Guan, "Sailing Past Singapore", in Miksic and Low (eds.), *Early Singapore*, pp. 95–105. For disputes concerning early sea routes and the possible identification of the Lung-ya-men, or Dragon's Teeth Gate, with the modern Keppel Harbour, see J.V. Mills, "Arab and Chinese Navigators in Malaysian Waters in about A.D. 1500", *JMBRAS*, XLVII, 2 (1974), pp. 1–82; C.A. Gibson-Hill, "Singapore Old Strait and New Harbour, 1300–1870", *Memoirs of the Raffles Museum*, No. 1 (Singapore, 1956), pp. 11–115; C.A. Gibson-Hill, "Singapore: Notes on the History of the Old Strait, 1580–1850", *JMBRAS*, XXVII, 1 (1954), pp. 163–214; R. Braddell, "Lung-ya-men and Tan-ma-hsi", *JMBRAS*, XXIII, 1 (1950), pp. 37–51; reprinted in *JMBRAS*, XLII, 1 (1969), pp. 10–24.

17. Captain Daniel Ross's "Chart of Singapore, February 1819", in John Bastin, *Sir Stamford Raffles's Account of the Founding of Singapore* (Eastbourne, 2004), p. 8.

18. John Crawfurd's eyewitness report from *The Singapore Chronicle* of November 1825; reprinted in J.H. Moor, *Notices of the Indian Archipelago* (Singapore, 1837; reprinted London, 1968), I, pp. 269–71 and Tassin's map opposite, p. 268.

19. D.E. Sopher, "The Sea Nomads", *Memoirs of the National Museum*, No. 5 (Singapore, 1965), p. 105.

20. J.R. Logan, "The Orang Biduanda Kallang of the River Pulai in Johore", *JIA*, I (1847), pp. 299–302; J.R. Logan, "The Orang Sletar of the Rivers and Creeks of the Old Strait and Estuary of the Johore", *JIA*, I (1847), p. 302; J.T. Thomson, "Remarks on the Seletar and Sabimba Tribes", *JIA*, I (1847), pp. 342–44; W.W. Skeat and H.N. Ridley, "The Orang Laut of Singapore", *JMBRAS*, XXXIII (1900), pp. 247–50, reprinted *JMBRAS*, XLII, 1 (1969), pp. 114–16.

21. W. Hartley, "Population of Singapore in 1819", *JMBRAS*, XI, 2 (1933), p. 177; reprinted *JMBRAS*, XLII, 1 (1969), pp. 112–13.

22. J.R. Logan, "The Piracy and Slave Trade of the Indian Archipelago", *JIA*, III (1849), p. 632.

23. Quoted in John Bastin, *William Farquhar First Resident and Commandant of Singapore* (Eastbourne, 2005), pp. 22–23.

24. Chief Secretary to Raffles, 28 November 1818, reprinted in Bastin, *Sir Stamford Raffles's Account of the Founding of Singapore* (Eastbourne, 2004), p. 46.

25. Supplementary instructions, Chief Secretary to Raffles, 5 December 1818, reprinted in Bastin, *Raffles's Account*, pp. 48–49.

26. Bastin, *Raffles's Account*, p. 13.

27. Raffles to Farquhar, 16 January 1819, quoted in John Bastin, *William Farquhar*, p. 23. Instructions reprinted in full, in Bastin, *Raffles's Account*, pp. 16–19.

28. Captain Daniel Ross (1780–1849), the son of a prosperous Scottish planter in Jamaica and a freed quadroon slave, Ross joined the East India Company's navy at the age of fourteen, spent many years surveying the South China coast, Macau, and Hong Kong, and eventually rose to be the Company's Marine Surveyor General in 1823.

29. Raffles's despatch to the Governor-General of 13 February 1819, reproduced in John Bastin, *Sir Stamford Raffles's Account of the Founding of Singapore* (Eastbourne, 2004), Preface and pp. 24–25, shows that the first landing was made on the evening of 28 January and not the morning of 29 as hitherto accepted.

30. R.O. Winstedt, "Abdul-Jalil, Sultan of Johore (1966–1719), 'Abdu'l Jamal, Temenggong (ca) 1750, and Raffles' Founding of Singapore", *JMBRAS*, XI, 2 (1933), p. 165.

31. John Bastin draws attention to Raffles's report on this expedition, in *Sir Stamford Raffles's Account*, Preface and p. 31.

32. J.A.E. Morley, "The Arabs and the Eastern Trade", *JMBRAS*, XXII, 1 (1949), p. 155.

33. A.H. Hill (ed. and trans.), "Hikayat Abdullah", *JMBRAS*, XXVII, 3 (1955), p. 142; reprinted Kuala Lumpur, 1970.

34. J. Bastin (ed.), "The Journal of Thomas Otho Travels, 1813–1820", *Memoirs of the Raffles Museum*, No. 4 (Singapore, 1957), pp. 142–56.

35. The reconstruction and layout are described and illustrated in H.F. Pearson, "Singapore from the Sea, June 1823", *JMBRAS*, XXVI, 1 (1953), pp. 43–55; reprinted *JMBRAS*, XLII, 1 (1969), pp. 133–44; and "Lt. Jackson's Plan of Singapore", *JMBRAS*, XXVI, 1 (1953), pp. 200–4; reprinted *JMBRAS*, XLII, 1 (1969), pp. 161–65.

36. C.M. Turnbull, "John Crawfurd" in *Oxford Dictionary of National Biography* (Oxford, 2004), Vol. 14, pp. 90–2.

37. *Singapore Chronicle*, 8 April 1830.

38. Raffles to Minto, in 1811, quoted in Syed Mohd Khairudin Aljunied, *Raffles and Religion: A Study of Sir Thomas Stamford Raffles's Discourse on Religion among the Malays* (Kuala Lumpur, 2004), p. 17.

39. W. Milburn, *Oriental Commerce*, 2 vols. (London, 1813), I, p. 320.

40. The text is given in Buckley, pp. 106–7, and is also to be found in IOL, Raffles to Government of India, 7 June 1823, Enclosures to Secret Letters from Bengal (12 March 1824), L/P&S/5/103.

41. Roderick MacLean, *A Pattern of Change: The Singapore International Chamber of Commerce from 1837* (Singapore, 2000), p. 17.

42. H.E. Miller (trans.), "Extracts from the Letters of Col. Nahuijs", *JMBRAS*, XIX, 2 (1941), p. 195.

43. Advocate General to Secretary to Government of India, 16 August and 13 October 1823, IOL, L/P&S/5/103, No. 9 (12 March 1824).

44. Crawfurd to India, 10 January 1824 & Secretary to Government of India to Crawfurd, 5 March 1824, IOL, L/P&S/5/103, No. 9 (12 March 1824).

45. Crawfurd to India, 3 August 1824, P/BEN/SEC/328, no. 9 (4 March 1825); reprinted in full, Braddell, "Notices", *JIA*, VII (1853) pp. 350–54; Buckley, pp. 170–73. Text of treaty in J.

de Vere Allen, A.J. Stockwell and L.R. Wright, *A Collection of Treaties and other Documents affecting the States of Malaysia, 1761–1963*, 2 vols. (London, 1981), pp. 30–32.

46. Text of the Anglo-Dutch Treaty in Allen, Stockwell and Wright, *Treaties*, I, pp. 288–93; Article XII on Singapore and the Riau-Lingga archipelago, p. 291.

47. Directors to Bengal, 4 August 1824, F/4/878, Board Collections, 1826–27. B.C. 22996, December 1825.

48. Crawfurd to Sec to Govt, Fort William, 1 October 1824, P/BEN/SEC/328 & B.C. 23009, p. 4.

49. Sec to Govt to Crawfurd, 4 March 1825, IOL, P/BEN/SEC/328.

2 "This Spirited and Splendid Little Colony", 1826–1867

1. J. Kathirithamby-Wells, "Early Singapore and the Inception of a British Administrative Tradition in the Straits Settlements (1819–1832)", *JMBRAS*, XLII, 2 (1969), pp. 48–73, deals with early administration in Singapore.

2. J.R. Logan, "The Orang Binua of Johore", *JIA*, 1 (1847), p. 300.

3. C.A. Gibson-Hill, "The Orang Laut of the Singapore River and the Sampan Panjang", *JMBRAS*, XXV, 1 (1952), pp. 161–74; reprinted *JMBRAS*, XLII, 1 (1969), pp. 118–32.

4. N.H. Wright, *Respected Citizens: The History of the Armenians in Singapore and Malaysia* (Victoria, Australia, 2003), p. 45.

5. J. Crawfurd, *Journal of an Embassy from the Governor General of India to the Courts of Siam and Cochin China*, 2 vols. (London, 1828; reprinted Kuala Lumpur, 1967), II, p. 383.

6. Sharom Ahmat, "American Trade with Singapore, 1819–65", *JMBRAS*, XXXVIII, 2 (1965), pp. 241–57; Sharom Ahmat, "Joseph Balestier: The First American Consul in Singapore, 1833–52", *JMBRAS*, XXXIX, 2 (1966), pp. 108–22.

7. *ST*, 10 January 1865.

8. *Singapore Free Press* (hereafter *SFP*), 6 January 1854.

9. For the construction of Horsburgh Lighthouse see J.T. Thomson, "Account of the Horsburgh Lighthouse", *JIA*, VI (1852), pp. 376–498, and J.A.L. Pavitt, *First Pharos of the Eastern Seas: Horsburgh Lighthouse* (Singapore, 1966).

10. F. Pridmore, "Coins and Coinages of the Straits Settlements and British Malaya, 1786 to 1951", *Memoirs of the Raffles Museum*, No. 2 (Singapore, 1955), pp. 28–40; C.H. Dakers, "Some Copper Tokens in the Raffles Museum, Singapore", *JMBRAS*, XV, 2 (1937), pp. 127–29; E. Wodak, "Some Coins and Tokens of Malaya", *JMBRAS*, XXIII, 3 (1950), pp. 143–47.

11. "Oriental Pirates", *United Service Journal*, III (1835), pp. 31–42; "The Malay Pirates", *United Service Journal*, I (1837), pp. 450–65; E.G. Festing (ed.), *Life of Commander Henry James, R.N.* (London, 1899), p. 262.

12. J.R. Logan, "The Piracy and Slave Trade of the Indian Archipelago", *JIA*, IV (1850), p. 145.

13. *SFP*, 17 March 1854.

14. *SFP*, 18 January 1866. H. Miller, *Pirates of the Far East* (London, 1970) gives a readable general account of piracy in the region.

15. G.F. Davidson, *Trade and Travel in the Far East* (London, 1846), p. 69.

16. Quoted in *SFP*, 6 August 1852.

17. J.R. Logan, "Sago", *JIA*, III (1849), pp. 288–313.

18. J. Cameron, *Our Tropical Possessions in Malayan India* (London, 1865; reprinted Kuala Lumpur, 1965), p. 168.

19. J.T. Thomson, "General Report on the Residency of Singapore Drawn up Principally with a View of Illustrating Its Agricultural Statistics", *JIA*, III (1849), pp. 618–28, 744–55, IV (1850), pp. 27–41, 102–6, 134–43, 206–19; J. Balestier, "View of the State of Agriculture in the British Possessions in the Straits of Malacca", *JIA*, II (1848), pp. 139–50; T. Oxley, "Some Account of the Nutmeg and Its Cultivation", *JIA*, II (1848), pp. 641–60; J. Crawfurd, "Agriculture of Singapore",

JIA, III (1849), pp. 508–11, reprinted from *Singapore Chronicles*, 1824.

20. J.C. Jackson, *Planters and Speculators: Chinese and European Agricultural Enterprise in Malaya, 1786–1921* (Kuala Lumpur, 1968), pp. 7–30; J.C. Jackson, "Chinese Agricultural Pioneering in Singapore and Johore", *JMBRAS*, XXXVIII, 1 (1965), pp. 77–105; P. Wheatley, "Land Use in the Vicinity of Singapore in the 1830s", *Malayan Journal of Tropical Geography*, II (Singapore, 1954), pp. 63–66.

21. C.M. Turnbull, "The Johore Gambier and Pepper Trade in the Mid-nineteenth Century", *JSSS*, XV, 1 (1959), pp. 43–55.

22. E.A. Brown, *Indiscreet Memories* (London, 1935), pp. 257–58.

23. G.W. Earl, *The Eastern Seas* (London, 1837; reprinted Kuala Lumpur, 1971), p. 145.

24. Munshi Abdullah bin Abdul Kadir gave an eyewitness description of the 1830 fire in *Shaer Singapura Terbakar* and of the 1847 fire in "Shaer Kampong Gelam Terbakar oleh Abdullah b. Abdul-Kadir", romanized version, edited with notes by C. Skinner, *JMBRAS*, XLV, 1 (1972), pp. 21–56.

25. K.S. Sandhu, "Tamil and Other Indian Convicts in the Straits Settlements. A.D. 1790–1873", *Proceedings of the First International Conference Seminar of Tamil Studies, Kuala Lumpur, Malaysia, 1966* (Kuala Lumpur, 1968), I, pp. 197–208; C.M. Turnbull, "Convicts in the Straits Settlements, 1826–1867", *JMBRAS*, XLIII, 1 (1970), pp. 87–103.

26. J.P. Mialaret, *Hinduism in Singapore* (Singapore, 1969) describes the Hindu temples of Singapore and their past history.

27. B.W. Hodder, "Racial Groupings in Singapore", *Malayan Journal of Tropical Geography*, I (Singapore, 1953), pp. 25–36.

28. C.A. Gibson-Hill, "Singapore Old Strait and New Harbour, 1300–1870", *Memoirs of the Raffles Museum*, No. 3 (Singapore, 1956), pp. 11–115; C.A. Gibson-Hill, "Singapore: Notes on the History of the Old Strait, 1580–1850", *JMBRAS*, XXVIL, 1 (1954), pp. 163–214; and C.D. Cowan, "New Harbour,

Singapore and the Cruise of H.M.S. "Maeander", 1848–49", *JMBRAS*, XXXVIII, 2 (1965), pp. 229–40, discuss the development of New Harbour.

29. J. Crawfurd, "Remarks on the Revenue", 21 October 1825, *JIA*, VIII (1854), p. 414.
30. SSR, H13, 24 December 1824.
31. R. MacLean, *A Pattern of Change* (Singapore, 2000).
32. G.W. Earl, *The Eastern Seas*, p. 383.
33. M. Freedman, *Lineage Organisation in Southeastern China* (London, 1958) and M. Freedman, *Chinese Lineage and Society: Fukien and Kwangtung* (London, 1966), provide valuable background studies.
34. Yen Ching-hwang, *A Social History of the Chinese in Singapore and Malaya 1800–1911* (Singapore, 1986), p. 177.
35. Yen, *Social History*, p. 42.
36. Yen Ching-hwang, *Coolies and Mandarins: China's Protection of Overseas Chinese During the Late Ch'ing Period 1851–1911* (Singapore, 1985); and Yen, *Social History*, p. 112.
37. Yen, *Social History*, p. 113.
38. SSR, R17, pp. 65–66.
39. SSR, V37, p. 155.
40. See vivid descriptions in J.T. Thomson, *Some Glimpses into Life in the Far East* (London, 1864); reprinted as *Glimpses into Life In Malayan Lands* (Singapore, 1984), pp. 307–11; H. Keppel, *A Sailor's Life under Four Sovereigns*, 3 vols. (London, 1899), III, p. 13.
41. *ST*, 21 December 1869.
42. L. Oliphant, *Narrative of the Earl of Stain's Mission to China and Japan*, 1 vols. (Edinburgh and London, 1859; reprinted Kuala Lumpur, 1970).
43. *SFP*, 29 December 1859.
44. *SFP*, 25 July 1851.
45. *SFP*, 21 July 1854.
46. RC Penang to Governor, 26 June 1861, SSR, DD 34, Item 86.
47. Belcher, *Voyage of the Samarang*, II, pp. 184–85.
48. SSR, W27, Item 231A.

49. C.K. Byrd, *Early Printing in the Straits Settlements, 1806–58* (Singapore, 1971), pp. 13–17.

50. Annual Report on the Administration of the Straits Settlements for 1862–63.

51. Y.K. Lee, "Medical Education in the Straits, 1786–1871", *JMBRAS*, XLVI, 1 (1973), pp. 101–22.

52. *ST*, 17 August 1861.

53. *SFP*, 29 March 1849.

54. SSR, S25, Item I 52.

55. R. Little, "On the Habitual Use of Opium in Singapore", *JIA*, II (1848), pp. 1–79; T. Braddell, "Gambling and Opium Smoking In the Straits of Malacca", *JIA*, New Series, I (1857), pp. 66–83.

56. Cheng U Wen, "Opium in the Straits Settlements", *JSEAH*, II (1961); Carl A. Trocki, *Opium and Empire* (Ithaca, 1990).

57. SSR, V37, p. 52; SSR, W46, Item 247.

58. *ST*, 18 June 1864.

59. F.S. Marryat, *Borneo and the Indian Archipelago* (London, 1848), p. 213; E. Belcher, *Narrative of the Voyage of H.M.S. "Samarang" during the Years 1843–6*, 2 vols. (London, 1848), II, pp. 179–80; J.D. Ross, *Sixty Years: Life and Adventure in the Far East*, 2 vols. (London, 1911; reprinted London, 1968), I, pp. 58–59.

60. F.S. Marryat, *Borneo and the Indian Archipelago* (London, 1848), pp. 213–18.

61. *ST*, 14 January 1865.

62. *SFP*, 3 October 1851.

63. Correspondent "ZZ" to *SFP*, November 1850.

64. C.A. Gibson-Hill, "The Singapore Chronicle, 1824–37", *JMBRAS*, XXVI, 1 (1953), pp. 175–99.

65. Y.K. Lee, "The Grand Jury in Early Singapore, 1819–1873", *JMBRAS*, XLVI, 2 (1973), pp. 55–150.

66. *ST*, 3 July and 7 August 1855.

67. *SFP*, 14 May 1857; C.M. Turnbull, "Communal Disturbances in the Straits Settlements in 1857", *JMBRAS*, XXXI, 1 (1958), pp. 96–146.

68. SSR, W25, Item 339; *ST*, 7 July 1857; *SFP*, 23 July 1857.
69. *SFP*, 17 September 1857; *ST*, 22 September 1857.
70. *PP*, 1862, xl (H. of C.), 259, pp. 585–88.
71. *PG*, 19, 26 September, 10 October; in *SFP*, 1, 8, 22 October 1857.
72. CO correspondence and minutes, 7–10 July 1860, CO 144/18.
73. *PP*, 1861, XIII, No. 423, pp. 69–373.
74. J. Cameron, Our Tropical Possessions in Malayan India, p. 48.

3 High Noon of Empire, 1867–1914

1. Ord to Parker (CO), 6 July 1866, Carnarvon Papers, PRO 30/6 (The National Archives, London).
2. *London and China Telegraph*, 26 January 1867.
3. *ST*, 21 March 1867.
4. For a satirical sketch of these early years see G. Dana, *Letters of "Extinguisher" and Chronicles of St. George* (Singapore, 1870).
5. Ord to CO, 15 July 1867, GD 1, No. 61.
6. COD 2, No. 71.
7. For early colonial impressions about the inefficiency of the Indian administrative system, see A. Anson, *About Others and Myself* (London, 1920).
8. Legislative Council minutes, 18 December 1867, 1 E 1, p. 41.
9. Minutes of meeting to form the Straits Settlements Association in Napier to Buckingham, 7 February 1868, in Buckingham to Ord, 17 February 1868, COD 3, No. 27.
10. Straits Settlements Association, *Memorandum Regarding the Government of the Straits Settlements*, 26 April 1869, in S. of S. to Ord, 1 June 1869, COD 7, No. 95.
11. P.C. Campbell, *Chinese Coolie Emigration to Countries Within the British Empire* (London, 1923; reprinted London, 1971), pp. 6–7.
12. S. of S. to Ord, 1868, COD 4, Nos. 77, 99, 119, and 166.
13. *ST*, 15 September 1873; CO 273/70, Nos. 290 and 291.
14. *SFP*, 24 April 1936.

15. *ST*, 12 January 1874.

16. Extract of report of 1 January 1873, in CO to Ord, 11 June 1873, COD/C 5.

17. Lim Joo Hock, "Chinese Female Immigration into the Straits Settlements, 1860–1901", *JSSS*, XXII, 2 (1967), pp. 58–110.

18. R.N. Jackson, *Pickering: Protector of Chinese* (Kuala Lumpur, 1965), p. 97.

19. Quoted in Ng Siew Yoong, "The Chinese Protectorate in Singapore, 1877–1900", *JSEAH*, II (1961), p. 95.

20. Wong Lin Ken, *The Malayan Tin Industry to 1914* (Arizona, 1965).

21. K.G. Tregonning, *Straits Tin: A Brief Account of the First Seventy-five Years of the Strait Trading Company Ltd., 1887–1962* (Singapore, 1962).

22. J.H. Drabble, *Rubber in Malaya, 1876–1922* (Kuala Lumpur, 1973).

23. Chiang Hai Ding, "The Origin of the Malayan Currency System", *JMBRAS*, XXXIX, 1 (1966), pp. 1–18; W.A. Shaw and Mohammed Kassim Haji Ali, *Paper Currency of Malaysia, Singapore and Brunei, 1849–1970* (Kuala Lumpur, 1971); and F. Pridmore, "Coins and Coinages of the Straits Settlements and British Malaya, 1786 to 1951", *Memoirs of the Raffles Museum*, No. 2 (Singapore, 1955).

24. *ST*, 16 May 1872.

25. The history of the firm of Guthrie is told in S. Cunyngham-Brown, *The Traders* (London, 1970).

26. B. Cable, *A Hundred-Year History of the P. & O. (Peninsular and Oriental Steam Navigation Company), 1837–1937* (London, 1937).

27. G. Blake, *The Ben Line, 1825–1955* (London, 1956).

28. E. Jennings, *Mansfields: Transport and Distribution in Southeast Asia* (Singapore, 1973). The early struggles of the firm are poignantly described in the "Diary of George John Mansfield, 1863–1866", MSS Ind. Ocn. r 11 (Rhodes House, Oxford).

29. R. Kipling, "The Song of the Cities", in *The Seven Seas* (London, 1896), p. 175.

30. Quoted in J. Morris, *Pax Britannica* (London, 1968), p. 148.
31. See Yip Yat Hoong, *The Development of the Tin Mining Industry of Malaya* (Kuala Lumpur, 1969).
32. Philip Loh Fook Seng, *The Malay States: Political Change and Social Policy, 1877–1895* (Kuala Lumpur, 1969), pp. 104–5.
33. *PG*, 20 August 1908.
34. *PG*, 7 June 1906.
35. W.R. Roff, *The Origins of Malay Nationalism* (New Haven and Kuala Lumpur, 1967), p. 37.
36. Ibid., p. 35.
37. I.L. Bird, *The Golden Chersonese and the Way Thither* (New York, 1883; reprinted Kuala Lumpur, 1967), p. 119.
38. E.W. Birch, "The Vernacular Press in the Straits", *JMBRAS*, IV (1879), pp. 51–55, reprinted in *JMBRAS*, XLII, 1 (1969), pp. 192–95; W.R. Roff, *Guide to Malay Periodicals, 1876–1941* (Singapore, 1961).
39. Yen Ching-hwang, *A Social History of the Chinese in Singapore and Malaya 1800–1911* (Singapore, 1986), pp. 178–79.
40. Tan Jiak Kim, Lim Boon Keng and Song Ong Siang (eds.), *Duty to the British Empire during the Great War* (Singapore, 1915).
41. C.E. Ferguson-Davie (ed.), *In Rubber Lands* (London, 1921).
42. F. Caddy, *To Siam and Malaya in the Duke of Sutherland's Yacht "Sans Peur"* (London, 1889), p. 84.
43. J.B. Elcum, Director of Public Instruction, in *Straits Settlements Annual Report for 1906*.
44. Yen, *Social History*, pp. 287–89.
45. Yen Ching-hwang, "Ch'ing's Sale of Honours and the Chinese Leadership in Singapore and Malaya, 1877–1912", *JSEAS*, I, 2 (1970), pp. 20–32; M.R. Godley, "The Late Ch'ing Courtship of the Chinese in Southeast Asia", *JAS*, XXIV, 2 (1975), pp. 361–65.
46. Wu Lieh-teh, *Plague Fighter: The Autobiography of a Modern Chinese Physician* (Cambridge, 1959).
47. Wang Gungwu, "Sun Yat-sen and Singapore", *JSSS*, XV, 2 (1959), pp. 55–68.

48. Yen Ching-hwang, *The Overseas Chinese and the 1911 Revolution* (Kuala Lumpur, 1976), p. 55–56.

49. Yong Ching Fatt, *Chinese Leadership and Power in Colonial Singapore* (Singapore, 1992).

50. H.Z. Schiffrin, *Sun Yat-sen and the Origins of the Chinese Revolution* (California, 1968). The early revolutionary movement in Singapore is discussed in Png Poh Seng, "The KMT in Malaya", *JSEAH*, II, 1 (1961), pp. 1–32; and in K.G. Tregonning (ed.), *Papers on Malayan History* (Singapore, 1962), pp. 214–25.

51. *ST*, 25 January 1912.

52. Discussed in Yong Ching Fatt, "A Preliminary Study of Chinese Leadership in Singapore, 1900–41", *JSEAH*, IX, 2 (1968), pp. 258–85.

53. W. Feldwick (ed.), *Present Day Impressions of the Far East and Prominent and Progressive Chinese at Home and Abroad* (London, 1917), pp. 836–37.

54. Gov. to S. of S., 19 September 1887, GD 25.

55. Caddy, *To Siam and Malaya*, p. 227.

56. H. Norman, *The People and Politics of the Far East* (London, 1895).

57. E.A. Brown, *Indiscreet Memories* (London, 1935), p. 17.

58. K.G. Tregonning, *The Singapore Cold Storage, 1903–1966* (Singapore, 1966).

59. Chan Kwok Bun and Tong Chee Kiong (eds.), *Past Times: A Social History of Singapore* (Singapore, 2003), p. 141.

60. Y.K. Lee, "A short history of K.K. Hospital and the maternity services of Singapore", *Singapore Medical Journal*, XXX (1990), pp. 599–613; Chan Kwok Bun and Tong Chee Kiong, *Past Times*, p. 76.

61. C.A. Trocki, *Opium and Empire: Chinese Society in Colonial Singapore, 1800–1910* (Ithaca, 1990), p. 210.

62. E. Wijeysingha, *A History of Raffles Institution, 1823–1963* (Singapore, 1963), pp. 83–107.

63. C.M. Turnbull, *Dateline Singapore: 150 Years of the Straits Times* (Singapore, 1995).

64. Zainal Abidin bin Ahmad (Za'ba), "Malay Journalism in Malaya", *JMBRAS*, XIX, 2 (1941), pp. 244–50; W.R. Roff, *Bibliography of Malay and Arabic Periodicals in the Straits Settlements and Peninsular Malay States, 1876–1941* (London, 1972).

65. Chen Mong Hock, *The Early Chinese Newspapers of Singapore, 1881–1912* (Singapore, 1967), p. 52.

66. *Straits Settlements Legislative Council Proceedings*, 13 February 1890, GD 28, 19 February 1890.

67. Quoted in A. Lovat, *The Life of Sir Frederick Weld* (London, 1914), p. 383.

68. A. Wright and H.A. Cartwright, *Twentieth Century Impressions of British Malaya* (London, 1908), p. 49.

69. A. Wright and T.H. Reid, *The Malay Peninsula*: A Record of Progress in the Middle East (London, 1912), p. 236.

4 "The Clapham Junction of the Eastern Seas", 1914–1941

1. F. Swettenham, *British Malaya* (London, 1948; reprinted London, 1955), p. 142.

2. See T.M. Winsley, *A History of the Singapore Volunteer Corps* (Singapore, 1937).

3. For example journalist Tsukada, quoted in M.H. Murfett, J.N. Miksic, B.P. Farrell and Chiang Ming Shun, *Between Two Oceans: A Military History of Singapore* (Oxford, 1999), pp. 135–36.

4. Sho Kuwaijima, *The Mutiny in Singapore* (New Delhi, 2006), pp. 9–10.

5. Quoted in F.M. Luscombe, *Singapore, 1819–1930* (Singapore, 1930), p. 66.

6. Yong Ching Fatt, *Chinese Leadership and Power in Colonial Singapore* (Singapore, 1992).

7. J.F. Warren, *Rickshaw Coolie: A People's History of Singapore, (1880–1940)* (Singapore, 1986), p. 114.

8. Discussed in Y. Akashi, "The Nanyang Chinese Anti-Japanese and Boycott Movement, 1908–1928", *JSSS*, XXIII, 2 (1968), pp. 89–96.

9. A.H.C. Ward, Raymond W. Chu and Janet Salaff (eds. and trans.), *The Memoirs of Tan Kah Kee* (Singapore, 1994).

10. Yong Ching Fatt, *Chinese Leadership*, p. 203.

11. C.M. Turnbull, "Sir Cecil Clementi and Malaya: The Hong Kong Connection", *Journal of Oriental Studies* (University of Hong Kong), 22, no. 1 (1984), pp. 33–60.

12. J.N. Parmer, *Colonial Labor Policy and Administration: A History of Labor in the Rubber Plantation Industry in Malaya, 1910–1941* (New York, 1960), p. 93.

13. Naosaku Uchida, *The Overseas Chinese* (Stanford, 1959), p. 48; Tan Ee Leong, "The Chinese Banks Incorporated in Singapore and the Federation of Malaya", *JMBRAS*, XXVI, I (1953), pp. 113–39; reprinted in *JMBRAS*, XLII, 1 (1969), pp. 256–81; D. Wilson (assisted by S.Y. Lee and others), *Solid as a Rock: The First Forty Years of the Oversea Chinese Banking Corporation* (Singapore, 1972).

14. R.H. de S. Onraet, *Singapore: A Police Background* (London, 1947), p. 33.

15. Manicasothy Saravanamutu, *The Sara Saga* (Penang, 1970), p. 48.

16. *ST*, 16 July 1934.

17. M. Saravanamutu, *The Sara Saga*, p. 54.

18. Vividly revealed in James Warren's accounts of rickshaw pullers (*Rickshaw Coolie* [Singapore, 1986]), and prostitutes (*Ah Ku and Karayuki-san: Prostitution Singapore* [Singapore, 1993]).

19. M. Freedman, "Colonial Law and Chinese Society", *Journal of the Royal Anthropological Institute*, LXXX (1950), pp. 114–15; W. Woods and C.A. Wills, *Report of the Commission on Mui Tsai in Hong Kong and Malaya* (London, 1937); E. Picton-Turbervill, *Report of the Commission on Mui Tsai in Hong Kong and Malaya* (London, 1937) (minority report).

20. Chu Tee Seng, "The Singapore Chinese Protectorate, 1900–1941", *JSSS*, XXVI, 1 (1971), pp. 5–45.

21. Colonial Office, *Higher Education in Malaya: Report of the Commission appointed by the Secretary of State for the Colonies, June 1939* (London, 1939) (the McLean Report).

22. T.R. Doraisamy (ed.), *150 Years of Education in Singapore* (Singapore, 1969), p. 38.

23. C.M. Turnbull, *Dateline Singapore: 150 Years of the Straits Times* (Singapore, 1995), p. 96.

24. See Radin Soenamo, "Malay Nationalism, 1900–45", *JSEAH*, I, 1 (1960), pp. 9–11.

25. Chen Ta, *Immigrant Communities in South China: A Study of Overseas Migration and Its Influence on Standards of Living and Social Change* (Shanghai, 1939; and New York, 1940), p. 118.

26. C.M. Turnbull, "The Malayan Connection", in Lau Chan Kit Ching and P. Cunich (ed.), *An Impossible Dream* (Hong Kong, 2002), p. 99.

27. Y. Akashi, *The Nanyang Chinese Anti-Japanese National Salvation Movement, 1937–41* (Kansas, 1970), p. 74.

28. Described in R.O. Winstedt, *The Constitution of the Colony of the Straits Settlements and of the Federated and Unfederated Malay States* (Royal Institute of International Affairs, London, 1931); and War Office, *Malaya and Its Civil Administration Prior to the Japanese Occupation* (London, 1944).

29. L. Guillemard, *Trivial Fond Records* (London, 1937), p. 99.

30. Report of Brigadier General Sir Samuel Wilson, G.C.M.G., K.C.B., K.B.E., *Permanent Undersecretary of State for the Colonies on His Visit to Malaya 1932* (London, 1933).

31. A. Wright and T.H. Reid, *The Malay Peninsula: A Record of Progress in the Middle East* (London, 1912), p. 232.

32. W. Churchill to Guillemard, 24 June 1922, CO 273/510, quoted in Yeo Kim Wah, *Political Development in Singapore, 1945–1955* (Singapore, 1973).

33. *ST*, 14 November 1930.

34. President's speech, annual general meeting, *Association of British Malaya Minute Books*, I, 26 July 1922.

35. Annual report for 1926–27, *Association of British Malaya Minute Books*, II.
36. A. Scott-Ross, *Tun Dato Sir Cheng Lock Tan* (Singapore, 1990) is a "personal profile" by his daughter; Tan Cheng Lock's career is discussed in Soh Eng Lim, "Tan Cheng Lock", *JSEAH*, I, 1 (1960), pp. 29–55.
37. *Proceedings of the Straits Settlements Legislative Council*, 1928, pp. 147–48.
38. Printed also in *ST*, 23 December 1932.
39. Arthur Creech-Jones Papers, Rhodes House, MSS Brit. Emp. S 332, Box 26, File 11.
40. *Malaya Tribune*, 20 December 1930.
41. R. Emerson, *Malaysia: A Study in Direct and Indirect Rule* (New York, 1937; reprinted Kuala Lumpur, 1964), p. 287.
42. Ibid., p. 306.
43. Ibid., p. 519.

5 War in the East, 1941–1942

1. J. Neidpath, *The Singapore Naval Base and the Defence of Britain's Eastern Empire 1919–1941* (Oxford, 1981), pp. 153–54.
2. General Sir Ian Hamilton, *The Times*, London, 24 March 1924, quoted in L. Wigmore, *Australia in the War: The Japanese Thrust* (Canberra, 1957), p. 3 .
3. *Sydney Morning Herald*, 14 February 1938, quoted in Wigmore, *Australia in War*, p. 47.
4. John Gunther, *Inside Asia* (London, 1939), who according to Fujii, editor of the (Japanese owned) *Singapore Herald*, was "prize fool of them all".
5. Extract from Malaya Combined Intelligence Summary, No. 8/1940, October 1940, in CO 273/666, 50336.
6. D. Russell-Roberts, *Spotlight on Singapore* (London, 1965), p. 29.
7. *SFP*, 7 January 1941.

8. Although the Netherlands was occupied by Nazi Germany at this time, the London-based Dutch government-in-exile continued to administer the Netherlands East Indies.

9. J.H. Brimmell, *Communism in South East Asia* (London, 1959), p. 148.

10. *Malaya Tribune*, 5 May 1939.

11. S. of S. to Governor, 28 February 1941, CO 273/668, 50695/41.

12. Virginia Thompson, "Japan Frozen out of British Malaya", *Far Eastern Survey*, X, 20 (20 October 1941), p. 238.

13. W. Churchill, *The Grand Alliance*, III, p. 522.

14. C. Brown, *Suez to Singapore* (New York, 1942), p. 280.

15. M. Shinozaki, *My Wartime Experiences in Singapore* (Singapore, 1973), p. 5.

16. Yamashita's diary, 3 January 1942, in Yoji Akashi, "General Yamashita Tomoyuki: Commander of the 25th Army", in B. Farrell and S. Hunter (eds.), *Sixty Years On: the Fall of Singapore Revisited* (Singapore, 2003), p. 193.

17. B. Ash, *Some One Had Blundered* (London, 1960), p. 151.

18. D. Cooper, *Old Men Forget* (London, 1957), p. 300.

19. Quoted in Wigmore, *Australia in the War: the Japanese Thrust*, p. 103.

20. Pownall "Comments" for Churchill, 2 January 1949, in CHUR 4/258, Churchill Archives, Cambridge.

21. G.A. Weller, *Singapore is Silent* (New York, 1943), p. 65.

22. C. Brown, *Suez to Singapore*, p. 210.

23. Letter to Editor, *ST*, by "Asian", 2 January 1942.

24. A. Bowden to Australian Department of External Affairs, 10 January 1942, quoted in Wigmore, *Australia in the War: The Japanese Thrust*, p. 204.

25. *ST*, 29 December 1941.

26. *ST*, 12 January 1942.

27. W.S. Churchill, *The Second World War, IV* (London, 1951), p. 47.

28. A.G. Allbury, *Bamboo and Bushido* (London, 1955), p. 13.

29. A.H.C. Ward, Raymond W. Chu and J. Salaff (eds. and trans. with notes), *The Memoirs of Tan Kah Kee* (Singapore, 1994), pp. 153–57.

30. Governor to S. of S. telegram, 3 January 1942, CO 273/668, 50695/41.

31. Hu Tien Jun, "An account of the war fought by the Singapore Overseas Chinese Volunteer Army", in Foong Choon Hon (comp.), *The Price of Peace: True Accounts of the Japanese Occupation* (in Chinese, Singapore, 1995; English translation, Singapore, 1997), pp. 264–73.

32. Governor to S. of S., 4 February 1942, CO 273/669, 50750.

33. Yong Ching Fatt, *Chinese Leadership and Power in Colonial Singapore* (Singapore, 1992), p. 318.

34. A.H.C. Ward, Raymond W. Chu and J. Salaff, *The Memoirs of Tan Kah Kee*, pp. 158–59.

35. B. Bond (ed.), *Chief of Staff: The Diaries of Lt. General Sir Henry Pownall*, 2 vols. (London, 1972 and 1974), II, p. 81.

36. S.A. Field, *Singapore Tragedy* (Auckland, 1944), p. 230.

37. B. Bond, *The Diaries of Lt. General Sir Henry Pownall*, II, p. 76.

38. J.D. Potter, *A Soldier Must Hang* (London, 1963), p. 84.

39. Y. Akashi, *Sixty Years*, p. 197.

40. A.E. Percival, *The War In Malaya* (London, 1949), p. 260.

41. I. Morrison, *Malayan Postscript* (London, 1942), p. 159.

42. M. Tsuji, *Singapore: The Japanese Version* (Sydney, 1960; reprinted Singapore, 1988), p. 60.

43. Y. Akashi, *Sixty Years On*, p. 195.

44. W. Churchill, *Second World War*, IV (London, 1951), pp. 87–88.

45. L. Allen, *Singapore 1941–1942* (1st Edition, London 1977; revised edition 1993).

46. L. Allen, *Singapore 1941–1942*, quoting Major C.H.D. Wild's "Note on the Capitulation of Singapore".

47. M. Tsuji, *Singapore: The Japanese Version*, p. 215.

48. H. Gordon Bennett, *Why Singapore Fell* (Sydney, 1944), p. 21.

49. Colonel Ian Stewart of the Argylls to Major-General Sir N. Malcolm, New Delhi, 14 November 1942, in CO 273/671, 50790.

50. Sir John Pratt, *War and Politics in China* (London, 1943; reprinted New York, 1971), p. 152.

51. M. Murfett, *Between Two Oceans*, p. 175.

52. M. Tsuji, *Singapore*, p. 269.

6 Syonan: Light of the South, 1942–1945

1. K.G. Tregonning, *The Singapore Cold Storage, 1903–1966* (Singapore, 1966).

2. M. Shinozaki, *My Wartime Experiences in Singapore* (Singapore, 1973), p. 14.

3. M.C. ff Sheppard, *The Malay Regiment, 1933–1947* (Kuala Lumpur, 1947); Foong Choon Hon (comp.), *The Price of Peace: True Accounts of the Japanese Occupation* (in Chinese, Singapore, 1995; English translation by Clara Shaw, Singapore, 1997).

4. A.J. Sweeting, "Prisoners of the Japanese", in L. Wigmore, *Australia in the War: The Japanese Thrust* (Canberra, 1957), p. 511.

5. F.A. Reel, *The Case of General Yamashita* (Chicago, 1949), p. 53.

6. P.H. Kratoska, *The Japanese Occupation of Malaya: A Social and Economic History* (London, 1998), p. 95.

7. K. Blackburn, "Memory of the Sook Ching Massacre and the Creation of the Civilian War Memorial of Singapore", *JMBRAS*, LXXIII, 2 (2000), pp. 71–90.

8. Chin Kee Onn, *Malaya Upside Down* (Singapore, 1946), p. 8.

9. M. Tsuji, *Singapore: The Japanese Version* (Sydney, 1960; reprinted Singapore, 1988), p. 175.

10. *Good Citizen's Guide* (Singapore, 1943), p. 4.

11. *Syonan Times*, 25 February 1942.

12. Ibid., 25 April 1942.
13. He Wen-lit, *Syonan Interlude* (Singapore, 1992), pp. 131–33.
14. E.J.H. Corner, *The Marquis: A Tale of Syonan-to* (Singapore, 1981).
15. Jeyamalar Kathirithamby-Wells, *Nature and Nation: Forests and Development in Peninsular Malaysia* (Copenhagen and Singapore, 2005), pp. 233–34.
16. C. McCormac, *You'll Die in Singapore* (London, 1954), autobiographical. Told at second hand in P. Brickhill, *Escape or Die* (London, 1952).
17. Yap Pheng Geck, *Scholar, Banker, Gentleman, Soldier: The Reminiscences of Dr. Yap Pheng Geck* (Singapore, 1982) quoted in Kratoska, *Japanese Occupation*, p. 101.
18. M. Shinozaki, *My Wartime Experiences in Singapore* (Singapore, 1973), p. 35.
19. Toru Takase, *Principles and Policies Governing towards the Chinese*, 19 April 1942; English translation in H. Benda et al., *Japanese Military Administration in Indonesia: Selected Documents* (New Haven, 1965).
20. *Good Citizen's Guide*, 3 March 1942, pp. 17–18.
21. Chin Kee Onn, *Malaya Upside Down*, p. 197.
22. Ibid., p. 89.
23. Ibid., p. 46.
24. Article by T. Fujimori of Propaganda Department Military Administration Singapore in *Syonan Times*, 5 September 1942.
25. M. Shinozaki, *Wartime Experiences*, p. 52.\
26. H.E. Wilson, *Educational Policy and Performance in Singapore, 1942–1945* (Singapore, 1973).
27. T.R. Doraisamy (ed.), *150 Years of Education in Singapore* (Singapore, 1969), p. 45.
28. W.H. Elsbree, *Japan's Role in Southeast Asian Nationalist Movements, 1940–1945* (Harvard, 1953), p. 105.
29. Chin Kee Onn, *Malaya Upside Down*, p. 156.
30. P. Kratoska, *Japanese Occupation*, pp. 347–48.
31. Chin Kee Onn, *Malaya Upside Down*, p. 172.
32. Tan Thoon Lip, *Kempeitai Kindness* (Singapore, 1946), p. 81.

33. Tie Yi and Zhong Cheng, "An account of the Anti-Japanese War fought jointly by the British government and MPAJA", in Foong Choon Hon (comp.), *Price of Peace*, chap. 3.

34. D. Russell-Roberts, *Spotlight on Singapore* (London, 1965), p. 229.

35. Zhou Mei, *Elizabeth Choy: More than a War Heroine: A Biography* (Singapore, 1995); Elizabeth Choy, "A Shameful Past in Human Memory: A Verbal Account", in Foong Choon Hon (comp.), *Price of Peace*, chap. 14.

36. R. McKie, *The Heroes* (Sydney, 1960); B. Connell, *Return of the Tiger* (London, 1960); P. Thompson and R. Macklin, *Kill the Tiger* (Sydney, 2000).

37. Quoted in F.C. Jones, *Japan's New Order in East Asia: Its Rise and Fall, 1937–45* (London, 1954), p. 383.

38. J.C. Lebra, *Jungle Alliance* (Singapore, 1971), p. 36.

39. A.C. Bose, *Indian Revolutionaries Abroad* (Patna, 1971).

40. M.K. Durrani, *The Sixth Column* (London, 1955), p. 74.

41. Quoted in Lebra, p. 118.

42. Supreme Allied Commander's Meetings, 4, 5, 27 February and 22 April 1945, WO 203/469.

43. Cheah Boon Kheng, *Red Star over Malaya: Resistance and Social Conflict during and after the Japanese Occupation of Malaya, 1941–1946* (Singapore, 1983; 2nd edition Singapore 1987), p. 141.

7 The Aftermath of War, 1945–1955

1. C.A. Trocki, *Singapore: Wealth, Power and the Culture of Control* (London, 2006), p. 185.

2. A.J. Stockwell, "Colonial Planning during World War II: The Case of Malaya", *Journal of Imperial and Commonwealth History*, II, 3 (May 1974), pp. 333–51; C.M. Turnbull, "British Planning for Postwar Malaya", *JSEAS*, V, 2 (1974), pp. 239–54.

3. Colonial Office comment on Sir Shenton Thomas's visit to the office while on home leave in 1936.

4. Albert Lau, *The Malayan Union Controversy 1942–1948* (Singapore, 1991), p. 39.

5. CO Memorandum, 28 July 1942, CO 825/35.

6. Colonial Office, "Future Constitutional Policy for British Colonial Territories in South-east Asia", C.M.B. (44) 3 of 14 January 1944, CO 825/43.

7. It was left to Lord Hailey, distinguished expert on Africa and India, and chairman of the Colonial Committee on Post-War problems, but not a specialist on Malaya, to point out that the racial imbalance was likely to become the main problem. Hailey to Gent, 19 April 1943, CO 825/35, quoted in Lau, *Malayan Union*, p. 49.

8. Exchange of minutes, 30 November and 1 December 1943, CO 825/35 I.

9. Tan Cheng Lock, *Memorandum on the Future of British Malaya* (Bombay, 1943), and CO minute, 11 July 1945, CO/825/42A.

10. John Laycock, Tan Chin Tuan, Tunku Abu Bakar and Oliver Holt, *Memorandum on Proposals for Political Changes in Malaya* (Bombay, 1944); and CO minute, 29 July 1944, CO/825/42A.

11. Report on "Maintenance of Operations after the Capture of Singapore", Adv. H.O. ALFSEA 151/AQP, 11 June 1945, WO 203/888; War Office Plan, 26 June 1945, W0203/1105.

12. Supreme Allied Command South-East Asia to FO, 3 September 1945, CO 273/675.

13. Shenton Thomas, Memorandum, Formosa, 29 February 1944, CO 273/677; Thomas to Gent, 20 October 1945, and CO minutes CO 273/675.

14. Clementi, "Comments at meeting at the Colonial Office, February 1946, and Colonial Office, Notes for Guidance of Secretary of State at Meeting, February 1946", CO 273/676.

15. CO minutes, March 1943, CO 825/35 I.

16. "Constitutional Reconstruction in the Far East", 21 July 1943; and revised Colonial Office memorandum, 30 July 1943, CO 825/35 I.

17. C.M. Turnbull, *Dateline Singapore: 150 Years of The Straits Times* (Singapore, 1995), pp. 131–36.

18. McKerron and others, "Memorandum on Constitution for Singapore", 1 May 1945; McKerron to Gent, 30 November 1945; Hone to Gent, 5 December 1945, CO 273/675.

19. Sir Ralph Hone, "Papers Relating to the Military Administration of the Malayan Peninsula, 5 September 1945–1 April 1946", Rhodes House, MSS Brit. Emp. S 407/3; British Military Administration, *Singapore Advisory Council Proceedings*, 14 November and 12 December 1945 and January 1946.

20. F.S.V. Donnison, *British Military Administration in the Far East, 1943–46* (London, 1956).

21. Colonial Office, *British Dependencies in the Far East, 1945–1949*, Cmd. 7709 (London, May 1949), p. 33.

22. Ibid., p. 161.

23. A. Gilmour, *My Role in the Rehabilitation of Singapore: 1946–1953* (Singapore, 1973), p. 6.

24. C. Gamba, *The Origins of Trade Unionism in Malaya* (Singapore, 1962), p. 45.

25. T. Silcock and Ungku Aziz, "Nationalism in Malaya", in W.L. Holland (ed.), *Asian Nationalism and the West* (New York, 1953; reprinted New York, 1973), p. 300.

26. United Engineers, Hume Pipe Company, Singapore Cold Storage, Wearne/Borneo Motors, Fraser & Neave Breweries, Singapore Traction Company, in Singapore, and Malayan Collieries at Batu Arang, Selangor.

27. I. Ward, *The Killer They Called God* (Singapore, 1992).

28. Akashi Yoji, "General Yamashita Tomoyuki: Commander of the 25th Army", in B. Farrell and S. Hunter (eds.), *Sixty Years On: The Fall of Singapore Revisited* (Singapore, 2002), p. 199.

29. K. Blackburn, "Memory of the Sook Ching Massacre and the Creation of the Civilian War Memorial of Singapore", *JMBRAS*, LXXIII, 2 (2000), pp. 71–90.

30. Arthur Creech-Jones Papers, Rhodes House, MSS Brit. Emp. S 332, Box 26, File 11.

31. *Malayan Union and Singapore: Statement of Policy on Future Constitution*, Cmd. 6724 (London, January 1946).

32. New Democracy, 24 January 1946 (also *Chung Hwa* and *Sin Chew*, 24 January 1946), *Malayan Press Comment on the White Paper on Malayan Union, Special supplement to Malayan Press Digest* 1/MPD, 15/16, 2.

33. P. Hoalim, *The Malayan Democratic Union: Singapore's First Democratic Political Party* (Singapore, 1973).

34. Malayan Union, *Constitutional Proposals for Malaya: Summary of a Report of the Working Committee Appointed by a Conference of the Governor of Malayan Union, the Rulers and the Representatives of the United Malays National Organization* (Kuala Lumpur, 1946).

35. Albert Lau, *The Malayan Union Controversy 1942–1948* (Singapore, 1991), p. 212, No. 3.

36. PUTERA and All-Malaya Council of Joint Action, *The People's Constitutional Proposals for Malaya* (Kuala Lumpur, November 1947).

37. Colonial Office, *British Dependencies*, pp. 30, 41. The infant mortality rate was 80.79 in 1948, compared with 191.30 in 1931 and 285 in 1944.

38. S.S. Awberry and F.W. Dalley, *Labour and Trades Union Organization in the Federation of Malaya and Singapore* (Kuala Lumpur, 1948), p. 27.

39. M.V. del Tufo, *A Report on the 1947 Census of Population* (London, 1949).

40. Department of Social Welfare, *A Social Survey of Singapore* (Singapore, 1947), pp. 114, 119–21.

41. Kernial Singh Sandhu, *Indians in Malaya* (Cambridge, 1969), p. 151.

42. Tan Chin Tuan, quoted in *ST*, 4 July 1947.

43. Yeo Kim Wah, *Political Development in Singapore 1945–1955* (Singapore, 1973), p. 103.

44. Department of Social Welfare, *A Social Survey of Singapore* (Singapore, 1947), p. 75.

45. Quoted in Colonial Office, *British Dependencies*, p. 35.

46. This thesis was forcibly argued in D.D. Chelliah, *A History of the Educational Policy of the Straits Settlements* (Kuala Lumpur, 1947; 2nd edition, Singapore, 1960). Based upon a Ph.D. thesis submitted to the University of London in 1940, this work was published by the Malayan Union government and was very influential in post-war thinking on education policy.

47. Singapore Advisory Council, *Education Policy in the Colony of Singapore: Ten Years' Programme* (Singapore, 1948), pp. 36–37, 40–42, 50.

48. The University opened a division in Kuala Lumpur in 1958, and in 1961 split into two separate institutions: the University of Malaya (in Kuala Lumpur) and the University of Singapore.

49. Tan Ern Ser, "Balancing State Welfarism and Individual Responsibility: Singapore's CPF Model", in C. Jones Finer and P. Smyth (ed.), *Social Policy and the Commonwealth: Prospects for Social Inclusion* (Basingstoke, 2004), pp. 125–37.

50. F.C. Carnell, "Constitutional Reform and Elections in Malaya", *Pacific Affairs*, XXVII, 3 (1954), p. 219.

51. *Report of the Constitutional Commission* (The Rendel Report) (Singapore, 1954).

52. Vividly described in D. Bloodworth, *The Tiger and the Trojan Horse* (Singapore, 1986; reprinted Singapore, 2005).

53. *Report of the Singapore Riots Inquiry Commission* (Singapore, 1951); Tom Eames Hughes, *Tangled Worlds: The Story of Maria Hertogh* (Singapore, 1980); Haja Maideen, *The Nadra Tragedy: The Maria Hertogh Controversy* (Kuala Lumpur, 1989); C.M. Turnbull, *Dateline Singapore: 150 Years of the Straits Times* (Singapore, 1995).

54. Homer Cheng, "The Network of Singapore Societies", *Journal of the South Seas Society*, VI, 2 (1950), p. 12; Sikko Visscher,

The Business of Politics and Ethnicity: A History of the Singapore Chinese Chamber of Commerce and Industry (Singapore, 2007).

55. Quoted in Yeo Kim Wah, *Political Development in Singapore, 1945–1955* (Singapore, 1973), p. 161.

56. Melanie Chew, *Leaders of Singapore* (Singapore, 1997), pp. 19–22.

57. Colonial Office, *Organization of the Colonial Service*, Cmd. 197 of 1946 (London, 1946).

58. Lam Peng Er and Kevin Tan (eds.), *Lee's Lieutenants: Singapore's Old Guard* (London, 1999); Tan Jing Quee and K.S. Jomo (eds.), *Comet in Our Sky: Lim Chin Siong in History* (Kuala Lumpur, 2001).

59. D.N. Pritt, *Autobiography, Vol. III. The Defence Accuses* (London, 1966).

60. Goh Keng Swee, *Urban Income and Housing* (Singapore, 1954).

61. K.S. Jomo, in Tan and Jomo (eds.), *Comet in our Sky*, p. ix.

62. J. Drysdale, *Singapore: The Struggle for Success* (Singapore, 1984), p. 95.

63. Melanie Chew, *Leaders of Singapore*, p. 86.

8 The Road to Merdeka, 1955–1965

1. People's Action Party, *The Tasks Ahead* (Singapore, 1959), p. 6.

2. *ST*, 29 March 1955.

3. Actually the Malay Union Alliance, which was a parliamentary coalition of UMNO and the Malayan Chinese Association.

4. Tan Jing Quee and K.S. Jomo (eds.), *Comet in Our Sky: Lim Chin Siong in History* (Singapore, 2001).

5. Lee Kuan Yew, *The Singapore Story: Memoirs of Lee Kuan Yew* (Singapore, 1998), p. 184.

6. Sit Yin Fong, *I Stomped the Hot Beat* (Singapore, 1991), pp. 104–23, gives a graphic eyewitness report.

7. Singapore Legislative Assembly, *Report of the All Party Mission to London, April/May 1956*, Cmd. 31 of 1956 (Singapore, 1956).

8. Singapore Legislative Assembly, *Report of the All Party Committee of the Singapore Legislative Assembly on Chinese Education*, Cmd. 9 of 1956 (Singapore, 1956).

9. Singapore Legislative Assembly, *White Paper on Education Policy*, Cmd. 15 of 1956 (Singapore, 1956).

10. Singapore Legislative Assembly, *Singapore Chinese Middle Schools Students Union*, sessional papers, Cmd. 53 of 1956 (Singapore, 1956).

11. Singapore Legislative Assembly, *Singapore Constitutional Conference, March/April 1957* (Singapore, 1957).

12. Singapore Legislative Assembly, *The Communist Threat in Singapore*, Sessional Cmd. Paper No. 33 of 1957 (Singapore, 1957).

13. Ministry of Education, *First Triennial Survey of Education*, 1955–57 (Singapore, 1959).

14. Great Britain, *State of Singapore Act 1958*, Chapter 59, 6 & 7 Eliz. II (London, 1958); *Singapore (Constitution) Order in Council*, laid before Parliament 27 November 1958, Gazette Supplement No. 81 of 27 November 1958 (Singapore, 1958). See also Creech-Jones Papers, Rhodes House, MSS. Brit. Emp. S 332, Box 26, File 11.

15. Great Britain, *Exchange of Letters on Internal Security Council of Singapore*, Cmd. 620 of 1958 (London, 1958).

16. Singapore Legislative Council, *Report on the Reform of Local Government* by L.C. Hill, November 1951 (Singapore, 1952).

17. Singapore Legislative Assembly, *Report of the Committee on Local Government* (the McNeice Report) (Singapore, 1956).

18. Lim Choon Meng (Liberal Socialist) in *Singapore Legislative Assembly Proceedings* (Singapore, 1956–7), Vol. 2, Col. 2452.

19. Melanie Chew, *Leaders of Singapore* (Singapore, 1996), p. 86.

20. Singapore, *Minutes of City Council Proceedings*, 30 July 1958.

21. W.A. Hanna, *Sequel to Colonialism* (New York, 1965), p. 31.

22. Toh Chin Chye in People's Action Party, *The Tasks Ahead*, February 1959, p. 2.

23. Ibid., April 1959, pp. 8–9; Goh Keng Swee in People's Action Party, *The Tasks Ahead*, March 1959, p. 19.

24. For detailed commentary on the elections see Ong Chit Chung, "The 1959 Singapore General Election", *JSEAS*, VI, 1 (1975), pp. 61–86.

25. F. Thomas, *Memoirs of a Migrant* (Singapore, 1972), p. 99.

26. J.B. Perry Robinson, *Transformation in Malaya* (London, 1956), p. 66.

27. S. Rajaratnam, *The Tasks Ahead*, April 1959, p. 12.

28. Singapore Ministry of Culture, *The Socialist Solution: An Analysis of Current Political Forces in Singapore* (Singapore, 1960).

29. People's Action Party, *Sixth Anniversary Celebration Souvenir* (Singapore, 1960).

30. Othman Wok, journalist, trade unionist, Cabinet minister, diplomat, businessman; born in Singapore 1924, educated Raffles Institution, journalist *Utusan Melayu*, MP 1963, Minister of Social Affairs 1963–77; subsequently Singapore Ambassador to Indonesia.

31. International Bank for Reconstruction and Development, *The Economic Development of Malaya* (Singapore, 1955), p. 28.

32. Lee Kuan Yew, *The Tasks Ahead*, March 1959, p. 24.

33. *Straits Budget*, 21 November 1962.

34. Lee Kuan Yew, *The Singapore Story: Memoirs of Lee Kuan Yew* (Singapore, 1998), p. 373.

35. Ibid.

36. Lord Selkirk in letter to author, 12 December 1973.

37. D. Bloodworth, *The Tiger and the Trojan Horse* (Singapore, 1986 and 2005), p. 243.

38. Pang Cheng Lian, *The People's Action Party* (Singapore, 1971), p. 15.

39. Singapore government, *Comments on the Memorandum by Nineteen Singapore Opposition Assemblymen to the United Nations Committee on Colonialism* (Singapore, 1962).

40. Ministry of Finance, *State of Singapore Development Plan, 1961–1964* (Singapore, 1961).

41. Hon Sui Sen (1916–1983), born in Penang, graduated from Raffles College with distinction and joined Straits Settlements Civil Service 1938; Land Commissioner after World War II; chairman Economic Development Board 1961–68; chairman Develop-ment Bank of Singapore 1968–70; Minister of Finance 1970–83.

42. Economic Development Board, *The Jurong Story* (Singapore, 1967).

43. Sheikh Azahari bin Sheikh Mahmud (A.M. Azahari) (1928–2002), Arab-Malay, born in Labuan, educated in Java, fought against the Dutch colonial regime, leader of radical Brunei Parti Rakyat (Brunei People's Party).

44. Said Zahari, *Dark Clouds at Dawn: A Political Memoir* (Kuala Lumpur, 2001)

45. Singapore Legislative Assembly, *Malaysia Agreement Concluded between the U.K., Federation of Malaya, North Borneo, Sarawak and Singapore*, Cmd. paper 24 of 1963 presented to Legislative Assembly, 30 July 1963 (Singapore, 1963); *Malaysia Agreement: Exchange of Letters between Prime Minister and Ministers of Singapore, Deputy Prime Minister and Ministers Federation and British Colonial Office*, Misc. 5 of 1963, presented to Singapore Legislative Assembly by Prime Minister, 26 July 1963.

46. *Malaysia Act No. 26 of 1963* (Kuala Lumpur, 1963); *Sabah, Sarawak and Singapore (State Constitutions) Order in Council*, 29 August 1963; *State of Singapore Government Gazette, Subsidiary Legislation Supplement*, 16 September 1963, No. 1493 Malaysia.

47. Discussed in Wang Gungwu, "Traditional Leadership in a New Nation: The Chinese in Malaya and Singapore", in G. Wijeyewardene (ed.), *Symposium on Leadership and Authority* (Singapore, 1968), pp. 209–26; and in S.T. Alisjahbana (ed.), *The Cultural Problems of Malaysia in the Context of Southeast Asia* (Kuala Lumpur, 1966).

48. Colony of Singapore, *Report on the Reform of Local Government* (Singapore, 1952).

49. Lim Kim San (1916–2006), born in Singapore, educated at Anglo-Chinese School and Raffles College, businessman and bank director, appointed to Housing and Development Board 1960; MP 1963–81; Minister for National Development 1963–65; Minister of Finance 1965–67; Minister of Interior and Defence 1967–70; Chairman Public Utilities Board 1971–78; Chairman Port of Singapore Authority 1979–94; Executive Chairman Singapore Press Holdings 1988–2002; Chairman Council of Presidential Advisers 1992–2003; died in Singapore July 2006.

50. Singapore Legislative Assembly, *Report of the Select Committee on the Women's Charter Bill* (the Oehlers Report), L.A. 16 of 1960 (Singapore, 1960).

51. Chan Choy Siong (1934–81), PAP City Councillor 1957; PAP Assemblywoman and MP 1959–70; killed in car crash 1981; wife of Ong Pang Boon.

52. Ministry of Finance, *State of Singapore First Development Plan, 1961–64, Review of Progress for the Three Years Ending 31 December 1963* (Singapore, 1964).

53. F.L. Starner, "The Singapore 1961 Elections", in K.J. Ratnam and R.S. Milne, *The Malayan Parliamentary Election of 1964* (Singapore, 1967).

54. International Bank for Reconstruction and Development, *Report on the Economic Aspects of Malaysia* (Rueff Report) (Kuala Lumpur, July 1963) supported the proposed common market.

55. *ST*, 23 May 1963.

56. *ST*, 10 September 1961; Tun Abdul Razak was then Deputy Prime Minister of Malaysia.

57. *Sunday Times*, 15 March 1964.

58. Singapore Ministry of Culture, *The Socialist Solution* (Singapore, 1960).

59. *ST*, 8 March 1965.

60. See M. Leifer, "Singapore in Malaysia: The Politics of Federation", *JSEAH*, VI, 2 (1965), pp. 54–70; and P. Boyce, "Policy without Authority: Singapore's External Affairs

Power", *JSEAH*, VI, 2 (1965), pp. 87–103, for contemporary comment.

61. See W.A. Hanna, "Go-ahead at Goh's Folly", *American Universities Field Staff Inc., Southeast Asia Series*, XII, 3 (New York, 1964) for these difficult early years.

62. Colony of Singapore, *Information on Singapore for 1949 transmitted to the United Nations* (Singapore, 1949).

63. *Straits Budget*, 1 November 1964.

64. Lee Kuan Yew, *The Singapore Story*, p. 551.

65. Quoted in C.M. Turnbull, *Dateline Singapore* (Singapore, 1995), p. 255.

66. Lee Kuan Yew, *The Singapore Story*, p. 572.

67. *ST*, 22 May 1965.

68. *ST*, 2 and 3 June 1965

69. Harold Wilson, *The Labour Government, 1964–1970* (London, 1971), p. 131.

70. Lee Kuan Yew, *The Singapore Story*, p. 625.

71. Quoted in Albert Lau, *A Moment of Anguish: Singapore in Malaysia and the Politics of Disengagement* (Singapore, 1998), p. 257.

72. *Independence of Singapore Agreement in Singapore Government Gazette Extraordinary*, VIII, No. 66, 9 August 1965.

73. Lee Kuan Yew, *The Singapore Story*, p. 653.

74. *Sunday Times*, 8 August 1965.

75. C.M. Turnbull, *Dateline Singapore*, p. 258.

76. Patrick Keith, Ousted! An Insider's Story of the Ties that Failed (Singapore, 2005), pp. 190–91.

9 The New Nation, 1965–1990

1. State of Singapore, *Comments of the Singapore Government on the Memorandum by Nineteen Singapore Opposition Assemblymen to the United Nations Committee on Colonialism* (Singapore, 1962).

2. *ST*, 25 May 1965.

3. Melanie Chew, *Leaders of Singapore* (Singapore, 1996), p. 97.

4. Harold Wilson, *The Labour Government 1964–1970: A Personal Record* (London, 1971), p. 131.

5. ST editorial, 11 August 1965, quoted in C.M. Turnbull, *Dateline Singapore: 150 Years of the Straits Times* (Singapore, 1995), p. 261.

6. Felix Abisheganaden, *Sunday Times*, 15 August 1965.

7. Lee Kuan Yew, *Singapore Parliamentary Debates*, Vol. 24, 14 December 1965.

8. Detailed in Lau Teik Soon, "Malaysia-Singapore Relations: Crisis of Adjustment, 1965–68", *JSEAH*, X, 1 (1969), pp. 155–76; Background in R.S. Milne, "Singapore's Exit from Malaysia: The Consequences of Ambiguity", *Asian Survey*, VI, 3 (1966), pp. 175–84.

9. *ST*, 20 October 1965.

10. *Utusan Melayu*, 20 March 1967.

11. G. Alexander, *Silent Invasion: The Chinese in Southeast Asia* (London, 1973), p. 214; reprinted as *The Invisible China* (New York, 1974).

12. M. Leifer, *Singapore's Foreign Policy: Coping with Vulnerability* (London & New York, 2000), p. 8.

13. Contemporary information and comment in H. Hughes and You Poh Seng (eds.), *Foreign Investment and Industrialization in Singapore* (Canberra and Wisconsin, 1969); P.I. Drake, *Financing Development in Malaya and Singapore* (Canberra, 1969); Economic Development Board, *The Jurong Story* (Singapore, 1967).

14. The then novel thesis presented in Stephen Fitzgerald, *China and the Overseas Chinese: A Study of Peking's Changing Policy, 1949–1970* (Cambridge, 1970).

15. Singapore Constitution 1966, *Republic of Singapore Government Gazette Reprints Supplement (Acts)*, No. 14, March 1966.

16. M.H. Murfett, J.N. Miksic, B.P. Farrell, and Chiang Ming Shun, *Between Two Oceans: A Military History of Singapore from First Settlement to Final British Withdrawal* (Oxford, 1999), p. 291.

17. K. Hack, *Defence and Decolonization in Southern Asia: Britain, Malaya and Singapore 1941–68* (London, 2001), p. 259.
18. ANZAM – Australia, New Zealand and Malaya.
19. Ministry of Defence, *Defence: Outline of a Policy*, Cmnd. 124 of 1957, April 1957.
20. Ministry of Defence, *Report on Defence: Britain's Contribution to Peace and Security*, Cmnd. 363, February 1958.
21. Ministry of Defence, *Report on Defence, 1960*, Cmnd. 952, February 1960.
22. Ministry of Defence, *Statement on Defence: the Next Five Years*, Cmnd. 1639, February 1962.
23. Ministry of Defence, *Statement on Defence 1963*, Cmnd. 1936, February 1963.
24. Ministry of Defence, *Defence Statement 1964*, Cmnd. 2270, February 1964.
25. Murfett, Miksic, Farrell and Chiang, *Between Two Oceans*, p 316.
26. Ministry of Defence, *Statement on Defence Estimates 1965*, Cmnd. 2592, February 1965.
27. Ibid., February 1965.
28. Ministry of Defence, *Statement on the Defence Estimates 1966: Part I The Defence Review*, Cmnd. 2901, February 1966.
29. Ministry of Defence, *Statement on Defence Estimates 1966: Part II Defence Estimates 1966–67*, Cmnd. 2902, February 1966.
30. Ministry of Defence, *Supplementary Statement on Defence Policy 1967, Part I*, Cmnd. 3357, July 1967.
31. Murfett, Miksic, Farrell and Chiang, *Between Two Oceans*, p. 315.
32. Ministry of Defence, *Statement on the Defence Estimates 1967* Cmnd 3203, February 1967.
33. Murfett, Miksic, Farrell and Chiang, *Between Two Oceans*, p. 319.
34. Ibid., p. 322.
35. Melanie Chew, *Leaders of Singapore* (Singapore, 1996), p. 142.

36. Tim Huxley, *Defending the Lion City The Armed Forces of Singapore* (Sydney, 2000), p. 9.

37. Murfett, Miksic, Farrell and Chiang, *Between Two Oceans*, p. 318.

38. Cmnd. 3515, 16 January 1968.

39. Ministry of Defence, *Statement on the Defence Estimates, 1968–69*, Cmnd. 3540, February 1968.

40. Murfett, Miksic, Farrell and Chiang, *Between Two Oceans*, p. 323.

41. A. Josey, *Lee Kuan Yew in London* (Singapore, 1968).

42. Hon Sui Sen (1916–83), born in Penang; Raffles College graduate 1938; Straits Civil Service; 1st Chairman Ecoomic Development Board 1961–68; Chairman Development Bank of Singapore 1968–70; Finance Minister 1970–83.

43. Ministry of Defence, *Defence Estimates 1970*, Cmnd. 4290, February 1970.

44. Yang Di-Pertuan Negara's opening speech, 8 December 1965, *Singapore Parliamentary Debates*, Vol. 24.

45. Text of industrial and political speeches in A. Josey, *Labour Laws in a Changing Singapore* (Singapore, 1968); see also W.E. Chalmers, *Crucial Issues in Industrial Relations in Singapore* (Singapore, 1967) for contemporary background.

46. Chiang Hai Ding, "*The Early Shipping Conference System of Singapore, 1897–1911*", *JSEAH*, X, 1 (1969), pp. 50–68.

47. *Financial Times*, London, 1 October 1973.

48. Murfett, Miksic, Farrell and Chiang, *Between Two Oceans*, p. 324.

49. Ministry of Defence, *Supplementary Statement on Defence Policy 1971*, Cmnd. 4521, October 1970.

50. Ministry of Defence, *Statement on the Defence Estimates 1971*, Cmnd. 4592, February 1971.

51. Ministry of Defence, *Statement on the Defence Estimates 1995*, Cmnd. 5976, March 1975: Ministry of Defence, *Statement on the Defence Estimates 1976*, Cmnd. 6432, March 1976.

52. *New Nation*, 1 November 1971.

53. Yong Nyuk Lin, April 1959, People's Action Party, *The Tasks Ahead* (Singapore, 1959), p. 2.

54. Lee Kuan Yew, *New Bearings in Our Education System* (Singapore, 1966).

55. Singapore Legislative Assembly, *Commission of Inquiry into Education (final report)* (Lim Tay Boh Report), Cmd. 8 of 1964 (Singapore, 1964).

56. Ong Pang Boon, born in Kuala Lumpur, attended primary Chinese school, Confucian Middle School, English-medium secondary Methodist Boys School, English-medium University of Malaya (in Singapore), B.A. Hons degree in geography; PAP MP 1959–84, Minister for Home Affairs 1959–63; Education Minister 1963–70; Minister of Labour 1970–80; Environment Minister 1980–84; retired from politics 1984. Married to Chan Choy Siong (MP 1959–70).

57. Lee Kuan Yew, quoted in *The Asian*, 19 November 1972.

58. Chan Kwok Bun and Tong Chee Kiong (eds.), *Past Times: A Social History of Singapore* (Singapore, 2003).

59. Johnny Sung, *Explaining the Economic Success of Singapore: The Development Worker as the Missing Link* (Cheltenham, UK, 2006).

60. Goh Keng Swee in speech to annual meeting, International Monetary Fund and World Bank, Washington, October 1969.

61. *The Mirror*, Vol. 12, No. 27, 4 July 1977.

62. Chan Heng Chee, *Singapore: The Politics of Survival, 1965–1967* (Singapore, 1971).

63. *Report of The Constitutional Commission* (Singapore, August 1966).

64. *ST*, 18 March 1967, Editorial comment.

65. Constitution (Amendment) Act No. 19 of 1969.

66. Chan Heng Chee, *Politics in an Administration State: Where has the Politics Gone?* (Singapore, 1975).

67. Seah Chee Meow, *Community Centres in Singapore: Their Political Involvement* (Singapore, 1974).

68. Yang Di-Pertuan's speech, 8 December 1965, *Singapore Parliamentary Debates*, Vol. 24.

69. Lee Kuan Yew at the International Press Institute, Helsinki, 9 June 1971.

70. Editorial: "A Lot of Room", *ST*, 20 November 1972.

71. Simmons to Harry Miller, 13 February 1975 (Singapore Press Holdings archives, LJH Box 3), quoted in C.M.Turnbull, *Dateline Singapore: 150 Years of the Straits Times* (Singapore, 1995), p. 301.

72. Tisa Ng and Lily Tan, *Ong Teng Cheong: Planner, Politician, President* (Singapore, 2005).

73. Singapore National Trades Union Congress, *Why Labour Must Go Modern* (Singapore, 1970); Singapore National Trades Union Congress, *Towards Tomorrow* (Singapore, 1973).

74. Lee Kuan Yew at Rural East District Citizens' Consultative Committee, reported in *New Nation*, 7 September 1971.

75. A. Josey, *The Singapore General Elections 1972* (Singapore, 1972) gives a detailed, pro-PAP account.

76. Lee Kuan Yew, *The Battle for Merger* (Singapore, 1961), p. 166.

77. *The Asian*, 20 August 1972.

78. Goh Keng Swee, speech, *The Mirror*, Vol. 13, No. 27, 4 July 1977.

79. The thesis of Iain Buchanan's controversial *Singapore in Southeast Asia* (London, 1972).

80. S. Rajaratnam, *Malaysia and the Changing Patterns of World Politics* (Singapore, 1964).

81. S. Rajaratnam, *The Asian*, 20 August 1972.

82. Brunei became a member of ASEAN in 1984, Vietnam in 1995, Myanmar and Laos in 1997, and Cambodia in 1999.

83. Author's interview with Thanat Khoman, 17 February 1983.

84. *The Asian*, 10 December 1972.

85. Statement read in Colombo, 18 August 1976, in *The Mirror*, Vol. 12, No. 35, 30 August 1976.

86. Government of Singapore, *Ministry of Foreign Affairs, Havana and New Delhi: What's the Difference?* (Singapore, 1983); Singapore delegate's speech at Non-Aligned Movement Conference in Cuba, September 1988.

87. *Singapore Bulletin*, Vol. 15, No. 13, September 1987.

88. *The Mirror*, Vol. 18, No. 4, 15 February 1982.
89. Singapore Bulletin, Vol. 13, No. 12, August 1985.

10 The New Guard, 1990–2005

1. Goh Chok Tong interview, *The International Herald Tribune*, 12 November 1990.
2. Chew Soo Beng, *Fishermen in Flats* (Melbourne, 1982).
3. Detailed in Hadijah Rahmat, *Portraits of a Nation – British Legacy on the Malay Settlement in Singapore* (Singapore, 2007), pp. 16–19.
4. Lee Hsien Loong, "The National Identity – a direction and identity for Singapore", 11 January 1989, *Speeches*, XIII, 1 (January–February 1989), p. 29.
5. Government of Singapore, *The Next Lap* (Singapore, February 1991), p. 159.
6. George Yeo Yong Boon, born Singapore 1954, President's scholar and Singapore Armed Forces Scholar, Cambridge and Harvard; Singapore Armed Forces 1985–88, Brigadier-General; resigned from the army in 1988 to enter Parliament; Minister of State for Finance and Foreign Affairs 1988–90; thereafter held a variety of Cabinet posts as Minister for Information and the Arts, Health, Trade and Industry, and Foreign Affairs; Chairman of Young PAP 1991–2000.
7. Tommy Koh Thong Bee, born Singapore 1937; University of Malaya, Harvard, Cambridge; Law Faculty, University of Singapore 1962–74; Prof. Law, NUS, from 1977; permanent representative, UN 1968–71, 1974–84; Ambassador to US 1984–90; Director, Institute of Policy Studies 1990–97, 2000–04; Chairman, National Arts Council 1991–96; Ambassador-at-large 1990– .
8. *South China Morning Post*, 31 July 1991.
9. Low Thia Khiang, born 1956; Chinese- and English-educated, B.A. Nanyang University 1980; BA National University of Singapore 1981; Diploma Institute of Education 1982;

teacher and businessman; joined Workers' Party 1982; entered Parliament 1991; re-elected MP 1997, 2001, 2006; secretary-general, Workers' Party 2001– .

10. Ong Teng Cheong (1936–2002); architect and urban planner; Hokkien, grandfather a manager in Tan Kah Kee's rubber factory, father a colonial official; educated Chinese High School, Adelaide Technical School, Adelaide University and Liverpool University; Singapore State and City Planning 1967–71; joined PAP 1972; Minister of State for Communications 1975; Minister for Communications 1978, (and Labour) 1980; secretary general of the National Trade Union Congress 1983–93; Second Deputy Prime Minister 1985–93; President 1993–98.

11. Lisa Ng and Lily Tan, *Ong Teng Cheong: Planner, Politician, President* (Singapore, 2005).

12. Walter Woon Cheong Ming; born in Singapore 1956; educated NUS and Cambridge; Professor of Law, NUS 1988–95; Legal Adviser to President and Council of Presidential Advisers 1995–97; Nominated MP 1992–96; Ambassador to Germany and later Belgium 1998–2006; Solicitor-General 2007.

13. Dr Kanwaljit Soin, orthopaedic surgeon; born in India 1942; came to Singapore 1952; educated NUS and Australia; consultant surgeon in government and subsequently private practice; founder member AWARE (Association of Women for Action and Research) 1985 and president of AWARE 1991–93; Nominated MP (two terms) 1992–96; executive committee and board member, (London-based) HelpAge International.

14. *International Herald Tribune*, 12 November 1990.

15. K. Hewison, R. Robison and G. Rodan (eds.), *Southeast Asia in the 1990s: Authoritarianism, Democracy and Capitlaism* (St. Leonards, NSW, 1993), p. 87.

16. Lee Kuan Yew, *From Third World to the First: The Story of Singapore 1965–2000: Memoirs of Lee Kuan Yew* (Singapore, 2000), p. 223.

17. Singapore's permanent representative at the UN 1968–71, and 1974–84; Ambassador to the United States 1984–90; President of the UN Conference on the Law of the Sea 1980–82, and other UN appointments.

18. Chan Heng Chee; educated University of Singapore and Cornell; formerly Director of the Institute of Southeast Asian Studies; founding Director of the Institute of Policy Studies; Singapore's permanent representative to the UN 1989–91; Ambassador to the United States from 1996.

19. Eu Chooi Yip died in Singapore in 1995.

20. Lee Kuan Yew, *From Third World to First: The Singapore Story, 1965–2000: Memoirs of Lee Kuan Yew* (Singapore, 2000), pp. 138–39.

21. Preface to Chee Soon Juan, *Dare to Change: An Alternative Vision for Singapore* (Singapore Democratic Party, Singapore, 1994).

22. The number of elective parliamentary seats had been increased to 84, of which 47 were uncontested.

23. For the election and its aftermath see Derek da Cunha, *The Price of Victory: The 1997 Singapore General Election* (Singapore, 1997).

24. Lee Kuan Yew, *Third World to First*, p. 148.

25. E. Kay Gillis, *Singapore Civil Society and British Power* (Singapore, 2005).

26. AWARE, *Small Steps, Giant Leaps: A History of AWARE and the Women's Movement in Singapore* (Singapore, 2007).

27. That is, a country that no longer qualified for international aid.

28. Sellapan Ramanathan (S.R. Nathan), born in Singapore 1924; University of Malaya (in Singapore), Social Studies diploma 1954; Singapore Civil Service 1955–82 (Permanent Sec Min of Defence 1971–79; Permanent Sec Min Foreign Affairs 1979–82); Executive chairman of Straits Times Press 1982–88; Ambassador to Malaysia 1988–90; Ambassador to USA 1990–96; Ambassador-at-large 1996–99; President of the Republic 1999–2016 .

29. Formerly a branch of the Malayan Nature Society (established 1954), it became the Nature Society (Singapore) in 1991.

30. Geh Min, eye surgeon, educated NUS, granddaughter of Lee Kong Chian; president of the Nature Society 2000, Nominated MP 2004.

31. Aline Wong, B.A. Hong Kong, Ph.D. Berkeley; lecturer University of Singapore 1971; MP 1984–2001; founder member and chairman, PAP Women's Wing 1988–2004; Minister of State 1990; Senior Minister of State 1995; chairman Housing and Development Board.

32. Cherian George, *Contentious Journalism and the Internet: Towards Democratic Discourse in Malaysia and Singapore* (Singapore, 2006), p. 42.

33. The theme of C. George's *Contentious Journalism*.

34. C. George, *Singapore: The Air-Conditioned Nation* (Singapore, 2000), p. 38.

35. A term adopted cheerfully by Singapore from an apparently disparaging remark made by President Habibie of Indonesia in 1999, and the title of Tommy Koh and Chang Li Lin (eds.), *The Little Red Dot: Reflections by Singapore's Diplomats* (Singapore, 2005).

36. G. Rodan in Hewison, Robison and Rodan (eds.), *Southeast Asia in the 1990s*, p. 77.

37. For example, C.A. Trocki, *Singapore: Wealth, Power and the Culture of Control* (New York, 2005).

38. As in the stimulating collection, M.D. Barr and C.A. Trocki (eds.), *Paths Not Taken: Political Pluralism in Postwar Singapore* (Singapore, 2008).

39. Quoted in Han Fook Kwang, Warren Fernandez and Sumiko Tan (eds.), *Lee Kuan Yew: The Man and his Ideas* (Singapore, 1998).

40. C. George, *Air-Conditioned Nation*, p. 45.

41. Quoted in Chapter 9, p. 325.

42. Lee Kuan Yew, *Third World to First*, pp. 741–43.

43. With the exception of the very brief period in 1957 when the extreme left wing took control.

Further Reading

This not an exhaustive bibliography but a guide to the major archival sources and mainly English-language publications relating directly to Singapore, including contemporary descriptions, academic books (which often carry comprehensive bibliographies) and articles relating to topics of special note. References to other sources are to be found in the *Notes* section. See also Tim Yap Fuan et al. (comp.), *A Sense of History: A Select Bibliography on the History of Singapore* (Singapore, 1998; Internet ed., 2002).

Official records

The major holdings of official archives relating to the history of Singapore are held in the National Archives of Singapore; The National Archives (formerly the Public Record Office) and the British Library in London; and the National Archives of India in New Delhi.

Founded in 1968 the National Archives of Singapore (NAS) is the official custodian of public records in Singapore and also holds collections of private papers. Unclassified official records are normally open for inspection after twenty-five years, but classified documents may be subject to a longer restriction. The NAS also holds archives of the colonial era. Most pre-Second World War official records were destroyed during the Pacific War, with the exception of the documents of the pre-1867 period, when Singapore was under administration from India, that were housed in Raffles Museum during the Japanese Occupation. Under an

Acquisitions programme the NAS obtained copies of records which are relevant to Singapore from Australia, the United Kingdom, the United States, and Japan.

The NAS incorporates the Oral History Department, created in 1979, which conducts an ongoing programme of interviews and has built up a substantial collection of tapes and transcripts. NAS, *Memories and Reflections: The Singapore Experience – Documenting a Nation's History through Oral History* (1st ed. 1988/1992; 2nd ed. 2007).

NAS also published a *Guide to the Sources of History in Singapore*, 2 vols. (Singapore, 1991) and a series of excellent illustrated publications in conjunction with exhibitions, notably *Road to Nationhood: Singapore 1819–1980* (Singapore, 1984).

The National Archives (TNA) (of the United Kingdom) (formerly the Public Record Office) at Kew, London, has the most comprehensive holdings of official documents relating to Singapore in the period from 1867 (when the Straits Settlements became a crown colony) up to independence in 1965 and much relating to the subsequent years leading up to the withdrawal from the military bases early in the 1970s. Many documents have been reproduced by the British Documents on the End of Empire Project (BDEEP). The five volumes in Series A on general imperial policy provide valuable background, and of special interest are the two volumes devoted to Malaya/Malaysia in the Series B country series: Series B, Vol. 3 (in 3 parts), A.J. Stockwell (ed.), *Malaya* (HMSO London, 1995), which covers the period from 1942 to Malayan independence in 1957); and Series B, Vol. 8, A.J. Stockwell (ed.), *Malaysia* (HMSO, London, 2004).

The British Library (BL) holds various collections of private papers (notably those of Crawfurd and Raffles) and the BL's Oriental and India Office Collections are the most comprehensive holdings of official documents relating to Singapore before 1867, when the Settlement was administered by India. They are more complete than the archives for this period in NAS, which suffered loss and damage from climate and insects over the years.

Proceedings and Consultations of the East India Company and the India Office period (before 1867) are also to be found in the National Archives in New Delhi.

The US National Archives and Records, US Army Center of Military History Records holds US Military Intelligence translations of Japanese monographs, personal accounts and other records relating to the Malayan campaign and the Occupation.

Parliamentary records

Singapore

With the exception of the Japanese Occupation and the first few weeks after liberation, there is a complete record of council, assembly, or parliamentary records since 1867, i.e.

- Straits Settlements Executive Council and Legislative Council Proceedings, 1867–1941.
- British Military Administration Advisory Council Proceedings, November 1945–March 1946.
- Singapore Advisory Council, Public Sessions, 1946–48.
- Singapore Legislative Council Proceedings, 1948–55.
- Singapore Legislative Assembly Proceedings, 1955–65.
- Singapore Parliamentary Debates, 1965 onwards.

United Kingdom

Singapore was the subject of various Parliamentary proceedings recorded in Hansard's Parliamentary Debates; British Parliamentary Accounts and Papers; and British Sessional Papers.

India

In the 1850s–1860s Singapore affairs were occasionally discussed in the Proceedings of the Legislative Council of India, 1854–61 (1st series) and 1862–67 (2nd series).

Private papers

Apart from the NAS, TNA and BL holdings, the largest collections of private papers relating to Singapore are to be found in the Royal Commonwealth Society library, now part of Cambridge University Library; and in Rhodes House (Bodleian) Library in Oxford. Of the records of Western Christian missionaries, most British society records are held in the School of Oriental and African Studies in London while the American societies' archives are housed mainly in Harvard University, in the United Mission Library, New York, and in Philadelphia. A number of other relevant private papers are to be found elsewhere, including the Arkib Negara in Kuala Lumpur, the Churchill Archives Centre (Churchill College, Cambridge); Durham University (the Malcolm MacDonald papers) and Murdoch University, Western Australia (the Peet Collection). See James F. Warren, *A Guide to the George L. Peet Collection on Singapore and Malaysia* (Perth, 1986).

Newspapers

The main English-language press sources are:

- *Malaya Tribune*, Singapore, 1914–51.
- *Singapore Chronicle*, Singapore, 1824–37.
- *Singapore Free Press*, Singapore, 1st ser. 1835–69; 2nd ser. 1884–1962 (incorporated into *Malay Mail*, in 1962).
- *Singapore Herald* (1) (Japanese-owned), Singapore 1939–41.
- *Singapore Herald* (2) Singapore, 1970–71.
- *Singapore Standard*, Singapore, 1950–59.
- *Straits Times*, Singapore, 1845–1942, 1945 onwards.
- *Syonan Times* (later the *Syonan Shimbun*), Singapore, 1942–45.

Details of holdings of the *Straits Times* and certain other English-language newspapers and Directories are given in C.M. Turnbull, *Dateline Singapore: 150 Years of the Straits Times* (Singapore, 1995). See also P. Lim Pui Huen, *Newspapers Published in the Malaysian*

Area: With a Union List of Local Holdings, Institute of Southeast Asian Studies, Occasional Paper No. 2 (Singapore, 1970).

For details of the pre-war Malay vernacular press, see W.R. Roff, *Bibliography of Malay and Arabic Periodicals in the Straits Settlements and Peninsular Malay States, 1876–1941* (London, 1972). The major post-war Malay language newspaper was the *Utusan Melayu* (Singapore, 1939–57 and Kuala Lumpur from 1957).

The emergence of the Chinese press is traced in Chen Mong Hock, *The Early Chinese Newspapers of Singapore, 1881–1912* (Singapore, 1967). The leading Chinese language newspapers were the *Nanyang Siang Pao* (Singapore, 1923–83) and *Sin Chew Jit Poh* (Singapore, 1929–83), which were replaced by *Lianhe Zaobao*, and *Lianhe Wanbao* in 1983.

Treaties

J. de Vere Allen, A.J. Stockwell and L.R. Wright (eds.), *A Collection of Treaties and Documents Affecting the States of Malaysia, 1761–1963*, 2 vols. (New York, 1981) includes text and commentary on the 1819 and 1824 Singapore treaties, the Straits Settlements Repeal Act 1946, and the Malaysian Treaties 1963.

Books and articles

General

Traditionally Singapore's history has been merged with the Malay Peninsula, as in Barbara Watson Andaya and Leonard Y. Andaya, *A History of Malaysia* (London, 1982; 2nd revised ed. Honolulu, 2002). Singapore's story was entwined with Penang and Melaka for 120 years, but there is no complete history of Penang or of the Straits Settlements colony (1826–1946), and this era figures only briefly in Paul Wheatley and Kernial Singh Sandhu (eds.), *Melaka: The Transformation of a Malay Capital, c 1400–1980*, 2 vols. (Kuala Lumpur, 1983).

The celebration of Singapore's centenary in 1919 led to the publication of W.E. Makepeace, G.S. Brooke and R. St. J. Braddell (eds.), *One Hundred Years of Singapore*, 2 vols. (London, 1921; reprinted Singapore, 1991), which explored particular aspects of Singapore's first century; and to a companion volume by Song Ong Siang, *One Hundred Years' History of the Chinese in Singapore* (London, 1923; reprinted Kuala Lumpur, 1967 and Singapore, 1984). The first history of Singapore as a separate island was H.F. Pearson's short *Singapore: A Popular History, 1819–1960* (Singapore, 1961; reprinted and briefly updated Singapore, 1985). It was only after she became an independent republic in 1965 that writers began to view Singapore as a distinct entity.

The *Journal of Southeast Asian History*, X, 1 (1969) and *Journal of the Malaysian Branch, Royal Asiatic Society*, XLII, 1 (1969) were special issues commemorating the 150th anniversary of the founding of modern Singapore, while Donald and Joanna Moore, *The First 150 Years of Singapore* (Singapore, 1969), viewed her history largely through the medium of contemporary accounts.

The first full-length narrative was C.M. Turnbull, *A History of Singapore, 1819–1975* (Kuala Lumpur, 1977); 2nd ed., *A History of Singapore, 1819–1988* (Singapore, 1989). Ernest C.T. Chew and Edwin Lee (eds.), *A History of Singapore* (Singapore, 1991) was a collaborative history by Singaporean historians. In the early twenty-first century a younger generation of historians presented a stimulating challenge to the conventional narrative: Carl A. Trocki, *Singapore: Wealth, Power and the Culture of Control* (Routledge, 2006); Hong Lysa and Huang Jianli, *The Scripting of a National History: Singapore and its Pasts* (Hong Kong and Singapore, 2008).

There is no comprehensive economic history of Singapore, but Wong Lin Ken's "Singapore: Its Growth as an Entrepôt Port 1819–1941", *JSEAS*, IX, 1 (1978), pp. 50–84, is a useful article for the period up to the Second World War, and the twentieth century is covered authoritatively in W.G. Huff, *The Economic Growth of Singapore: Trade and Development in the Twentieth Century* (Cambridge, 1994). Other economic histories treated Singapore as part of Malaya, as in Lim Chong Yah, *The Economic Development of Modern Malaya* (Kuala Lumpur, 1967), which covered the period 1874–1963; and Chiang Hai Ding, *A History of Straits Settlements*

Foreign Trade, 1870–1915 (Memoirs of the National Museum No. 6, Singapore, 1978). C.D. Cowan (ed.), *The Economic Development of South-East Asia* (London, 1964) was a collection of papers weighted heavily on Malaya and Singapore.

Economic studies relating to specific periods are noted in the following sections, but some works cover a wider span of time. These include histories of institutions and companies. Roderick MacLean, *A Pattern of Change: The Singapore International Chamber of Commerce from 1837* (Singapore, 2000) is a record of the Chamber's first 160 years. K.G. Tregonning, *Home Port Singapore* (London, 1967), is a substantial history of the Straits Steamship Company from 1890 to 1965; S. Cunyngham-Brown, *The Traders: A Story of Britain's South East Asian Commercial Adventure* (London, 1971), concerned Guthrie's, Singapore's longest surviving firm. Shorter works include K.G. Tregonning, *The Singapore Cold Storage Company, 1903–1966* (Singapore, 1966) and *Straits Tin: A Brief Account of the First Seventy Five Years of the Straits Trading Company Ltd., 1887–1962* (Singapore, 1962); Emil Helfferich, *Behn Meyer & Co. and Arnold Otto Meyer Hamburg* (1981); The Hongkong and Shanghai Banking Corporation, *A Century In Singapore, 1877–1977* (Hong Kong, 1978); Eric Jennings's handsomely illustrated books: *Mansfields: Transport and Distribution in Southeast Asia* (Singapore, 1973); *Wheels of Progress: Seventy Five Years of Cycle and Carriage* (Singapore, 1975); and *Cargoes: A Centenary Story of the Far Eastern Freight Conference* (Singapore, 1980); and Austin Coates, *The Commerce in Rubber: The First 250 Years* (Singapore, 1987).

Demographic information is contained in official census reports: notably C.A. Vlieland, *Census of British Malaya, 1931* (London, 1932) which gave a detailed analysis of Singapore's population and also in the pre-war *Straits Settlements Annual Reports, Singapore Annual Reports* 1947–63, and *Singapore Yearbooks* from 1964. Statistician Saw Swee Hock's impressive body of publications over the past forty years has built up a comprehensive picture of Singapore's population from the early nineteenth century and particularly since the Second World War. Saw has provided authoritative surveys and analyses from *Population in Transition* (Philadelphia, 1970), through to *The Population of Singapore* (Singapore, 1999; 2nd ed., Singapore, 2007), which covers the whole period from 1819 into the twenty-first century, and extensive bibliographies from Saw Swee-Hock and Cheng Siok-Hwa, *A Bibliography of the Demography of Singapore* (Singapore, 1975) through to Saw Swee Hock, *Bibliography of Singapore Demography* (Singapore, 2005).

Studies of the major Chinese community in specific periods are listed accordingly. Song Ong Siang's anecdotal *One Hundred Years' History of the Chinese in Singapore* spanned a wider time. Other works put the Singapore Chinese in a broader setting, such as Wang Gungwu, *A Short History of the Nanyang Chinese* (Singapore, 1959) and the volumes by Victor Purcell, a former colonial official with working experience of the Chinese community: *The Chinese in Malaya* (London, 1948; reprinted Kuala Lumpur, 1967); *The Chinese in Modern Malaya* (Singapore, 1956; 2nd revised ed., Singapore, 1960); and *The Chinese in South-East Asia* (Oxford, 1951; 2nd ed., 1965; reprinted Singapore, 1981); Maurice Freedman, *Lineage Organisation in Southeastern China* (London, 1958) and *Chinese Lineage and Society: Fukien and Kwangtung* (London, 1966) were pioneer anthropological background studies.

W.L. Blythe, *The Impact of the Chinese Secret Societies in Malaya* (London, 1969), expanded and challenged M.L. Wynne's pioneer *Triad and Tabut* (Singapore, 1941), Leon Comber's *Chinese Secret Societies in Malaya* (New York and Singapore, 1959), and Comber, *The Traditional Mysteries of Chinese Secret Societies in Malaya* (Singapore, 1951). Mak Lau Fong, *The Sociology of Secret Societies: A Study of Chinese Secret Societies in Singapore and Peninsular Malaysia* (Kuala Lumpur, 1981) provided a new insight, based on field-work in addition to documentary data.

Whereas most early Western historians – and particularly former colonial administrators – tended to be preoccupied with the Chinese as a law-and-order or labour problem, later writers looked at the wider social organization of the Chinese community, notably Yen Ching-hwang, *A Social History of the Chinese in Singapore and Malaya 1800–1911* (Singapore, 1986). Sikko Visscher, *The Business of Politics and Ethnicity: A History of the Singapore Chinese Chamber of Commerce and Industry* (Singapore, 2007) was the first full-length history of the Chinese Chamber of Commerce, which celebrated its centenary in 2006 and played such an important political and social as well as economic role in Singapore's story.

Kernial Singh Sandhu, *Indians in Malaya* (Cambridge, 1969), and S. Arasaratnam, *Indians in Malaysia and Singapore* (Bombay and Kuala Lumpur, 1970; revised ed., Kuala Lumpur, 1979) incorporate comprehensive accounts of the Singapore community. Sharon Siddique and Nirmala Puru Shotam, *Singapore's Little India: Past, Present and Future* (Singapore, 1982) deal specifically with the Indian enclave. Minority groups were considered in S. Durai Raja Singam, *A Hundred Years of Ceylonese in Malaya and Singapore, 1867–1967* (Kuala Lumpur, 1968); Manuel Teixeira, *The Portuguese Missions in Malaya and Singapore 1511–1958*, 3 vols. (Lisbon, 1963), of which Volume III, *Singapore*, has material about Portuguese and some prominent Eurasian families; J. Vredenbregt, "Bawean Migration: Some Preliminary Notes", *Bijdragen Tot de Taal-, Land-, en Volkenkunde*, CXX (1964), pp. 109–37, looks at the Boyanese community; Hans Schweizer-Iten, *One Hundred Years of the Swiss Club and the Swiss Community in Singapore, 1871–1971* (Singapore, 1981); William Gervase Clarence-Smith's two articles about Arab migration, "Hadramaut and the Hadhrami Diaspora in the Modern Colonial Era" and "Hadrami Entrepreneurs in the Malay World c. 1750 to c. 1940" in U. Freitag and W.G. Clarence-Smith (eds.), *Hadhrami Traders, Scholars, and Statesmen in the Indian Ocean, 1750s–1960s* (Leiden and

New York, 1997); Eze Nathan, *The History of Jews in Singapore 1830–1945* (Singapore, 1986); Jim Baker, *The Eagle in the Lion City: America, Americans and Singapore* (Singapore, 2005); and a very substantial work by Nadia H. Wright, *Respected Citizens: The History of the Armenians in Singapore and Malaysia* (Victoria, Australia, 2003).

T.W. Doraisamy (ed.), *150 Years of Education in Singapore* (Singapore, 1969) looked at the history of education up to the early years of independence. The development of education before the Second World War is discussed in D.D. Chelliah's influential *A History of the Educational Policy of the Straits Settlements* (Kuala Lumpur, 1947; reprinted Singapore, 1960), and post-war development in S. Gopinathan, *Towards a National System of Education In Singapore, 1945–1973* (Singapore, 1974). Harold E. Wilson, *Social Engineering in Singapore: Educational Policies and Social Change, 1819–1972* (Singapore, 1978) emphasizes the period 1918 to 1959. Headmaster Eugene Wijeysingha, *A History of Raffles Institution, 1823–1963* (Singapore, 1964) and *The Eagle Breeds a Gryphon: The Story of Raffles Institution, 1823–1985* (Singapore, 1989) told the story of Singapore's premier English-medium school.

R. St. J. Braddell, *The Law of the Straits Settlements: A Commentary,* 2 vols. (Singapore, 1916; 2nd ed., Singapore, 1931; reprinted Kuala Lumpur, 1982) included an important chapter on the reception of English law. W.N. Kyshe, *Cases Heard and Determined in H.M. Supreme Court of the Straits Settlements, 1808–84, 3* vols. (Singapore, 1885) gives a valuable introduction to the early history of legal development in Singapore, and Kevin Y.L. Tan, *An Introduction to Singapore's Constitution* (Singapore, 2005) is authoritative on the modern constitution.

Malcolm H. Murfett, John N. Miksic, Brian P. Farrell and Chiang Ming Shun, *Between Two Oceans: A Military History of Singapore from First Settlement to Final British Withdrawal* (Oxford, 1999) examined the island's strategic significance from the thirteenth century to 1971.

Bobby Sng Ewe Kong, *In His Good Time: The Story of the Church in Singapore 1819–1978* (Singapore, 1980), and Eugene Wijeysingha, *Going Forth: The Catholic Church in Singapore, 1819–2004* (Singapore, 2006) span the Christian missions from early days.

Singapore's changing landscape and architecture have been handsomely recorded, as in Gretchen Liu, *Singapore: A Pictorial History, 1819–2000* (Singapore, 2001) and her earlier *Pastel Portraits: Singapore's Architectural Heritage* (Singapore, 1984; re-issued 1996); and Evelyn Lip, *Chinese Temple Architecture in Singapore* (Singapore, 1983). Jane Beamish and Jane Ferguson, *A History of Singapore Architecture: The Making of a City* (Singapore, 1985) trace architectural history from 1819. A number of informative, and often well-illustrated, publications have described individual historic buildings and neighbourhoods and in particular Raffles Hotel. Raymond Flower, *Raffles: The Story of Singapore* (Singapore, 1984) is a handsomely-illustrated popular history of Singapore, using the focus of Raffles Hotel, whose fortunes are chronicled in another well-illustrated book by Ilsa Sharp, *There is Only One Raffles: The Story of a Grand Hotel* (Singapore, 1982), and Gretchen Liu, *Raffles Hotel Singapore* (Singapore, 1992). Ilsa Sharp, *The Journey: Singapore's Land Transport Story* (Singapore 2005) traces road and rail systems from the earliest days.

C.M. Turnbull, *Dateline Singapore: 150 Years of the Straits Times* (Singapore, 1995) is the history of the first 150 years of Singapore's leading English-language newspaper founded in 1845.

1 The New Settlement, 1819–1826

Singapura/Temasek

John N. Miksic and Cheryl-Ann Low Mei Gek (eds.), *Early Singapore 1300s–1819* (Singapore, 2004) is a comprehensive collection of essays and excellent illustrations presenting archaeological, cartographic and historical evidence about pre-colonial Singapore. Aileen Lau and Laura Lau (eds.), *Maritime Heritage of Singapore* (Singapore, 2005) is a handsome production, with useful text and illustrations about the pre-colonial activity in the Straits of Singapore, including Peter Borschberg, "Mapping Singapore and Southeast Asia", pp. 43–46. A further important article by Peter Borschberg, "The Straits of Singapore: Continuity, Change and Confusion", is included in Irene Lim (ed.), *Sketching the Straits: A Compilation of the Lecture Series on the Charles Dyce Collection* (Singapore, 2004), pp. 33–48.

These modern works update the portrayal of fourteenth-century Temasek in P. Wheatley, *The Golden Khersonese* (Singapore, 1961), a pioneer historical geography of early Malaya, and P. Wheatley, *Impressions of the Malay Peninsula in Ancient Times* (Singapore, 1964).

The major part of *JMBRAS*, XLII, 1 (1969), the Singapore 150th Anniversary Commemorative Issue [reprinted as M. Sheppard (ed.), *Singapore 150 Years* (Singapore, 1982)], is devoted to reprints of articles appearing in past issues of the *JMBRAS* and *JSBRAS* concerning pre-colonial Singapore and the early years of the modern settlement. O.W. Wolters, *The Fall of Srivijaya in Malay History* (Ithaca, 1970) is a stimulating interpretation of Temasek's history in the fourteenth century.

The earliest indigenous history of Temasek/Singapura is the *Sejarah Melayu* (*Malay Annals*), probably written in the early seventeenth century, the most outstanding and colourful of

Malay histories. The best English version is C.C. Brown (trans.), "Sejarah Melayu or 'Malay Annals'; A Translation of Raffles MS 17", *JMBRAS*, XXV, 2 and 3 (1953); reprinted as *Sejarah Melayu: "Malay Annals"* (Kuala Lumpur, 1970).

The founding of modern Singapore

The best Malay source is the vivid description given by Munshi Abdullah bin Abdul Kadir, *The Hikayat Abdullah* (Singapore, 1849), translated and annotated by A.H. Hill, *JMBRAS*, XXVIII, 3 (1955), and reprinted as *The Hikayat Abdullah* (Kuala Lumpur, 1970). Munshi Abdullah, who was born in Melaka of Malay/Arab/Tamil descent, came to Singapore about 1820 and remained there for most of his life until he died in 1854. His colourful autobiography provides the only detailed Asian eyewitness account of Singapore's first thirty years.

The *Tuhfat al-Nafis* (or *Precious Gift*), written by Raja Ali Al-Haji bin Raja Ahmad of Riau in 1865, covering the history of Riau and South Malaya from the seventeenth to the mid-nineteenth centuries, gives the Malay/Bugis interpretation. Virginia Matheson and Barbara Andaya (eds.), *The Precious Gift* (*Tuhfat Al-Nafis*) (Kuala Lumpur, 1982) provides an annotated English translation. A romanized version was published as *Tuhfat al-Nafis: Sejarah Melayu dan Bugis* (Singapore, 1965). The Jawi text with an English summary appears in R.O. Winstedt (trans. and ed.), "A Malay History of Riau and Johore", *JMBRAS*, X, 2 (1932), pp. 1–320.

C.H. Wake, "Raffles and the Rajas: The Founding of Singapore in Malayan and British Colonial History", *JMBRAS*, XLVIII, 1 (1975), pp. 47–73 places the foundation of modern Singapore in the setting of Malay politics. Anthony C. Milner, *Kerajaan: Malay Political Culture on the Eve of Colonial Rule* (Tucson, 1982) gives useful background, while Carl A. Trocki, *Prince of Pirates: The Temenggongs and the Development of Johor and Singapore, 1784–1885* (Singapore, 1979; 2nd ed., Singapore 2007) is an original and important study based on English and Malay sources.

Extensive work on Raffles and this period is being carried out by John Bastin, who contributed Introductions to modern reprints of T.S. Raffles, *Statement of the Services of Sir Thomas Stamford Raffles* (London, 1824; reprinted Kuala Lumpur, 1978); and to Sophia Raffles, *Memoir of the Life and Public Services of Sir Thomas Stamford Raffles FRS* (London, 1830), and as 2 volumes (London, 1835; reprinted Singapore, 1991). Bastin also printed privately a number of booklets, which throw light on the founding of Singapore: *Sir Stamford Raffles's Account of the Founding of Singapore* (Eastbourne, 2004), comprising commentary and original documents, including Raffles's unpublished despatch to the Supreme Government of India, 13 February 1819, reporting his taking of Singapore; *Sir Stamford Raffles's Historical Sketch of the Settlement of Singapore* (Eastbourne, 2000); *John Leyden and Thomas Stamford Raffles* (Eastbourne, 2003); *Lady Raffles's Memoir of the Life and Public Services of Sir Thomas Stamford Raffles* (Eastbourne, 2004). *William Farquhar, First Resident and Commandant of Singapore* (Eastbourne, 2005) is a privately printed revised version of the biography of Farquhar in John Bastin, Ivan Polunin and Kwa Chong Guan (eds. and introduction), *The William Farquhar Collection of Natural History Drawings*, 2 vols. (Singapore, 2000), and suggests that in many ways Farquhar had a better claim than Raffles to be the founder and certainly the father figure of Singapore.

The definitive biography of Raffles remains to be written. Of existing biographies the best and most meticulously researched is C.E. Wurtzburg, *Raffles of the Eastern Isles* (London, 1954; reprinted

Singapore, 1984). Older studies tended to be uncritically admiring: D.C. de K. Boulger, *The Life of Sir Stamford Raffles* (London, 1897; reprinted London, 1973); H.E. Egerton, *Sir Stamford Raffles: England in the Far East* (London, 1900); and R. Coupland, *Raffles, 1781–1826* (London, 1926); 3rd ed. reprinted as *Raffles of Singapore* (London, 1946). Emily Hahn, *Raffles of Singapore* (London, 1946; reprinted Kuala Lumpur, 1968) is a racy account but more perceptive than M. Collis, *Raffles* (London, 1966). Syed Hussein Alatas, *Thomas Stamford Raffles, 1781–1826: Schemer or Reformer* (Sydney, 1971), and Syed Muhd Khairudin Aljunied, *Raffles and Reform A Study of Sir Thomas Stamford Raffles's Discourse on Religion among the Malays* (Kuala Lumpur, 2004) offer revisionist, more critical interpretations.

The diplomatic background to the founding of modern Singapore is covered in detail in H. Marks, "The First Contest for Singapore: 1819–1824", *Verhandelingen van het Koninklijk Instituut voor Taal-, Land-, en Volkenkunde*, XXVII (The Hague, 1959), and N. Tarling, *Anglo-Dutch Rivalry in the Malay World, 1780–1824* (Cambridge and Queensland, 1962). There are two excellent collections of documents relating to early Singapore: T. Braddell, "Notices of Singapore", *JIA*, VII (1853), pp. 325–57; *JIA*, VIII (1854), pp. 97–111, 329–48, 403–19; *JIA*, IX (1855), pp. 53–65, 442–82; and C.D. Cowan, "Early Penang and the Rise of Singapore", *JMBRAS*, XXIII, 2 (1950), 210 pp.

J. Crawfurd, *Journal of an Embassy from the Governor-General to the Courts of Siam and Cochin China* (London, 1828; reprinted Kuala Lumpur, 1967 and Singapore, 1987) describes his visit to Singapore in 1822 and some aspects of Crawfurd's period as Resident from 1823–26.

C.B. Buckley, *An Anecdotal History of Old Times in Singapore, 1819–1867* (Singapore, 1902; reprinted Kuala Lumpur, 1965 and Singapore, 1984), uses mainly contemporary newspapers and personal memories to describe the early years. Buckley's *History* is not entirely trustworthy but an invaluable source, since many of the original journals have been lost.

K.G. Tregonning, *The British in Malaya: The First Forty Years, 1786–1826* (Tucson, 1965) has a final chapter on the origins of modern Singapore. Brian Harrison, *Holding the Fort: Melaka under Two Flags, 1795–1845* (Kuala Lumpur, 1985) has a chapter on early Singapore, upholding Farquhar's claims.

Several works deal with missionary activities and the plans for the Anglo-Chinese College in Singapore. Elizabeth Morrison, *Memoir of the Life and Labours of Robert Morrison D.D. Compiled by His Widow*, 2 vols. (London, 1839), describes her husband's visit to Singapore in 1823. See also Brian Harrison, *Waiting for China: The Anglo-Chinese College at Malacca, 1818–1843, and Early Nineteenth-century Missions* (Hong Kong, 1979); R. Lovett, *The History of the London Missionary Society, 1795–1895* (1899); and H.E. Wilson, "An Abortive Plan for an Anglo-Chinese College in Singapore", *JMBRAS*, XL, 2 (1972), pp. 97–109.

David Marshall Lang, *The Armenians: A People in Exile* (London, 1981) includes the Armenian community in early Singapore and their background.

2 "This Spirited and Splendid Little Colony", 1826–1867

The period is covered by L.A. Mills, "British Malaya, 1824–67", *JMBRAS*, III, 2 (1925), revised as *JMBRAS*, XXXIII, 3 (1960), reprinted as *British Malaya 1824–67* (Kuala Lumpur, 1966); and by C.M. Turnbull, *The Straits Settlements, 1826–67* (London and Kuala Lumpur, 1972), both of which have comprehensive bibliographies.

The *Journal of the Indian Archipelago and Eastern Asia*, edited by J.R. Logan, 12 vols. (Singapore, 1847–59), has many valuable articles on contemporary affairs in Singapore.

A.H. Hill (ed. and trans.), *The Hikayat Abdullah* (Kuala Lumpur, 1970) is particularly valuable for this period. Munshi Abdullah also left descriptions of two big Singapore fires: *Shaer Singapura Terbakar* about a fire in February 1830, and *Shaer Kampong Gelam Terbakar*, concerning a disastrous fire which destroyed Kampong Glam in 1847, of which a romanized annotated version appears in C. Skinner (ed.), *JMBRAS*, XLV, 1 (1972), pp. 21–56.

Buckley's *Anecdotal History* is based mainly on excerpts from the *Singapore Free Press* for the post-1835 period. This era is particularly rich in contemporary writings on maritime Southeast Asia. Of those directly relating to Singapore, the widely travelled G.W. Earl, *The Eastern Seas* (London, 1837; reprinted Kuala Lumpur, 1971) gives the best eyewitness view of the settlement in the 1830s, while P.J. Begbie, *The Malayan Peninsula* (Madras, 1834; reprinted Kuala Lumpur, 1967); and T.J. Newbold, *Political and Statistical Account of the British Settlements in the Straits of Malacca*, 2 vols. (London, 1839; reprinted Kuala Lumpur, 1971) each have a chapter on Singapore. Unfortunately a second volume of J.H. Moor (ed.), *Notices of the Indian Archipelago and the Adjacent Countries* (Singapore, 1836; reprinted London, 1968), which was to contain material on Singapore in the 1830s, was never published.

The most comprehensive contemporary description of Singapore in the last years of Indian rule is J. Cameron, *Our Tropical Possessions in Malayan India* (London, 1865; reprinted Kuala Lumpur, 1965). Further factual information about this period is given in T. Braddell, *Singapore and the Straits Settlements Described* (Penang, 1858) and *Statistics of the British Possessions in the Straits of Malacca* (Penang, 1861).

J.T. Thomson, *Some Glimpses into Life in the Far East* (London, 1864) and *Sequel to Some Glimpses into Life in the Far East* (London, 1865) reprinted as John Hall-Jones (ed.), *Glimpses into Life in Malayan Lands* (Kuala Lumpur, 1985) are lively but scathing about the Straits administration and Governor Butterworth in particular. For Thomson's career as architect, artist, and government surveyor, see John Hall-Jones and Christopher Hooi, *An Early Surveyor in Singapore: John Turnbull Thomson in Singapore, 1841–1853* (Singapore, 1979). John Hall-Jones, *The Thomson Paintings: Mid-Nineteenth Century Paintings of the Straits Settlements and Malaya* (Singapore, 1983) reproduces sixteen of Thomson's paintings. Irene

Lim, *Sketching the Straits: A Compilation of the Lecture Series on the Charles Dyce Collection* (Singapore, 2004) was inspired by Dyce's watercolours of this period.

Orfeur Cavenagh's autobiography, *Reminiscences of an Indian Official* (London, 1884) includes a detailed but uninspired account of his governorship. W.H. Read, *Play and Politics: Reminiscences of Malaya by an Old Resident* (London, 1901) is a disappointing book, the ramblings of an old man who had played a prominent part in commercial and public affairs in mid-nineteenth century Singapore. J.F.A. McNair, *Prisoners Their Own Warders* (London, 1899) is a valuable first-hand account of the convict system which he supervised under the Indian regime.

J.D. Vaughan, *The Manners and Customs of the Chinese of the Straits Settlements* (Singapore, 1879; reprinted Kuala Lumpur, 1971) is a sympathetic account. Seah Eu Chin, "The Chinese in Singapore; General Sketch of the Numbers, Tribes and Avocations of the Chinese in Singapore", *JIA*, II (1848), pp. 283–9, was contributed by a leading Chinese. Other useful studies by well-informed contemporaries are T. Braddell, "Notes on the Chinese in the Straits", *JIA*, IX (1855), pp. 109–24; W.A. Pickering, "The Chinese in the Straits of Malacca", *Fraser's Magazine* (October 1876); and W.A. Pickering, "Chinese Secret Societies and Their Origin", *JSBRAS*, I (1878), pp. 63–84, and II (1878), pp. 1–18.

J. Crawfurd, *A Descriptive Dictionary of the Indian Islands and Adjacent Countries* (London, 1856; reprinted Kuala Lumpur, 1971), pp. 395–402, has a long entry on Singapore.

There are a number of important contemporary missionary references to Singapore in the earlier part of this period, including David Abeel, *Journal of a Residence in China and the Neighbouring Countries from 1829 to 1833* (New York, 1834; 2nd ed., New York, 1836); Jacob Tomlin, *Missionary Journal Kept at Singapore and Siam from May 1830 to January 1832* (Malacca, 1832); Walter H. Medhurst, *Journal of a Tour through the Settlements on the East Side of the Peninsula of Malacca, 1828* (Singapore, 1828); Daniel Tyerman and George Bennet, "Report on the Mission at Singapore", Morrison Collection,

Hong Kong University; J. Montgomery (comp.), *Journal of Voyages and Travels* (by Tyerman and Bennet), 2 vols. (London, 1831); and Singapore Christian Union, *The First Report of the Singapore Christian Union* (Singapore, 1830).

Turning to more modern works, Yen Ching-hwang, *A Social History of the Chinese in Singapore and Malaya 1800–1911* (Singapore, 1986) shed valuable insight into Chinese associations in this still shadowy time. Lee Poh Ping, *Chinese Society in Nineteenth Century Singapore* (Kuala Lumpur, 1978) was an original socio-political study, based on indigenous as well as English-language sources. M. Freedman threw valuable light on Chinese society at that time in "Immigrants and Associations: Chinese in 19th Century Singapore", *Comparative Studies in Society and History*, III (The Hague, 1960–61), pp. 25–48, and "Chinese Kinship and Marriage in Early Singapore", *JSEAH*, III, 2 (1962), reprinted in *The Study of Chinese Society: Essays by Maurice Freedman*, selected and introduced by G. William Skinner (Stanford, 1979). See also Wong Choon San, *A Gallery of Chinese Kapitans* (Singapore, 1964), pp. 27–37; Lea E. Williams, "Chinese Leadership in Early British Singapore", *Asian Studies*, II, 2 (1964), pp. 170–79; and an early article by Yong Ching Fatt, "Chinese Leadership in Nineteenth Century Singapore", *Journal of the Island Society (Hsin-she Hsueh-pao)*, I (1967), pp. 1–18, which studies the background of fifteen important community leaders.

Some interesting insights into perceptions in China itself of Singapore's role in this period are given in Jane Kate Leonard, *Wei Yuan and China's Rediscovery of the Maritime World* (Harvard, 1984).

Nicholas Tarling, "British Policy in the Malay Peninsula and Archipelago, 1824–71", *JMBRAS*, XXX, 3 (1957), reprinted as *British Policy in the Malay Peninsula and Archipelago, 1824–71* (Kuala Lumpur, 1970) deals in meticulous detail with the relations between Singapore and the neighbouring regions. This theme is developed further in relation to piracy in N. Tarling, *Piracy and Politics in the Malay World: A Study of British Imperialism in the Nineteenth Century* (Melbourne, 1963).

Wong Lin Ken, "The Trade of Singapore, 1819–69", *JMBRAS*, XXX, 4 (1960), 315 pp. (reprinted as MBRAS Reprint No. 23,

2003) is a thorough study of Singapore's trade before the opening of the Suez Canal.

Lee Yong-kiat, *The Medical History of Early Singapore* (Tokyo, 1978) is a substantial work on the 1819–74 period based on primary sources.

3 High Noon of Empire, 1867–1914

Many aspects of this period are dealt with in W.E. Makepeace, R. St. J. Braddell and G.S. Brooke (eds.), *One Hundred Years of Singapore*, 2 vols. (London, 1921). Edwin Lee, *The British as Rulers: Governing Multiracial Singapore, 1867–1914* (Singapore, 1991) portrays the colonial government in its most confident years.

The leading English-language newspapers, the *Straits Times* and the *Singapore Free Press*, flourished during much of this period, and the first vernacular newspapers begin to throw light on some of the activities of the Muslim and Chinese communities. But there were no outstanding contemporary books.

G.M. Reith, *Handbook to Singapore* (1907) (Singapore, 1907; reprinted Singapore, 1986), the second edition of a guidebook first published in 1892, is interesting not only as a description but showing European attitudes at that time.

J.D. Ross, *Sixty Years: Life and Adventure in the Far East*, 2 vols. (London, 1911; reprinted London, 1968) is a colourful story about the author and his relatives in Singapore, Borneo and the region in the second half of the century. But, while the port is not specifically named, the most evocative picture of Singapore in the 1880s appears in the stories of Joseph Conrad, and in particular "The End of the Tether" in *Youth: A Narrative, and Two Other Stories* (Edinburgh, 1902), and *The Shadow Line* (New York and London, 1917). These are discussed in N. Sherry, *Conrad's Eastern World* (Cambridge, 1966).

Conrad had more opportunity to study Singapore's port life than upper-class casual visitors who left brief impressions, such as Isabella Bird, *The Golden Chersonese and the Way Thither* (New York, 1883; reprinted Kuala Lumpur, 1967 and 1980) or Florence Caddy, *To Siam and Malaya in the Duke of Sutherland's Yacht "Sans Peur"* (London, 1889). There are brief comments by Kuo Sung-T'ao and Sir Halliday Macartney in John D. Frodsham (trans.), *The First Chinese Embassy to the West: The Journals of Kuo Sung-T'ao, Liu Hsi-Hung and Chang Te-Yi* (Oxford, 1974) on their visit to Singapore in 1876.

J.A. Bethune Cook, *Sunny Singapore* (London, 1907) has useful information about mission activities, E.A. Brown, *Indiscreet Memories* (London, 1935), a detailed diary of European social life at the beginning of the twentieth century, contains much trivia with some revealing glimpses, R.O. Winstedt, *Start from Alif: Count from One* (Kuala Lumpur, 1969) describes his brief first impressions of Singapore when he arrived as a Malayan Civil Service cadet in 1902.

Weighty "pride of empire" books published at the turn of the century tended to give potted histories and factual descriptions of Singapore but reflected the confident atmosphere of the time, such as N.B. Dennys, *A Descriptive Dictionary of British Malaya* (London, 1894), which was designed as a follow-up to Crawfurd's *Dictionary*; C.C. Wakefield, *Future Trade in the Far East* (London, 1896) which has four pages on Singapore as part of "the Minor East", i.e. Southeast Asia; A. Wright and H.A. Cartwright, *Twentieth Century Impressions of British Malaya* (London, 1908), a monumental tome which devoted a section to Singapore's background, pp. 20–48; or A. Wright and T.H. Reid, *The Malay Peninsula: A Record of Progress in the Middle East* (London, 1912), a complacent work with a chapter on contemporary Singapore, pp. 217–36.

Paul Kratoska (ed.), *Honourable Intentions: Talks on the British Empire in South-East Asia Delivered at the Royal Colonial Institute 1874–1928* (Kuala Lumpur, 1983) contains a lecture given by Governor Sir Frederick Weld in 1884 on "The Straits Settlements and British Malaya".

There is a wealth of literature on Singapore's relations with the Malay States and the spread of British rule, starting with the partly autobiographical work by Frank Swettenham, *British Malaya* (London, 1948; reprinted London, 1955). The theme was taken up later in academic studies based on original research into contemporary sources. Khoo Kay Kim, *The Western Malay States,*

1850–1873 (Kuala Lumpur, 1972) shows the involvement of the Straits Settlements with the Malay States before the British formally intervened. The intervention is the subject of C.D. Cowan, *Nineteenth Century Malaya: The Origins of British Control* (London, 1961) and C.N. Parkinson, *British Intervention in Malaya, 1867–77* (Singapore, 1960), W.D. McIntyre, *The Imperial Frontier in the Tropics, 1865–75* (London and New York, 1967) and J.S. Galbraith, "The 'Turbulent Frontier' as a Factor in British Expansion", *Comparative Studies in Society and History*, II, 2 (1960), pp. 150–68, put the Malay States frontier problem in its imperial setting. E. Sadka, *The Protected Malay States, 1874–1895* (Kuala Lumpur, 1968) and E. Thio, *British Policy in the Malay Peninsula, 1880–1910, Volume I: The Southern and Central States* (Singapore, 1969) are excellent studies of the extension and consolidation of British rule.

E.M. Merewether, *Report on the Census of the Straits Settlements Taken on the 5th April 1891* (Singapore, 1892) and J.R. Innes, *Report on the Census of the Straits Settlements taken on 1st March 1901* (London, 1901) contain vital information concerning Singapore's population.

Song Ong Siang, *One Hundred Years' History of the Chinese in Singapore* is a major source of information on this period. The *Straits Chinese Magazine* (Singapore, 1897–1907) has many pertinent articles. Gwee Thian Hock, *A Nonya Mosaic: My Mother's Childhood* (Singapore, 1985) gives a fascinating vignette of the life and customs of a well-to-do Singapore Baba family in the early twentieth century. Wu Lien-Teh, *Plague Fighter: The Autobiography of a Modern Chinese Physician* (Cambridge, 1959) portrays Straits Chinese life at the turn of the century, although it relates primarily to Penang.

Eunice Thio, "The Singapore Chinese Protectorate: Events and Conditions leading to Its Establishment 1823–1877", *JSSS*, XVI, 1 and 2 (1960), pp. 40–80, is a careful study of the origins of the Chinese Protectorate. Cheng Siok-Hwa, "Government Legislation for Chinese Secret Societies in the Straits Settlements in the Late 19th Century", *Asian Studies*, 10, 2 (1972), pp. 262–71 deals with the subsequent years. R.N. Jackson, *Pickering: Protector of Chinese* (Kuala Lumpur, 1965) is a short but interesting biography of the first

Protector of Chinese by a former Chinese Secretariat administrator. R.N. Jackson, *Immigrant Labour and the Development of Malaya, 1786–1920* deals mostly with the Malay States but sets the work of the Protectorate in context.

Png Poh Seng, "The Straits Chinese in Singapore: A Case of Local Identity and Socio-Cultural Accommodation", *JSEAH*, X, 1 (1969), pp. 95–114, investigates problems facing Singapore Chinese society at this time.

Studies on opium in this period include Cheng U Wen, "Opium in the Straits Settlements, 1867–1910", *JSEAH*, II, 1 (1961), pp. 52–57: and Carl A. Trocki, "The Rise of Singapore's Opium Syndicate, 1840–86", *JSEAS*, XVIII, 1 (March 1987), pp. 58–80, followed by his stimulating but controversial *Opium and Empire: Chinese Society in Colonial Singapore, 1800–1910* (Ithaca, 1990) arguing the crucial role of opium in the colonial economy.

Using mainly Chinese-language sources, a good deal of research has been devoted to the study of the changing character of the Chinese community in the late nineteenth/early twentieth centuries, and its relationship with late imperial China. Michael R. Godley, *The Mandarin-Capitalists from Nanyang: Overseas Chinese Enterprise in the Modernization of China 1893–1911* (Cambridge, 1981). Yen Ching-hwang's work has concentrated on this period: notably *The Overseas Chinese and the 1911 Revolution: With Special Reference to Singapore and Malaya* (Kuala Lumpur, 1976), the major part of Yen's *A Social History of the Chinese in Singapore and Malaya 1800–1911* (Singapore, 1986), and his *Coolies and Mandarins: China's Protection of Overseas Chinese in the Late Ch'ing Period* (Singapore, 1985) although the latter relates primarily to North America.

Yong Ching Fatt, *Chinese Leadership and Power in Colonial Singapore* (Singapore, 1992) examined leadership in the Chinese community. In contrast James F. Warren, *Rickshaw Coolie: A People's History of Singapore (1880–1940)* (Singapore, 1986) used untapped coroner's court reports to portray a poignant picture of coolie life, although the major focus of the book is on the inter-war period.

Png Poh Seng discussed the early Chinese revolutionary movement in "The KMT in Malaya", *JSEAH*, II, 1 (1961), pp. 214–25.

There are a number of economic studies, notably Francis E. Hyde, *Far Eastern Trade, 1860–1914* (London, 1973); G. Bogaars, "The Tanjong Pagar Dock Company, 1864–1905", *Memoirs of the Raffles Museum*, III (Singapore, 1956), pp. 117–266; Chiang Hai Ding, "Sino-British Mercantile Relations in Singapore's Entrepôt Trade, 1870–1915" in J. Ch'en Chi-Jang and N. Tarling (eds.), *Studies in the Social History of China and South-East Asia* (Cambridge, 1970), pp. 247–66: G. Bogaars, "The Effect of the Opening of the Suez Canal on the Trade and Development of Singapore", *JMBRAS*, XXVIII, 1 (1955), pp. 99–143; D.R. Sardesai, *British Trade and Expansion in Southeast Asia, 1830–1914* (Bombay, 1977) and his *Trade and Empire in Malaya and Singapore l869–74* (Ohio, 1970); and Chiang Hai Ding, "A History of Straits Settlements Foreign Trade, 1870–1915", *Memoirs of the National Museum*, No. 6 (Singapore, 1978).

John G. Butcher, *The British in Malaya, 1880–1941: The Social History of a European Community in Colonial South-East Asia* (Kuala Lumpur, 1979) is mainly devoted to the Malay Peninsula but has relevance to Singapore. Chan Kwok Bun and Tony Chee Kiong (ed.), *Past Times: A Social History of Singapore* (Singapore, 2003) includes a description of the changing lifestyle among wealthy Asians.

4 "The Clapham Junction of the Eastern Seas", 1914–1941

The English-language press, joined in 1914 by the *Malaya Tribune*, and the Chinese newspapers, notably the *Nanyang Siang Pao* and the *Sin Chew Jit Poh*, both founded in the 1920s, are an invaluable source of material for this period.

On-the-spot investigation by a number of able North American scholars produced some admirable studies of British colonial administration on the eve of the Second World War. R. Emerson, *Malaysia: A Study in Direct and Indirect Rule* (New York, 1937; reprinted Kuala Lumpur, 1964), although considered controversial in its day, is the most acute analysis and commentary on government and society in the Straits Settlements in the 1930s. L.A. Mills,

British Rule in Eastern Asia (London, 1942) was a balanced and sober assessment, based on a pre-war 1936–37 visit and documentary study. Virginia Thompson, *Postmortem on Malaya* (New York, 1943) is a scholarly, well-researched and substantial analysis but highly critical of the colonial system in the light of the 1941–42 debacle. See also R. Emerson, L.A. Mills and V. Thompson, *Government and Nationalism in Southeast Asia* (New York, 1942).

From Government House, Laurence Guillemard's appropriately-titled *Trivial Fond Records* (London, 1937) gives a disappointing description of his governorship from 1919 to 1927, and H.A. Gailey, *Clifford: Imperial Proconsul* (London, 1982) has only a brief section about his successor Clifford's unhappy time as Governor. Brian Montgomery, *Shenton of Singapore: The Life of Sir Shenton Thomas, Governor and Prisoner of War* (London, 1984) is useful mainly for the war years.

Apart from a host of superficial or frivolous recorded impressions of the inter-war years, there are a number of interesting contemporary accounts. George L. Peet, *Rickshaw Reporter* (Singapore, 1985) which records Peet's memories of his first tour of duty from 1923 to 1927 as a young newspaper reporter; R.C.H. McKie, *This Was Singapore* (London, 1950), the colourful account of another young journalist's life in the late 1930s; Roland St. J. Braddell, *Lights of Singapore* (London, 1934; reprinted Kuala Lumpur, 1982) by a third-generation British Singaporean lawyer; R.H.B. Lockhart, *Return to Malaya* (London, 1936), which compares the Singapore of the mid-1930s with the pre-First World War era. Two police officers published worthwhile reminiscences: R.H. de S. Onraet, *Singapore: A Police Background* (London, 1947), written by an Inspector-General of Police of the inter-war years: and A. Dixon, *Singapore Patrol* (London, 1935), describing a junior policeman's work in the mid-1920s. Victor Purcell, *The Memoirs of a Malayan Official* (London, 1965) are the experiences of a Malayan Civil Service official, who served from 1921 to 1946, becoming Adviser on Chinese Affairs to the British Military Administration in 1945–46. In the inter-war years Purcell worked with the Chinese Protectorate, mainly in the Straits Settlements and part of the time in Singapore.

A. Gilmour, *An Eastern Cadet's Anecdotage* (Singapore, 1974) gives some glimpses into a junior official's life, although his reminiscences relate mainly to up-country Malaya.

Of contemporary descriptions by Asian writers, Janet Lim, *Sold for Silver* (London and New York, 1958; reprinted Singapore, 1985 and 2004), is the fascinating autobiography of a *mui tsai* of the 1930s, who subsequently became a hospital matron. Low Ngiong Ing, *Chinese Jetsam on a Tropic Shore* (Singapore, 1974) is a vivid autobiographical portrayal of life among the Chinese poor in this period, and was later reprinted as part of *Recollections* (Singapore, 1983). J.B. van Cuylenburg, *Singapore: Through Sunshine and Shadow* (Singapore, 1982) tells his story as a second-generation Singaporean born in 1895 of Ceylonese burgher stock, who became a medical doctor and pre-war municipal councilor. Yap Pheng Geck, *Scholar, Banker, Gentleman, Soldier: The Reminiscences of Dr. Yap Pheng Geck* (Singapore, 1982) is the autobiography of a Johor village boy born in 1901, who became a Singapore banker in the 1930s and a post-war stalwart of the Straits Chinese British Association.

David L. Kenley, *New Culture in a New World: The May Fourth Movement and the Chinese Diaspora in Singapore, 1919–1932* (New York, 2003) explored the intellectual background to the political upheavals among the Singapore Chinese in the inter-war years.

The Singapore Chinese Chamber of Commerce, *Fifty Years of Enterprise* (Singapore, 1964), had interesting material about Chinese leaders. Yong Ching Fatt, *Tan Kah-kee: The Making of an Overseas Chinese Legend* (Singapore, 1987) is a well-researched biography, and Tan's autobiography was translated by A.H.C. Ward, Raymond W. Chu and Janet Salaff (eds. and trans.), *The Memoirs of Tan Kah Kee* (Singapore, 1994). Yong Ching Fatt, "Emergence of Chinese Community Leaders in Singapore, 1890–1941", *Journal of the South Seas Society*, 30, 1 and 2 (1975), pp. 1–18; and Yong Ching Fatt, "Leadership and Power in the Chinese Community of Singapore during the 1930s", *JSEAS*, VIII, 2 (1977), pp. 195–209.

On the political activities of the Singapore Chinese, Y. Akashi, *The Nanyang Chinese Anti-Japanese National Salvation Movement, 1937–41* (Kansas, 1970) was a valuable pioneer study, based on

Japanese, English and Chinese sources, and Akashi continued to research on Japanese activities in Singapore and Malaya during the wartime Occupation. Pang Wing Seng, "The Double Seventh Incident, 1937: Singapore Chinese Response to the Outbreak of the Sino-Japanese War", *JSEAS*, IV, 2 (1973), pp. 269–99, offers an insight into leadership and institutions among the Singapore Chinese. See also Tsui Kuei-chiang, "The Response of the Straits Chinese to the May 4th Movement" (in Chinese). *Journal of the South Seas Society*, XX (1966), pp. 13–18; Stephen Leong, "The Malayan Overseas Chinese and the Sino-Japanese War, 1937–1941", *JSEAS*, X, 2 (1979), pp. 293–520; and Wang Gungwu, "The Limits of Nanyang Chinese Nationalism, 1912–1937", in C.D. Cowan and O.W. Wolters (eds.), *Southeast Asian History and Historiography: Essays Presented to D.G.E. Hall* (Ithaca, 1976), pp. 405–23.

J. Chesneaux, *The Chinese Labor Movement, 1919–1927* (French original edition, 1962; trans. by H.M. Wright, Stanford, 1968) is invaluable as a background study. There are several useful works on the inter-war labour movement in Singapore, which mainly affected the Chinese: C. Gamba, *The Origins of Trade Unionism in Malaya: A Study of Colonial Labour Unrest* (Singapore, 1962) is a substantial well-researched work. J.N. Parmer, "Attempts at Labour Organization by Chinese Workers in Certain Industries in the 1930s", in K.G. Tregonning (ed.), *Papers on Malayan History* (Singapore, 1962), pp. 239–55, gives an interesting insight into the labour movement in Singapore among seamen, pineapple industry and building workers.

A number of studies of the Overseas Chinese and their ancestral home background throw valuable light on the Singapore Chinese as the major Nanyang community, notably Chen Ta, *Emigrant Communities in South China: A Study of Overseas Migration and Its Influence on Standards of Living and Social Change* (Shanghai, 1939; and New York, 1940), based upon field-work carried out in China in the mid-1930s. See also H.F. MacNair, *The Chinese Abroad, Their Position and Protection: A Study of International Law and Relations* (Shanghai, 1925; reprinted Taipeh, 1971).

Although not directly concerned with Singapore, two autobiographical works throw light on contrasting Baba Chinese lifestyles in this period. Queeny Chang, *Memoirs of a Nonya* (Singapore, 1981) gives a vivid picture of traditional Straits Chinese home life in Penang and Medan in the first quarter of the century. Ruth Ho, *Rainbow Round My Shoulder* (Singapore, 1975) portrays the different family background of a third-generation Straits Chinese girl in a Christian, Westernized, English-speaking Malacca family in the 1930s.

James Warren's *Rickshaw Coolie* (Singapore, 1986) is particularly useful for this period, together with his study of Japanese prostitutes: James F. Warren, *Ah Ku and Karayuki-san: Prostitution in Singapore* (Singapore, 1993).

Kuomintang activities are discussed in Png Poh Seng, "The KMT in Malaya", *JSEAH*, II, 2 (1961), pp. 1–32, reprinted in K.G. Tregonning (ed.), *Papers on Malayan History* (Singapore, 1962); and Yong Ching Fatt and R.B. McKenna, *The Kuomintang Movement in British Malaya, 1912–1949* (Singapore, 1990).

J.D. Brimmell's excellent *Communism in South East Asia* (London, 1959) looks at the movement in Singapore in the context of the region, while C.B. McLane, *Soviet Strategies in Southeast Asia: An Explanation of Eastern Policy under Lenin and Stalin* (Princeton, 1966) sets Singapore in the Communist International background. J.D. Brimmell, *A Short History of the Malayan Communist Party* (Singapore, 1956) is very brief. Harry Miller, *Menace in Malaya* (London, 1954) has a good readable account of the early communist movement in Singapore.

D.D. Chelliah's seminal *A History of the Educational Policy of the Straits Settlements* (Kuala Lumpur, 1947; 2nd ed., Singapore, 1960), completed before the Japanese war, is the most comprehensive treatment of education in this period, while Harold E. Wilson, *Social Engineering in Singapore: Educational Policies and Social Change, 1819–1972* (Singapore, 1978) concentrates on the post-1918 era. Victor Purcell, *Problems of Chinese Education* (London, 1936) is a substantial and useful book by an official directly involved, I.S. Nagle, *Educational Needs of the Strait Settlements and Federated Malay States* (Baltimore, 1928) contains much detailed information about the system, and R.O. Winstedt, *Education in Malaya* (Singapore, 1924), a booklet written when the author was Director of Education, is a useful summary.

British Foreign Office documents on the opium trade were published as *The Opium Trade, 1910–1941*, 6 vols. (Delaware, 1974).

R.W.E. Harper and Harry Miller, *Singapore Mutiny: The Story of a Little "Local Disturbance"* (Kuala Lumpur, 1984); and Nicholas Tarling, "The Singapore Mutiny, 1915", *JMBRAS*, LV, 2 (1982), pp. 26–59, describe the mutiny of 1915. Rhodes House, Oxford, and the Royal Commonwealth Society Library, Cambridge, house some personal reminiscences. Lauterbach's role is described in a dated but once popular book by Lowell Thomas, *Lauterbach of the China Sea* (London, 1930), and in a chapter of Dan van der Vat, *The Last Corsair: The Story of the Emden* (London, 1983). A.C. Bose, *Indian Revolutionaries Abroad* (Patna, 1971) refers to the mutiny and the attempts to build up anti-British feeling in Japan in the First World War, which Sho Kuwajima, *The Mutiny in Singpore: War, Anti-War and the War for India's Independence* (New Delhi, 2006), describes in detail.

Noel Barber, *Tanamera: A Novel of Singapore* (London, 1981) used the author's background knowledge as a journalist in pre-war Singapore.

5 War in the East, 1941–1942

There is a daunting array of publications about defence policy in the Far East and the campaign leading to the fall of Singapore. Malcolm H. Murfett, John N. Miksic, Brian P. Farrell and Chiang Ming Shun, *Between Two Oceans: A Military History of Singapore* (Oxford, 1999) carries several chapters about this period. The sixtieth anniversary of the capitulation encouraged historians to reassess the events in measured perspective, as in Brian P. Farrell, *The Defence and Fall of Singapore 1941–1942* (Stroud, UK, 2005), and Karl Hack and Kevin Blackburn, *Did Singapore Have to Fall? Churchill and the Impregnable Fortress* (Singapore, 2004). These books carry comprehensive bibliographies, including archival sources, private papers, regimental histories and detailed accounts of the campaign, which are too numerous to be included in this Further Reading. Brian P. Farrell and Sandy Hunter (eds.), *Sixty Years On: The Fall of Singapore Revisited* (Singapore, 2002) is a substantial collection of papers which were presented at a large conference held in Singapore in February 2002.

Pre-war defence policy

The voluminous literature on defence policy in the Far East leading up to the Pacific War includes important studies on the Japanese and British background to the Pacific war such as Ian H. Nish, *Alliance in Decline: A Study of Anglo-Japanese Relations, 1908–23* (London, 1972); and Nish (ed.), *Anglo-Japanese Alienation 1919–1952: Papers of the Anglo-Japanese Conference on the History of the Second World War* (Cambridge, 1982); Peter Lowe, *Great Britain and the Origins of the Pacific War: A Study of British Policy in East Asia 1917–1941* (Oxford, 1977); Malcolm Murfett, *Fool-proof Relations: The Search for Anglo-American Naval Co-operation during the Chamberlain Years 1937–1940* (Singapore, 1984); Paul Haggle, *Britannia at Bay: The Defence of the British Empire against Japan 1931–1941* (Oxford, 1981); A.J. Marder, *Old Friends New Enemies, Vol. 1: Strategic Illusions, 1936–1941* (London, 1981); Paul M. Kennedy, *The Rise and Fall of British Naval Mastery* (London, 1983); Ong Chit Chung, *Operation Matador: Britain's War Plans against the Japanese, 1918–1941* (Singapore, 1997); W.R. Louis, *British Strategy in the Far East, 1919–1939* (Oxford, 1971), Brian P. Farrell, *The Basis and Making of British Grand Strategy, 1940–1943: Was there a Plan?* (New York and Lampeter, 1998). The Australian aspect is dealt with in Ian Hamill, *The Strategic Illusion: The Singapore Strategy and the Defence of Australia and New Zealand, 1919–1942* (Singapore, 1981) and David Day, *The Great Betrayal: Britain, Australia and the Onset of the Pacific War 1939–42* (New York, 1989).

Much attention has been given to the naval base. Stephen W. Roskill, *Naval Policy between the Wars*, 2 vols. (London, 1968 and 1976) put the base in the context of general British strategic policy in the Far East. Vaughan Cornish, "Singapore and Naval Geography", in Paul Kratoska (ed.), *Honourable Intentions: Talks on the British Empire in South-East Asia Delivered at the Royal Colonial Institute 1874–1928* (Kuala Lumpur, 1983), pp. 382–400 was a lecture given in June 1925; postwar historians studied the base: C.N. Parkinson, *Britain in the Far East: The Singapore Naval Base* (Singapore, 1955); W. David McIntyre, *The Rise and Fall of the Singapore Naval Base 1919–1942* (London, 1979); J. Neidpath, *The Singapore Naval Base and the Defence of Britain's Eastern Empire, 1919–1941* (Oxford, 1981).

For air defences see N. Shorrick, *Lion in the Sky: The Story of Seletar and the Royal Air Force in Singapore* (Kuala Lumpur, 1968) and Henry A. Probert, *The History of Changi* (Singapore, 1965; 2nd ed., Singapore, 2006).

Eric Robertson, *The Japanese File: Pre-war Japanese Penetration in Southeast Asia* (Hong Kong, 1979) was an official British account compiled in India in 1942 from Straits Settlements

Police Special Branch information taken out of Singapore shortly before the surrender.

The military campaign

The official Commonwealth histories are based on original documents, but they suffer from the inevitable limitations of authorized accounts: S. Woodburn Kirby (ed.), *The War Against Japan, Vol. I: The Loss of Singapore* (London, 1957); L. Wigmore, *Australia in the War: The Japanese Thrust* (Canberra, 1957); K.D. Bhargava and K.N.V. Sastri, *Campaigns in South-East Asia, 1941–42*, in B. Prasad, (ed.) *Official History of the Indian Armed Forces in the Second World War, 1939–45* (Combined Inter-Services Historical Section, India and Pakistan, 1960). Woodburn Kirby also published a good independent study, *Singapore: The Chain of Disaster* (London, 1971).

Of the leading participants' accounts, the most essential reading are Lt-Gen. A.E. Percival, *The War in Malaya* (London, 1949) and *Operations of Malaya Command, from 8th December 1941 to 15th February 1942* (HMSO, London, 1948); and Lt-Gen. H. Gordon Bennett, *Why Singapore Fell* (Sydney, 1944). Sir Henry Pownall, *Chief of Staff: The Diaries of Lieutenant-General Sir Henry Pownall,*

Vol. II, 1940–44, Brian Bond (ed.), (London, 1974) includes his brief command in Singapore, and the Churchill Archives, CHUR4/258, 2 January 1949 carries Pownall's postwar reflections on the Singapore debacle. Winston Churchill gives his own account in *The Second World War, Vol. IV: The Hinge of Fate* (London, 1951). John Connell (ed. and completed by Brigadier Michael Roberts), *Wavell, Supreme Commander, 1941–1943* (London, 1969) contains many documents; Brigadier I. Simson, *Singapore: Too Little, Too Late* (Singapore, 1970) is a bitter commentary by the Chief Engineer, Malaya Command; the autobiography of Duff Cooper (Viscount Norwich), *Old Men Forget* (London, 1957) contains a chapter on his time as Resident Cabinet Minister in Singapore in 1941–42.

Frank Legg, *The Gordon Bennett Story* (Sydney, 1965) has five chapters on the Malayan campaign and the aftermath. Sir John Smyth, *Percival and the Tragedy of Singapore* (London, 1971) and Clifford Kinvig, *Scapegoat: General Percival of Singapore* (London, 1996) attempted to clear Percival's reputation.

The Japanese commanders left no comparable memoirs, apart from Colonel Masanobu Tsuji, *Singapore: The Japanese Version* (Sydney, 1960; reprinted Singapore 1988), which was first published in Japanese in 1952 and is a gripping account by a senior but controversial military leader. Lt-General Iwaichi Fujiwara recorded his activities in collecting intelligence and promoting the formation of the first Indian National Army in *F Kikan: Japanese Army Intelligence Operations in Southeast Asia during World War II*, Yoji Akashi (trans.), (Hong Kong, 1983). Yoji Akashi, "General Yamashita Tomoyuki, Commander of the 25th Army", [*Sixty Years*, pp. 185–207] was based on Yamashita's diary, but very few of the other papers at that conference dealt with the Japanese side. This is still under-represented in the literature, although recent work sets out to redress the balance, as in Brian Bond and Kyoichi Tachikawa (eds.), *British and Japanese Military Leadership in the Far Eastern War 1941–45* (London, 2004); and Henry Frei, *Guns of February: Ordinary Japanese Soldiers' Views of the Malayan Campaign in 1941* (Singapore, 2003).

There is no definitive biography of Yamashita in English. He is included in Arthur Swinson, *Four Samurai* (London, 1968). J.D.

Potter, *A Soldier Must Hang: The Biography of an Oriental General* (London, 1963) is a favourable, rather simplistic view, an interesting early attempt at reassessing Yamashita. Two studies by authors who were involved with Yamashita's trial relate mainly to his later years but provide interesting insight to his character: F.A. Reel, *The Case of General Yamashita* (Chicago, 1949) and A.S. Kenworthy, *The Tiger of Malaya* (New York, 1953).

A number of servicemen described their own experiences, including: K. Attiwill, *The Singapore Story* (London, 1959), a vivid account of the last days before the city's fall by a former soldier and prisoner of war, which was written in reaction to the bland official histories; A.G. Donahue, *Last Flight from Singapore* (London, 1944), on the experiences of an American fighter pilot with the RAF in the last days before the fall of Singapore; D.C. Eyre, *The Soul and the Sea* (London, 1959) in collaboration with Douglas Bowler, an RAF wireless operator, telling the story of the small ships which fled at the fall of Singapore. Geoffrey Brooke, *Singapore's Dunkirk: The Aftermath of the Fall* (London, 1989; reprinted London, 2005), by a survivor from *The Prince of Wales* who recounted other escape stories.

Journalists on the spot produced a number of reports, notably: Ian Morrison, *Malayan Postscript* (London, 1942) a short but perceptive book by the (London) *Times* correspondent; Cecil Brown, *Suez to Singapore* (New York, 1942), a blistering indictment of the colonial regime by an American journalist and *Prince of Wales* survivor in the form of a detailed diary kept until he was expelled in mid-January 1942; G.A. Weller, *Singapore is Silent* (New York, 1943), by the last American war correspondent to leave Singapore; O'Dowd Gallagher, *Retreat in the East* (London, 1942), the bitter impressions of a South African correspondent of the London *Daily Express* who was on the *Repulse* when she sank; E.M. Glover, *In 70 Days* (London, 1946; rev. ed. London, 1949) by the general manager of the *Malaya Tribune* who had worked in Malaya as a journalist since 1927. The story is told from the opposite side in (Johnny) Tatsuki Fujii, *Singapore Assignment* (Tokyo, 1943) by an American-educated Japanese journalist who worked with the English-language, Japanese-owned *Singapore Herald* from 1939 to 1941, and edited the *Syonan Shimbun* during the Occupation.

Other expatriate civilians left eyewitness impressions of everyday living during the last weeks before Singapore's fall, including G. Playfair, *Singapore Goes Off the Air* (London, 1944), the diary of a newly recruited Malayan Broadcasting Corporation employee who arrived in Singapore the day the Pacific war broke out and escaped three days before the capitulation; and O.W. Gilmour, *Singapore to Freedom* (London, 1943), the account of the Deputy Municipal Engineer, who had lived in Singapore for over twenty-five years. Noel Barber, *Sinister Twilight: The Fall and Rise Again of Singapore* (London, 1968), reprinted as *The Fall of Singapore* (London, 1985) set the real life reminiscences of a group of expatriate residents within the framework of the general story. This made compelling reading, as did J.G. Farrell, *The Singapore Grip* (London, 1978), a much-acclaimed novel set in wartime Singapore.

Among the many secondary accounts of the military campaign (which are listed in detail in Brian Farrell, *Defence and Fall*, and in Hack and Blackburn, *Did Singapore Have to Fall?*), Louis Allen, *Singapore, 1941–1942* (London, 1977; rev. ed. 1993), is a particularly stimulating work that used Japanese sources to break new ground. Romen Bose, *Secrets of the Battlebox: The History and Role of Britain's Command HQ in the Malayan Campaign* (Singapore, 2005) provides detailed insight into command headquarters.

Captain Russell Grenfell, *Main Fleet to Singapore* (London, 1951; reprinted Singapore, 1987) is a good account of the naval war background, starting from the rise of Japan in the early twentieth century to the Battle of Midway in May 1942. G.M. Bennett, *The Loss of the Prince of Wales and Repulse* (London, 1973), and Martin Middlebrook and Patrick Mahoney, *Battleship: The Loss of the Prince of Wales and the Repulse* (London, 1977) describe this episode in detail. H.M. Tomlinson, *Malay Waters: The Story of Little Ships Coasting out of Singapore and Penang in Peace and War* (London, 1950) recounts the activities of small ships during the Japanese campaign.

The full story of the part played by official local forces remains to be written: M.C. ff (later Mubin) Sheppard, *The Malay Regiment*,

1933–1947 (Kuala Lumpur, 1947) has some interesting material but is brief, and there is no specific account of the Singapore Volunteers' role to update T.M. Winsley, *A History of the Singapore Volunteer Corps* (Singapore, 1937).

In a panoramic study, Christopher Bayly and Tim Harper, *Forgotten Armies: The Fall of British Asia, 1941–1945* (London, 2004) looks at the Pacific war not from the conventional military angle but as a political and social revolution, which swept up the Asian inhabitants throughout the whole crescent of British Asia and was the death knell for imperialism.

6 Syonan: Light of the South, 1942–1945

There is a voluminous literature written by and about military prisoners of war, most of whom were sent away as slave labour, but the following concentrates mainly on the experiences and reminiscences of Asians and of expatriate civilians, who spent all the war years in Singapore.

Breaking away from the usual treatment of the Occupation as a chapter of Second World War history, Paul H. Kratoska, *The Japanese Occupation of Malaya: A Social and Economic History* (London, 1998) focuses instead on the impact on Malaya's economy, society and population. While looking primarily at the peninsula, the book also covers Singapore, making extensive use of interviews and memoirs, and it includes an excellent bibliography.

Syonan, *The Good Citizen's Guide, Handbook of Declarations, Orders, Rules and Regulations etc. issued by Gunseikan-bu (Military Administration Department), Syonan Tokubetu-si (municipality) and Johore Administration between February 2602 (1942) and March 2603 (1943)* (Singapore, 1943) is a good source for Japanese rule in the early months of the Occupation.

Two valuable studies by Japanese writers set official policy in the wider Malayan context: Yoichi Itagaki, (who served in wartime Malaya), "Some Aspects of the Japanese Policy for Malaya under the Occupation, with Special Reference to Nationalism", in K.G.

Tregonning (ed.), *Papers on Malayan History* (Singapore, 1962), pp. 256–73; and Yoji Akashi, "Japanese Policy towards the Malayan Chinese, 1941–45", *JSEAS*, I, 2 (1970), pp. 61–89, which contains much detail about Singapore. See also three essays by Yoji Akashi, "Bureaucracy and the Japanese Military Administration, with Specific Reference to Malaya", in William H. Newell (ed.), *Japan in Asia, 1942–1945* (Singapore, 1981), pp. 46–82; "Education and Indoctrination Policy in Malaya and Singapore under the Japanese Rule, 1942–1945", *Malaysian Journal of Education*, 1978; and "The Koa Kunrenjo, 1942–45: A Case Study of Cultural Propagation and Conflict under the Japanese Occupation of Malaya", Paper presented at the *Conference on South-East Asian Studies*, Kota Kinabalu, 1977. The Singapore training school is also described in Alfred W. McCoy (ed.), *Southeast Asia under Japanese Occupation* (New Haven, 1980).

Mamoru Shinozaki, *My Wartime Experiences in Singapore* (Singapore, 1973); *Syonan—My Story* (Singapore, 1975) and *Three and a Half Years of Occupation in Singapore* (Singapore, 1982) are fascinating reminiscences by a Japanese official who played an important role in Singapore before, during, and after the war.

Other works deal with Japanese policy in Southeast Asia as a whole, notably J. Lebra (ed.), *Japan's Greater East Asia Co-Prosperity Sphere in World War II: Selected Readings and Documents* (Kuala Lumpur, 1974), a valuable collection and commentary, taken mainly from Japanese sources; W.H. Elsbree, *Japan's Role in Southeast Asian Nationalist Movements, 1940–1945* (Cambridge, Mass., 1953); F.C. Jones, *Japan's New Order in East Asia: Its Rise and Fall, 1937–45* (London, 1954).

In the immediate post-war years, several Singaporeans wrote vivid and bitter first-hand accounts about the Occupation: notably Chew Hock Leong, *When Singapore was Syonan* (Singapore, 1945), the earliest, brief, and hurriedly written narrative; Tan Yeok Seong, "History of the Formation of the Oversea Chinese Association and the Extortion by Japanese Military Administration of $50,000,000 from the Chinese in Malaya", *JSSS*, III, 1 (1946), pp. 1–12; Tan Thoon Lip, *Kempeitai "Kindness"* (Singapore, 1946), a poignant account, written by an English-educated lawyer, grandson of Tan

Tock Seng; Chin Kee Onn, *Malaya Upside Down* (Singapore, 1946) which is mostly about Perak but is relevant to Singapore; Chin Kee Onn, *Ma-Rai-Ee* (London, 1952), a novel set in Japanese-occupied Perak and Singapore, based on the author's personal experience; N.I. Low and H.M. Cheng, *This Singapore: Our City of Dreadful Night* (Singapore, 1947) describing the experiences of a teacher and a civil servant. N.I. Low, *When Singapore was Syonan-to* (Singapore, 1973) is largely a duplication of this work, with additional chapters about other people's experiences. This was reprinted, together with Low's *Chinese Jetsam on a Tropic Shore*, in *Recollections* (Singapore, 1983).

For the next two decades Singaporeans put the Occupation behind them. But a new wave of more detailed and less emotional reminiscences started to appear from the late 1960s, beginning with Chen Su Lan, *Remember Pompong and Oxley Rise* (Singapore, 1969), the personal experiences of a prominent doctor. Many later autobiographies devote pride of place to wartime and Occupation reminiscences, such as J.B. van Cuylenburg, *Singapore: Through Sunshine and Shadow* (Singapore, 1982) and Yap Pheng Geck, *Scholar, Banker, Gentleman, Soldier: The Reminiscences of Dr. Yap Pheng Geck* (Singapore, 1982). Edward Phua, *Sunny Days in Serangoon* (Singapore, 1981) is a simple little book about childhood in rural Singapore during the Occupation, whereas Lucy Lum, *The Thorn in the Lion City: A Memoir* (London, 2007) presents a grim contrast of wartime hardship and neglect. Ruth Ho, *Rainbow Round My Shoulder* (Singapore, 1975) recounts the trauma of a brief period as a refugee in Singapore at the time of the capitulation, E.H. Corner, *The Marquis: A Tale of Syonan-to* (Kuala Lumpur, 1981) describe the unique experience of a European botanist who continued to work under the Japanese regime. He Wen-lit, *Syonan Interlude* (Singapore, 1992) is the memoirs of a Chinese hospital doctor.

Lee Geok Boi, *Syonan Years: Singapore under Japanese Rule, 1942–1945* (Singapore, 2006) uses many photographs and oral interviews, as in P. Lim Pui Huen and Diana Wong (eds.), *War and Memory in Malaysia and Singapore* (Singapore, 2000). Some recollections make grim reading, notably Foong Choon Hon (comp.), *The Price of Peace: True Accounts of the Japanese Occupation* (Chinese version, Singapore 1995; English translation by Clara Shaw, Singapore 1997); Foong Choon Hon (comp.) *Eternal Vigilance: The Price of Freedom*, Yuen Chen Ching (trans.) (Singapore, 2006) and Zhou Mei, *Elizabeth Choy: More than a War Heroine: A Biography* (Singapore, 1995).

Many military prisoners of war and civilian internees described their experiences. D. Russell-Roberts, *Spotlight on Singapore* (London, 1965) was written by one of the few military prisoners who remained in Singapore throughout the Occupation. T.P.M. Lewis, *Changi: The Lost Years: A Malayan Diary, 1941–1945* (Kuala Lumpur, 1984) recorded a British headmaster's experiences as a Volunteer in the retreat from Perak and subsequent internment in Singapore. Tan Sri Dato Mubin Sheppard, *Taman Budiman: Memoirs of an Unorthodox Civil Servant* (Kuala Lumpur, 1979) has a vivid chapter about his imprisonment in wartime Singapore. Penrod Dean, *Singapore Samurai* (NSW Australia, 1998), who was one of ten Australian witnesses at the Tokyo War Crimes Trials, attempted escape and was imprisoned in Outram gaol.

R. McKie, *The Heroes* (Sydney, 1960) described the audacious Operation Jawick, which had such horrific consequences for civilian internees and Singaporean suspects, while the disastrous Operation Rimau sequel was recorded by B. Connell, *Return of the Tiger* (London, 1960) and, more controversially, in Peter Thompson, *Kill the Tiger: Operation Rimau and the Battle for Southeast Asia* (Sydney, 2002; reprinted London, 2007).

A number of women internees published reminiscences, notably Freddy Bloom, *Dear Philip: A Diary of Captivity, Changi 1942–1945* (London, 1980), the diary of an American journalist and camp newsletter editor, written in the form of letters to her British doctor husband, who was interned in the men's camp. Sheila Allan, *Diary of a Girl in Changi, 1941–45* (3rd ed., NSW Australia, 2004) updates the internment diary of a seventeen-year old girl with stories of other former internees.

Biographies were written of prominent Westerners who were allowed to work for a time in town and were subsequently arrested by the *Kempeitai*. A. Dally, *Cicely, the Story of a Doctor* (London, 1968), a paediatrician and women's camp leader, who came to Singapore in 1937; and R. McKay, *John Leonard Wilson, Confessor for the Faith* (London, 1973), the bishop of Singapore.

Kevin Blackburn, "Memory of the Sook Ching Massacre and the Creation of the Civilian War Memorial of Singapore", *JMBRAS*, LXXIII (2) 2000, pp. 71–90, examines in detail the latest evidence about the notorious Chinese massacre and its aftermath. This had been discussed by Lord Russell of Liverpool, *The Knights of Bushido: A Short History of Japanese War Crimes* (London, 1958; reprinted London, 2005) and by Hsu Yun-Ts'iao (comp.), "Introduction of the Record of Malayan Chinese Victims during the Japanese Occupation", *JSSS*, XI, 1 (1955), pp. 1–112 (in Chinese with English introduction) listing 7,000 names.

Two books covered the "Double Tenth" trial: B.A. Mallal (ed.), *The Double Tenth Trial* (Singapore, 1947); and the full proceedings in C. Sleeman and S.C. Silkin (eds.), *Trial of Sumida Haruzo and Twenty Others: The Double Tenth Trial* (London, 1951).

Among many studies of the Indian community and the Indian National Army, C. Kondapi, *Indians Overseas, 1828–1949* (New Delhi, 1951) has a section on the Azad Hind movement and Japanese Occupation. Gurchan Singh, *Singa: The Lion of Malaya* (London, 1949), told by a Sikh ex-police inspector, is only partly about Singapore but gives unusual insight into life among the Indian community during the Occupation. B. Prasad (ed.), *Official History of the Indian Armed Forces in the Second World War, 1939–45, Vol. II, The Reconquest of Burma* (India and Pakistan, 1959) and K.K. Ghosh, *The Indian National Army: Second Front of the Indian Independence Movement* (Meerut, 1969) deal with the Indian National Army. Joyce C. Lebra, *Jungle Alliance: Japan and the Indian National Army* (Singapore, 1971) and Joyce C. Lebra, *Japanese Trained Armies in Southeast Asia: Independent and Volunteer Forces in World War II* (Hong Kong, 1977) put the movement in the wider context.

Written in 1945 from wartime notes and later revised for publication, K.R. Menon, *East Asia in Turmoil: Letters to My Son* (Singapore, 1981) recorded the author's personal experiences of the fall of Singapore and the Indian National Army. Shah Nawaz Khan, *My Memories of I.N.A. and its Netaji* (New Delhi, 1946) was written by an ex-INA officer and great admirer of Subhas Chandra Bose. A contrasting view is given by Mahmood Khan Durrani, *The Sixth Column* (London, 1955), which is a fascinating autobiographical story by an Indian Muslim army officer who infiltrated the Indian National Army.

The story of Subhas Chandra Bose attracted many writers: Hugh Toye, *The Springing Tiger* (London, 1959) by a British army colonel; Tatsuo Hayashida, *Netaji Subhas Chandra Bose: His Great Struggle and Martyrdom* (Bombay, 1970) is a short Japanese eyewitness account in English translation; Sisir K. Bose (ed.), *A Beacon across Asia: A Biography of Subhas Chandra Bose* (New Delhi, 1973; reprinted 1996), which was also published in German and Japanese; M.I. Bhargava, *Netaji Subhas Chandra Bose in South-East Asia and India's Liberation War, 1943–45* (New Delhi, 1982); H.N. Pandit, *Netaji Subhas Chandra Bose* (New Delhi, 1988); through to Ratna Ghosh (ed.), *Netaji Subhas Chandra Bose and Indian Freedom Struggle*, 2 vols. (New Delhi, 2006).

Of European neutrals in Japanese-occupied Singapore, Hans Schweizer-Iten, *One Hundred Years of the Swiss Club and the Swiss Community in Singapore, 1871–1971* (Singapore, 1981) is particularly interesting about life among the Swiss community; and H.E. Wilson, *Educational Policy and Performance in Singapore, 1942–1945* (Singapore, 1973) is largely based on the unpublished diary of an Irish teacher priest.

S. Woodburn Kirby (ed.), *The War Against Japan, Vol. V: The Surrender of Japan* (London, 1969) is the official British history of the last stages of the Pacific War. Cheah Boon Kheng, *Red Star Over Malaya: Resistance and Social Conflict during and after the Japanese Occupation of Malaya 1941–1946* (Singapore, 1983; 2nd ed., Singapore, 2003) is an important and original study, which focuses on the peninsula but includes Singapore's "Whispering Terror".

7 The Aftermath of War, 1945–1955

By the turn of the century historians were becoming increasingly interested in the immediate post-war years and in the initiative of the local population in beginning to shape their own destiny, as in the revisionist work of Christopher Bayly and Tim Harper, *Forgotten Wars: The End of Britain's Asian Empire* (London, 2007), the sequel to their *Forgotten Armies*; Yong Mun Cheong, *The Indonesian Revolution and the Singapore Connection, 1945–1949* (Leiden, 2003); Tim Harper, *The End of Empire and the Making of Malaya* (Cambridge, 1999); and Michael D. Barr and Carl A. Trocki, (eds.), *Paths Not Taken: Political Pluralism in Postwar Singapore* (Singapore, 2008).

The standard official work on the British Military Administration was F.S.V. Donnison, *British Military Administration in the Far East, 1943–46* (London, 1956). The official view of the immediate post-war years was given in *British South East Asia Recovers* (Singapore, 1949) which was a *Straits Times* reprint of Colonial Office, *British Dependencies In the Far East, 1945–49*, Cmd. 7709 (London, 1949), together with Great Britain, *Information on Singapore for 1949 Transmitted to the United Nations* (London, 1949). Romen Bose, *The End of the War: Singapore's Liberation and the Aftermath of the Second World War* (Singapore, 2005) is based on recently-released British documents.

S.W. Jones, *Public Administration in Malaya* (London and New York, 1953) was a useful description of the political and administrative framework of Malaya and Singapore by a pre-war Colonial Secretary. M.V. del Tufo, *A Report on the 1947 Census of Population* (London, 1949) shows the changed structure of population in the post-war years.

O.W. Gilmour, *With Freedom to Singapore* (London, 1950) is an interesting personal commentary on newly liberated Singapore. The final chapter of E.M. Glover, *In 70 Days* (first published London, 1946; rev. ed. 1949) concludes with brief post-war impressions.

A number of politicians and officials published interesting personal recollections, notably: MDU Chairman Philip Hoalim, *The Malayan Democratic Union* (Singapore, 1973); Malayan Civil Service officer Andrew Gilmour, *My Role in the Rehabilitation of Singapore, 1946–1953* (Singapore, 1973); David Marshall, "Singapore's Struggle for Nationhood, 1945–59", *JSEAS*, I, 2 (1970), pp. 99–104, reprinted as *Singapore's Struggle for Nationhood, 1945–1959* (Singapore, 1971); Francis Thomas, *Memoirs of a Migrant* (Singapore, 1972), a refreshingly candid short autobiography. Thio Chan Bee, *Extraordinary Adventures of an Ordinary Man* (London, 1977) is the vivid reminiscences by a leading political figure of the period. There is no definitive biography of Tan Cheng Lock but two daughters published tributes: Agnes Tan Kim Lwi's, short *Tun Dato Sir Cheng Lock Tan SMN, DPMJ (Johore) CBE KBE JP: A Son of Malacca* (Singapore, 1985); and Alice Scott-Ross, *Tun Dato Sir Cheng Lock Tan: A Personal Profile* (Singapore, 1990), which includes family background. Tan Cheng Lock, *Malayan Problems: From a Chinese Point of View*, C.Q. Lee (ed.), (Singapore, 1947) is a collection of his pre-war, wartime and immediate post war speeches and pamphlets. The Straits Chinese leader's private papers are divided between the Arkib Negara, Malaysia, and the Institute of Southeast Asian Studies, Singapore.

Yeo Kim Wah, *Political Development in Singapore, 1945–1955* (Singapore, 1973) remains the most detailed and thorough study, although Yeo came to modify some of his views, particularly on student politics, as in "Joining the Communist Underground: The Conversion of English-educated Radicals to Communist in Singapore, June 1948–January 1951", *JMBRAS*, LXVII, 1 (1994), pp. 29–59. Most other studies of politics in this period concentrate on peninsular Malaya, notably A.J. Stockwell, *British Policy and Malay Politics during the Malayan Union Experiment, 1942–1948* (Kuala Lumpur, 1979); J. de V. Allen, *The Malayan Union* (New Haven, 1967); T.H. Silcock and Ungku Aziz, "Nationalism in Malaya", in W.L. Holland (ed.), *Asian Nationalism and the West* (New York, 1953; reprinted New York, 1973); K.J. Ratnam, *Communalism and the Political Process in Malaya* (Singapore, 1965); and R. Emerson, *Representative Government in Southeast Asia* (Cambridge, Mass., 1955). S. Rose, *Socialism in Southeast Asia* (London, 1959) devoted considerable attention to Singapore's politics between 1945 and 1957 in a chapter on Malaya. Rajeswary Ampalavanar (Brown), *The Indian Minority and Political Change in Malaya, 1945–1957* (Kuala Lumpur, 1981) is a detailed study of a minority that played a particularly important role in the politics of Singapore and West Malaysia in this period.

The origins of Singapore's immediate post-war separation are considered in A.J. Stockwell, "Colonial Planning during World War II: The Case of Malaya", *Journal of Imperial and Commonwealth History*, II, 3 (May, 1974), pp. 333–51; and C.M. Turnbull, "British Planning for Postwar Malaya", *JSEAS*, V, 2 (1974), pp. 239–54. And the whole period is covered in Mohamed Noordin Sopiee, *From Malayan Union to Singapore Separation: Political Unification in the Malaysia Region, 1945–65* (Kuala Lumpur, 1974; 2nd ed., Kuala Lumpur, 2005).

Two valuable official reports describe social conditions at this time, namely Department of Social Welfare, *A Social Survey of Singapore* (Singapore, 1947) and Goh Keng Swee, *Urban Incomes and Housing* (Singapore, 1956), a report on the 1953/4 social survey. C. Gamba, "Some Social Problems in Singapore", *Australian Quarterly*, XXVI, 2 (1954) gave a grim picture of poverty and overcrowding.

Education policy is detailed in Singapore Advisory Council, *Education Policy in the Colony of Singapore: Ten Years' Programme Adopted in the Advisory Council on 7th August 1947* (Singapore, 1948); and S. Gopinathan, *Towards a National System of Education in Singapore, 1945–1973* (Singapore, 1974). Harold E. Wilson, *Social Engineering in Singapore: Educational Policies and Social Change, 1819–1972* (Singapore, 1978) stresses this period.

A number of excellent field studies were carried out by anthropologists and sociologists in Singapore in the 1950s. M. Freedman, *Chinese Family and Marriage in Singapore* (London, 1957); Barrington Kaye, *Upper Nankin Street Singapore* (Singapore, 1960); M. Freedman and M. Topley, "Religious and Social Realignment among the Chinese in Singapore", *JAS*, XXI, 1 (1961), pp. 3–23; M. Topley, "The Emergence and Social Function of Chinese Religious Associations in Singapore", *Comparative Studies in Society and History*, III (1960–61), pp. 289–314; A.J.A. Elliott, *Chinese Spirit and Medium Cults in Singapore* (London, 1955), and Judith Djamour, *Malay Kinship and Marriage in Singapore* (London, 1959) based on field-work carried out in 1949–50.

The Hertogh riots were examined by the Director of Social Welfare, Tom Eames Hughes, *Tangled Worlds: The Story of Maria Hertogh* (Singapore, 1980); and by A.J. Stockwell, "Imperial Security and Moslem Militancy, with special reference to the Hertogh Riots in Singapore (December 1950)", *JSEAS*, XVII, 2 (1986), pp. 322–35. The story from the Malay perspective is told by Haja Maideen, *The Nadra Tragedy (Maria Hertogh Controversy)* (Kuala Lumpur, 1989).

There are numerous studies of labour unrest leading up to the outbreak of the Communist Emergency in Malaya. Of particular relevance to Singapore are: M.R. Stenson, *Repression and Revolt: The Origins of the 1948 Communist Insurrection in Malaya and Singapore* (Ohio, 1969), a small but interesting paper; M.R. Stenson, *Industrial Conflict in Malaya: Prelude to the Communist Revolt of 1948* (London, 1970), an important study of the labour background; Richard Clutterbuck, *Riot and Revolution in Singapore and Malaya, 1945–1963* (London, 1973), by a senior British army officer serving in Malaya during part of this time and updated as *Conflict and Violence in Singapore and Malaysia 1945–1983* (Singapore, 1985); G.Z. Hanrahan, *The Communist Struggle in Malaya* (New York, 1954; rev. ed. Kuala Lumpur, 1971); V. Thompson and R. Adloff, *The Left Wing in Southeast Asia* (New York, 1950) which has a chapter on Malaya, the growth of the Malayan communist movement and Singapore politics.

In a detailed study, Charles Gamba, *The Origins of Trade Unionism in Malaya: A Study in Colonial Labour Unrest* (Singapore, 1962), took the story up to the formation of the Singapore Trade Union Congress in 1951. Alex Josey, *Trade Unionism in Malaya* (Singapore, 1954; rev. ed. Singapore, 1958) was a shorter account by a left-wing journalist. Virginia Thompson, *Labour Problems in Southeast Asia* (New Haven, 1947) deals with immediate post-war strikes. S.S. Awberry and F.W. Dalley, *Labour and Trades Union Organisation in the Federation of Malaya and Singapore* (Kuala Lumpur, 1948) reported an investigation carried out in 1947–48 at the invitation of the Malayan and Singapore governments. C. Gamba, *Labour Law in Malaya* (Singapore, 1955) gives a brief synopsis of labour law. George Sweeney, "Singapore, 1945–57", in Mohamed Amin and Michael

Caldwell, *Malaya: The Making of a Neo-Colony* (Nottingham, 1977) offered a radical left-wing interpretation.

A more recent evaluation, Kua Busan, *Teachers Against Colonialiam in Post-war Singapore and Malaya* (Kuala Lumpur, 2007) portrays the low morale, poor pay, and discrimination in education, which led to the formation of anti-colonial teachers' unions in the late 1940s.

International Bank for Reconstruction and Development, *The Economic Development of Malaya* (Singapore, 1955), the report of a mission to Malaya and Singapore in 1954, is a weighty and valuable commentary not only on the economy but on education, social welfare, and health.

8 The Road to Merdeka, 1955–1965

By the early twenty-first century this decade, together with the early years of independence, came to be seen as the most crucial and controversial period in the making of modern Singapore. Historians began to examine aspects of the colonial legacy. Brenda S.A. Yeoh, *Contesting Space in Colonial Singapore: Power Relations and the Urban Built Environment* (Singapore, 2003) studied the social conflict which arose from urban expansion in colonial times. E. Kay Gillis, *Singapore Civil Society and British Power* (Singapore, 2005) traced the development of civil society from 1819 to 1963.

Under the Labour Front governments, Legislative Assembly papers provided valuable discussions of major issues, notably *The Report of the All Party Committee of the Singapore Legislative Assembly on Chinese Education*, Cmd. 9 (Singapore, 1956); *White Paper on Education Policy*, Cmd. 15 of 1956 (Singapore, 1956); *The Communist Threat in Singapore*, Sessional Paper, Cmd. 33 of 1957 (Singapore, 1957).

Singapore was included in N. Ginsburg and C.F. Roberts, *Malaya* (Seattle, 1958; rev. ed. 1960) which provided a useful factual background; in L.A. Mills, *Malaya: A Political and Economic Appraisal* (Minneapolis, 1958); and J.N. Parmer, "Malaysia", in G. McT. Kahin (ed.), *Governments and Politics of Southeast Asia* (2nd ed., Ithaca,

1964), pp. 281–365. S.C. Chua, *State of Singapore: Report on the Census of Population in 1957* (Singapore, 1964) analysed population statistics. Michael Leifer, "Politics in Singapore: The First Term of the People's Action Party, 1959–63", *Journal of Commonwealth Political Studies*, II (1963–64), pp. 102–19, was a balanced commentary.

In addition to Francis Thomas, *Memoirs of a Migrant* (Singapore, 1972) and David Marshall, *Singapore's Struggle for Nationhood, 1945–1959* (Singapore, 1971), personal reminiscences of this period include: Lim Yew Hock, *Reflections* (Kuala Lumpur, 1986); Gerald De Cruz, *Rojak Rebel: Memoirs of a Singapore Maverick* (Singapore, 1993), the aptly titled reminiscences of an ex-Communist, who flitted through Singapore politics in the 1950s; and, in a quite different vein, D.J. Enright, *Memoirs of a Mendicant Professor* (London, 1969) by a university professor who came into conflict with the PAP authorities.

Chan Heng Chee wrote a balanced political biography of Singapore's first Chief Minister in *A Sensation of Independence: A Political Biography of David Marshall* (Singapore, 1984; reprinted Singapore, 2001). Alex Josey, *David Marshall's Political Interlude* (Singapore, 1982) was drawn largely from Singapore Legislative Assembly debates, and Alex Josey, *The David Marshall Trials* (Singapore, 1982) gave a verbatim reporting of the court proceedings, which conveyed the social "feel" of Singapore and illuminated Marshall's character.

From the outset the PAP leadership was very vocal, both in opposition and later in office. The party issued annual reports and anniversary souvenirs from 1955, and *Petir*, the PAP's official organ, began publication in 1956. *The Tasks Ahead* (Singapore, 1959) gave a comprehensive statement of the party's policy prior to the 1959 election. From that time the Ministry of Culture issued numerous booklets detailing the ruling party's policy: *Towards a More Just Society* (Singapore, 1959); and *Towards Socialism* (Singapore, 1960–61), a seven-part analysis of policy. *Democratic Socialism in Action, June 1959–April 1963* (Singapore, 1963) summed up the party's first ministry, followed by *Social Transformation in Singapore* (Singapore, 1964); and People's Action Party, *Tenth Anniversary Celebration Souvenir* (Singapore, 1964).

Many of the political leaders' speeches from this period were published, notably Lee Kuan Yew, *Towards a Malaysian Malaysia* (Singapore, 1965); *Malaysia – Age of Revolution* (Singapore, 1965); *and Malaysia Comes of Age* (Singapore, 1965). Goh Keng Swee, *Some Problems of Industrialization* (Singapore, 1963), which was based on a series of radio talks; S. Rajaratnam, *Malayan Culture in the Making* (Singapore, 1960), *Challenge of Confrontation* (Singapore, 1964), and *Malaysia and the World* (Singapore, 1964).

Contemporary writers described Singapore's political turmoil, set against the background of the Malayan Emergency, China and the Cold War in Asia. This was the era of a lively local press and the golden age of the Singapore-based Southeast Asia foreign newspaper correspondent. Sit Yin Fong, *Dateline Malaya and Singapore 1939– 1971: I Stomped the "Hot" Beat* (Singapore, 1991), a collection of the *Straits Times* star reporter's columns, brought the excitement of the past to life, particularly his classic report of the 1955 Hock Lee riots: "The Night that Singapore went Mad", pp. 104–123. Veteran journalist Dennis Bloodworth, with long experience of communism in Europe and Vietnam, told the story of intrigue and violence in the battle between the PAP and the left wing in *The Tiger and the Trojan Horse* (Singapore, 1986; reprinted Singapore, 2005). Bloodworth's vivid narrative was based on extensive personal contacts with the participants but was later unfairly underrated. John Drysdale, *Singapore: The Struggle for Success* (Singapore, 1984) was built on comprehensive research and interviews about the 1946–65 period. Journalist Robert Shaplen, *Time out of Hand: Revolution and Reaction in South East Asia* (New York and London, 1969) contained an interesting commentary on Singapore's experience in Malaysia and during the early years of independence.

Lee Ting Hui, "The Communist Organization in Singapore: Its Techniques of Manpower Mobilization and Management, 1948–66", *Institute of Southeast Asian Studies, Field Report Series*, No. 12 (Singapore, 1976) used ex-detainees' reports. See also Lee Ting Hui, "The Communist Open United Front in Singapore: 1954–66" in Lim Joo-Jock and S. Vani (eds.), *Armed Communist Movements in Southeast Asia* (London, 1984), pp. 109–29. At the other end of the Chinese-educated socio-political scale, Sikko Visscher, "Actors and Arenas, Elections and Competition: The 1958 Election of the Singapore Chinese Chamber of Commerce", *JSEAS*, XXXIII (2003), pp. 315–32; and Hong Liu and Wong Sin-kiong, *Singapore Chinese Society in Transition: Business, Politics, and Socio-Economic Change, 1945–1965* (Chinese version Singapore, 2004; English translation 2006).

Richard Clutterbuck, *Riot and Revolution in Singapore and Malaya, 1945–1963* (London, 1973), updated as *Conflict and Violence in Singapore and Malaysia, 1945–1983* (Singapore, 1985), is relevant to this period, as is A.C. Brackman, *Southeast Asia's Second Front: The Power Struggle in the Malay Archipelago* (London, 1966). R.S. Elegant, *The Dragon's Seed: Peking and the Overseas Chinese* (New York, 1959) conveys the view which was prevalent at that time in Singapore of China's involvement with the overseas Chinese and local politics. As does J.M. Van der Kroef, *Communism in Malaysia and Singapore* (The Hague, 1967) and J.M. Van der Kroef, "Nanyang University and the Dilemmas of Overseas Chinese Education", *China Quarterly*, 20, (October-December 1964), pp. 96–127. This view was challenged in Stephen Fitzgerald, *China and the Overseas Chinese: A Study of Peking's Changing Policy, 1949–70* (Cambridge, 1972), a stimulating re-interpretation of PRC policy, based largely on Chinese official sources.

The Barisan Sosialis published *The Plebeian* fortnightly (1962–63), which continued at irregular intervals as *The Plebeian Express* (1963/4–68) and reverted to *The Plebeian* (1968–70). But it was many years before the radical left had further opportunity to present their side of the story in Singapore/Malaysia: most importantly Tan Jing Quee and K.S. Jomo (eds.), *Comet in our Sky: Lim Chin Siong in History* (Kuala Lumpur, 2001). Lim Chin Siong was also among the interviewees for Melanie Chew, *Leaders of Singapore* (Singapore, 1996) and was included – rather controversially – in Lam Peng Er and Kevin Y.L. Tan (eds.), *Lee's Lieutenants: Singapore's Old Guard* (Sydney, 1999). Liew Khai Khun, "The Anchor and the Voice of 10,000 Waterfront Workers: Jamit Singh in the Singapore Story (1954–63)", *JSEAS*, XXXV, 3 (2004), pp. 459–78; the autobiography, Said Zahari, *Dark Clouds at Dawn: A Political Memoir* (Kuala Lumpur, 2001); and the testimony of the Malayan Communist Party leader: (Alias) Chin Peng, *My Side of History, as told to Ian Ward & Norma Miraflor* (Singapore, 2000); and C.C. Chin and Karl Hack (eds.), *Dialogues with Chin Peng: New Light on the Malayan Communist Party* (Singapore, 2004).

Singapore's incorporation into and subsequent separation from Malaysia attracted widespread contemporary commentary, as in R.C.H. McKie, *Malaysia in Focus* (Sydney, 1963), a readable personal impression of events and prominent personalities on the eve of the formation of Malaysia; and W.A. Hanna, *Sequel to Colonialism: The 1957–1960 Foundations for Malaysia* (New York, 1965). The friction and growing tensions in the relationship were shown in

Michael Leifer, "Singapore in Malaysia: The Politics of Federation", *JSEAH*, VI, 2 (1965), pp. 54–70; and Peter Boyce, "Policy without Authority: Singapore's External Affairs Power", *JSEAH*, VI, 2 (1965), pp. 87–103; the shock of separation in R.S. Milne, "Singapore's Exit from Malaysia: The Consequences of Ambiguity", *Asian Survey*, VI, 3 (1966), pp. 175–84, and Nancy Fletcher, *The Separation of Singapore from Malaysia* (Ithaca, 1969; reprinted 1971).

A good deal of information was released at the time in the form of newspaper interviews and official notices, as in Government of Singapore, *Separation: Singapore's Separation from the Federation* (Singapore, 1965). Detailed scholarly studies were made when the official archives were opened, notably Albert Lau, *A Moment of Anguish: Singapore in Malaysia and the Politics of Disengagement* (Singapore, 1998). Matthew Jones, *Conflict and Confrontation in South East Asia, 1961–65: Britain, the US, and the Creation of Malaysia* (Cambridge, 2002) set the story in the wider international context. The participants themselves recorded their memories: the first volume of Lee Kuan Yew's memoirs, *The Singapore Story* (Singapore, 1998); Melanie Chew, *Leaders of Singapore* (Singapore, 1996), a collection of nearly forty short biographies, largely derived from personal interviews; Patrick Keith, *Ousted! An Insider's Story of the Ties that Failed* (Singapore, 2005), by the Deputy Director of External Information in Malaysia at that time; British Prime Minister

Harold Wilson, *The Labour Government, 1964–1970: A Personal Record* (London, 1971); Tunku Abdul Rahman, *Viewpoints* (Kuala Lumpur, 1978); and Ooi Kee Beng, *The Reluctant Politician, Tun Dr Ismail and his Time* (Singapore, 2006).

9 The New Nation, 1965–1990

By the end of the twentieth century, the early years of independence were to come under close scrutiny, but for contemporaries this was a time to look forward; to examine the existing situation and current trends, not to reflect on the past.

A spate of publications about the new republic concerned politics, the economy, population, ethnicity, fertility, urban development, foreign policy, and other aspects. Some were in the form of Occasional Papers, Field Reports, Working Papers, Research Notes and Discussion Papers, issued by the Institute of Southeast Asian Studies in Singapore and by university departments (the University of Singapore, Nanyang University, and after 1980 the National University of Singapore). These and longer studies were to become the historical records for the future.

Basic sources of official information were presented in the *Singapore Yearbook*, first published in 1964 to replace the former *Annual Reports*; and in *Singapore Facts and Figures* from 1974. Articles on contemporary Singapore appeared in the annual *Southeast Asian Affairs*, published by the Institute of Southeast Asian Studies.

Ooi Jin Bee and Chiang Hai Ding (eds.), *Modern Singapore* (Singapore, 1969) was a collection of essays, published to celebrate Singapore's 150 years. Seah Chee Meow (ed.), *Trends in Singapore* (Singapore, 1975) took stock of prospects at the end of the first decade of independence.

Two studies were made of the People's Action Party at this stage: T.J. Bellows, *The People's Action Party of Singapore* (New Haven, 1971); and Pang Cheng Lian, *Singapore's People's Action Party* (Singapore, 1971). Fong Sip Chee, *The PAP Story: The Pioneering Years (November 1954–April 1968): Diary of Events of the People's*

Action Party, Reminiscences of an Old Cadre (Singapore, 1979) was an unvarnished personal account.

American Universities Field Staff Reports, *Southeast Asia Series*, published a number of useful commentaries, in particular, W.A. Hanna, "Success and Sobriety in Singapore", Vol. 16, No. 2–5 (New York, 1968). Iain Buchanan, *Singapore in Southeast Asia* (London, 1972), was sharply critical and stirred up a great deal of controversy at a time when most other writing exuded positive optimism.

Political scientist and later diplomat Chan Heng Chee provided a perceptive guide to political development and increasing PAP control: Chan Heng Chee, *Singapore: The Politics of Survival, 1965–1967* (Singapore, 1971); *The Dynamics of One Party Dominance: The PAP at the Grass Roots* (Singapore, 1976); and articles including "Nation Building in Southeast Asia: The Singapore Case", in B. Grossman (ed.), *Southeast Asia in the Modern World* (Wiesbaden, 1972), pp. 165–79; "Politics in an Administrative State: Where have the politics gone?" in Seah Chee Meow (ed.), *Trends in Singapore* (Singapore, 1975); and "In the Middle Passage: The PAP Faces the Eighties", University of Singapore, Politics Department, Occasional paper series, No. 36 (Singapore, 1979).

See also Raj K. Vasil, *Politics in a Plural Society* (Singapore, 1971); Seah Chee Meow, *Community Centres in Singapore: Their Political Involvement* (Singapore, 1973); Wu Teh-yao (ed.), *Political and Social Change in Singapore* (Singapore, 1975); Stanley S. Bedlington, *Malaysia and Singapore: The Building of New States* (Ithaca, 1978); Charles Ng Sen Ark and T.P.B. Menon (eds.), *Singapore—A Decade of Independence* (Singapore, 1975).

Great attention was focused on the economy: Goh Chok Tong, *Industrial Growth in Singapore, 1959–68* (Ministry of Finance, Singapore, 1968), an informative official paper by Singapore's future prime minister; P.J. Drake (ed.), *Money and Banking in Malaya and Singapore* (Singapore, 1966); R. Ma and You Poh Seng, *The Economy of Malaysia and Singapore* (Singapore, 1966); P.I. Drake, *Financial Development in Malaya and Singapore* (Canberra, 1969); H. Hughes and You Poh Seng (eds.), *Foreign Investment and Industrialization in*

Singapore (Canberra, 1969); You Poh Seng and Lim Chong Yah (eds.), *The Singapore Economy* (Singapore, 1971); Lee Soo Ann, *Papers on Economic Planning and Development in Singapore* (Singapore, 1971); Wong Kum Poh and M. Tan (eds.), *Singapore in the International Economy* (Singapore, 1972); P.P. Courtenay, *A Geography of Trade and Development in Malaya* (London, 1972); Lee Soo Ann, *Industrialization in Singapore* (Melbourne, 1973); Lee Sheng-yi, *The Monetary and Banking Development of Malaysia and Singapore* (Singapore, 1974); Kunio Yoshihara, *Foreign Investment and Domestic Response: A Study of Singapore's Industrialization* (Singapore, 1976); Tan Chwee Huat, *Financial Institutions in Singapore* (Singapore, 1978). Lim Joo-Jock et al, "Foreign Investment in Singapore: Some Broader and Socio-Political Ramifications", Institute of Southeast Asian Studies, *Field Report Series* No. 13 (Singapore, 1977) had more general bearing. Lim Chong-Yah (ed.), *Learning from the Japanese Experience* (Singapore, 1982) and Wee Mon-Cheng, *The Chrysanthemum and the Orchid: Observations of a Diplomat* (Singapore, 1982) illustrated the "learn from Japan" movement. You Poh Seng and Lim Chong-Yah (eds.), *Singapore: Twenty Five Years of Development* (Singapore, 1984) was a celebratory collection of essays mainly concerned with the years since independence.

Interesting comparisons between development in Singapore and Hong Kong at that stage were made in M. Herrmann, *Hong Kong Versus Singapore* (Stuttgart, 1970); T. Geiger, *Tales of Two City States: Development Progress of Hong Kong and Singapore* (Washington, 1973); and Peter Hodge (ed.), *Community Problems and Social Work in Southeast Asia: The Hong Kong and Singapore Experience* (Hong Kong, 1980).

Alex Josey, *Industrial Relations: Labour Laws in a Developing Singapore* (Singapore, 1976) updated his *Labour Laws in a Changing Singapore* (Singapore, 1968). Alex Josey (ed.), *Asia Pacific Socialism* (Singapore, 1973) comprised mainly speeches made at the Socialist International Asia-Pacific Bureau in Singapore in 1972, including a speech by C.V. Devan Nair and a PAP policy paper on "Singapore's Concept of Socialism". C.V. Devan Nair (comp. and ed.), *Socialism that Works: The Singapore Way* (Singapore, 1976) comprised articles by political leaders and other Singaporeans. C.V. Devan Nair, *Inlook and Outlook* (Singapore, 1977) included reports on trade unions.

R. Nyce, *The Kingdom and the Country: A Study of Church and Society in Singapore* (Singapore, 1970; 2nd ed., 1972) gave an interesting insight into the social change of the 1960s.

Substantial sociological studies were undertaken in the 1970s: R. Gamer, *The Politics of Urban Development in Singapore* (Ithaca, 1972); Stephen H.K. Yeh (ed.), *Public Housing in Singapore: A Multi-disciplinary Study* (Singapore, 1975), which was officially commissioned by the Housing and Development Board; Riaz Hassan (ed.), *Singapore: Society in Transition* (Kuala Lumpur, 1976); Riaz Hassan, *Families in Flats: A Study of Low Income Families in Public Housing* (Singapore, 1977); Peter Chen Shou-jen and Hans-Dieter Evers (eds.), *Studies in ASEAN Sociology: Urban Society and Social Change* (Singapore, 1978), which was heavily weighted on Singapore.

Government of Singapore, *Census Report for 1970* (Singapore, 1973) is a valuable source of information. Chang Chen-tung, *Fertility Transition in Singapore* (Singapore, 1974) examined the National Family Planning Programme's role. Peter S.J. Chen and James T. Fawcett, *Public Policy and Population Change in Singapore* (New York, 1979), and Saw Swee Hock, *Population Control for Zero Growth in Singapore* (Singapore, 1980) put the controversial population policy into context.

The situation of the Malay minority came under scrutiny. The legal position of the Malay minority had been considered by the State Advocate-General of Singapore Ahmad Ibrahim, in "The Legal Position of Muslims in Singapore", *Intisari*, I, 1 (1962), pp. 40–50, and *The Status of Muslim Women in Family Law in Malaysia, Singapore and Brunei* (Singapore, 1965). Judith Djamour, *The Muslim Matrimonial Court in Singapore* (London, 1966) was based on field-work. Sharom Ahmad and James Wong (eds.), *Malay Participation in the National Development of Singapore* (Singapore, 1971); political scientist Ismail Kassim, *Problems of Elite Cohesion: A Perspective from a Minority Community* (Singapore, 1974) looked particularly at Malay PAP leaders. Chew Soo Beng, *Fishermen in Flats* (Melbourne, 1982) investigated the impact of social change on a Malay fishing village.

The place of women still received little attention, but Eddie C.Y. Kuo and Aline K. Wong, *The Contemporary Family in Singapore* (Singapore, 1979) was followed by various reports and papers by Aline Wong on divorce, fertility and women in economic development. Joyce C. Lebra and Joy Paulson, *Chinese Women in Southeast Asia* (Singapore, 1980) compared women's roles in Singapore, Kuala Lumpur and Bangkok. See also Linda Y.C. Lim, *Women in the Singapore Economy*, Occasional Paper No. 5, Economic Research Centre (Singapore, 1982).

At that time the troubled history of Nanyang University was viewed primarily as a political problem: Malaysian Government, *Communism in the Nanyang University* (Kuala Lumpur, June 1964). A.W. Lind, *Nanyang Perspectives: Chinese Students in Multiracial Singapore* (Hawaii, 1974) was a detailed study, based on field-work carried out in 1969. The emphasis on a national system of education for modernization and development is seen in Goh Keng Swee, *Report on the Ministry of Education 1978* (Singapore, 1979); and Pang Eng Fong, *Education, Manpower and Development in Singapore* (Singapore, 1982).

The final phase of decolonization and the British withdrawal from their bases was of crucial importance for both the early republic and Britain. A number of historians wrote about British defence policy: Philip Darby, *British Defence Policy East of Suez, 1947–1968* (London, 1973); D. Lee, *Eastward: A History of the Royal Air Force in the Far East 1945–1972* (London HMSO, 1984); M. Murfett, *In Jeopardy: The Royal Navy and British Far Eastern Defence Policy 1945–51* (Kuala Lumpur, 1995); Jeffrey Pickering, *Britain's Withdrawal from East of Suez: The Politics of Retrenchment* (New York, 1998); Saki Dockrill, *Britain's Retreat from East of Suez: The Choice between Europe and the World?* (Basingstoke, 2002). Chin Kin Wah, *The Defence of Malaysia and Singapore: The Transformation of a Security System 1957–1971* (Cambridge, 1983); and the final section of Murfett et al., *Between Two Oceans* (Oxford, 1999) concentrated on Singapore. Michael

Leifer, *Malacca, Singapore and Indonesia* (Netherlands, 1978) set modern international navigation problems in the historical context of left-over colonial rivalries. Karl Hack, *Defence and Decolonisation in South East Asia: Britain, Malaya and Singapore, 1941–68* (London, 2001) examined the wider canvas in depth, with a comprehensive bibliography. Marc Frey, Ronald W. Pruessen and Tan Tai Yong (eds.), *The Transformation of Southeast Asia: International Perspectives on Decolonization* (New York, 2003) looked at the impact from the Asian angle.

On foreign policy, P. Boyce, *Malaysia and Singapore in International Diplomacy: Documents and Commentaries* (Sydney, 1968); Chan Heng Chee, "Singapore's Foreign Policy, 1965–68", *JSEAH*, X, 1 (1969), pp. 177–91; and Singapore featured prominently in the prolific writings of Michael Leifer about post-colonial international relations in Southeast Asia. There were pertinent points in F.H.H. King, "The Foreign Policy of Singapore", in R.P. Barston (ed.), *The Other Powers; Studies in Foreign Policies of Small States* (London, 1973), pp. 252–86. Lau Teik Soon (ed.), *New Directions in the International Relations of Southeast Asia: The Great Powers and Southeast Asia* (Singapore, 1973).

By the early 1980s Singapore was taking stock of what had been achieved and celebrating some anniversaries: Alex Josey, *Singapore: Its Past, Present and Future* (Singapore, 1979) which took a strongly pro-PAP stance; Jackie Sam (ed.), *The First Twenty Years of the People's Association* (Singapore, 1980); S. Jayakumar (ed.), *Our Heritage and Beyond: A Collection of Essays on Singapore, its Past, Present and Future* (Singapore, 1982) which included essays by the Prime Minister and senior civil servants; Raj K. Vasil, *Governing Singapore* (Singapore, 1982); Jon S.T. Quah, Chan Heng Chee and Seah Chee Meow (eds.), *Government and Politics of Singapore* (Singapore, 1985; rev. ed. Singapore, 1987) which was a comprehensive collection of articles on the historical background since 1945 and the contemporary scene. Aline Wong and Stephen H.K. Yeh, *Housing a Nation: 25 Years of Public Housing in Singapore* (Singapore, 1985) was commissioned by the Housing and Development Board. Jon Quah Siew-Tien, "Meeting the Twin Threats of Communism and Communalism: The Singapore

Response", in Chandran Jeshurun (ed.), *Governments and Rebellions in Southeast Asia* (Singapore, 1985), pp. 186–217.

A number of biographical works were written about Lee Kuan Yew during this quarter of a century, when he reached the peak of his power. Most important was the second volume of Lee's own memoirs, *From Third World to the First: The Singapore Story, 1965–2000* (Singapore, 2000). In the early days of independence he was portrayed from opposing angles: on the one hand by friend and adviser, Alex Josey, *Lee Kuan Yew* (Singapore, 1968; rev. ed. 1971) and *Lee Kuan Yew: The Struggle for Singapore* (Sydney, 1974; 3rd ed. Sydney, 1980); and on the other by T.J.S. George, *Lee Kuan Yew's Singapore* (London, 1973); hatchet-work by an Indian journalist, James Minchin, *No Man is an Island: A Study of Singapore's Lee Kuan Yew* (Sydney, 1986) attempted to steer a middle course but was critical overall.

The activities of the Old Guard generation continued to be important to the end of the 1970s. Several spoke for themselves in personal and often very frank and illuminating interviews for Melanie Chew, *Leaders of Singapore* (Singapore, 1996), which included the most outstanding figures in various spheres of public life. Melanie Chew, *Biography of President Yusuf bin Ishak* (Singapore, 1999) was the biography of the first president of the republic, who died in office in 1970.

Apart from these interviews and the stimulating studies in Lam Peng Er and Kevin Y.L. Tan (eds.), *Lee's Lieutenants: Singapore's Old Guard* (Sydney, 1999), most other members of that generation of leaders left a record chiefly in their speeches and writings. The evolution of Goh Keng Swee's economic philosophy was seen in two collections of essays, letters and speeches: *Economics of Modernisation and Other Essays* (Singapore, 1972), covering the period 1959 to 1971; and *The Practice of Economic Growth* (Singapore, 1977), collected in the years 1972–77; and in Goh Keng Swee, "Economic Development and Modernization in South-East Asia", in H.D. Evers (ed.), *Modernisation in South East Asia* (Singapore, 1973). Tan Siok Sun, *Goh Keng Swee: A Portrait* (Singapore, 2007) was written by his daughter-in-law.

S. Rajaratnam, *The Prophetic and the Political: Selected Speeches and Writings of S. Rajaratnam*, Chan Heng Chee and Obaid ul Haq (eds.), (Singapore and New York, 1987; 2nd ed. with a new epilogue, Singapore, 2007) gives a good insight into the veteran political leader's thinking, together with Kwa Chong Guan (ed.), *S. Rajaratnam on Singapore: From Ideas to Reality* (Singapore, 2006), which was published following his death. See also Ang Hwee Suan, *Dialogues with S. Rajaratnam, Former Senior Minister in the Prime Minister's Office* (Singapore, Shin Min Daily News, Singapore 1991).

A. Roland, *Profiles from the New Asia* (London, 1970) included a chapter on Lim Kim San and his Singapore background. Hon Sui Sen's daughter produced a personal tribute: Joan Hon, *Relatively Speaking* (Singapore, 1984); and Linda Low and Lim Beng Lum (arranged and ed.), *Strategies of Singapore's Economic Success, Speeches and Writings by Hon Sui Sen* (Singapore, 1992). C.V. Devan Nair, *Towards Tomorrow: Essays on Development and Social Transformation in Singapore* (Singapore National Trades Union Congress, Singapore, 1973); *Socialism That Works: The Singapore Way* (Singapore, 1976); and *Not by Wages Alone: Selected Speeches and Writings of C.V. Devan Nair, 1959–1981* (Singapore, 1982) which was published by the Singapore NTUC to celebrate his becoming President of the republic. Othman Wok, *Never in My Wildest Dreams* (Singapore, 2000) was autobiographical.

There was also testimony from those who fell afoul of the regime in that period: Tan Wah Piow, *Let the People Judge: Confessions of the Most Wanted Person in Singapore* (Kuala Lumpur, 1987); and Francis Seow, *To Catch a Tartar: A Dissident in Lee Kuan Yew's Prison* (New Haven, 1994).

A number of attractive books illustrated Singapore as it was then and in the past. Ray K. Tyers, *Singapore Then and Now*, 2 vols. (Singapore, 1976); and Singapore Ministry of Culture, Daljit Singh and V.T. Arasu (eds.), *Singapore: An Illustrated History, 1941–1984* (Singapore, 1984); Eric Jennings, *Singapore Panorama: 150 Years in Pictures* (Singapore, 1969); Ilsa Sharp (ed.), *This Singapore* (Singapore, 1975) commemorating ten years of independence; Yeo Soh Choo, *Singapore Memento* (Singapore, 1984); *A Salute to*

Singapore (Singapore, 1984); V. Gopalakrishnan and A. Perera (eds.), *Singapore: Changing Landscapes: Geylang, Chinatown, Serangoon* (Singapore, 1983).

10 The New Guard, 1990–2005

While the latest phase in Singapore's story is too recent to allow historical perspective, the last decade of the twentieth century was well served by two very different publications: Ross Worthington, *Governance in Singapore* (London and New York, 2003); and Cherian George, *Singapore: The Air-Conditioned Nation: Essays on the Politics of Comfort and Control, 1990–2000* (Singapore, 2000). Worthington's work is a weighty academic treatise, with a comprehensive bibliography, which concentrates on the first eight years of Goh Chok Tong's premiership and examines the executive as a "Westminster state". George's lively collection of essays offers a Singapore journalist's acutely observed portrait of the republic in the final years of the century.

Despite the "out-of-bounds" markers and disciplined political system, the feeling was that the new millennium would bring in a new age encouraged fertile discussion, fuelled by the impressive expansion of education from the 1980s, particularly in the tertiary sector. The growing intelligentsia reviewed the present and looked back over the past half century to see how far Singapore had come and in what direction it was moving; how to reconcile the anomalies of tight political control with the revolution in education, and great economic wealth with social change and higher expectations.

The PAP itself continued to be vocal, to issue policy documents, and to publish volumes of ministerial speeches and celebratory party issues: People's Action Party, *For People through Action by Party* (Singapore 1999); Irene Ng (ed.), *PAP 50: Five Decades of the People's Action Party* (Singapore, 2004).

Kernial Singh and Paul Wheatley (eds.), *Management of Success: The Moulding of Modern Singapore* (Singapore, 1989) ranged across politics, the economy, population, education and language.

In the field of politics, Kevin Tan and Lam Peng Er (eds.), *Managing Political Change in Singapore: The Elected Presidency* (London, 1997); Ho Khai Leong, *The Politics of Policy-Making in Singapore* (Singapore, 2000); revised and expanded as *Shared Responsibilities, Unshared Power: The Politics of Policy Making in Singapore* (Singapore, 2003), examined unilateral policy making by the elite since 1959. Hussin Mutalib, *Parties and Politics: A Study of Opposition Parties and the PAP in Singapore* (Singapore, 2003; 2nd ed., 2004) is a perceptive discussion ranging from colonial to contemporary times. Diane K. Mauzy and R.S. Milne, *Singapore Politics under the People's Action Party* (London, 2002); Derek da Cunha (ed.), *Debating Singapore: Reflective Essays* (Singapore, 1994); *The Price of Victory: The 1997 Singapore General Election* (Singapore, 1997); and da Cunha (ed.), *Singapore in the New Millenium: Challenges facing the City State* (Singapore, 2002); Michael Hill and Lian Kwen Fee, *The Politics of Nation Building and Citizenship in Singapore* (London and New York, 1995).

The politics of control attracted much criticism: Christopher Tremewan, *The Political Economy of Social Control in Singapore* (New York and Basingstoke, 1994); Carl A. Trocki, *Singapore: Wealth, Power and the Culture of Control* (London, 2006); and the works of Garry Rodan: *The Political Economy of Singapore's Industrialization: National State and International Capital* (Basingstoke, 1989); Rodan (ed.), *Singapore Changes Guard: Social, Political and Economic Directions in the 1990s* (Melbourne and New York, 1993); Rodan (ed.), *Political Oppositions in Industrialising Asia* (London and New York, 1996); Rodan (ed.), *Singapore* (Aldershot, 2001); Rodan, *Transparency and Authoritarian Rule in Southeast Asia: Singapore and Malaysia* (London and New York, 2004); and as joint editor, Kevin Hewison, Richard Robison and Garry Rodan (eds.), *Southeast Asia in the 1990s: Authoritarianism, Democracy and Capitalism* (Sydney, 1993); Rodan, Hewison and Robison (eds.), *The Political Economy of South-East Asia: An Introduction* (Melbourne, 1997); 2nd ed. as *The Political Economy of South-East Asia: Conflicts, Crises and Change* (Melbourne, 2001); and a further new edition as *The Political Economy of South-East Asia: Markets, Power and Contestation* (Melbourne, 2006).

Lee Kuan Yew continued to command attention. Lee's own two volumes of memoirs appeared in 1998 and 2000. Three senior journalists from the *Straits Times* combined a series of interviews with speeches, to produce a virtual autobiographical picture in Han Fook

Kwang, Warren Fernandez and Sumiko Tan (eds.), *Lee Kuan Yew: The Man and his Ideas* (Singapore, 1998). A more critical appraisal was made in Michael D. Barr, *Lee Kuan Yew: The Beliefs behind the Man* (London, 2000); and in Hong Lysa, "The Personal is Political: The Lee Kuan Yew Story as Singapore's History", *JSEAS*, XXXIII, 3 (2002), pp. 545–57.

Of the presidents of this era, Tisa Ng and Lily Tan, *Ong Teng Cheong: Planner, Politician, President* (Singapore, 2005) was a biography, and Ong's predecessor, Wee Kim Wee, *Glimpses and Reflections* (Singapore, 2006) autobiographical.

The voices of opposition politicians were expressed too: Chee Soon Juan, *Dare to Change: An Alternative Vision for Singapore* (Singapore, 1994); *Singapore My Home Too* (Singapore, 1995); and *The Power of Courage: Effecting Political Change in Singapore Through Non-Violence* (Singapore, 2005). Veteran Workers' Party leader, J.B. Jeyaretnam, *Make it Right for Singapore: Speeches in Parliament, 1997–1999* (Singapore, 2000); and *The Hatchet Man of Singapore* (Singapore, 2003). Dana Lam, *Days of Being Wild: GE 2006 Walking the Line with the Opposition* (Singapore, 2006) about the Workers' Party and the 2006 general election. James Gomez (ed.) *Publish and Perish: The Censorship of Opposition Party Publications in Singapore* (Singapore, 2001); and non-constituency MP (2001–2006) Steve Chia, *Called to Serve: A Compilation of Parliamentary Speeches and Questions* (Singapore, 2006).

Michael Leifer, *Singapore's Foreign Policy: Coping with Vulnerability* (London, 2000) looked back to independence in 1965, and Joseph Chinyong Liow and Ralf Emmers (eds.), *Order and Security in Southeast Asia: Essays in Memory of Michael Leifer* (New York, 2005) included a number of contributions about Singapore. N. Ganesan, *Realism and Dependence in Singapore's Foreign Policy* (London, 2005), from early independence onwards. Singapore's small but diverse diplomatic corps began to record their experiences: Ho Rih

Hwa, *Eating Salt: An Autobiography* (Singapore, 1991) by a former ambassador to Thailand; Maurice Baker, *A Time of Fireflies and Wild Guavas* (Singapore, 1995); Lee Khoon Choy, *On the Beat to the Hustings: An Autobiography* (Singapore, 1986); and *Diplomacy of a Tiny State* (Singapore, 1993); Joe F. Conceicao, *Flavours of Change: Destiny and Diplomacy – Recollections of a Singapore Ambassador* (Singapore, 2004), former MP and ambassador to Moscow and Indonesia; Tommy Koh and Chang Li Lin (eds.), *The Little Red Dot: Reflections by Singapore's Diplomats* (Singapore, 2005); and a handsome volume by Gretchen Liu, *The Singapore Foreign Service: The First 40 years* (Singapore, 2005).

The economy was well covered by academic economists W.G. Huff, *The Economic Growth of Singapore: Trade and Development in the Twentieth Century* (Cambridge, 1994); and Gavin Peebles and Peter Wilson, *The Singapore Economy* (Cheltenham, 1996); and by former Director of the International Monetary Fund's Singapore Regional Training Institute, Henri Ghesquiere, *Singapore's Success: Engineering Economic Growth* (Singapore, 2007).

Tim Huxley, *Defending the Lion City: The Armed Forces of Singapore* (Sydney, 2000) is an authoritative work, showing the evolution since the 1950s. See also Peter H.L. Lim, *Navy: The Vital Force* (Singapore, 1992); and Melanie Chew, *The Sky Our Country: 25 Years of the Republic of Singapore Air Force* (Singapore, 1993); Felix Soh Wai Ming, *Phoenix: The Story of the Home Team* (Singapore, 2003) traced the history of internal security from 1819 to twenty-first century anti-terrorism.

There was an abundance of social studies. Some were historical, such as Chan Kwok Bun and Tong Chee Kiong (eds.), *Past Times: A Social History of Singapore* (Singapore, 2003), "the social backdrop to Singapore's faded years", and Stephen Dobbs, *The Singapore River: A Social History, 1819–2002* (Singapore, 2003). Others are sociological studies of modern times: Ong Jin Hui, Tong Chee Kiong, Tan Ern Ser (eds.), *Understanding Singapore Society* (Singapore, 1997); Chua Beng Huat, *Communitarian Ideology and Democracy in Singapore* (London, 1995); and *Life is not Complete without Shopping: Consumption Culture in Singapore* (Singapore, 2003). Many focused on ethnicity, such as Raj K. Vasil, *Asianising Singapore: The PAP's Management of Ethnicity* (Singapore, 1995); John R. Clammer, *Race and State in Independent Singapore, 1965–1990: The Cultural Politics of Pluralism in a Multi-ethnic Society* (Aldershot, 1998); Lai Ah Eng, *Meanings of Multi-ethnicity: A Case Study of Ethnicity and Ethnic Relations in Singapore* (Kuala Lumpur, 1995); Lai Ah Eng, *Beyond Rituals and Riots: Ethnic Pluralism and Social Cohesion in Singapore* (Singapore, 2003); Lian Kwen Fee (ed.), *Race, Ethnicity and the State in Malaysia and Singapore* (Leiden, 2006).

Some writers were concerned with the growing doubts about welfare: Linda Low and Aw Tar Chean, *Social Insecurity in the New Millennium: The Central Provident Fund in Singapore* (Singapore, 2004); Tan Ern Ser, "Balancing State Welfarism and Individual Responsibility: Singapore's CPF Model", in Catherine Jones Finer and Paul Smyth (eds.), *Social Policy and the Commonwealth: Prospects for Social Inclusion* (Basingstoke, 2004), pp. 125–37; John Gee and Elaine Ho (eds.), *Dignity Overdue* (Singapore, 2006), on the condition of foreign domestic workers in Singapore.

Many publications discussed the impressive expansion of education in the late twentieth/early twenty-first century. John Yip Soong Kwong and Sim Wong Kooi (eds.), *Evolution of Educational Excellence: 25 Years of Education in the Republic of Singapore* (Singapore, 1990) celebrated what had been achieved since independence. S. Gopinathan et al (eds.), *Language, Society and Education in Singapore: Issues and Trends* (Singapore, 1994; 2nd ed., 1998) looked to the present and future, as did Jason Tan and Ng Pak Tee (eds.), *Thinking Schools, Learning Nation: Contemporary Issues and Challenges* (Singapore, 2008). Janet Shepherd, *Striking a Balance: The Management of Language in Singapore* (New York, 2005) discussed bilingual schooling. Edwin Lee and Tan Tai Yong, *Beyond Degrees: The Making of the National University of Singapore* (Singapore, 1996); National University of Singapore, *Transforming Lives: NUS Celebrates 100 Years of University Education in Singapore* (Singapore, 2005); and Raffles Institution, *Under the Banyan Tree: Collected Memories of*

Some Inspiring Rafflesians (1961–1964) (Singapore, 2007) hailed the successes of the English-dominated bilingual system. On the darker side, the problem of Malay schooling loomed large in Lily Zubaidah Rahim, *The Singapore Dilemma: The Political and Educational Marginality of the Malay Community* (Kuala Lumpur, 1998), and the unhappy saga of Chinese-medium education in mid-twentieth century Singapore is re-awakening interest among some younger scholars. Some of those involved in the Nanyang University story have given their views in recent years: Rayson Huang (Vice chancellor 1969–72), *A Lifetime in Academia: An Autobiography* (Hong Kong, 2000); and Wang Gungwu (author of the 1965 Nanyang Curriculum Report), Gregor Benton and Hong Liu (eds.), *Diasporic Chinese Ventures: The Life and Work of Wang Gungwu* (London, 2004). Wong Ting-hong, *Hegemonies Compared: State Formation and Chinese School Politics in Postwar Singapore and Hong Kong* (New York, 2002) makes an interesting comparison, but a full comprehensive history of education in Singapore since independence remains to be written.

Saw Swee Hock, *Changes in the Fertility Policy of Singapore* (Singapore, 1990) looked at the changes in the 1980s, and Saw's *Population Policies and Programmes in Singapore* (Singapore, 2005) traced policies since the 1950s.

On the situation of the Malay minority, Saat A. Rahman (ed.), *In Quest of Excellence: A Story of Singapore Malays* (Singapore, 2002) celebrated the twentieth anniversary of Mendaki. More in-depth and less sanguine were Tania Li, *Malays in Singapore: Culture, Economy and Ideology* (Singapore, 1989), and Lily Zubaidah Rahim, *The Singapore Dilemma: The Political and Educational Marginality of the Malay Community* (Kuala Lumpur, 1998). Hadijah Rahmat, *Portraits of a Nation—British Legacy on the Malay Settlement in Singapore* (Singapore, 2007) chronicled the fate of the Malay reservations.

By the late twentieth century more interest was shown in the situation of women in Singapore with the publication in 1993 of two books edited by Aline K. Wong and Leong Wai Kum: a short study, *A Woman's Place: The Story of Singapore Women* (Singapore, PAP Women's Wing, 1993); and a more detailed, *Singapore Women: Three*

Decades of Change (Singapore, 1993). This was followed by Stella R. Quah, *Family in Singapore: Sociological Perspectives* (Singapore, 1994); Lenore Lyons, *A State of Ambivalence: The Feminist Movement in Singapore* (Leiden, 2004); and Arora Mandakini (ed.), *Small Steps, Giant Leaps: A History of AWARE and the Women's Movement in Singapore* (Singapore, 2007).

Francis T. Seow, *The Media Enthralled: Singapore Revisited* (Boulder; US, 1998) was very critical of the press in this period. Cherian George, *Contentious Journalism and the Internet: Towards Democratic Discourse in Malaysia and Singapore* (Singapore, 2006) was a stimulating study of the current and potential effect of the Internet on politics.

Compared with earlier periods, labour relations became unexciting in the very modern era, and writing on the subject has been largely historical, as in Raj K.Vasil, *Public Service Unionism: A History of the AUPE (Amalgamated Union of Public Employees) in Singapore* (Singapore, 1979); Singapore Port Workers Union, *The Port Worker and his Union: The First 40 Years of the Singapore Port Workers' Union* (Singapore, 1986); Singapore Port Workers Union, *Portside: A Celebration of the 50th Anniversary of the Singapore Port Workers' Union* (Singapore, 1996).

By the last decade of the twentieth century historians were beginning a radical reinterpretation of Singapore's past, and this interest gathered momentum from the backlash against the government's attempt to instil what was seen as an authorized propaganda version; history as written by the victors: Ban Kah Choon, Anne Pakir and Tong Chee Kiong (eds.), *Imagining Singapore* (Singapore, 1992; 2nd ed., 1994); Loh Kah Seng, "Within the Singapore Story: The use and narrative of history in Singapore", *Crossroads*, 12 (1998); Abu Talib Ahmad and Tan Liok Ee (eds.), *New Terrains in Southeast Asian History* (Athens, Ohio and London, 2003); Albert Lau, "Nation Building and the Singapore Story" in Wang Gungwu (ed.), *Nation Building: Five Southeast Asian Histories* (Singapore, 2005), pp. 221–50. Several articles by Hong Lysa were incorporated together with new material into Hong Lysa and Huang

Jianli, *The Scripting of a National History: Singapore and its Pasts* (Singapore, 2008); and Michael D. Barr and Carl A. Trocki (eds.), *Paths Not Taken: Political Pluralism in Postwar Singapore* (Singapore, 2008), a wide-ranging collection of conference papers, which should stimulate debate. The study of Singapore history entered the twenty-first century alive and well.

Index